THEORY
OF
MOTIVATION

Second Edition

Robert C. Bolles

University of Washington

HARPER & ROW, PUBLISHERS
New York, Evanston, San Francisco, London

Harper's Experimental Psychology Series

UNDER THE EDITORSHIP OF H. Philip Zeigler

Sponsoring Editor: George A. Middendorf
Project Editor: Cynthia Hausdorff
Designer: Jared Pratt
Production Supervisor: Will C. Jomarrón

THEORY OF MOTIVATION, Second Edition

Library of Congress Cataloging in Publication Data
Bolles, Robert C
      Theory of motivation.

      Bibliography: p.
      Includes index.
      1. Motivation (Psychology)   I. Title.
[DNLM: 1. Motivation.   BF683   B691t]
BF683.B6   1975   156'.2'5   74–28083
ISBN 0–06–040793–X

CONTENTS

Preface to the Second Edition   *vii*

1   Introduction   1

     The explanation of behavior   *1*
     Mechanism   5
     Empirical determinism   6
     The evaluation of theories   *10*
     The constructs of a theory   *14*

2   Historical Origins of Motivational Concepts   21

     The rationalistic era   *22*
     The intellectual revolution   *24*
     Associationism   *29*
     The reactionary counterrevolution   *32*
     The advent of determinism   *36*
     Empirical determinism   *44*
     Summary   *50*

3   Dynamic Psychology   52

     The origins of psychoanalysis   *54*
     Explanatory principles   *56*
     Psychoanalytic theory of instinctual drives   *59*
     Psychoanalytic explanation of behavior   *62*
     Formal adequacy as a theory of behavior   *66*
     Energy versus structure   *68*

Lewin's theory of motivation 70
Lewin's motivational constructs 72
Formal adequacy of Lewin's theory 76
Murray's concept of need 80
Summary 84

4 Instincts 86

William James' instincts 87
Instincts as universal motivators 89
The outcome of the controversy 99
The ethologist's instincts 101
Energy models 103
Summary 107

5 The Drive Concept 108

Stimuli as drives to action 109
Drives as stimuli to activity 115
Definitions of drive 124
Associative account of motivation 127
Hull's drive theory 129
Summary 133

6 Antecedent Conditions 135

Hunger 136
Thirst 157
Sexual motivation 170
Other kinds of motivation 179
Summary 186

7 Energizing Effects 188

The energizing of consummatory behavior 189
The energizing of instrumental behavior 210
The energizing of general activity 217
Some new approaches to general activity 229
Summary 234

8 Associative Aspects of Motivated Behavior   235

The independence of D and H   *236*
The effects of irrelevant drive   *247*
The reinforcing function of drive reduction   *257*
The stimulus concomitants of drive   *270*
Summary   *279*

9 Motivation and Learning   280

Acquired-drive models   *281*
Incentive motivation models   *291*
Reinforcement models   *304*
Cognitive models   *313*
Summary   *321*

10 Avoidance   323

Two-factor theory   *323*
The properties of S+   *337*
The properties of the response   *350*
Species-specific defense reactions   *357*
Summary   *366*

11 Punishment and Frustration   367

Varied effects of punishment   *368*
Behavioral effects of shock   *371*
Theories of punishment   *381*
The response contingency problem   *393*
Frustration   *400*
Summary   *409*

12 The Conditions of Reinforcement   411

Amount of reinforcement   *412*
Quality of reinforcement   *423*
Delay of reinforcement   *426*
Percentage of reinforcement   *436*
The response contingency problem   *437*
Summary   *444*

13 Secondary Reinforcement   446

Early experiments on secondary reinforcement   447
The behavioral effects of secondary reinforcers   448
The establishment of secondary reinforcers   466

References   479
Index   557

PREFACE

The second edition is like the first in many respects. The topic of motivation is still approached from a historical perspective, and it is still related primarily to animal learning. But because history has moved on and the theory of animal learning has moved with it, there are a number of changes. The first part of the book, which attempts to show how the concept of motivation arose, is virtually unchanged from the first edition. I still believe that the concept of motivation became popular because so many people thought it would help explain behavior. Therefore, we will examine rather carefully just what "explaining" behavior means. We will also become involved to some extent in the history of psychology because the roots of the motivation concept lie in this history rather than in any contemporary analysis of behavior. It is only by viewing the concept of motivation in historical perspective that we can understand why people thought it would help explain behavior.

The middle part of the book, which analyzes the drive concept, is reduced in size because drive is no longer a popular concept and no longer needs detailed criticism; it is also reorganized to some extent because the emphasis is now on the various kinds of behavior that drive was supposed to explain rather than on the drive concept itself.

The last part of the book, which analyzes motivational concepts other than drive, is almost wholly reorganized and rewritten to take into account current issues, new explanatory models, and a great many new aspects of behavior that have been discovered recently. The determinants of behavior appear to be more complicated than they seemed just a few years ago, and so do our theories. For example, theorists used to postulate general-process or universal mechanisms; now we are beginning to see that motivation and learning operate rather selectively.

I still view science not as a search for imperishable truth but more as a kind of game. We play the game partly for the fun of it, but partly also because we believe it will increase our understanding. This book is dedicated to those rare men, like Tolman and Hull, who taught us how to play the game in psychology and who made it seem worth playing. It is addressed to all those who would do research to improve our understanding of behavior.

I am indebted to the National Science Foundation, which has supported my research for several years, enabling me to do research and write during the summer, and has borne some of the cost of preparing the manuscript. I am also grateful for permission generously granted by a number of authors and publishers to reproduce quotations and figures.

ROBERT C. BOLLES

1

INTRODUCTION

The notion of cause is replaced by the notion of law. Instead of causal relation, we have the conception of a continuous succession of events logically connected with one another by an underlying principle . . .
Sir Edmund Whittaker

Only rarely is motivation said to be a fact of human experience, that is, a mental event, which determines the course of action. The idea of motivation does not originate from what men say either about their own experience or about their own behavior. It is not one of the "indigenous problems" of psychology.

Nor is motivation a fact of behavior. There is not one feature or aspect or characteristic of behavior to which we invariably have reference when we say that some behavior is motivated. Although some writers have suggested behavioral criteria to define motivation, these attempts to specify what is meant by motivation are not very compelling. There is little agreement among the different proposals about what the defining criteria should be. We may say, for example, that an animal that has been deprived of food is hungry or that it has a hunger drive or that it "looks" motivated. But even though we may agree on this, it is not so clear that we can agree on what characteristic of its behavior makes the animal look motivated.

What one proposes as a definition of motivated behavior seems to depend more upon his theoretical commitments than upon anything in the behavior itself. Any solution to the problem of what it is about a particular behavior that makes it appear motivated will therefore depend upon how we regard behavior in general and how we explain it in general. Thus motivation seems to be neither a fact of experience nor a fact of behavior, but rather an idea or concept we introduce when we undertake to explain behavior.

The explanation of behavior

Sometimes we are fortunate enough to observe behavior occurring as a direct response to prevailing stimulus conditions in the environment. In such cases no very elaborate explanation is necessary; we may simply cite the eliciting conditions. In these cases of reflexive responses, the behavior of the organism becomes nearly as predictable as the behavior of simple physical systems, and our explanation can be correspondingly simple. More frequently, though, no identifiable external stimulus can be specified for a certain act. In this case behavior might be explained indirectly as the result of stimuli that have been effective in the past or it might be explained indirectly as a result of the physical structure of the individual, or of its prior experience. But all such explanations would be relatively indirect compared with the simple idea that there is a single active internal agency that, if it could be located, would provide a direct explanation. If such an internal agency or cause of behavior could be found, our explanation of all behavior could then be as simple as it is in the case of the reflex. Typically, the search for such an agency is fruitless, and it is then that we take the much easier course of hypothesizing the existence of an appropriate agency.[1] Different theories of motivation are distinguished primarily by the different kinds of motivation agencies that they hypothesize.

In this sense the most enduring theory of motivation is that which attributes a man's behavior to the results of his own mental processes. We can designate this traditional approach to the problem of explaining behavior by any name we wish, since it has no accepted name (prevailing doctrines often do not). Let us call it rationalism or, more precisely, traditional rationalism.

Traditional rationalism. The naïve and traditional explanation of human behavior is that we act because we have reasons for acting. Because we have free will, our reasons constitute a sufficient account of the whole matter. Such was the common view of the Greek philosophers, and such is the common view of the layman today. Traditional rationalism, of course, receives considerable support from our continuing use of it in our day-to-day contact with people. We hold our fellow man personally responsible as the author of his actions, and society expects him to describe his own actions in terms of intention, awareness, and purpose. We teach our children to use these words by making our transactions with them contingent upon what we consider to be their proper usage. We all do this, even the most behavioristic of us, because that is, in turn, what we have learned to do.

[1] Skinner makes the point this way: "A rat does not always respond to food placed before it, and a factor called its 'hunger' is invoked by way of explanation. The rat is said to eat only when it is hungry. It is because eating is not inevitable that we are led to hypothesize an internal state to which we may assign the variability. Where there is a no variability, no state is needed. Since the rat usually responds to a shock to its foot by flexing its leg, no 'flexing drive' comparable to hunger is felt to be required" (Skinner, 1938, p. 341).

We attribute a man's behavior to events going on in his mind. This is the common and familiar variety of explanation that provides the point of departure for all other theories of motivation. All alternative conceptions of motivation and all alternative motivation constructs arise as reactions to this traditional rationalistic doctrine.

There are two distinguishing characteristics of traditional rationalistic explanations of behavior. These explanations are almost invariably (1) teleological and (2) untestable.

Teleology. When we speak in everyday language about the reasons for some behavior or about its purpose, we usually have reference to the mind and, more specifically, to the conscious intentions of the person behaving. And to the extent that the individual has some purpose or intention that is focused upon the future, such an explanation is said to be teleological. Today we tend to restrict teleological explanations to human behavior because of our conviction that only man can foresee the consequences of his actions. The idea that purpose always implies intention and that some reasoning intellect, either man's or God's, must be the author of the intention is a feature of Christian philosophy; it was formalized by Augustine and the other codifiers of Christian theology.[2] By contrast, Greek philosophers found it possible to consider purpose and even reason as characteristics of nature quite apart from any conscious intention on the part of man. Thus Aristotle proclaims that in some cases an event is explained when we know what end it serves.

> Another sort of cause is that on account of which a thing is done. For example, bodily health is a cause of walking exercise. Why does a man take exercise? We say it is in order to have good health; in this way we mean to specify the cause of walking.[3]

This earlier teleological concept, the idea of final cause as something apart from intention, was most suited to processes of growth, development, and fulfillment. For example, a block of stone becomes a statue with the sculptor as a causal agent or a child grows up and becomes a man. The stone and the child represent the unfulfilled but potential matter to which the statue and the man give form and fulfillment. They are in turn the final causes of their respective developments.

Whether we speak of purpose in the sense of final cause or

[2] The idea that man is personally, morally responsible for his own acts is also due to the early Church Fathers. The blamable part of the human personality was called the soul. The Greeks, on the assumption that man always seeks to do good, attributed evil to human error or ignorance.

[3] Aristotle's views on causation are given in *Physics*, Book 2, ch. 3, and *de Anima*, Book 2, ch. 4. He believed a phenomenon was not fully explained until its purpose, final form, and physical cause had each been accounted for.

purpose in the sense of intentions, both usages have a common element; some events are explained for some people when a justification for them is found. Justification is one variety of explanation. Some, like Aristotle, insist that there are certain events in the world that can be given meaning only in terms of the reasons for which they occur. But the meaning that is found in these instances is invariably evaluative; it is justification. Consider as an example the ancient argument that the appearance of purpose throughout nature is proof of the existence of a Creator. Aside from the difficulty that the argument presupposes what it purports to prove (i.e., the existence of purpose), it has the additional difficulty that after invoking a Creator such an explanation, or justification, stops with its account of nature as though nothing more were of interest. Invoking a Creator perhaps justifies creation but tells us nothing about creation; it has only restated the problem.[4] So, too, when we demand of a person the reason for his actions, his statement that he behaved as he did for such and such a reason only restates the problem; at best, we still must explain why he had the reason he had. In the meantime, however, we may attach blame or praise to his purposes, and, indeed, it is probably just the evaluative freedom we have with another person's motives that gives us such a sense that his purposes are important. If we were to give up the notion of purpose as the cause of action, we would lose the principal objects of our own affections and aggressions.

Untestability. The most serious limitation of traditional rationalism is not that its explanations are teleological but that they are inherently untestable. The events that are presumed to explain behavior are supposed to occur in the mind and be available only to the individual himself. Others have no ready or certain access to the hypothesized events. Moreover, there are no explicit hypotheses about how the mind is supposed to work so as to produce behavior; the relationships between these inaccessible mental events and observable behavior are so ill-defined and elusive that we cannot lay down any rules to indicate how the mind itself works. How does an intention to act (granting that an intention to act can produce the action) itself arise from the individual's perceptions, knowledge, feelings, and so on? There are no rules to guide us.

We should note that it is not just the case that such rules have not been found; typically, the proponents of traditional rational-

---

[4] The point was made by Hume (1779) when he said that the argument (for the existence of God) from design was invalid because it involves the assumption that the existence of a Creator was a sufficient cause of creation, whereas at most the existence of a Creator is only necessary. The argument itself is that the world presents endless indications of means adapting themselves to ends, which could only have occurred as the deliberate action of a powerful intellect.

ism insist that there are no such rules. They say that the mind of man cannot be bound by lawfulness; it operates creatively and dynamically rather than according to fixed, predictable principles. Plato said that the psyche is that which moves itself; it has laws of its own being and needs no others. Similar statements about the inherent unpredictability, the untrammeled freedom of the human mind have come rattling down the ages. These assertions are, in fact, a crucial part of the traditional rationalistic doctrine, and it is for this reason, as we will see later in this chapter, that traditional rationalism does not constitute a "theory" of motivation; nor does it provide an explanation of behavior in any real sense. That is, it is not a coherent, consistent, testable set of propositions about behavior; indeed, it is in large measure a denial that such a set of propositions can be found.

Mechanism

In his restless quest for understanding and certainty man has sought to find the causes of all natural events, including, sometimes, human behavior. One of the oldest and most time-honored alternatives to the traditional rationalistic approach to explanation is mechanism. Briefly, this is the doctrine that all natural events have physical causes and that if we knew enough about physical and mechanical systems, we would then be able to explain, at least in principle, all natural phenomena. The mechanist has the faith that when all the mechanical factors have been accounted for, there will be nothing else left to explain.

This faith is supported in part by the predictability of physical objects in everyday life. We throw rocks and we observe that they behave in a reasonably predictable manner. If we make our observations on a billiard table, we find that the predictability of the balls appears to be limited only by our skill in applying energy to them. The mechanist starts on the basis of a number of such observations and proceeds by analogy to the hypothesis that all events in nature have a similar machinelike predictability.

The doctrine of mechanism is based upon several distinct precepts, and it is important not to confuse them. The mechanist views all the phenomena of nature in the same light, whereas the rationalist makes a special case of man's ability to reason, the mechanist is concerned with finding principles that will include the behavior of man among the other phenomena of nature. Man's ability to reason provides no grounds for introducing exceptions to the laws of nature. His intellectual activity must be derived somehow from other, simpler principles.

The mechanist is also a determinist. Whereas the rationalist assumes free will, the mechanist assumes that there are systematic laws of behavior that can be discovered. He assumes that if these laws were known, they would permit behavior to be predicted. He may or may not involve the mind of man in his explanatory schemes, but if the mind is included, then it too must follow determinate laws.

The third distinguishing characteristic of the mechanist is his assumption that the world of physical events not only provides the pattern of what is natural and what is lawfully determined in nature but also provides the substance for all phenomena. Thus he is a materialist. Behavior is not only a natural phenomenon, and lawfully determined, but it is determined by precisely the same physical laws and forces that apply throughout nature. The ultimate and only reality, it is assumed, is physical in character.

There were Greek mechanists, but they were a minority group, and their influence was small compared with that of either Plato or Aristotle. Any substantial gains for the mechanistic position had to await its development and success in the physical realm itself; this occurred only in the seventeenth century through the work of such giants as Galileo and Newton. Wider scientific acceptance of mechanism had to wait still longer until it had been applied to the biological sciences.

Faith in the mechanistic doctrine has usually extended far beyond its usefulness in explaining the phenomena to which it has been applied. For example, most and perhaps all of our motivational concepts, such as drive and incentive, were developed and popularized during the interval between the introduction of mechanistic assumptions into psychology and the time when these concepts were put to empirical test. As a consequence, our theorizing made considerable use of drives and incentives and their postulated properties long before the usefulness of these concepts had been demonstrated by their ability to explain behavior. Indeed, virtually the entire history of motivation theory is devoted to declarations by this or that theorist that we must find the forces underlying behavior and the physiological causes of behavior if we are ever to explain it. The urgency with which this program has been proclaimed has, unfortunately, not always been matched by the development of what we now consider to be the proper fruits of science, namely, adequate explanatory theories. We will consider shortly what is meant by an adequate explanatory theory, but first we must note some objections that have been raised to the mechanistic doctrine.

Empirical determinism

The traditional difference of opinion regarding what constitutes an adequate explanation of any natural phenomenon has centered on purpose and teleology. The scientist has always been reluctant to admit that there are purposes operating in nature, preferring to rely upon what he views as the "real" or physical causes of things. On the other hand, rationalists, humanists, the clergy, and most thoughtful laymen have felt most at ease with, or even insisted upon, teleological accounts of certain natural phenomena, such as human behavior. The question at issue has traditionally been whether physical causes provide a total explanation, or whether teleological principles had to be added for some phenomena. Before David Hume (1739) did so, no one seemed to question whether physical causes were necessary but only whether they were sufficient. Hume asked: How can we know the nature of causation? How can we know if causes really produce their effects? Hume's skeptical epistemology led him to the realization that the best evidence we can ever obtain is that two events invariably occur together, one preceding the other, always in the same order, and neither occurring alone. The imputation of causation, the abstract conception that the prior event necessitates the subsequent event, is an inference that goes beyond the evidence. There may be physical or material causation, of course, but we can never be sure whether nature operates mechanistically, since all we can know is the successive experience of successive events. It is in the nature of the human mind, Hume asserted, to transcend the data and infer a causal relationship between the two events if we invariably experience them one before the other.

Although scientists have characteristically operated in an empirical and pragmatic manner, philosophers, even philosophers of science, have tended to lag behind conceptually. Hence for many years Hume's point was regarded as undue skepticism or as mere sophistry. Most men felt bound to commit themselves metaphysically to either a rationalistic position, a mechanistic position, or some dualistic combination of the two.

As far as science is concerned, its object is not to discover the ultimate nature of reality, but rather to explore empirical relationships and derive useful generalizations from them. The question of what kind of causation is involved in explanation is an unnecessary impediment, a philosophical encumbrance, to the conduct of science. It is futile for the scientist to be concerned with whether an event occurred because some other event made it occur; much more to the point is that an event occurs and its occurrence can be correlated with certain sets of conditions. Of course, we wish to refine our observations and improve our ability to control conditions until a point is reached where perfect or near perfect correlations are possible and where very powerful general descriptive laws can be found.[5]

---

[5] Scholars have sought to analyze more carefully the meaning of terms like "cause," "effect," and "necessitate" (Bunge, 1959; Smith, 1960). Usually, the conditions of temporal and spatial contiguity between cause and effect call for their most serious consideration. These considerations are serious, weighty, and highly involved logically—particularly when contrasted with the simple elegance of the empirical laws to which they are purported to be relevant.

But science cannot wait for the final solution of the causation problem. We must proceed to view empirical correlations as the subject matter of science without committing ourselves to either a teleological, purposive, or materialistic philosophy. Nor do we need to go as far as Hume and say that we can never transcend empirical correlations. We may believe that, or we may take the more optimistic position that the empirical correlations we observe will ultimately be undergirded by a more profound understanding of causation. By adhering to a descriptive or correlational approach we may at least leave the way open for such a possibility.

The empirical approach is noncommittal; it provides a convenient vantage point from which we may survey other, more highly committed approaches. Psychology, particularly the area of motivation, is confused enough by the practice of regarding motives, or drives, or instincts, or needs, as the causes of behavior. If we are to describe behavior from a point of view that does not restrict us to any particular theoretical or philosophical position, then we should adopt a terminology that leaves these questions open. Thus the relationship that exists, for example, between a stimulus and a response will be described throughout this book, not in causal terms, but in neutral and descriptive terms. We will say that deprivation and stimulus conditions *determine* behavior or that some behavior is under the *control* of some stimulus.

The crucial insight here is that the empirical attitude does not imply a rejection of the principle of determinism. Quite the contrary; it will be argued that behavior is determined, not because forces act on the organism to make it behave, nor because the behavior was willed by some reasoning intellect, but simply in the sense that it is intrinsically predictable. Behavior is determined in that it is lawful.

Therefore, the doctrine that I have called empirical determinism keeps the first two propositions of the mechanistic doctrine, namely, that behavior is a natural phenomenon and that it is determined, and rejects only its materialistic bias. It will be argued that a "causeless" account of a phenomenon can explain it even though it fails to provide any justification or indicate its physical basis. It will also be argued that correspondence with an empirical law constitutes just the kind of explanation we want, provided only that the empirical law is contained in a systematic theory. Before proceeding with this argument let us digress briefly to consider some objections that might be raised to this position.

Hempel and Oppenheim (1948) have discussed a number of such objections. They consider, for example, the argument that a strictly empirical explanatory system is not applicable to behavior in humans because of the enormous complexity of the human subject and the unique character of his behavior. Hempel and Oppenheim contend that the only real question is whether phenomena as complex as human behavior are susceptible to adequate explanation. This is an empirical question; can laws of sufficient breadth and generality be discovered and can sufficient precision be obtained in specifying the appropriate antecedent conditions? The uniqueness and the irrepeatability of observations do not distinguish behavior from other observable phenomena. Irrepeatability is no less a problem in physics, or even astronomy, than it is in psychology; all observations are unique. The only strategy by which science can proceed at all is to concern itself with common features of and abstractions from unique observations.

Is such a system of explanation applicable to psychological phenomena in view of the fact that so many of the theoretical entities in psychology are not directly observable? The answer, again, is that psychological phenomena and theoretical constructs do not differ appreciably from those in physics or any other science in this respect. As long as there are methods for determining with reasonable clarity and precision the hypothesized variables, there is no special problem here at all. The only real question is whether psychological theories are to be based entirely upon empirical observations or whether they are to be based partly upon other, "transempirical," sources of knowledge.

Another question is whether psychological explanations, which have historically involved reference to purposive behavior, call for a different mode of explanation. If "purposive" pertains to divine purpose or to some inscrutable intention on the part of the individual, then, it is true, the approach fails to provide an adequate explanation. But if these kinds of purpose really have no empirical reference, then behavior that is purposive in this sense is probably not susceptible to any sort of explanation. On the other hand, if we mean by "purposive behavior" only that form of behavior that is highly correlated with its consequences—that is, if we use the phrase in a purely descriptive or empirical manner—then there is no difference in principle between purposive behavior and any other kind of phenomena.

Perhaps the most fundamental practical objection that might be raised to empirical determinism is that it fails to tell *why* an event occurs; it only describes how and when events occur. But in the last analysis, a phenomenon is explained when it is put into terms with which we are familiar and shown to be an instance of a principle with which we are familiar. As Bridgman (1932) has said, an explanation is that kind of account that puts the curiosity at rest.[6] We may ask what is the frame of mind of a man whose curiosity is only "put at rest" by an account of why things happen. What are such men really looking for? In the case of behavior, there

---

[6] ". . . an explanation consists in reducing a situation to elements with which we are so familiar that we accept them as a matter of course, so that our curiosity rests" (Bridgman, 1932, p. 37).

seem to be two different kinds of accounts that men may be seeking when they ask "why?" One is justification, and the other is an application of the mechanistic doctrine. Thus some of the time when someone is asked "why did you do that?" what is expected is a justification of the action. At other times it seems clear that what is demanded is an understanding of the physiological or neurological machinery that produced the effect.

In general, a satisfactory answer to a why question is a statement involving terms with which the inquirer is familiar. The difficulty of explanation in psychology is that those who ask why of the psychologist come to him quite familiar with justifying action and quite familiar with the reality of the physical body, and they seek some explanation in these terms. On the other hand, the scientist, who is familiar with the empirical regularities in his science, does not seek the why of them. Insofar as the psychologist asks why, it is because he is curious about moral questions of justification or about the mysteries of neurology, either of which he may have legitimate reasons for wanting to relate to behavior. But the psychologist asks why only when he wants to transcend or extend the boundaries of his science and not when he is working within them.

The evaluation of theories

It was noted previously that if an empirical law is to provide an explanation of a phenomenon, it must be part of a systematic theory. All this means in effect is that explanation in science requires that a phenomenon be systematically related to other phenomena. When we have a model for producing such a systemization, then we have a theory. Since there is ample opportunity for confusion about what does and what does not constitute a theory, let us consider in some detail just what is involved.

Formal properties of theories. From a logical point of view a theory involves at least (1) a number of terms and (2) a number of relational rules tying the terms together or interrelating them in some way. In purely formal systems, such as the different branches of mathematics, the terms are undefined. However, if a theory is to have empirical usefulness and testability, it must have a third property: Its terms must be defined or related in some way to empirical events. There are a few examples of theories in psychology in which the primary emphasis is placed upon formal structure and in which little interest is attached to the problem of relating to empirical events. One example is Lewin's topological psychology (1936). Lewin went to considerable effort to develop a formal (or what might be called a preexperimental) structure that would be able to encompass the full richness and complexity of human behavior as the facts became known. The terms that constitute the formal language of the theory—that is, terms like "valence," "force," and "tension"—are explicitly related to each other but are only poorly tied to observable events in the empirical world. Lewin's theory demonstrates a remarkable degree of sophistication, complexity, and internal coherence quite apart from the empirical question of whether people actually behave as the system prescribes. One could entertain oneself at length with the purely formal properties of the theory without applying it to the explanation of behavior.

Another example of a theory that provides a certain measure of formal adequacy is Hull's hypothetico-deductive theory of rote learning (Hull et al., 1940). This theory was admittedly only a model to describe the "behavior" of an idealized "subject" learning a list of nonsense syllables, and, again, it would be of considerable formal interest even if it should turn out that no actual subject ever demonstrated such behavior. What makes these formal systems interesting, apart from their empirical possibilities, is that they contain sets of relational rules that together give structure to the theory. Such a structure is called the *syntax* of a theory. The syntactical rules indicate how the terms of the theory fit together to provide an explanatory network; they describe how to operate with the theoretical terms in order to relate them to each other.

The syntax of a theory may be precise and formally rigid, as in Hull's hypothetico-deductive theory, in which mathematical relationships were formulated between all of the terms; or it may be left loose and qualitative; and terms may be left undefined, as in mathematical systems. All gradations occur. But since it is by relating the terms of the theory to each other (and to the data) that a theory is used, a theory without adequate syntactical rules is no theory at all. For example, the traditional view that man's behavior is explained by his rationality lacks any syntax because it assumes that man's behavior cannot be described by any set of rules. And this, the most serious limitation of traditional rationalism, is why this doctrine cannot properly be called a theory of behavior. One property we may require of a theory, then, is that it should have an explicit syntax.

Empirical base of a theory. Philosophers of science and model builders may be chiefly interested in the structure of a theory considered just as a formal system. But to the scientist a much more interesting and important matter is the tying down of the logical or formal structure of the theory to empirical data so that the theory may be tested. This tying-down process is often called anchoring. It is a different kind of process from the construction of the formal structure of the theory and in many instances occurs quite independently of it. The branch of logic that deals with such definitions is called *semantics.* One difficulty in semantics is that a theory will ordinarily possess two kinds of terms: those that are theoretical, or not directly observable, and those that are empirical, or more or less directly observable. The theoretical terms of a theory (which I will call its *theoretical constructs*) are known by the fact that they are interrelated syntactically; they constitute the terms in the formal theory. But they must also be given empirical reference by being tied semantically to empirical terms (which, for reasons that follow, I will call the *empirical constructs* of the theory).

From the point of view of the formal purist, some of the most popular theories have unfortunately been developed by theorists who have not paid enough attention to the empirical roots of theory making. For example, in psychoanalysis the semantic linkages of the theoretical constructs to empirical observations are so weak that it sometimes appears as though only the theorist himself could possibly know what he is theorizing about. Psychoanalysts seem at times to make a deliberate effort to create a mystique: The empirical anchoring of the terms of the theory is supposed to be left intuitive and loose. Freud believed that the rigid definition of theoretical terms should be the end rather than the means of theoretical advancement.

> The view is often defended that sciences should be built up on clear and sharply defined basal concepts. In actual fact no science, not even the most exact, begins with such definitions. The true beginning of scientific activity consists rather in describing phenomena and then in proceeding to group, classify and correlate them. Even at the stage of description it is not possible to avoid applying certain abstract ideas to the material in hand, ideas derived from various sources and certainly not the fruit of new experience only. Still more indispensable are such ideas—which will later become the basal concepts of the science —as the material is further elaborated. They must at first necessarily possess some measure of uncertainty; there can be no question of any clear delimitation of their content. So long as they remain in this condition, we come to an understanding about their meaning by repeated references to the material of observation, from which we seem to have deduced our abstract ideas, but which is in point of fact subject to them. . . . It is only after more searching investigation of the field in question that we are able to formulate with increased clarity the scientific concepts underlying it, and progressively so to modify these concepts that they become widely applicable and at the same time consistent logically. Then, indeed, it may be time to immure them in definitions. (Freud, 1915, pp. 60–61)

Although some might despair at such laxity, Freud always put difficult problems into historical perspective, and here he has indicated quite realistically how a scientific theory develops. We find that the logical analysis of the formal structure of a theory into its syntax and semantics does not tell us all about it, and such an analysis may, in fact, have little historical or practical validity.

Still, the most useful theories of behavior are those in which theoretical constructs are coordinated at least tentatively with behavioral data. A theory must contain hypothetical relationships that tie together the empirical and theoretical terms. A second property we may require of a theory is that it have an explicit semantics.

Data language. It should be noted that the specification of the empirical terms of a theory, the selection of facts that it is to explain, is not entirely arbitrary but is dependent also upon usage and habits of observation. "Response" is usually considered an empirical term, but it is not purely empirical. Its meaning is determined as much by the theory in which it is designated an "empirical observation" as by what happens in the real world. Thus it is only relatively empirical. It is empirical by comparison with the theoretical constructs, but it is theoretical compared with the more basic terms of everyday language. To emphasize the quasi-empirical–quasi-theoretical nature of such terms we will call them *empirical constructs*. The empirical constructs, taken together, constitute what we will call the *data language*.

Data language serves as a foundation for a theory by tying it down empirically; it is also the language that scientists use to talk among themselves. As Estes has put it,

> the data language . . . includes the terminology needed for the description of observations and operations. In psychology the chief function of the data language is the description of behaviors and of the situations in which they occur. The terms used in description must be limited to those for which agreement upon usage can be obtained from workers in the field regardless of theoretical biases and which are free of any reference to theory (that is, to the theory for which the set of terms in question functions as data language). (Estes, 1954, p. 321)[7]

Some writers (e.g., Skinner) define the data language of their theory explicitly, but more often they leave it unanalyzed, implicit (e.g., Lewin or the Gestalt psychologists).

One of the difficulties in assessing different theories of behavior is that they have tended to isolate themselves by the use of data languages that are unintelligible to theorists of other persuasions.

---

[7] I have taken much of the language Estes uses in the logical analysis of theories for the present discussion. I cannot agree with one point that Estes makes, however—that a data language is theoretically neutral. It seems to me that much of a data language is determined in the same way as the other contents of a theory, namely, by the constraints of our own experience and by our previously established habits of speculation and observation. In the storybooks the scientist is able to study a perfectly arbitrary selection from among possible phenomena, but, in fact, this selection is determined in large part by what he believes to underlie what he observes. Stevens says: "There are *only* constructs. . . . A datum *is* a construct" (1935, p. 523). Margenau (1950) has examined thoroughly the implications of this position for physical theory.

Thus it is only with considerable effort that a S-R learning theorist and a psychoanalyst can communicate with each other. The difficulty is that what one accepts as an empirical observation the other may not. Each has no difficulty in a linguistic community that accepts the same data language, but the mixture of data languages from two independent sets of workers can be disastrous. Some of the great conflicts in the history of theoretical psychology can be traced to the problem of mutually unintelligible data languages. For example, the continuing lack of harmony between molar and molecular points of view may be attributed to the use of the word "response" for very different kinds of events for which very different kinds of psychological theories seem appropriate.

Consequently, we must consider that the semantic problems in a theory of behavior extend not only from the theoretical constructs down to the empirical constructs of the data language, but from there on down to facts of experience upon which anyone speaking the language can agree—what Carnap (1936) has called the physical-thing language. Ideally, the data language would be linked to the thing language, the language of common perceptual experience, through operational definitions. As an alternative to such rigid linkages, the theorist may use the technique commonly employed in the physical sciences, *sets* of reductions. That is, he might identify a term by means of several functional properties.

An important question is whether the ultimate language to which the data language is reduced *must* be the physical-thing language. This question lies at the very heart of the traditional difficulty of studying complex human behavior. In the rationalistic variety of explanation the language of human experience is asserted to be the only one that is valid for the study of man. To be sure, there may be a perfectly good language of human experience that is more or less independent of the language of physical things, but this language has shown itself to be of relatively little use for the purpose of developing a theory of human behavior. There is so much difficulty communicating with such languages that we cannot test assertions stated in them. And perhaps above all else we require that a theory of behavior be testable. Therefore, we may require of a theory that it have a precise and explicit data language, precise enough and explicit enough that it is possible to test assertions derived from the theory.

Fig. 1-1 depicts some of the formal properties of theories we have been considering.

The constructs of a theory

Viewed solely as part of a conceptual model, the set of theoretical constructs in a theory are all of the same kind, namely, symbols to be put down on paper. But imbued with the purposes and presuppo-

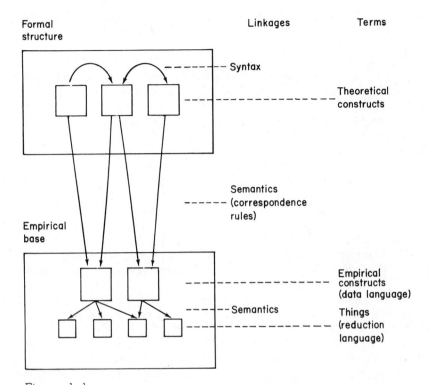

Figure 1–1
An analysis of the kinds of terms and linkages between terms that occur in a theory.

sitions (and biases) of the theorist, the theory takes on new dimensions, and all its constituent constructs acquire conceptual properties of their own. They differ in temporal duration; some are enduring, like "dispositions," while others are temporary state variables, like "drive," while still others are fleeting determinants of behavior, like "percepts." They differ also in temporal order; the consequences of stimulation precede the final determinants of the response. Constructs also differ with respect to their causal relationships; stimuli are sometimes assumed to cause the responses they control.

Empirical reference of constructs. Perhaps the most striking way in which constructs differ is with respect to their hypothetical or actual empirical reference. Spence (1944) has suggested a fourfold classification of the referents commonly used in psychological theories: animistic, neurophysiological, response-inferred, and intervening. With constructs of the animistic variety there is no anchoring to empirical observables. Presumably, everyone is just supposed to know the signs of these intuitive psychological variables. The reason these kinds of constructs are called animistic is clear: They operate on the individual as though they had reason and will of their own, and these cognitive and volitional powers are not subject to further analysis.

Physiological reference. The neurophysiological type of construct is another favorite; its empirical reference is most frequently to a hypothetical neurological mechanism that is not now directly observable but that, at least in principle, could be observed. One example is the concept of decreased synaptic resistance as a basis of learning. As a mechanism it sounds plausible, but as an empirical fact it has the status of a "promissory note"; that is, we invoke it hoping that some day the physiologist will confirm its existence for us.

It is not clear that either the physiologist or the psychologist has gained much by the one telling the other what he should look for. It is also not certain that the surplus meaning that the psychologist attaches to his constructs by means of these promissory notes makes them any more valuable. Certainly, they become no more useful for describing the facts of behavior; their only possible utility would seem to be to establish a true bridge science of physiological psychology. But their major application is not ordinarily as constructs in new physiological theories but as ancillary elements in behavioral theories. In this application they would seem to be something like status symbols.

The theorist may be simply indicating his faith in a mechanistic variety of explanation when he posits neurophysiological constructs; he may simply be showing that he believes that ultimately the facts and laws of psychology will be reducible to the facts and laws of physiology. But if the theorist would validate a theoretical construct in terms of, say, neural synapses, then neural synapses must be included in the data language of his theory, and he would then have a theory *about* neural synapses rather than one *invoking* them. He still would not have validated the original behavioral construct; that can only be done empirically. If the theorist attempts a reductionistic coup by translating all his data language into the language of physiology, then he is thrown back by the fact that physiology lies no closer to "reality" but is itself only an organization of empirical correlations. The reductionistic psychologist might just as well have stayed where he started. Translation of the stimulus into its neurological correlate and the response into its neurological correlate has brought him no nearer to demonstrating that the stimulus really causes the response. After the translation the psychological theorist (who has now become a physiological theorist) may observe a correlation between this neural activity and that, but he is no closer to having shown that the one causes the other.

Mentalistic reference. In an earlier day it was more frequent for the psychologist to seek validation of his constructs by shifting to quite another level, that of "human experience." Again, this sort of validation of a theoretical construct is inadmissible. If human experience can be included in the data language, then so much the better, but it cannot be invoked to lend ancillary validity to a construct that is otherwise anchored to behavioral phenomena. Because its reference is outside the theory, introducing human experience does nothing to bind together the structure of the theory. Its surplus meaning must always remain surplus.

Response-inferred constructs. The other two categories of theoretical constructs that Spence lists, response-inferred and intervening, are the bread and butter of psychological theorizing. Response-inferred constructs are those that are linked by coordinating definitions to only one kind of empirical construct—some single response phenomenon. Now there is a hazard in relying upon a single semantic linkage. It means that, in one sense, the construct cannot be used to explain the phenomena with which it is linked because such an explanation would be circular. Theorists are rarely so naïve, however, and certainly they rarely work with such uninteresting constructs, and perhaps the theorist has in mind some more or less implicit secondary linkages that give further conceptual properties to his constructs. The theorist may simply not feel ready to incorporate them into the definition (the primary linkages) of the construct, preferring to leave them tentative. The onus of circularity that is often put on response-inferred constructs is really only justifiable in those cases in which the theoretical construct is used to explain exactly the same features of behavior from which its existence is inferred. To the extent that a variable is used across different situations or different subjects or different behavioral events, it acquires some practical sort of validity.

Intervening constructs. Constructs of the intervening-variable type are those that are embedded in a network involving several empirical constructs, and, in particular, they intervene between the stimulus and the response.[8] If they are given semantic and/or syntactical linkages to both the stimulus and the response, then they are said to be anchored on both the antecedent and the consequent side. Spence has tried to make a sharp distinction between the intervening-variable and the response-inferred types of construct, and he has made clear his preference for the intervening variety. However, I doubt that the distinction can be maintained as sharply as Spence would like. It frequently turns out that the stimulus is not empirically independent of the response; we sometimes do not know what the effec-

---

[8] The designation "intervening variable" was coined by Tolman (1936). Skinner has pointed out, however, that this designation is not a particularly good one unless what is meant is some sort of transempirical, that is, mentalistic or physicalistic, intervention between stimulus and response (Skinner, 1959, p. 320). Tolman probably had no such intention.

tive stimulus is until the response occurs. Consequently, an intervening-variable construct is often logically reducible to one of the response-inferred variety.

But the point of Spence's argument remains, and it is critically important: Our theoretical constructs must be tied by two or more semantic relationships (possibly via some further syntactical linkages) to two or more empirical constructs. The whole set of theoretical and empirical constructs may then be visualized as a sort of network. Sometimes it is called a nomological net. A theory in which there is a simple one-to-one correspondence between empirical and theoretical constructs is hardly better than a theory with none. Such a theory would consist merely of a restatement of empirical relationships that had been obtained, and it would contribute no economy, power, or possibility of further insight to a purely empirical description.

Radical empiricism. One way to adhere to the formal criteria of science is to exclude all theoretical constructs from consideration, that is, to use no terms that cannot be immediately reduced operationally to the physical-thing language. This means a dedication to finding lawfulness among empirical constructs. This approach may be called radical empiricism. The scientist who adheres to the program of radical empiricism gains some safety from it, since he never has to revise his theoretical constructs or his syntactical structure— because he does not have any. But there is relatively little else to recommend this approach.

Of course, those who speak loudest against theories may only be voicing their distaste for the animistic and neurophysiological kinds of constructs that so frequently occur in them.[9] Or the advocates of atheorism may be against the kind of causation that tends to be implied in some psychological theories. But one does not have to abandon theory altogether to overcome the limitations of animistic and neurological constructs. In fact, the formal and empirical struc-

---

[9] I am referring here particularly to Skinner's disavowal of theory (1950). He said that he would have theory excluded from a science of behavior if that word refers to "any explanation of an observed fact which appeals to events taking place somewhere else, at some other level of observation, described in different terms, and measured, if at all, in different dimensions" (p. 193). Skinner clarifies further the object of his dissatisfaction: theories incorporating real and conceptual mental and neural terms. "When we attribute behavior to a neural or mental event, real or conceptual, we are likely to forget that we still have the task of accounting for the neural or mental event. When we assert that an animal acts in a given way because it expects to receive food, then what began as the task of accounting for learned behavior becomes the task of accounting for expectancy. The problem is at least equally complex and probably more difficult. We are likely to close our eyes to it and to use the theory to give us answers in place of the answers we might find through further study" (p. 194).

ture of most of our theories of behavior may be quite easily divorced from the surplus meaning that is characteristically associated with them. It is certainly possible to have a theory of behavior involving terms with no surplus meaning, terms that do not commit the theorist to a particular variety of explanation or betray his personal belief in one.[10]

Radical empiricism is too big a price to pay. All that it buys can be purchased more cheaply by demanding that constructs be validated solely by being tied syntactically and semantically to the data language. This demand appears simple and straightforward, but it is contrary to the common practice of attempting to validate a construct or give it more status by transcending the data or by going to another level of discourse. What makes one construct "better" than another is not that it is more real but that it is tied in more different ways to empirical constructs, that it has what Koch (1941, p. 30) has called a plurality of observable symptoms.[11] It is not the theorist's inclusion of a neurological or mentalistic construct that is bad but his attempt to give a construct status within a theory by going outside the theory. He is subscribing to a belief in some transempirical validation. He believes that he has somehow really gotten hold of the causal agencies when he refers to a synapse or a S-R connection or a drive or a cell assembly or an expectancy. But at our present stage of understanding we can know no more than that our observations correlate. The fourth and final requirement we should make of a theory, then, is that its theoretical terms be validated solely by their empirical usefulness. We will give no weight to any sort of claimed transempirical validation.

Compromise character of a theory. We have come to a point where logical analysis fails us. We want to require of a theory that its terms

---

[10] Undeniably, there is a correlation between what variety of explanation a theorist favors and the sort of constructs he puts into his theory. But there is no necessary connection between the two. Thus animistic constructs tend to be teleological, but they are not necessarily so. Neurophysiological constructs may indicate the theorist's faith in physical causation, but they may have reference only to the empirical regularities in physiology. The response-inferred and intervening types of constructs tend more than the others to be of a purely empirical or mathematical nature, but they too may be based upon other varieties of explanation. Thus Hull generally believed that the constructs in his theory had physiological reality, and Tolman believed that behavior was intrinsically teleological. A response-inferred or intervening type of construct may be proposed by a theorist with an acausal view of nature, or by one who, for some other reason, prefers a purely empirical approach.

[11] The plurality of empirical symptoms is a measure of the *fruitfulness* of the construct, as opposed to the commonness of the symptoms, which is a measure of its *generality*. Another way to state the importance of a plurality of empirical symptoms is to say that a construct should be "overdetermined" by its empirical coordinations.

be anchored to empirical observations as definitively as possible, but at the same time we must recognize that these linkages are always tentative; theories are always in a process of formulation—or should be. The skill of a theorist is shown by his ability to alter the semantic structure of his theory as new evidence becomes available. And at the same time, the structure of the theory dictates to some extent what observations will be made and even how they will be made and recorded. So a theory must specify its constructs with some precision, but it must also allow for further conceptual reorganizations. We want to require of a theory that it provide some measure of economy over a raw description of certain phenomena, but it must not be too economical; it must provide for some syntactical complexity if it is to prove useful. We want to require that a theorist speak out as plainly and explicitly as possible, but we must recognize that the formal statement of a theory must always remain somewhat behind the insight of the theorist.

So our portrait of the useful theory begins to take shape. A good theory is a tentative compromise between economy and complexity, explanatory power and mere descriptive tautology, precision and richness. We require that a theory meet certain standards of formal adequacy: Its syntax, semantics, and data language must be set forth with some precision and explicitness. But we may wish to relax these formal standards if doing so can lead to further theoretical gains in the long run. We can expect an occasional departure from these standards, particularly with the more interesting and important theories.

2
HISTORICAL ORIGINS OF MOTIVATIONAL CONCEPTS

the hope of progress—moral and intellectual as
well as material—in the future is bound up
with the fortunes of science, and every obstacle
in the way of scientific discovery is a wrong
to humanity.

J. G. Frazer

The experimental psychologist today assumes with little question that systematic laws of behavior can be discovered. This deterministic outlook would seem to be established firmly enough that we would not have to examine it further. We might just acknowledge that we have arrived at this position and pass on quickly to other problems. But the idea of universal determinism is new and exciting, even today. We who regard behavior as determined by natural law occupy a unique position. The present chapter celebrates our arrival at this position and is a testimonial to some of those who have led us to it.

The gradually growing confidence in the power of some form of determinism to explain human behavior must be considered against the perennial background of the rationalistic doctrine. Our brief history will show that rationalism has provided a continuing challenge, first to the mechanist and then to the more empirically oriented scientist. We will see that naïve forms of the mechanistic philosophy have been advanced with fond hopes and great faith and that mechanism has been extended to encompass an ever-widening range of topics, only to be replaced in turn by a more subtle variety of determinism. We should be able to discover in the course of this history not only the origins of the general concept of motivation but also the beginnings of such specific concepts as instinct, drive, incentive, and reinforcement.

The rationalistic era

For Plato, as for most of the other Greek philosophers, what we would call the motivational determinants of behavior had little direct bearing on a man's behavior because they could always be overridden by his faculty of reason. As long as the intellect is free to decide upon a course of action, a man's ability to select goals makes his choice of goal the determinant of his subsequent course of action. The will is free because it is always directed toward the future; it is not constrained by the situation (except insofar as a man's reason is limited by his education). Plato did recognize "forced" movements, those produced by emotion or by the animal passions, but he considered them awkward, graceless, and lacking in purpose. He thought of them as essentially random or lawless in character and surely not like man's usual, natural activities.[1]

Plato's position is noted here, not only because of its enormous significance in the history of ideas but also because it provides an interesting example of a comprehensive philosophy of man that includes no motivational concepts. The reason for this omission is clear: No such concept was necessary because man was viewed as an active and rational agent; he was free to do what he wanted to do. Man's intellect and will were felt to provide a sufficient account of his actions. Such an attitude, of course, shuts the door to further possible investigation. Shut long ago, the door has been very difficult to open.

The evaluative elements of Greek rationalistic philosophy have also endured. They have dominated not only Western philosophical thought but, via Christian theology, have permeated our whole culture to a degree that is difficult to overestimate. Consider the following quotation:

> . . . man has sensuous desire, and rational desire or will. He is not absolutely determined in his desires and actions by sense impressions as is the brute, but possesses a faculty of self-determination, whereby he is able to act or not to act. . . . The will is determined by what intelligence conceives to be the good, by a rational purpose. This, however, is not compulsion; compulsion exists where a being is inevitably determined by an external

---

[1] Here I have followed Zeller (1883)—a particularly useful source because he seemed to be remarkably aware of the problems inherent in explaining behavior and of the Greeks' failure to cope with them. Another useful classic, for similar reasons, is Lange (1873).

cause. Man is free because he is rational, because he is not driven into action by an external cause without his consent, and because he can choose between the means of realizing the good or the purpose which his reason conceives.

This quotation sounds as though it could have been taken directly from Plato or perhaps Aristotle. It is, however, from a discussion of the philosophy of Thomas Aquinas, who wrote 1500 years later. Moreover, it is the position taken today by most Catholic writers on the question of psychological determinism.[2]

The first mechanists. From the earliest times there was a small group of thinkers who dissented from this position. Democritus, a contemporary of Plato, based his elaborate philosophical system upon the mechanistic principle that all substances, animate as well as inanimate, were reducible to atoms of different sizes and shapes. Events in both the physical world and the mental world occur because of the constant motion of the respective atoms. The atoms of the psyche are smooth and round, which enables them to interpenetrate other, coarser atoms; and it is because of this penetrating power of its atoms that the psyche can get in contact with and come to have knowledge about the physical world.

   This philosophy was all the more remarkable for its time because it was supplemented by a principle that has become known as ethical hedonism. There had always been agreement that pleasure and pain were related in some way to man's conduct and that pleasure sprang from the exercise of the animal passions, for example, eating, drinking, and sex. Rationalists, like Plato, had dealt with this persistent fact by asserting that such pleasures were ethically or morally inferior to those obtained through the exercise of the higher mental capacities. What Democritus argued was that all of the pleasures were equally good and that the rational and virtuous man is simply one who regulates his life so that in the end he would have obtained the greatest possible total of pleasure. The problem of the animal appetites in this view is not that they are intrinsically evil or less desirable than the intellectual pursuits, but rather that they entail

[2] The quotation is from Thilly and Wood (1957, pp. 232–233). This is another useful history of philosophy for our purposes because the writers pay particular attention to the problem of determinism. For the Catholic the question of free will is not just academic; it is an important theological matter. The Catholic's salvation depends upon his choosing good instead of evil. Confronted with this special problem, most Catholic psychologists hold the will to be free axiomatically (see, e.g., Harmon, 1951). For a further discussion of this problem and of the research done by Catholic psychologists to demonstrate the existence of the will and how to train it, see Misiak and Staudt (1954). The best discussions of theories of the will (like the theory that it is awareness of effort) is still James (1890). The clearest sympathetic treatment of Aquinas is Gilson (1956).

certain dangers. The wise man, therefore, will seek to satisfy his bodily needs and to attain physical pleasures only in moderation.[3]

Epicurus, following Democritus, proposed an improved atomistic system, but he held what appears to be an incongruous view of determinism. He argued that there was a chain of mechanical causation from the atoms of the soul to the atoms of the body. But he allowed for the atoms of the soul to "swerve" slightly through volition so that the subsequent chain of movements of the atoms would pursue the desired end. The causal chain of events could be altered by volition. This inconsistency was deliberately installed into the system in order to make moral responsibility more plausible.

Epicurus' solution to the problem of moral responsibility was symptomatic of the treatment the problem was to receive for the next 2000 years. During this long interval there was no real opposition to the doctrine that man is a free agent and, therefore, morally responsible for his acts.[4] For most of this period dissension was held in check by self-appointed keepers of revelation who crystallized what they called knowledge.

The intellectual revolution

The established orthodoxies were not shattered by any single blow. But gradually man began to enter a new age, an age of discovery. He discovered himself (the Renaissance) and the outer world (the Copernican revolution). Some of the participants in this great awakening were concerned with overthrowing Aristotle's philosophy, others with reforming the Church. Still others were dedicated to the new scientific methodology; Bacon, for example, attributed the success of the new science to the collection of data, while Galileo was concerned primarily with determining the empirical laws that would best provide a concise mathematical account of certain facts he hoped to explain.[5]

[3] Watson (1895) and Bailey (1928) give specialized accounts of this period.

[4] However, the glorious autonomy we appear to have gained through the rationalistic doctrine has been bought at a considerable price. We may hold man to be free, but we also hold him to be responsible. And, therefore, because he is free and responsible, he is liable to punishment. Someday we may be able to show that men consider themselves free *because* they are held responsible (Bolles, 1963a). Thus it may not be that the burden of responsibility attaches to the glory of freedom; rather, it may be that a sense of freedom is all that can be salvaged from the bondage of being held responsible!

[5] A great deal has been written on the scientific reawakening of the sixteenth and seventeenth centuries. Perhaps the best introduction is Crombie (1959). Crombie is especially interested in the divergent views about causation entertained at this time. Crombie, and most recent students of this period, have emphasized that the awakening was a gradual process that took many centuries and was marked by many setbacks.

With the decline in prestige of Aristotelian philosophy, other philosophers were inspired to propose bold new world views based upon the new physicalistic account of the heavens. Rather than despair because Copernicus had displaced man from the station he had assumed at the center of the universe, philosophers of that day, at least some of them, found a new optimism.

René Descartes. Descartes (1649) introduced a bold new dualism of mind and matter to replace the prevailing scholastic philosophy. He held that all physical phenomena could be adequately explained mechanically. The solar system, Descartes observed, could be likened to a great clockwork. Descartes contended that it was not necessary to suppose divine intervention in the solar machinery. Divine creation was assumed to be necessary to create and set the system in motion, but once in motion it could be assumed to proceed by its own purely physical laws.

According to his view, animals, lacking rational souls, were merely automata. Their behavior was held to be due to the physical forces acting upon them. Some forces were external, but other forces were internal, caused by agitations within the physical organism. For example, if an animal was without food, its physiology would be disturbed in such a way that it would eat; it was compelled to eat by its physical structure. Although Descartes' physiology has failed to survive, it was important for establishing a break with traditional scholastic doctrines and for its postulation of explanatory mechanisms where previous analysis had been in terms of Aristotelian capacities and functions. As Descartes saw it, organisms functioned largely through agitations entering the brain and being reflected (reflect = reflex) back out into the muscles (Fearing, 1930). In the case of animals, reflection was entirely automatic; what went in completely determined what came out. But in the case of man, reasoning intervened between input and output so that man was free to choose, to select, to determine his behavior according to his knowledge. Because man possessed a reasoning soul, his nature transcended the physical realm.

The popularity of Descartes' dualism derived from the fact that it retained rationality where it was important, that is, in man, but espoused determinism in the physical realm, where it was becoming increasingly hard to deny it. This dualism of mind and matter constitutes the starting point for any discussion of the mind-body problem; indeed, it may be said that Descartes created the problem.

Descartes presented his own solution to the mind-body problem in *The Passions of the Soul* (1649). He held that man's conduct was mediated through complex interactions of mind and body in which the body as much as the mind could be said to initiate action. The mind is subject to certain passions (literally, agitations), which might come to it either from its own reflections or from the body. Agitations from the body might come from the receptors or might depend upon bodily conditions like hunger and sexual appetite, or they might arise from other internal disturbances such as the emotions, for instance, joy and anger.

Descartes believed that the emotions were critically important because of the way they can change the flow of animal spirits, which, in turn, determine action. He was concerned with showing how six primary emotions in combination could give rise to the large number and gradation of feelings that are known introspectively. The modus operandi of the emotions was complex. The passions

> dispose the soul to desire those things which nature tells us are of use, and to persist in this desire, and also bring about that same agitation of spirits which customarily causes them to dispose the body to the movement which serves for the carrying into effect of these things. (Descartes, 1649, article 52)

The emotions appear from this to have four functions. They cause: (1) an appropriate flow of animal spirits in the body, (2) the body to be ready for certain goal objects, (3) the soul to desire the objects (which nature tells us are of use), (4) persistence of the desire for these objects.

Descartes' optimistic theorizing stands as the first real attempt to build a theory to correlate physiological, behavioral, and experiential events. He was quite explicit in stating that it was not sufficient to look merely to the mind itself in order to understand its activity; appropriate behavior must be accounted for as well as the underlying substrate of physiological events. Thus he broke with and went considerably beyond the old rationalism. His account was deterministic in spirit, although it still left considerable room for the free play of man's rationality. Although Descartes still retained teleological elements (e.g., he viewed the nature of man as organized in such a way as to serve his natural ends), he made some effort to rid his system of teleology, and he said (1677), "All the phenomena of nature may be explained by their means." On the other hand, Descartes assumed that it was God who had so built man and given him his rationality and his wondrously adapted biological nature.

Here Descartes had seized upon a new concept, one that was to have considerable impact, for in discussing man's God-given nature, which guides him to satisfy his appetites and which is organized in such a marvelous way as to make behavior adaptable, Descartes was talking about the seventeenth-century concept of instinct. Instinct was, at first, the source of the forces that impel man to satisfy his appetites. It should be noted that in this early usage instincts were not the impelling forces themselves but the source of such forces. It should also be noted that in this early usage there was no implication of a mechanical principle; quite the contrary, instinct (the word was used in the singular) was evidence of the hand of

God, of His divine plan. Instinct, being God given, was considered to be perfectly normal and natural. Instinct was thus the natural origin of the biologically important motives.

Although the word "instinct" was first used in this sense in English at the end of the sixteenth century (Shakespeare, *Henry IV*, 2), the concept had a much earlier origin. Aquinas had said,

> There are some things which act not from any choice, but, as they are moved and made to act by others; just as an arrow is directed to the target by the archer. Others act from some kind of choice, but not from free choice, such as irrational animals, for the sheep flies from the wolf by a kind of judgment whereby it considers it to be hurtful to itself; such a judgment is not a free one but implanted by nature.

Thus nature has given animals (and man, according to Descartes) a remarkable constitution that produces the right kind of behavior and the right kind of mental attitude and a readiness to do just those things that will promote their welfare.

Thomas Hobbes and materialism. The pinnacle of seventeenth-century scientist optimism was reached by Hobbes (1651) who sought to build upon the materialism of Democritus a philosophy of great breadth and subtlety that accepted little of traditional doctrines.[6] Hobbes was a resolute materialist for whom the explanation of all things was to be found in their physical motions. Hobbes supposed that there were two kinds of motion in the body. One kind, vital motion, was concerned with the circulation of the blood, breathing, nutrition, and other biological processes. The other kind of motion, animal or voluntary motion, manifested itself in locomotion, in speaking, and so on. Animal or voluntary motion was asserted to be "first fancied in our minds." But these contents of the mind, together with thinking and the other intellectual activities, were held to follow the same physical laws of motion as corporal bodies. The unique nature of mental activity was due entirely to its location in the head. The appetitive life and the life of the emotions and feelings were held to be merely motions in the head that are produced by motions in the heart.

Pleasure, in Hobbes' system, was due to a speeding up of the flow of blood, while pain was attributed to an impediment of the blood. The changing rate of these physiological processes was alleged to produce not only these emotional feelings but, more importantly, general bodily reactions that augmented or inhibited a tendency to action. An action was initiated, however, in Hobbes' psychology by an "endeavor." Endeavors were hypothesized to be small, incipient actions, or beginnings of actions. Whenever an endeavor was directed

[6] A useful discussion of Hobbes, particularly since it is written by a motivation psychologist, is Peters (1956).

toward an object known by experience to be pleasant, an appetite was aroused; and with an appetite the vital motion of the body is enhanced, the endeavor gains energy, the blood is speeded up, and the action must necessarily follow. On the other hand, if an endeavor was directed toward an object known by experience to be painful, then an aversion was aroused, the vital motions were impeded, and the blood congealed to prevent action directed toward the object. This crude physiological scheme is interesting because it is the forerunner of a number of similar schemes, and, like them, it proposes a singularly important role for pleasure and pain: They or their physiological correlates are the essential agents for motivating the organism or else for governing what it learns.

By endeavor Hobbes did not mean just a readiness or desire to act—it was not a mental event—he meant a small incipient motion. This remarkable concept of endeavor is clearly in the same spirit and is implemented with many of the same hypothetical properties that we attribute today to the anticipatory goal response, r_G. Hobbes' startling innovation appears to have had no precedent; it evidently arose out of what he considered to be the necessity to explain mechanistically what had always been one of the principal tenets of the rationalistic position, namely, that man can anticipate what he is about to do.

Hobbes was also the originator of a new kind of hedonism. He said that no matter how much we may deceive ourselves, all our actions are motivated by the desire for pleasure or the desire to avoid pain. In contrast to ethical hedonism, which is based upon the premise that man's tendency to pursue pleasure and avoid pain is ethically good, psychological hedonism, which was what Hobbes was proposing, strips the pleasure-pain principle of all ethical implications and makes it a principle of motivation. According to psychological hedonism, the pursuit of pleasure and the avoidance of pain are the only agencies that can move an organism to action. Thus whether the hedonistic nature of man is good or bad is inconsequential for the psychological hedonist; the ethical question is transcended by a law of nature: Men are hedonistic.

As a group, the proponents of psychological hedonism stand in opposition to the rationalistic tradition. Whereas the rationalist is willing to admit that men do indeed tend to pursue pleasure, he usually insists that man ought to exercise his higher mental capacities to overcome this tendency. A psychological hedonist, on the other hand, argues that the will cannot be free if man invariably chooses that course of action having the most pleasant or the least painful consequences.

Hobbes believed that the will was simply an idea that man has about himself. What are the facts of the will? Hobbes asked. We deliberate. We alternately think of fear and pride; we are alternately given to aversion and appetite; we alternately experience anticipated pleasure and pain. The last of these conditions to be present prior to action is presumably the strongest, and we think of it in retrospect as our own volition. Hobbes admitted that during the deliberation prior to an act many ideas (all governed by the laws of association, to be sure) may come to mind. Many of these ideas will have associated with them separate endeavors and the associated ideas of pain and pleasure.

Hobbes made many contributions to the history being described here. Descartes had offered a mechanistic explanation of the behavior of animals. The next logical step—a step Descartes had perhaps been afraid to take—was that man too could be viewed as a machine. That step was taken by Hobbes, awkwardly perhaps but bravely. By taking that step he became the first thoroughgoing opponent of rationalism and the first thoroughgoing determinist. Hobbes' psychology provided an impetus for the subsequent development of British associationism, and it contributed appreciably to the secularization of the study of man. One issue Hobbes raised that subsequent thinkers could not ignore was whether it was advisable, or even possible, to conceive of man purely as a biological-mechanical entity. Correlated with Hobbes' determinism was the concept that man's motives must be prior to his actions (this was the principle that led him to postulate a device such as endeavor). Hobbes was perhaps the first to see that the explanation of human behavior did not have to be teleological. The goal of an action influenced that act only through its anticipation and only through previous experience. He contended that man's actions were determined by his knowledge of how his ends were to be achieved and by his knowledge of the pleasure to be derived from his acts. Descartes had hinted that teleology could be rejected, but he could not do it himself. Hobbes could.

Associationism

Descartes and Hobbes had presented the case for a mechanistic philosophy in which the behavior of animals, and some of the behavior of man, could be understood in terms of mechanical principles alone. They thus shared in launching one of the critical movements against the traditional rationalistic view of man.

A second and perhaps even more devastating movement was associationism, which was based on the premise that there are psychological laws that, like Newton's law of gravity (see p. 45), need not commit one to materialism or to dualism or to any particular theological position but that describe what a man would think, what he could know, and what he might do. It should be emphasized that the mechanistic doctrine and the associationistic idea are logically independent, and although they do often occur together (for example, in Hobbes and later in Hartley and in Watson), it is possible to endorse one without endorsing the other.[7] One may, like Hume, be an associationist without being a mechanist; or one may be a mechanist without being an associationist, like La Mettrie, for example, who based his materialism entirely upon Descartes' prior speculations by simply omitting the theological dogma. Sometimes the separation is not clear. With Freud, for instance, we invariably find strong associationistic principles that are sometimes accompanied by a mechanical model but that stand alone at other times. The most important point is that the mechanist and the associationist share a common denial of free will and a common espousal of determinism.

John Locke. Although Hobbes might be said to be the father of British associationism, Locke (1690) is usually credited with being its founder. Like Hobbes, Locke was an opponent of the traditional rationalism, but he was not a materialist. On the assumption that the innate mind is a *tabula rasa* (cleared slate) and that all knowledge is attributable to experience, Locke sought to understand the contents of the adult mind in terms of the gradual building up of ideas from experience. He conceived the mind to be passive, capable only of receiving sensations and of remembering them as ideas. The mind, he contended, cannot create original ideas, nor are ideas given to it innately; it can only form simple ideas from sensations, and complex ideas from simple ones.

On the question of what moves man to action, Locke contended that the will is always determined by some pressing "uneasiness" that not only establishes the will but also initiates action. The will is strictly determined by the particular uneasiness that is most pressing. The uneasiness was said to be a desire, "an uneasiness of the mind for want of some absent good. . . . God has put into man the uneasiness of hunger and thirst, and other natural desires . . . to move and determine their wills for the preservation of themselves and the continuation of their species."[8] The emotions and the will, like pleasure and pain, were said to be merely ideas that arise from sensations in the body and present themselves to the mind. That a man knows his own will tells us only that he can have an idea of his action or his preference for a particular action, and nothing more.

For Locke the virtuous man was characterized by his ability to deliberate on the consequences of alternative actions so that he

[7] Even though a commitment to determinism does not necessarily commit one to physicalism, or preclude a belief in mentalism, many writers mistakenly see free-willist mentalism and deterministic physicalism as the only possible alternatives. For example, Krutch (1956), by rejecting determinism, finds nature full of teleology; and Farrer (1959), by rejecting determinism, finds God.

[8] This passage from Locke (1690, Book 2, ch. 21, No. 31, 34) makes it rather clear that he espoused the instinct concept.

might choose that which offered the greatest pleasure in the long run. The man without virtue lacks this ability to deliberate. Not having the advantage of a suitable education and not having established suitable habits, the virtueless man chooses a course of action that leads to the greatest immediate pleasure. For example, when the virtuous man deliberates on the pleasure of intoxication and the pain of the subsequent hangover, he abstains, whereas the man without virtue, imagining only the short-term pleasure, indulges. (Locke noted in this connection that if the hangover were to precede the intoxication, few men would drink.) Both the man with virtue and the man without it, however, follow the same general hedonistic principle of acting so as to maximize their expected pleasure; they differ only in what they expect.

After Locke, others offered alternative solutions to the problem of how to account for moral or ethical behavior in view of man's natural hedonistic tendencies. Psychological hedonism had become by this time a well-accepted psychological precept. Hutcheson (1728), for example, proposed that men have two basic motives, one egotistical, which seeks pleasure for themselves, and a second, altruistic, which seeks pleasure for others.

Hutcheson was also concerned with the instinct concept. He noted that we often have a propensity to act "without any prior conception of good, which is neither a desire nor a sensation, and which determines our actions before we can think of the consequences, indeed before we could have learned about the consequences." Recall that just 30 years before, Locke had retained the original theological flavor of instinct; it was a source of motivation that "God had put into man to determine his will." Hutcheson was changing the emphasis here so that instinct became the force itself rather than the natural origin of the motivating force. Hutcheson was also adding to the concept of instinct the idea that instinct produces action prior to any thought of the consequences of action. This too was a clear break with earlier tradition. Thus in Hutcheson we find the first really modern view of instinct as a force that impels to action without the idea of the object of the action. The other clause of Hutcheson's definition, which asserts that instincts occur prior to learning about the consequence of an action, was not new. In fact, this is about the only common strand linking the diverse early interpretations of instinct.

Hutcheson was not an intellectual descendant of Locke; quite the contrary. He invoked instinct at this point to attack British associationism, which was then beginning to gain some favor and according to which man does what he does because he knows and desires the consequences of his act. Hutcheson was primarily attacking Locke's *tabula rasa* doctrine. It was only the seriousness of Hutcheson's opposition to that doctrine that made plausible the introduction of a mechanistic instinct concept into a philosophy that was otherwise in the rationalistic tradition. The incongruous blind impulse type of instinct was evidently a sort of concession to some of the strength of Locke's position; it was a small price to pay to avoid confronting the main force of Locke's argument.

David Hume. Hume (1739) gave the concept of will a new and different treatment, first by recognizing that much of what man calls his will may really be just an impression of effort, and second by his famous treatment of the problem of causation, which was outlined in the previous chapter. Hume's determinism, like that of Locke, was mentalistic. That is, the determining conditions for man's actions were his ideas, his sensations, and his desires. He made no reference to an underlying physiological or materialistic causal substrate. Perhaps Hume's greatest contribution was to question the validity of traditional ways of explaining man's thoughts, feelings, and behavior. It is a man's experience, that is, his history of sensations, that governs his thoughts and his behavior, not some fixed unalterable "human nature." A man's experience not only limits his thoughts and behavior but even imposes limits upon the knowledge he may have of himself and the world he lives in. This was Hume's great message.

The mentalistic determinism of Locke and Hume might have given rise to a viable psychology of the mind or even a psychology of behavior, but it did not. It did, however, have considerable impact upon the philosophers of the Enlightenment. The importance of this early deterministic movement, therefore, lay not in the growth of a science of psychology, but rather in the development of sociological reform through the efforts of wise political leaders, and an aroused citizenry.[9]

The reactionary counterrevolution

There was a rationalistic reaction against these developments. The reaction was led in Scotland by Reid and was derived mainly from a moral conception of man designed to combat the materialistic view of Hobbes and the French philosophers. Reid also sought to salvage certain aspects of the associationism of Hobbes, Locke, and Hume that appealed to common sense. Reid sought to establish a new realism by making the final authority on all empirical matters the intuition of the ordinary man. The result of such analysis was a multiplication of the faculties and powers of the mind, each of which was held to be more or less discrete and incapable of analysis. Faculty psychology admitted faculties of the will, courage, nobility,

[9] See Bury's (1913) enthusiastic treatment of this subject. The best overall history of associationism is Warren (1921).

and so on—in short, all of the "noble" motives. The variety of faculties that arose appeared to be limited only by the philosopher's verbal agility.

The concept of instinct as an impulse to action prior to thought or to knowledge about its consequences played an important part in this commonsense or faculty psychology. And again we may note the incongruity of the notion of a blind force to action in Reid's otherwise rationalistic philosophy. To understand this it is important to note that here, as with Hutcheson, motivational concepts had a compromise character. The admission of instinct is the concession that tender-minded writers have made.[10] In comparison with the tough-minded principle of hedonism, instinct represents a somewhat smaller concession, somewhat less of a compromise, on the part of the tender-minded, since they usually admit that only some behavior is determined by instinct, whereas the tough-minded mechanist usually holds hedonism to be a universal principle. The tender-minded, by invoking instincts and making some concessions in the direction of determinism, may still retain in his philosophy some spirituality, some purposes, and some rationality.

Within the framework of faculty psychology man did what he did because he wanted to, except on those occasions when he was moved by instinctive forces. The will was free again, and man's motives were considered to be of concern not so much to the psychologist as to the moralist. Man's motives were viewed as reflecting his choice of action and hence were not subject to such questions as how they arose.[11]

The counterrevolution spread to France. French thinkers, who had a generation or two before been leaders in the original intellectual revolt and had espoused a variety of naturalistic ideologies, suddenly reverted to earlier orthodoxies. Early in the nineteenth century there appeared what Robertson (1930) has called a sentimental return to religion and to the thinking of a much earlier era.[12] The effects on French psychology in particular were disastrous. The

[10] James (1914) suggested that psychologists tended to be either tender-minded, or tough-minded. The tender-minded were supposed to be rationalistic, idealistic, optimistic, religious, free-willist. In contrast, the tough-minded were supposed to be empiricalistic, empiricistic, sensationistic, materialistic, pessimistic, irreligious, and fatalistic. It is too much to expect that these traits would always go together so that men could be divided neatly into two groups, but they go together well enough to make this a useful distinction.

[11] The principal works of the Scottish school were Reid (1785, 1788), Stewart (1792–1827), Brown (1820), and Hamilton (1858). The whole movement has been discussed by one of the last of their number, McCosh (1874); Warren (1921) is more objective.

[12] That there is a historical connection between the rationalistic position and religiousness (or at least piety) seems inescapable (see Bury, 1913).

French spiritualism that evolved led to a sort of pervasive, uncritical dogmatism that did little to advance psychology, and French psychology has not yet, 150 years later, managed to escape from a sort of complacent unsystematic attitude toward man.[13]

Experimental psychology. It is not certain that the explanation of behavior was proceeding any better in Germany, where the "new psychology" was being developed. At first sight, it might appear surprising that Boring's *History* (1950), which is so rich an account of the early experimental psychology, would contain almost no mention of how behavior was explained in this system. This is scarcely an oversight on Boring's part; it is an indication of the nature of that early science. Structuralism was a marriage of two deterministic traditions, one physiological and the other the mentalistic associationism of Locke and Hume. The marriage appears to have been one of convenience, however, for the structuralists never allowed it to be consummated. Man's action was always viewed entirely as a physiological problem; it could not be illuminated by any knowledge of how the mind functions. At the same time, the activity of the mind was assumed to depend upon and to be determined by its underlying neural substrate. But the laws of its activity were never to be found by recourse to physiological observables, much less to behavioral data; they were always to be revealed by an introspective analysis of the mind's own contents. Utter dedication to this schematic program precluded such questions as what motivates man's actions. The traditional explanatory devices, hedonism, free will, emotions, were treated just as the ideational contents of the mind were treated; that is, they were analyzed into more elemental sensations, and their relationships to action were wholly ignored.

Abnormal psychology. In his *History of Medical Psychology* Zilboorg (1941) has provided evidence of a parallel in abnormal psychology to this paradoxical attitude toward determinism in experimental psychology. In the medical world there was little doubt that behavior was physiologically determined and that physiological research could discover the determinants of all behavioral phenomena. Curiously, though, medical men were reluctant to apply the same sort of positivistic attitude to the problems of mental illness. Up until the eighteenth century insanity had been explained by means of demonic

---

[13] This indictment follows Baldwin (1913). The same situation also prevailed for a time in this country. Baldwin said "Early American psychology was written by theologians or educators or both in the same person" and thus laconically dismissed a large part of our history. He was right though; counting just some of the educators who were college presidents and also theological psychologists we have: Bascom at Wisconsin, Hill at Rochester, Hopkins at Williams, McCosh at Princeton, Porter at Yale, and Wilson at Cornell. This era, fortunately, ended about 1890 (see Fay, 1939).

possession. But when that was gradually abandoned during the Enlightenment, no alternative account of mental illness was proposed. The problem of insanity became, to a surprising degree, a purely legalistic matter. Medical men were, to be sure, in charge of mental institutions, and they promoted the use of various kinds of restraint and shock therapy, but they did little in an attempt to understand or explain the behavior of their patients. The law enters the picture because it is obliged to have some criterion for meting out the judgments it has to make; the law must cope with behavior—particularly abnormal behavior—and the working assumption that has stood unquestioned in the legal profession from the earliest times down to our own is that man is morally responsible for his actions.[14]

The new rationalism. The Enlightenment was over. And as it ended, a new rationalism emerged that was similar in some respects to the old Greek rationalism. Man's reason still had its sovereignty; it was still held to be unanalyzable. Man was still assumed to have an autonomous will. The faculty psychologists were, of course, in the forefront of the new rationalistic movement. One contribution of the later psychologists in this tradition was their popularization of the faculty of conation. By the turn of the century British writers such as Stout and Ward, and in this country, James, were emphasizing that man strives for his goals. James said, "Desire, wish, will, are states of mind which everyone knows, and which no definition can make plainer" (1890, II, p. 486).[15] Stout (1903) said behavior was to be explained in terms of either (1) "the motive for" our actions (i.e., the reasons we assign for choosing to do the things we do) or (2) "the motive of" our actions (i.e., the factors that influenced the deliberation or choice of action).

This revised rationalism has continued with some vitality to the present day. One spokesman, Peters (1958), has written "the most obvious and usual answer to the question 'Why' about human actions is to find the goal or end towards which an action is directed or the rule in accordance with which it is performed" (p. 149). In this view the goals and ends in question are to be found by asking a

---

[14] Zilboorg further observed that the freedom of the will was so incontestable that during the sixteenth-century witch hunts it led "to its most terrifying, although most preposterous, conclusion. Man, whatever he does, even if he succumbs to an illness which perverts his perceptions, imagination, and intellectual functions, does it of his own free will; he voluntarily bows to the wishes of the Evil One. The devil does not lure and trap man; man chooses to succumb to the devil and he must be held responsible for this free choice. He must be punished; he must be eliminated from the community. More than that, his soul, held in such sinful captivity by the corrupted, criminal will within the body, must be set free again; it *must* be delivered. The body must be burned" (Zilboorg, 1941, p. 156).

[15] This is not really fair to James. I will try to straighten accounts in discussing his theory of instinct in Chapter 4.

man why he performed the act. Whereas Peters recognizes that the man's stated reasons and the "real" reasons for his actions may not be the same, still, he insists, they do correspond most of the time. Men are assumed to be rational and to direct their behavior to their own ends. Peters insists that it is only when this purposive approach to the explanation of behavior fails that we seek to explain behavior deterministically (we will consider Peters' discussion of psychoanalysis on p. 64).

The new rationalists are eclectic. They are willing to accept the occurrence of an occasional unconscious act; they may recognize automatisms of behavior; they acknowledge the existence of reflexes and habitual behavior governed by external or internal stimuli; but they are not willing to accept any sort of universal law of behavioral determination. Man's behavior may be determined some of the time, or even most of the time, but a place must be left for the operation of man's higher moral and creative activities.[16]

The challenge of rationalism. It must be admitted that while rationalism is not likely to take us very far in the explanation of behavior, it does provide stimulation in one respect. The rationalist's conception of man's free and fluid mind and of the loose ties between man's mental activity and his behavior lead to a very pat and simple account of many kinds of complex behavior. The great challenge to the modern behaviorist is how can he design scientifically acceptable explanatory mechanisms that allow the human organism the same flexibility that the rationalist can allow him. How can the behaviorist build a model to explain the behavior of man, a model that is congruent with the phenomena that the rationalist is talking about when he speaks of purpose, thinking, and creativity? This is the challenge of rationalism that has only recently been squarely faced.

The advent of determinism

By the beginning of the nineteenth century the appeal and the practical utility of the deterministic assumption were becoming apparent.

[16] Evidently, the rationalist feels able to explain behavior without having to tie the behavior mechanistically, empirically, or in any other way to its determinants. The explanation of behavior simply does not involve behavior. A nice illustration of this is found in Moslem theology. The Moslem philosophers liked to concern themselves with the attributes of God, and frequent lists were drawn up of properties and powers that a god would have to have in order to fulfill his godly functions as revealed in the Koran. One popular list included the following attributes: life, knowledge, hearing and sight, will, and speech. The point is that speech was the only motor possibility allowed Allah. This did not mean that he was powerless to act except to speak to his prophets but that in the tenth and eleventh centuries no one conceived it necessary to have any rules translating knowledge and will into action.

It seems clear that educated men, at least, were ready to accept some forms of determinism, or some more sophisticated form of materialism. Witness the popularity of a number of naturalists and the remarkable acceptance of phrenology in France and England.[17] In classical mechanics, and in physiology, in the newly successful chemical sciences, and in the newly formulated economic philosophies men could see their success in applying deterministic principles.

Charles Darwin. At mid-nineteenth century there were apparently limits to how far determinism was supposed to extend, however, and Darwin's biological determinism exceeded accepted bounds. He contended (1859) that the variety of living forms that we see before us could be explained entirely in terms of random variation and natural selection. There was no need for teleology or divine intervention in evolution, nor for revelation as a source of knowledge about evolution. For the rationalistic philosophers, and for the clergy, such a position was deplorable; but for the scientist new realms of nature were now open for systematic investigation. This was Darwin's great contribution. The problem of creation was, at least in large measure, now solved, and the naturalistic approach that had yielded the solution now strongly suggested itself as the way to solve other age-old problems.

　　To appreciate fully Darwin's contribution it is necessary to contrast his ideas with the prevailing background of thought. Prior speculation about evolution tended to interpret phylogenetic development as evidence of a divine plan. The existence of the higher animals and man was taken to be evidence for a teleological principle of evolution. This view was consonant with the older idea of instinct as the guiding hand of nature that directs impulses. Early in the nineteenth century as distinguished a scientist as Magendie could define instincts as "propensities or inclinations or wants by which animals are constantly excited and forced to fulfill the intentions of nature."[18]

　　It had become clear by this time that a sharp line could not be drawn between intelligence, such as found in man, and instinct, such as found in animals. Lamarck (1809) had emphasized that the mark of instinctive behavior in animals was not its stereotypy (this was a late nineteenth-century contention that arose when the mechanistic philosophy had become more highly developed and widely applied), but rather its adaptiveness or apparent intelligence.

　　　[17] It is quite evident that uneducated men have always been far more willing to attribute their behavior to bumps on their skulls, wrinkles in their hands, their body chemistry, or the location of the planets, than to their own psychological experience.

　　　[18] Quoted from Drever, 1917 (p. 74). Magendie (1831) was by no means a conservative thinker; he was perhaps the first experimental biologist in the sense that he was the first to use live animal preparations —much to the horror of his peers. Biology before and biology after Darwin have been nicely contrasted by Eiseley (1958).

Theory of motivation

Lamarck proposed that this appearance of intelligence represented the gradual accumulation over many generations of the slight learning that was possible with a low level of intelligence. Adaptiveness, when it became habitual and was passed on to succeeding generations as part of the evolutionary heritage could, after a sufficient number of generations, take on the appearance of intelligent behavior. This was an optimistic theory; it carried the implication that man or beast could help his descendants through his own efforts, slight though they might be. Thus the life and effort of an animal have purpose. The species learns so that the individual may react instinctively.

Darwin's idea of evolution was characterized by quite a different spirit. He contended that instinct that looked like blind impulse was indeed just that. It was present because the animal that had it, out of a random variation of possible blind impulses, had been lucky enough to survive and procreate.

> . . . if it can be shown that instincts do vary ever so little, then I can see no difficulty in natural selection preserving and continually accumulating variations of instincts to any extent that may be profitable. It is thus, as I believe, that all the most complex and wonderful instincts have originated. (Darwin, 1859, p. 209)

It is unnecessary, Darwin tells us, to suppose that nature has purpose—the only criterion is whether a particular aspect of behavior promotes survival. If it does it will persist in evolution, and if it does not it will disappear. As wondrous as the variety of instinctive adaptations appears to be, we must recall that there are multitudes of different animal forms, that they are prolific, and that they have been evolving for an immense period of time. It is therefore perhaps not surprising that a variety of remarkable adaptations have survived.

Darwin went on to argue that if random variation and natural selection suffice to account for the diversity of the lower animal forms, the same principles are logically extendable to account for the evolution of the entire animal kingdom, including man. It is only necessary to suppose, Darwin asserted, that intelligence in lower animal forms has survival value. It then follows that evolution is likely to proceed along this line and that more and more intelligent members of the animal kingdom will evolve. Given the perpetual adaptive value of higher intelligence it is likely that animals as intelligent as man (or even more so) will eventually evolve.

Biological determinism. Darwin's theory of evolution involved four precepts, each of which was to have widespread implications for research and theory. First, there is a constant struggle for survival. Nature is a battlefield on which the species compete for space, food, and the necessities of life. This competition leads to a natural selection of some species and the elimination of others.[19] Those that survive the competition do so by possession of some specialized adaptation. This idea bears the crucial burden in Darwin's theory of accounting for selection. If it were not for natural selection, presumably all kinds of different forms would survive. But as it is, we find in nature's realm only those forms that are specialized in their own peculiar ways, while their forebears, generally speaking, have all been superseded.

A second but closely related aspect of Darwin's theory is that whenever a characteristic of an animal is found to be strikingly limited to only closely related species, or, contrarily, whenever it is strikingly general across species, we may suppose that it has played some crucial role in survival. If the characteristic had not been important in survival, it would not have become so specific or, as the case may be, so general. For example, Darwin makes it clear that the relatively general characteristic of birds to build nests facilitates their survival. But, at the same time, he points out that the idiosyncratic way birds of a given species build their particular nests is also adaptive for that species. Survival has become a criterion against which we may judge all behavior. How does any instinctive behavior aid the survival, maintenance, and adaptation of the organism? The great animal psychologists of the past century and the learning theorists of the past few generations have nearly all invoked this criterion of survival at one time or another, and certainly no theory of motivation or learning can afford to ignore it.

The third precept of Darwin's theory that demands our attention is his utter rejection of his predecessors' teleology. This aspect of his theory provided biology, and indeed, all the Western world, with a new outlook on nature. Darwin supposed that nature has neither purpose nor plan. The only mechanisms that are required to explain the diversification of animals is some random variation in original characteristics and then the continued operation of natural selection. Random variation and natural selection produce the entire realm of nature without cause or purpose, without insight or guidance, without foresight or hindsight. Whether this brand of biological determinism provides a sufficient account of the awe-inspiring spectacle of nature has been hotly debated, but we cannot pursue that subject here.[20]

[19] The full title of Darwin's *Origin* pretty well tells the story: *On the Origin of Species by Means of Natural Selection or the Preservation of Favoured Races in the Struggle for Life.*

[20] The effect of modern discoveries in genetics has not been to change the force of the argument but merely to speed up the process, to allow for more change in the same time, or the same change in less time. Because of genetics we have an explanation of variation without having to suppose, with Darwin, that it is "random." Darwin later made considerable concession to the Lamarckian proponents; this was particularly true of his treatment of instinctive and emotional behavior (Darwin, 1872), but even so there was no more purpose or teleology in evolution.

Theory of motivation

The fourth aspect of Darwin's theory follows if the first three are granted: Phylogeny is continuous. The point is simply that the Darwinian theory of evolution implies the continuity of man and beast. Biologists and psychologists, regardless of how they may feel about the metaphysical or moralistic problems involved, have found it most useful to accept the continuity assumption. Even though some psychologists (e.g., Allport, 1947) feel that their science would be better off if the gap were not bridged, the acceptance of continuity has proved to be one of the most crucial points in the history of human thought. It was a point that had to be passed in order for the explanation of behavior to pass from philosophy to science, from theology to naturalism, and from speculation to investigation.

Animal psychology. One group of writers, working from the assumption of phylogenetic continuity, sought to develop an animal psychology by looking for the mental faculties of man in animals. The advocates of this approach, writers such as Carus (1866) and Romanes (1882), expected to find the same kind of mental faculties in animals as in man, although developed to a lesser extent.[21] The fate of this enterprise was doomed by the weakness of the methodology that was used. Carus relied primarily upon allegories to demonstrate the gradual growth of consciousness in the animal mind, and Romanes relied perhaps too heavily on anecdotal evidence, although he himself was evidently a very competent observer.

More conducive to a successful inquiry was the experimental method developed by the great German physiologists and the animal psychologists at the end of the last century whose approach was, in effect, to downgrade man to the level of animals by seeking to explain all behavior mechanistically. These workers gave great impetus to the development of conceptions of reflex and instinct that could be applied equally to man and to animals.

The continuity assumption also opened up a number of purely quantitative problems. For example, if we assume that intelligence does not emerge suddenly with man but is present to some degree in lower animals, then it is natural to ask to what extent it is present in any given animal species. A great deal of experimental work has been addressed to just this problem, and for a while the issue of intelligence versus instinct became a favorite for both theorists and experimenters.[22]

[21] Keller (1937) has observed that Darwin closed the Cartesian gap; he gave animals back their minds—with interest.

[22] The instinct vs. intelligence debate, which really began long before the Darwinian revolution and continued on into the present century, might appear from here as a great waste of words. However, it was symptomatic of profound changes occurring in man's view of himself and his fellow creatures. And directly out of it came much of the animal research of the period, research with a genuinely comparative outlook.

Darwin initiated the modern era in instinct theory. It was he who proposed the first objective definition of instincts in terms of animal behavior; his predecessors had derived their concept of instinct from the subjective emotional experience of man.[23] He was also one of the first to come to grips with the question of how instincts arise. Darwin treated instincts as though they were merely complex reflexes, hoping thereby to be able to analyze them into units that were compatible with the assumed mechanisms of random variation and natural selection. Evolution must proceed in small steps. Therefore, the evolved instinct must be constituted of small parts. In his later writing (e.g., 1872) Darwin made bold attempts to analyze instinctive and emotional reactions into their basic elemental and inheritable units.

One important consequence of this molecular approach was that men began to think of behavior in man as well as in animals as dependent upon a number of specific stimulus-response reflexes. This interpretation of instinctive behavior as merely complex reflexes, and indeed the whole approach of analyzing behavior in terms of elemental units, provided a clear alternative to traditional modes of thought. Such an account of behavior, being free from intellectualistic bias, is inherently deterministic and antirationalistic. Darwin thus indirectly gave a tremendous boost to the mechanistic position.

By the turn of the century animal psychology had developed a very powerful explanatory concept, a concept that would in time totally change the content and even the definition of psychology: the reflex arc. We need not dwell upon the central position that this concept held in the behavioristic revolution. The success of that revolution is evidence enough that psychologists had finally addressed themselves to the question of behavior and how to explain it mechanistically. Before turning to these developments and the beginning of the experimental psychology of motivation it is necessary to note briefly a final crucial contribution by a philosopher.

Herbert Spencer and the new hedonism. Up to this point hedonism had always referred to the seeking of pleasure and the avoidance of pain. Spencer proposed a new and conceptually powerful form of hedonism that shifted the attempt to explain behavior hedonistically out of philosophy and into biology and psychology. For Spencer pain

---

Some of the best surveys of this research and of the theoretical positions that marked the age are Morgan (1894), Hobhouse (1901), Washburn (1908), Holmes (1911), and Warden et al. (1936). One outcome of this work, of course, has been the realization that the distinction between instinct and intelligence is not a useful one.

[23] This nice distinction between objective and subjective definitions of instinct is due to Drever (1917). He has written a valuable history of the subjective instinct concept. Wilm (1925) is a better history of the objective instinct concept.

and pleasure were critically important determinants of behavior, not because they are what we seek but because they control what we learn. Here was a materialistic and hedonistic determinism that would have delighted old Thomas Hobbes.

Spencer suggested that if Darwin's naturalistic conception of the survival of the fittest works so well for biological phenomena, it might be applicable to psychological and sociological phenomena as well. Hence Spencer argued that during the course of evolution a correlation must develop between those behaviors that yield pleasure and those behaviors that promote survival.

> If we substitute for the word Pleasure the equivalent phrase—a feeling which we seek to bring into consciousness and retain there, and if we substitute for the word Pain the equivalent phrase—a feeling which we seek to get out of consciousness and to keep out; we see at once that, if the states of consciousness which a creature endeavours to maintain are correlatives of injurious actions, and if the states of consciousness which it endeavours to expel are the correlatives of beneficial actions, it must quickly disappear through persistence in the injurious and avoidance of the beneficial. In other words, those races of beings only can have survived in which, on the average, agreeable or desired feelings went along with activities conducive to the maintenance of life [and in which disagreeable feelings went along with detrimental activities]. (Spencer, 1880, I, p. 280)

With the survival of species accounted for by means of the hedonistic principle, Spencer went on to account for the survival of the individual organism. An animal in an uncomfortable situation, Spencer supposed, goes through a series of random movements. The pleasurable ones are beneficial, and the painful ones are injurious; after many repetitions whenever by chance an organism happens to make a movement that leads to pleasure, there will be a concomitant increase in nervous activity involving those nerves that have just participated in the movement. Thus stimulated, the nerves are rendered "more permeable" than before. When these circumstances recur, those muscle movements that were followed by success are likely to be repeated so that what was initially an accidental motion will acquire considerable probability.

Physiological speculation, reminiscent of Hobbes', follows:

> For when on such subsequent occasion the visual impressions have produced nascent tendencies to the acts approximately fitted to [attain some end], and when through these there are nascently excited all the states, sensory and motor, which accompany [that end], it must happen that among the links in the connected excitation there will be excitations of those fibres and cells through which on the previous occasion, the diffused discharge brought about the actions that caused success. The tendency for the diffused discharge to follow these lines will ob-

viously be greater than before; and the probability of a success-fully modified action will therefore be greater than before. Every repetition of it will make still more permeable the new channels, and increase the probability of subsequent repetitions; until at length the nervous connections become organized. (Spen-cer, 1880, I, p. 545)

There are a number of respects in which this remarkable the-ory of Spencer's has proved to be important. First of all, it is built upon a new type of psychological hedonism: Man's actions are gov-erned by pleasure and pain, not because they serve as goals or as motives but because they have served as reinforcement in the past. Pleasure and pain explain action by accounting for what has been learned. All teleology is rejected. The "purpose" of action was not egotistical for Spencer; it is not pleasure qua pleasure that rules the behavioral domain but only survival. Only that behavior survives that has proved its survival value; the explanatory principle of survival of the fittest applies to responses as well as to species. The antecedent effects of pleasure and pain are real, and effective, but they are histori-cal rather than immediate or teleological.[24]

Spencer's explanation of behavior was in the deterministic tradition of Hobbes, but it added to the tradition some evolutionary considerations, the concept of habit, and some nineteenth-century physiology. Before we condemn Spencer's overzealous physiological speculation, we should ask what we have to replace it with today. If we substitute for Spencer's term "pleasure" the modern phrase "drive reduction" and if we substitute for his "lines of nervous communica-tion" the modern term "S-R association," we arrive at this position: Drive reduction strengthens S-R associations. This is not to say that Spencer's theory of learning was the same as Hull's; the point is that the assumed physiological mediation was not appreciably different.

Spencer's concept of nascent excitation is particularly interest-ing. It was clearly a revival of Hobbes' notion of endeavor, but it is also reminiscent of the modern concept of mediating response. Note, in this latter connection, that the nascently excited states were asserted to be both sensory and motor, just as mediating responses are supposed to have both sensory and motor properties. The flexible properties of these nascent excitations, or endeavors, or mediating responses, were particularly emphasized by Bain (1864). Bain, follow-ing the central lines of Spencer's theory, said that when pleasure occurs, a number of things become associated. The association includes not only a situation and the successful act but also the idea of the situation, the idea of the successful act, and the idea of the pleasurable consequences. Thus when any one of these components

[24] The hedonisms of Epicurus, Locke, and Spencer have been characterized by Troland (1928) as hedonisms of the future, present, and past.

occurs in the future, any of the others may be reinstated by virtue of the laws of association.

Bain's psychology retained a good deal of traditional rationalism: Man's actions were still largely governed by events occurring in the mind. The crucial acquisition in learning was the idea of the successful act. Thus Bain was in no real sense a behaviorist; that important step was taken by Thorndike and by others in the twentieth century.

Most of our motivational concepts have stemmed from the materialistic tradition, the tradition that includes Darwin and Spencer, and excludes Bain. Darwin had initiated the modern era of instinct theory, which, as we will see in Chapter 4, was the direct and immediate ancestor of our modern drive concept. Spencer, too, made a crucial contribution. We have just seen that he supplied us with most of the ingredients for a law of reinforcement and a behavioristic account of learning. Spencer had also suggested in his concept of nascent excitation all of the important ingredients for an incentive theory of motivation. Thus we find in the materialistic tradition the roots of the incentive theory and the reinforcement theory of our own era. The instinct concept had an earlier and more tender-minded origin. It seems that by as early as about 1880 we had fairly clear expositions of the motivational constructs that were eventually to dominate contemporary theories of motivation.

Empirical determinism

At the end of the century one essential element still had to be supplied before we could have theories of motivation. Theorists had to learn to view their constructs as constructs rather than as approximations to an underlying reality. The origins of this development may be traced to a small rebellion that took place within the scientific community toward the end of the nineteenth century. This rebellion was directed against mechanism and, more specifically, against the physicalistic bias that had played such a prominent role in the development of mechanistic ideas. What was wanted was a determinism that was not mechanistic in character, that is, an empirical determinism. This rebellion was not touched off by any one person, and it had no single leader. Rather, the idea has grown slowly and has gradually accumulated support and status until today, still growing, it is one of the leading contenders along with rationalism and materialism as an explanatory position.

Empirical determinism is primarily a protest against the assumption that there must be some material (or mental) basis for causation. It is opposed to the ancient precept underlying materialism that was formulated by the Greek philosophers—"action at a distance is impossible." An event cannot occur, it was said, unless there is some medium or material through which energy that makes the event occur can be transferred. The mover must "touch" the moved. The action-at-a-distance-is-impossible principle would seem to be so obvious that no one could question it.

Yet it turns out that it is just in physics, where the principle might seem, naïvely, to have the highest validity, that it was most hotly debated and most quickly abandoned. The battle raged over Newton's law of gravitation. Here was a case of action at a distance that had to be accepted because of its descriptive utility, even though the law of gravity required forces acting through empty space. Newton ended the *Principia* (1687) with the words, "I have not been able to discover the cause of these properties of gravity, and I make no hypotheses. . . . It is enough that gravity act according to the laws which we have found." Newton had constructed what we could call a mathematical model that accounted for a variety of observations, and he would make no hypotheses regarding the physical reality that underlay the observations. This attitude was not new with Newton; it had also been characteristic of Galileo. It is interesting to note that at its outset classical mechanics could dispense with a materialistic or mechanistic interpretation of nature and use a purely mathematical or empirical explanation of its findings.

Materialistic varieties of explanation were not abandoned so easily, however. Many physicists, and particularly philosophers writing about physics, insisted upon maintaining a mechanistic outlook. The late, great historian of science, Charles Singer, observed that

> The course of the new science, as a progression from the observation of a few phenomena to a world-outlook, was transmuted into a world-outlook imposed on those phenomena. . . . No sooner was the conception of inert bodies passively following the dictates of blind forces seen to be applicable to the motion of mass-points, than it was immediately generalized into a world-philosophy. Instead of being accepted as what it was [a model] it became a principle of universal . . . materialism . . .

Singer went on to note the irony in the misapplication of the empirical nature of science. The mathematical, empirical *method* of Galileo and Newton was what was revolutionary, not that they were studying physical systems. The mechanistic philosophy that was later superimposed on the method totally ignored the principal lesson to be learned from the scientific revolution.

> It is to this cause that we owe the great conflicts between science and religion, and science and humanistic feeling, that reached their culmination in the second half of the nineteenth century. Science was justified by its success, and it was incompatible with religion and with art; therefore religion and art were illusions or fancies. What was not realized was that the success of science was due to the faithfulness of its practice, while its destructiveness arose from the error of its philosophy. . . . (Singer, 1959, pp. 419–420)

For 200 years after Newton the mechanistic view of nature gradually gained currency, as we have seen, leaving behind the real contribution of the seventeenth century to the methodology of science. A crisis for the concept of material causation and for the mechanistic doctrine finally came when it was deemed necessary to postulate a medium through which light waves could travel in space. The "ether" was accepted as a necessary compromise, and it really was a compromise because the hypothesized ether was required to have properties quite unlike anything that had ever been observed.

By the turn of the century the physicist Mach (1900) could outline a philosophical basis for explanation in science in which virtually no part was played by traditional concepts of causation; explanation was simply an ordering of our sense data. Karl Pearson could observe: "Step by step men of science are coming to recognize that mechanism is not at the bottom of phenomena, but is only the conceptual shorthand by aid of which they can briefly describe and resume phenomena" (Pearson, 1911, viii).[25] Even before Planck and Einstein had destroyed the mechanical world view, we had begun to see that it was inadequate.

Reductionism. In spite of the lesson to be learned from the history of physics, psychologists seem reluctant to abandon the concept of material causation. This reluctance may be attributable to the plausibility of reductionism in psychology. The physicist has had to cope with the problem of matter in one way or another; he could not relegate the responsibility to another discipline. But the psychologist has been able to postpone facing the problem by arguing that the material underlying his studies is the subject matter of biology or physiology or neurology. The behaviorist, especially, has grown up with the belief that eventually he would be superfluous because of the promised success of the biological sciences in explaining at the material level any phenomenon that he might explain at the empirical level.

However, it is purely an article of faith for the psychologist to believe that the biologist can do any better with his substrate of phenomena than the physicist has done with his. The biologist, of course, faces the same problem: whether to reduce his science to the terms of organic chemistry, or to accept it for what it is, that is, sets of laws or principles for relating diverse biological phenomena. We may doubt if the biologist will prove to be in any position to provide the material substrate for the psychologist's requirements of material causation. However successful reductionism may eventually prove to be, it seems clear that the psychologist will continue to have a place in science as long as it proves to be more economical to explain

[25] It seems likely that Pearson worked so hard to develop tools of correlational analysis just because he believed correlation rather than causation should be the guiding principle in science.

psychological phenomena with psychological terms than to reduce them to biological ones.

Meteorology is in a similar situation: No meteorologist would deny that the subject matter of his science is directly reducible to classical, well-worked-out problems of hydrodynamics and thermodynamics. Yet scientists in the latter fields have little interest in the phenomena that the meteorologist has managed to explain in his more molar terms. With molarity goes economy. The specialized applications of science do not lead to reductionism but to the establishment of bridge sciences such as physical-chemistry, biochemistry, astrophysics, and physiological psychology. What has happened throughout science is not the breaking down of interdisciplinary boundaries through the success of reductionism, but rather the establishment of new sciences, bridge sciences, at the boundaries.

Despite the poor prospects for an effective reductionism, psychologists persist in the faith that whatever they can find at an experiential or behavioral level will have its correlate in the physiological and especially in the neurological substrate. No one seems to question that the nerves are the material cause of behavior. There is, of course, some justification for this belief in the high correlations obtainable between neural activity and behavior. But both the nerves and behavior have properties that have made it difficult to benefit very much so far from the observed correlations. Of course, such correlations provide the phenomena for another bridge science, physiological psychology, but they are not part of psychology qua psychology, that is, as the science of behavior. While it might be possible to sharpen a psychological definition of "response" so that it corresponded precisely with what a neurologist means by "response," it cannot be guaranteed that such a definition would have any use in a psychological theory of behavior.

Distinguishing sharply between psychological and physiological varieties of behaviorism, Tolman observed:

> Science demands, of course, in the end, the final development of both sorts of behaviorism. And the facts and laws of physiological behaviorism, when obtained, will presumably provide the explanation for the facts and laws of psychological behaviorism. But the psychological facts and laws are also to be gathered and established in their own right. A psychology cannot be explained by a physiology until one has a psychology to explain. (Tolman, 1936, p. 118)[26]

[26] See also Woodworth (1924) and Skinner (1938, especially ch. 12) on the question of why psychology does not need reductionism. Perhaps the most urbane rejection of reductionism is Kantor (1947). What it all comes down to is not whether the terms and laws of psychology can be reduced to those of physiology but whether they would be deduced from them.

But Tolman was too generous and perhaps too optimistic with respect to the future potentialities of reductionism. Singer was perhaps more realistic:

> science, true to its principle of limited attacks and limited objectives, has its own working rules of causality. It follows Galileo in agreeing to discuss only certain particular types of sequence and treating them as related, the relation being regarded as cause and effect. Thus the physicist will deal only with physical, the chemist only with chemical sequences, the biologist only with biological sequences. In the course of this process new relationships may be discerned or become more apparent, as for instance in the physical state of the heavenly bodies or the relative constitution of parents and offspring. Thus will arise new sciences—astro physics and genetics—which will limit their scope to the relations in their particular fields. (Singer, 1959, p. 258)

Psychological forces. When physics gave up the materialistic doctrine, it still retained the concept of force. But modern physics has given the term "force" a meaning somewhat different from its historical connotation and quite different from the layman's use of the term. Force is given a very elegant mathematical definition as the second derivative with respect to time of the displacement of a mass. Technically, this is all force means, whether we are speaking of gravitation, magnetism, kinetics, or whatever. But the separation of this mathematical abstraction from the older historical connotation of a causal agency has taken a long time and has required a great deal of discussion (Jammer, 1957).

In psychology the concept of force has sometimes been used as though it were nothing but an analogy from the modern physicist's use of the term, that is, as a term that describes changes in behavior. More often, however, force is given surplus meaning; it is used to imply some sort of internal agency or mechanical causation. Perhaps the same promise of an effective reductionism in psychology that maintains our faith in physical causes also leads us to perpetuate the idea that the motivating agents (motives, tensions, drives, etc.) goad or force or drive the organism into action.

A good example of such mechanistic thinking is provided by the etymology of the word "drive," which was introduced into American psychology by Woodworth in 1918.[27] Woodworth was primarily concerned with showing that a large part of behavior could be thought of as the product of the psychophysical machinery, machinery that revealed itself in innate and habitual dispositions to action. Like any other machine, Woodworth contended, it will not operate without fuel, without some source of motive power or force. Woodworth

---

[27] Young (1936) has published an interesting letter from Woodworth discussing how he came to use the word and how that usage caught on among animal psychologists.

sought a word to denote this psychological force and, disliking the mentalistic connotations of "impulse" and "desire," he suggested "drive," which he felt conveyed the proper mechanistic connotation, Subsequently, drives have always been assumed to have the ability to goad an organism into action. A drive makes itself known to the observer—it is asserted—through its power of raising the subject's activity level.

This conception of force was implicit in psychology, however, long before Woodworth helped popularize the word "drive" for it. The idea that behavior occurs when psychological forces exist stood pretty much unquestioned until 1949, when Hebb suggested that motivation might better be thought of as an organization of behavior or as a coordination of behavior in a particular direction, rather than in the mere production of behavior. Hebb pointed out that even at the neural level the "motivated" animal shows no more overall activity than the "unmotivated" animal; the most one might hope to observe would be a difference in the *pattern* of neural activity of the two animals.[28]

We have now traced the history of motivational concepts and the idea of motivation itself up to about 1900. We have seen the concepts that gave rise to the modern explanatory constructs of drive, incentive, and reinforcement. There was still one impediment, however, to the application of deterministic principles to the explanation of human behavior, namely, that no one except a very small minority believed it could be done. The rationalist still reigned supreme; he could argue that the reflex-arc concept and the encroaching deterministic attitude, particularly the mechanistic variety, had no bearing upon what went on in the human mind. The reality of the soul and the freedom of the will could not be changed by what the mechanist said.

The case for the rationalist ultimately rests on the argument that man's will must be free so that he can be held responsible for his

---

[28] The idea that motives supply the energy for behavior has been spoofed by Littman (1958) and Kelly (1958). Kelly says that in school counseling teachers often make the complaint that some pupils just are not motivated. "Often the teacher would insist that the child would do nothing—absolutely nothing—just sit! Then we would suggest that she try a nonmotivational approach and let him 'just sit.' We would ask her to observe how he went about 'just sitting.' Invariably the teacher would be able to report some extremely interesting goings on. An analysis of what the 'lazy' child did while he was being lazy often furnished her with her first glimpse into the child's world and provided her with her first solid grounds for communication with him. Some teachers found that their laziest pupils were those who could produce the most novel ideas; others that the term 'laziness' had been applied to activities that they had simply been unable to understand or appreciate" (pp. 46–47). Kelly observed further: "There is no doubt that the construct of motives is widely used, but it usually turns out to be a part of the language of complaint about the behavior of other people" (p. 46).

behavior. It is probably not just a historical accident that the evidence that provided the breakthrough, the insights from which Freud deduced his theory of motivation, came from neurotics, that is, people who are not held wholly responsible for their behavior. Freud's contribution is so great that we will consider it in some detail in the following chapter. But there is one aspect of Freud's contribution that needs to be brought out here in order to complete our historical outline: the shattering of man's faith in his own rationality. Freud contended that the rationality that is supposed to guide our actions is only a façade with which we keep ourselves from knowing what we are really doing and why we are doing it. He made it plausible to suppose that there are always real reasons for our actions, although they can sometimes only be known through psychoanalysis.

Parallel to the history of determinism is a history of man's loss of his own high regard for himself. Man's elevated self-regard has suffered three blows. The first was the cosmological blow administered by Copernicus. Man no longer occupied the center of the universe. But he still had an advantage over other animals; he surely had acquired a dominant position over them. "Not content with this supremacy, however, he began to place a gulf between his nature and theirs. He denied possession of reason to them, and to himself he attributed an immortal soul, and made claims to a divine descent."[29] Darwin, in doing away with this bit of arrogance, delivered the second, the biological, blow to man's elevated regard for himself. But man still retained his rationality and his high moral nature. Freud found, however, that the ego is not master in its own house and thereby delivered the third and most wounding, the psychological, blow to man's self-esteem. Man had to start conceiving of himself as a natural phenomenon.

Summary

Originally, behavior was explained by events going on in the mind of the man who behaved. This primitive philosophy was often applied not only to the behavior of man but, in the animistic tradition, to the behavior of inanimate objects as well. They, too, were considered to be motivated either by the will of gods and demons for particular purposes or by the possession of these faculties themselves. One ancient alternative was that everything was mechanical, including, according to some theorists, the mind of man itself. Everything followed physical laws. This was the great dichotomy, the great schism between mind and matter that Descartes made famous.

[29] Original authorship of the idea of three blows, or revolutions, has been attributed to several writers. Here I am paraphrasing Freud's own version (1917).

From our vantage point in history we can see that these classical alternatives are but two of a number of ways to explain observable events. For some a particular piece of behavior may still be explained in terms of the machinery that makes it occur. For others it is explained in the traditional manner when the mind of man or of some other thinking being has produced it. But the doctrine of empirical determinism maintains that a piece of behavior is explained when it can be related in a lawful manner to *any* other kind of observation. Behavior may be explained when its survival value has been determined, when the motivational or instinctive forces producing it have been specified, when its history of reinforcement has been discovered, or when its goal and purpose have been indicated. Empirical determinism is the only system that provides a broad enough frame of reference to explain the greatest puzzle: the mind of man and how it works.

3

DYNAMIC
PSYCHOLOGY

*no therapist or, indeed, anyone who has to
deal in a practical way with human
beings, can get along without some notion
of motivational force . . .*
Henry Murray

In the preceding chapter the growth of the deterministic attitude was described, and we saw how this attitude gradually became applied to the explanation of human behavior, replacing traditional rationalistic and mentalistic explanations. The following chapters will be concerned primarily with the study of animal behavior, in which the deterministic attitude has become strongly established, in which theories of behavior have been stated with considerable precision, and in which, consequently, we may hope to find some promising models for theories of human motivation. But in the present chapter we must consider another sort of theory that has arisen primarily from the very practical need to assess human motives. We will be concerned here with theories written by men who had to build their theoretical structures because of pressing commitments to provide usable tools for everyday human problems without waiting for fundamental *research* findings.

The theories that resulted from this practical need to deal with human affairs show some strain from the lack of a firm empirical base, but they can be readily recognized, nonetheless, as transitional between the traditional rationalistic approach to human behavior and modern behavior theory. We shall see first how Freud shattered the widespread complacent reliance upon traditional rationalism. The rationalist doctrine maintains that man acts in any particular instance because he has reasons for acting as he does, and although we may often be able to discover his reasons by asking him what they are or were, more often his reasons are forever lost in the privacy of his own mind—he alone may know why he acts as he does. This doctrine accepts that some behavior may be due to emotion (passion), or habit, or instinct, or reflex, but it insists that all of the important reasons for action are intellectual in nature, which makes them something apart from all of the mechanical causes just noted. It sets them apart by exempting them from natural law.

Freud also maintained that men act because they have reasons for their action, but there is a difference. Freud would not accept what a man gives as the reasons for his own actions; so the purely intellectual reasons, to which the rationalist is accustomed, are not allowed. In their place we find a new explanatory principle: The reasons for an action can be found by certain procedures of psychological analysis ("psychoanalysis," for short), which can disclose the pattern of forces and energies that led to the action. A man's private intellectual reasons are replaced by a theoretical array of forces and energies that constitute the real reasons for his actions. The potential advantage of this approach is that *all* behavior now becomes subject to psychological law. This was the sense in which Freud was a determinist. We will discover that psychoanalysis is inadequate as a formal theory of behavior because, while Freud elaborated a systematic account of the reasons for action, he paid little attention to how these reasons became transformed into behavior. The lawfulness in psychoanalysis pertains to the reasons for, or the motives of, behavior and not to behavior itself.

We will consider next Lewin's theory of motivation. Lewin also postulated that behavior is a result of forces and tensions, but the nature and origin of these dynamic factors are very different from what they are in psychoanalysis; and the time perspective is quite different for the two theories. Although Lewin, in contrast to Freud, devoted considerable attention to the relationships between the hypothetical dynamic causes of behavior and their behavioral consequences, he unfortunately neglected the equally important explanatory task of accounting for the forces and tensions themselves, so that, again, we do not have a strictly deterministic system nor one that is acceptable as a theory of behavior. Although we have to grant that Freud and Lewin both handed down to us a variety of conceptual tools to enrich our understanding of behavior, we also recognize that they each retained a little too much of the traditional rationalism.

Finally, we will consider briefly Murray's theory of motivation partly just to present a third variation on the dynamic-psychol theme, and partly to illustrate the versatility of the motivation cor Murray applied this concept, with considerable success, to the r of analyzing personality, which is surely the most intractabl in all of psychology.

These three theorists—Freud, Lewin, and Mur contrasting points of view; they were interested in kinds of behavior, and, of course, their total syst quite different. Our concern in this chapter is ' or even to survey their complete theoretic only at the motivational aspects of the theories, paying particular attention to the evolution of the concept of drive in the context of human motivation. In succeeding chapters we will see that there has been a parallel evolution of a similar drive concept in the context of animal motivation. In both cases we will find that motivation theorists have tried to maintain a sharp distinction between energy and structure. Freud, Lewin, and Murray have all argued that the explanation of psychological phenomena requires more than an account of the conditions under which an event occurs, more than merely a description of the observed relationships between events. Such structural accounts must be supplemented, it is argued, by the postulation of psychological forces that make the necessary conditions *produce* the observed event and *bring about* the observed relationships between events. Each theorist can cite some psychological phenomena that, he insists, cannot be explained in terms of structure alone; it is necessary to adopt some form of energy conception for these phenomena, and the logical extension of postulating an energy or force for all behavior follows. This is what makes a theory motivational. Let us begin by seeing how this energy versus structure distinction first came into psychology with Freud.

The origins of psychoanalysis

It has become customary in tracing the history of psychoanalysis to start with the development of hypnosis in the eighteenth and nineteenth centuries. This history usually runs up to Charcot and emphasizes his use of hypnosis in treating hysteria. The beginnings of psychoanalysis are then attributed to the impact of Charcot's work on Freud. Certainly, some of the phenomena and concepts of psychoanalysis—namely, the concept of the unconscious mind, the idea of getting at unconscious material through hypnosis, and the underlying importance of sex—are evident in Charcot's work. It is also certain that some of the data of psychoanalysis and some of its hypotheses about underlying processes were derived from the phenomena of hypnotism and neurotic hysteria. There was nothing motivational about Charcot's treatment of these phenomena, however. If they contributed to the origin of psychoanalysis, it was by providing it with structural content. Nor is either hypnosis or hysteria generally given a motivational interpretation except in the context of psychoanalysis. Freud must have derived his dynamic concepts from another source.

Although neither hypnosis nor hysteria might seem therefore to have a place in a history of motivation, they do quite properly belong to our narrative simply because they both were phenomena that demonstrated the inadequacy of traditional explanations of behavior. As Cofer and Appley have described the situation:

. . . when hypnotism and psychoneurosis came to be regarded as natural phenomena, involving neither magnetic, spiritual nor willful aspects, they yet remained phenomena requiring explanation. The great systems of philosophy, in general, and in their psychological principles, had almost always been constructed by and with a view to normal, rational men. Their principles, even the motivational ones . . . could not easily accommodate the phenomena of mental disorder and hypnotism. (Cofer & Appley, 1964, p. 51)

In short, toward the end of the last century it was no longer acceptable to deal with hypnosis or hysteria by means of any accustomed variety of explanation. The challenging problem for Freud was that these phenomena had to be explained naturalistically, and there were at that time no adequate conceptual tools for doing it. If he did not get a motivational model from Charcot, where did Freud's idea of motivation come from? The answer is to be found in his continuous commitment to determinism.

At first Freud adhered to the only kind of determinism then available, materialism, and only later did he become a psychological determinist, a variety of determinism he virtually had to construct himself. Freud trained as a medical student from 1876 to 1881 under Ernst Brücke, who was the arch-materialist of his day. Brücke was the man who had pledged with Du Bois-Reymond to fight vitalism by demonstrating that "no other forces than common physical chemical ones are active within the organism," and Brücke's students were trained in the same spirit.[1] This background was apparent as a strong physicalistic bias in Freud's early work. In 1895 Freud wrote a radically reductionistic psychology, his *Project for a Scientific Psychology*, in which physical and physiological bases for psychological phenomena were boldly hypothesized. Although he had no sooner committed these ideas to writing than he repudiated them (they were not published during his lifetime), it is interesting to note that many of his earliest explanatory principles survived his subsequent efforts to translate this early work into purely psychological terms. As this transition occurred, his determinism changed from being physicalistic to psychological, and as his system became no longer mechanical, it became motivational. Freud's biographer, Jones (1953), has given very little indication of how Freud's earlier physicalistic, materialistic, and reductionistic psychology became transformed into a psychological system. Jones said only that he became emancipated. Freud himself commented only that the mechanistic view is intellectually crippling (1925, p. 166).

If we seem to be laboring the point that Freud shifted from a physical to a psychological variety of determinism, it is because

---

[1] See Bernfeld (1944) and Jones (1953). Brücke's pledge is quoted from Boring (1950, p. 708).

the point is so crucial in understanding the origin of the idea of motivation. It is characteristic of all of our motivational concepts, whether they be drive, incentive, or reinforcement, that they are initially visualized in physical or physiological terms, and only later conceptualized in behavioral terms. What makes Freud's case so interesting is that while this transition has usually occurred only as one theorist superseded another, Freud made the transition himself. In the following section we shall look at the evolution of some of the basic motivational concepts of psychoanalysis. We will see how the evolution of these concepts reflected Freud's growing conception of psychological determinism.

Explanatory principles

The concept of equilibrium. Throughout the years when Freud developed his theory, certain concepts kept recurring. One such perennial concept is *equilibrium* (probably more literally translated as "constancy"). Equilibrium is the tendency of the nervous system to discharge any increase in excitation. In 1892 Freud and Breuer declared:

> The nervous system endeavours to keep constant something in its functional condition that may be described as the "sum of excitation." It seeks to establish this necessary precondition of health by dealing with every sensible increase of excitation along associative lines or by discharging it by an appropriate motor reaction. (Freud & Breuer, 1892, p. 30)

Freud elaborated the concept of equilibrium in the *Project for a Scientific Psychology*, where it was put into strict physicalistic and reductionistic form. The nerves were said to function to maintain a constant amount of energy; if they are stimulated, they will seek to discharge the input energy. At this point there was nothing very psychological in the equilibrium concept, but by 1900 the situation had changed. In *Interpretation of Dreams* Freud abandoned the earlier mechanistic orientation when he wrote that the work of the primitive psychic apparatus

> . . . is regulated by the effort to avoid accumulation of excitation, and as far as possible to maintain itself free from excitation. For this reason it was constructed after the plan of a reflex apparatus; motility, in the first place as the path to changes within the body, was the channel of discharge at its disposal . . . the accumulation of excitation . . . is felt as pain, and sets the apparatus in operation in order to bring about again a state of gratification, in which the diminution of excitation is perceived as pleasure. Such a current in the apparatus, issuing from pain and striving for pleasure, we call a wish. (Freud, 1900, p. 533)

Then, in 1915, he referred to the great complexity introduced into a reflexive conception of the nervous system by the instincts, that is, internal sources of stimulation. Although the task of the nervous system was still considered to be the mastery of stimulation, internal stimuli lend an aspect of purpose to how this is accomplished, since the individual must adapt its means to the end of abolishing stimulation.[2]

Thus over a period of 20 years Freud stated in somewhat different ways his belief in the concept of equilibrium, and the different statements indicate profound changes in orientation. Later, the maintenance of equilibrium served as a prototype for what was called the primary process. Before the child finds out how to cope with the problems of the real world, tension may be discharged through hallucinatory images in the absence of appropriate motor activity. A direct but unrealistic discharge of energy also occurs in adults in wish-fulfilling dreams.

We may note another aspect of Freud's theoretical treatment of the equilibrium concept. He always made the implicit assumption that stimuli were "bad," not just because the organism sought to maintain a condition of equilibrium but also because stimuli by their very nature in some way posed a threat to the continued health of the organism. He observed that, historically,

> . . . the concept of *stimuli* and the scheme of the reflex arc, according to which a stimulus applied *from the outside world* to living tissue (nervous substance) is discharged by action *towards the outer world*. The action answers the purpose of withdrawing the substance affected from the operation of the stimulus, removing it out of range of the stimulus. (Freud, 1915, p. 61)

Then early animal physiologists had indeed arrived at the concepts of stimulus and reflex arc on the basis of their observations that animals would react to avoid externally applied irritations; these withdrawal reactions (e.g., the flexion reflex in mammals) formed the experimental basis of their early work. In all of Freud's examples stimuli are assumed to have the same aversive nature. For example, he speaks of a strong light striking the eye and of certain stimuli that can be avoided, and even more explicitly he says that "external stimuli impose on the organism the single task of withdrawing itself from their action." It seems that Freud invoked the concept of instinctual drive as a stimulus to action in large measure because he had taken such a narrow definition of stimulus. Stimuli were ipso facto dangerous or threatening to the welfare of the organism. It is no wonder then that he discovered that the organism was dedicated

---

[2] These ideas were remarkably similar to those being developed quite independently by Tolman and other instinct theorists about 1920 (see Chapter 4).

to minimizing stimulation. This view of stimuli was not idiosyncratic of Freud. In fact, we must wait another whole generation to find writers proposing that some stimuli are "good" and to be sought.[3]

The concept of structure. Freud's *Project* emphasized another concept that was adopted from physics but given a characteristically Freudian twist. While it is possible to hold that neurons (or states of awareness) tend to discharge their excitation, it must also be recognized that discharge is only possible through specific preestablished channels. A neuron can only discharge its energy through other neurons with which it is connected. The tendency of excitation to be discharged according to some established pattern is recognizable as a prototype of what Freud later called the *secondary process;* that is, tension can only be reduced by finding an outlet through the constraints and inhibitions that the structure of the ego places upon its discharge. To extend the analogy, it may be supposed that such an outlet, once found to be useful in the discharge of excitation, would come to be used habitually. The individual might even develop a fixation on the particular means of relieving excitation.

Here we have come to the all-important distinction between energy and structure. In order to explain what the individual does the psychoanalyst must determine not only what energy or motive force lies behind the behavior but also what structure of the ego enables the motivating forces to be expressed in ways that are characteristic of a particular individual. We have also come to another characteristic of Freudian theory, namely, Freud's tendency to view any consequence of a man's psychological make-up as the result of conflict. Excitation is never just discharged; it is always met with some opposition—from the external world, from the structure of the ego, from the superego, from some contrary primitive instinct, or from some other conceptual barrier, so that what is manifest in behavior is never a direct consequence of the motivating energy but is always a resultant, a compromise, or a disguised consequence of the underlying excitation.

To explain behavior, then, it is necessary to look first for the motivating force, and then for a counterforce, before the details of the explanation can be filled in. At first, Freud viewed the balance of the effects of the equilibrium principle and the limitations of the neuronal circuitry as a type of conflict. Later, he emphasized the constant conflict between libidinal impulses and the structure of the ego. Neurotic symptoms, dreams, slips of the tongue, and other kinds of behavior that have no apparent motivation were regarded as the

---

[3] The realization that stimuli might be sought, that there could be a "stimulus hunger," first occurred to Fenichel (1934), Lashley (1938), and Lorenz (1937). This more or less independent formulation of the concept by at least three men provides an interesting example of simultaneous discovery.

effects of conflict. In cases in which there is no superficial motive or in which the motive is not known to the individual himself some motive must be postulated, and its apparent absence is explained by postulating countermotives that hide it from view.

Freud argued that the nature of these repressed motives was revealed clinically when the resistance of the patient was overcome. In neurotic patients these repressed motives invariably turned out to be sexual. Hence, according to Freud, a systematic picture of the neurotic may be formulated as follows: (1) a powerful sexual wish as the basic motivation that strives to flood the patient with stimulation but that is inhibited by (2) powerful counterforces originating from the demands of the real world; the result is (3) a loss from awareness of the initial sexual wish and (4) a disguised expression of the initial wish in the form of a neurotic symptom. We will see shortly how the counterforces were characterized and how they were assumed to develop. But first let us look at the nature of the assumed motivating forces.

Psychoanalytic theory of instinctual drives

Freud's most important paper on motivation was "Instincts and their vicissitudes," written in 1915. In it Freud distinguished between instincts and stimuli and asserted that the former were the principal (or at least the most interesting) motivators of behavior. Stimuli were regarded as necessarily (or by definition) external to the organism and necessarily to be avoided. Freud admitted to considerable difficulty in arriving at a choice of a word to describe the internal counterpart of stimulus before deciding on the German word *Trieb*. At the time the early translations of Freud's works were being made into English, *Trieb* was rendered as "instinct"; today "drive" would be more accurate. Literally, *Trieb* means a mechanical provocation to action. Probably the best semantic strategy is to speak of these psychoanalytic motivators as "instinctual drives."

By 1915 Freud had completely given up his early physiological model with its reductionistic philosophy and adopted a very broad outlook on drive and instinct, transcending even the relatively broad mentalistic viewpoint he had assumed in the *Interpretation of Dreams* (1900). According to his 1915 essay, an instinct or instinctual drive could be characterized by its impetus, its aim, its object, and its source.[4]

[4] It may be of some significance that some 40 years earlier Freud had been a student of Brentano. Barclay (1959) has suggested that Freud's theory of motivation owes a great deal to the influence of Brentano's teaching. Brentano's "act psychology" was built in large part upon the philosophy of Aquinas and Aristotle taught at that time by Catholic scholars. Evidence for Barclay's argument is suggested by the parallel

By the *impetus* of an instinct we understand its motor element, the amount of force or the measure of the demand upon energy which it represents. The characteristic of impulsion is common to all instincts, is in fact the very essence of them . . .

The *aim* of an instinct is in every instance satisfaction, which can only be obtained by abolishing the condition of stimulation in the source of the instinct. . . . this remains invariably the final goal of every instinct . . .[5]

The *object* of an instinct is that in or through which it can achieve its aim. It is the most variable thing about an instinct and is not originally connected with it, but becomes attached to it only in consequence of being peculiarly fitted to provide satisfaction. . . .

By the *source* of an instinct is meant that somatic process in an organ or part of the body from which there results a stimulus represented in mental life by an instinct. We do not know whether this process is regularly of a chemical nature or whether it may also correspond with the release of other, e.g., mechanical, forces. The study of the sources of instinct is outside the scope of psychology; although its source in the body is what gives the instinct its distinct and essential character, yet in mental life we know it merely by its aims. (Freud, 1915, pp. 65–66)

Instincts thus have some of the same properties as external sources of stimulation: They have the same aim (to be rid of stimulation) and a comparable impetus (motivational). The differences lie in the source and in the necessity of realizing a particular relationship with some particular external goal object. Flight is of no avail against the internal stimulation of an instinct. Hence, the instinct provides a steady and continuing source of stimulation, whereas external stimuli are reduced to momentary disturbances by reflex action.

The alteration of the instincts. Having stated that instinctual drives are the universal motivators in psychoanalytic theory, it is necessary to point out immediately that there are some qualifications that must be attached to the statement. The vicissitudes of the original instinct

---

between Freud's discussion of the impetus, aim, object, and source of an instinct and Aristotle's distinctions among the efficient, final, formal, and material causes of an event. Indeed, a better modern exemplar of Aristotle's fourfold approach to explanation can hardly be found. The point was also made by Merlan (1945). Boring (1950) seems intrigued by the possibility of Brentano's being one of Freud's intellectual fathers; however, Jones (1953), after noting that Freud took courses under Brentano, observes that so did everyone in Vienna! Jones does not entertain the possibility of any influence.

[5] But Freud sometimes (even in the 1915 paper) used "aim" to refer to the particular consummatory activity through which the stimulating condition is abolished, rather than the abolition itself.

may carry it so far from its initial manifestation that it becomes practically unrecognizable. The object of an instinct and its means of expression may become so changed that only a historical tie with the original remains. Freud devoted the last part of his *instincts* paper to a discussion of how instincts may change in their object and in their aim and how they may become reversed or inverted, repressed or sublimated.[6] The way that this sort of change is assumed to occur has been outlined by Rapaport:

> When an instinctual drive reaches threshold intensity and the drive object is absent, and therefore no consummatory action can take place, a change in threshold is assumed to occur. This change is conceptualized as a heightening of threshold by means of a superimposed cathetic barrier termed "anticathexis." When such anticathexes structuralize, we speak of them as defenses. . . . Anticathexis, like any other energy, manifests itself as a force. (Rapaport, 1960, p. 212)

For example, altruism may result from frustrated aggression. These defenses result in differentiation of the original motives into a variety of derivative motivations, that is, motivations with displaced objects and with diversified means of object attainment. The original instinctive force may become increasingly hampered as these defense structures continue to ramify and diversify. It may even be the case that the initial drive becomes devoid of its initial emotional potential; it may be said then to have become neutralized or sublimated. Sufficient energy may even get bound up in these anticathectic structures that they become semiautonomous, running on their own borrowed energy. These ego structures, whether they be activated by diverted instinctual energy or by their own bound energy, may be said to be determinants of behavior every bit as much as were the primal sexual instincts. To this extent, the behavior of the adult can be virtually independent of its original motivational source, that is, independent in all senses except the historical.

Perhaps the Freudian view of instinctual drives can be restated as follows: Instinctual drives are characterized by their energy or impulse to action. Men learn to attain certain objects, or goals, that make possible the discharge of this energy. This discharge makes the goals more valuable and reduces the original impulse to action. Psychoanalysis is a theory about the goals of behavior, what they are, and how they become goals.

[6] In 1920 Freud reorganized his view of the instincts and their incessant struggle. Roughly, he grouped the ego and id instincts together, calling them life instincts, and opposed them by the newly conceived death instinct. There has been a good deal of dissension among psychoanalysts about the value of this reorganization. The reorganization affected only the details, however, and not the general nature of what Freud considered to be an adequate explanation of human behavior.

Theory of motivation

Psychoanalytic explanations of behavior

Although the theory incorporates a vast explanatory network to deal with the establishment of motives and goals, psychoanalysis provides a dearth of explanatory hypotheses to account for how goals are attained. Freud's psychology deals with the wish and goal object and proclaims that we can understand the individual if we know these components of his mental life. But the motility component (the regulation of behavior) is only given in barest outline. Freud tells us *why* but not *how* a man does what he does. The actual behavior of the individual is viewed by the psychoanalyst principally as a means of inferring the underlying structure of the personality. But a complete account of behavior requires something more than this. It requires a complimentary theory of the ego, some explanation of how the ego goes about its business.[7]

Passivity of the ego. Allport, among others, has criticized psychoanalysis for the passive role it gives the ego. Allport has said that in psychoanalysis, egoism

> . . . is not ascribed to the ego, but to the urges arising from the id. For Freud the ego proper is a passive percipient, devoid of dynamic power, "a coherent organization of mental processes" that is aware of the warring forces of id, superego, and external environment. The ego, having no dynamic power, tries as well as it can to conciliate and to steer the warring forces, but when it fails, as it often does, it breaks out in anxiety. (Allport, 1943, pp. 455–456)[8]

There is a major fallacy, however, in Allport's analysis: There is only one limited sense in which the ego has been dethroned, namely, that it has no autonomy for establishing its own goals. The goals it serves are established at best through principles of expediency and compromise. Nor can the ego produce its own energy; ultimately its dynamic power is derived. In these matters the ego is legislated to by the other components of the personality. Nonetheless, the ego is, for good reason, called the executive of the personality. "The ego is said to be the executive of the personality because it controls the gateways to action, selects the features of the environment to which it will respond, and decides what instincts will be satisfied and in what manner" (Hall & Lindzey, 1957, p. 34).

[7] A number of psychoanalytic writers in the last 20 years have tended to give much more attention to the ego than Freud did, even in his later years (e.g., Hartmann, 1958). To the end, Freud provoked ego psychologists with statements like: The ego develops "as an *intermediary* between the id and the external world" (italics mine) (Freud, 1940, p. 15).

[8] Allport takes offense at psychoanalysis, not only because of its denial of the ego's autonomy but also because of its insistence upon historical explanations of men's motives (Allport, 1937) and its failure to recognize the uniqueness of the individual (Allport, 1937a).

How can Allport designate as passive any agency that controls, selects, and decides and that is essentially autonomous in performing these functions? The behaviorist sees a limitation of psychoanalytic theory opposite that which Allport sees: The ego is too active, too removed from explanatory mechanisms. and too free of lawful determination. The behaviorist suspects that a psychoanalytic explanation of behavior is considered complete when the psychoanalyst has discovered the motive and the goal of the behavior.

Defense mechanisms. According to some writers on psychoanalytic theory (e.g., Anna Freud, 1936), the nature of the ego is best revealed by analyzing the way in which it learns to cope with anxiety. The first confrontation with reality is the birth trauma; since the ego is essentially passive at this point, it has no means of coping with the flood of external stimulation with which it is suddenly faced. This initial overpowering excitation presents a model for all subsequent traumatic experience. To cope with the fear of too much stimulation, the ego may acquire further mechanisms of defense, further techniques for dealing with the threat of being overwhelmed.

In acquiring and using these defense mechanisms the ego is going beyond a passive role and taking a hand in the regulation of the total personality. Some of the mechanisms that Freud stressed were repression, projection, fixation, and regression. Each of these is a technique for coping with anxiety. Each of these modes of adjustment may, if used exclusively, lead to personality abnormalities. On the other hand, it is just the characteristic limited use of these mechanisms that provides the structure of the individual personality. It is important to note that the defense mechanisms are not motivational concepts per se. In every case the motivational components of behavior lie beneath the ego and dictate to it what it must do. Defense mechanisms are essentially structural conceptions—they are descriptive of how the ego handles its task of warding off anxiety.

Freud did not even regard anxiety itself as a motivational force, but he emphasized its role as a signal or a cue (1926). Little Hans was anxious about horses; he was frightened of them. Freud's interpretation of Little Hans' phobia was based on the assumption that the boy unconsciously feared his father for the threat of castration that the father represented. This fear of damage at the hands of his father was symbolized as a fear of being bitten by a horse. The function, therefore, served by the anxiety about horses was a cue, a signal to the ego to repair or strengthen the defense (in this case repression) against fear of the father. If Little Hans could keep away from horses, he could keep away from the to-be-repressed fear of the father and the oedipal reasons for the fear. Anxiety is thus a signal to the ego to get to work to avoid a potentially more dangerous situation; it is not in itself, according to Freud, a motive or a source of energy.

Specifying when the ego must act and what it must do is

about as far as Freud went in developing an ego psychology. Beyond this, psychoanalysis has very little to say about how the ego works and how it serves its executive role. We may note again that the psychoanalytic theory of motivation is essentially a *theory of the structure and historical development of motives.* A complete theory of motivation would encompass not only these aspects of the determination of behavior, it would also include an explanatory account of behavior itself, that is, how behavior is mediated. In this respect psychoanalysis represents very little gain over the traditional rationalistic explanation that men do what they want to do.

The scope of psychoanalysis. Another serious limitation to psychoanalytic theory is that it was never intended to apply to all behavior.[9] Although the unconscious libidinal strivings, particularly those associated with sex, are in one sense universal, it is a misinterpretation to suppose that Freud wanted to explain all behavior in the same way he explained neurotic symptoms. He formulated the concept of unconscious instinctual drives to make sense out of a relatively small class of clinical phenomena. The phenomena that were to be included were (1) certain pathological phenomena (like hysteria), (2) certain irrational ideas or behavior that are not necessarily pathological, (3) the origin of certain phenomena that are subjectively felt as being beyond voluntary control, and (4) "spontaneous" ideas and behavior that are not obvious responses to known stimuli.[10] These categories clearly do not encompass all behavior; they probably exclude the majority of the things people do.

Peters (1958, pp. 53–61) has made the same point quite insistently. Peters argues that outside his specialized field of interest Freud accepted traditional varieties of explanation:

> . . . there are a great number of cases . . . which have such an obvious and acceptable explanation in terms of conscious reasons that it seems absurd to look around for unconscious motives. This, I think, Freud would have been perfectly prepared to accept; for, though he held that much of the ego was unconscious, he thought that the ego-instincts, concerned with self-preservation, were more influenced by the reality principle and less subject to repression than the sex instincts. In such cases the conscious reasons are obviously sufficient to explain what a man does. (Peters, 1958, pp. 60–61)

[9] Psychoanalysis "has never dreamt of trying to explain 'everything,' and even the neuroses it has traced back not to sexuality alone but to the conflict between the sexual impulses and the ego" (Freud, 1922, p. 127).

[10] This analysis of the scope of psychoanalysis is taken from Rapaport (1960), which is one of the best analyses of the psychoanalytic theory of motivation.

Perhaps Peters is right in saying that psychoanalysis is only suitable for explaining the bizarre, the pathological, and the inexplicable and that it falls back upon other, mundane rationalistic principles for explaining the bulk of things that men do.

This is a serious indictment of Freudian psychology, and I should hasten to add that there are some outstanding respects in which psychoanalysis is far from impotent in dealing with normal behavior. Much behavior that appears to be motivated by ordinary, reasonable, and time-honored interests and attitudes can be explained developmentally or historically in terms of more basic, primitive, and unifying motives. For example, the ordinary virtue of tidiness can frequently be traced back (by a psychoanalyst) to an individual's adjustment to the stresses of his anal period.

Moreover, there seems to be no limit to the circumstances under which psychoanalytic principles can be invoked. Our appreciation of literature, our understanding of social structure, of family relationships, and of religion and art have all been enriched by the introduction of psychoanalytic concepts. It may be that in explaining the abnormal Freud had discovered new principles of explanation and that having become acquainted with these new principles we can no longer accept the old ones. One such feature of Freud's view of man is that it emphasizes underlying sources of motivation and denies the importance of superficial motives, particularly those that the individual cites in explanation of his own behavior. It is difficult to accept any longer as an explanation of a man's behavior that he had "no reason" for it or that he "just felt like it." Still another feature of psychoanalysis that cannot be dismissed in the explanation of everyday behavior is its emphasis upon the historical and developmental determinants of behavior. Characteristically, what is attributable to structural features of the individual's adult personality may often be understood in terms of the energetic features of his earlier personality. An adult motive, functionally autonomous though it may be, may often only be explained in terms of its motivational origins; and, in many cases, to ignore its origins may be to eliminate the only grounds on which a motive can be explained. We have to conclude that although Peters' point is well taken, he is wrong in dismissing psychoanalysis as a serious challenge to the rationalistic position. After Freud the student of behavior can no longer accept a rationalistic account for the explanation of any behavior.

Freud's paradox. There is still another aspect of psychoanalytic theory that deserves comment in relation to the traditional rationalistic account of behavior. We have emphasized that one of the enduring contributions of psychoanalysis was Freud's demonstration that man's sense of rationality and will power are essentially illusory. Now we are confronted by a paradox: While a central tenet of psychoanalysis had been a denial of man's rationality and will, at the same time these

same faculties have been retained and pressed into service as tools of
the ego. Put another way, behavior is explained deterministically, but,
at the same time, the ego is free to get along in any way it can in
meeting the demands placed upon it. Freud said repeatedly that the
ego learns, perceives, remembers, imagines, thinks, and so on. In
short, the ego seems to have all of the powers that a nineteenth-
century faculty psychologist might suppose it to have. And yet it
would also be fair to conclude that people do the things they do
because of powerful unconscious sexual motives; and even though
these be disguised during the course of individual development, their
motive power can be discerned by the use of appropriate analytic
techniques.

A resolution of the paradox can be based upon the fact that
Freud felt that his own contribution to human thought was primarily
a humanitarian one.[11] The classical picture of man as a rational being
had attributed all mental functioning to a conscious ego (or mind
or soul) and had set the conscious ego apart from unconscious instinctive activities such as eating and sexual behavior. Freud complicated this dichotomous scheme by inserting a third level. There were
instincts to be sure, and also a conscious part of the ego, but there was
a third part of the mind, which obeyed determinate laws of mental
organization as though it was conscious but which was, in fact, not
conscious. This third element of the mind represented a limitation
upon the sovereignty of rationality and the will, even though it functioned like the volitional and rational part of the mind. All of us to
some extent, but especially the neurotic, suffer a grim tyranny of the
mind that prevents us from being wholly rational or completely in
command of our actions. Freud viewed psychoanalysis as a technique
for minimizing the power of this third realm, for liberating man, for
restoring him to the dichotomous condition depicted by the
traditionalist.

Formal adequacy as a theory of behavior

Our final concern with psychoanalysis is not with its status as a new
political, social, or humane philosophy, but rather with its status as a
formal theory of behavior. As an explanatory model it is much in need
of a firmer empirical foundation and more explicit rules for the use of
its theoretical constructs. That is, we need to know how to relate the

[11] See, for instance, Zweig (1932) and Zilboorg (1951). Zilboorg
said "One always feels an undertone of pessimism, or a cold rejection of
fate, circumstances, society, whenever one reads Freud very carefully.
Freud set very little store in possible changes of mankind in general, in
man's social structures, or in any other set of environmental forces . . .
they always seemed to him to interfere with the inner freedom of man"
(p. 25). According to Zilboorg, Freud conceived of mental health as a
"new, special kind of strength and freedom."

theoretical terms both to each other (the syntactical problem) and to observable events (the semantic problem). Psychoanalysts have concerned themselves primarily with inferring central events or structures of a nondirectly observable character from certain manifestations of overt behavior, but they have not told us the rules for such inferences. The trouble here, of course, is that the analyst is not very interested in explaining behavior itself or in constructing a theory that would permit him to do so. The traditional belief seems to prevail that it is sufficient to explain an individual's motives or reasons for acting; this done, the behavior follows as a matter of course. Therefore, dream analysis, associative recall, catharsis, and all of the other behavior-eliciting techniques of the analyst are considered to be merely means for getting at the all-important motivational factors of the individual. As Janis (1959) and others have pointed out, it is possible for the psychoanalytic interview to be a useful research tool, and some steps in realizing this promise have already been taken, but there is a great deal of work yet to be done to establish an unambiguous set of principles and hypotheses.

Historically, the behavioral observations upon which psychoanalysis was built did not come from the laboratory or even from systematic work in a clinical setting, but rather from case histories, from Freud's own self-analysis, and partly also from the fields of art and literature. Freud attached little importance to external verification of the events his patients described; it was much more important that his patient's reports held together in a pattern that was consistent with psychoanalytic principles than that they be empirically verifiable. When the analyst comes to the conclusion, for example, that a patient's symptoms, associations, and emotional characteristics can be best interpreted in terms of an unresolved oedipal problem, he is quite concerned that all of the patient's current behavior is consistent with this interpretation, but he is relatively unconcerned with whether the individual has, in fact, always loved his mother and feared his father. In part, this bias reflects the demand, mentioned in the introduction to this chapter, put upon the analyst to adjust the patient's current behavior to his current situation.

On the other hand, it seems unlikely that psychoanalysis is wholly without empirical content. Freud and others have assured us that during a series of psychoanalytic interviews the structure of the patient's mental world becomes clear. And the analyst assures us that during this process he is discovering the determinants of the patient's behavior in an empirical manner. Freud insisted that his conclusions were in many cases "forced" upon him by his clinical findings, often in contradiction to his prior conceptions. Unfortunately, Freud has not told us how to arrive at an empirically compelling confirmation of the theory. It is commonly said that verification of the hypotheses of psychoanalysis requires considerable clinical sophistication and experience. If this is true, it indicates the seriousness of the inherent semantic difficulties of the theory.

The theory also presents certain problems of syntax. There is rarely an unequivocal way of fitting the theoretical terms of the theory together to constitute an explanation of behavior. More often, there is a diversity of possible interpretations of a given phenomenon; and the rules of syntax are not clear enough to permit us to say which of the alternative interpretations is preferable, much less to permit us to test between them. Discrepant and even contradictory interpretations are often possible. More often than not, psychoanalytic theory "under-determines" the phenomena it is expressly designed to explain. Thus although psychoanalysis provides a deterministic account of behavior and lends itself to an ad hoc account of any behavioral happening, where in Freud's writing can we find a prediction of behavior?

The value of psychoanalysis lies in its challenge to the traditional rationalistic interpretations of behavior. For centuries we had come to accept the proposition that a man does what he wants to do because he wants to do it. Psychoanalysis impressed upon us that men frequently act for reasons that are quite different from those they articulate. But a psychoanalytic explanation of behavior still adheres to the principle that a man does what he is motivated to do, and it is addressed not so much to explaining behavior as to explaining the motives that are assumed to underlie behavior. The syntactical rules of psychoanalysis rarely, if ever, include overt behavior in their terms. They tell us what a man wants to do and why he wants to do it but never how he does it. This limitation of psychoanalytic theory is, of course, not unique among the theoretical accounts of human behavior. Indeed, it seems to be symptomatic, and perhaps it is too easy to criticize Freud for attempting to explain no more than why a man has the motives that he has.

Pratt has aptly summarized for us the essence of Freud's contribution:

> Freud will be remembered long after the names of most scientific psychologists have been forgotten. . . . [He was] a brilliant artist whose glamorous perceptions and piercing intuitions have held the modern intellectual world enthralled. The tremendous sweep of his imagination has enabled him to see connections where narrower minds see nothing. Whether the connections are *really* there or not, no one knows, not even Freud himself; or if he does, he has committed an unpardonable scientific sin by not revealing to the rest of the world the secret of his knowledge. Many generations of psychologists will spend their lives trying to translate the poetry of Freud into the prose of science. (Pratt, 1939, p. 164)

Energy versus structure

In German psychology at the turn of the century the dominant viewpoint was Wundt's structuralism, which was based on the premise that psychology could solve all its problems through an investigation of the mind. It was supposed that the functioning of the mind would be revealed by an analysis of its contents. Of course, the easiest elements of awareness to investigate were sensations, and accordingly the bulk of the structuralists' research involved sensations. But emotions, feelings, acts of will, and automatic impulses to action were all supposed to yield to the same introspective mode of analysis. The basic belief was that to understand the mind (which implied an understanding of the whole individual) it is necessary only to know what is associated with what in the mind.

The discoveries at Würzburg. This purely structural approach was extended to the problem of the higher mental processes (thinking) by a dedicated group of psychologists at Würzburg under the leadership of Külpe. But although these investigations were initiated in complete faith in structuralism, they soon led to the demise of the structuralistic position.

In the first place, it was found that thinking could occur without any mental content at all; that is, so-called imageless thoughts were discovered. Later, these contentless elements or processes were held to be the fundamental elements of thinking.[12] Secondly, and more importantly, the Würzburgers found that they had to introduce other, new, and nonassociative explanatory terms. For example, they began to concern themselves with the effects of instructions (Aufgabe) in producing a set (Einstellung). The Würzburg psychologists began to consider the selectivity of attention and the importance of experimentally induced sets in the selection of associations. Of course, instructions might be viewed as stimuli, as particular stimuli that are presented prior to the stimulus that actually elicits the response.[13] The Würzburgers did not handle the problem this way, however; instead they contended that an Einstellung was a new kind of mental process.

According to Ach (1905) and Watt (1905), a subject could have a "determining tendency," which could operate upon the associative structure of the mind by selecting among available associations. Watt contended, therefore, that the selective principle, the

[12] This was the view of Messer (1906). The best account of the Würzburg school in general is Humphrey (1951). Boring (1950) gives a shorter survey of Würzburg but relates it better to the stream of history. Thus he cites not only the Würzburgers but also the men in the tradition of Leibnitz and Herbart as the creators of the dynamic principle. I mention the former and slight the latter. Earlier in the chapter I ignored (also in defiance of Boring's example) the psychopathologists prior to Freud on the grounds that they had little or no influence upon him, at least as far as his motivational concepts were concerned.

[13] A stimulus interpretation of set and other attitudinal concepts is possible (Graham, 1950). The best overall review of the tortured concepts of set is Gibson (1941).

determining tendency, must have a different nature from the processes that it governed. Because focusing attention and maintaining a set were largely under voluntary control, a function of the will, this additional principle was held to be a "dynamic" factor in mental processes. This dynamic factor was viewed as something distinct from the purely structural features of the mind. Humphrey has observed that for Watt,

> . . . this is a dichotomy separating the mechanical from the non-mechanical factors in thinking. . . . Watt assumes as a groundwork the conventional associational theory that if experience A has occurred together with experience B, then if either A or B occurs later, there is a tendency for the other to recur. This theory Watt has overlaid with the stipulation that before this tendency can be realized, there must be a task present, which will itself contribute energy that may reinforce or inhibit any particular association. (Humphrey, 1951, pp. 98–99)

Humphrey further notes that the assumption by the Würzburgers of a dynamic factor, an energizing force, which activates the associative content and causes an event in our mental experience to occur, is the root idea behind the modern theory of drive or motive. The implication is that the material of past experience, the associative structure of the mind, is simply the material to be *used by* the energizing task and does not itself have any power to cause a mental event.

In spite of some differences of opinion regarding the interpretation of the Würzburg findings, psychologists of that time generally concluded that a purely structuralistic psychology would not suffice because (1) certain mental processes (e.g., thinking) could occur in the absence of any associative content and (2) such a system failed to provide the energy needed to make the mental processes operate.

It should be emphasized that structuralism was not rejected on empirical grounds, or at least not on these empirical grounds. Actually, the dynamic principle upon which the psychologists at Würzburg (and later those at Berlin) insisted is necessary only to the extent that one insists upon having it. There are no compelling logical or empirical reasons for rejecting a psychological theory just because it lacks a dynamic principle. We will see in the present chapter and in succeeding ones that the theorist assumes the concept of energy as necessary to complement the concept of structure. It never emerges from a survey of the facts, and it never emerges from the theoretical structure; it is always lurking in the background as a basic presupposition.

Lewin's theory of motivation

No one made more of the energy versus structure distinction than did Kurt Lewin. He began by extending and giving a broader interpretation to the work of Ach and Watt. Whereas the Würzburg investigators had argued that determining tendencies (produced by appropriate instructions) could either facilitate or interfere with associative tendencies, Lewin (1917, 1922) contended that the conflict was not between associative and determining tendencies, but rather between different determining tendencies. He also maintained that all mental processes, even those that appeared to be entirely under associative control, are in fact caused by some tension or psychic energy. In the laboratory the subject is always following some task, either one set for him or else one he sets himself. And in the course of everyday life, again, the individual's behavior is always governed by some intention to do one thing or another. In other words, all behavior is motivated. Lewin always adhered to this basic postulate.

A second postulate to which Lewin held consistently was that if psychology hopes to find causal laws to explain its phenomena, these laws must be based upon psychological "realities" and not just fictions. He contrasted realities with what he called achievement concepts (1926a). Achievement concepts, when applied to behavior, are definitions of behavior in terms of its consequences. Lewin cited as an example the case of learning to type, in which, he says, the beginner and the expert are engaged in psychologically different activities. The beginning typist is really hunting for letters, whereas the expert typist is really punching out words. It is only when we have determined what the psychologically real processes are that we can hope to explain them adequately. When we miss the real phenomena, we are concerning ourselves with mere semblances of the underlying processes. In some cases such semblances might be valid indications of their underlying causes, but we can never assume that they are, so we should not build our theories upon them.[14]

A third important postulate, or axiomatic assumption, in Lewin's work was that conventional associationism was inadequate to the task of explaining man's behavior. He distinguished between "controlled" and "intentional" actions. Controlled actions, being those controlled by direct associative connections, may depend upon simple linkages between the occasion for an action and the action itself; but intentional or voluntary or willed behavior follows "field" principles. In a willed action the organism brings his whole psychological being into the production of his behavior. It is not sufficient to look for simple associative links or direct forces; we must look for more global factors (i.e., field factors). This position, long a part of the rationalistic doctrine, did not mean to Lewin that voluntary behavior

---

[14] See also Lewin (1927) for his further views on explanation. This point in Lewin illustrates one of those "polarized" issues about which it is difficult to be indifferent; one reacts with either "what a good way to put it" or else "what a lot of nonsense." The issue basically is whether science should properly be concerned with realities or with conventionalisms, that is, constructs. If we are to deal with realities, then *whose* should we accept?

was not lawful. Quite the contrary, as we will see, he attempted to furnish a much needed syntactical structure to fill the void the rationalists had left between man's mind and his behavior.

There is a fourth characteristic feature of Lewin's motivation theory that should be mentioned before we proceed to consider his theoretical constructs in any detail. He believed there was little doubt about the basic facts of motivation and little question about how they should be explained. He never claimed to have a "theory"; an explanatory theory was really not necessary. Lewin was concerned with representing and clarifying the understanding of behavior that was already in the public domain. He said that "the main objective of [his 1938 book] is to bring into the open some of the basic concepts and assumptions which objectively are presupposed in practically all psychological research in this field" (1938, p. 18). Lewin's attempts to find a satisfactory representation consumed a large part of his theoretical efforts, and he was evidently never thoroughly satisfied with any of his representational schemes. The logical structure of the theory and particularly the conceptual properties of its constructs are what concern us here, however, and it is quite possible to deal with these features of the theory without becoming involved with the arrows, Easter eggs, and gerrymanders to which Lewin himself was so devoted.[15]

Lewin's motivational constructs

In brief, Lewin asserts that a man's actions are to be explained on the grounds that he perceives particular ways and means of discharging certain tensions. Those activities that an individual perceives as making possible the release of tension will attract him; they will have positive valence for him, and he will experience a force moving him to engage in these activities. Certain other activities may have the opposite effect; they are seen as increasing tension; they are said to have a negative valence and to generate repulsive forces. Heider says of Lewin's theory:

> Essentially, this is an explication in systematic terms of the simple fact that when I think that I can reach goal y by doing x, I will do x in order to get what I want. It is not an explanation; it is a representation in a language which is supposed to help in disentangling more complicated means-end situations, and which

[15] Some writers have said that the representations cannot be given up without losing the theory, but we will follow the example of others who have done so. Cartwright (1959) and Heider (1960) are recent sympathetic reviews; Leeper (1943) is more critical; Estes (1954) is very critical, especially of the failure of Lewin's theory to meet acceptable standards for explanatory models. Only Leeper of these four writers found it necessary to make extensive use of diagrams, and Heider used none at all.

also is supposed to help in spotting relevant variables. (Heider, 1960, p. 158)

Later, Heider sketches it ". . . tension induces valence and valence directs behavior . . ." (p. 164).

We can already see illustrated in this summary outline all of the characteristics of Lewin's theorizing noted previously. All behavior, or at least all intentional behavior, is motivated; it is driven by tensions, moved by forces, directed by valences, and addressed to goals. Lewin does not question the reality status of these terms; they are not constructs but facts of behavior as far as he is concerned. For Lewin, behavior is not just an associative response to a stimulus—it is potentially subject to influence by anything the individual may perceive, feel, or think. Finally, we may note that there is little that is inconsistent between Lewin's account of behavior and the traditional rationalist's account. Certainly, the kinds of determinants Lewin introduced were acceptable to the traditionalist. Where Lewin went beyond the rationalist was in attempting to supply syntactical rules for the determination of behavior. The important question as we proceed is whether the syntactical and semantic linkages of Lewin's theoretical constructs meet the criteria given in Chapter 1 that would make the theory scientifically acceptable. Let us look at the four motivational constructs—tension, need, valence, and force.

Tension. Lewin's basic explanatory premise was that a voluntary intention to perform some act creates in the organism a state of tension that persists until the tension can be dissipated by the performance of the intended act.

> For instance, someone intends to drop a letter in the mailbox. The first mailbox he passes serves as a signal and reminds him of the action. He drops the letter. The mailboxes he passes thereafter leave him altogether cold. . . . According to the laws of association, dropping the letter into the first mailbox should create an association between the mailbox and the dropping of the letter; the forces, whether associative or any other kind, which lead to dropping the letter, should also be reinforced by it. This is a stumbling block for association psychology; moreover it casts doubt upon whether the coupling between occasion and consummation . . . plays really the essential role here. If the effect of the act of intending is that a tendency toward consummation arises when the occasion implied by the act of intending occurs, then it is hard to see why on a second occasion this tendency should not appear to the same and even to a greater degree. . . . Thus, the cause of the process does not seem to be simply that the coupling between the [mailbox and consummation] drives toward action when the occasion arises. (Lewin, 1926, pp. 97–98)

Some other sort of explanation besides associationism is required, Lewin believed; and he suggested that we view the causal factor in the mailbox example as a tension that is aroused by the intention to mail the letter.

There was a second class of phenomena that seemed to Lewin to require a tension concept, namely, that in the absence of a suitable goal object the tension to fulfill an intention may be discharged by a substitute action that attains the same end. For example, if a person has the intention to write to a friend, this establishes a certain tension that would ordinarily persist until the letter was written. But seeing a telephone might remind him to communicate with his friend; the substitute activity of phoning discharges the tension aroused by the intention to write.

Third, a task that has been interrupted is likely to be subsequently resumed. Were the coupling between the occasion and consummation decisive, nothing would happen without a repeated recurrence of the occasion. In point of fact though, as Ovsiankina had shown (reported in 1928), an interrupted task is more likely to be resumed than one that was allowed to go to completion.

Fourth and finally, Lewin noted that frequently we forget our intentions. This occurs generally either because the occasion for the consummatory activity is not perceived or because the tension to consummate the intention is swamped by some greater demand upon psychic energy. Lewin concluded that

> The experiments on forgetting of intentions, and even more those on resumption of interrupted activities, prove that . . . intention is a force. . . . *There exists rather an internal pressure of a definite direction, an internal tension-state which presses to carry out the intention* even if no predetermined [associatively established] occasion invites the action. (Lewin, 1926, pp. 113–114)

So here, as early as 1926, is a clear statement of the motivational idea, the dynamic principle.[16]

Need. In this same 1926 paper Lewin defined the concept of need and distinguished between genuine needs and quasi-needs. The genuine needs arise from conditions such as hunger, relief from which serves the organism biologically. Tensions arising from intentions, acts of will, and other more or less arbitrary commitments of the individual person are quasi-needs; they are purely psychic needs. This distinction is approximately the same as that which was current in this country at about the same time between primary and secondary (or acquired)

---

[16] Lewin's intention here was evidently to be able to arrive at an inductive definition of tension. This strategy calls for making many loosely tied linkages between data and construct, no one of which can be held to be a strict definition. Compare this strategy with that of Murray, to be described shortly. Brown (1932) reported that the rate of tension discharge depends upon the structure of the system. In 1938 Lewin had added this as well as Zeigarnik's finding (1927) that tension diffuses with time to his earlier "evidences" of tension.

drives (e.g., Tolman, 1926). It might just be noted that now, 50 years later, we are in no better a position than Lewin was in making or defending such a distinction.

This distinction does not turn out to play a very important part in Lewin's theorizing, however, because of his insistence upon the principle of contemporary action. It does not make much difference, except for purposes of historical analysis, where a need comes from or how it arises, because the causes of action must be contemporary with the action. Wherever a need may have come from, the principle of contemporary action makes it functionally equivalent to all other needs.

For Lewin one of the important classes of motivating tensions is that arising from needs that characterize a given individual. Every person has a characteristic need structure that may be more or less stable but which may also vary somewhat from moment to moment. The needs of an individual may be real or quasi; they may arise as the result of any circumstance that gives the individual a reason for acting in a particular way.

Lewin's failure to delimit more precisely how tensions are induced provides at once both theoretical strength and weakness. On the one hand, by leaving open the question of how needs arise Lewin was free to consider the effects on the individual of any reason at all that he might have for acting. But on the other hand, by neglecting the antecedent conditions that produce tensions we are immediately deprived of the opportunity to investigate a large important class of determinants of behavior. Furthermore, by ignoring these antecedents, tension becomes, in effect, a response-inferred type of construct, with all the problems that attend such constructs.

The hypothetical relationship between need and tension is described in terms of conceptual properties: ". . . whenever a psychological need exists, a system in a state of tension exists within the individual" (Lewin, 1938, p. 99). And another: A tension is a "state of a system which tries to change itself in such a way that it becomes equal to the state of surrounding systems . . ." (p. 98). It seems clear that tensions are supposed to be caused by needs (or quasi-needs) and that they persist until the needs are alleviated.

These conceptual distinctions would suggest that we could distinguish empirically between needs and tensions. Both constructs, however, are so poorly linked operationally to experimental variables that the hypothetical connections between them can hardly be confirmed. For example, it is not clear how one might demonstrate a need in the absence of a corresponding tension or a tension without an underlying need. Moreover, in Lewin's writings, need and tension are frequently referred to almost interchangeably. For example, Lewin sometimes equated the psychic reality of tension with the experimentally manipulated variable hours of deprivation. But neither need nor tension was systematically anchored to a set of experimental conditions or to a specific behavioral phenomenon. Lewin always left the linkages between constructs and the data language loose and intuitive.

Force and valence. In addition to generating tensions and thereby providing the "push" in behavior, needs also set the occasion for the two "pulling" constructs, force and valence, to take effect. As a general rule, the perception of the possibility of engaging in some activity, the desirability of that activity (its valence), and the tendency to engage in it (the force it exerts) all go together. The conceptual differences emerge principally as a matter of emphasis. Valence helps to account for choice, but force may be more useful if we are concerned with the speed or persistence of behavior.

Lewin tells us that when a need exists there will arise a force or a field of forces signifying a valenced activity. If an individual has no need, then the environment registers no valences for him, nor does it generate any forces for him. The attainment of goals is typically perceived as possible only by engaging in certain intermediary activities. Each of these intermediaries may hold a valence itself, and all the valences may be viewed as generating forces directed either toward or away from the particular activities. The resulting behavior is assumed to be determined by some sort of psychological summation of these different forces.

It should be easy to separate force from valence conceptually, but it is not. Force is given three explicit attributes. It has magnitude (but so does valence), direction (a valence has location, which is topologically equivalent to direction), and it has a point of application (and so does valence). These conceptual properties of the construct justify the designation "force," by analogy with "force" in physics. There is a fourth, implicit, property of force that is also relevant, namely, that forces are what make things go. A force makes something happen, whereas a valence is passive; it is an abstract value that is merely correlated with action.

In conclusion it seems that both in the case of need and tension and in the case of valence and force there is an unnecessary redundancy of constructs. Moreover, there seems to be further redundancy between the pullers and the pushers of action. If all four constructs are merely different manifestations of the same underlying principle, then it would be valuable to know what the underlying principle is. And if the four constructs are to be viewed as four more or less independent agencies, then perhaps a more parsimonious account would be more valuable.

Formal adequacy of Lewin's theory

Although Lewin claimed he did not have a theory, he did formulate specific constructs and indicate how they might be linked to empirical phenomena. There are also hypothetical syntactical linkages, that is, hypotheses to interrelate the different constructs. The system as a whole deals with the individual, his tensions, and his perceptions, indicating how they determine behavior. The "laws and definitions are a network of statements which only as a whole can be viewed as right or wrong" (Lewin, 1938, p. 16). And it is as a whole that we shall consider them.

Lewin's variety of explanation. What did Lewin consider to be an explanation of behavior? He made no reference to physical or physiological causation; quite the contrary, his network of terms and laws, like that of Freud, was expressly designed to apply to psychological phenomena. And the causes in Lewin's system, as in Freud's, are invariably analogous to mechanical causes—they are tensions and forces. Needs and tensions both are necessary for action, although they are not in themselves sufficient. An additional component is required, namely, a perception of certain behavioral possibilities, certain goals. The goals of behavior play an explanatory role, but their action in behavior is transferred to the construct of force. When Lewin speaks of goals, there is nothing teleological in the account. In this he broke sharply with the rationalist tradition. A goal does not have a future reference; rather it has its effect by changing the individual's contemporary perception. He sees or feels or knows what he wants to do. Unfortunately, the simple elegance of the motivational model is purchased at a terrible cost; all of the vague, lawless, inherently untestable, and rationalistic characteristics that have been kept out of the motivational hypotheses pop up immediately in the perceptual hypotheses, that is, in the structural properties of the life space. Lewin can tell us precisely how a man's perceptions go over in a determinate manner to fix his behavior, but what can he tell us about the man's perception? The trouble is that all we can know of another's perception must be inferred from his behavior.

Lewin was a determinist. Whereas he frequently spoke of the organism choosing between one course of action and another or choosing between one goal and another, choice was always a metaphor, since the behavior in question was always assumed to be strictly determined by the resolution of conflicting forces. Choice was recognized as a kind of activity that the organism may perceive himself engaged in, but this was as much reality status as it was given. Lewin was clearly a determinist of the psychological variety, inasmuch as the determining conditions for behavior are explicitly stated to be dynamic and structural psychological occurrences.

Semantic problems. The major inadequacy of Lewin's theory is its uncertain semantics. There is little indication of how one could possibly validate the constructs of the theory. How do we know what the needs of an organism are? How can we tell whether these needs

Theory of motivation

have created tension? How do we know that the tension is recipro-
cated in a force or in a valence perceived by the individual? How can
we know how the individual perceives his behavioral possibilities? The
constructs of the theory are not even provisionally tied to empirical
observations; there are no semantic rules for translating between the
construct language of the theory and the data language.

This problem is somewhat greater for the Lewinian than for
most other theorists because he claims (1) to know reality and (2) to
have discovered laws that are universal and determinate. If a theorist
leaves a certain margin of fuzziness either in the definition of his constructs (as Freud did) or in the linkages between constructs (as
Tolman did), then the theory is open to improvement. But when the
theory remains rigid from construct to construct, then fuzziness at
the level of linking the theory to the data would seem to leave the
theory itself untestable.[17] To the extent that Lewin was not building
a theory but only attempting to represent what he regarded as the
generally accepted facts of behavior, he might have been willing to go
along with this charge of untestability.

Syntactical problems. Lewin's theory presents some syntactical problems, too. It has an overabundance of what can be called accessory
hypotheses, that is, hypotheses that are not deductions from the basic
hypotheses of the theory but that seem to have been added to the
theory as afterthoughts. For example, Lewin said that with an increase
in tension (or need) there will be a force to quit an ongoing activity.
This is evidently a translation into the terms of the theory of the
"generally accepted knowledge" that the motivated organism becomes
restless. A more formally adequate theory than Lewin's would, of
course, either deduce this hypothesis as a "theorem" from more fundamental hypotheses or state it as a fundamental hypothesis. A more
empirically adequate theory would indicate, in addition, how we
might go about confirming or rejecting the hypothesis.

As another example, when Lewin (1938) discussed the possibility that motivation might influence the speed of learning, he
observed that learning is speeded up when force (or valence) is
increased. But then he said, "If the force in the direction toward the
goal is too great, a decrease in learning probably will result, because
learning requires a *sufficient survey* of the total situation" (italics
mine) (pp. 160–161). This assertion seems intuitively plausible, but
how would one test it empirically; in particular, how can one know if
a "sufficient survey" has been taken?

Data-language problems. The Lewinian psychologist typically refers
to the structure of the organism's private world (his life space) as

---

[17] Brunswik (1952) said of Lewin's theory that it was "encapsu-
lated."

though he could observe it himself. The structuralists (e.g., Titchener) occasionally spoke this way also—and surely the psychophysical dualism of that era led psychologists to believe that their statements about the sensations of the subject were statements in the data language—but Titchener told us in more or less operational terms how we might train a subject and how we could establish a stimulus situation in precise physical terms so that sensations were empirically anchored antecedently.

Lewin refers to energy, tension, force, and the rest as "psychological facts." He says in defense,

> The reality of the psychological forces is the same as that of the "biological forces governing the brain." . . . It is often asked whether psychological force is something "real" or only an "analogy." The problem of the reality of a dynamic construct is a peculiar one in any science. . . . It will suffice here to emphasize that a psychological force is as real as any other kind of dynamical construct in psychology and certainly as real as a physical force. The situation is not merely one in which the person *appears* to locomote in the direction to a goal. A change in the position of the goal easily proves that the dynamical interrelation between person and goal expressed in the term force is a real one. . . . (Lewin, 1938, p. 87)

So Lewin's theory can be seen as a system in which the linkages between constructs and experimentally manipulable physical conditions are either ignored or intuited.[18]

As promising as the syntactical features of Lewin's theory are, the semantic problems and the data-language problems are so serious that the theory cannot really be put to empirical test. This is not to say that there is no relation between the theory and the empirical world but only that most of those who have tried to work with Lewin's theory have been forced to intuit the coordination between the level of the formal model and the level of behavioral data as best

---

[18] At first glance, Lewin might seem to have been a phenomenologist. He was not. Indeed, one might complain that Lewin failed to take sufficient account of immediate experience and that he did not use it enough to check out his theoretical formulations. For example, does an individual really perceive a variety of possible activities and decide upon a course of action on the basis of their various attractivenesses? Or does the individual more nearly only perceive one possibility, that which is a consequence of some unconscious decisional process? In any case, only one possibility at a time can be registered, as any good introspectionist could have told Lewin. Consequently, the life space, which Lewin assumed to be fixed at one time point, must be more nearly the summation of processes occurring over a short period of time. One wonders if the order in which these sequential processes occur is a factor itself in the determination of behavior. However that may be, the point should be emphasized that Lewin used intuition, not introspection. Lewin's orientation was logical rather than empirical.

they could. It seems likely that Lewin's own, highly imaginative laboratory work flowed primarily from his abundant supply of "accessory" hypotheses rather than from the systematic or formal properties of the theory.

In spite of the limitation of untestability, the motivational model has enjoyed considerable popular acceptance. Perhaps one reason for this acceptance is that Lewin's account of behavior was so compatible with the traditional rationalistic mode of thought. Indeed, the only serious departure from the rationalistic position was Lewin's "postulate" (see page 71) that all behavior was a result of forces acting upon the individual. Because force was said explicitly to be merely analogous to physical force and because Lewin emphasized the necessity of "field factors" to explain human behavior, there was no danger that his theory would be mistaken for a mechanical explanation. What he gave us then was the promise of a deterministic calculus of forces with which we could describe the psychological causes of behavior—provided only that we could measure the forces.

Lewin's three other postulates have not fared so well. In fact, his insistence upon speaking about realities (implying that other people's constructs are illusory), his utter rejection of associationism (on the grounds that it was too mechanical, rather than because of any empirical shortcomings), and his extravagant dedication to representational problems (when theoretical problems might more profitably have occupied his time) may have kept Lewin's work from being as widely regarded as it might otherwise have been. The first two of these postulates have given us field theory, and the third has been even less consequential.

Murray's concept of need

It is perhaps appropriate to conclude this brief sampling of human motivation theories with a sketch of Henry Murray's position. Because Murray is an extremely eclectic motivation theorist, his views encompass pretty well those of many modern workers, and he summarizes many of the implicit views of others regarding how behavior should be explained. Many of his concepts are derived from Freud, from Lewin, and particularly from Tolman (see Chapter 4).

According to Murray, the behavior of an individual person reveals rhythms of rest and activity. The cycles are interwoven in a dense network of total behavior, and the task of the psychologist is to discover the individual threads that make up the whole fabric. If we consider just one cycle of activity, we may observe that the organism will invariably react in such a way that its behavior shows a "unitary trend." The trend may not be noticed if the reactions are analyzed simply into muscle movements because muscle movements are not themselves organized so as to display purposiveness or adaptability.[19] But viewed in molar terms, particularly if the behavior is analyzed in terms of its effects upon the organism and upon the environment, its adaptive unity will be apparent. This molar analysis of the units of behavior has the practical advantage of permitting us to deal directly with the biological usefulness of behavior; it also has the convenience of providing units that are nearly universal across individuals and across time.

Behavior, defined in these molar terms, generally serves to take the organism from some prior state into some consequent state—that is what the unitary trend of behavior consists in. These trends are assumed to be due to a hypothetical force (a drive, need, or propensity), which operates homeostatically. That is, a motivating force carries the organism away from the prior or initiating condition into a state like satiation in which the force disappears. Because motivating forces are not directly observable, we have to infer them from observations of and communications with the individual. Sometimes the needs or drives of the individual can be related to specific physiological disturbances; this is true in the case of hunger, thirst, sex, and the avoidance of various kinds of harmful stimulation. But Murray felt that the physiological conditions underlying these viscerogenic drives, and their subsequent effects upon behavior were fairly well understood, and he argued that much more relevant for human psychology were the psychogenic drives or needs, of which he has listed about 30.[20] The psychogenic needs are also, of course, less crucial to the survival and the long-term adaptation of the organism, but they are, perhaps just for this reason, all the more important in understanding human behavior and experience. Both psychogenic and viscerogenic drives are viewed as central states of the organism ultimately localizable in the brain.

Homeostatic nature of needs. Needs, in Murray's system, may arise from physiological disturbances, but more typically they are aroused by particular events in the environment that offer certain threats or promises to the individual. These stimulus actions upon the organism Murray calls "presses."

The purposive motivational model includes the following sequence of events: (1) some stimulus feature in the environment

[19] Thus Murray summarily dismissed simple associationistic and mechanistic approaches to the explanation of behavior. I am following here Murray's *Explorations in Personality* (1938), which seems to have escaped critical reviewers except for Hall and Lindzey (1957).

[20] The distinction between need and drive for Murray is not very clear-cut. Needs are somewhat more on the antecedent or perceptual side of the organism, whereas drives are more directly related to motor behavior (similar to Lewin's distinction between need and tension).

promises to have some effect upon the organism, either desirable or undesirable; (2) a drive or need is aroused; (3) the organism is activated to engage in certain kinds of activity, which may be motor, verbal, merely ideational, or even unconscious; (4) this activity has the effect of causing a trend in the overall behavior of the organism that tends to restore equilibrium; (5) the achievement of a demotivated state is only possible in many cases through the attainment of some particular goal object. Goal objects acquire, through learning, a value, or valence, or cathexis. Finally (6), this reestablishment of equilibrium, dispelling the drive, arouses a pleasurable affect. (Murray did not emphasize this affective element nor indicate what it might mean for learning.) We can recognize in this simply stated homeostatic scheme the same conception of equilibrium that Freud had proposed and the same sequence of tension-force-release of tension that Lewin had proposed. In Chapter 4 we will discover that the concepts of instinct and drive were also largely based upon the same paradigm. Our interest in it here is that it arose from the consideration of such different behavioral events in Murray's case. What it was designed to accomplish was to account for the uniqueness of integration of human personalities. This purpose could not be achieved immediately, however; first it was necessary to embellish the homeostatic model with a number of syntactical properties.

Functional properties of needs. Murray admits that one could translate motivational constructs into purely behavioral terms; but he insists that there are good reasons, at least ten of them, for not making such a translation. (Again, we may observe the similarity of his arguments to those that had been advanced by McDougall, Lewin, Freud, Lorenz, and others.) (1) There is the problem of the persistence of behavior, particularly in the face of barriers to its realization. Overall trends may be found in behavior even when the details of the muscle movements are without apparent significance. The unitary trend is not given in the behavioral data, but it is assumed to be a property of an underlying agent, the need. (2) The organism will persist in a variety of attempts to get at its goals or to fulfill its purposes. Again, the motive lends a unity to what would otherwise be simply a variety of different behaviors. (3) Even in an experimental context it is found that what response a particular stimulus will evoke depends upon the needs of the individual. (4) Occasionally, behavior will go off in the absence of an appropriate goal object (so-called vacuum activity). (5) Behavior frequently occurs not because it was elicited by a stimulus but because a stimulus is absent (i.e., there may be seeking for a stimulus).

Murray continued the list with evidence of a more subjective sort: (6) Fantasy is evidence of the direct action of some need. (7) Subjective experience of desire or feeling of an urge helps to corroborate and validate the construct. (8) Needs are more important in an explanation of behavior than S-R associations because they are more closely linked with the emotions of the organism. (9) Needs may interact either by summation or in conflict to yield effects that are not predictable on the basis simply of the available stimulation. (10) Most of the phenomena of abnormal psychology—compulsion, conflict, repression, conversion, displacement—would be wholly unintelligible without a concept of motivating force. This list of ten arguments does not seem to be so much evidence of needs as an enumeration of the sort of phenomena that Murray intends to explain by invoking needs. Whether they can be explained without invoking needs is quite a separate question, which Murray begs. It might be a worthwhile exercise to see if it could be done, or in how many different ways it could be done.

A lexicon of human needs. After demonstrating the need for the need concept (or the drive for the drive concept), Murray proceeds by classifying and cataloging the different needs and indicating some relationships among them. Murray's characterization of the different needs evolved from his clinical studies of the needs underlying the activities of his subjects. The needs discovered in these clinical cases range alphabetically from need-abasement (the need to surrender, to self-deprecate) and the now-popular need-achievement down to need-understanding (which is the need to analyze experience, to define relations, to synthesize ideas). These needs were discovered in a wide variety of behavior situations: casual interviews (and the subject's subsequent recollection of them); autobiographical writings; childhood memories; questionnaires; highly structured interviews; casual conversations; interest and ability tests; aesthetic tests; a hypnotism test: a level-of-aspiration test; tests of memory for failure, ethical standards, and emotionality. The subjects were also observed at play and were given TAT and Rorschach tests.

The assumption underlying the assessment of motives is that if an individual is characterized by a few salient needs, then these needs should keep reappearing in a number of different contexts. The different contexts thus provide a means of cross-validating the motivational structure (and consequently the analysis of the personality) of the individual. At the same time, enough observations of the subject are made to ensure that some of his less salient needs would also be disclosed.

Murray's position does not really constitute a theory of behavior because it provides so few syntactical rules telling us how to operate with the theoretical terms. Consequently, we do not know how to fit them together to form an explanatory network. We are not told how different individuals come to react differently to environmental presses. Why, for example, does failure characteristically induce need-abasement in one person and need-achievement in another? Even though Murray tells us that such differences constitute the basic source of difference between individual personalities, he provides no analytical tools for explaining them. Nor does he consider the question of how a given pattern of needs comes to characterize a given individual. Still more serious is that we are not told how these particular needs, once given as part of the individual, are expressed in ways characteristic of him; we do not know from Murray's scheme how to predict any particular behavior from the knowledge that an individual is subject to or has been previously subjected to a particular press.

The semantics of Murray's formulation, on the other hand, provides a considerably improved set of constructs over those proposed by his predecessors, Lewin, for example. He admits that the ties between the data language and construct language are rather loose. But this looseness obtains only within a single observational context, and certainly we cannot demand that the observation of a single bit of behavior within a single environmental context be itself of particular interest, scientific or otherwise; ". . . it is an outcast fact begging to be understood and to be accepted with others of its kind" (1938, p. 127). If we would know what motivates a person, then we must make use of a diversity of indices. Even though the linkages between empirical data and the constructs are not defined operationally, nor tied down in any rigid way, the psychologist has an opportunity in Murray's system to use a variety of semantic tricks. He may use, in effect, any behavioral measure he wishes. Whatever variety of evidence is available, it is used to "converge" upon the organism's needs. Thus a potent safeguard was provided against the too facile and too simple postulation of drives to account for particular instances of behavior. With Murray human motivation theory began to lose its linear or simple this-causes-that character and began to assume the form of a network of functional relationships.

Summary

The motivational theories of Freud, Lewin, and Murray present many points of difference. The three men had different points of view and different philosophical commitments; their backgrounds and the times in which they lived were different. They concerned themselves with quite different kinds of problems, and they certainly had in mind quite different applications for their theories. Nonetheless, there are certain areas of basic correspondence. In each case the theorist was a determinist and attempted to explain behavior in determinate ways by means of certain psychological constructs. In each case behavior is partly "pushed" through the action of motivating drives and partly "pulled" through the perception of valuable objects, valences, or goals in the environment. In each case an individual is to be described by his characteristic drives and by the characteristic goals he uses to discharge the tension his drives produce.

The drive construct, as it is formulated by Freud, Lewin, or Murray always operates homeostatically; the individual is constantly seeking to rid himself of tension that threatens his well-being. The greater the threat, the greater the drive and the more likely the individual is to seek and find a suitable goal. For Freud, behavior ultimately depends upon one drive, sex; for Murray, there are a large number of social as well as biological drives; and for Lewin, there is nearly an infinite number of possible tension systems that could stir an individual to action. However, Freud's unitary drive is found by viewing the subject historically; even a Freudian sees a large number of energy systems when he views the subject more contemporaneously. This is what Murray sees from his viewpoint. Lewin, by freezing his subject in time and attributing energy to whatever he sees happening, sees it everywhere. Nothing just happens; for each of our three theorists there must always be some force of energy or drive that makes it happen. Where they find the drive depends mainly on where they look for it. It may be back in the repressed memories of the individual, or it may be lurking in the most inconsequential movement, but it must be there somewhere. These three theorists share a common belief: Behavior is to be explained by discovering the underlying forces that make it happen.

4

INSTINCTS

*There are reflexes—then vastly more important
and complex are instincts—emotionally
toned activities which are inborn reaction
tendencies. They furnish a fundamental basis
for likes and dislikes—they are the great
primitive drives in our lives.*
William McDougall

As a general rule the concept of instinct is introduced to account for the apparent intelligence of behavior when it does not seem reasonable to attribute intelligence to the organism. The problem arose originally because intelligence was considered to be a faculty of man alone. Therefore, the adaptiveness and apparent intelligence of animals had to be explained by a special faculty, instinct. After the Darwinian revolution it became reasonable to attribute intelligence, at least in some measure, to animals; but careful naturalistic observation indicated that the adaptability of behavior, especially the behavior of the lower animals, far exceeded the amount of intelligence that could be afforded them, so the instinct concept was retained.

The next step is that the theorist, in defense of the instinct concept, studies behavior and discovers still more marvelous adaptations that cannot be accounted for except by assuming the operation of instinctive forces.

But the instinct concept does not have a cohesive and consistent form that fixes its conceptual properties; it changes shape to suit the circumstances, the problem, and the range of alternatives that are acceptable at a given time. For example, when James or McDougall wrote about instincts, it was permissible to make subjective experience an important part of the definition of instincts, and they did. Later writers could not.

When the mentalist talks about instinct he is admitting that at least some behavior, that which is instinctive, is not due to mental causes but is governed instead by other, mechanical-like principles of some sort. When the tough-minded mechanist or empiricist talks about instinct, he is admitting that at least some behavior is innately organized along functional lines, or that at least some behavior is not learned.[1]

In the present chapter we will discover that instincts have been invoked and defended mainly by tender-minded theorists in protest against mechanistic theories because they consider such theories to be lacking in the proper appreciation of either the adaptability of behavior, its goal directedness, its energetic properties, or its emotional concomitants. Different instinct theorists differ largely in what they consider to be the strongest attack upon the mechanistic position.

It might be expected that because the instinct concept has such flexible conceptual properties, explanations of behavior couched in terms of instincts would come to acquire considerable popular acceptance, and that is just what happened. Indeed, after McDougall such explanations became so popular, so universal, and so all-encompassing that the instinct concept could no longer be used by the serious student of behavior. We will see how some theorists, most notably Tolman, began to transform the instinct concept into what we now know as the drive concept. Finally, we will note the contribution of a new discipline, ethology, which has recently revitalized the instinct concept, changing and sharpening it considerably but not altogether altering its basic character. As the story proceeds, we will see that various conceptual properties have gradually been stripped away from instinct—first its opposition to intelligence, then the subjective experience component, then the emotional component, and, most recently, the idea of instinct energy.

William James' instincts

The early development of the instinct concept was outlined in Chapter 2. We noted there that it had gained considerable acceptance by the proponents of the commonsense or faculty psychology of the nineteenth century. In that school of thought instinct was still sharply contrasted with intelligence, instinct supposedly being the source of adaptive behavior in animals (and occasionally in man) while intelligence was regarded as the principal source of adaptive human behavior. Toward the end of the century the ancient dichotomy between the animal mind and the human mind had begun to evaporate, mainly as a consequence of Darwin's influence; and some type of conceptual reorganization was desperately needed. This was the problem to which William James addressed himself.

James (1890) defied the popular view that since man has a superior intellect, he possesses few instincts. Quite the contrary, James argued, man has many more different instincts than the other animals;

[1] James' distinction between tough- and tender-mindedness was described on page 33.

they are merely more apt to be obscured by the operation of his superior mental apparatus. Man's great facility for learning can readily disguise or modify his native instinctive endowment. Moreover, he argued, the traditional interpretation of instinct as a blind impulse or force, as something opposed to intelligence, is valid only at a very shallow level of analysis; there are many tangled relationships between learning and instinctive impulses. For example, he noted that an instinct could only properly be said to be blind on its first occurrence; after that it must be accompanied by some amount of foresight of its end.[2]

James stressed that with an instinct appropriate objects capture the organism's attention at the appropriate time. This is the hypothesis of "instinct meaning" or "instinct interest," which suggests that when the organism is being acted upon by instinctive forces, these forces will make known what is the appropriate goal object and will give the goal object a value appropriate for the instinct. Thus James suggests that a hen sits on an egg because the egg looks to the hen as though it is just right for sitting on; we should not ask why it does, it just does. ". . . to the animal which obeys it, every step of every instinct shines with its own sufficient light, and seems at the moment the only eternally right and proper thing to do" (1890, II, p. 387).

Instinct was defined as "the faculty of acting in such a way as to produce certain ends, without foresight of the ends, and without previous education in the performance" (1890, II, p. 383). Although this definition of instinct seems clear enough, James did not adhere to it in his examples; he included as instincts simple reflexes such as sneezing and coughing, some much more complex motor adjustments such as walking, and some emotional dispositions like fear and love. He also listed as instincts some very complicated patterns of behavior, such as hunting and kleptomania, where there was certainly little likelihood of meeting his defining criteria of no previous education and occurrence without foresight.

We can see in James, transitional figure that he was, the merging of a number of apparently disparate viewpoints encompassing both the old and the new: Darwin's conception of biological adaptation, the prevailing mentalism, a tough-minded dependence upon the underlying neural basis of behavior and consciousness, and a tender-minded acceptance of spiritual values and of the then popular faculty

---

[2] James anticipated two phenomena that have attracted much attention recently in connection with imprinting. He proposed a law of inhibition of instincts: Sometimes only the first object of an instinct can occupy the central role on its subsequent performance. After the first object of an instinct has become associated with it, other objects could not readily take its place. His law of nonuniformity was a clear anticipation of the modern critical-period hypothesis. James tells us that if an instinct has not found a suitable object by some certain time, it may never find one.

psychology. For example, his famous treatment of emotions in terms of the feedback from bodily reactions was frankly materialistic, but on the free will versus determinism issue, he took the side of free will (this was clearer in some of his later writings, e.g., 1914, than in *The Principles*).

Atkinson (1964) has observed that in the gradual transition between traditional, mentalistic accounts of behavior and the more scientifically adequate models we have today, James stands among the last of the traditionalists. To put his contribution into proper perspective it is necessary to note that the doctrine of instincts constituted only a minor part of James' total view of behavior. James proposed three distinct devices to explain behavior: (1) the ideomotor theory of voluntary action in which the idea of the consequence of a voluntary act is sufficient to make the act occur; (2) habit, which was a sort of short circuiting of consciousness that occurs with repetition of a voluntary act; and (3) instinct.

If we think of instinct as Lamarck did (and as did most other theorists of the times), as a sort of short circuiting of habit that occurs over evolutionary time, then we have the following overall scheme for the explanation of behavior: All behavior is originally voluntary, but after sufficient exercise of the voluntary act it becomes habitual, and after sufficient exercise of the habit it becomes hereditary or instinctive. Even Darwin (1872) subscribed to this position. Thus none of James' three explanatory devices was, strictly speaking, original with him, but he spelled them out, especially the ideomotor theory, so clearly that everyone knew what they meant. James was a mentalistic psychologist and to that extent among the last of the traditionalists; his use of three mediating devices to explain behavior prevents us from classifying him as a rationalist, and to that extent he belonged to the new era rather than the old.

Instincts as universal motivators

William McDougall. It would be possible to cite a number of theorists after James who had a hand in the development of the instinct concept, but none of their contributions compares with that of McDougall. Even though James had broken with the traditional view that instinct applied to animals and intelligence applied to man, he still gave instincts a role secondary to that of ideation and habit in the determination of behavior. James only used instincts to explain certain bits and pieces of behavior. McDougall went much further; for him *all* behavior had an instinctive origin. He contended that if it were not for instincts, man would lie inert, like an intricate clockwork with a broken mainspring. He believed that it was not sufficient to explain a man's actions in terms of his having an idea to act in a certain way; it was much more important and basic to explain *why* he wanted to act as he did. For McDougall the part of psychology that is of the greatest importance is

> . . . that which deals with the springs of human action, the impulses and motives that sustain mental and bodily activity and regulate conduct; and this, of all the departments of psychology, is the one that has remained in the most backward state. . . . It is the mental forces, the sources of energy, which set the ends and sustain the course of all human activity—of which forces the intellectual processes are but the servants, instruments, or means—that must be clearly defined . . . before the social sciences can build on a firm psychological foundation. . . . (McDougall, 1914, p. 3)[3]

We have seen earlier that Stout (1903) had recognized the importance of men's motives in the explanation of behavior, but it had not occurred to Stout to make motivation a universal principle; that was where McDougall parted with the long line of rationalists who had come before him. The importance that McDougall attached to active or dynamic principles in human behavior was all the more remarkable because he had little precedent for it. Few theorists (Freud was one exception) had proposed that men always acted because they were made to do so by particular forces acting upon them.

For McDougall these psychological forces were definitely not to be conceived as mechanical in operation. He stood in violent opposition to the application of the mechanistic philosophy to psychological problems, and he was, accordingly, opposed to the idea that instincts were merely complex reflexes. He was, in fact, the leading critic in his day of this idea. Reflexes are immutable and unchanging, he asserted, while instinctive behavior is modifiable and adaptable to changing circumstances. An instinct is to be defined and recognized not by the kind of movements in which it finds expression, but by its goal, that is, by the kind of change in the organism's environment that brings the sequence of behavior to a close. Behavior manifests a striving toward its natural goal, and if the behavior is frustrated by an obstacle, the striving merely intensifies until the appropriate end process of the instinct is finally achieved. This type of action, striving toward a goal, is characteristic of psychological phenomena and is to be contrasted with mechanical action; mechanical laws are not applicable here, McDougall tells us.

Instincts, in McDougall's view, not only regulated behavior, they also provided the basis of the subjective experience of striving and goal directedness; all of our wants and desires were supposed to stem from the instincts. In addition, each instinct had associated with

---

[3] I have quoted the 8th edition of McDougall's *Social Psychology,* but the other 28 editions, starting with the first in 1908, were all quite similar. So were most of his other books.

it a characteristic emotion. Indeed, McDougall sometimes asserted that the emotional aspect of the instinct was its most important and constant feature. The emotion, together with the sense of striving and desire, constituted the subjective aspect of the instinct, while the resulting behavior that achieved the goal was the objective aspect of the instinct, the part that man shared with other animals.

Putting these different features of McDougall's concept together, we can say that an instinct is an innate predisposition "to perceive, and to pay attention to, objects of a certain class, to experience an emotional excitement of a particular quality upon perceiving such an object, and to act in regard to it in a particular manner" (McDougall, 1914, p. 29).

It would seem that McDougall made what may have been an indispensable contribution to the development of our thinking about motivation. It seems possible that motivation theory would bear little resemblance to its current form if McDougall had not held the theoretical position he did nor written as persistently as he did about his position. To appreciate his contribution it must be remembered that he wrote at a time when Watson's behaviorism was beginning to consume behavior theory. Conditioning, both the physiological concept and the method, was coming to occupy a central position in psychological theory. Psychologists were entering a self-confident materialistic era in which teleology had no place and in which man's mental life was to be excluded. What men thought were their motives for action could be dealt with in terms of physiological constructs and conditioning. In this setting it was McDougall who reminded us that man can be characterized by his purposiveness and his emotional life. And it was he, as much as Freud or anyone else, who popularized the idea that we act because of forces operating on us: All behavior is due to motivating forces, or energies, that push us toward some goal.

The decline of instinct. The increasing popularity of explaining behavior in terms of instincts rapidly led to the crisis that may be called the Great Instinct Controversy. During the second decade of the century, sociologists and economists as well as psychologists began to invoke instincts to explain any and all kinds of human activity. It became fashionable to introduce an instinct to explain all kinds of behaviors. No criteria were employed to determine if the allegedly instinctive behavior was unlearned or universal or done without foresight or if it was purposive. Instincts were invoked ad hoc and ad lib. If the connotation had been purely descriptive, little harm would have been done; however, the attitude common in these accounts was that nothing more needed to be said of any behavior to explain it once an instinct had been invoked.

It was clear that such a state of affairs could not endure, and a lively critical movement was soon underway. Ayres (1921) was provoked to write a paper subtitled "The instinct of belief-in-instincts";

Theory of motivation

Dunlap (1919) wrote one titled "Are there any instincts?" and there were others in a similar vein. The best review of the controversy has been written by Tolman (1923). Tolman presented the issues fully and fairly and attempted to reconstruct a serviceable conception of instinct.

Tolman began by noting some of the objections the critics had raised to the instinct concept. First, they contended that the arbitrary and ad hoc designation of instincts deprived the concept of explanatory value. This criticism was valid insofar as all existing lists of the principal instincts had been drawn up on the basis of the most casual sort of observation. Nothing stood in the way of a systematic investigation of just what constituted the instinct repertoire of animals (including man), but unfortunately the lack of systematic observation was only part of the trouble. Equally serious was the lack of generally acceptable criteria for distinguishing between what was instinctive and what was not; the proponents of the instinct concept had failed to embellish it with adequate semantic and syntactical rules for its proper scientific use. As Tolman noted in defense of the concept, the critics could be disarmed on this point by the development of adequate theories and observational techniques. There was, he concluded, nothing necessarily erroneous in the basic conception of instinctive behavior.

Second, some critics thought the instinct concept had come to look like a modern version of the doctrine of preestablished harmony or the doctrine of innate ideas. Tolman argued that this charge was largely fallacious, since ultimately it is an empirical question whether instinctive reactions are so adaptive that they make the animal appear to have intelligence or some special form of knowledge.

Third, according to some critics the instincts were no more than class names for certain kinds of behavior; they were just new names for the old and discredited "mental faculties." If there was any further implication, it was that the behavior in question was caused by some sort of drive or mystical force. The assumption of an instinct adds nothing to a descriptive account of the behavior. Tolman observed, and certainly we must agree, that the same charge could be leveled against any theoretical position; theories are necessarily tautological to some extent. But a theoretical statement offers a possibility of economy and order and added perspective beyond that given by a bare description of the data—which is just why we entertain theories.

Finally, it was frequently pointed out that the instincts were often confused with habits. McDougall had argued, for example, that the widespread occurrence of combat and war could be taken as evidence of an aggressive instinct in man, that is, an innate disposition common to all men. This argument is far from compelling. We have only McDougall's assurance of the universality of combatitiveness. We cannot tell if the peaceful men we know have learned to overcome their original combatitive dispositions, or whether, perhaps, the aggressive men we know have learned to overcome an originally peaceful nature. Surely few of the arguments about man's original nature have been based upon substantial data. Tolman's reaction to this criticism was that it had merit but that the critics went too far with it, for in the absence of the appropriate data it took just as much faith to maintain that a particular behavior was learned as to hold that it was instinctive. His opinion was, as on all these issues, that more data were needed to settle the question.

All of these criticisms had some validity when directed against the interpretation of instincts which identifies them as direct sensory-motor mechanisms, that is, complex reflexes. However, the mechanistic theorist who advances this interpretation gains very little by classifying some behavior as instinctive. His recognition of such a classification is no more than a concession that at least some behavior is innately organized. This is not to say that the mechanist should not make the concession and attempt to distinguish between native and acquired behavior, but only that once he has made the distinction he has extracted all the meanings from the broader conception of instinct that he can use in his system. None of the other features of the instinct concept, namely, those which we have just seen attacked, are compatible with the mechanist's account of behavior. This is why, on the one hand, the mechanists attacked the concept, and on the other hand, why the concept was so ardently defended by McDougall and Tolman; they stood in opposition to the mechanists, men like Pavlov, Watson, and Thorndike. How else was one to defend the idea of motivation, emphasize the importance of psychological forces in human conduct, and explain the apparent purposive character of behavior except by promoting the instinct doctrine?

Tolman's behavioral teleology. Tolman proposed that if the instinct concept was to be reconstructed usefully it had to be based upon teleological principles; a mechanistic orientation simply would not do. On this point he followed McDougall. Tolman thought that a new, empirically well-founded, teleological interpretation could meet all of the objections that had been raised against the older instinct doctrines. There are different possible teleological frames of reference that could be employed, but our choice is pretty much determined by our dedication to the problem of behavior. First, Tolman argued, we may reject the possibility of a biological teleology, one that stresses the biological utility of instinctive behavior. Some of the most important instincts, for instance, those that promote racial preservation, lack behavioral purpose for the individual. Racial continuity may very well be served by sexual behavior, but in what sense is the individual animal served? Tolman's basic assumption was that *the ends of behavior must be found in the organism that behaves.*

A mentalistic teleology, like that proposed by McDougall,

meets the previous requirement but is empirically inadequate. Consider, as an example, McDougall's position that we infer the "pugnacious instinct" when the emotion of anger occurs. Tolman asks: Is this not just the opposite of what we actually do? Is it not more nearly correct to say that we infer the emotion of anger from the observation of pugnacious behavior? We observe the persistence of pugnacious behavior; the supposition of an underlying explanatory instinct and the associated emotion is an inference (Tolman, 1923).[4]

Tolman concluded that the only acceptable possibility would be a purely behavioral teleology, according to which behavior is to be understood in its own terms, by its own ends. Behavior, in this view, is characteristically purposive, which means that it can be best defined in terms of its goals or consequences, rather than in terms of its mediating processes. As individual psychologists, we may elect to focus our attention either upon the goal and its effect upon the mediating processes or upon those processes themselves; but the entire initiation-means-end relationship is to be taken as the inherent and defining function of an instinct. Once the instinct is initiated, either by internal or external stimulation or by some physiological condition of the organism, it determines what adjustments the organism must make to reinstate a neutral condition. The instinct does not determine, however, how the final adjustment or end is to be brought about; that is governed by environmental conditions, by previous training in particular means-ends relationships, by the influence of competing instincts, and so on. Thus Tolman arrived at the proposition that behavioral ends are fixed, but behavioral means are variable. This point, fundamental to his whole approach to motivation, marks a critical turning point in the history of the instinct concept at least as important as any we have noted so far.

Today we might wonder why this behavioral teleology was couched in terms of instincts when it could have been stated in terms of motives, drives, tensions, or more simply just in terms of purposive behavior itself. The answer is that it was really only a matter of historical accident. The explanatory concept of the day was instinct; motivational ideas were either formulated in terms of instincts or not at all. Tolman was concerned with maintaining a theory of motivation, and his use of the instinct idea was simply a means toward that end. As it turned out, his theory of motivation came to occupy a

---

[4] I will have nothing more to say here about emotion except to recommend Beebe-Center's (1951) brilliant historical analysis of the problem and to note that in recent years the provocative research begun by Schachter and Singer (1962) has stirred up new interest, new theories, and new research on the difficult problem of emotion. These and other recent developments are summarized by Arnold (1970). At this point, too, having moved from McDougall's mentalism to Tolman's behaviorism, we will leave human motivation, rarely to return. To see what has been happening recently in human motivation see Weiner (1972).

prominent historical position, while his reconstructed instinct concept, as such, was neglected. In contrast with James and McDougall, whose conceptions of instinct were frankly mentalistic, since their times required that behavior be explained by events going on the mind, Tolman cast the functional properties of instincts into behavioral language. Wants, desires, and the subjective sense of striving became simply persistent behavior. Tolman was known as a cognitive theorist, but it is wrong to suppose on that account that he was not a behaviorist. The mentalistic language he adopted (1932) was to be considered no more than a heuristic device to build a better theoretical model for the explanation of behavior. Even then, all his mentalesque terms were carefully defined behaviorally.

Tolman, in his review of these events, modestly minimized his own contribution to them. The fundamental idea of behavioral teleology, the idea that behavior could be explained in terms of its behavioral consequences, Tolman attributed to his teacher Perry (1918).[5] Tolman also acknowledged that the essential features of his teleological account of behavior had been proposed by three other men, namely, Craig, Woodworth, and Dunlap, all more or less independently; and he pointed out that there had emerged a surprising degree of agreement among the different positions in spite of their differences in detail and nomenclature. The consensus was that instincts are aroused by certain physiological conditions of the organism that signify some biological distress, like a sexual or food need. Instincts also characteristically involve particular kinds of motivated behavior: a sequence of restless seeking behavior that may be highly variable but that is invariably terminated by a fixed innate reaction that has the effect of relieving the initiating condition. In 1923 this conception was called instinct; five years later, and ever since, it has been called drive. Let us look at some of the variations of this new instinct concept.

Wallace Craig. One variation was formulated by the naturalist Wallace Craig (1918). He noted that the overt behavior of adult animals (Craig spoke principally about birds) occurs not so much in fixed stimulus-response elements, but rather in flexible cycles or chains of behavior, only some parts of which may be fixed. We should not let the fixed part of an instinct prevent us from seeing that for each instinct there is a characteristic appetitive or aversive sequence of

[5] Tolman's new teleology was introduced in 1920. Students of E. A. Singer have told me that in his lectures Singer had anticipated both Tolman and Perry by about ten years; I have not been able to find the anticipation in print, however. Tolman might also have cited Russell (1916), and particularly Holt (1915). But questions of historical priority should not obscure the fact that it was Tolman who developed the idea, made it popular, built it into a general theory of behavior, and, above all, tried to put it to empirical test.

behavior that is not fixed. Appetitive behavior (or appetence, as Craig preferred to call it) is a state of agitation that continues as long as a certain stimulus, the appeted stimulus, is absent. When the stimulus is present, it stimulates a *consummatory reaction*, which terminates the behavior cycle. When the appeted stimulus is absent, there will still be a "readiness" to make the innate consummatory reaction. The best evidence for its fixity and innateness is the occurrence (even on the first manifestation) of incipient consummatory action when the appeted stimulus has not yet been presented. (This is called vacuum activity by present-day ethologists and is rather common in the sexual behavior of birds but occurs elsewhere as well.)

Aversion was treated in an analogous way; whenever a stimulus evokes in an animal an agitation, a particular restlessness, which continues until the animal takes flight, we may say that the animal is showing aversion to that stimulus. In this case flight is the instinctive consummatory reaction. For either appetence or aversion the agitation consists of (1) phasic and static contractions of skeletal and dermal muscles, giving rise to body postures and gestures that are readily recognizable "signs" of the appetite or aversion; (2) restlessness; (3) activity; (4) varied effort; and (5) the readiness to engage in the consummatory activity.

Craig admitted that there were probably a number of gradations between true reflexes and a mere readiness to act in a certain way. Instinctive readiness patterns, though, differ in principle from reflexes in that they may involve trial-and-error learning: A number of trials takes place until one response pays off. Those modes of behavior that were immediately followed by the appeted stimulus are later repeated while the other behaviors drop out. Sometimes, of course, such trial and error is not evident, but even in this case it is useless to seek the environmental stimuli that elicit the behavior because appetitive behavior is characterized by its variability in the absence of the appeted stimulus, rather than by fixed stimulus-response relationships. Thus for Craig instinctive behavior was defined by the kind of consummatory reaction it involves and by the occurrence of variable, restless, agitated behavior that precedes the consummatory reaction.[6]

Robert Woodworth. For many years Woodworth was concerned with what he called dynamic psychology, which he defined at one point as the study of cause and effect in psychology. The study of cause and

---

[6] Craig perhaps placed even greater reliance upon behavioral data than Tolman did. He also put less weight on the energy versus structure distinction than any of the other theorists we have considered here. He was thus much more in the spirit of modern behaviorism than were his contemporaries. Craig supposed, interestingly, that it was necessary to assume the existence of internal stimuli to help account for appetitive behavior, since it is not regularly elicited by external stimulus conditions.

effect is the "attempt to gain a clear view of the action or process in the system studied . . . noting whatever uniformities occur, and what laws enable us to conceive the whole process in an orderly fashion" (Woodworth, 1918, p. 35[7]).

This approach introduces two problems, one the problem of mechanism, that is, how a thing is done, and the other the problem of drive, that is, what induces us to do it. It may be noted that *how* questions are relevant to mechanisms whereas *why* questions lead us to inquire about drives. In the case of a machine, the mechanism is the machine itself, which is inert until power is supplied to it to make it go. On the other hand, the energy supplied to the machine— its drive—requires the machine to guide, channel, and direct it. Now if all behavior were of a simple reflex type, dynamic psychology would be relatively simple: The mechanisms would be the whole organism, and the drive would be the stimulus to which it responds. The situation is complicated, however, by the fact that once a neural center is aroused by an external stimulus, it stays in a state of activity that outlasts its excitation.

The principal justification of dynamic psychology, and the main reason for distinguishing between mechanisms and drives, is the phenomenon of instinctive behavior, which, following Sherrington (1906), Woodworth characterized in terms of preparatory and consummatory reactions.

> A consummatory reaction is one of direct value to the animal— one directly bringing satisfaction—such as eating or escaping from danger. The objective mark of a consummatory reaction is that it terminates a series of acts, and is followed by rest or perhaps by a shift to some new series. Introspectively, we know such reactions by the satisfaction and sense of finality that they bring. The preparatory reactions are only mediately of benefit to the organism, their value lying in the fact that they lead to, and make possible, a consummatory reaction. Objectively, the mark of a preparatory reaction is that it occurs as a preliminary stage in a series of acts leading up to a consummatory reaction. Consciously, a preparatory reaction is marked by a state of tension. (Woodworth, 1918, p. 40)

Some preparatory reactions, like looking and listening, may occur when the animal is in a passive state; but a more interesting set

---

[7] Compare McDougall, 1932, p. 9. He tells us that so long as any science is content merely to describe, it does not require the conception of energy. The energy concept introduces order and system into an explanation of events when we seek the causal laws of a science. It seems as though the notion of force, or energy, arises in psychology when a theorist wants to disavow mechanistic explanations but does not have a sound alternative. James did not do this because he had mentalism to rely upon, but most of the theorists we are considering here discovered the dynamic principle when they gave up mechanism. So did Freud; and so did the psychologists at Berlin, including Lewin, as we saw in the preceding chapter.

of preparatory reactions are those that arise only when the mechanism for a consummatory reaction has been aroused, as when the animal is hungry. Then we find that while each preparatory reaction is in part a response to some external stimulus, it is also dependent upon the drive toward the consummatory reaction.

Woodworth parted company with McDougall most emphatically on the question of the universality of instincts as motivating agents. McDougall had posited that all behavior was directly or indirectly motivated by the instinct. Woodworth, denying this view, held that "any mechanism—except perhaps some of the most rudimentary that give the simple reflexes—once it is aroused, is capable of furnishing its own drive and also of lending drive to other connected mechanisms" (p. 67).

Thus Woodworth denied the proposition that all the mechanisms of the human adult, all the things he is capable of doing, are wholly passive, requiring the drive of a few instincts, like sex, hunger, curiosity, and so on, to put them into action. Sometimes, especially upon their first occurrence, instincts do drive these mechanisms into action; but after a time they become more or less autonomous. Typically, we find that any mechanism that is habitually exercised tends to behave as though it were itself a drive and comes to acquire the ability to drive other mechanisms so that the latter are freed from the direct dependence upon the primitive instincts. "Mechanisms can become drives."

Dunlap and others. The third theorist who had also arrived at a similar position regarding the new teleology, Tolman felt, was Dunlap (1922, 1923). Historically, his contribution has not been as important as the contributions made by Craig, Woodworth, or Tolman. What Dunlap did was to draw up a list of fundamental desires. These desires had reference to some of the physiological disturbances of the organism and provided the springs of social conduct.

Dunlap was just one of a number of writers urging that the current conception of instinct should be discarded or replaced. All of these men shared certain broad theoretical commitments. Like all instinct theorists, they sought to account for the seeming intelligence, adaptability, and goal directedness of behavior without invoking rationalism or mentalism. They all had the conviction that the task could not be accomplished by the mechanists, because behavior was a different type of realm from the world of physical laws. Some, like Tolman, retained mentalistic-sounding concepts to help do the job, while others, like Craig, were able to see enough lawfulness in behavior itself that they could accept this lawfulness as providing a sufficient account. However, most instinct theorists have insisted upon adding "something else," such as energy, to explain purposive behavior.

The outcome of the controversy

With the added perspective of 50 years we can see the Great Instinct Controversy somewhat more clearly than the participants could.[8] It appears that three distinct issues were involved, although they were not always sharply distinguished at the time. The issues in contention were (1) whether adaptive behavior is learned or innate, (2) whether adaptive behavior is best explained with purely structural concepts or with dynamic ones, and (3) whether the explanation of behavior should be mechanistic or mentalistic.

McDougall was the leading spokesman for the extreme tender-minded position on all these questions. He argued that both biological and social motivations were innate, that behavior had to be explained in terms of instinctive forces, and that psychology should retain its mentalistic terms, particularly those referring to feelings and emotions. Watson (1919) and Kuo (1924) were the outstanding extremists for the tough-minded side of these issues. They argued that what were called instincts were either just reflexes or else involved learning, that the explanation of behavior should be exclusively in associationistic terms without reference to dynamic forces or energies, and that a mechanistic account of behavior was sufficient to encompass all the facts. The critics of the instinct concept also attacked it on the grounds that it lacked scientific rigor. For example, Kuo (1924) argued that the propositions of the instinct theorists were untestable; instinct psychology was a "finished psychology," discontinuing its study of behavior just at the point where behaviorism would wish to begin. It proposed answers when questions were more in order. Had he adhered to this position, Kuo's attack upon the instinct theorists might have had a better reception. As it was, he overstated his case and defended with great passion (and largely in the absence of experimental support) the position that there were no instincts, nor indeed any evidence of hereditary factors in psychology. He argued not only that there was no innate organization of behavior but even that there was no predetermination of behavior in the structure of the nervous system. This latter position could not bear up under the first reports of the empirical work of Carmichael (1926) or even the work of Kuo himself (1929).

As might be expected, neither extreme position won a clear victory; the outcome was mixed. In 50 years we have not resolved the question of what is learned and what is innate. However, it has become apparent that the truth of the matter does not lie anywhere

[8] Judging from contributions to the *Psychological Review*, 1923 was the year of crisis. See, for example, Perrin (1923), Tolman (1923a), Wells (1923), Zigler (1923), and the remarkable paper of Thurstone (1923).

between Kuo's and McDougall's positions but somewhere off to the side. We have discovered that there are species-specific constraints on what animals can learn and, at the same time, that much species-specific behavior involves unique kinds of learning. Hence, one writer (Verplanck, 1955) has been led to wonder "Since learned behavior is innate, and vice versa, what now?" But this is a recent dilemma and for many years the initial deadlock was considered to have been resolved by means of a compromise: There are a few basic innate drives such as hunger and thirst, while the other varieties of motivation, for example, those in social situations, derive from (are learned on the basis of) the basic ones (see Chapter 9).

The tender-minded carried the day on the question of structure versus energy.

> The psychology of instincts was a dynamics of imaginary forces and the anti-instinct movement was primarily a crusade against such a conceptual dynamism. Somehow the argument got twisted. Heredity was made the scapegoat and the hypostatization of psychic energies goes merrily on. (Lashley, 1938, p. 447)

Of the three theoretical issues of the 1920s, the most important was probably the third, which was whether man's behavior could be explained mechanistically (and if it could, whether it should) or, on the other hand, whether the traditional rationalistic variety of explanation had to be retained. Indeed, the instinct controversy of the 1920s could only have occurred if men saw mentalism and mechanism as the only real alternative explanatory systems. This controversy has gradually become resolved as we have begun to see that behavior can be explained in its own terms without recourse to either mentalism or mechanism. This was, of course, the change that Tolman, Craig, and Woodworth sought to bring about. However, this solution was not generally seen as the proper course, and this final resolution is still being brought about, its slowness perhaps resulting from the seeming appropriateness of mechanistic and mentalistic approaches to our problems. At the time, neither side won a clear victory on this question. Mentalism was dethroned; Watson had won that much. But Watson's stark physicalistic alternative to mentalism was not widely accepted. The definition of psychology changed from the study of the mind to the study of behavior, but this too was only accomplished gradually.

The only obvious immediate outcome of the Great Instinct Controversy was that the word *instinct* was banished; it virtually disappeared from the psychological literature for the next 15 or 20 years. When it began to reappear (e.g., Lashley, 1938), it was purely as a descriptive term designating unlearned behavior. It had been stripped of its prior connotations of emotion, biological adaptiveness, unconscious impulses, and teleology. These connotations did not perish when the word was banished, however; they merely became attached, with varying degrees of persistence, to the new word *drive*.

Drive was an even better compromise concept than instinct had been. It gave the mechanist just the principle of mechanical causation he wanted; and the drives promised to have objective physiological or physical bases, which the instincts lacked. Drives also permitted the vitalist and the mentalist to keep at least a descriptive teleology of the kind Craig and Tolman had proposed. Drives were manifest in behavior, had physiological correlates, and gave rise to man's desires. Thus they bridged all of the interdisciplinary gaps that instincts were supposed to bridge.

In England and in Germany the instinct idea became embodied in a new set of theoretical trimmings. It is undoubtedly not just a coincidence that the new revitalized instinct concept arose from a relatively new realm of behavioral data to which neither the mechanistic nor the mentalistic philosophy had previously been applied in a wholesale manner. This new area emphasized the behavior of submammalian forms, primarily birds and fishes. This new subject matter and the new approach of its students led to the rapid growth of a new discipline, ethology. In later chapters we will consider the development, the vogue, and the subsequent decline of the drive concept, all primarily as the result of research in animal laboratories in this country. It will not be digressing too far, however, to look at the rise and decline in popularity of some ethological concepts, because that story provides some very nice parallels.

The ethologist's instincts

Ethology may fairly be said to have begun with the publication in 1935 of Lorenz's paper "Companions in the life of birds." Lorenz begins this paper by calling our attention to the principle that different animals have different perceptions of objects. Man, by virtue of his good sensory equipment and highly differentiated nervous system, can perceive and respond to many different aspects of a stimulus situation. By contrast, most animals tend to respond only to a given aspect or to some fixed feature of objects in their world. Lorenz proceeds then to note a further restriction on the behavior of animals, namely, that the response to the limited perception is again limited, restricted by the animal's particular nervous organization. In the most characteristic cases the response that occurs is innately organized into adaptive patterns. When these responses occur, they are not so much elicited by the appropriate stimulus events as they are *released* by them. Lorenz observes that in order for an animal's behavior to be adaptive, it is sufficient that an appropriate fixed action pattern be released by the appropriate stimulus.

Theory of motivation

What gives individuality and specificity to each animal species is that both the particular releasing stimulus and the particular response that it releases are highly specific to a given species. We may credit evolution with producing both the diversity of particular instinctive behaviors observed in nature and the development of structures and behaviors in other members of a species that serve as releasers for the appropriate behavior (appropriate in the sense of being biologically adaptive). Thus, for example, birds mate with members of their own species because both the male and female, under the proper hormonal conditions, engage in behavior that presents stimulation that releases just the appropriate behavior in the mate; and these mechanisms are specific enough that the corresponding behavior is not produced except by animals of the proper sex and the proper species. The specificity of these instinctive mechanisms gives them a certain general improbability in much the same way that a key fits only a particular lock and has a low probability of fitting locks in general.

Lorenz distinguishes sharply between the final act of instinctive behavior, which he assumes is innately organized and released by appropriate stimuli, and all of the prior, more or less motivated, behavior that precedes it. It is only the final fixed action pattern that is properly referred to as the instinct. Whatever other behavior precedes it, including whatever instrumental (i.e., learned) behavior there may be that makes it possible for the instinct to run off, this behavior is not to be confused with the instinct itself but is, instead, to be referred to as appetitive behavior. It is only the final act, the behavioral end point, that is necessarily fixed because it is innately given. Lorenz denies emphatically that the instinct itself is modifiable through experience.

Lorenz cites as an example of instinctive behavior the "following" response of geese and other birds. Ordinarily, the young goose follows its mother in a characteristic manner that provides some safety for the individual and some integrity for the family group. This behavior turns out, however, not to be purely instinctive, nor to be learned, but to be a unique blend of the two processes. The following response itself is assumed to be fixed, but the particular releaser is not. Rather, it depends upon what objects happen to occupy the bird's world at a particular stage in its development. If the young animal is surrounded by members of its own species at a certain critical period in its development, then it will follow in a normal manner. But if it is isolated from members of its species, it will follow other objects, including people, that happen to be present during the critical period. Lorenz argued that this flexibility in the behavior is not an instance of learning since (1) it is irreversible; for example, having been imprinted on a human, the duck will always follow the human and may even direct sexual behavior toward the human rather than to members of its own species; and (2) plasticity in the behavior is limited to a very short period lasting only a few hours early in the animal's development.

Lorenz gave ample credit to his forerunners. His idea of an animal's unique and limited perception of objects was based largely on von Uexküll's profound and often poetic appreciation of the perceptual worlds of animals (1909). The distinction between the modifiable appetitive component in a sequence of behavior and the fixed end point was attributed to Craig (1918). His description of imprinting followed that of Heinroth (1911).

The picture we get, then, of adaptive behavior is that such behavior, crucial for the survival and normal functioning of the animal, is innately organized into fixed action patterns that normally occur when released by certain specific stimuli. However, the integrated and coherent nature of the fixed action pattern, Lorenz argues, is most convincingly demonstrated by its tendency to go off "in a vacuum" in the absence of the characteristic releasing stimuli if it has not been released appropriately for a long period of time. In fact, it is this separation of the innate releasing mechanism from the normal releaser that tells us what part of the behavior is fixed and innately organized as an instinctive pattern (Lorenz, 1937).

One of the great values of the ethological approach for the psychologist is the wealth of descriptive material about animal behavior it has produced. The ethologist insists, moreover, that behavior is seen at its best in its natural setting, that is, in nature, so that its appearance will be governed by the characteristics of the animal rather than by the constraints of the laboratory situation. Ethology makes the constant discovery that the behavior of one species is often no more than analogous to the behavior of another. Each animal form has its own characteristic ways of solving its problems. It may share its manner of solution to some extent with other species, but the range of generalizability must always be determined empirically. We cannot expect the psychology of the rat to apply immediately to the stickleback, or to the jackdaw, or to man. The psychologist, with his great haste to generalize, can learn a valuable lesson from the ethologist's respect for the diversity of behavior.

Energy models

Up to this point the account of behavior Lorenz had given us was purely structural; dynamic or motivational elements played little part in it. Moreover, much of subsequent ethological theory and research has developed along purely structural lines. For example, there has been considerable discussion of the conditions under which imprinting occurs, the variety of species in which it may be found, the variety of objects upon which birds may be imprinted, and the determination of the other behavioral effects that the imprinted object may have.[9] All such questions can be put in structural form without introducing motivational concepts, and perhaps that is the best way to put such questions if we wish to get answers to them.

However, Lorenz's theoretical model was soon motivationalized, both by Lorenz himself and by Tinbergen. For Lorenz (1937, 1950) each fixed action pattern, that is, each instinct, was motivated by its own source of energy, its own action-specific energy. Lorenz likened the source of energy for each instinct to a reservoir in which the energy specific to a given instinct would gradually accumulate in the absence of the appropriate releaser and then be discharged when the releasing stimulus was presented. This analogy illustrated several hypothetical properties of the fixed action pattern: the specificity of the fixed action pattern, its weakening with continued elicitation, its strengthening with the withdrawal of the appropriate releaser, and even the overflow of energy in vacuum activity when the organism is sufficiently aroused but the appropriate releasing conditions are absent.

Tinbergen (1951) elaborated this model by proposing first that the different sources of action-specific energy were arranged in a hierarchical system so that the energy pertinent to one basic class of functional activity, such as reproduction, would motivate a number of different but related behaviors, such as mating, aggression, nest building, and tending the young. Each of these specific patterns of behavior was assumed to be organized around and motivated by energy associated with a particular center, presumably localizable somewhere in the central nervous system. Tinbergen further elaborated this model by supposing that a surplus of energy in any one center, if blocked or prevented from being discharged, or in the absence of the appropriate releaser, could "spark over" to other centers, even centers controlling quite unrelated behaviors (Tinbergen, 1940, 1951). It had been noted by a number of ethologists that instinctive behavior patterns often occur out of context and that this is most apt to happen in situations where the behavior of another instinctive pattern is blocked or frustrated in some way. This out-of-context occurrence of behavior has been called *displacement activity* (Armstrong, 1947, 1950). Most characteristically, displacement activity takes the form of some sort of grooming behavior. For example, if an animal is thwarted in mating, it may groom. Grooming, itself an innately organized behavior, is supposed to occur in this instance because it is motivated by the displaced energy normally residing in the center controlling mating.[10]

[9] Subsequent research (reviewed by Bateson, 1966) has given us a picture of imprinting that is considerably different from Lorenz's.

[10] The theoretical importance of displacement is further emphasized by Tinbergen in terms of the concept of ritualization. This concept arises from the problem of attempting to account for the evolutionary development of fixed action patterns. Why is it that a bird of a particular

The view of behavior that we have just described has been criticized on several grounds, and it should be noted that partly as a result of this criticism ethology, which was at its inception characterized by an extremely naturalistic approach (i.e., an approach that maximizes the richness of descriptive observation while minimizing experimental intervention in the natural order of events to be observed), has proceeded to become less naturalistic in orientation. For example, recent work in this field has tended to become more analytical both with respect to the physiological determinants of behavior and with respect to the immediate psychological conditions that govern the behavior. Moreover, there has been increasing concern about the genetic basis of instinctive behavior, and considerable progress has been made in the direction of manipulating the genetic substrata (Fuller & Thompson, 1960). At the same time, there has been an increasing concentration upon the details of the behavior itself, and as a consequence of this analysis we have come to realize that no real distinction can be made between innate and learned behavior (Lehrman, 1970). Even the most innate of behaviors is likely to be expressed only if certain developmental and other experiential conditions are met. And even the most learned of behaviors requires for its expression that there be an appropriate genetic background.

Our concern here is not with the criticisms that have been made of these structural aspects of the ethologist's instinct theory, but rather the criticisms that have been made of the ethologist's use of motivational concepts and, more specifically, of the energy concept of motivation. Some of this criticism has been directed at the motivation idea itself. (Hebb, 1955; Hinde, 1959, 1960). Some critics have stressed that motivational models, especially the one proposed by Tinbergen, do not correspond with what is known about the workings of the central nervous system (Hinde, 1954, 1956). Hinde observes that we know of nothing in the field of neurology that corresponds with Tinbergen's sparking-over phenomenon.[11]

The most telling argument against Tinbergen's motivational model is that which has arisen from the recent experimental analysis

---

species displays in a particular manner? Tinbergen's answer is that particular forms of behavior, such as grooming, that occur as displacement behavior early in the evolutionary history of the animal become, through the pressure of natural selection, a necessary part of the releaser in later evolutionary time. Hence the importance of plumage, spectacular colorations, and display patterns found in mating. Displacement behavior can be viewed, therefore, as a source of variation in the process of evolution.

[11] Hinde recognizes that a model need not necessarily represent everything about the system being modeled. But he argues that since Tinbergen speaks about neural centers, his model should at least not be inconsistent with what is known in neurology. The history and current status of the motivation concept in ethology have been ably surveyed by Beer (1963–1964).

of displacement activity. Recall that displacement and vacuum activity are the two principal sources of support for the motivation idea in ethology. These are the phenomena that cannot be explained, it has been argued, without recourse to motivational or dynamic concepts; how else are we to account for the sudden occurrence of grooming or aggression when the animal has been frustrated in the midst of mating?

Quite recently, however, it has become apparent that a purely structural or associative account of displacement behavior can be formulated. The necessary assumption is that displacement activities, such as grooming, are very high in the animal's repertoire of available responses because the stimulus conditions that ordinarily elicit them are nearly always present (Andrew, 1956). It is certainly the case that grooming constitutes one of the most common behavior patterns under normal circumstances, and it is precisely this sort of behavior that is most frequently observed as a displacement activity. If the animal has nothing else to do, if it is not responding to some more insistent stimulus, it grooms. However, grooming is easily supplanted by other kinds of behavior. In conflict situations when a response such as a part of the mating ritual is simultaneously evoked and inhibited, the response that would ordinarily take precedence over grooming is blocked and then grooming proceeds as the next most probable response. So-called displacement activities, therefore, can be viewed simply as the occurrence of the next strongest response in the animal's repertoire on those occasions when the strongest response or responses are prevented from occurring.

Rowell (1961) has given experimental support to this competing response interpretation of displacement grooming. Rowell varied the presence of conflict and the presence of the external stimuli that ordinarily produced grooming (water was sprayed on the feathers of a chaffinch, or sticky material was placed on the bird's bill). By varying the kind and intensity of stimuli to elicit characteristic forms of grooming (preening or bill wiping) Rowell demonstrated that both the amount of grooming and the form it took were appropriate to the stimulus conditions and the experimentally produced conflict conditions. Thus displacement behavior, which was supposedly inexplicable simply in terms of stimulation, appears to be readily explained in structural terms.

The way now seems clear to give vacuum activity a similar systematic structural interpretation. Thus, for example, mounting of inappropriate objects when an animal is "sexually aroused" does not necessarily have to be understood in motivational terms as an "overflowing" of the reservoir. We might also regard it merely as an instance of stimulus generalization (Beach, 1942a), or we might conceive of it as indicating the breadth of stimulus and hormonal conditions that ordinarily produce it. It is only if we think of mounting as a response released by, or given exclusively to, the female of the species that its occurrence in the absence of the female appears incongruous. If we think of mounting as a response that occurs whenever there are enough stimuli from a pool of possible stimulation including the female, hormonal effects upon the nervous system, gonadal tension, and the animal's postural and kinesthetic feedback, then there is nothing at all incongruous about its occurrence in the absence of one of these potential sources of stimulation.

Some writers (Hinde, 1960; Zeigler, 1964) have seen an object lesson in the doubt suddenly cast upon the utility of energy models in ethology by the experimental work of Andrew and Rowell. Tinbergen's theoretical account of displacement had a great deal of appeal—it was simple and elegant, but it did not foster an empirical attack upon the problems presented by the displacement phenomenon. Hinde and Zeigler have both suggested that Tinbergen's energy model was too pat, too facile—it discouraged an experimental analysis of the behavior. Like McDougall's analysis of instinctive behavior a generation before, it proposed answers when questions would have been more valuable.

We know enough about behavior now to find no explanation satisfactory unless it describes the structural or associative facts of the case. But when these facts are known in any specific instance, the further attribution of motivating agencies may add nothing more to our understanding of it. Our concern should be with discovering the controlling mechanisms, whether these be associative, hormonal, or whatever, and with whether they derive from the experience of an animal, its genetic history, or some combination of the two. This approach is nicely illustrated by Hinde's (1970) book *Animal Behaviour*. Although some contemporary writers (e.g., Eibl-Eibesfeldt, 1970) continue to use a motivational approach much like Tinbergen's (1951), ethology is becoming increasingly devoted to the search for controlling mechanisms and less of a defense of the idea that behavior is to be explained by motivating instincts.

Summary

At this point we may begin to wonder whether instincts (or drives) are invoked to explain some behavior only when too little is known about the behavior to explain it structurally.

5
THE
DRIVE
CONCEPT

We believe, however, that spontaneous activity
arises from certain underlying physiological
origins. We shall attempt to show from
studies chiefly on the white rat what some
of these origins are. . . .
C. P. Richter

The concept of drive was recognized, even from the first, as being similar to the concept of instinct; but drives were supposed to have certain theoretical advantages over the discredited instincts. Drives were like instincts in that they were believed to motivate behavior. They were also like instincts in that they were supposed to provide a substantial and scientific basis for the subjective aspects of motivation; they were supposed to explain men's wants. Finally, drives were like instincts in that they were considered to be biologically important. The drive concept had one theoretical advantage in that it was based upon a new conceptual distinction between energy and structure to replace the time-worn distinction between vitalism and mechanism that had supported the concept of instinct.

But the principal virtue of the early conception of drives was that they were assumed to have a discernible, tangible, easily accessible physiological basis. Instincts were assumed to have physiological bases too, of course, but these bases were not immediately accessible; they were bound up in the intricacies of the genetic mechanisms. The only tangible reference for the instincts was the relatively permanent nature of hereditary behavior traits. Certainly, one reason for the widespread acceptance of the drive concept was the general belief that physiological research would soon disclose the real roots of motivation. The drive concept, which was already gaining considerable currency in the explanation of both human and animal behavior, needed only to be tied down empirically to physiological observables to be thoroughly acceptable to all parties. Some of the first experimental reports looked encouraging; they were eagerly seized upon as scientific proof of the motivational ideas that few psychologists doubted. We were so convinced of the legitimacy of the concept that supporting evidence was accepted quite uncritically.

In the present chapter we will consider some of these early attempts to get at the real roots of motivation. We will find that four kinds of evidence, originating from different laboratories, focused upon quite different aspects of motivation, and involving initially entirely different conceptions, began to converge upon a unifying set of ideas that gave the drive concept its present form. The first of these sources of ideas was the failure of the "local" theory of hunger and thirst proposed by Cannon. Cannon attempted to defend the position that hunger and thirst were merely stimuli, certain special localized sensations to be sure, but nonetheless stimuli, to which motivated behavior became associated. As data began to accumulate that indicated that Cannon's particular local theory was incorrect, the most attractive alternative was the position that hunger and thirst were dynamic central states, definitely something other than stimuli.

At about the same time, Richter and his collaborators were discovering that animals became more active as biological needs were imposed upon them. This result suggested that an animal's drives not only were directed toward specific goals, such as food and water, but that drives had a diffuse and generalized effect as well. Drives not only led to specific adaptive behavior, they were also reflected in general activity level.

Third, the discovery of specific hungers helped to shape the drive concept. Animals appeared to be motivated for just those things they needed for their well-being. For example, an animal maintained on a salt-free diet seemed to develop a specific motivation for salt.

The fourth, and in some ways the most exciting, development was the belief that Warden and his co-workers at Columbia had actually measured the strengths of the animal drives.

Some of these early research findings were pressed into service as a means of establishing operational definitions of drive. But we will see that these proposed definitions failed to survive because they could not cope adequately with the broad range of facts that were becoming known about motivated behavior. An adequate theoretical anchoring of the drive concept had to await a more detailed and sophisticated analysis. But in the interim there was little question that this either had been or soon would be accomplished. Nearly everyone believed in the validity of the drive concept.

Stimuli as drives to action

In the early days of behavior theory "stimulus" nearly always referred to events external to the organism. But it soon occurred to some theorists that it might be useful to consider the possibility of internal stimuli. They began to conceive of certain events in the organism's internal environment that could register on the nervous system and to which the organism could react.[1]

We have already seen that Freud had developed a similar view in 1915 and had called attention to the fact that until that time stimuli had always been regarded as noxious as well as external. Freud's theory of motivation was built on the fact that an organism cannot escape noxious internal stimuli in the same way it can flee external ones. A noxious internal stimulus requires some special arrangement with the environment in order to bring about an adequate adjustment.

Local theory of motivation. At about the same time, certain physiologists, most notably Walter B. Cannon, were beginning to develop similar ideas about the importance of internal stimulation. Cannon guessed from internal noises that hunger sensations, "pangs," were caused by stomach contractions.[2] He persuaded Washburn to swallow a balloon on the end of a tube that was connected to a pneumatic kymograph on which were also recorded marks made by pushing a button whenever Washburn felt a hunger pang. The correlation of contractions with hunger sensations indicated that Cannon's guess had been correct (Cannon & Washburn, 1912). Substantiation for this conclusion came from Carlson's laboratory and from X-ray observation (Carlson, 1912; Rogers & Martin, 1926). Carlson (1916) then came out strongly in support of a local theory of hunger.

More recently, some doubt has arisen regarding the legitimacy of Cannon's conclusion that hunger pangs can be identified with stomach contractions; but for nearly a half century it was generally accepted that Cannon had found the source of those stimuli we perceive as hunger pangs.[3] On the other hand, there has been a

---

[1] Verworn (1889) was one of the first to suggest that internal stimuli should be considered in the explanation of behavior. Others, for example, Morgan (1894) and Jennings (1906), also emphasized the importance of internal stimulation and physiological conditions for the behavior of lower animals.

[2] This was not an entirely novel conception, nor was Cannon by any means the originator of the local theory. The long history of these matters has been nicely surveyed by Rosenzweig (1962).

[3] Davis et al. (1959) measured gastric motility in terms of electric activity measured by electrodes placed externally on the upper abdomen. They found no evidence of the classical gastric activity cycle demonstrated in balloon studies until *after* a balloon had been inflated in the stomach. Essentially the same results have been reported by Penick et al. (1963) using a miniature pressure-sensitive telemetering device taken into the stomach. It would appear that the contractions reported by Cannon, and others, are *produced* by filling the stomach with a balloon and are not just a phenomenon measured by the balloon. This wonderful illustration of the principle that a measuring device can distort the phenomenon to be measured should not obscure the fact that many people do

great deal of discussion about the wisdom of Cannon's next step, which was to label these sensations hunger. He defined hunger as a ". . . disagreeable ache or pang or sense of gnawing or pressure which is referred to the epigastrium, the region just below the tip of the breast bone" (1934, p. 248).[4] Cannon said that he had made the identification of hunger with the sensations from stomach contractions mainly to combat the notion that hunger was a "general" sensation, a sort of diffuse awareness, which was not based upon any particular localizable sensation.

Cannon was well aware that people eat without being goaded into eating by hunger pangs; he said: "In any discussion of hunger and thirst it is important at the outset . . . to distinguish carefully between these sensations [of hunger] and appetite" (1934, p. 247). Cannon paid very little attention to appetite, however; he indicated only that it depends upon previous experience with sensations that are so agreeable that we desire to repeat them. He acknowledged that appetite was an important determinant of how and when people eat and particularly of what they eat; but he was almost exclusively concerned with showing that hunger was a local sensation.[5]

In 1918 Cannon developed a similar local theory of thirst. He adduced a variety of evidence to support the view that the sensation of thirst arose from a dry, parched mouth and throat. Some of the relevant observations are that a small mouthful of water, anesthetic drugs, or saliva produced by acid in the mouth all abolish the thirst sensation.[6] He observed at one point that "All accounts of well-marked thirst agree that its main characteristic is the dry mouth" (1934, p. 254). We may wonder how Cannon could have failed to

---

report having hunger pangs or cramps. Moreover, it is certain that many people eat in order to stop these sensations. See Hoelzel and Carlson (1952) and Hoelzel (1957) on the question of whether these sensations disappear with continued food deprivation—the sensations do but hunger does not.

[4] An expert introspective study of hunger and appetite was conducted by Boring and Luce (1917). The closest agreement with Cannon's perception came from the subject Dimmick: Hunger is a "bright burny thing at the base of the stomach" (p. 445). Boring concluded that hunger differed from appetite in many ways: certain stomach sensation, certain oral factors (like salivation), presence of imagery, and the general attitude or disposition. Thus for some subjects the main component of appetite was the desire to grab the food and eat it.

[5] Cannon never made clear who he thought his opposition was. Perhaps he was opposing Bernard (1878) but, if so, the charge was unjustified because Bernard believed thirst was a general *need*, not a general sensation. In other words, Cannon may have been attacking a straw man (see also Fitzsimons, 1972).

[6] Cannon (1918) gives only a short account; Cannon (1929, 1934) gives fuller accounts and attempts to deal with some of the criticisms that had come up.

note that all accounts of thirst agree that its main characteristic is that the individual wants a drink.

There are two distinct questions here: One is the semantic question of whether the subjective experiences of hunger and thirst are actually due to local sensations arising from the stomach and the oral cavity. The second question, a syntactical one, is perhaps more interesting. Granted for the moment that Cannon really found the psychophysical correlates of what we call hunger and thirst, what can we say then about the behavior of hungry or thirsty organisms? Cannon himself was so busy defending his answer to the first question that he neglected the second. On the other hand, it now seems clear that those who most bitterly attacked Cannon did so because they were primarily interested in developing concepts of hunger and thirst that would permit them to deal with the second question rather than with the first. Even if Cannon had provided an answer to the first question, the semantic rigidity with which hunger and thirst were tied down made them virtually useless for explaining what or how or when the organism will eat or drink. Cannon's sensations from the stomach or the mouth could only tell the organism it was hungry or thirsty and never how much to consume or how to get consumable commodities.

The syntactical poverty of Cannon's local theory was not recognized at first. From the point of view of the early animal psychologists it was easy to suppose that an internal noxious stimulus such as a hunger pang or a parched throat would stir the organism to action and lead it to do something to relieve the condition. Experimental psychologists had generally been so preoccupied with problems of sensation and perception and so committed to the traditional structural account of behavior that for them too the problems of hunger and thirst were largely solved once stimulus correlates for each could be found. But psychologists eventually began to distrust Cannon's theory as they came to develop the notion that drives were something other than stimuli and, particularly, as they gained more insight into the behavioral facts of motivation, that is, as they began to see that motivation was a problem in the organization and explanation of behavior rather than a problem in perception. At the same time, physiologists became dissatisfied with Cannon's local theory, first, as they probed further into the brain and found more central mechanisms in motivated behavior, and second, as they began to accumulate evidence that was incompatible with the theory. Let us look at some of this evidence.

Evidence against local theory. Hoelzel (1927) and Wangensteen and Carlson (1931) had patients who had the stomach removed and the esophagus tied directly to the intestine. These patients' eating habits and experience of hunger were said to be normal, even to the experience of hunger pangs. More systematic observations of a similar kind were made by Tsang (1938), who surgically removed the stomachs of rats. Again, except for the fact that the animals ate somewhat more frequently than usual (due no doubt to their limited storage capacity), they ate normally and showed the normal pattern of activity in an activity wheel. Wolf and Wolff (1943) found that a patient with a stomach fistula, which permitted gastric activity to be observed directly, showed no correlation between stomach activity and subjective hunger. Other experimenters (Bash, 1939; Morgan & Morgan, 1940) found that cutting the neural pathway from the stomach had little effect either upon a rat's consummatory behavior or its instrumental food-getting behavior.

Cannon's local theory of thirst was not faring any better. According to Weir et al. (1922), in cases of diabetes insipidus drugs such as pilocarpine and atropine (which have the effects of facilitating and inhibiting salivation respectively) had little effect either upon the patients' reports of thirst or upon their drinking behavior. Moreover, extensive application of cocaine to the throat (which Cannon had found eliminated the sensation of dryness) failed to alleviate the craving for water characteristic of the disease. Similar studies with dogs (e.g., Montgomery, 1931) have failed to show that dryness or wetness of the mouth has a determining effect upon water consumption. Studies by Bruce (1938) and Morgan and Fields (1938) showed that animals were more motivated for food or water, in the sense that they ran faster for it, if they were prefed or prewatered a small part of their daily ration just before running. The optimum amounts for the fastest running turn out to be large enough that they would be expected to stop stomach contractions and alleviate the parched throat.[7]

Perhaps the studies that were the most damaging to Cannon's local theory, and at the same time the most interesting in terms of methodology, were those reported by Adolph (1939) and Bellows (1939) with fistulated dogs. These dogs were allowed to drink, but the water was prevented from getting to the stomach by a fistula connected to the esophagus that drained it all back out. Such dogs "sham drank" great quantities of water each day, keeping the mouth wet, but evidently not reducing the desire to drink. These studies also indicated that if water is poured into the dog's stomach directly through the fistula without letting it enter the mouth, subsequent drinking would be inhibited provided some time elapsed between the stomach loading and the subsequent drinking test. The interesting finding was that a lapse of 10 to 15 minutes was sufficient to obtain a marked inhibition of drinking, and this is ordinarily considered to be too short a time for an appreciable amount of water to be absorbed from the stomach.

[7] Carlson (1916) reported that stomach contractions stopped with the first mouthful of food. This reaction is evidently conditionable, since Lorber et al. (1950) found that the first mouthful of food stopped contractions even when the food was sham eaten.

It was inevitable that the local theory of motivation would be extended to sexual motivation. However, Bard (1935) and Root and Bard (1937) showed that cutting the afferent pathways from the genital region of female cats failed to disrupt their sexual behavior. So it seemed that this behavior was like eating and drinking in that it too could not be explained solely in terms of unique localizable eliciting stimuli.

The systematic importance of all these studies was soon overshadowed, however, by the excitement that followed application of the Horsley-Clarke stereotaxic technique in making hypothalamic lesions. Bard (1940) found that there was a region of the hypothalamus that appeared to be critical for the appearance of sexual behavior. He showed that if this region was destroyed or if appropriate hormones were not present, female cats could not be brought into heat; normal behavior required both. Other "centers" controlling other kinds of motivated behavior (sleep and eating) were located about the same time by Ranson (1939) and Hetherington and Ranson (1940).

This sort of evidence made it plain that Cannon's spit-and-rumble theory of motivation would not suffice. Finding a motivating stimulus simply would not account for the animal's consummatory or instrumental behavior. For such an explanation it seemed more profitable to seek mechanisms, or explanatory constructs, that would have more generalized, widespread, and organizing effects upon the organism.

Central theory of motivation. Beach (1942) surveyed the evidence then available on male sexual behavior and postulated that there is what he called a central excitatory mechanism, which, once aroused by stimulus and hormonal factors, acts to initiate and sustain the variety of behavior patterns that constitute the male's sexual activity. Morgan (1943) proposed a similar concept; he suggested that there were a number of "central motive states," each of which governed one of the different kinds of motivation. The hypothetical properties of a central motive state (CMS) were:

1. Persistence—a CMS endures in a more continuous form than either the initiating conditions or the consequent behavior.
2. General activity—the motivated animal has a heightened level of bodily activity.
3. Specific activity—a CMS evokes specific forms of behavior that do not seem to depend upon any special environmental conditions.
4. Preparatory condition—the most important feature of a CMS is that it "primes" the organism for appropriate consummatory behavior when the right environmental conditions appear.

This view of the motivated organism, emphasizing the central state, has dominated subsequent physiological research. Typically, the neural and hormonal bases of the state are discovered, their effects upon behavior noted, and the controlling antecedent conditions hunted down. Explanations of specific behaviors result that may quite legitimately be considered to constitute a theory of motivation. The physiologist's concern here, however, is ordinarily not with explaining behavior, but rather with elucidating the nature of the central state. The consequent linkages to behavior are often considered as more properly of concern to the psychologist. Thus it has been fairly common to follow Adolph (1943) and speak of hunger and thirst as the "urges" to eat and drink.[8] Work in this area has progressed at a remarkable rate in the 30 years since these pioneering discoveries. We have now begun to get a rather good, albeit complex, picture of the various physiological factors that control specific behaviors such as eating, drinking, and mating. Although it is not the purpose of this book to describe our present understanding of the physiological mechanisms underlying motivated behavior, we will have occasion in subsequent chapters to look at some of this material.

Drives as stimuli to activity

If a rat is put in a revolving wheel (first used by Stewart, 1898) or a cage mounted on tambours (first used by Szymanski, 1914), then it will engage in different kinds of behavior that result in turning the drum or tilting the tambour cage. Munn (1950) has observed that this behavior sometimes seems random because it is

> . . . without the kind of specific direction that we observe when an animal runs toward food, toward water, or toward a sexual partner. What the animal does is run around in its cage or run in a revolving drum. Two terms have been used to designate this apparently random activity. One of these is *spontaneous activity*, and the other, *general activity*. The first term involves the assumption that no external stimulation, or at least no experimentally varied external stimulation, is responsible for eliciting or regulating the behavior. It has also been used to mean that the

[8] The urge is measured, ordinarily, only in terms of the animal's consummatory behavior. Hence the construct is not particularly well anchored behaviorally, and the psychologist may become a bit uneasy when such a basically mentalistic term is bandied about by men who he may feel have a better claim than he does to being called scientists. We have become accustomed to thinking of psychology as issuing promissory notes to physiology, and we are a little shocked to find that physiologists may also at times use the same currency. When a physiologist speaks of an urge, he seems to be revealing a faith that psychology either knows all about urges or soon will.

stimulus for the activity is unknown. The second term makes no assumptions about stimulation and, being just as descriptive as the first, is to be preferred. (Munn, 1950, p. 52)

Further justification for calling it *general* activity is that it is usually not analyzed; we count wheel revolutions when we do not care to know or do not bother to find out what animals do under some particular condition or what the controlling stimuli are. Recent work has confirmed Munn's suspicions that the stimuli that control general activity are more complex and more external than was thought at first.

The effect of deprivation on general activity. The historical importance of the early studies of general activity was that they called attention to the internal and constitutional determinants of behavior. No one played a larger part in this movement than Curt Richter. Richter first discovered that general activity tended to occur periodically rather than continuously (1922, 1927). He then attempted to correlate the periodic activity of different animals, including humans, with periodic physiological disturbances, such as stomach contractions. Richter (1927) has described the technical difficulties and disappointing initial results of trying to get stomach balloons to stay down. But when Wada (1922) managed to obtain records from medical students while they were sleeping, gross bodily movements were indeed found to occur more or less simultaneously with stomach contractions as registered by balloons swallowed just before retiring. Further supporting evidence of a somewhat more circumstantial nature was obtained from rats living in a tambour cage attached to an eating cage, also mounted on tambours. Kymograph records were obtained of bodily general activity, which showed not only more or less periodic bursts of activity at approximately 4-hour intervals but also that these active periods correlated with the times when food was taken.[9]

Richter reported further that activity records of very young rats showed their activity to be more or less continuous, and that only after the age of two weeks or so does the continuous activity pattern break up into discrete periods of activity. This change in pattern was attributed to learning. Richter supposed that through more or less continuous activity and by virtue of reflexive sucking in the young animal an association will be learned between stomach contractions and nursing. In the adult rat the same preliminary restlessness, due

---

[9] It is clear even from Wada's and Richter's published records that stomach contractions do not necessarily precede the overt activity. Powelson (1952) has made a special point of this and has suggested that perhaps waking up and running around stimulates stomach contractions, rather than the other way around. This interpretation has been defended by Richards (1936). Bolles (1960) has also reported that when rats wake up in their home cages, they typically do not start to eat until after they have groomed or engaged in some other activity.

to contractions, also becomes diverted into specific food-seeking activities, which again lead to quiescence.

Wang (1923), also working in Richter's laboratory, showed that there was a similar correlation between activity in a rotating drum and phases of the female rat's estrous cycle. When the female rat is in heat (approximately every four days, as judged either by her receptivity to males or by histological examination of the vagina), she may run three to ten times as much as normally. Slonaker (1924), confirming this, was also able to show that this cyclicity persists from puberty to menopause. This vivid cyclicity was said to be destroyed and the level of activity markedly reduced during pregnancy, lactation, or in pseudopregnancy.

In the male rat, too, there seemed to be a hormonal contribution to general activity in rotating cages, inasmuch as castration markedly reduced activity level (Hoskins, 1925). The dependence of activity upon hormones is not as clear in the case of the male as it is for the female, since injection of testosterone does not reestablish a high activity level. Transplantation of ovaries to male rats, however, has been reported (Wang et al., 1925) to lead to heightened activity with a 4-day rhythm. Also, whereas sexual consummatory activity immediately reduces general activity in the female, it has little effect in the male (Slonaker, 1924).

Other studies from Richter's laboratory indicated that there were also periodicities in drinking, elimination, and nest-building activity (Richter, 1927). It should be emphasized, however, that when Richter speaks of cyclic or periodic behavior he sometimes means behavior with a fixed period, as in the case of the estrous cycle, and sometimes he means merely behavior that does not occur continuously. In the case of eating, which he calls periodic, the data he gives for the time intervals between feedings reveal a very broad distribution of intervals. Bash (1939) and Baker (1953) have also demonstrated that there is no strict periodicity of the order of 2 to 4 hours in eating in rats (see page 196). There is abundant evidence for a 24-hour periodicity, however, as we will see later. But in any case, Richter's contention that drives have a basically cyclic character was widely accepted for many years.

Another important implication of Richter's work is the idea that if an animal is deprived of anything necessary for its well-being, it responds by becoming more active. In support of this hypothesis Hitchcock (1928) reported that rats became more active on a low-protein diet (although their activity level soon drops as they become progressively weakened). Wald and Jackson (1944) found that deprivation of water, or food and water, or thiamine increased running in activity wheels. How could anyone doubt the validity and power of the drive concept?

Specific hungers. In 1916 Evvard reported that hogs permitted to select their own diet from a variety of foods showed far better growth than animals maintained on normal fixed diets. Evvard's study was soon followed by similar self-selection studies with chickens (Pearl & Fairchild, 1921), human infants (Davis, 1928), and rats (Richter et al., 1938), all testifying to the ability of organisms to select for themselves diets appropriate for their needs. Subsequent work (reviewed by Young, 1959; Rozin & Kalat, 1971), using more sophisticated controls, has revealed a number of complicating factors in self-selection diet experiments. But these early studies aroused a great deal of initial interest; they were seen as illustrating the important new phenomenon of specific hungers and as adding an important new dimension to the drive concept.

Animals had been balancing their diets, of course, for some time before there were any commercially prepared foods or any nutritionists, but the discovery of such dietary balancing under laboratory conditions was something new, and the new concept of specific hungers was proposed to handle it. The old idea of instinct was that nature had put into animals marvelous devices so that they could promote their welfare without knowing that they were doing so. Specific hunger was the twentieth-century variant of this idea: If an animal needed a particular dietary component, then it would become hungry for that component. Green (1925) had shown that cattle deficient in phospherous tend to dig up bones and eat them. Richter (1936) showed that adrenalectomized animals (which rapidly develop a need for salt) show a preference for salt in concentrations that normal animals find totally intolerable. Richter (1939, 1942) generalized from these findings to arrive at the principle that appetites for particular substances always come from some physiological need, and that the preference for the needed object arises innately through an automatic adjustment of the sensory receptors. Richter's principle means that the animal in need of salt, for example, is more likely to detect salt in its food. Subsequent research has indicated, however, that, at least as far as salt is concerned, normal rats have thresholds of detection at least as low as adrenalectomized rats (Harriman & MacLeod, 1953).

Young began a long series of food preference experiments quite in sympathy with Richter's emphasis on innate food preferences, but his findings led him to change his opinion (compare Young, 1941 and 1948 with Young, 1959). Young found that rats could develop strong learned food preferences that might or might not serve their needs. Thus Young concluded that an animal's preference for particular food substances is a complex interaction of experiential and innate factors. In the case of preference for salt in salt-deficit rats, the importance of learning factors has been clearly shown by Scott and Verney (1949), Smith et al. (1958), and Smith (1972). On the other hand, Bolles et al. (1964), Rozin (1965), Krieckhaus and Wolf (1968), and others have shown that there are strong salt preferences in the absence of any opportunity for learning. Perhaps the best conclusion is that there is an unlearned initial preference for salt when it is needed but that this preference is further increased with experience. In retrospect, it appears inappropriate to treat the specific hunger phenomena as a single, unified phenomenon that must be based upon either an innate or a learning factor. In their excellent review of specific hungers Rozin and Kalat (1971) conclude that while there is an innate need-related preference for salt, the specific hungers for thiamine and most other needed substances are based on quite different mechanisms.

Rozin and Kalat (1971) emphasize that two problems have marred much of the research done on specific hungers. One problem is that virtually all of the research has been done with animals (usually rats) deficient in salt or thiamine. Because the mechanisms involved with these two substances are so different, neither one can be accepted as the general pattern for whatever other specific hungers may exist. The second problem is methodological. Consider a common experimental procedure, which first makes the animal thiamine deficient and then offers it a choice between a new distinctively flavored diet containing thiamine and the old deficient diet. Rodgers and Rozin (1966) have shown that under these conditions the animal chooses the new diet not because of a preference for the thiamine food, but rather because it avoids the old diet on which it became ill. In short, the animal has no initial preference for the taste of thiamine; it has an aversion to the familiar diet on which it became ill. If the animal is given two new foods, only one of which contains thiamine, it is indifferent in its initial choice between the two new foods. Such findings virtually destroy the conception of specific hungers as automatic regulating mechanisms by which animals take care of their dietary needs.

Rozin's work on specific hungers is a very new development, and it should be emphasized that for many years the concept was widely accepted. The early research on specific hunger, together with the early research with activity wheels, was seen as providing two broad conclusions. The first, clearly derived from the instinct idea, was that a condition of need in an organism leads it to engage in just that behavior that will alleviate the need. If the animal needs food, it will eat; if it needs water, it will drink; if it needs salt, it will eat salt; if it is cold, it will build a nest for warmth; and so on through the whole gamut of biological necessities. The biological needs of animals lead to appropriate behaviors that occur with little or no training when the appropriate occasions for them arise. The second general conclusion that was drawn from these early studies of specific hungers and general activity was unique to the drive concept; it was that in the absence of appropriate objects the organism will be motivated to engage in general or diffuse activity. In the absence of food, for instance, the animal will run in an activity wheel, as will the animal that has no mate, the thirsty animal, and the animal that is cold or that has specific dietary deficiencies.[10] During the 1920s and 1930s when this evidence was first becoming available, it was eagerly seized upon as supporting the notion that an animal's needs determine its drives and its drives in turn determine its behavior.

The drive concept also gave apparent substance to the idea that all of the organism's biological needs could be directly and simply translated into motivational terms. Thus it would be easy for Hull in 1943 to *equate* drive with the animal's needs. Moreover, the early research on the drive concept gave it an aspect of tangibility and empirical testability, which the instinct concept had never enjoyed. To help press the concept into active service, just one more thing needed to be done: The different drives had to be quantified. Warden (1931) was foremost among those psychologists who optimistically set out to measure drive strength.

The Columbia obstruction-box studies. Warden objected to activity-wheel measures as indices of the strength of motivation on the grounds that while they may have provided a valid index of the general tendency of animals to be active, they failed to differentiate among the different drives and to indicate the directionality of motivated behavior.

> Certainly, the knowledge that a hungry rat is excited by food in the offing and is bending its energies to secure the food, to the exclusion of other types of activity, presents a more adequate biological and psychological picture of its behavior than the knowledge that, when equally hungry the same rat will turn a wheel round and round so many times per hour. (Warden et al., 1931, p. 5)

To meet this objection, the well-known Columbia obstruction box was developed (Jenkins et al., 1926). With this apparatus, Warden argued, it would be possible to define and measure the strength of the animal's drive in terms of its tendency to approach a particular goal.[11]

[10] Further support for the idea that animals react adaptively to their needs was reported by Dashiell in 1925 in a paper entitled "A quantitative demonstration of animal drive." Dashiell reported that animals deprived of food would explore more in a complex maze he had designed than would animals that were satiated. These results were so reasonable and Dashiell's interpretation of them so intellectually satisfying that for nearly 30 years Dashiell's study was accepted as definitive. Finally, in the early 1950s the bubble burst (see Chapter 7). But for approximately a generation the drive concept was held to be valid because it embodied the idea that animals' behavior adjusts automatically to their needs.

[11] The method had been developed a little earlier by Morgan (1916, 1923) and Moss (1924). Their studies were highly imaginative but rather casually conducted, for which Warden scorned them severely. Warden attributed the origin of the basic idea that the strength of a motive can be measured in terms of how hard the animal will work for an incentive to Lubbock (1882), but the connection seems dubious.

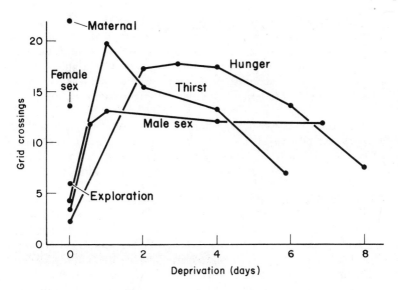

Figure 5–1

Grid crossings in the Columbia obstruction box as a function of deprivation of food, water, or sexual behavior. The number of grid crossings is also indicated for female animals returning to their nests and young (maternal), crossing for a male animal (female sex), and for animals given no incentive (exploration).
(From Warden et al., 1931)

Warden and his co-workers ran a series of studies measuring the number of times an animal under a given deprivation condition would cross an electric grid in a 20-minute observation period in order to have momentary contact with the incentive. The results for a number of different drives—hunger, thirst, sex (both male and female), exploration (no incentive), and maternal (returning to the litter and nest)—are summarized in Fig. 5-1.

These systematic investigations provided some information about the effects of different deprivation conditions upon the strength of a single drive (e.g., that the maximum strength of hunger occurred with a deprivation of about three days). The guiding idea behind the Columbia obstruction-box studies, however, was to make possible the comparison of different drives within a single experimental context; and it was certainly this possibility of comparisons across drives (e.g., the strongest thirst is stronger than the strongest hunger) that caught the imagination of subsequent psychologists. (Witness the studies by Simmons, 1924; Tsai, 1925; Stone & Sturman-Huble, 1927; and Stone & Ferguson, 1938, all attempting to compare hunger and sex.) Unfortunately, it is just at the point of comparing different drives, where the Columbia obstruction-box studies offered the greatest promise, that the results are most subject to criticism.

The difficulty of interpreting the results of these studies comes from the unique definition that had been given to the term "drive." For most psychologists around 1930, drive referred to a physiological state of the organism that was aroused by a particular goal or by a particular deprivation condition. But for Warden et al. drive meant just the behavioral tendency that resulted from such an arousal. It was recognized, of course, that approach behavior depends not only upon the conditions of deprivation but also on the fact that the organism's activity is always directed toward or away from some incentive, that is, toward or away from some object such as food or water or an animal of the opposite sex, which is capable of arousing and then satisfying the animal's seeking tendency. In all of the Columbia studies, then, the strength of approach behavior, which was said to be drive strength, was really a measure of both drive and incentive factors combined in some unknown proportion. After recognizing the important distinctions between deprivation and incentive conditions, Warden and his collaborators proceeded to study deprivation conditions almost to the exclusion of incentive factors.[12]

We cannot deny that Warden et al. did good and important work, but at such an early date it would have perhaps been more valuable had they mapped out a wider variety of experimental variables, even if this meant that the work had to be done with less precision. Let us see what some of the implications might have been. Their own data show that early in the test session the results are markedly different from what they are over the whole session; such changes are found both in the effect of deprivation upon the strength of a single drive and also in apparent relative strengths of different drives. Thus with 5-minute test sessions quite a different picture of drive strength is obtained from that with the standard 20-minute tests.

Second, consider the effects of pretraining. In all of the obstruction-box studies, animals received 5 pretraining trials, 4 without shock, and 1 with the shock grid activated. We wonder whether different strengths of learning under the different motivation conditions were obtained with the use of a fixed number of pretraining trials and whether 5 trials provides a "normal" drive, as Warden claimed. We wonder, too, whether the performance that was measured during the immediately following 20-minute test should be thought of as extinction of the approach tendency built up in the pretraining trials, or whether it is better to think of it as a learned aversion of the shock grid. It may be noted in this connection that the rate of grid crossing falls off during the 20-minute test; that is, the response does extinguish.

Thirdly, Warden et al. went to some trouble to maximize the stimulus properties of the incentive; the experimental apparatus was

---

[12] Hamilton (1929) is a notable exception. She studied the effect of delay of reinforcement upon the rate of crossing.

arranged so that the animal could see and smell the food, mate, litter, and so on. But we must wonder how one can equate the stimulus values of these diverse incentives. Finally, we must wonder how one equates the effect of contact with the different incentive objects—that is, how does one ensure that a comparable amount of consummatory activity has been guaranteed by permitting the animal a "nibble of food," or a "lick of water," or a "nosing of the female."

The concept of drive presents both semantic and syntactical problems. Warden's approach was to solve the semantic problems in one stroke with an operational definition: Strength of drive equals the number of grid crossings. But the equally important syntactical properties of the drive construct remained in the dark, and no amount of definitional rigidity or experimental precision could shed any light on them. Clarification could only come from discovering how behavior is dependent upon the many variables that affect it. Thus the standardization of conditions under which the Columbia studies were conducted, which made them so outstanding for their day, was also their greatest limitation.[13]

The trouble with the Columbia obstruction-box studies was that the same word, drive, was used on the one hand by Warden to designate grid crossing behavior and on the other hand by most psychologists to designate hypothetical motivational or physiological states of the organism. It was popularly believed that Warden had measured the intensity of these motivational states and not just a particular behavior tendency motivated by them. Had Warden et al. studied the effect of different incentives under the same deprivation conditions, we now know that he would have found marked differences in what he called drive, and the confusion between what he called drive and what others called drive could not have occurred. Most psychologists were no more ready to accept Warden's explicit definition of drive than they were to accept Richter's implicit definition in terms of activity level or Cannon's in terms of localized sensations; drive always meant something more. All of these early investigators began by bravely defining drive in ways they thought would be convenient, but their efforts came to naught because they

---

[13] It might be objected that the use of operational definitions under "standardized conditions" has proved of great value in the physical sciences, so we ought to emulate the practice of standardization. The difference is that reference to a physical standard (such as a platinum meter in Paris) is only useful when we have a very good understanding of what the variables are that affect the construct (in this case length). The arbitrariness of the standard meter is only defensible to the extent that we can refer to it after making a correction for temperature without worrying about how it may change as a function of other physical manipulations. We know the variables of which length is a function, and we know how it depends upon them. In short, semantic rigidity of the length construct pays off because it also has a well-established syntax. Drive does not.

had not come to grips with the diversity of phenomena the concept was supposed to explain.

Definitions of drive

Sometimes a scientific term can be defined operationally in a way that arouses virtually no opposition. The principal reason for the success of the operational definitions in these cases is that they are applied to new phenomena with which no one had been concerned until they had been discovered and named. Consider, for instance, proactive and retroactive inhibition. No one but the verbal-learning psychologist means anything by these terms or knows anything about the phenomena. Consequently, these labels can mean precisely what the specialist wants them to. But more often science must cope with concepts that have been thought about and talked about a great deal, concepts for which there is a rich background of prior associations. To the extent that such concepts enjoy common usage, they must have some intrinsic primitive meaning. Such meaning is simply not fixed by an explicit definition. Each person "knows what he means," even though he cannot quite explain it to anyone else's satisfaction. Such terms ordinarily lack syntactical rigor; their conceptual properties are not agreed upon. The concept of drive went through this kind of phase, as we have seen.

Freud, Tolman, Woodworth, and many others proposed dynamic or motivating principles. And although their different principles and concepts had some common semantic and syntactical features, the essence of the drive concept eluded them—and so did an adequate definition. In this section I will summarize some of the strategic choice points, or kinds of conceptual issues, that confronted the early theorists in formulating a definition of drive.

One issue was whether drives contribute only to the energy of behavior or only to the directionality of behavior or to both the energy and the directionality of behavior. The phenomenon of specific hungers, and Warden's studies with the obstruction box, in which the animals work for specific goals, reflected a directional mode of thought. Richter's work on general activity represents the nondirectional or purely energizing mode of thinking. Freud and Lewin embodied both modes; energy once directed toward a certain goal could become diverted or diffused and hence become manifest in the motivation of different kinds of behavior. Looking further back in our history, it is clear that instincts implied specific directionality. At the other extreme, drive in the form that Hull gave it in 1943 was nothing but energy. Drive itself lent no directionality to behavior. Thus for Hull the motivation that characterizes the hungry animal is identical to the motivation that characterizes the frightened animal. If the hungry one acts differently from the frightened one, it is because the stimulus situation, the associative or structural determinants of behavior, are different and not because they have distinguishable kinds of motivation.

A related question is whether drives should be conceived to be an antecedent determinant of behavior or thought of as an aspect or dimension or quantity of behavior. Again, the ancestral concept of instinct implied that motivated behavior should take a particular form, that the animal should search for food, recognize a mate, or flee to safety, as the case might be. The different drives in each case were hypothetical mechanisms that produced and motivated appropriate behaviors. Thus instincts were the causes of behavior, not the behavior itself. The alternative approach was clearly illustrated by those like Warden and Richter, who, in the attempt to be scientifically objective, proposed operational definitions for drive, in effect equating the strength of drive with the strength of behavior. This type of approach has not been successful. What it gains in objectivity, it loses in failing to recognize the primitive meaning of the term. The primitive concept of drive has both semantic and syntactic implications, and an approach like Warden's, which attempted to solve the semantic problems in one stroke with an operational definition, must necessarily ignore the equally important syntactical implications. No amount of definitional rigidity or experimental precision can shed any light on the other motivational properties that drives, by common consensus, are supposed to have. The implicit primitive syntax of the drive concept could only become clarified by observing a diversity of motivational phenomena. Like Cannon's attempt to define drive a few years earlier, Warden's attempt only demonstrated again that a useful theoretical construct must be given both syntactical and semantic properties if it is to do the explanatory work that we need it to do.

A closely related question is whether drive should be a central event, as Beach and Morgan had proposed and as the instinct theorists had been advocating all along, or whether it should be defined peripherally in terms of a stimulus event (Cannon) or some behavioral measure (Warden). The centralists ultimately had their way, largely as a result of Hull's influence. For Hull drive was not directly observable; it was central in locus and only indirectly available for observation.

Another question is whether there should be a multiplicity of drives (the drive for food, water, a sex object, etc.), or whether there should only be a single drive—drive itself—which could have different sources and different objects. The question is whether we should regard drives as the motivators of specific kinds of behavior or make drive synonymous with motivation in general. If we assume a multiplicity of specific drives, so that we can refer to a drive for this or that object or a drive from this or that disturbance, we retain much of the earlier concept of instinct. Just as there was a plurality of instincts, so there could be a plurality of drives. This historical ancestry was quite apparent in the early days of drive theory, and drives usually were plural, although a few writers referred to a singular "animal drive" (e.g., Dashiell, 1925; Young, 1936).

Drives in the plural are not very secure logically. Their very specificity deprives them of the functional properties that give value to the singular construct. For example, consider hunger and sex. The primary evidence of the sexual drive is a single consequent relationship; namely, it motivates sexual behavior. The sex drive may also be related on the antecedent side to various hormonal and stimulus conditions that have been found to be related to sexual behavior. On both the antecedent and consequent sides, then, the sex drive is tied by functional properties that are different from those of food deprivation and the motivation of eating, which constitute the primary evidence of the hunger drive. We are left in the very difficult position of having an explanatory concept that is empty in the sense that invoking it contributes nothing beyond specifying the original empirical relationships. Under these circumstances, we are free to invoke a drive to explain all conceivable kinds of behavior: a drive for activity, a drive to explore, a drive to perceive, a drive for competence (these are all examples of drives that have hypothesized by different theorists to explain particular kinds of behavior). In the case of some of these hypothetical drives there is evidence for additional semantic linkages; hence, they have some explanatory value. But the danger is clear; there is nothing to prevent us from invoking drives to explain twiddling the thumbs or not twiddling the thumbs or even believing in drives. Perhaps the solution to this problem of circularity is obvious: To make the concept of multiple, specific drives useful it is necessary to anchor them on the response side in more than one way. That is, a specific drive must have two or more behavioral consequences. Not only must a drive for food motivate eating, it must also increase activity in a running wheel or facilitate learning about the location of food or have some other behavioral effect.

All of these issues were finally resolved by Hull (1943). His approach was bold, provocative, and, as it turned out, decisive as far as the theoretical development of the drive concept was concerned. For Hull drive contributes merely to the energy of behavior and not to its direction; it is an antecedent of behavior rather than a property of behavior; it is central; it is singular. Drive is manifest in general activity, in consummatory behavior, and in learned instrumental behavior. Hull's basic strategy was to embed the drive construct in a network of many semantic and syntactic relationships no one of which could be directly proved and no one of which provided an operational definition of drive, but all of which taken together constituted a definitional network. After Hull drive was no longer an implicit concept; it was a well-defined theoretical construct with a number of explicit, testable properties.

Before we see how Hull brought all this about, let us consider briefly one of the most basic of all definitional questions, namely, whether the concept of drive is necessary for the explanation of behavior.

Associative account of motivation

While the early drive theorists were flourishing, a small but vocal group of theorists had been arguing that there was no need for special dynamic concepts such as instincts or drives to handle the facts of motivation.

To illustrate the thinking of this group, let us see how they might have dealt with the arguments advanced by Morgan (1943) in support of his central motive state construct. Recall that his CMS construct was based upon four sets of phenomena, which, he said, could not be explained by a purely associative or structural account. These were: (1) persistence of motivation after the initiating conditions were removed, (2) increased activity level, (3) occurrence of specific consummatory responses, and (4) preparation of the organism to make appropriate consummatory responses. The question here is whether Morgan was really justified in his contention that stimuli alone cannot have these behavioral effects.

Let us conceive of a consummatory response as being innately connected to an internal stimulus that persists until the occurrence of certain supporting external stimuli make possible the particular consummatory response. And let us suppose further that the internal stimulus in question is abolished only as a consequence of this consummatory response. Such a stimulus would then be persistent. It might also well be that if it were intense enough it could increase general activity. It has specific responses innately connected to it by definition, so that the continual presence of such a stimulus would "set" the organism for making the consummatory response when the goal object was presented. Such a stimulus would then seem to have all of the properties that Morgan attributed to his central motive state. All that would distinguish such a stimulus from any other type of stimulus would be its innate association with a particular consummatory response and its persistence.

Even if we grant that because of these special properties it would be desirable to call this state of affairs by some name other than stimulus, still, logically, such a state would have its effect upon the nervous system by initiating particular patterns of nerve impulses; and at that point it would become the adequate stimulus for its neurological consequences. Thus the only real criterion for distinguishing between such a "motivating stimulus" and any other stimulus is that we do not yet know if it has a unique psychophysical correlate (Cannon's proposals, as we have seen, will not do). But the inability to identify corresponding physical stimulus objects has not deterred psychologists from hypothesizing stimuli. So there seems to be nothing to prevent us from proposing that stimuli are the motivators of behavior as long as we admit that such stimuli would have to have properties that other stimuli lack, such as persistence and innate association with particular consummatory responses.

This purely associationistic point of view has been given its best-known (and most enduring) formulation by Smith and Guthrie (1921). For many years Guthrie insisted that what we call hunger, for example, is just the effect of some stimulus (he never subscribed to any particular theory of its somatic source) which he called a *maintaining stimulus* because, until terminated by eating, it persists and maintains whatever behavior makes the animal act hungry.

Guthrie argued that if a hungry animal makes energetic movements in running to food, it must be because it has learned to do so; these energetic movements are the ones that have become conditioned to the hunger stimulus; without it they would not occur. The same principle is held to account for the apparent purposefulness of the preparatory responses; they too have all become conditioned to the maintaining stimulus and will persist as long as it does. Guthrie has been charged with ignoring the obvious purposive character of behavior; the animal "wants" to get to the goal box and "tries" to get there. The answer to the charge is that the "want" and the "try" are inferences the observer makes. Such inferences are evidently based upon some feature of the animal's behavior, sometimes just the occurrence of the learned response that gets the animal to the goal box. In more complicated situations the animal may be said to "try" to get to the goal box when it makes responses that are similar to the responses that would get it there.

According to Guthrie, motivated behavior is identical in principle to any other behavior except that it is characterized by the presence of this persistent maintaining stimulus. This kind of argument deals with the phenomena of motivation in terms of stimulation but without making the additional assumption that the stimulus is good or bad, that is, that it must be reacted to either appetitively or aversively.[14] This purely associative account of motivated behavior has been defended over the years by Guthrie (1935, 1952), Copeland (1926), Kuo (1928), Hollingworth (1931), Rexroad (1933), Wolpe (1950), and Estes (1958), among others.[15]

[14] The neutrality-of-stimuli plank of Guthrie's theoretical platform was really a by-product of his particular view of association by contiguity. Miller and Dollard (1941) also promoted the idea that stimuli maintain behavior and can be drives, but their commitment to a drive reduction theory of reinforcement had the consequence that for them, as for Freud, stimuli had to be noxious.

[15] The best systematic statement of the associationistic position is Brown's (1961). Brown's account is particularly valuable, since, being a drive theorist, he is most concerned with drive theory and associationistic theory as competitive positions.

Such an amotivational approach to the phenomena of motivation offers the obvious advantages of parsimony and elegance. It explains the phenomena with a simple conditioning model. However, in higher animals, in which the effect of stimulation cannot generally be traced through to response consequences, it is common practice to infer the eliciting stimulus from the occurrence of the response. The specification of the stimulus then raises all of the problems of circularity that invoking a drive or an instinct would. In the last analysis if we are to have theories with constructs (and we should not call them theories otherwise), it would seem to be pretty much optional whether our constructs are maintaining stimuli or central motive states or drives.

Hull's drive theory

Hull's major theoretical statement regarding drive and its theoretical properties appeared in his book *Principles of behavior* (1943). Drive was tentatively equated with the total need of the animal. Although an experimenter might attempt to activate an animal's behavior by imposing a particular need such as hunger, additional activation was assumed to come from other sources: a little fear, a little unresolved sexual tension, a little thirst. These irrelevant needs (irrelevant to the experimental situation) contribute to the animal's total drive level. Therefore, one implication of Hull's definition of drive is that drive must be a generalized motivator. The animal's motivation conditions, or needs, do not give directionality to behavior. Different needs constitute different *sources of drive*, but in each case the produced drive, D, is the same.[16] Therefore, Hull's D is singular not plural, general not specific, and motivational not directional.

The most basic property of Hull's drive construct is that it activates behavior—it energizes or augments whatever behavior the animal may be engaged in. According to Hull, if an animal is more active, it is more likely to make an adaptive response in a particular situation. The hungrier a rat is, for example, the more active it will be and the more likely it will be to make some response that finds food. Hull further postulated that eating food reduces drive and that as a consequence of this reduction in drive *reinforcement* occurs. Therefore, there will be a strengthening of whatever response the animal happens to make that obtains food. Thus we see the animal activated to make a variety of responses. The response that solves the immediate biological problem (need) and reduces drive will become learned so that upon a recurrence of the biological problem

[16] We will use the designation D to refer to Hull's version of the drive concept, thereby distinguishing his concept from earlier, more primitive drive concepts. The phrase "sources of drive," originally suggested by Brown (1961), helps clarify the D concept. Brown is one of the clearest, most able, and most recent spokesmen for Hullian drive theory.

the appropriate adaptive response will be more likely to occur. Once an appropriate response is learned, then it will simply increase in likelihood as the animal becomes more motivated. Consequently, the dual principles of reinforcement and motivation work together to ensure that the animal will learn adaptive behavior.

There had been a substantial amount of work done in Tolman's laboratory and elsewhere showing the important effects of both practice factors and motivational factors on behavior, so Hull's distinction between learning and performance was not a new idea. Such a distinction is actually an inherent part of any motivational system. But it remained for Perin (1942) and Williams (1938), two of Hull's students, to determine what happens to the strength of a response when practice and motivational variables are manipulated at the same time. Perin and Williams provided, in effect, a map of the strength of a bar-press response as a joint function of practice and motivation. Their results were especially important because they constituted empirical justification for many of Hull's theoretical assertions about drive.

Perin (1942) trained four groups of 40 rats to press a bar for food. The groups were all trained under 23-hour food deprivation but with different numbers of reinforced trials (5, 8, 30, or 70). The response was then extinguished in all animals under 3-hour deprivation. The results are given in the lower curve of Fig. 5-2. The results from Williams' (1938) study are given in the upper curve. He also trained four groups under 23-hour food deprivation with varying numbers of reinforcement (5, 10, 30, and 90), but extinction was carried out while his animals were all under 22-hour deprivation. For both sets of data the dependent variable was the number of bar presses the animals made before meeting a criterion of 5 minutes with no responding.

Three features of these curves should be noted. One is the regular growth of resistance to extinction as a continuous increasing function of the number of reinforcements that the response received during training. Although the level of performance was a function of the motivation existing at the time behavior was tested, the relative rate of growth was not.[17] This finding led Hull to conclude that behavior strength was a function of a construct *habit*, which he designated $_sH_R$, which presumably reflected a more or less permanent change in the organism's nervous system and which was independent of the animal's transient state of deprivation. That is, the strength of the habit did not depend upon whether subjects were

[17] Both curves can be represented by equations of the same form, $A(1 - 10^{-BN})$, in which A indicates the asymptote of performance reached for a given drive intensity, N is the number of reinforcements, and B is the growth constant. The Perin and Williams data are fitted by curves whose growth constants are 0.0185 and 0.0180, that is, very nearly the same.

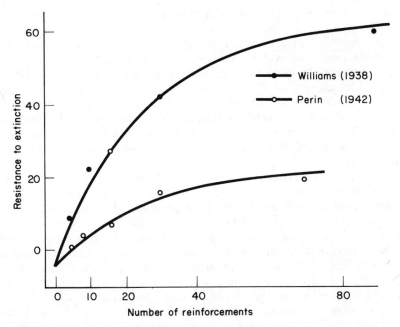

Figure 5–2

The Perin-Williams data showing how resistance to extinction depends upon both deprivation conditions (D) and the number of reinforcements ($_sH_R$). Williams' animals were 22 hours deprived, Perin's only 3 hours. (Adapted from Perin, 1942) Copyright (1942) by the American Psychological Association. Reproduced by permission.

tested under high or low motivational conditions but only upon the number of prior reinforcements. The second crucial feature of these curves is that they differ as a function of test deprivation conditions, so that a second construct, drive, symbolized D, may also be assumed to contribute to the strength of behavior. Third, it is apparent from the independence of these learning and motivational effects that $_sH_R$ and D must combine multiplicatively to determine overt behavior.

Perin ran four other groups. They were all trained with 16 reinforcements under 23-hour deprivation, but they were extinguished under differing hours of deprivation. The results, again measured in terms of resistance to extinction, are presented in Fig. 5-3.

In view of the multiplicative equation just established, this curve represents the general relationship describing behavior strength as a function of hours deprivation. This function should therefore, be independent of the number of reinforcements. Increasing or decreasing the number of reinforcements from 16 should simply generate a family of curves of the same form lying above or below the given one.

In order to understand properly much of the material discussed in the following chapters, it is necessary to be quite clear about the different conceptual properties Hull attributed to drive. All of these properties will be spelled out in more detail and put into their appropriate theoretical contexts later, but it may be useful to summarize them here.

1. ANTECEDENT CONDITIONS OF DRIVE. Drive is to be anchored by tying it on the antecedent side directly to the animal's biological needs. The only specific need Hull worked out in any detail was hunger, by which he usually meant some number of hours of food deprivation.

2. DRIVE STIMULI. Conditions of need that produce drive are also credited with producing characteristic stimuli. Although these need-related stimuli are called drive stimuli (symbolized S_D), they are assumed to have no effect upon the organism's motivation; that is, they do not contribute to drive. In short, while drive is a motivational factor, drive stimuli are purely associative. Thus while drive itself cannot direct behavior, these drive stimuli can. They can do so because, like any other stimuli, particular responses, such as food-getting responses, can become conditioned to them.[18]

3. INDEPENDENCE OF DRIVE AND HABIT. D and $_sH_R$ are independent, and although neither one alone is manifest in behavior, their multiplicative combination determines behavior. Hull's primary evidence for this principle was the Perin-Williams data.

4. ENERGIZING EFFECT OF DRIVE. On the consequent side drive is to be tied by several effects upon behavior. The most fundamental effect is the energizing of behavior. The difference in response strength found by Perin and Williams under 3-hour and 22-hour deprivation, respectively, represents a difference in activation of the same habit. The activating or energizing role of drive can be manifest in any behavior—in the performance of learned instrumental acts, such as running in a maze; in the readiness to engage in some form of consummatory activity, such as eating; and in an increase in the organism's general activity level, such as running in an activity wheel.

5. REINFORCING EFFECT OF DRIVE REDUCTION. On the consequent side drive is also to be tied to behavior by the phenomenon of

---

[18] Note that the distinction between the response-eliciting power of drive stimuli and the energizing effect of drive is conceptual rather than empirical. It is never possible to have more than circumstantial evidence for it. Some circumstantial evidence is provided by the part of Perin's results shown in Fig. 5-3. Hull assumed that approximately one-half of the behavior strength obtained under 22-hour deprivation was due to the contribution the drive stimulus makes to the total stimulus situation. When performance is tested under the lower hours of deprivation, the contribution would be proportionally less. Moreover, the test involves somewhat different stimulus conditions than applied during training, so we should expect some curvature of the function because of a generalization decrement. This is what I call circumstantial evidence.

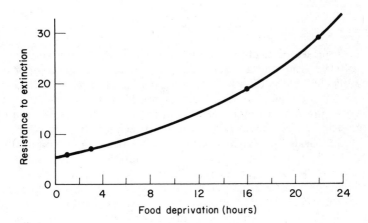

Figure 5–3

*Perin's data showing how resistance to extinction depends upon
deprivation conditions (D). (From Perin, 1942) Copyright
(1942) by the American Psychological Association. Reproduced
by permission.*

reinforcement. Drive reduction is the underlying basis of all
reinforcement.

    6. GENERALIZED CHARACTER OF DRIVE. Drive is nonspecific;
there is only one drive, D, and although it may be produced by food
deprivation, water deprivation, electric shock, or whatever, and even
though these different drive-producing conditions may produce different stimuli, they all contribute alike (but probably in different
degrees) to D. Hence drive cannot direct behavior; it can only energize. All steering of behavior is done associatively by stimuli. Hull
cited Perin (1942) once again in support of the generalized drive
effect.[19]

    It is important to recognize that no one of these six functional
properties taken by itself provides a definition of drive. The different
hypothetical relationships comprise a network that interrelates all of
the theoretical constructs of the theory—D and $_sH_R$ and several
others—so that the whole set of constructs must be defined at once.
For example, neither D nor H is directly observable, and nothing can
be asserted about either D or H without making at least some tentative assumptions about the other. But the Perin-Williams data portray
the functional properties of D and H acting together.

    [19] Note that extrapolating from Perin's data points (Fig. 5-3)
back to 0-hour deprivation we can expect that there would still be some
resistance to extinction. Hull attributed this residual behavior strength to
the miscellaneous sexual, fear, and exploratory sources of drive that would
persist and maintain the hunger-learned behavior in the absence of
hunger.

Summary

All of the pre-Hullian attempts to define drive that have been noted here suffered from the difficulty that they defined it too simply and too rigidly. Drive was identified as a particular kind of behavior or as the strength of behavior, as if the theorist viewed behavior as the direct result of some simple motivating force. By Hull's time more of the complexity of behavior was recognized. Because a distinction had to be made between learning and performance, for example, Hull had to devise a model in which the associative effects of learning, tentatively identified as habit, were separated by the motivational construct drive from direct behavioral expression. Whereas earlier theorists could propose that motivational factors could be directly expressed in behavior, Hull was required to introduce another layer of complexity. The constructs in his theory were not anchored to observable behavior by one semantic linkage but by a *network* of both syntactical relationships (e.g., D and H combine multiplicatively) and semantic relationships (D is related to the animal's needs). The validity of Hull's treatment of drive therefore cannot be tested with any one experiment; it takes a variety of experiments producing different kinds of evidence to test the theoretical network.

In the next three chapters we will examine the evidence that has accumulated on all of these questions. Chapter 6 will be concerned with the relationships that have been discovered between the antecedent conditions of need and the animal's resulting drive strength. This analysis will not only permit us to evaluate one of Hull's theoretical assertions about drive but will provide the additional benefit of summarizing a great deal of research that has been done on the regulation of eating and drinking and on the physiological basis of motivation. Chapter 7 will be concerned with the energizing effect of drive. We will consider the energization of instrumental behavior, consummatory behavior, and general activity. Again, we will be concerned both with assessing Hullian drive theory and also the broader issue of how one goes about explaining these different kinds of behavior. Chapter 8 will survey the other functional properties Hull attributed to drive. After examining the relevant literature, we will stop to take stock of the current status of D and then move on to consider some alternative motivational constructs.

6

ANTECEDENT CONDITIONS

*It has been assumed that behavior goes off,
in the last analysis, by virtue only of
certain final physiological quiescences,
which are being sought, or of certain final
physiological disturbances which are
being avoided.*

E. C. Tolman

The conventional view of animal behavior attributes all behavior to certain basic needs. In the absence of all biological problems there is not supposed to be any behavior. The generation of behavior is usually assumed to be a two-step process. First, the existence of some need, such as for food or water or reduced body temperature, is said to produce motivation, or drive, or to arouse an instinct. Second, the animal's motivation generates behavior. In other words, behavior does not proceed directly from the initiating need; it comes about as a reaction, typically a learned reaction, to the intermediary motivation.

The conceptual separation into two steps is quite explicit in Hull's theory. All needs serve as sources of drive, but neither the need itself nor the resulting drive is immediately manifest in behavior. Behavior results from the combined action of drive and particular habit structures, that is, particular responses to specific stimuli. Thus Hull postulated that drive was to be connected on the antecedent side to conditions of need and on the consequent side to various manifestations of motivated behavior. One could, of course, construct a theory in which behavior was tied directly to the conditions of need, thereby obviating the assumption of a two-step process, but such a theory would not be a motivational theory, nor would it, according to Hull, provide the distinction that must be made between changes in behavior that are due to need and those that are due to other factors such as learning.

In a broader sense the study of antecedent conditions is of basic importance in any biological approach to behavior. Whether one attempts to explain behavior in terms of drives or instincts or selection pressures or by probing into the nervous system, the antecedent conditions of need must be found to be an important class of behavior correlates. Ultimately, all behavior depends upon the physiological functioning of the body, and no explanation of behavior can be complete until the details of the underlying machinery are known. Although, fortunately, we need not examine in detail what is known about the physiological basis of motivation, the present chapter will survey a variety of different physiological approaches. We will consider some of the directions in which contemporary research is going. At the same time, we will gain a better perspective of what it means to say that some behavior is motivated. We will see that each kind of motivation seems to have its own pattern and to govern behavior by its own set of rules. In some cases it is difficult to see any underlying need, and in other cases even though a need exists, it does not seem to be reflected in motivated behavior. In the case of hunger, which perhaps fits the classical view best, we will see that there does not seem to be any one simple mechanism that translates the need for food directly into hunger-motivated behavior.

Hunger

Basically, an animal becomes hungry, psychologically speaking, when it needs food, physiologically speaking. This simple statement hides many complexities, however. When an animal is deprived of food, there are changes in the blood, in the nutritional state of the body's cells, and in a number of metabolic processes. There are also changes in the central nervous system, which lead to further alterations in the animal's body chemistry. Moreover, these physiological changes produce a variety of psychological effects. We will refer here to the state of need as deprivation and use the word "hunger" to refer to the psychological effects of deprivation. Hunger may mean that food begins to taste good to the animal; food becomes interesting; the animal likes food, wants food, and is willing to work for food. The analysis is complicated by the fact that neither the physiological events following food deprivation nor the different behavioral manifestations of hunger vary together in a uniform manner. Any definitive statement about hunger motivation must indicate what physiological effects of deprivation are most simply and directly tied to what changes in the animal's behavior. Only when this complex analysis is completed will we be able to say what the antecedent conditions of hunger are.

Deprivation schedules. Hunger is produced by limiting an organism's food intake. Deprivation may be continuous; that is, food may be totally withheld until the animal is later tested or until it dies (terminal deprivation). Under these conditions the animal's deficit increases continuously so that it can be tested only once at a given degree of deprivation. The animal's hunger also presumably increases continuously, but with most behavioral measures there is a deterioration of performance if deprivation is continued too long. The generality of this debilitation effect led Hull (1952) to postulate an "inanition factor," which progressively reduced the effective value of drive. Unfortunately, there have been almost no systematic studies of such effects.

Deprivation may also be intermittent; that is, food may be alternately withheld and made available on some kind of schedule. With an appropriate "maintenance schedule" of feeding, animals can be kept more or less indefinitely at a more or less constant level of deprivation and tested repeatedly. Thus maintenance schedules make it possible to test animals, for example, every day under 23 hours of food deprivation. The practical advantage of such a procedure is apparent, and it should not be surprising that maintenance schedules are widely used in experimental work. However, such schedules leave the animal's state of deprivation rather inadequately defined. It is now apparent that providing an animal with food, for instance, for an hour a day, gives no assurance that the animal will be in the same state of deprivation day after day. Whereas one animal may starve to death on such a routine, another will thrive. And, of course, the motivation of the two animals is likely to be quite different. Perhaps in recognition of this variability, it has become the custom to put animals on a maintenance schedule for several days prior to putting them into the experimental situation. This custom is said to adapt or habituate the animal to the feeding cycle. While this procedure guarantees that the animal will be motivated, it unfortunately disguises the nature of the motivation. Is the result of being on an hour-a-day schedule merely the elimination of prior eating habits? Does it provide the opportunity for eating to become conditioned to stimuli like those of the test situation? Is the animal merely being brought down to a consistent weight-loss figure? Does it permit the animal's weight to stabilize at a new lower value? How much of the animal's subsequent motivation is a result of its particular drive level, and how much is attributable to incentive factors? We will consider all of these questions in the next few chapters.

The phenomenon of regulation. The marvelous thing about feeding and hunger motivation is that animals can prosper by eating intermittently even while they expend energy more or less continuously. Prior to a meal the animal may be somewhat in need of energy, while after a meal it may be somewhat on the credit side. It is remarkable that under normal circumstances neither the credits nor the debits become very large, and the animal regulates its energy intake to its expenditure exceedingly accurately over a period of time (Adolph, 1943).

All of the body's various demands for energy have to be supplied in the form of food (Kleiber, 1961). A convenient unit to measure energy is the calorie, since it measures all expenditures whether they involve mechanical work done by the muscles, heat generated by the body (which may amount to 1000 calories a day in man), or chemical energy involved in the operation of body processes, such as maintaining body temperature (which may amount to 1500 calories a day) as well as growing, excreting, and digesting food (another 500 calories a day). All of these functions (except muscular work, which is variable) are obligatory in the sense that they are carried out even when the organism cannot afford the expenditure of energy and even when food is withheld.

One major source of energy for all kinds of cellular functioning in the body is glucose carried in the blood. This blood sugar is the "pocket money" of the system. It is immediately available, but there is not much of it, rarely more than 20 calories at any one time. Even when glucose is ingested, it is promptly converted to glycogen and stored away for later reconversion to glucose. Even the body stores of glycogen rarely amount to more than about 500 calories, so that the liver frequently must draw on the much larger reserve banks of body fat and convert this to glycogen. When food again becomes available, the liver converts it back into fat to pay off the debt. Thus to meet the more or less continuous demands for various forms of energy, the liver must be constantly converting energy stores in the body into blood glucose.[1]

One way to think of the problem of regulation is in terms of *set point*, which can be defined as the weight at which an organism tends to maintain itself over a period of time. A number of writers (e.g., Brody, 1945; Kleiber, 1961) have emphasized the accuracy with which animals usually regulate their weight around a set point. Other writers have put it somewhat differently by saying that in the long run the organism eats for calories (Adolph, 1947). This conclusion is supported by a number of investigations. For example, if an animal's food is diluted with water, it will eat an increased amount

---

[1] A 150-pound man is approximately one-third solid and two-thirds water. In terminal deprivation he will metabolize about a third of his solid body weight, about 18 pounds. These 18 pounds represent the total fuel or energy reserves of the body. These energy stores provide approximately 60,000 calories, sufficient to maintain the man at his minimal obligatory caloric requirement of 1,500 a day for approximately 40 days, which is about how long the average man can fast before perishing. By contrast, a full-grown rat weighing 1 pound has about 2 ounces of reserve fuel in the body, which can provide 400 calories. Since the rat's minimum requirement is 50 calories per day, it can survive about 8 days. (Survival in each case is somewhat longer than indicated because the caloric requirement decreases toward the end.) Note that the man's daily requirement for calories is only 30 times the rat's, even though he is 150 times the rat's weight. The fivefold increase in needed calories per unit weight for the rat is primarily a function of its smaller size, which makes body-temperature maintenance a much more serious problem.

and simply pass the excess water. When food is diluted with non-digestable cellulose, the animal will eat a larger amount of that also and pass the residue (Adolph, 1947; Harte et al., 1948; Janowitz & Grossman, 1949).[2] If animals are given access to alcohol, which has caloric content among its other values, they tend to drink it moderately and to reduce the intake of their regular food so as to maintain constant caloric intake (Cowgill, 1928; Hausmann, 1932). Collier and Bolles (1968, 1968a) maintained rats on a variety of diets with food, water, and different sugar solutions. The animals' consumption varied widely in terms of total amount consumed, amounts drunk and eaten, and the proportion of food to sugar. Indeed, all measures varied—except total caloric content, which was constant. On the other hand, some foods, particularly high-fat foods, are evidently palatable enough to induce some overeating (e.g., Corbit & Stellar, 1964).

Granting then that animals typically do regulate, the question is how they do it. How does the animal maintain its weight, and hence its total energy reserves, at a remarkably constant value even though it eats sporadically and eats meals of different sizes and qualities? How does the animal reduce the size and/or frequency of its meals when it is over its set point, and how does it take more frequent and/or larger meals when it is below its set point? Let us see how the Hullian drive construct, which relates the probability of eating to the animal's need for food, suggests itself as a suitable homeostatic mechanism.

Weight loss as an index of drive. The idea that the weight of an animal might be manipulated as an antecedent condition to control its motivation has become widely accepted recently. But although the possibility of this kind of experimental control was recognized some time ago by Stone (1929), it gained acceptance rather slowly. Skinner has indicated that the technique was used consistently with pigeons from the beginning of his work with these animals (in 1941), but he could not say how the practice arose (personal communication). Stolurow (1951) manipulated motivation in rats by maintaining them at a fixed percentage of their ad lib. body weight. He found,

[2] The dietary dilution procedure is a potentially powerful technique for studying caloric regulation, but so far it has not been widely used. A couple of curious findings can be cited: Rozin (1968) found that when the rat's diet is separated into different components, protein, fat, and sugar, and then these components are individually diluted, the rat increases its intake to compensate for the dilution of the protein and fat components but not the sugar component. Snowdon (1969) has reported that under a variety of conditions the rat's adjustment to dilution requires about four to six meals. Thus the adjustment is too slow to be based upon an immediate reaction to, say, change in the palatability of the diet, and too fast to be based upon a change in the animal's need state. It appears to reflect some special kind of learning (see also Fitzsimons & Le Magnen, 1969; Booth, 1972).

of course, that instrumental behavior increased in strength with the amount of weight loss. He also discovered that although it made some difference in the animal's ultimate survival, it made little difference in instrumental behavior whether the animal was maintained for long periods of time at a fixed percentage of normal ad lib. weight, brought down suddenly to that level, or switched from some other long-maintained level.[3]

In the next few years several investigators began to consider the relationship between weight loss and what was then the established maintenance-schedule procedure for manipulating hunger motivation. Eisman (1956) ran five groups of animals on a discrimination problem. Three of these groups were on a 48-hour feeding cycle but were run 45, 22, or 4 hours after the last feeding. A fourth group was on a 24-hour cycle and was run after 22-hours deprivation; the fifth group was deprived 4 hours (after 44 hours ad lib.). There was no difference in the discrimination performance of the first three groups, which differed markedly in deprivation time but which had comparable total deprivation experience. The fourth and fifth groups, which were matched to two of the previous groups in terms of deprivation time but under conditions of less severe total deprivation, showed poorer performance. Eisman presents no weight data, but it seems likely that discrimination performance was correlated with weight loss.[4] Similar findings were reported by Eisman et al. (1956).

Other studies (Hall et al., 1953; Lawrence & Mason, 1955; Reid & Finger, 1955) indicate that the naïve animal needs a period of at least two weeks to reach a stable level of activity wheel running and/or food intake. During this two-week period the animal's food consumption rises sharply at first and then more gradually until a

---

[3] It is assumed, of course, in speaking of weight loss that the critical part of the total body weight is that which reflects the animal's energy stores. The animal could increase its weight appreciably, perhaps by 5 percent, by consuming large quantities of water, or it could reduce its weight a like amount by losing water, without appreciably affecting its hunger. Our convention of referring to weight loss in terms of the weight of the whole animal is simply a convenient approximation. Fortunately, most animals do not materially alter their body weight one way or another by drinking when they are hungry. We will proceed, then, simply keeping in mind the idea that the animal's total body weight is not itself regulated; it merely provides a useful index to the size of the animal's energy stores, which are regulated.

[4] Eisman proposed a two-factor theory of hunger motivation, one factor involving whether the stomach is full or empty, and the other depending upon the animal's immediate long-term food deprivation experience. The short-term effect, lasting perhaps four hours after ingestion of a full meal, may act to inhibit the second and principal motivational factor, which is evidently highly correlated with, if not the same thing as, weight loss (see also Eisman et al., 1960). Further evidence for such an interpretation is given on page 211.

stable maximum is reached. At the same time, the animal's weight drops off sharply and then more slowly until, in about two weeks, it too reaches a relatively stable value.

In contrast with these findings, Brownstein and Hillix (1960) reported a study in which only 5 days were necessary to stabilize running performance in an alley. Two groups were compared, a group with 15 days prior deprivation experience and a group with 5 days prior experience. No weight data are reported except that the authors noted that the 15-day and the 5-day prior deprivation conditions did not produce a difference in weight! Perhaps this is why only 5 days were necessary to accommodate to the deprivation conditions. We may presume that Brownstein and Hillix were more generous with food than Reid and Finger (1955), whose animals showed a close parallel between performance and weight loss.

Bolles and Petrinovich (1956) found that it was loss in body weight—rather than the nature of the deprivation, the nature of the consummatory activity, or the particular incentive—that determined an apparent difference in alternation behavior between hungry and thirsty rats. Several investigators have reported that the rat's behavior in an activity wheel appears to be directly (and highly) correlated with its percentage weight loss (Moskowitz, 1959; Treichler & Hall, 1962; Duda & Bolles, 1963). Ehrenfreund (1960) has confirmed Stolurow's earlier finding that instrumental performance can be controlled by controlling weight. In addition, he has developed an apparatus for precisely and systematically maintaining an animal at a given desired weight.

It looks, then, as though the motivation of behavior can be meaningfully manipulated in terms of the animal's weight loss and that this procedure is more meaningful than the older procedure of imposing some number of hours of deprivation. Whether the new procedure will continue to enjoy an advantage over the older one in terms of more consistent functional behavioral relationships remains to be seen, for there are already some interpretive difficulties. For one thing, as we will see in Chapter 7, when an animal is maintained at a given weight loss, the amount of food it consumes and its rate of consumption at the next eating opportunity are not related to its need state (Bousfield & Elliott, 1934; Baker, 1955; Moll, 1959). We will also see in Chapter 7 that when rats are maintained with minimal deprivation, for example, when they have food constantly available, eating appears to become quite independent of the need state and to follow other kinds of rules (Collier et al., 1972).

It is also true that the motivating potential of a given weight loss can be balanced against other motivational variables. In particular, the animal's prior experience with a given level of deprivation may partly determine how effective that level is in motivating the animal's behavior. Moll (1964a) maintained rats 1, 5, 10, or 20 days at either 80 percent or 90 percent of normal body weight and found increasing bar-pressing rate with increasing experience of deprivation. This effect was small, however, and did not obscure the overall difference between 80 percent and 90 percent animals. On the other hand, McMahon and Games (1964) gave their animals much more handling and apparatus experience and found that the difference between 80 percent and 90 percent animals had dissipated. Such findings are not inconsistent, however, with the proposition that percentage weight loss is the best antecedent index of the hungry rat's drive strength; they may only show that no single antecedent index of hunger can be expected to be perfectly correlated with behavior strength. After reviewing a number of studies of the effects of prior maintenance conditions on hunger motivation, Weinstock (1972) concluded that although weight loss is not the only determinant, it is the primary determinant of the rat's hunger motivation.

Another problem arising from considering weight loss as the basis of hunger is whether the reference point for weight loss should be the animal's weight prior to deprivation (which is the usual reference) or the weight of the animal had it been allowed to grow at the normal rate. The available evidence is not entirely consistent. When Davenport and Goulet (1964) adjusted the weights of their animals to 80 percent or 90 percent of an ad lib. (and growing) control group, they found a gradual loss of motivation over an extended period of testing (see also Capaldi, 1972). On the other hand, Ehrenfreund (1960) and Marwine and Collier (1971) held animals at a fixed percentage of their initial weight and found a gradual long-term increase in apparent motivation. Perhaps the optimum adjustment procedure for constant motivation is some compromise between initial weight and the normal growth weight.

A potential problem in using weight loss as the antecedent motivating condition is that there are gross differences as a function of age in the weight lost under a given set of deprivation conditions (Stone, 1929). A small animal is more seriously affected by a given loss of weight than a big animal. Campbell et al. (1961) weighed rats of different ages after a given number of hours deprivation and found that younger animals do lose weight at a faster rate than the older ones and that younger animals die much sooner in terminal deprivation. But Campbell et al. found that all animals died at about the same *relative* weight loss, namely, 43 percent. If their raw data, which are shown in Fig. 6-1, were translated into time relative to ultimate survival time, it is clear that the weight loss curves for the different populations of animals would all fall on top of each other. Campbell's solution to the problem of differential weight loss with age was also validated by using another measure of motivation, namely, acceptance of quinine in the food (Williams & Campbell, 1961). See Fig. 6-2.

These data may be refined somewhat by separating the

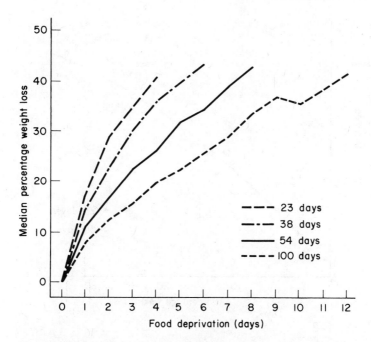

Figure 6–1

Percentage weight loss of rats of different ages as a function
of continuous food deprivation. Weight loss is taken relative
to initial weight. (From Campbell et al., 1961) Copyright (1961)
by the American Psychological Association. Reprinted by
permission.

results of males and females; the irregularity in the lowest curve in
Fig. 6-1 can be attributed to the survival of males after the smaller
females had perished. Accordingly, size would seem to be a more
useful parameter than age simply because older males and females
differ so much in size. Weight loss data of this sort (Bolles, 1965)
are shown in Fig. 6-3. The values shown are for weight loss relative
to the weights of undeprived (growing) control animals rather than
to the weights of the animals before deprivation. Note that females
lose weight considerably more slowly than do males of the same
weight (but faster than males of the same age). The curious reversal
between the top two curves results from the fact that 27-day-old
rats grow much faster than 19-day-old ones.

It is tempting to fit equations to such data: The percentage
weight loss is given by $\dfrac{260}{W_o}h^{0.71}$ for males and $\dfrac{190}{W_o}h^{0.71}$ for females,
where W_o is the normal weight and h is hours deprivation (Bolles,

Theory of motivation

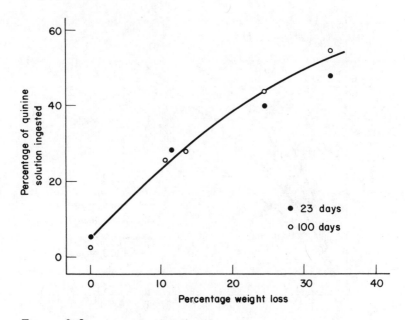

Figure 6–2

Ingestion of quinine-flavored food relative to the amount of unflavored food consumed by control animals with the same weight loss, as a function of weight loss. (From Williams & Campbell, 1961) Copyright (1961) by the American Psychological Association. Reprinted by permission.

1965).[5] It seems, therefore, that by the simple expedient of measuring the animal's need for food in terms of *percentage weight loss* we may obtain an index of need and, hopefully, of hunger, an index that is independent of the size of the animal. Thus this appears to be the most useful way to anchor a drive type of construct to the animal's need for food.

Physiological basis of hunger. The search for the underlying physiological determinants of hunger logically divides itself into two parts. First, there must be some means whereby the body's general need for food, the general caloric deficit, is communicated to the nervous system; that is, somewhere there must be a stimulus—some specific event that occurs in the body as a consequence of caloric deficit and that is detected by the nervous system. The second part of the search

[5] We must expect some species-by-species variation in these constants, too. For example, Myer and Kowell (1970) report an exponent of 0.32 for snakes; snakes lose weight more slowly than rats. We can anticipate that because of their higher metabolism birds would lose weight more quickly, that is, have an exponent greater than 0.71.

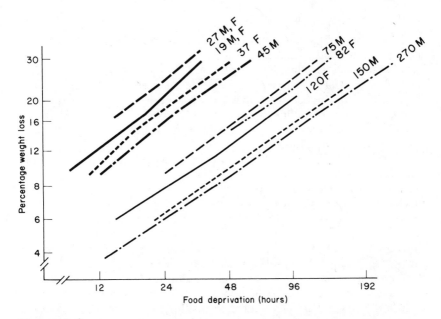

Figure 6–3

Weight loss of male and female rats of different ages as a function of continuous food deprivation. Weight loss is taken relative to the weight of undeprived controls, and age in days is indicated. (From Bolles, 1965) Copyright (1965) by the American Psychological Association. Reprinted by permission.

is to locate that part of the central nervous system where the messenger or stimulus is detected and where the signal is translated into behavioral consequences. Let us see where this kind of an approach has brought us in the past several years.

In the preceding chapter we considered Cannon's ill-fated conjecture that hunger becomes known first to the stomach, either because the stomach itself detects nutritional deficits or merely because it is empty. The stomach was said to respond in terms of muscular contractions, and this activity was supposed to produce stimulation that went to the central nervous system, where it became known to the organism as the sensation of hunger. This interpretation is not consistent with the facts. Both the sensations of hunger in human subjects and adaptive eating behavior in animals occur when the nerves to the stomach are cut, in the absence of stomach contractions, and even in the absence of the stomach itself. Thus we are forced to reject Cannon's conjecture about the stimulus for hunger and begin to search elsewhere for it.

It might seem reasonable to suppose that hunger would be signaled by some metabolic consequence of deprivation, such as lowered concentration of sugar in the blood. This proposition seems all the more plausible because glucose is the principal source of energy for all bodily activities. However, verbal reports of hunger in people are not correlated with changes in blood sugar level (Janowitz & Ivy, 1949); there is no systematic change in blood sugar level with continued deprivation (Scott et al., 1938); and intravenous glucose injections do not alter stomach contractions as measured with a stomach balloon (Morrison et al., 1958). Furthermore, intraperitoneal administration of glucose has no more effect upon subsequent food consumption than the administration of the same amount of a nonnutritive substance (Janowitz & Grossman, 1948). The injection of insulin, which produces a rapid and marked drop in blood sugar level and a prompt onset of stomach contractions, does not lead to reports of increased hunger in humans (Janowitz & Ivy, 1949). A number of investigators have attempted to produce hunger in animals by injecting insulin, and although this procedure is not always effective, some workers have gotten rats to overeat by maintaining them for long periods of time on high doses of insulin (Hoebel & Teitelbaum, 1966; Booth & Brookover, 1968). But Campbell and Fibiger (1970) found that insulin injections have no effect upon running in activity wheels, which should be the case if it is the stimulus for hunger. According to a report by Booth and Pain (1970), insulin does not have a direct motivating effect by the usual criteria, such as a tendency to approach food. Rather, it seems to make the animal eat a larger meal, perhaps by increasing the retention of food in the stomach. Recall that blood sugar is normally maintained at a relatively constant level in the body by the liver. If the level falls much below normal values, the liver, presumably through some kind of hormonal control, immediately starts drawing upon energy reserves to restore it; and if the level is appreciably higher than normal, as it is following the ingestion of sugars, then the liver rapidly converts the surplus to glycogen. Since one or another of these processes is almost constantly going on without affecting the animal's motivation, it is perhaps not surprising that manipulation of the blood sugar level by means of insulin injections should have little effect upon the animal's motivation.[6]

Many writers appear to have accepted the idea that there is a hormone liberated into the bloodstream that triggers the physio-

---

[6] A further complication in the insulin-blood glucose system is that blood glucose is subject to a number of nonregulatory effects. For example, Woods et al. (1969) reported that blood glucose levels are conditionable. They gave rats a small number of insulin injections in a particular experimental situation; later the animals became hypoglycemic when placed in the situation. It is also possible to get conditioned hyperglycemia under essentially the same conditions (Siegel & Nettleton, 1970; Siegel, 1972), perhaps because the situation elicits an emotional response, including hyperglycemia, which overrides the hypoglycemic reaction.

logical adjustments to deprived states and the behavior (hunger) appropriate to it. Luckhardt and Carlson (1915) had provided early evidence to support a hormonal theory of hunger with the report that transfusing blood from a hungry dog to a satiated one produced stomach contractions in the recipient animal. A number of subsequent investigators have reported, however, that such transfusions fail to affect consummatory behavior. Bash (1939) reported that normal activity of the stomach of a hungry dog was inhibited by blood transfusion from a sated animal. Other investigators (e.g., Bulatao & Carlson, 1924) had shown that stomach contractions were affected differently by injections of glucose and by insulin. Unfortunately, none of these early experimenters had been able to show that such transfusions (or, for that matter, the injection of sugar or insulin) had any effect upon the animal's consummatory behavior; so when Cannon's stomach-contraction theory of hunger began to be replaced by better alternatives, the hunger hormone idea collapsed.[7]

Perhaps the psychological effect of a hunger hormone is proportional to its concentration in the blood, so that injection of a small amount of hormone or the transfusion of a small amount of blood should not be expected to have an appreciable effect upon an animal's behavior. If this is the case, then it would be necessary to effect a massive transfer of blood between the donor and the recipient animals. Davis and his collaborators (1969), using a cross-circulation procedure in which virtually the entire blood supply of two animals is intermixed, have now obtained substantial evidence indicating, not that there is a hunger hormone, but that there is a satiety hormone, that is, a blood-borne factor that terminates eating. Thus while the initially sated animal could not be induced to eat by receiving the blood of a hungry animal, the opposite effect was found. Rats were trained to eat at a certain time each day until their daily intake had stabilized. Then when they were cross-circulated with sated animals, they ate less. A procedure like Davis' carried out with rhesus monkeys, however, failed to produce any effect on eating, on stomach contractions, or on anything else that was measurable (Walike & Smith, 1972). Hervey (1959) had reported earlier that when a normal rat was cross-circulated with one having VMH lesions (described below), the normal animal got skinny while the lesioned one got fat.

[7] At the same time, it has been discovered that much of the activity of the gastrointestinal tract is under hormonal control—for example, the passage of food from the stomach into the intestine is regulated by hormones; so too, judging from the evidence just reviewed, is the activity of the stomach itself. Although no very clear picture has yet emerged regarding the action of these various digestive hormones, several of them have been identified and their modes of action more or less demonstrated (Morgane & Jacobs, 1969). It should be emphasized, however, that in only one case (see page 148) has any of these hormones been shown to affect hunger, that is, the animal's motivation for food.

This result also suggests that there is a satiety factor carried in the blood (such a factor, hormone, or whatever would presumably have no effect upon the operated animal but would inhibit eating in the normal animal).

A major breakthrough in this area is the report of Gibbs et al. (1973) that one of the intestinal digestive hormones, cholecystokinin (CCK), seems to inhibit eating. Relatively modest doses of CCK promptly reduced food intake in deprived rats by as much as 50 percent. CCK is normally produced by the duodenum when food enters it from the stomach, and Gibbs et al. describe a variety of evidence indicating that the satiating effect of CCK is not an artifact, for example, because it makes the rat ill.

But while the case for a satiety hormone has come to look quite promising in recent years, the original search for a complementary hunger hormone has not been so fruitful. Kennedy (1953) has argued that caloric regulation would be optimized if a hunger hormone were also actively involved in the conversion of the body's fat deposits. But the attempts to correlate the level of free fatty acids (which should rise during deprivation as the fat stores are called upon to provide energy) have yielded no consistent pattern (e.g., Walker & Remley, 1970). There are a number of further negative reports with regard to other blood-borne factors. To mention just one example, Beaton (1969) reported that the pH of the blood (which might be thought of as a possible stimulus to hunger) fails to show a correlation with hunger.

A basic problem in conceiving of the bloodstream as the conveyor of information about the general nutritional state is that this information is so apt to be lost in the flood of other information carried in the bloodstream. For example, the bloodstream can undergo a change in glucose level not only as a result of changes in the nutritional state but also in response to emotional activity, general arousal, muscular movement, and so on. How is the gradually lowered glucose level arising from a deficient nutritional state to make itself known to the central nervous system when other factors are constantly producing short-term alterations in circulating glucose levels? An interesting proposal to explain this dilemma has been suggested by Woods and Porte (1975). They suggest that nutritional information is communicated to the brain by way of the cerebrospinal fluid. This system is not subject to the same momentary changes as the bloodstream because the short-term changes due to emotion, exercise and so on are filtered or buffered out, so that only the long-term, slow changes associated with nutrition are passed on to feeding centers in the brain. This hypothesis would explain why caloric intake is regulated only over substantial periods of time, rather than moment by moment. It would explain also why the long search for a blood-borne factor controlling hunger has been so unproductive.

Another possibility regarding the stimulus for hunger is, of course, that it is not peripheral at all. Perhaps the stimulus does not arise from the gut or the fat stores: Perhaps it arises within the brain itself. There is no reason why there could not be specialized receptors within the brain, perhaps within the hypothalamus, that monitor their own nutritional state and initiate impulses whenever some critical value is reached. Although we know that just such a mechanism is part of the story of thirst, no one seems to have seriously proposed it for hunger. All that can really be concluded at the present time regarding the search for the stimulus for hunger is that it has not yet been found.

Hypothalamic mechanisms. Whatever the stimulus for hunger turns out to be, it must be detected somewhere in the brain if it is to initiate behavior. It is customarily assumed that the central detector is in the hypothalamus. The hypothalamus is certainly implicated in a host of regulatory functions served by the immediately adjacent pituitary gland. Its involvement in hunger awaited only the discovery of Hetherington and Ranson (1940) that discrete lesions in the ventromedial area of the hypothalamus (VMH) produced a disturbance in normal food-regulatory behavior. Hetherington and Ranson found that bilateral VMH lesions made their animals emotional, difficult to handle, and made them overeat so as to become enormously fat. The ventromedial area was said to be a "feeding center," the integrity of which was necessary for normal food-regulatory behavior. The VMH animal eats two or three times the normal amount of food during a dynamic phase that lasts about a month. During this dynamic phase, the animal may double its normal weight. Then food intake declines somewhat, and body weight stabilizes at the abnormally high value during a relatively permanent static phase.

One might think that the VMH animal is characterized by intense hunger. But Miller et al. (1950) found that VMH animals show *decreased* motivation in terms of their performance for food in an instrumental situation. Teitelbaum (1957) found that such animals do not run in activity wheels as they should if they were suffering from severe hunger. Teitelbaum (1955) also observed that the hyperphagic (fat) rat is actually quite finicky about its food. It is less tolerant of quinine added to its diet, and will not increase its intake when its diet is diluted. Teitelbaum and Campbell (1958) have shown that the hyperphagic rat eats approximately the same number of meals a day as the normal animal but that each meal is larger than normal. It is as though the principal disturbance is the loss of the animal's normal satiety mechanisms. That is, although hunger as measured in terms of most behavioral criteria is not increased, once the animal starts eating, it cannot stop. One is therefore tempted to view the ventromedial area as some kind of satiety center.

This interpretation was supported by discoveries about another area of the hypothalamus. Anand and Brobeck (1951) discovered that bilateral lesions made in the lateral area of the hypothalamus (LH) eliminated all eating and drinking. The animals die in a few days unless kept alive by forced feeding. About the same time, it was discovered that electrical stimulation of this area in normal, satiated animals would elicit apparently normal eating or drinking behavior if food or water were available (Andersson, 1951). This then surely looked like a hunger center. It was also discovered that if both the ventromedial and lateral areas were removed, animals would starve. Thus it began to appear that the lateral area generates hunger but that the ventromedial area can inhibit hunger under the appropriate conditions. With both areas missing, the animal simply has no hunger and therefore does not eat. Sclafani and Grossman (1969) found that cutting through the brain between the two areas had the same effect.

Teitelbaum and Epstein (1962) reviewed a long series of studies investigating the recovery of rats from lateral lesions. There are definite stages of recovery that may be observed if animals are kept alive by forced feeding. Initially, the animal eats or drinks nothing. After a time it will eat wet food but not enough to maintain itself. Later, it can again regulate its intake of highly palatable wet foods, and, finally, it will regulate its intake with dry food, provided water is always available with meals. Normal thirst never recovers, and the animal can only be induced to take fluids by mixing water into its food, by making water available with dry food, or by putting food, such as sugar, in its water supply.

For a few years it looked as though the discovery of these hypothalamic lesion effects had located feeding and satiation centers and that all of the neural machinery involved in food regulation would soon be discovered. But then this simple picture began to become more complicated. For one thing, it was noted that these lesions had a number of effects, not only upon drinking and all of the complications that that introduced, but upon other kinds of behavior as well. It was discovered that the lateral areas were essentially the same as the areas of the brain in which electrical stimulation was reinforcing (see Chapter 8). At the same time, it was found that the VMH areas implicated in the satiation of feeding were precisely those in which brain stimulation was found to be aversive (Krasne, 1962). We have already noted that animals with such lesions display a variety of emotional disturbances. More recently, Marshall et al. (1971) have reported that the lateral lesion produces profound sensory disturbances. Lesioned animals appear unresponsive to a wide range of stimulation in several modalities. We must begin to wonder whether these animals do not eat because they cannot taste their food or appreciate appropriately the other sensations normally arising from food near at hand or in the mouth.[8]

[8] A variety of evidence, not yet published, is just now being discovered by Marshall and Zeigler and others that many of the effects of LH lesions can be mimicked by purely sensory deficits of various kinds.

Any such account of the function of the hypothalamus in food regulation is rather heretical in view of the established orthodoxy that the VMH contains a satiety center and the LH contains a hunger center. One heresy is Panksepp's (1971) intriguing idea that the VMH animal is distinguished by an inability to detect its need state rather than by a disruption of the normal satiation mechanisms. One of the greatest heresies is the idea suggested (but not actually endorsed) by Carlisle and Stellar (1969) that lesions in the VMH and the LH areas have their effects primarily by altering the palatability of foods. Thus the hyperphagic rat might be thought of as being fat because it so relishes its preferred foods (the VMH rat will not get fat unless it is given preferred foods). The LH animal is just the opposite; nothing tastes good, so it starves. None of these accounts explains why the LH animal will not drink, however. Another novel idea is that VMH animals are characterized primarily by emotional difficulties (Grossman, 1966). And at least one modern writer (Wampler, 1973) is able to defend the idea that VMH lesions really do produce greater hunger motivation. It is obvious that the primary effects of these hypothalamic lesions are not agreed upon.

One of the most interesting recent findings was reported by Hoebel and Teitelbaum (1966). They showed that VMH lesions do not disrupt satiety or regulatory mechanisms per se; they simply raise the animal's set point. Hoebel and Teitelbaum maintained rats on insulin until they were obese, some more obese than lesions would have made them. Then lesions were made in the VMH area, and they were permitted to regulate their own intake. These animals did not overeat; actually, they appeared to be regulating their intake quite accurately to a point substantially above the normal set point. More recently, Powley and Keesey (1969) showed that although previously starved animals that had lost a great deal of weight before receiving LH lesions ate less than normal, they ate enough to maintain their weight at a drastically subnormal set point. In short, it appears that lesions in these two areas have the effects of raising or lowering the set point rather than giving direct control over either the hunger-initiated eating or satiety-produced termination of eating found in normal animals. Just as a fat person and a skinny person both show all of the normal phenomena of food preferences and the normal evidence of sometimes being hungry and sometimes being full, so lesioned rats regulate their intake in normal ways. It is only the set point that is abnormal. Thus as interesting and provocative as the hypothalamic lesion literature is, it does not seem to tell us much about the regulation process; it only seems to tell us once again that animals do regulate their intake.

Satiety mechanisms. Caloric regulation requires that there be mechanisms to terminate eating as well as mechanisms to initiate eating. There are, as we will see, two different kinds of factors that can produce satiety. There are *gut factors*, which concern the stomach and which are relatively mechanical in their operation. Then there are *head factors*, which come into play when food is taken into the mouth and swallowed; these latter factors are also much more psychological in their operation, and hence they can be called head factors for this reason as well. Normally, of course, both kinds of factors work together to limit the size of an animal's meal. But it is possible to by-pass the head altogether by running a tube through the animal's mouth and tubing material directly into the stomach (this "preloading" is sometimes done with the animal lightly anesthetized, so the head is by-passed in that sense too).

Loading the stomach with food given through a tube or inflating a balloon in the stomach inhibits eating (Janowitz & Grossman, 1948, 1949a; Kohn, 1951; Share et al., 1952; Berkun et al., 1952). It is commonly reported that the regulation of eating by preloading the stomach is only relatively effective, since there is only a partial reduction in the amount of food subsequently consumed. The animal eats less than it would if the preload were not given, but the total intake may be appreciably greater than the animal would have otherwise consumed. The animal must be preloaded with an amount larger than a normal full meal if the inhibition of subsequent eating is to be complete. When Share et al. gave dogs a 30 percent preload, there was virtually no inhibition of eating; animals subsequently ate as much as controls that had not had the prefeedings.

There is now an impressive accumulation of evidence that the inhibition of eating following stomach preloading depends upon the osmotic pressure that it produces (McCleary, 1953; Smith & Duffy, 1957; Smith et al., 1959; Schwartzbaum & Ward, 1958; Mook, 1963). Mook (1963), using an elegant double-fistula technique, was able to produce a very effective separation of head and gut factors. His rats could sham drink one substance, for example, a concentrated glucose solution, while an equivalent amount of another substance, perhaps water, was tubed directly into the stomach. Mook found that the consumption of foods as a function of their concentration was dependent almost wholly upon the osmotic pressure of the substance tubed into the stomach. For example, rats sham drank huge quantities of 40 percent sucrose solutions when pure water was tubed, but they inhibited their drinking when concentrated sugar or concentrated saline solutions were tubed. Mook obtained preference data that are markedly different from those obtained when taste factors are confounded by postingestion factors, as they usually are (see also Rabe & Corbit, 1973). For example, he found that rats would sham drink appreciable quantities of rather concentrated salt solutions when they were tubed with water, that is, when it cost the animal nothing in terms of the consequences of drinking. It was already known that the rat's preferred concentration of sugar is much lower if the preference is measured in terms of consumption over a long period of time, such as 24 hours, than if it is measured in terms of an initial choice or short-term preference test—conditions that minimize the amount consumed.

There is some question about the precise nature of the osmotic satiety mechanism. McCleary (1953) and Smith et al. (1959) found that inhibition of eating could be obtained by sub-cutaneous injection of hypertonic salt solutions. The result of such injections is cellular dehydration, an osmotic block on water moving into the stomach, and a subsequent inability to normalize ingested food. In short, the animals are thirsty. So perhaps the termination of eating occurs because thirst interferes with hunger. A conceptually neat, but not very defensible, hypothesis is that hunger is basically the opposite of thirst: Thirst is due to increased osmotic pressure (see the discussion of thirst mechanisms on page 157), whereas hunger is due to decreased osmotic pressure, presumably, of the blood-stream. It is true that shifts in osmotic pressure, for instance, as produced by hypertonic injections, affect drinking and eating oppositely in accordance with this hypothesis (Harper & Spivey, 1958; Schwartzbaum & Ward, 1958; Smith et al., 1959). But the inhibition of eating produced by injecting animals with a substance that increases osmotic pressure evidently depends upon what the substance is, not merely on its osmotic properties. Smith et al. (1961) found that injecting nutritive glucose inhibited eating much more than a nonnutritive but equimolar saline injection. These data and others (e.g., Jacobs, 1964) argue strongly against the idea that eating is controlled osmotically. For example, Smith (1966, 1966a) found that the osmotic inhibition of eating is quite short-lived and follows a time course different from the facilitation of drinking (see also McFarland & L'Angellier, 1966). Apparently, osmotic tension in the bloodstream inhibits eating, but it is a much more widespread osmotic factor that produces thirst. The lack of parallelism between osmotically controlled hunger and thirst is found both with measures of consumption and with various other behavioral measures of motivation (Balagura, 1968). Hsiao (1967) has reported that when a given amount of salt is taken in by voluntary drinking of saline solutions, there is less subsequent inhibition of eating than if the same amount of salt is tubed into the animal. Even more peculiar is that there is no inhibition of eating if the salt is mixed in with the animals' food (Hsiao, 1970). Furthermore, Gutman and Krausz (1969) have reported that eating is inhibited by hypovolemic thirst (see the following). Thus the inhibition of eating produced by salt loads must involve much more than just an osmotic effect.

Since water is necessary for both digestion and reducing the tonicity of ingested foods, the availability of water should be expected to affect food intake. Bing and Mendel (1931), Strominger (1946), Adolph (1947), Finger and Reid (1952), Verplanck and Hayes (1953), Gilbert and James (1956), and Collier and Levitsky (1967) all report that rats deprived of water reduce their food intake to roughly one-half the normal amount over a 24-hour period. Similar results have been reported for men. (Adolph, 1947a), rabbits (Cizek, 1961), dogs (Pernice & Scagliosi, 1895; Cizek, 1959) and doves (McFarland, 1964). With deprivation of water continued past 24 hours it is generally found that the consumption of food drops even further. Moreover, the inhibition effect is apparently continuous in the sense that rats kept for 23 days on a half-normal water ration reduced their food intake to 75 percent of the normal value, and rats kept on one-fourth to one-eighth normal water ration reduced their food consumption accordingly still further (Adolph, 1947; Collier & Levitsky, 1967). The availability of water is thus an important determinant of how much an animal eats.[9]

Another stomach-related satiety mechanism is the sheer bulk of stomach contents. Mook (1963) found that when rats sham drank water but were tubed with a 3 percent saline solution, they consumed (sham drank) large quantities of water. Under these conditions it was obviously impossible for the animal to sham drink enough water to dilute its ever-mounting salt load. We may ask why the animal ever stopped sham drinking. The answer is evidently that stomach distention was produced by the bulk of material that had been tubed. Smith and Duffy (1957) have demonstrated rather nicely that rats given preloads of insoluble material, cellulose or kaolin, reduce their food consumption accordingly (see also Smith et al., 1962; Towbin, 1949). Whether stomach distention plays much of a role in the normal regulation of food intake is quite another matter. Chances are it is not important in the rat; Harper and Spivey (1958) measured the stomach contents of rats after meals of different osmolarities and found that the total content was (1) far less than the animal's capacity and (2) only slightly dependent upon the osmotic potential of the meal. However, the results of James and Gilbert (1957) and others suggest that stomach distention may normally be an important satiety factor in the dog.

When we consider head factors, the situation evidently becomes more complicated. An animal will eat more following preloading than following the oral ingestion of the same amount of food (Janowitz & Grossman, 1951; Kohn, 1951), but not if a different test food is used (Smith, 1966). Janowitz and Hollander (1955) found that, with experience, dogs become more accurate in regulating how much they eat following a preloading. They learn not to overeat as much, although they still overeat to some extent.

<hr>

[9] In this connection Hamilton (1963) has shown that the rat's failure to eat at high ambient temperature (above 90° F.) is due to its failure to take enough water. After a day or two of high temperature, water consumption rises sharply and increased food consumption follows. Hainsworth et al. (1968) have proposed that heat poses no added water need on the rat except for the extra water lost in licking the fur. Their desalivate rats did not drink more at higher temperatures. This idea is difficult to accept (Budgell, 1970).

Perhaps the most remarkable event that puts an end to eating is eating itself. What makes this mechanism remarkable is that if we think of the existence of a need as causing eating, then we have no way of explaining the termination of eating because the animal stops eating when virtually the entire meal is still in the stomach, that is, before the general state of need throughout the body has been appreciably alleviated—hence the continuing interest in factors such as osmotic tension, which could have an effect while the ingested food is still in the stomach. Even more remarkable is that eating ultimately stops even when ingested food is not allowed to get to the stomach. When dogs are prepared with esophageal fistulas so that food taken into the mouth does not reach the stomach, they sham eat an amount of food that is considerably larger than they would need to make up their deficit but that, nonetheless, varies continuously with the magnitude of the deficit (James, 1963).[10] It is as if the dog can monitor the calories or at least the quantity of food passing through its mouth; it is as if it had a "mouth meter" that tells it approximately when enough has been consumed. Le Magnen (1969) has suggested that the metering is based upon learned associations between the cue properties of a food—that is, its taste, smell, and texture—and its nutritional consequences. Le Magnen cites evidence from dilution experiments indicating that the rat makes some kind of learned adjustment to dilution.

It would be wrong to conclude that the stomach plays no part in the satiation of sham eating, that is, that the fistulated dog's behavior has become totally disassociated from its stomach. We have known since the turn of the century, when Pavlov (1902) did his classic work with sham eating, that food taken into the mouth produces a copious flow of digestive juices into the stomach. This "psychic secretion" may play a part in the termination of sham eating either because the secretion fills the stomach, makes the animal thirsty, or in some other way triggers the normal satiation mechanisms. Hence it does not seem to be possible to separate the stomach experimentally from the rest of the animal in order to determine how it contributes to the satiation of eating.

Epstein and Teitelbaum (1962) have described a procedure that seems to separate the mouth from the rest of the organism, so that its participation in satiation can be assessed. They trained rats to press a bar for food; then the food delivery mechanism was replaced by a pump system that pumped small amounts of food through a

---

[10] There are some discrepancies in the sham-eating literature. For example, Hull et al. (1951) reported that a dog would eat tremendous amounts of food before stopping. Hull also concluded that stomach tubing was more reinforcing than sham eating, whereas James (1963) came to the opposite conclusion. It is unfortunate that for various technical reasons sham-eating fistulas cannot be used with rats, at least not if the fistula is put in the neck. Rats will sometimes sham drink (e.g., Mook, 1963), but they will not sham eat.

stomach tube whenever the bar was pressed. The rats lived in the experimental situation and were required to obtain all their food in this manner. The bar-press rate was found to vary correspondingly when the caloric payoff for bar pressing was varied. But Snowdon (1969), who has replicated the main features of these results, reported that when food is diluted, the compensatory increase in bar pressing does not occur immediately, as might be expected if the stomach alone were governing meal size, but rises gradually over four to six meals, that is, the same number as intact animals eating normally require to adjust to dilution of their food. Since normal animals have the use of head factors, we may suppose that somehow Epstein's animals did too. Holman (1969) has shown how difficult it is to eliminate all head stimulation even when food is tubed in, and all investigators using this kind of preparation have noted that it poses a number of serious problems. Evidently, even when the animal's mouth is eliminated as part of the normal sequence of events in food ingestion, the head is still critically involved in one way or another (see page 266).[11]

To summarize this discussion of satiety mechanisms, it can be said that there are a number of fairly well-investigated but still somewhat controversial physiological mechanisms, the best established of which seems to be increased osmotic pressure, secretion of digestive fluid, stomach distention and cellular dehydration, all of which are caused by the ingestion of food and all of which are accompanied by an influx of water into the stomach. It is not yet clear how these factors are interrelated—whether, for example, they may be just different aspects of a single mechanism. We have noted too that under certain circumstances factors such as the amount of consummatory behavior can serve to terminate ongoing consummatory behavior. It is interesting to note that there is no evidence to indicate that the alleviation of need has anything to do with the termination of eating. Thus although need may have something to do with the initiation of eating (and even this is not certain), the end of the meal is determined by a completely different set of factors.

To summarize the entire discussion of hunger and the conditions that produce it, a few points should be emphasized. Hunger is basically a psychophysical phenomenon in which the animal's continuous need for energy in the form of calories is met by the animal's occasional motivation to consume calories. It is possible to deceive an animal with nonnutritive food for short periods of time (Taylor &

[11] The head was implicated in satiation in another way by Brobeck (1960), who emphasized the fact that the digestion of food, especially high-protein food, generates heat. This effect, called the specific dynamic action of food, was suggested to cause satiety; in effect, the animal becomes too warm to continue eating. This hypothesis has now been disposed of (Rampone & Shirasu, 1964; Abrams & Hammel, 1964; Peters & Kent, 1970).

Bruning, 1967), but in the long run the rat, and probably most other animals, will eat just enough of whatever is available to regulate body weight rather precisely around a natural set point. It is easy to demonstrate (see Chapter 7) that the rat's readiness to eat and willingness to work for food increases systematically with its need for food if need is defined as percentage of body-weight loss. It is tempting, therefore, to conceive of body-weight loss both as the most relevant antecedent condition of hunger and as the best way to relate it to a homeostatic motivating concept, such as Hull's D. How the animal's need for calories is detected by the body so that it makes itself known to the nervous system, that is, what the stimulus is for hunger, remains very much a mystery. How the animal knows how much to eat, that is, what kind of mechanism signals satiety and produces the termination of eating, also remains a mystery. It cannot be satisfaction of the initiating need because eating stops when most of the meal is still in the stomach and the initial condition of need still prevails throughout the body. It is becoming increasingly apparent that both the initiation and the termination of eating depend upon a number of psychological factors, about which we will have more to say in Chapter 7.

Thirst

There is always an obligatory water loss, that is, a fairly constant loss of water, in respiration, in perspiration and other cooling mechanisms, and in urination and defecation. If an animal fails to take in as much water as its obligatory loss, either in fluids it drinks or food it eats, then it becomes water deprived. We will refer to this physiological need state simply as deprivation and use the word "thirst" to refer to the psychological effects of deprivation, that is, the motivation for water, the desire for water, the readiness to drink or to work for water. The problem of thirst might then be thought of as a matter of psychophysical equivalence: A certain amount of physiological deprivation produces a certain amount of psychological thirst. But while this simple picture of thirst has some merit as a rough first approximation, it turns out that the true picture is considerably more complicated.

One complication is that thirst can be produced not only by depriving an animal of water but also by injecting it with any of a number of substances, the most noteworthy of which is salt, NaCl. A somewhat better model of thirst might, therefore, be one in which thirst is a function of the animal's osmotic balance, the water-salt balance. The problem of regulating water intake would then reduce to regulating tonicity, that is, total saltiness. This alternative model of thirst also has some merit as a very rough approximation, but it is quantitatively inadequate; it fails to describe how much the animal

Theory of motivation

will drink. This defect of the model was illustrated in a classic study by Gilman (1937). Gilman injected dogs with quantities of either NaCl or urea, which were calculated to produce the same osmotic effect, and found that the dogs drank much more water following a salt injection than following a urea injection. Gilman had discovered a new complication. The relevant difference between these two substances is that when urea goes into solution in the body, it freely passes into the body cells and becomes uniformly distributed throughout the body, whereas NaCl cannot pass through cellular membrances, and so it remains concentrated in what is called the extracellular space, that is, in the bloodstream and in the spaces between cells.[12] When a hypertonic salt solution is injected, water rapidly leaves the cells and enters the extracellular space to dilute it (Corbit, 1965; Hatton & Thornton, 1968). This movement of water restores osmotic balance to the extracellular space, but at the cost of cellular dehydration. Gilman's drinking data suggest that thirst is not due to an overall osmotic imbalance, but rather to the loss of cellular water. Gilman's study was replicated by Holmes and Gregersen (1950), who used other substances like salt, which cannot enter the cells, and glucose, which can. The same basic findings have also been obtained with rats (Adolph et al., 1954).

Adolph et al. reported additional data that create further trouble for the idea that osmotic pressure is the crucial factor in thirst. They noted that although NaCl caused more drinking than other substances, even NaCl injections produced relatively little drinking— nowhere near enough to restore normal tonicity of the extracellular space. They also observed that if the opportunity to drink was delayed for a period of 8 hours, rats drank as much as they would if offered water shortly after the salt injection, even though in 8 hours the entire extra salt load had been excreted in the animals' urine. Here then we have another complication: The animal's excretory system can participate in the regulation of osmotic imbalances by helping get rid of excess salt. There are limits upon what the excretory system can do, however, because the kidneys have a limited ability to concentrate salt. Thus if a great deal of salt is to be excreted in this manner, it can cost the animal a considerable amount of water, so that even though the excess salt is gotten rid of, the animal may end

[12] NaCl is normally found in body fluids in a concentration that can be reckoned as .14 molar or 140 mEq./l. or 0.8 percent. According to Gamble (1953), the body of a typical mammal is constituted by weight of approximately 70 percent water, of which about five-sevenths, or 50 percent of the total body weight is cellular water. The remainder is in the extracellular spaces, about a quarter of which is the bloodstream. Recall that in the food-energy regulation system, the liver serves as a buffer between the source of food in the stomach and the body's need for energy in the form of glucose. The extracellular water spaces serve a similar buffering function in that all water and all solutes entering or leaving the body do so through the extracellular space, normally, the bloodstream.

up with a net loss of body water. Evidently, the animals used by Adolph et al. were compensating for this loss of cellular water when they accepted water 8 hours after a salt injection. The effect of the injection is, therefore, much like the effect of water deprivation in that it creates a loss of cellular water, and it is this loss then that appears to produce thirst.

It might be supposed that the critical factor following salt injection is not loss of water from the cells, but rather the osmotic pressure gradient established between extracellular and cellular spaces. But this does not seem to be the case. Experimenters who have measured the tonicity of extracellular fluids, for instance, the blood, following the injection of solutes, find a sharp rise in osmotic pressure, but within only a few minutes pressure begins to drop as water is drawn out of the extracellular spaces. Yet even though the salt load is diluted and the excess salt is largely excreted in an hour or two (Hatton & O'Kelly, 1966), the animal remains thirsty. Therefore, it appears that the real stimulus to thirst produced by this procedure is the loss of cellular water.[13]

This hypothesis accounts for a number of findings that have previously been rather difficult to explain. Lepkovsky et al. (1957) found that, following water deprivation, water was lost from certain organs, predominantly the skin and muscles, but that there was no lasting change in the volume or tonicity of the blood (see also Heller, 1949). Adolph had calculated that water deprivation should produce very large changes in osmotic pressure, but he and others (e.g., Fitzsimons & Oatley, 1968) find very little osmotic change in the blood—perhaps only one-tenth of the predicted values. Therefore, the stimulus to thirst cannot be purely osmotic but must be a consequence of water being drawn out from the cells.

Animals that have had their kidneys surgically removed can survive for several hours, long enough to conduct an experiment of the sort that has been described. Because such surgically prepared animals cannot eliminate excess salt, they are dependent upon water intake to relieve the imbalance produced by salt injections. Fitzsimons (1961, 1969) repeated the experiment originally done by Gilman using nephrectomized rats and a variety of substances, some of which could pass into the cells and some of which could not. Over the ensuing 6-hour test period Fitzsimons' animals drank amounts of water that just matched the amounts calculated to be lost by cellular dehydration. His animals drank a great deal following injection of substances like NaCl and only about 20 percent as much

---

[13] The reader should be warned that thirst produced by hypertonic solutions is sometimes called osmotic thirst, and while this is not really a misnomer (because the thirst is produced by osmotically produced shifts in water), the deficit is most immediately a result of cellular dehydration and only an indirect result of osmotic factors. It is best to think of the thirst as being due to cellular dehydration or cellular shrinkage.

Theory of motivation

following the injection of urea. It can also be shown mathematically that the amount of water drunk under these conditions is a function of the amount of solute injected and does not depend upon the size of the animal. Corbit (1969) has confirmed this surprising prediction. Corbit (1965, 1967), Corbit and Tuchapsky (1968), and Hsiao and Trankina (1969) have also shown that injection of isotonic fluids into the bloodstream does not inhibit drinking. The reason must be that the cells cannot derive water from the extracellular space if the latter is isotonic. The conclusion that must be drawn is that following the injection of hypertonic substances, the rat drinks in order to replace water lost from the cells of the body. The cellular dehydration model is much more adequate than any that we have discussed so far. But there is one more important complication to be dealt with; namely, thirst can be produced not only by the loss of cellular water but also by the loss of extracellular fluid.

Note that simply removing extracellular fluid does nothing to change osmotic conditions within the animal, since if what is removed is isotonic, then what remains must be isotonic also. It might be thought that removal of extracellular fluid would also cause water to flow from the cells to replace the extracellular loss, producing the same kind of thirst, but this does not seem to happen. Consider the procedure in which fluid is removed by injecting the animal just under the skin or in the peritoneal cavity with a mass of a substance such as polyethylene glycol, which is chemically inert and has very large molecules so that it cannot pass into the body by diffusion or osmosis. The substance then pulls large quantities of water, plus isotonic quantities of salts, including NaCl, out of the extracellular space. Following the treatment the animal is hypotonic as far as extracellular fluids are concerned. As a result of this lowered osmotic pressure, water goes *into* the cells, distributing the negative osmotic pressure throughout the body and depleting extracellular volume.[14]

The total situation is theoretically just the opposite of sodium-injection thirst; that is, cellular water levels are high and extracellular osmotic pressure is low, but the animal is thirsty (Fitzsimons, 1961a; Stricker, 1966). It will drink if offered water or even saline solutions (but ordinarily it does not take in enough salt to replace that lost). Other procedures that result in sodium depletion, including hemorrhage (loss of blood), also reduce extracellular fluid

---

[14] All of these different effects are postulated on logical grounds. It is a hazardous business, as we have already seen, to think of the live organism as a physical system in which ions pass here and are blocked there because the live animal has a large number of adaptive mechanisms to prevent all of these events from occurring or to counteract them. That is what life is all about. As the data begin to come in (e.g., Stricker, 1968; Almli, 1970, 1971) it is not so clear that these procedures produce hypoosmotic conditions within the extracellular space or that there is no accompanying cellular dehydration.

volume, increase cellular water levels, and reduce osmotic pressure (Fitzsimons, 1961a; Oatley, 1964; Falk, 1965). It is now clear that this state, which is called *hypovolemia* (reduced blood volume) induces thirst. Therefore, there appear to be two quite different thirst mechanisms: (1) reduction in cellular fluid volume and (2) reduction in extracellular fluid volume. Experimenters have recently shown that the two sources of thirst have independent, or noninteracting, and additive effects upon total thirst (Fitzsimons & Oatley, 1968; Corbit, 1968; Almli, 1970; Blass & Fitzsimons, 1970). For example, deprivation plus NaCl injections produces total subsequent water drinking equal to that produced by the deprivation alone plus the injection alone. Hsiao (1970a) has shown not only additive effects on the facilitation of drinking but also additive effects on the inhibition of eating.

Evidence for the independence of the two thirst mechanisms also comes from studies that have attempted to localize brain mechanisms of thirst. It has long been thought that osmotic receptors located in the preoptic area of the hypothalamus were involved in thirst. One reason for this belief was the early finding of Andersson (1953) that minute quantities of salt injected into this area would promptly induce drinking. Andersson (1951) had also found that electrical stimulation of this area would elicit drinking or drinking-related reactions. More recently, Blass (1968) has found that lesions in the preoptic area disrupt thirst due to cellular dehydration but not hypovolemic thirst (see also Margules, 1970; Peck & Novin, 1971, for further evidence for preoptic involvement). Fitzsimons (1971) has argued persuasively that while cellular dehydration thirst may be detected by specialized hypothalamic receptors, hypovolemic thirst is a result of a hormone, probably renin, which is released by the kidneys, presumably as a result of the drop in extracellular fluid pressure. Renin facilitates secretion of the hormone angiotensin, which is known to increase blood pressure.[15] These developments, and many others, are discussed in Fitzsimons' outstanding review (Fitzsimons, 1972).

Our analysis of the antecedent conditions of thirst is just about complete. We have a picture of two compartments of the body in which water is normally abundant: the cellular and extracellular

---

[15] Stricker (1971) has argued that the renin-angiotensis system has no direct connection with hypovolemic thirst. Part of his evidence is that drinking is relatively short-lived, stopping long before the animal is restored to a normal state. One difficulty here is that hypovolemia produces a peculiar kind of thirst; the animal cannot return to normal just by drinking water. The animal is in the unusual predicament of needing both water and salt and will drink water or saline solutions or whatever else is available; compared with the osmotically thirsty rat, it is an indiscriminate drinker (Burke et al., 1972). There are essentially no data indicating that hypovolemia motivates instrumental behavior because the test for thirst typically consists only of a drinking test.

spaces. Fluid can be lost from either compartment, producing a distinctive thirst in each case. These two thirst conditions can be produced experimentally by different operations, for example, by salt injection on the one hand and by salt depletion on the other hand, so that it is possible to study the contributions each makes to total thirst. There still remain two complications, however. One is that as Adolph (1964) made clear in an earlier summary of the experimental evidence, ordinary water deprivation, the most familiar method of producing thirst, produces both cellular and extracellular fluid loss in some unknown combination. When a rat is deprived of water, we do not know for certain how much of its subsequent thirst is attributable to cellular dehydration and how much of it is due to extracellular dehydration. The recent results of Hsiao and Trankina (1969) suggest that the major component is cellular. These results, together with the observation of Almli (1970) that while hemorrhage may produce hypovolemia, it can also result in increased osmotic pressure, suggest that there may not be two thirst mechanisms after all but just one: cellular dehydration (or cellular shrinkage). The issue remains unsettled.

The second complication is that following extensive water deprivation, deprivation severe enough to produce considerable weight loss in the animal, there is very little if any relative dehydration. The reason is that in the absence of water, the rat reduces its food intake. Indeed, the reduction in food intake is so great that the animal appears to be as much in need of food as it is of water (Collier, 1964; Collier & Knarr, 1966). The body simply shrinks with continued water deprivation. Most of the body organs, as well as the body as a whole shrink while maintaining the same proportion of water (65 to 70 percent) that characterizes the undeprived animal (Schmidt-Nielsen et al., 1948; Collier & Levitsky, 1967). Why then is the animal thirsty? Let us give a name to this dilemma; let us call it the Shrinkage Paradox. Perhaps the critical factor in thirst is actually cellular shrinkage rather than cellular dehydration.

Having at least tentatively settled that the antecedent condition for thirst is cellular and/or extracellular dehydration, there is still the practical problem of how to measure it.

Weight loss as an index of drive. The technique originally advocated by Adolph (1939) and subsequently used by many physiologists working with thirst is to assess the severity of the need state by measuring the animal's loss in body weight. Weight loss can be related much more directly to hours of water deprivation than it can to hours of food deprivation. The reason is that a 24-hour water deficit can be made up in a single drinking session, whereas, at least for an animal as small as the rat, a 24-hour food deficit cannot be made up in a single meal. Successive food deprivations leave a cumulative deficit. Therefore, one of the serious shortcomings of hunger maintenance schedules does not seriously limit thirst maintenance schedules. In making up the water deficit the rat typically drinks and eats alternately for about an hour. If it is allowed this much time, its per meal consumption stabilizes and its weight stabilizes at a slight loss in 2 or 3 days; if less than an hour is allowed or if food is not available with water, more weight will be lost and stabilization may take longer (Dufort et al., 1966; Kutscher, 1966).

Weight loss during terminal water deprivation for rats of different ages has been studied by Campbell and Cicala (1962); their data are summarized in Fig. 6-4. Note the similarity between these data and those obtained by Campbell et al. (1961) for weight loss during terminal food deprivation (Fig. 6-1). Note also that if these raw thirst data are converted from absolute time to time relative to the animal's expected survival time, all of the curves will fall on top of each other again, just as they did in the case of terminal food deprivation. The similarity in weight loss between thirsty and hungry rats does not stop here. If the raw data are converted to percentage

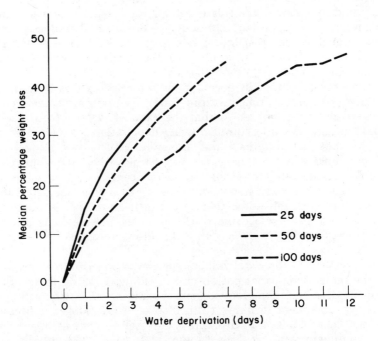

Figure 6–4

Weight loss of rats of different ages as a function of continuous water deprivation. Weight loss is taken relative to initial weight. (From Campbell & Cicala, 1962) Copyright (1962) by the American Psychological Association. Reprinted by permission.

weight loss and if this percentage and the deprivation time are plotted on logarithmic scales, then the data appear as a set of closely parallel lines like those obtained with food deprivation (Fig. 6-3). Moreover, if the weight-loss data with continued water deprivation subsequently reported by Dufort (1963) and Collier and Levitsky (1967) are plotted in the same manner, more parallel lines are found and each of these data lines can be closely approximated with a function of the same form as for food deprivation, namely, $C\,h^{0.71}$, where C is constant and h is hours of deprivation. Dufort (1963) made a direct comparison of groups of rats terminally deprived of water, food, or both water and food. The differences in weight loss among the three groups was never more than 2 percent. If we discount the small amount of water or food that may have been in the digestive system of animals that had water or food available, we can conclude that weight loss was identical under the three different conditions!

These results indicate that weight loss produced by water deprivation may be an optimal measure of thirst. And we have as a bonus that the weight-loss function for continuous water deprivation is not only of the same type as for continuous food deprivation, it is the same function. While this is a far more elegant conclusion than might have been expected, it presents the Shrinkage Paradox in a new form. Consider Dufort's three groups again: One had only water to drink; one had only food to eat; and the third had nothing to consume. The group with food did not eat much, but it ate some, perhaps one-eighth, of its normal daily intake. Why was it not larger or heavier than the groups with no food? We know from the data of Collier and Levitsky (1967) that the ratio of water to body solids does not change with continued water deprivation, so we must wonder in what way the thirsty animal is different from the hungry one. To put the paradox in the most stark terms, when the animal has been deprived so that it has lost, say, 25 percent of its body solids and 25 percent of its body water, and if either food or water deprivation can reduce it to this state, then how can it know if it is hungry or thirsty? It does know because it will eat in the one case and drink in the other; but what is the basis for this discrimination?

The satiation of drinking. Drinking appears to be terminated by many of the same factors that put an end to eating. Loading the stomach without oral ingestion, for example, by means of a stomach tube, reduces subsequent drinking (Miller et al., 1957; Moyer & Bunnell, 1962). This inhibition of drinking occurs before there is appreciable assimilation of water. If water is pumped intravenously, either during or just preceding the opportunity to drink, the amount consumed is reduced by an amount that very closely matches that pumped directly into the system. This matching has been found in the dog (Holmes & Gregersen, 1950) and the rat (Fitzsimons, 1961; Corbit, 1965). In addition, Corbit (1965) has shown that if isotonic saline is pumped in, the amount subsequently consumed remains unchanged; whereas if hypertonic saline is pumped in, intake of water is increased. All of these events have a short time course, indicating that any sudden change in the animal's water balance is very rapidly detected and intake adjusted accordingly.

Towbin (1949) and Miller et al. (1957) have shown that filling the stomach with a balloon will also inhibit drinking, but the inhibition produced with this procedure is relatively slight unless the stomach is entirely filled. Similarly, Adolph (1950) and Mook (1963) have shown that the size of the stomach imposes an upper limit upon the amount of water that can be drunk. Although stomach size obviously limits the amount of drinking that can occur following a severe deprivation, it cannot affect the regulation of intake in which the animal matches a small deficit, so most of the time stomach size is not a limiting factor.

It has frequently been proposed that the tonicity of the extracellular space (specifically, the bloodstream) satiates thirst. Hatton and Bennett (1970) have measured circulatory osmotic pressure and find that drinking ceases when osmotic tension in the bloodstream returns to normal. There are difficulties in interpreting these findings, however (see also the report of Gutman & Krausz, 1969). There is the further difficulty that hypovolemic thirst cannot be sated in this manner. After reviewing a number of such problems, Adolph (1964) concluded that the hypothetical osmotic satiation mechanism alone cannot account for the termination of drinking. In its place Adolph emphasized the anticipatory quality of regulatory drinking. Because water can be taken in so quickly, drinking generally stops before there is any relevant change in the need state. Even so, the animal seems to know about how much water it needs, and it drinks accordingly. Vivid evidence for this argument comes from the early sham-drinking studies of Adolph (1939), Bellows (1939), and Adolph et al. (1954), who found that a dog will sham drink just slightly more than its deficit. Thus the dog appears to have a very accurate "mouth meter." Although many animals may have a mouth-metering mechanism, it is evident that not all animals do. Thus McFarland (1969) has reported that in the barbary dove, the amount drunk is totally governed by the amount in the crop, whether it arrives by a tube or is ingested orally.

The relationship between drinking and eating. Much of some animals' drinking occurs in association with eating. In the rat the diurnal course of drinking closely follows that of eating (Siegel & Stuckey, 1947; Fitzsimons & Le Magnen, 1969). If food is withheld from a rat, its total daily water consumption drops to approximately one-half the normal intake (Verplanck & Hayes, 1953; Bolles, 1961). This voluntary reduction of water intake is also found in the dog (Kleitman, 1927; Gregersen, 1932; Robinson & Adolph, 1943).

Theory of motivation

Gregersen (1932) suggested that the digestion of food creates a direct and immediate need for water, which is met by drinking if water is available. If water is not available, the digestive system will make its demand anyway, producing cellular dehydration. Lepkovsky et al. (1957) confirmed this speculation. They fed dry food to rats, either with or without water available during the meal. At various periods of time after eating, the animals were sacrificed and the contents of their stomachs determined. It was found that whether or not water had been available with the meal, the stomach content was approximately 50 percent water. We can conclude that when dry food is ingested, water is transported to the stomach at the expense of other body tissues. (Lepkovsky et al. assayed the water content of various body tissues and found them, particularly the skin, to be dehydrated in those rats that had not been allowed water with their food.) Some of this water is, of course, later returned as food is digested and metabolized; meanwhile, the animal is dehydrated, and since the ultimate overconsumption of water costs it nothing, it will drink in order to alleviate the short-term need.

This discovery has important implications for understanding what is called hunger-thirst interaction. Interaction creates a methodological problem because when an animal is deprived of water it not only becomes thirsty as intended, it also becomes hungry in some sense. We can also say that although the reduction in food intake by thirsty rats is nearly the same as the reduction in water intake by hungry rats (approximately one-half), the underlying mechanisms are quite different in the two cases. In the first place, the animal needs all of the food it consumes to meet its various metabolic requirements, and its intake, as we have seen, is primarily governed by the caloric content of its food. On the other hand, water intake is regulated by long-term metabolic requirements, plus short-term demands, the most important of which is the digestion of dry food.

Hence the nominally hungry animal drinks less because it needs less. As it is allowed more food to eat, there is a proportional increase in water consumption. On the other hand, if an animal is deprived of water, its food requirements remain unchanged, so that its reduced food intake must represent some sort of inhibition of eating. The nature of this inhibition is not yet clear. It could be that eating becomes aversive with increased thirst, or it could be that food loses palatability when the mouth is dry. In support of this latter interpretation there is the finding (Pliskoff & Tolliver, 1960) that thirsty rats avoid a stimulus that has previously been associated with food. Collier (1964) has suggested that animals reduce their food intake in order to lose weight and thereby help maintain water balance. But whatever it is that prevents the consumption of food in thirsty animals, this inhibition is removed when water is again made available, so that the animal will first drink what it needs and then eat freely and rapidly make up its self-imposed food deficit, provided the deficit is not too great (Hamilton & Flaherty, 1973).[16] An over-simplified summary then would be that the thirsty animal does not want to eat and the hungry animal does not need to drink.

The reduction of drinking when food is withheld probably occurs in most animals, but certainly not in all. Schmidt-Nielsen et al. (1956) report that the camel is nearly immune to this problem, and Cizek (1961) found that the rabbit shows tremendously increased water intake when food is withheld. Kutscher (1969) has conducted a comparative study to look at the interaction of hunger and thirst in several species of rodents. Gerbils showed a great increase in water intake without food, much like Cizek's rabbits (see also Reynierse et al., 1970). Hamsters showed a slight increase in water consumption, but the guinea pig stopped drinking almost entirely when food was withheld. All of these animals were like the rat in showing a sharp reduction in food intake in the absence of water (Kutscher, 1969).

The pattern of drinking with meals also varies from species to species. Gregersen (1932) reported that dogs consume a great deal of water, perhaps as much as half of their total daily intake, in a single large draft following their daily meal. In the rat, when both food and water are available for an hour a day, the animal alternates between eating and drinking. Some of this food-associated drinking occurs, no doubt, because the rat is typically fed a very dry food, which has the effect of drying out the mouth. But Hatton and Almli (1969) found that rats will quit eating and start drinking when the blood osmotic pressure rises by 2 percent, which is essentially the same figure at which deprivation-produced drinking begins. Fitzsimons (1957) has reported, however, that rats will drink a considerable amount of water during a meal even when water is automatically infused into the mouth. Again, the reason is probably that it costs nothing and makes food more palatable. Fitzsimons and Le Magnen (1969) have noted that the interaction of hunger and thirst is a function of what the food is. When the diet is changed to one requiring more water, rats adjust their correlated water intake immediately. But when the diet is changed to one requiring less water, the correlated water intake only declines slowly. It looks, in other words, as though the demand for more water produces cellular dehydration, which in turn produces an immediate drinking response; but the response to decreased water need is the result of a slower-acting learning mechanism.

The regulation of water is quite different from the regulation of food in one respect. In food regulation an animal has two prob-

---

[16] The whole situation is different, of course, if the food provides its own water content (Collier & Bolles, 1968a; Hsaio & Pertsulakes, 1970). And if calories are available in the form of sugar solutions, the rat readily maintains its normal caloric intake.

Theory of motivation

lems: It must not take too little food or its energy stores will remain depleted, but it also must not eat too much food or it will become fat. Water regulation presents only the problem of shortage because excessive consumption of water costs the animal nothing. The excess is simply excreted. Because it costs an animal relatively little to overdrink, we can expect there to be circumstances in which animals will drink more water than they need to meet their minimal body water requirements. Such cases of nonregulatory drinking are theoretically interesting because they show that while the animal's need state can produce consummatory behavior, consummatory behavior can also occur in the absence of a need. Let us consider briefly some cases of nonregulatory drinking.

Nonregulatory drinking. Recall that in our earlier discussion of the effects of lateral hypothalamic (LH) lesions on eating, such lesions were also said to disrupt drinking (Epstein & Teitelbaum, 1964). During recovery from the effects of LH lesions, the rat eventually reaches a stage at which it consumes approximately normal quantities of both food and water. Kissileff (1969, 1969a) has shown, however, that only food consumption returns to a normal pattern; the approximately normal water consumption is strictly tied to eating. Through a series of experiments Kissileff has shown that the recovered LH rat has a unique drinking pattern, which he calls prandial drinking. The animal eats a few bites and then takes a brief drink of water. It will not drink if water is presented at times when food is not available, even at the conclusion of a meal. Evidently, the animal's mouth is too dry to swallow laboratory rat food comfortably, and so it takes a small draft of water after each bite of food. There is no drinking in the absence of food, but there is a constant mouth watering, which defines the prandial drinking pattern in the presence of food. The rat drinks in this case, not in any regulatory sense, but simply to relieve the local oral discomfort. Although the LH-recovered rat can, in effect, be tricked into consuming enough water to meet its various body needs, it is not really regulating its water intake but merely drinking in order to eat. Kissileff (1969a) has found that this prandial drinking could be markedly reduced by injecting small amounts of water directly into the animal's mouth while it was eating. It has also been found that neurologically intact animals will adopt a prandial drinking pattern if salivation is prevented by surgical removal of the glands (Kissileff, 1969) or by the action of the drug atropine (Chapman & Epstein, 1970).

Another curious type of nonregulatory drinking was noted previously: Some animals, notably rabbits (Cizek, 1961) and gerbils (Kutscher, 1969), drink great quantities of water when deprived of food. Such drinking appears to serve no useful function (perhaps just filling the stomach does something for these animals when they are hungry). Another interesting instance of drinking in the absence of a need for water is that reported by Williams and Teitelbaum

(1956) and Crawford (1970) that rats will drink water if avoiding an electric shock is made contingent upon drinking. The rats can be induced to consume enormous quantities. Again, if an animal is given a reason for drinking, then it will drink even though such behavior serves no regulatory function.

Sometimes the rat will drink without a reason or at least without an apparent reason. Falk (1961) reported that if water was made available in a Skinner box while rats were working for food on a VI schedule, they would consume a tremendous quantity of water. The drinking typically occurs immediately after food reinforcement, so it does not seem appropriate to regard it as superstitious behavior reinforced by the ultimate delivery of food (Schaeffer & Salzberg, 1973). A variety of experimental manipulations have indicated that there is no physiological basis for the great quantity of water drunk (Falk, 1969); the behavior can, therefore, be properly designated psychogenic polydipsia. This polydipsia is relatively lawful. Falk (1969) has summarized a variety of functional relationships that have been discovered in his laboratory and elsewhere. The excessive drinking depends upon the food-reinforcement schedule; hence it can be called schedule-induced polydipsia. It is greatest when the VI interval is approximately 2 minutes. It is a function of hunger, reaching a maximum with 15 percent weight loss; it is a function of the physical characteristics of the food reinforcer, being maximal with small, dry pieces. It has been found that LH lesions abolish this polydipsia without eliminating prandial drinking and also that phenibarbital, essentially a tranquilizer for rats, abolishes the effect. There should be no great mystery about why the rat drinks under these conditions. It seems that the rat nearly always drinks after it eats a piece of food and has nothing else to do. If pieces of food are doled out on a fairly lean schedule, the rat will drink a little (about 0.3 ml) after each piece and consume in this way a substantial amount of water (Lotter et al., 1973).

Peculiar nonregulatory "drinking" behavior has also been reported by Hendry and Rasche (1961). They discovered that a thirsty rat will "drink" from a small jet of air. On the one hand, this behavior may cool off the mouth, thereby producing some of the stimulation characteristic of water drinking, but, at the same time, the air jet produces evaporation of whatever moisture is in the mouth, thereby increasing the animal's dehydration. Nonetheless, this behavior is extremely persistent. It is relatively lawful; Treichler and Hamilton (1967) have shown, for example, that it increases with the severity of water deprivation.

Finally, Weijnen (1972) has discovered that when a drinkometer that provides a small electric current, say, 10 μA, is connected to an empty drinking tube, this slight electrical stimulation will maintain licking behavior. The phenomenon is seen best when the animal is previously trained to drink water and receives the small electric current in addition to its water. Then with the water discontinued, the weak current flowing through the drinkometer will maintain the drinking response more or less indefinitely. If Hendry and Rasche showed that rats will drink air, then Weijnen has shown that they will drink electricity.

In this discussion thirst was first considered to be a homeostatic regulatory system. But then we discovered that there were several different kinds of nonregulatory drinking. Consequently, we must conclude that although an animal's need for water (or in the case of hypovolemia, its need for water plus salt) is an important factor in its drinking behavior, animals may have a variety of reasons for drinking besides regulating their water intake. To that extent a homeostatic model fails to explain drinking behavior. Fitzsimons (1972) has stressed the fact that *most* of the rat's normal day-to-day drinking is associated with eating and is governed by the time of day and other kinds of stimulus factors quite independently of any tangible need for water. To that extent too a homeostatic model fails to explain drinking behavior. We will have more to say about the importance of these need-independent factors in Chapter 7.

Sexual motivation

As soon as we leave hunger and thirst and look at other types of motivation, we encounter considerable difficulty applying a homeostatic type of drive concept, such as Hull's D. There is little that is regulatory or homeostatic about sexual behavior. It seems to require an entirely different type of motivational model. Consider the following. Suppose we have a healthy male animal alone in an observation arena. The animal is busy doing all of the things characteristic of its species—grooming, exploring, and so on. He does not look very sexually motivated. But we know that if we were to put a female animal of the same species in the arena, we could get startling changes in behavior. The grooming and the exploration could suddenly be replaced by courting and sexual responses. The question is, then, what sense does it make to attribute a sexual drive to the animal when it is alone? If drive is produced by the stimulus conditions (the sight and smell of a female in heat) that control the motivated behavior, then what sense does it make to introduce a drive concept to explain the behavior? Is it not sufficient to explain the behavior in terms of the stimulus and hormonal conditions under which it occurs in a particular species of animal?[17]

---

[17] Beach (1970) calls motivation the phlogiston of psychological theorizing; he suggests that motivational concepts delay our search for the mechanisms that control sexual behavior. The old reviews by Beach (1956) and Ford and Beach (1951) are still of fundamental importance and provide an excellent introduction to the literature. Beach (1965) and Bermant and Davidson (1974) are more recent and provide extensive accounts of the physiology of sex.

The reproductive cycle. The primary sexual response, copulation, which has been so extensively studied, is only a small part of an animal's total pattern of reproductive behavior. Hinde (1965) has indicated for one species, the canary, the complexity of factors that when combined, organized, and integrated constitute the total reproductive cycle. It all starts in the spring when increased day length stimulates pituitary hormones. These hormones, in turn, stimulate the secretion of estrogen in the female and androgen in the male canary. Courtship behavior occurs when the female, because she is a female, violates the territorial defenses of the male (which in itself is a complicated activity). These violations of his territory stimulate the male to engage in sexual displays, or courting displays, which are characteristic of his species and to which the female, if her estrogen level is high enough, responds by her own species-characteristic displays. It is only after a considerable period of such displaying (which in many species of birds stimulates further production of hormones) that mating, that is, copulation, will occur (see also Bastock, 1967). Having mated, the birds are still dominated by the same hormonal factors but now proceed to build a nest (in some species nest building precedes mating; that is, it is part of the courtship behavior). As a result of having built the nest, having courted, and having copulated, there is a change in the hormonal balance so that the female is now predominantly governed by progesterone rather than estrogen. If everything has been timed correctly, fertilized eggs will be laid and the young mother bird will lay on the eggs and will confine herself to the nest until they hatch. Note that at this stage the female, who no longer engages in courting, nest building, or mating, can be returned to these earlier parts of the reproductive cycle by artificially raising the level of estrogen.

Ordinarily, the progesterone phase predominates long enough for the eggs to hatch, at which point altered body chemistry, together with the changed stimulus situation, leads to a second alteration in the hormonal balance so that behavior is now governed by a new hormone, prolactin. In this stage of the cycle the female is no longer interested in the earlier activities or in laying on eggs; she becomes a feeder of young (which in itself is another rather complicated activity). Complete new sets of behaviors occur, including feeding and caring for the young, protecting the nest, and eventually inducing the young to leave the nest. All of these behaviors are complex integrations that are governed in part by the stimulus situation presented by the young themselves and in part by the predominance of prolactin over other hormones. (Many male birds also share in the housekeeping and other parental duties, and in them too such behavior is presumably under the control of prolactin.) When the young finally fledge, there is a sudden reversion back to the predominance of estrogen, and the whole cycle may repeat itself.

The picture we should have of the reproductive cycle is that it involves an enormous number of highly coordinated and well-timed changes in the animal's predominant behaviors. While these behaviors are fixed action patterns, the behavior as a whole has enough flexibility so that each segment of the total cycle has a high likelihood of occurrence even though life in the wild involves a fair amount of unpredictability regarding what the other animals are doing at a given instant, how many there are, where the nest happens to be located, and so on. The point is that none of the pieces of the whole behavior sequence is reflexive in character, and it is even probably a serious distortion to think of copulation as reflexive, except in a rather limited context. It is also a gross distortion to think of sexual behavior as involving simply the primary sexual act without considering how mating fits into the larger picture. One intriguing aspect of reproductive behavior is that while segments of it depend upon specific hormones, the production of these hormones in mammals, and particularly in birds, depends upon the animal's behavior and upon the behavior of its mate and offspring (Lehrman, 1962), so that not only do hormones control behavior, as we would expect, but behavior controls the production of hormones too.

The whole series of species-specific reproductive behaviors has an entirely different temporal pattern and biological purpose from those that characterize eating and drinking. With hunger the animal is always either digesting its last meal or looking for the next one; the hunger-eating pattern is a continuing adjustment to a continuing problem. The antecedent conditions that motivate food-seeking behavior are accordingly relatively easy to find and specify. Sexual behavior is an interlude, an episode, that occurs in a particular context when both the occasion for it and the hormonal background necessary for it happen to occur.

A unique feature of reproductive behavior is that all parts of the total reproductive cycle depend upon a dual set of factors: a background of hormones and the presence of appropriate stimulus patterns. Both are necessary. If the hormonal balance is wrong, then the stimulus cannot be counted on to produce the response. If an appropriate releasing stimulus is not presented, then no amount of appropriate hormone can make the behavior occur.[18] A second point to be noted is that the stimuli that release various segments of reproductive behavior are typically the result of other organisms' behavior, so the ethological model of innate releasers and fixed-action patterns is applicable. The proper study of reproductive behavior almost necessarily involves us in ethological considerations.

[18] Ethologists like to argue, to the contrary, that sufficient motivation can lead to so-called vacuum behavior, that is, behavior occurring in the absence of the appropriate stimulus. But "appropriate" is a peculiar word in this connection because, as was noted on page 106, the releasing stimulus is often a complex pattern that may be partly present at the time the so-called vacuum behavior occurs. Thus vacuum behavior may not occur in a vacuum but only in the absence of an *entirely* appropriate stimulus.

Why then has the study of reproductive behavior been so preoccupied with copulatory behavior in male rats? It can be argued that the male rat's participation in the total reproductive pattern consists only of copulation. For the male rat there is no territory, little courtship, no nest building, and no tending of the young. It is also true, of course, that there is nothing to prevent one from isolating a segment of a larger pattern in order to study it extensively; it is not necessary to be concerned about the whole complex reproductive cycle in order to analyze a particular part of it. While all of these points have some validity and provide justification for studying sexual behavior in male rats, the most important consideration is still that the male rat's sexual behavior is a part of a total reproductive pattern and can only be properly understood as a part of that pattern. It is certainly a serious strategic error to think of sexual behavior as an instance of homeostatic regulation, which, historically, is how it has been considered. There is no sense in which the male rat "needs" sex, and there is no reason to suppose that in the continuing absence of sex, the need builds up so as to increase motivation for it.

One thin line of evidence to support such an interpretation is that noted in Chapter 5: The rat's level of running in activity wheels depends upon the level of sexual hormones. Another slim line of evidence, which we will consider in more detail in Chapter 8, is that contact with a female rat is reinforcing. Equipped with these relationships, some writers have attempted to force sexual motivation into the framework of generalized drive theory. Pursuing this approach for the moment, let us see if we can identify appropriate antecedent conditions for sexual motivation. But before turning to this question we should find out something more about the primary sexual response itself.

Mating pattern in the male rat. Once the male rat begins to mate (there are enormous individual differences in the initial latency), it will make a series of brief encounters involving mounting and intromission at irregular short intervals, until after approximately ten intromissions ejaculation occurs. Following ejaculation, there is a temporary refractory period during which the male appears to be sexually unmotivated.[19] But within a few minutes the male again begins to mount and thus initiates a second series of intromissions, which is shorter than the first and leads to a second ejaculation. This is followed by further refractory periods, which are progressively longer, and by further ejaculations, which occur after progressively fewer intromissions. Finally, the male leaves the female altogether. There is a minor paradox here in that successive refractory periods become longer, suggesting that the animal is becoming

[19] Barfield and Geyer (1972) have discovered that during this period the male rat emits a continuous high-frequency cry that is not audible to human ears but that evidently signals other rats to stay away.

unmotivated or satiated, but ejaculation occurs sooner following fewer intromissions, suggesting that the animal is becoming increasingly motivated. This apparent contradiction and the different consequences of deprivation for the different components of the consummatory act are interpreted by Beach (1956) as showing the existence of two separate mechanisms: (1) an arousal mechanism governing responsiveness to the female and (2) a consummatory mechanism having to do with intromission and the ability to ejaculate. (Similar proposals for dual mechanisms have been proposed by Soulairac (1952), Larsson (1956), and Young (1961). Even though both mechanisms must work together for mating to occur effectively, it is the arousal mechanism that motivates the consummatory behavior, and it is presumably this mechanism that is correlated with the animal's instrumental performance in getting to the female.

The time course of the consummatory mechanism can be altered by imposing an enforced interval between intromissions in the rat (Larsson, 1956, 1959; Bermant, 1964) and the guinea pig (Gerall, 1958). The intercopulatory interval in the early ejaculatory sequences is typically 20 to 30 seconds. When this interval is experimentally lengthened to approximately 2 minutes (by removing the female for that period of time), there is increased strength of both the arousal mechanism (mounting resumes sooner) and the consummatory mechanism (ejaculation occurs with fewer intromissions). If, on the other hand, the female is removed for a period as long as 7 minutes, the ejaculatory mechanism is depressed, even to the point where ejaculation may not occur at all. Apparently, intromission increases excitation for the consummatory mechanism, and following an intromission the level of excitation continues to increase for approximately 2 minutes before beginning to decline. When the level of excitation is high enough, ejaculation is triggered by the next intromission. Furthermore, it is apparent that following an intromission, the arousal mechanism recovers from its brief refractory phase much more rapidly than the ejaculatory mechanism reaches its maximum of excitation, so that the animal is aroused to make a new contact before it should for optimum ejaculatory performance. Hard and Larsson (1970) have shown that the male initiates a new intromission approximately eight times faster than it should for optimum consummatory performance. The temporal point of reference in such studies is generally the prior intromission, but Hard and Larsson (1968) and Sachs and Barfield (1970) have shown that the course of copulatory behavior is essentially the same if one counts mountings instead of intromissions (with an experienced male about three quarters of the mountings result in intromission).

It has been known for some time of domesticated cattle that a sexually satiated male can be "rejuvenated" by presenting him with a new female (Beach & Ransom, 1967). This effect was shown in rats by Fowler and Whalen (1961) and Fisher (1962). It is sometimes called the Coolidge effect (because President Coolidge is said to have noted the phenomenon in a barnyard), and it has now been reported by a number of investigators. It is not clear why the introduction of a new stimulus female should increase excitation for both the arousal mechanism and the consummatory mechanism, but it does. Bermant et al. (1968) have shown that the Coolidge effect involves more than rejuvenation of an apparently satiated male; it reflects the fact that at all times following an ejaculation the male rat is more responsive to a new female than to the familiar one. The effect makes sense for animals, such as cattle and sheep, that have a "harem" type of social organization, as well as socially promiscuous and polygamous animals, such as the rat.

It is apparent that there are two motivation mechanisms for sexual behavior in the male rat, not just one. But at this point our principal concern is with the arousal mechanism, since, as was noted previously, it is the male's readiness to initiate copulatory behavior with the female that can be expected to be most highly correlated with the strength of its instrumental behavior. The question can now be raised whether sexual arousal can be properly considered to be a source of drive. We can see analogies between sexual motivation and the more clearly homeostatic hunger and thirst sources of drive. There is something like a need (the species needs sex in about the same way that the individual needs food and water). On the antecedent side, it is possible to deprive the animal of sexual behavior by withdrawing potential mates. Let us turn to the relevant studies of sexual deprivation.

Sexual deprivation. Jenkins (1928) found that male rats segregated from female rats for 12 hours showed essentially full "drive strength" as measured by the Columbia obstruction-box method, and with deprivation greater than 24 hours a slight decrease began (Warner, 1927). Stone et al. (1935) pointed out that since the Columbia investigators had preselected potent males rather than looking at the performance of both potent and impotent animals, their results are not representative of sexual motivation in male rats in general. Furthermore, the exclusive use of potent males in the Columbia studies led to a poor correlation between instrumental and consummatory measures of sexual motivation. Stone et al. showed that when the whole range of individual differences in consummatory behavior was included, a much higher correlation between consummatory and instrumental behavior was found. In contrast with Jenkins' results, Seward and Seward (1940) found that sexual behavior in the male guinea pig increased in strength over several days of separation.

One difficulty with these early studies was their failure to control or specify the amount of consummatory behavior that had preceded deprivation. Hence it is not known how satiated the animals were at the start of the separation. Beach and Jordan (1956) have recommended placing males and females together and letting them mate until a criterion of exhaustion has been met (30 minutes elapsed without mounting). Using this criterion, Beach and Jordan tested male rats after 1, 3, 6, and 15 days of separation and found a clear increase in performance (see page 210).

No one seems to know what would be the result of depriving a female rat of sexual activity. In general, the study of sexual behavior in the female has lagged behind that of the male—as if it were relatively unimportant. But Doty (1974) has made a plea for the liberation of the female rodent. He notes that the female rat's behavior is of considerable importance in understanding the male rat's behavior, since it is primarily the female that times and paces copulation. Beach (1958) noted briefly that females fail to learn an instrumental response in order to get to a mate, and although Bolles et al. (1968) have confirmed Beach's finding that mating is not reinforcing for the female rat, Bermant (1961) came to the opposite conclusion. Bermant found that females would press a bar to have a male put in the test arena, but their latency of pressing was an increasing function of the completeness of the male's previous contact, that is, mounting, intromission, or ejaculation (see also Bermant & Westbrook, 1966; French et al., 1972).[20]

The hormonal background. Another approach to the antecedent anchoring of sexual motivation is based on the evidence that sexual behavior requires a background of appropriate hormones. Let us look at some of this evidence. Hormones are necessary, first, for the development of the physical characteristics that distinguish males and females and, second, for the fixed action patterns that make up the reproductive behaviors of the two sexes.

The nervous systems of both males and females evidently contain the basic circuitry for both male and female behavior patterns. The appropriate pattern of behavior is made to predominate by the action of hormones early in the life of the animal. Sexual patterns characteristic of both males and females can be found in fragmentary form in adult males and females, provided that the appropriate hormonal and developmental requirements are met. For example, when animals that are genetically female are castrated as infants and given testosterone injections, they later fail to show female behavior, even when given large doses of estrogen (recent research on this phenomenon is illustrated by the work of Hendricks, 1969, and Pfaff, 1970). Under normal circumstances, of course, the male

[20] It is necessary to distinguish clearly between the failure of reinforcement and the effects of the female's refractory period in these situations. Bermant's data, as well as those of Peirce and Nuttall (1961), have shown that the female will refuse to mate for a short period of time after an intromission and will leave the scene if permitted to do so.

acts like a male and a female acts like a female because of the differential action of testosterone and estrogen. The patterns of reflexive species-specific behavior that constitute copulation, as well as the stimulus conditions that control it, are well understood, at least for some animals such as the rat and the guinea pig.[21]

Sexual behavior in the female rat consists of a number of reflex patterns of courting or anticipatory behavior as well as the primary sexual behavior itself. Each component—the particular postures, specialized locomotory and grooming movements—occurs in a highly predictable way in response to particular features of the male animal's behavior. For example, when properly mounted, the female assumes a posture called lordosis, a sort of swaybacked crouch. Stone (1926) early emphasized the immediacy and apparent innateness of these reflex patterns in the female rat. He found that naïve females in heat would copulate within seconds of being placed for the first time with a male. A curious feature of these copulatory reflexes in the female is that they do not appear to depend upon any particular sense modality. Thus Bard (1936) found that decorticate cats show the complete sequence of female behaviors, although such animals appear to be disoriented and lacking in initiative. Later, Bard (1939) showed that the pattern of female behavior was still evident when the entire genital area was denervated and the sympathetic tracts cut. Another characteristic of many female animals is that their sexual behavior is completely dependent upon hormones. Without estrogen none of the females' behavior and none of the physiological changes necessary for the development of her reproductive machinery occur. After castration the female rats' "sex drive" appears nonexistent whether it is measured in terms of receptivity to the male, running in activity wheels, or by physiological indices (Beach, 1948). But with a normal estrogen level, produced either naturally or artificially by injection, the females' sexual behavior occurs in the normal pattern.

In some animals the predominance of estrogen is brought to an end, and the reproductive machinery is put in readiness for bearing young by mating; that is, copulation induces ovulation (Everett, 1961). Adler (1969) has shown that the rat follows the same pattern, at least to some extent. He found that the series of intromissions characterizing mating in the rat is a necessary part of the reproductive cycle, because if the male ejaculates without the female first experiencing a number of intromissions, the probability of her becoming pregnant is much reduced. On the other hand, Adler and

---

[21] In the past several years the sexual behavior of other animals has been studied more extensively, for instance, the dog (Hart, 1967), the cat (Whalen, 1963), the mouse (McGill, 1965), and the gerbil (Kuehn & Zucker, 1968). Although each species seems to have its own way of "doing its thing," in each case we find a comparable dual control by hormones and releasing stimuli provided by the mate.

Zoloth (1970) have reported that fertilization is less likely if too many intromissions precede the ejaculation. These circumstances could arise if the animals were living in a densely populated area.

In male rats there is a similar dependence upon the hormonal background, but the dependence is not as great as for the female. Male rats that have been castrated as adults gradually lose their potency and responsiveness (in that order), and it makes little difference whether they were sexually naïve or experienced at the time of castration (Stone, 1927). Males castrated before puberty, on the other hand, do not show normal sexual behavior as adults. Whether the reflexive patterns are destroyed by castration or prevented from developing by castration, they can be reinstated by the administration of testosterone. With such injections the male acquires normal responsiveness and potency, in that order (Stone, 1939). However, the early castrated male may never be as virile as animals with normal long histories of hormonal activity (Larsson, 1967).

Perhaps, then, since sexual behavior is so dependent upon gonadal hormones, the level of circulating hormones might provide a direct index of sexual motivation. For example, perhaps the more testosterone, the more motivated the male is. Some evidence to support such an interpretation was reported by Beach (1942a). Beach tested for stimulus generalization in male rats, giving them appropriate and inappropriate sex objects such as unreceptive females, males, and animals of other species. He found that large amounts of testosterone injected just before a copulatory test markedly broadened the range of acceptable sex objects. However, it should be noted that Beach used very large quantities of testosterone to produce these differences. At the same time, it is known that there are enormous individual differences in sexual responsiveness when there are only slight differences or perhaps no differences at all in hormonal level among normal animals. It has been found that both the rat (Beach & Fowler, 1959) and the guinea pig (Grunt & Young, 1952) show large individual differences in sexual activity and that these differences are only in small measure attributable to differences in hormonal level. Moreover, when animals are castrated and given fixed amounts of hormone, the precastration differences in sexual motivation are still evident (Grunt & Young, 1953; Larsson, 1966). It seems unlikely, therefore, that these individual differences are due to differences in hormone level; instead, they appear to be due to differences somewhere in the nervous system.[22] Consider too that the male becomes refractory after an ejaculation. Where would one look for a sudden drop and subsequent recovery of hormone concentration

[22] McGill and Blight (1963) undertook an extensive correlational analysis of individual differences in sexuality of male mice. They took 14 different behavioral measures and found multiple factors; that is, they did not discover one factor, such as a generalized drive concept would have predicted.

to account for the loss and recovery of motivation? The refractory period is evidently due to events occurring in the nervous system, rather than to hormone depletion. We might even wonder if the alleged deprivation effect for male sexual behavior has anything to do with hormonal level or whether it reflects some other mechanism of altered responsiveness, such as change in the total stimulus situation.

The male's behavior is characteristically more dependent upon sensory factors than the female's, although the male rat can also engage in normal sexual activity minus any one or several of his senses (Beach, 1947). Vision is apparently of little consequence (Hard & Larsson, 1968). Smell, as might be expected, is much more important for the rat (Larsson, 1969) and essential for mating in the male hamster (Murphy & Schneider, 1970). Finally, Adler and Bermant (1966) have reported that sensory feedback from the genitalia (which they eliminated with local anesthesia) markedly disrupts intromission and ejaculatory performance but has no effect upon arousal. Their anesthetized animals were just as quick to mount and attempt intromission as normal controls (see also Carlsson & Larsson, 1964).

In summary, sexual motivation in the male rat appears to depend as much as anything else on the context of the animal's behavior; what the animal will do next is determined primarily by what it has just done, where it is in the total pattern of reproductive and sexual behavior. Studies that have compared instrumental and consummatory behaviors, that is, running to a mate, find that in spite of the complexity of the copulatory response, it proceeds in a much more orderly and predictable manner than the instrumental response as the context of the behavior changes (Denniston, 1954; Schwartz, 1956). The level of circulating hormones seems to constitute a background that is necessary for sexual behavior but is hardly a sufficient condition for it. It is, as we said at the outset, an episode that occurs when the occasion for it and when the necessary hormonal background for it happen to occur.

Other kinds of motivation

As we move from hunger, thirst, and sex to other drives (or, in the Hullian framework, other sources of drive), the antecedent anchoring becomes distressingly insecure. Fortunately for the study of behavior, however, our loss of contact with the drive construct in these areas does not interfere seriously with our investigation or understanding of the behaviors themselves. We will see here that for some behaviors there seems to be no antecedent conditions; in other cases behaviors occur in the absence of any condition of need. Yet each of these kinds of behavior has at one time or another been said to constitute a basic drive, or source of drive. Let us look first at the case of exploratory behavior because the conception of an exploratory drive proved to be very important in the development of our overall thinking about motivation.

Exploration. Pavlov evidently considered exploration to be a reflex, for he spoke of investigatory reflexes. Then during the 1930s and 1940s exploration was generally regarded as a kind of general activity that was allegedly energized by the animal's drive state (in Chapter 9 we will consider whether such energization actually occurs). Suddenly, in 1950, exploration began to be regarded as a kind of drive in addition to being a kind of behavior (Harlow, 1950; Berlyne, 1950). Harlow et al. (1950) found that over a series of test sessions rhesus monkeys showed increased virtuosity in working mechanical puzzles, and they suggested that correctly solving a mechanical puzzle was satisfying or reinforcing for monkeys. Harlow (1953) rejected the idea that manipulatory behavior of this kind had any contemporary or historical connection with an animal's physiological motives, such as hunger and thirst. He also emphasized that monkeys performed better on the mechanical puzzles in the absence of food or other irrelevant rewards. In fact, Davis, Settlage, and Harlow (1950) found that hunger disrupted the monkeys' puzzle-manipulating ability. On these grounds Harlow (1953) postulated the existence of a new manipulation drive. He noted that it differed from the physiological drives of hunger and thirst principally in that the stimuli that arouse it are external (which makes it similar in some respects to sexual motivation).

Harlow's argument raises some interpretive issues. In his early studies he presented no evidence of learning other than the increased facility of the manipulatory behavior itself; that is, the learned behavior that was taken as evidence of the drive was not an instrumental response, as is the case in most instances of motivated learning, but what appeared to be a new class of consummatory behaviors. Although it is true that there is learning to eat and learning to drink, if these were the only phenomena that had been observed about eating and drinking, surely no one would have invented hunger and thirst drives. Subsequently, Harlow and other investigators have found that instrumental behavior can be reinforced by permitting an animal to explore (see the following), and, accordingly, exploration has subsequently been more often regarded as a kind of incentive than as a kind of drive.

Berlyne (1950) attempted to build a conceptual model for exploratory behavior that fits better with Hull's drive theory. Berlyne viewed exploration as a consummatory response for a source of drive he called curiosity, the antecedent condition of which was simply novel stimulation. In accordance with Hull's theory, Berlyne assumed that any behavior that led to the consummatory response of exploring would be reinforced. After a period of time something like inhibition of reinforcement would occur, and the consummatory behavior, exploration, would stop. Later, after the inhibition has dissipated, exploration would be renewed. Berlyne (1960, 1963) has elaborated this position and related it to a variety of neurological and behavioral findings.

Montgomery (1953) reported that exploration decreased rather than increased when rats were made hungry or thirsty. Confining animals before the exploratory test failed to change the incidence of exploration (Montgomery, 1953a). Similarly, fear inhibited rather than facilitated exploration (Montgomery, 1955; Montgomery & Monkman, 1955). Hence he concluded that since exploratory behavior could not be the result of a general activity drive, or hunger, thirst, or fear, it had to be based upon an autonomous exploratory drive. Although the logic of this conclusion left something to be desired, the conclusion was considerably strengthened by the additional finding that rats would learn an instrumental response in order to get into a complex novel situation that they could explore (Montgomery, 1954; Montgomery & Segall, 1955). Animals either learned a position habit or a black-white discrimination in a T-maze where the goal was a Dashiell-type maze, and they learned a reversal when the discriminanda were reversed. Reinforcing effects of giving an animal the opportunity to explore have subsequently been confirmed by several investigators (Chapman & Levy, 1957; Berlyne & Slater, 1957; Miles, 1958). Thus there seems little doubt that exploration can be properly considered a kind of consummatory behavior that can serve to reinforce instrumental behavior, and on this account we are perhaps justified in considering exploration as a source of drive.

In his important review of these matters Fowler (1965) has pointed out that prior to the discovery of the reinforcing value of exploratory activity, there was really little similarity between the newly hypothesized exploratory drives and Hull's generalized drive construct D. Harlow, Berlyne, and Montgomery had all been speaking about a specialized directive drive, a drive to explore, and not Hull's D. More compatible with the generalized drive construct were the formulations of Glanzer (1953, 1958), Myers and Miller (1954), and Brown (1955), which emphasized the aversive side of the coin. Boredom, it was contended, is a source of drive. If the animal is provided with constant stimulation, it becomes bored or satiated. Any response that takes the animal out of this state and puts into contact with new or different stimuli will be drive reducing. The discovery that novel stimuli were reinforcing, therefore, provided the first substantial link with Hullian drive theory.

But there still remained a question about the motivating function of boredom. According to drive theory, boredom must contribute to D and must motivate any and all behaviors, not just the single class of exploratory behavior that defines it. Moreover, Hullian drive theory requires that the strength of motivated behavior varies with the severity of the drive-producing condition. This requirement, in turn, demands that we be able to specify how much D is produced by particular antecedent conditions. Here is the principal problem with the concept of exploration as a source of D. The truth is that there do not seem to be any antecedent conditions for exploration. Recall Harlow's (1953) argument that exploration is aroused almost wholly by external events such as interesting and novel stimuli and not by internal events that would constitute appropriate antecedent conditions. Other writers (e.g., Berlyne, 1963) have emphasized that exploration has no physiological basis (actually, Berlyne suggested that the lack of physiological determinants may be a good defining property of exploration). It is certainly clear that the rat has no physiological *need* to explore or that the amount of exploration that the animal does must be regulated.

We have, then, a curious picture in which some theorists (e.g., Harlow) were maintaining that exploratory behavior was explained by an exploratory drive, probably because they thought that relating it to such a drive would in some way legitimize the behavior, while other theorists (e.g., Berlyne) were taking the position that the drive concept was of little use in explaining behavior because it failed to account for exploration. Some investigators attempted to tie up the loose ends by showing that rats deprived of the opportunity to explore, would subsequently do more of it. The argument is evidently that if a deprivation effect can be demonstrated, this would link the exploration phenomenon conceptually with the homeostatic drive model. However, early experimenters (Montgomery, 1953a; Charlesworth & Thompson, 1957; Montgomery & Zimbardo, 1957; Ehrlich, 1959) all reported negative results when rats were deprived of the opportunity to explore by confinement to small simple spaces for periods ranging up to several days.

On the other hand, Butler (1953) imposed a restricted visual environment upon monkeys for various periods of time ranging from 0 to 8 hours. The animals were then tested to determine how often they would make an instrumental response to open a window (which they had learned to do earlier) in order to view a rich visual environment (looking at Butler). Visual deprivation of this sort was found to be effective in increasing the rate of looking outside (see also Fox, 1962; Butler & Harlow, 1954).

One possible methodological difficulty with the earlier rat studies, and a reason they may have yielded negative results, may be that the deprivation times were of the wrong magnitude. Fowler (1963), using a runway, confined rats to a start box of one color for up to 15 minutes, then let them run to a goal box of a different color. Using such short-term stimulus-deprivation conditions (or boredom conditions) Fowler has reported a number of reliable deprivation effects (Fowler, 1965, 1967). Therefore, under the appropriate conditions, primarily external stimulus events of the appropriate quality, it is possible to produce a deprivation function even though it is hard to imagine a corresponding increase in a need to explore. Moreover, the opportunity to explore can reinforce instrumental behavior. Whether these empirical functions justify the assumption of an underlying drive is largely a matter of theoretical taste. If one thinks of drive as necessarily requiring conditions of bodily need and as being produced by certain antecedent physiological conditions, then the hypothetical motivation to explore cannot be a source of drive.

Miscellaneous motivation conditions. Probably related to exploration, but in ways that are by no means clear, are those kinds of behavior that are measured in certain kinds of apparatus and are called general activity. General activity is most commonly considered to be a symptom or an index of D, rather than a source of D. But being active can also be thought of as an autonomous kind of behavior for which animals can become motivated. Evidence that general activity, more specifically, running in an activity wheel, can be used to reinforce instrumental behavior comes from studies of Kagan and Berkun (1954) and Premack (1962). These investigators were able to show that rats would learn to press a bar or engage in other behavior in order to be able to run in an activity wheel when the latter was made contingent upon the former.

   Although a number of factors are recognized as increasing or decreasing the rat's activity (e.g., food deprivation, castration, etc.), the causal mechanisms are not understood. The rat runs sometimes and not other times, and the various conditions that play a part in its total activity only make running more or less probable; none of them can be said to control it. It is also not clear in what sense an animal has a need to be active. Presumably a certain minimal amount of exercise is prerequisite for the animal's general health and well-being, but it is not obvious that health and well-being are goals that, for the rat, motivate its activity. As was the case with exploratory behavior, a number of experimenters have attempted to obtain a deprivation effect. Animals were confined so they could not be active, and then were run in activity tests to see if they were not more active than normals. Hill (1956) is one of the few experimenters who has been able to obtain such a deprivation effect. He found that activity increased continuously as a function of confinement duration up to four days. Other experimenters, however, have found either minimal effects or effects in the wrong direction. Lore (1968), after reviewing these early studies, concluded that they do not demonstrate a drive for activity per se. Lore suggested instead that when animals are confined for periods of time in a very small space, they become emotionally disturbed so that when later put in the activity test situation, their behavior is likely to become unpredictable and more dependent upon the emotional state than a need for activity as such. We are left with the conclusion that activity, like exploration, is at best only slightly dependent upon conditions of prior deprivation, that it occurs in the absence of a relevant need state, and that the behavior cannot be adequately explained on the basis of a homeostatic model of drive.

There are physiological states other than food and water deprivation that represent clear dangers to the animal's welfare and for which we may suppose animals are motivated to take corrective measures. For example, animals are dependent upon a regular supply of oxygenated air. There can be no question about the need for air. When the need for it arises, the animal's problem is immediate and of the utmost urgency. Broadhurst (1957), among others, has shown that air deprivation (not being able to breathe) can motivate instrumental behavior that permits the animal to breathe. It is curious, however, that the need to breathe ordinarily plays so little a part in the psychological life of land animals (with sea animals the story is different), and that the kind of motivational stress produced and the kinds of instrumental behaviors that are learned on the basis of a "breathing drive" are of very little psychological interest. Similarly, the need to regulate sleep and the need to regulate ambient temperature can be critical considerations in the lives of many animals. Certainly, there are governing antecedent physiological conditions (Kleitman, 1963, is the classic work on sleep). Webb (1957) has reported a deprivation effect in sleep-deprived rats. It is regrettable that the work on sleep and temperature regulation has not been incorporated in the general corpus of literature on animal learning and motivation. It would be interesting to discover, for example, whether the kinds of learning and motivating factors that have been found by the extensive research on hungry rats are immediately applicable to the problem of the sleepy rat or the hot or cold rat. It is quite possible that entirely different sets of principles would be found. In any case, it is clear that these need states have been almost ignored as potential sources of drive by animal psychologists (however, see Matthew's, 1971, work on temperature regulation). Learning theory has also largely ignored other classes of behaviors that constitute an important part of animals' lives in normal circumstances. Examples are grooming, social behavior, and play. None of these behaviors depends upon a need state. It is true that if an animal fails to groom, it is likely to acquire skin disorders and other diseases, so that it is in its best interest to groom. But the necessity to groom, to interact, and to play does not have the immediate and urgent aspect of a caloric deficit or an air deficit, in which the animal has a limited amount of time to correct the deficiency. The pressures on the animal to groom, to arrange its social life, and to play are low priority, long-term payoff pressures.

Furthermore, while the nervous system obviously must be involved in the organization and integration of these behaviors, so that they can be disrupted by making lesions here and stimulating there, there is no apparent set of antecedent conditions that produces motivation for appropriate regulatory behaviors. Thus these kinds of behavior do not lend themselves readily to an explanation by a homeostatic model or a generalized drive construct. Like the other types of behavior that we have noted as lacking powerful internal determinants, they are governed primarily by external events: When the animal itches, it scratches; if it is provoked by another member of its species, it may play or it may engage in other kinds of social regulatory behavior, depending upon its age and a host of other factors.

Finally, we may consider defensive behavior, behavior that keeps animals out of danger, away from predators, and that presumably also enables them to avoid electrical shock in the laboratory.[23] The rat is quite capable of defending itself against loud noise (Campbell, 1955; Bolles & Seelbach, 1964), blasts of air (Ray, 1966), bright light (Kaplan, 1952; Cooper, 1963; Keller, 1966), cold (Carlton & Marks, 1958), mechanical agitation (Riccio & Thach, 1966; Wike & Wike, 1972), and water immersion (Woods et al., 1964). The list could be extended more or less indefinitely. But the motivating potential of all these stimuli is puny compared with what can be accomplished with electrical shock. Only shock reliably produces a great emotional reaction; only shock gets the rat really moving; and only shock lends itself to rapid avoidance learning in the laboratory. Shock is also unique in the ease with which it can be experimentally controlled and measured. It is little wonder then that studies using shock constitute by far the largest part of the experimental literature on defensive behavior.

Shock, like most other aversive stimuli, is a threat to the animal's welfare; it presents the animal with a condition of need. But note that this need is different from the need for food or the need for air because adaptive behavior eliminates rather than regulates it. That is, the needs created by aversive stimuli are not regulatory in character. Note too that the time scale is altogether different. The animal can solve its caloric problem now or later; it can even delay breathing for a short period. But shock, representing an immediate threat to the animal's existence, is dealt with immediately.

[23] There is a wide variety of conditions whose termination is reinforcing. Animals learn to terminate these conditions, and man, in addition, learns to call them unpleasant, painful, or aversive. Throughout the present book the basic definition of aversiveness will be in terms of negative reinforcement: That is, a stimulus will be said to be aversive if the organism can learn to escape it. Whether the organism can also learn to avoid it or will be punished by it or whether it elicits any particular emotional or other responses are all open questions that have to be answered empirically. As far as drive theory is concerned, it is only necessary to add the hypothesis that the presentation of aversive stimuli increases drive and that their removal reduces drive. The question we are concerned with here is whether some property of aversive stimuli, such as their intensity, can be systematically related to the strength of the motivation that they produce.

Theory of motivation

Defense is the highest priority problem; it must preempt all other behaviors, especially regulatory behaviors; and the motivation to defend the body must supersede other kinds of motivation. Note further that defensive motivation is itself entirely dependent upon external stimulation. Thus while exploration and sexual behavior are governed in large part by external stimuli, defensive behavior is even further over on the external side of the external-internal stimulation continuum.

Psychophysical techniques with human subjects have led to a number of quantitative scalings of the stimulus properties, if not the motivational properties, of aversive stimuli as a function of their intensity (e.g., Stevens et al., 1958). The best and most extensive work with animals is that described by Campbell and Masterson (1969). Campbell's basic procedure involves a standardized tilt cage in which shock (or noise) of one intensity is presented when the rat is on one side, and a different intensity is presented when it moves to the other side. With different sets of conditions on the two sides, rats quickly stabilize the proportion of time they spend on a given side. This choice tells us something about the aversiveness as well as the sensory aspects of the aversive stimulus.[24] Campbell and Masterson have reported: First, there is little difference between the sensory and aversive thresholds; that is, shock is aversive as soon as it is detected. Second, the rat's behavior is very stable over time; that is, the reaction to a given shock is the same after a few hours as after a few minutes. Third, the discriminability as well as the aversiveness of shock is directly proportional to its intensity; that is, the important consideration for the rat is the current in milliamperes flowing through it. Although there are some restraints and limitations on such a generalization, we can conclude that the current flowing through the rat is the principal factor in determining how aversive shock is.

Summary

We have come a long way toward the understanding of motivated behavior and its antecedents since the day Cannon listened to stomach rumblings. No attempt will be made to summarize what has been learned about the physiological basis of behavior, but it may be useful to survey where we stand with respect to the drive concept.

In general, it has been found that a variety of behavioral

[24] Campbell's technique could be used to construct ratio scales for a construct that, if it had the right behavioral properties, we might want to call drive. A similar methodology for scaling hunger is described by Bolles (1962a). Whether the attempts to quantify drive in this manner are going to be any more successful than the earlier attempt of Warden (1931) remains to be seen.

measures are closely correlated with the animal's physiological condition. In the case of hunger and thirst, motivated behavior appears to be better correlated with the need of the animal as measured by percentage weight loss than it is with any simple set of experimental manipulations, such as deprivation time, that produce the need condition. This finding should not be too surprising because it reflects the obvious fact that a given state of depletion can arise from a number of different experimental treatments. One implication is that a great deal of the research that has been done on animal motivation is either methodologically unsound or difficult to interpret because experimenters have tended to manipulate (and report) the wrong variables, for example, hours deprivation. If we are to interpret some of the experimental literature, we are required to deduce from the specification of experimental conditions what the animals' weight loss might have been.

Other sources of drive all seem to present special problems. Some of them, for instance, sex and exploration, grooming and social behavior, do not represent needs in any real sense. Nor do any of the relevant behaviors seem to serve any kind of regulatory function. There are other kinds of motivation for which the need is clear enough but for which a regulatory model seems inappropriate; bodily defense is one example. All of these behaviors appear to be episodic rather than regulatory in function. They are governed largely by momentary external stimulus events rather than by conditions inside the body that require regulation. Even thirst, for which we can find antecedent conditions of need, is not as regulatory as was once assumed.

We can conclude that the need for both calories and water is determined by percentage weight loss and that the need to be rid of electric shock is determined by its amperage. The question we must now consider is how these antecedent conditions of need are manifest in motivated behavior.

7
ENERGIZING
EFFECTS

*Psychology as a systematic science is
relatively young. As a consequence it is to be
expected that as time goes on marked changes
will continue to be made in the fundamental
assumptions underlying the systematizations.
The fearless performance of critical
experiments and the continuous quantitative
use of the relevant postulates and corollaries
will hasten the elimination of errors.*

C. L. Hull

In all versions of the drive concept it is given the role of energizing behavior. The unique feature of Hull's version is that drive is supposed to energize any and all behavior. In any given situation only that behavior occurs that has the strongest associative connections, and drive merely determines the strength of the dominant behavior. Thus, according to Hull, any source of drive is potentially able to energize any kind of consummatory behavior, any instrumental response, and any kind of general activity. In this chapter we will consider each of these kinds of behavior in turn.

We will start by examining whether the strength of a consummatory response varies systematically with the severity of the relevant drive-producing condition. For example, does eating increase in strength with percentage weight loss? Note that it is not enough to show that the response occurs in some strength in the presence of the drive condition; it must be shown that they vary in strength together. This may be taken as the definition of the hypothetical energizing effect.

The same basic question will then be asked of instrumental responses: Do they vary in strength with the strength of the relevant drive-producing condition? For example, does running to food increase in strength with percentage weight loss? Finally, we will ask the same question of general activity, behavior that occurs in spite of not affecting the drive-producing condition of the animal. Is such behavior also energized in the technical sense?

The present chapter attempts to do two things. First, it will consider the evidence bearing on the theoretical issue that was just defined; we will find that much of the evidence supports the energization hypothesis. Our second task will be to find out something about behavior itself, for example, how best to measure its strength. We will find that different explanatory principles seem to apply to different kinds of responses and even to different measures of a response. It will become clear that although the hypothetical energizing effect can be validated in many instances, it has little explanatory power. An adequate explanation of most behaviors must include an account of their associative characteristics.

The energizing of consummatory behavior

For years psychologists have tended to consider the strength of an animal's consummatory behavior as a direct measure of drive strength. Thus we have tended to think of hunger-produced drive as leading directly and immediately to the energization of eating. But a growing mass of evidence requires us to reject this conceptual shortcut. Recent investigations of consummatory activities have shown that, like any other responses, they are dependent upon controlling stimulus conditions and they are subject to reinforcement. We will see in the present section that it is necessary to distinguish among probability measures, amplitude measures, and persistence measures of eating. We will find that these different measures of the consummatory response are governed by different kinds of mechanisms. After we have gotten an overall view of eating behavior, we will be able to ask meaningfully whether hunger-produced drive energizes eating in the technical sense that eating increases monotonically with the severity of drive-producing conditions. This section will conclude with a look at some of the less well-studied consummatory behaviors, drinking, mating, and exploration, and we will then be in a position to arrive at some general conclusions about the energizing of consummatory behavior.

The problem of measurement. There are a number of ways in which the strength of consummatory behavior might conceivably be measured; it varies in probability and persistence and in the kinds of stimuli that will elicit it. The question is whether the different measures of consummatory behavior vary together in a consistent manner when the relevant antecedent conditions vary. If this were the case, it would be relatively easy to defend the idea that the strength of the consummatory response was determined by the intensity of an underlying motivating device, such as D. But, unfortunately, this is not the case. Miller (1956) has provided the classic demonstration of the lack of correlation when he compared three different measures of consummatory behavior and a physiological index presumably correlated with hunger. The measures were: (1) the concentration of quinine that would be tolerated in the food, (2) the rate of bar pressing on a variable-interval schedule, (3) the amount consumed during the test period, and (4) the occurrence of stomach contractions as measured by a permanently implanted stomach balloon. The results are shown in Fig. 7-1.

Miller's four measures are definitely not well correlated over the range of deprivation times, and his conclusion that we should not rely too much on any one measure of drive strength seems justified. But a little further analysis shows that these different measures are relatively lawful. Note that bar pressing and acceptance of quinine are response measures that tell us how likely the consummatory response is to be initiated. Both of these measures indicate the strength of the consummatory response before the animal has ingested enough food to affect its condition materially; they are *preingestion* measures of motivation. Miller's data suggest that these measures increase monotonically as deprivation becomes more severe. On the other hand, the third measure, amount consumed, depends not only upon the animal's starting to eat but, in addition, upon all of the new factors that come into play with ingestion, that is, all of the *postingestion* factors that are introduced by the consumption of

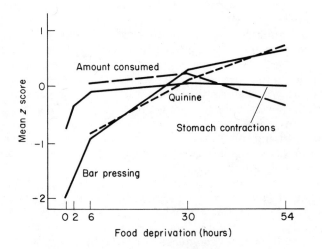

Figure 7–1

A comparison of four measures of "hunger." Each measure is plotted as a standard score derived from the average within-test-condition variability on the last three deprivation conditions; this makes the different measures directly comparable. (From Miller, 1965) Reprinted by permission of the New York Academy of Sciences and the author.

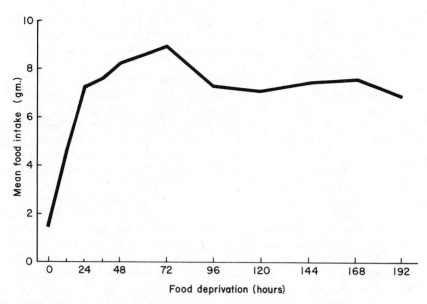

Figure 7-2

Food consumption as a function of deprivation time. (From Dufort &
Wright, 1962)

food. (It is not clear how the fourth measure, stomach contractions,
should be interpreted.)

More extensive data on amount consumed as a function of
deprivation were reported by Dufort and Wright (1962) and are
shown in Fig. 7-2. Their data are valuable because their animals were
naïve and subjected to a single test deprivation so that percentage
weight loss can be readily estimated from deprivation time and so
that there was minimal effect of associative factors, which, as we
will see shortly, have an important bearing upon consummatory
behavior.

One conclusion that can be drawn from these data is that
while the hungry animal's energy deficit increases monotonically
with deprivation time, its consumption in the test situation does not,
so that there is a lack of correspondence between the severity of the
drive state and this measure of the strength of the relevant motivated
behavior. There is, therefore, a failure of the principle that drive
energizes consummatory behavior. It could be argued that this lack
of correlation does not invalidate the functional relationship between
drive strength and consummatory response strength; it shows only
that other factors must also be considered. But this is still a very
serious qualification. Once it is admitted that it is necessary to postulate two kinds of factors, drive factors and associative factors, to

Theory of motivation

explain this straightforward aspect of motivated behavior, the way is open for an associative explanation of all aspects of motivated behavior. Let us turn then to the consideration of the different associative factors that appear to play a part in eating.

Associative factors in eating. When rats are deprived and offered food for the first time, they typically eat very little—not enough to make up their deficit and not enough to sustain them through to the next day without further weight loss. Ghent (1951, 1957) found that it required several days of successive testing before rats would eat enough at one time to maintain themselves. This conclusion is also indicated by the results of Lawrence and Mason (1955), Reid and Finger (1955), and Moll (1959). The effect of learning is confounded in these studies by the fact that when animals fail to eat enough, they become increasingly deprived on successive days. Thus the increased consumption may overestimate the amount of learning that is involved. Moll (1964) used a superior procedure in which animals were first brought down to reduced body weight, either 80 percent or 90 percent of normal weight adjusted for growth, before being run on consumption tests. Under these conditions Moll still obtained large learning effects measured either in terms of latency to start eating, amount consumed in the first 5 minutes, or the amount of time spent eating in the first 5 minutes. The rapidity of learning and the level of performance obtained also varied with the age of the animals, but the learning effect was evident in animals of all ages up to three months.

An interesting variation on this type of experiment has been reported by Williams (1968). In contrast to the findings of Ghent and Moll, Williams' well-controlled study revealed no evidence of learning to eat. The difference in methodology was that Williams tested her animals in their home cages, whereas Moll and others had tested theirs in a novel eating situation. Hence we must note that the important factor here appears to be familiarity with the *place* in which eating occurs and not prior familiarity with deprivation per se.

Another kind of learning that may be involved in consummatory behavior is familiarity with a particular test food. Young (1948) has surveyed some of the earlier studies showing that the rat's preference for particular foods depends in part upon its experience with them. Wetzel (1959) has reported that prior drinking of sugar solutions made them more reinforcing for rats.

Still another question is whether experience recovering from earlier deprivation facilitates recovery from a later deprivation. It is known that after being deprived for 24 hours and then being given food for 24 hours, the rat eats somewhat more than its normal ad lib. consumption (Adolph, 1947; Finger & Reid, 1952; Lawrence & Mason, 1955; Fallon, 1965; Levitsky, 1970), but this extra food intake ordinarily amounts to only 40 percent or 60 percent. The rat, therefore, does not make up its food deficit immediately; indeed, it takes an appreciable period of time for the animal to return to the weight it would have had if it had not been deprived, and Levitsky and Collier (1968) have indicated that it may never quite return to that point. Lawrence and Mason (1955) have shown that with repeated deprivation and recovery cycles the rat does not improve its ability to recover from food depletion. Nor when rats are thirsty does the compensatory increase in food consumption when water is returned rise appreciably above normal (Bolles, 1961). Beck and Horne (1964) found that when water was made available for only 30 minutes a day, the rat's food intake during and immediately after water presentation increased with experience. Thus the evidence is consistent in showing that, at least in a novel situation, the rat learns to eat more in a short eating session but that its consumption over a 24-hour period is relatively independent of its prior deprivation experience and even of its current accumulated deficit. It does not learn to increase its 24-hour food intake enough to compensate for its deficit, and, therefore, it requires a long time to recover fully.[1]

Le Magnen has advanced the idea that rats can learn to anticipate a forthcoming deprivation and increase their intake accordingly (Le Magnen & Tallon, 1963). In one experimental demonstration of this phenomenon Le Magnen (1959) first scheduled three meals a day. When the animals' consumption had stabilized, one of the meals was omitted. Subsequent intake data suggested that the rats were anticipating the long fast by consuming more at the preceding meal. However, Revusky (1970), using better counterbalancing of mealtimes across different times of day, failed to obtain such an effect.

In conclusion, it appears that the rat does not learn anything about deprivation per se but that learning to eat in a particular situation is a very important factor controlling its food intake. Feeding, as we will see next, is also very clearly a function of time parameters, which may also be considered a type of associative determinant.

Temporal factors controlling eating. The rat eats primarily on a 24-hour cycle, and the bulk of its eating ordinarily occurs during the dark part of the light-dark cycle (Bare, 1959; Bare & Cicala, 1960; Siegel, 1961). Siegel's data are shown in Fig. 7-3. Bare found that the rat's tendency to confine its eating to the evening is so strong that it

---

[1] There have also been studies of long-term effects of deprivation experience. It has been found that rats deprived in infancy will later, after being returned to normal weight, show an exaggerated reaction to subsequent deprivations, which can be observed not only in their consummatory behavior but in their instrumental and general activity as well (Marx, 1952; Levine, 1957; Mandler, 1958).

Theory of motivation

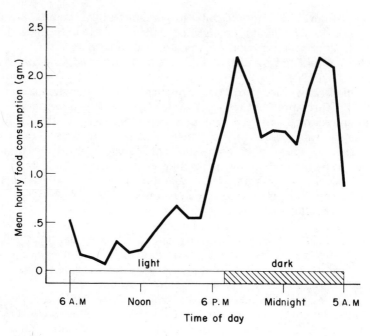

Figure 7–3

*The diurnal course of food consumption of rats maintained ad lib.
and on a natural light-dark cycle. (Adapted from Siegel, 1961)
Copyright (1961) by the American Psychological Association.
Reprinted by permission.*

can partially override a need to make up a previously incurred food
deficit. Thus rats that were deprived and then given food in the early
afternoon ate some food when it was presented, but they ate much
more later at the regular evening feeding time. Thus rats with food
constantly available tend to do the bulk of their feeding every 24
hours. The question is whether this concentration of eating occurs
because rats like to eat in the dark, because this is when they are
accustomed to eating, or because there is some inherent connection
between feeding and the natural 24-hour periodicity. The 24-hour
cycle appears to be the important factor. Baker (1955) compared the
food intake and rate of eating of animals fed every 24 hours with
animals fed randomly 12, 24, or 36 hours after the last meal. Baker
found that increased deprivation time led to *decreased* intake and
that the irregularly deprived group ate less on the average than the
regularly deprived group. In a related study Lawrence and Mason
(1955a) gave one group of rats a counterbalanced series of deprivations ranging from 4 to 48 hours, arranged so that feeding occurred
at different times of day. A control group first received a regular series
of 24-hour deprivations and was then tested with sessions at irregular

hours interspersed among feedings scheduled at the regular times. The control group therefore yielded consumption data for deprivations of 4 to 24 hours tested at the regular feeding time and also tested at unusual feeding times. Lawrence and Mason found that, for a given deprivation, intake was significantly greater at the regular feeding time than at the irregular feeding times and was maximal with 24-hour deprivation. The experimental group also showed maximum intake with 24-hour deprivation. Essentially the same findings have been reported by Bolles (1965a) when feeding animals randomly in time. Monti (1971) maintained animals for periods of 18 days, feeding them each day at the same time and then testing them at various hours after the last meal. Relative intake was sharply higher for deprivation times of 24 hours compared with all deprivations longer and shorter than 24 hours. The evidence seems to indicate, therefore, that rats eat more 24 hours after the last meal than at other times.

A second kind of cyclicity has been implicated in eating behavior, and this is the type of cycle originally reported by Richter (1922, 1927). Richter observed that rats having food continuously available take from five to ten meals a day; he suggested, therefore, that they have an eating cycle. The argument is presumably that when the stomach empties, when a certain threshold of weight loss has been reached, or when some other relatively fixed consequence of ingesting the last meal has occurred, the rat is ready to eat again and will do so if food is available. Richter suggested that the rat's ad lib. eating has an inherent cyclicity with a period of approximately 4 hours. Subsequent investigators (Baker, 1953; Teitelbaum & Campbell, 1958; Bolles, 1961; Fitzsimons & Le Magnen, 1969; Levitsky, 1970) have observed that the rat ordinarily eats 11 to 12 meals a day. This number appears to be remarkably constant across a wide range of conditions. It does not seem to depend upon whether water is available with the meal, whether the meal is given in liquid or solid form, or upon the age or sex of the animal.[2] Thus it would appear that if the rat has a short-term feeding cycle, it must have a period more like 2 hours than the 4-hour period Richter proposed.

The truth is that the rat's meals do not have any real periodicity; there is merely a mean inter-meal interval. The distribution

---

[2] The size of the meal does vary under these different conditions, which accounts for the different total intakes. It is not clear whether the number of meals increases with increased palatability of the diet (Gentile, 1970) or decreases (Levitsky & Collier, 1968; Levitsky, 1970). It is also not clear whether hyperphagic animals (made so by VMH lesions) eat the same number of daily meals as normals. Teitelbaum and Campbell (1958) report that they do, but Thomas and Mayer (1968) report that increased intake is a result of eating more meals as well as larger ones. Since the size of the meal, particularly for hyperphagic animals, is a function of the palatability of the diet and since relatively little is known about palatabilities of different foods, meaningful comparison may not be possible.

Theory of motivation

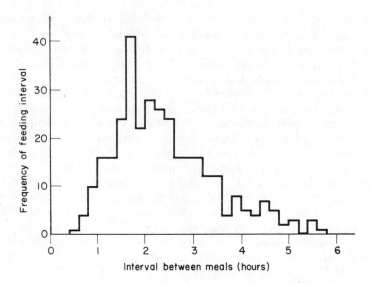

Figure 7–4

Distribution of time intervals between periods of eating in normal rats. (From Bash, 1939) © 1939 The Williams & Wilkins Co., Baltimore

function of intervals between meals invariably displays all the appearance of being random (Bash, 1939; Thomas & Mayer, 1968; Snowdon, 1969; Panksepp, 1973). The pattern obtained is always like that reported by Bash, shown in Fig. 7-4. Different methods of defining a meal make relatively little difference because the rat breaks up its consummatory behavior into distinct bouts of continuous eating with clear intermissions of 10 minutes or more. The question is whether the initiation of eating is really probablistic or whether it depends systematically upon some other variable, for example, weight loss, which varies in time. A homeostatic or regulatory motivation model requires that eating be triggered by the animal's nutritional state falling below some critical value.

But it is difficult to reconcile the idea that some antecedent condition, such as weight loss, governs the initiation of eating with the variability of mealtimes noted by many investigators. If the time of eating is as inherently unpredictable as, for instance, Fig. 7-4 suggests, then the size of the meal must also be unpredictable. Otherwise, there would have to be some real periodicity in the distribution of inter-meal intervals. To make the prediction of mealtimes even more uncertain, it has been discovered (Le Magnen & Tallon, 1963; Thomas & Mayer, 1968) that the size of a meal does not depend upon the time since the last meal, but is correlated with, and presumably determines, how long it will be until the next meal occurs. One possibility, then, is that the amount eaten in a given meal is a random variable that does not depend upon the rat's state of deprivation or the time since last eating. Then it would be possible for the time before the next meal to be random too, as suggested by Fig. 7-4, even though the onset of the next meal is causally determined by the animal's loss in body weight at that time. This interpretation ties up a number of loose ends. For example, it suggests that a rat deprived in the morning may hardly be deprived at all because it has spent most of the night eating, whereas one deprived in the evening may be suffering a much greater deprivation because it has not eaten all day, and hence the second rat can be expected to eat larger and more frequent meals. Siegel (1961) has shown that something like this happens; he found that rats would eat relatively little after a 4-hour morning deprivation and much more following a 4-hour evening deprivation.

But there are some problems with this interpretation. One difficulty is that rats do not seem to be at a constant point of weight loss at the time they start eating a meal; Booth (1970) has shown that there is more constancy of weight at the termination of meals than at the beginning. A second difficulty with a weight-loss threshold explanation of eating behavior is that such an account does not explain why the rat eats so little in the daytime when it is below weight and why it eats so much at night when it is considerably heavier. The basic consideration is not that the rat eats when it is below weight but that it eats at night (Panksepp, 1973). The situation with humans is the same, although the eating cycle is reversed; most of us have little appetite early in the morning when our weight is below average, and we have the heartiest appetites later in the day when our weight is likely to be already above average. The rat's pattern of eating, like our own, is governed primarily by the current cycle of eating itself and not by momentary weight loss or momentary nutritional state (Le Magnen et al., 1973).

It is clear that motivation theorists have put altogether too much emphasis upon the regulatory aspects of eating. Zeigler (personal communication) has suggested that our understanding of eating as a naturally occurring behavior might be much advanced if we could lay aside the idea that animals have to eat to maintain their weight and simply look at eating as important in the sense that animals do so much of it and interesting in the sense that it is relatively lawful (e.g., the rat eats mostly at night).

The most important and most interesting argument against a regulatory model of eating behavior is contained in a recent paper by Collier et al. (1972). They observed first that when a rat is maintained with food always available, the stomach is rarely if ever empty. That is, the ad lib, rat is in some sense never deprived; it is still obtaining the caloric benefit of the last meal at the time the next meal is initiated. Even though it may lose up to 1 percent of its body weight between meals, this loss may not represent a significant need,

Theory of motivation

and it is difficult to see how it can represent any need at all if calories are still being derived from the last meal. Why then does the rat begin eating again? The remarkable answer proposed by Collier et al. is simply that the rat has a preferred pattern of taking its meals. If food is readily obtainable, rats will eat approximately random amounts at approximately random times, but they will average about 12 meals a day and will average enough intake per meal to maintain their body weight. This is the rat's pattern: It does not depend upon any regulatory mechanisms dictating when eating should be initiated or when eating should be terminated—it is just the rat's pattern.

The regulatory mechanism itself, whatever it is, which has been traditionally regarded as the all-important factor controlling intake, appears to have little control over an individual meal; it must be a very gentle mechanism that exerts a subtle but persistent pressure on the animal to eat a little more or a little less, as the case may be, over a period of time.[3]

What kinds of factors affect the animal's preferred meal pattern? Recall that Richter (1927) found rats eating half a dozen meals a day, whereas subsequent investigators have reported approximately twice that number. According to Collier et al., the main procedural difference is that Richter's animals had to get up and leave their living quarters to get food, whereas subsequent investigators have made food more easily available. In other words, the critical difference may be the amount of instrumental-response effort involved in initiating a meal. Even pressing a bar for food (the procedure used by most investigators) imposes some effort, and by eliminating this small amount of effort the average number of meals can be further increased. What happens when the effort requirement is increased? The results shown in Fig. 7-5 indicate that the rat compromises its preferred pattern of eating when the effort requirement is raised. If sufficient effort is required, it will voluntarily drop to one meal a day. Consider that in its natural state the rat eats at its leisure from a large supply of available food. This style of eating can be contrasted with that of the large predator, which may expend an enormous amount of energy to consume an enormous meal that sustains it for a day or more. Zeigler et al. (1971) has reported that the pigeon is a more or less continuous eater, taking a large number of very small meals when food is continuously available. The meal-taking pattern of a given animal can, therefore, be expected to depend

---

[3] This conclusion, based primarily upon behavioral evidence, is consistent with the lack of physiological evidence, noted in Chapter 6, for any regulatory mechanism that controls intake on a moment by moment basis. At the same time, it provides further support for the proposal of Woods and Porte (1975) that caloric intake is regulated by hormonal factors operating through the slow-responding cerebrospinal fluid system rather than through the more direct and fast-responding circulatory system.

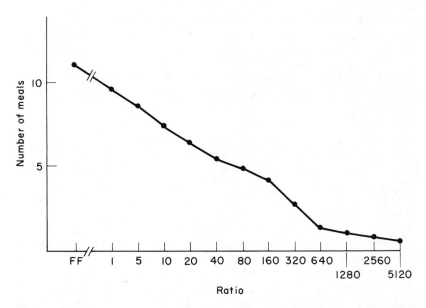

Figure 7–5

The preferred number of daily meals of rats with free food (FF) or with meals available on a fixed-ration schedule. (From Collier et al., 1972)

upon what kind of animal it is and what ecological niche it occupies.[4] The remarkable thing about both the rat and the pigeon is that their feeding systems are so adaptable to the artificial niches imposed on them by experimenters, who typically restrict them to one meal a day. That this is a relatively natural modification of the rat's normal eating pattern is shown by the fact it will do a tremendous amount of work for its one big meal, as Fig. 7-5 indicates, even though it has lost very little body weight.

Although many of the issues that have been raised in this section are relatively new and still unsettled, several conclusions can be suggested. One is that with food continuously available, the rat distributes its meals more or less randomly in time but has a preference for 11 or 12 meals a day. If the effort required for obtaining a meal is increased, then the preferred number of meals is sharply reduced and the rat will show a daily eating pattern characteristic of other types of animals. On top of all this is the rat's proclivity to do the bulk of its eating on a 24-hour cycle (the importance of this 24-hour cycle will be further substantiated when we discuss general activity). The temporal and other associative factors that govern the

[4] There is, as yet, no systematic comparative study of different animals' feeding patterns, but see Rozin's (1964) introduction to some of the relevant considerations.

rat's eating pattern appear to be such important determinants of its food intake that they severely limit the explanatory power of need and drive as determinants of eating behavior.

The energization of eating. All of the evidence discussed so far suggests that eating is much like any other behavior in being partly controlled by an animal's deprivation conditions and partly controlled by situational factors and by the animal's history of reinforcement. If the consummatory response is also like any other behavior in being conditionable to internal and external stimuli, then we surely cannot use it as an index of the strength of an underlying drive unless we are prepared to make some assumptions about the strength of the consummatory habit in the particular situation. More specifically, just because eating can be presumed to be of near maximal strength in some situations (e.g., in the animal's home cage in the evening), we cannot assume it would be of maximal strength in an arbitrary test situation. The experimenter who would use consummatory response as a measure of drive strength has the burden of showing that the stimuli occurring at the time of testing do in fact control the eating response and do so through a habit of near maximum strength.

The best evidence for an energizing effect of the need for food, in which the strength of the consummatory response is directly related to the severity of the need, is shown in studies that have measured the probability of the rat's beginning to eat. Zimbardo and Montgomery (1957) and Bolles (1962, 1965) have measured the latency to eat of naïve animals in a standard but novel situation, as a function of hours deprivation. The results, shown in Fig. 7-6, indicate that the strength of the eating response measured in terms of probability of occurrence is very nearly a power function of deprivation time. Expressing the latency to eat as a function of weight loss rather than deprivation time does not destroy the orderly relationship; indeed, it improves the regularity for it makes deprivation conditions comparable for animals of different sizes, as shown in Fig. 7-7. Similar relationships have now been obtained with other animals, for example, Megibow and Zeigler (1968) with the pigeon and Collier et al. (1968) with the guinea pig.

The relationship between the latency to eat and the animal's need for calories is undoubtedly a function of associative factors too, but the associative effects seem to be quite small relative to the impressive motivational effect (Bolles & Rapp, 1965). Welker (1959) and Candland and Culbertson (1963) have shown that rats show a considerable latency to eat even when they are tested in their own home cages. On the other hand, Myer and Kowell (1971) have shown that for one species of animal, the black rat snake, the latency to eat is only slightly dependent on deprivation and very dependent on prior experience. And Sclafani (1972) has shown that in rats

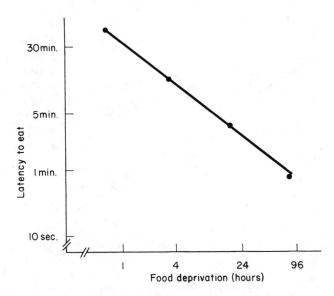

Figure 7–6

The latency to eat as a function of deprivation time. Note that both coordinates are on logarithmic scales. (From Bolles, 1962) Copyright (1962) by the American Psychological Association. Reprinted by permission.

with VMH lesions, the latency to eat depends less upon deprivation and more upon the palatability of the test food.

An alternative measure of the probability of eating was once suggested by Bousfield and Sherif (1932). They measured the speed with which eating is resumed after it is interrupted by a sudden loud noise. They found that rabbits and chickens resumed eating sooner if they had been deprived longer. A similar finding has been reported by Siegel and Correia (1963) for the rat. Bayer (1929) and Bousfield and Spear (1935) have reported that in chickens the *vigor* of the eating response increases with deprivation (the chickens peck harder). The rat, however, fails to show a vigor effect. Moll (1964) found that although rats had a higher probability of eating when maintained at 80 percent of body weight than when maintained at 90 percent of body weight, they ate significantly slower (see also Levitsky, 1970). Data on the amount consumed as a function of deprivation are shown in Fig. 7-2.

Finally, Allison (1964) and Timberlake and Birch (1967) have measured the proportion of time rats eat in a test arena or stay near food rather than stay near another rat or explore. This index of consummatory behavior was found to increase systematically with deprivation time (Allison & Rocha, 1965; Timberlake & Birch, 1967).

Theory of motivation

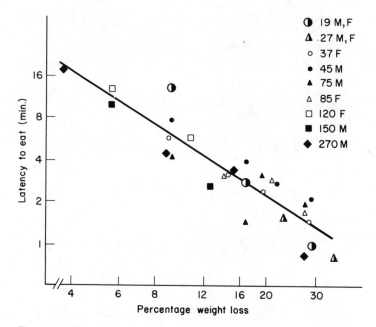

Figure 7–7

The latency to eat as a function of weight loss for male and female rats of different ages. (From Bolles, 1965) Copyright (1965) by the American Psychological Association. Reprinted by permission.

All of these measures of eating, particularly those involving the probability of eating, show the consummatory response increasing systematically in strength with the severity of the animal's need for food. We can conclude, therefore, that there is at least this much support for the hypothesis that hunger-produced D energizes eating.[5] It should be said once again, however, that the data do not justify the stronger conclusion that eating can be explained on the basis of the animal's drive strength. Eating behavior, and particularly how much is eaten, is too dependent upon too many associative factors for such an explanation to be convincing.

Perhaps the proper way to think of the energizing effect is that there are certain bodily states, or antecedent conditions, that have the effect of selectively facilitating or potentiating certain classes of behaviors. The most specific and relevant of the behaviors potentiated by food deprivation is, of course, eating. The more deprived

[5] There is peculiar irony in the fact that Hull's D, which was derived from homeostatic considerations, does not enable us to explain the amount consumed or the basic fact of regulation. The energizing effect appears to be limited to probability measures of consummatory behavior, such as the latency to eat.

the rat is, the more likely it is to eat. It must be emphasized, however, that this energizing effect upon the consummatory response only becomes an impressive feature of eating behavior when the deprivation is severe. The rat eats under ad lib. conditions, too, but probably not because of some minimal deprivation. The ad lib. animal, as well as the slightly deprived animal, may eat because it is time to eat, because food looks appetizing, because it is bored, or for a host of other nonregulatory reasons.

Drinking. Just as eating has often been taken to be an a priori measure of the animal's need for food, so the drive strength resulting from water deprivation has often been presumptively "measured" in terms of the amount of water an animal will drink. This approach turns out to be fraught with problems, just as it was with hunger. Drinking should be considered first as a response, and then its relationships to the antecedent conditions of deprivation and to other kinds of behavior can be determined in their own right. And again, as in the case of hunger, some cues to the nature of the drinking response can be obtained from considering normal drinking behavior.

Normal drinking behavior. Smith and Smith (1939) found that when the cat drinks, it does so at essentially a constant rate. It cannot drink quickly or slowly. Stellar and Hill (1952) showed that an approximately constant rate of drinking over a wide range of deprivation times is also characteristic of the rat. Their results are shown in Fig. 7-8. Note that over the course of a fairly long (2-hour) drinking session their animals showed increased intake but that this was due to greater persistence of drinking during the test rather than to an increased rate of drinking. Note that in contrast with the amount eaten, which is a nonmonotonic function of the animal's need for food, the results of Stellar and Hill (1952) suggest that the replacement of water is monotonic over an extensive range of deprivation conditions (see also Corbit, 1969).

The rat laps about six or seven times a second, consuming approximately 0.004 or 0.005 cc per lap, which results in a fixed intake of about 1 to 1½ cc per minute as long as drinking continues. The lick rate of rats and cats is apparently constant over a wide range of parameters, such as the age and experience of the animal (Schaeffer & Premack, 1961; Schaeffer & Huff, 1965). It also varies only slightly, if at all, as a function of what is drunk, whether it is sweet, salty, or plain (Davis & Keehn, 1959; Schaeffer & Huff, 1965; Allison, 1971). Keehn and Arnold (1960) and Keehn and Barakat (1964) have found that the constancy of lick rate is disturbed only very slightly, perhaps to the extent of one lap per second, by individual differences, by local variation, or by day-to-day variation in individual rats. Even when rats drink to avoid shock, their rate is constant (Crawford, 1970). In short, the lick rate appears to be quite constant over a considerable range of experi-

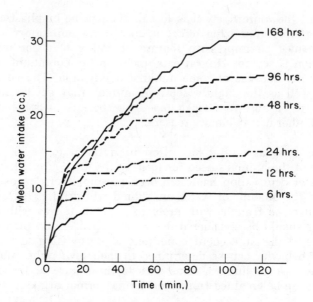

Figure 7–8

Mean cumulative water intake in a 2-hour test session following deprivations ranging from 6 to 168 hours. (From Stellar & Hill, 1952) Copyright (1952) by the American Psychological Association. Reprinted by permission.

mental parameters (see also Hulse & Suter, 1968; Corbit & Luschei, 1969).[6]

It is also known that rats drink approximately 20 times a day when both food and water are available (Bolles, 1961) and that this number is not much affected by withdrawing the food; what changes is the size of the drink. It was already noted (page 165) that drinking is most likely immediately following a meal, although it is apparent that drinking occurs at other times too. The occurrence of these bouts seems to be more or less random in time (Premack & Kintsch, 1970).

Associative factors in drinking. Ghent (1957) showed that when naïve animals are deprived of water and offered it for the first time,

[6] Sometimes drinking behavior is described in terms of a rate obtained by dividing the total number of licks by the duration of the test session. It is important to recognize that such indices are persistence or probability measures rather than speed or vigor measures. It has been found, however, that the first few licks of a drinking bout are appreciably faster (Collier & Bolles, 1968a), take in more water per lick, and involve more tongue pressure (Imada, 1964) than later steady licking. Boice (1967) has begun to study lick rates of other rodents.

they drink relatively little—only about one-half the amount that they will learn to consume after a series of daily tests (see also Hatton & Bennett, 1970). But Beck (1964) has argued from his findings that this phenomenon does not reflect true learning to drink, but rather the adaptation of emotional reactions occurring in the novel test situation. Recall that Williams (1968) had found that the learning-to-eat phenomenon was not apparent when animals were tested in a very familiar situation. Presumably, the same argument can be made here; what is learned is learning to drink in a particular situation and not learning to drink per se.

Collier (1962a) has reported that in a situation in which drinking is really well established, it may be so completely under the control of the test conditions that it is relatively independent of deprivation conditions. Further evidence of the importance of the associative control of the drinking response has been noted by Fink and Patton (1953). They found that rats drank less as the stimulus conditions in the test situation were changed from those they were accustomed to. We may also note that, just as in the case of hunger, whereas the rat's drinking behavior in a short test session is clearly a function of experience in the situation, its water consumption over a 24-hour period is relatively independent of its experience with deprivation (Bolles, 1961; Beck, 1962; Dufort & Blick, 1962).

It has been found that just as the hungry rat will not eat enough to pay off its food debt, so the thirsty rat does not drink enough to regain a normal water balance. However, other species do. Adolph (1950) proposes that the ratio of consumption to deficit is fairly constant over a range of deprivation conditions for a given animal species and that this ratio is relatively species-specific (see Fig. 7-9).[7]

The regularity of the time of testing has also been found to be an important factor in the control of drinking. Kessen et al. (1960) maintained rats on a regular 24-hour drinking cycle for five weeks. The animals were then tested under different deprivation times ranging from 0 to 47 hours. All tests were interspersed with drinking sessions scheduled at the regular accustomed times. Water consumption for a given deprivation time was greater at the regular test hour than at the irregular hours and was maximal at 24 hours deprivation (the same pattern of results Lawrence & Mason, 1955a,

---

[7] One feature of drinking behavior that is not shown in the figure is the threshold for the initiation of drinking. The dog drinks nothing at all until it has lost 0.5 percent of its body weight (Robinson & Adolph, 1943). The figure for the rat is perhaps 1 percent. Once over the threshold, the animal drinks an amount that bears some species-specific relationship to its deficit. This threshold in body-weight loss should not be confused with the threshold in change in osmotic pressure that is found when drinking is initiated (Hatton & Almli, 1969; Almli, 1970; Deaux et al., 1970) and which these writers assert is the cause for the initiation of drinking.

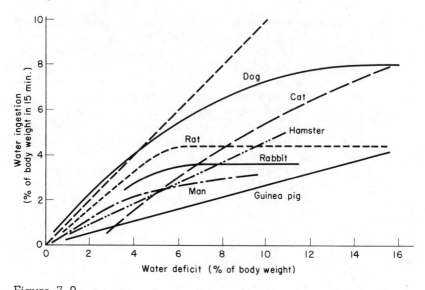

Figure 7–9

Water consumption as a function of water deficit for different species. (Adapted from Adolph, 1950)

found in eating). Kessen et al. interpreted their results as indicating the importance of drinking habits established on the basis of regularly scheduled drinking. The best evidence for the dependence of drinking upon temporal cues is the fact that all animals showed a sharp increase in drinking at or near 24 hours deprivation, a time of testing that would correspond to the regular time of drinking.

The energization of drinking. Collier (1969) has reviewed a number of studies done in his laboratory showing how thirst motivation varies with weight loss in different animals. Subsequently, Tang and Collier (1971) have reported that the thirst motivation function is path independent; that is, it matters very little how the rat has lost weight, for the amount consumed is determined wholly by the momentary loss in weight.

The latency to drink has also been investigated as a function of deprivation time (Siegel, 1947; Bolles, 1962, 1965a). See Fig. 7-10. These studies seem to be the only ones showing energizing effects of water deprivation upon drinking behavior, which are not confounded by possible postingestion and associative effects. There probably are associative effects in the latency to drink, but they are presumably minimal just as they appear to be in the case of eating. These results, like the similar results with hungry animals, support the hypothesis that the strength of the consummatory behavior increases systemati-

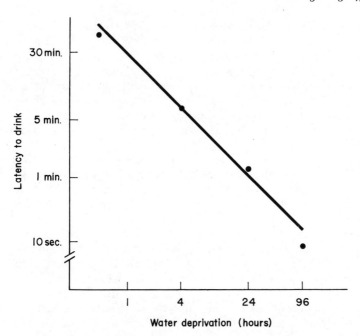

Figure 7–10

The latency to drink as a function of deprivation time. (From Bolles, 1962) Copyright (1962) by the American Psychological Association. Reprinted by permission.

cally with the severity of the relevant drive-producing conditions, that is, with the animal's need for water.

What if the need for water is produced by means other than deprivation? A number of studies on this question by O'Kelly and his students are noted by O'Kelly and Beck (1960). Water intake appears to increase monotonically with the amount of salt loaded directly into the animal, but the relationship is complicated. One reason is that if the salt is loaded into the stomach, extracellular water is immediately drawn into the stomach, filling it and prohibiting subsequent drinking even though the animal may be suffering substantial cellular dehydration. The kidneys begin excreting salt (getting rid of half the excess in about 20 minutes, according to Corbit, 1969) but at the cost of further cellular dehydration. A further complication in O'Kelly's experiments is that the salt-load-induced thirst is typically superimposed upon an existing 24-hour deprivation thirst and a previously established pattern of drinking (O'Kelly & Beck, 1960).

Corbit (1969) seems to have solved all these problems by introducing salt intraperitoneally so that there is no interference with drinking, treating initially satiated animals, and studying both normal and nephrectomized animals so that the regulatory contribution of salt excretion could be assessed. He found that within an hour rats consume an amount of water that very closely matches the cellular dehydration caused by the salt load. Hence we can say that hypertonically induced water deficits energize regulatory drinking. Hypovolemic thirst also energizes drinking (Stricker, 1966). Although the time course of this regulatory drinking has not yet been worked out in any detail, it evidently takes the rat much longer to restore water balance.

Other consummatory behaviors. The analysis of whether consummatory behaviors increase in probability or strength with the severity of their antecedent conditions bogs down at this point. For a variety of reasons, none of the evidence is very compelling one way or the other. The idea of a consummatory response does not seem applicable to defensive behavior, that is, escape from pain or aversive stimuli. An animal ordinarily does not engage in any specific kind of behavior in order to bring an end to aversive stimuli. How it may most appropriately cope with the situation is dictated almost entirely by the particular situation. Our analysis of defensive behavior cannot proceed, therefore, until we look at the motivation of instrumental behavior.

In the case of exploration, there is again no one kind of consummatory behavior, but a broad class of responses that might be said to consummate the motivating conditions. However, as we recall from Chapter 6, it is not clear what the motivating conditions are. There is a deprivation procedure. Fowler (1967) has shown that maintaining rats in one situation facilitates their getting to a different situation in which, presumably, they explore. But, again, Fowler's emphasis is upon the motivation of an instrumental response (running to the new situation) rather than the energization of exploration once it gets to the new situation.

Sleep is one case in which the consummatory behavior is well defined. Webb (1957) has shown that the probability of the rat's going to sleep is a monotonic function of the period of time since it last slept. Presumably, the probability of sleeping is an increasing function of whatever the stimulus is that signals the intensity of the need to sleep. Webb's results are shown in Fig. 7-11.

With sexual behavior we are confounded by our inability to find appropriate antecedent conditions, that is, a state of the organism that has the properties of a need and that builds up as a function of deprivation. Even so, Beach and Jordan (1956) have reported the results of a deprivation study in which the probability of initiating copulatory behavior was measured in male rats. Their results are shown in Fig. 7-12.

It is curious that the probability of a consummatory response is essentially the same kind of function of deprivation whether we

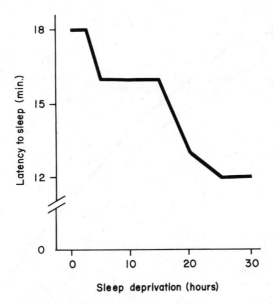

Figure 7–11

*Latency to sleep as a function of continuous
sleep deprivation. (From Webb, 1957)
Copyright (1957) by the American Psychological Association. Reprinted by permission.*

consider eating, drinking, mating, or sleeping as the consummatory
response. It is quite possible that were we able to say what we mean
by consummatory behavior and what we mean by deprivation, we
would be able to derive a family of functions, all of the same form,
relating the probability of any biologically important behavior to the
period of time in which its occurrence is prevented. We might be
able to accomplish this, for instance, for exploratory behavior, various kind of social behaviors, general activity, and, indeed, for the
whole gamut of behaviors that are thought of as motivated. With an
appropriately shortened time scale we might even be able to fit defensive behavior into the scheme. Perhaps deprivation itself rather than
the need state is the source of the animal's motivation. Indeed, the
question of need would seem to be irrelevant except for the fact that
there are functions, such as those shown in Fig. 7-7, in which the
strength of consummatory behavior is much more directly related to
the animal's need than it is to deprivation time.

If we take the right measure of the consummatory response
and the right measure of the animal's hunger state, we find a functional relationship, shown in Fig. 7-7, that looks like what Hull's
drive concept requires: Need determines motivation. But if we measure hunger in some other way or if we measure the animal's need

Theory of motivation

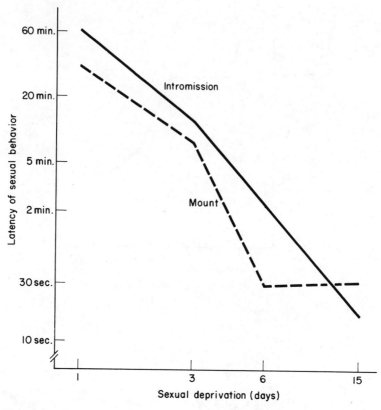

Figure 7–12

Median latency of mounting and intromission as a function of deprivation of sexual activity. Note that both ordinate and abscissa are on logarithmic scales. (Data reported by Beach & Jordan, 1956)

state in some other way, the relationship breaks down. The principal discovery we have made in this section is that eating and drinking and other consummatory behaviors depend upon a great host of associative and other factors, so that under most circumstances the animal's need to engage in these behaviors provides a very incomplete explanation of them.

The energizing of instrumental behavior

Probability measures—latency. The latency of a simple noncompetitive instrumental response becomes shorter when the drive-producing conditions are made more severe. This is the case for escape from shock (Trapold & Fowler, 1960) and for food deprivation (Kimble,

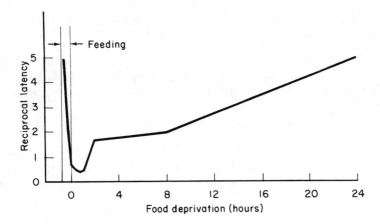

Figure 7–13

Speed of a panel-pushing response after an interruption in feeding or after a period of deprivation. (Adapted from Kimble, 1951) Copyright (1951) by the American Psychological Association. Reprinted by permission.

1951; Horenstein, 1951; Deese & Carpenter, 1951; Ramond et al., 1955).[8]

The most comprehensive data for hunger are Kimble's, shown in Fig. 7-13. Kimble trained rats to press a panel to obtain food and then tested them at various times after they had finished a regularly scheduled meal. Some very short deprivation periods were used; in fact, under some conditions the animals were interrupted during their meal and tested. Hence the declining speed scores shown on the left-hand side of Fig. 7-13 indicate what might be regarded as a decline in motivation as a function of prefeeding the animal a certain portion of its daily meal. It is interesting to note that the speed of responding decreases for some time after the animal has stopped eating, as though shortly after a meal an aversion to food develops, perhaps as a result of water going into and distending the stomach. Another interesting feature of the curve is the sudden rise in speed of responding, which occurs about 2 hours after the meal. Finally, the

[8] The expected relationship is not always found, however; Reynolds (1949a) reported an increase in latency with increasing food deprivation, and Woods et al. (1964) found that when amount of reinforcement was held constant, there was little effect of water temperature in a water-escape situation. By a noncompetitive instrumental response we mean merely a learned response that has a much higher probability of occurrence than any other response in the situation. It should be noted in passing that response speed, the reciprocal of latency, has been sanctioned by Spence (1954) and Logan (1952a) as a direct measure of effective excitatory reaction potential, that is, D × H.

instrumental response continues to gain in strength as deprivation is increased from 2 to 24 hours. This portion of the function indicates the principal relationship between hours deprivation and hunger motivation. A similar relationship, including the sharp rise between 1 and 2 hours, has been found in other studies involving short deprivation times (Horenstein, 1951; Koch & Daniel, 1945; Saltzman & Koch, 1948) using both latency and resistance to extinction measures. The shape of the curve above 24 hours is left open to question.

Resistance to extinction. It also seems likely that resistance to extinction in a simple noncompetitive situation increases with hours deprivation (Perin, 1942; Saltzman & Koch, 1948; Strassburger, 1950; Yamaguchi, 1951; Cotton et al., 1969). Sometimes negative results have been reported (Skinner, 1936; Sackett, 1939; Finan, 1940; Pavlik & Reynolds, 1963), but Barry (1967) has shown that some of these negative results can be attributed to the massing of trials. Some of the negative results may also be due simply to the tremendous variability typically found in resistance to extinction scores. Even at best the effects are small. For example, Yamaguchi (1951) used deprivations ranging from 3 to 72 hours and found that the median resistance to extinction scores varied only from 12 to 28, while the overall range under each condition was from 0 to 100 or more. Whatever it is that determines resistance to extinction, the conditions of deprivation do not seem to affect it very much.

Some writers (e.g., Atkinson, 1964) have emphasized that what really characterizes a motivated animal is its persistence in those activities upon which reinforcement is contingent. Persistence can be measured in a number of ways: as the number of unreinforced responses that occur, that is, resistance to extinction, or as the rate of responding in the presence of reinforcement. The latter provides a difficult measure to interpret, since the overall rate of responding depends not only upon the probability of responding but also upon the time spent in responding and the time spent taking reinforcement. Another possibility is to present reinforcement, but in very small amounts, so that little time is spent in consummatory activity. This was the approach of Warden et al. (1931) with the Columbia obstruction box; it is also the approach of those who use schedules of reinforcement.

With the judicious use of minimal reinforcement, for example, providing it on an intermittent schedule, animals can be differentially reinforced for persistence. Under these conditions the rate of responding increases with the severity of food deprivation (Skinner, 1936; Heron & Skinner, 1937; Weiss & Moore, 1956; Clark, 1958) and water deprivation (Collier, 1969). The performance of rats working for water on a fixed-ratio 20 schedule (Collier & Levitsky, 1967) are shown in Fig. 7-14.

Response-rate measures require a considerable amount of prior training before they become stable, and they are usually

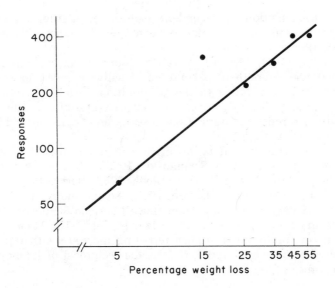

Figure 7–14

Bar presses for water in a 20-minute session on an FR-20 schedule under different degrees of weight loss. (From Collier & Levitsky, 1967) Copyright (1967) by the American Psychological Association. Reprinted by permission.

obtained by averaging the rate over a large number of responses. Hence it is difficult to relate such measures to measures of response probability and speed. Rate measures are sometimes assumed to be elemental or primary in their own right, and the functional differences between them and other response measures are attributed to deficiencies in the latter (Skinner, 1950). Sometimes there are anomalous differences between rate measures and other measures. For example, we have just seen that the rate of bar pressing for water may increase with deprivation up to a 25 percent weight loss, whereas obstruction-box scores reach a peak at about 24 hours (or about 10 percent weight loss), and other measures may reach a peak at other points. Sometimes, especially with pigeons, there is no apparent effect on variable interval bar pressing as a function of weight loss, deprivation time, or prefeeding (Powell, 1971).

Amplitude measures. All of the response measures just discussed— latency, resistance to extinction, and the like—may be taken as alternative indices of a common behavioral property, namely, the probability that the response will occur in a given interval of time. In contrast with all of these probability measures there are response measures that tell us something about the amplitude or strength or vigor of the response. The question then arises whether these measures are also functionally dependent upon drive conditions. The bulk of the evidence on this question indicates that they are (Notterman & Mintz, 1965).

Zener and McCurdy (1939) found that as hunger is increased, the strength of a conditioned salivary reflex in the dog becomes stronger relative to the unconditioned salivary reflex. In fact, Zener and McCurdy suggested that the ratio of conditioned to unconditioned reflex strengths (saliva secretion) could be used as an index of drive strength.

An energizing effect of drive conditions was first found with speed in a runway by Szymanski (1918). This effect was subsequently confirmed with hunger (Davis, 1957; Barry, 1958; Butter & Campbell, 1960; Lewis & Cotton, 1960), sexual motivation (Beach & Jordan, 1956a), and escape from shock (Trapold & Fowler, 1960). Trapold and Fowler's results are shown in Fig. 7-15. There are of course many, many other studies reporting increases either in running speed or in overall speed, that is, the reciprocal of latency plus running time.

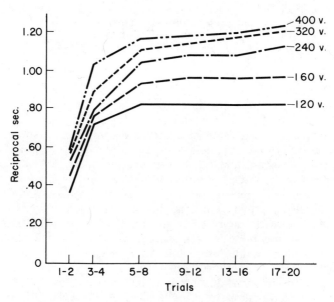

Figure 7–15

Acquisition of running speed in escape from shock as a function of shock intensity in the runway. (Acquisition of starting speed was generally more gradual, and the asymptotic speeds were not monotonically related to voltage.) (From Trapold & Fowler, 1960) Copyright (1960) by the American Psychological Association. Reprinted by permission.

Everything would seem to be in order with respect to the energizing of behavior and in accordance with the Hullian drive construct, but the situation is not quite that simple. The first serious challenge for the energization hypothesis that we will consider comes from the area of discrimination learning.

Discrimination performance. Performance on a discrimination problem is important for theories of motivation because of the arbitrary contingencies that can be esablished between the animal's behavior and reinforcement. The discrimination situation can be contrasted with the type of noncompetitive response situation we have been considering in that in the former we attempt to associate the response with specific stimuli, whereas in the latter the response may be associated with any stimulus on the situation. There is, accordingly, less obvious relevance between the hungry rat running to vertical stripes instead of horizontal ones, or to a white card instead a black card, than there is when the hungry rat merely runs or salivates where the vigor and the probability of the response seem appropriate in some intangible way to the drive condition.[9]

In Hull's system, whether or not increasing drive will facilitate discrimination performance, depends upon whether the habit strength of the correct response is greater than the habit strengths of competing responses. Thus if we were to compare the performance of high-drive and low-drive animals in a difficult discriminative-learning task, the percentage of correct responses under the two conditions should depend upon whether the comparison was made early or late in learning. The situation should be something like that diagramed in Fig. 7-16. If the correct response is governed by a relatively weak habit, then early in learning, discrimination should be worsened by the multiplicative effect of increasing drive, whereas later in learning, after the habit has become dominant, any increment in drive should lead to improved discrimination. Data to support such an analysis have been obtained by Ramond (1954).

In the usual discrimination-learning situation the relative frequency with which the animal responds correctly and incorrectly is a consequence of the initial strengths of the two habits. Spence (1956) has suggested that if the correct response is permitted to occur more frequently than the incorrect response, then when the discrimination is learned, a facilitory effect of drive upon performance is generally found (Dodson, 1917; Tolman & Honzik, 1930; Tolman & Gleitman, 1949; Hillman et al., 1953; Ramond, 1954; Eisman, 1956; Eisman et al., 1956). On the other hand, Spence observes, if animals are forced to make the correct and incorrect

[9] Kurtz (1970) has reported a study showing that more deprived rats are more willing to work harder for their food. Whether this effect can be interpreted as a simple energizing effect or whether it will require a more interesting explanation remains to be seen.

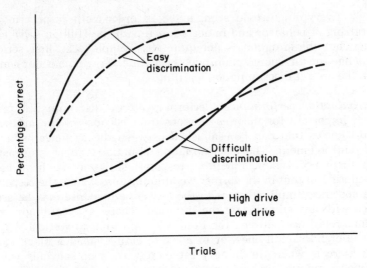

Figure 7–16

Hypothetical interaction between drive level and task difficulty in discrimination learning.

responses an equal number of times, then the expected facilitory effect is not found (Teel & Webb, 1951; Teel, 1952; Spence et al., 1959)[10]. But there are exceptions to this pattern. For example, Carper (1957), Armus (1958), and Jensen (1960) found drive conditions to have no effect in T-maze problems; and Lachman (1961) found no effect of drive conditions on the frequency of correct responding in a visual discrimination task. Sometimes (e.g., Champion, 1954; Carlton, 1955) no difference in performance as a function of deprivation conditions can be found at any point during the course of learning. This is especially true in the case of primates (Meyer, 1951; Miles, 1959). Sometimes deprivation produces effects in the unexpected direction (Birch, 1955; Bruner et al., 1955). To explain these latter anomalies Bruner suggests that too much drive might restrict the cognitive field (i.e., if the rat is too hungry, it will not see what is going on). Well-controlled studies illustrating such an effect have been reported by Cohen and Telegdy (1970) and Telegdy and Cohen (1971). Rats were trained with redundant two-dimensional cues and tested with the cues one at a time; if they were more severely deprived in the test, they were less likely to respond to both dimensions.

[10] This generalization is part of what led Spence (1956) to give up Hull's drive reduction hypothesis of reinforcement. Spence argued instead that it is the number of times the animal makes the correct and incorrect responses that determines their habit strengths.

All of the discrimination situations we have considered so far have involved spatial discrimination in which subjects are required to respond differentially in space, locomoting toward one stimulus and away from another. In the case of non-spatial discrimination, in which subjects are required to respond by, say, pressing a bar in the presence of one stimulus but not to press in its absence, Dinsmoor (1952a) and Coate (1964) have reported that the rate of responding increased both in the presence and in the absence of the discriminative stimulus but that the rate under the two conditions was always in a constant ratio, so that the accuracy of the discrimination was not affected by deprivation conditions.

It should be apparent that the important determinants of learning in complex situations are associative, attentional, cognitive, and so on, and that how hungry or thirsty the animal may be is a minor considertion in how rapidly it learns or how well it performs. The other side of the coin is that a motivational interpretation of animals' performance is most applicable to simple, noncompetitive learning situations. Certainly, most of the support for the energization of instrumental behavior comes from such situations. As long as the situation is simple enough, most measures of response probability and response vigor increase with the severity of the drive-producing conditions. This seems to be the case for hunger, thirst, sex, and escape; and it might be the case also for other varieties of motivation if appropriate antecedent conditions could be found. Thus there seems to be a substantial amount of evidence for the hypothesis that no one ever really doubted: Drive-producing conditions energize instrumental behavior. This conclusion, together with the conclusion reached earlier that drive-producing conditions energize consummatory behaviors, might appear to be so obvious as to be trivial. But it is important to hold them up to the light of day because it will turn out that these are about the only positive conclusions we will be able to draw regarding the drive concept. In the rest of this chapter we will see that the energization of general activity is a highly equivocal phenomenon; in the next chapter we will see that all of the other conceptual properties that have been given to the drive concept are clearly not supported by the evidence. In short, the energizing of certain classes of behaviors will be shown to be the *only* empirically defensible property of drive. In Chapter 9 we will see that the drive concept is easily dispensed with entirely because there are other ways to explain the energizing effect.

The energizing of general activity

General activity has traditionally been characterized and defined by the assumption that it occurs independently of reinforcement. It has always been considered irrelevant or goalless behavior. It is assumed to be elicited by randomly occurring stimuli and energized by whatever momentary drives the animal might have, but it is assumed to be unrelated to reinforcement. Thus general activity has been thought to be an immediate, unlearned, primitive kind of reaction to the animal's physiological need state. The early studies of general activity (which have been ably reviewed by Shirley, 1929; Reed, 1947; Munn, 1950) embodied the simple idea that the activity wheel measured the drive level of the animal and that its running indicated its general health and welfare. Since the antecedent conditions of general activity turned out to be the same conditions that motivate instrumental and consummatory behavior, there was a rather simple and popular picture of the relationship between drive and activity: Drive causes activity.

In the past several years this simple model has been destroyed, and all of the historically important conceptual properties of general activity have been discredited. For example, it is no longer considered to be goalless. We may, if we wish, now think of general activity as a reaction to its own drive state (see page 183) so that it becomes a kind of consummatory behavior. Or we may think of it as a kind of instrumental behavior, serving to alleviate some other drive state. Let us see how this revolution in thinking about general activity came about.

The Campbell-Sheffield studies. In 1954 Sheffield and Campbell suggested an interpretation of general activity that was quite different from the traditional one. They noted that when left to themselves, rats sleep much of the time and do not move about restlessly. Even when very hungry, rats only seem to be more active than when satiated if there is some external stimulation. Sheffield & Campbell's (1954) results indicated that hungry rats become most active when exposed to external stimulation that has regularly preceded feeding.

Earlier, Campbell and Sheffield (1953) had tested animals in stabilimeter-type cages, which were located in a room providing a relatively homogeneous auditory and visual environment. After four days ad lib. to provide a baseline, the animals were deprived for 72 hours. At noon of each of the seven days activity was recorded for the preceding 24 hours and also for a 10-minute "stimulation" period during which an environmental change was introduced (the continual masking noise was turned off, and the lights were turned on). It was found that activity (tilting of the cage) occurred at a much higher rate during the 10-minute stimulation period than during the remainder of the 24 hours. This effect, the arousal effect of stimulation, was significantly enhanced by the three days of deprivation. Although the total 24-hour activity counts increased during the deprivation period, there was a much greater relative increase in activity during the 10-minute stimulation tests.

In their second experiment Sheffield and Campbell (1954) gave animals daily feedings, which were immediately preceded for the experimental group by a 5-minute period of stimulus change (visual and auditory) and which were preceded irregularly an hour or two by a similar 5-minute stimulation period for the control group. The results are shown in Fig. 7-17. Note that the control animals, for which the stimulus change did not serve as a cue to feeding, showed a gradual adaptation to stimulation but that the experimental animals, for which the stimulus change was a cue for food, showed a marked increase in activity in response to it. Sheffield and Campbell (1954) conclude that the basic mechanism here must be the conditioning of the consummatory response to environmental cues. This behavior is subsequently reinforced by eating, and its frustration during the 5-minute test period generates the motivation that produces the observed activity in the experimental group. In the control group the consummatory response does not get conditioned to external cues, so there is no frustration and no increased activity. General activity is thus seen to be learned behavior. Progressive increases in activity, as shown in Fig. 7-17, reflect continued conditioning. A surprising feature of this analysis is that the stimuli that control general activity are said to be external environmental cues to food, not the internal need-related stimuli that Cannon and other early theorists had postulated.

Campbell and Sheffield's analysis has stood the test of time

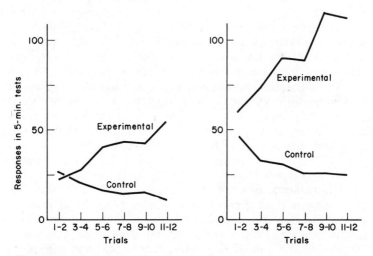

Figure 7–17

Acquisition of activity in response to a 5-minute change in the environment that regularly preceded daily feeding (experimental groups) compared with adaptation to the change when it was not correlated with feeding (control groups). For the groups on the left the change consisted of masking noise off and light on, and for the groups on the right noise on and light off. (From Sheffield & Campbell, 1954) Copyright (1954) by the American Psychological Association. Reprinted by permission.

rather well. Amsel and Work (1961) and Amsel et al. (1962) have replicated the main findings; Campbell (1960) has demonstrated the same phenomenon for water-deprived rats, and Hall (1956, 1958) found it using activity wheels instead of stabilimeter cages.

There are still a few interpretive difficulties, however. One is that most of these studies have shown that there is not only a learned responsiveness to cues preceding regular food and water but also a significant overall effect of deprivation on total daily activity scores. This finding suggests the action of a drive mechanism that motivates general activity in addition to whatever learning mechanism there may be. To counter this argument Teghtsoonian and Campbell (1960) tested rats in an isolated and homogeneous environment and found very little increase in tilt-cage activity in the absence of reinforcement (food) during the first few days of deprivation (activity did rise somewhat above the ad lib. baseline just before death). Animals maintained in the normal laboratory environment, where, presumably, there is far more heterogeneity of prevailing stimulus conditions, showed a much greater rise in activity, at least after the first few days. Teghtsoonian and Campbell propose, therefore, that there is no need for a drive mechanism, at least to explain most of the energization effects that have been reported with general activity.

Campbell and Sheffield's interpretation of general activity also embodies the idea that the effect of deprivation is to increase the animal's responsiveness to external stimuli. Unfortunately, it has never been made clear how this kind of hypothetical mechanism differs from the energizing mechanism that has traditionally been a part of general activity theorizing. If we think of increased responsiveness as a response characteristic, then there is very little difference. If, on the other hand, increased responsiveness means a higher probability of detecting external stimuli, then there are quite different implications. One implication is that the animal should show a lower threshold, that is, increased sensitivity, to external stimuli. In an attempt to test this possibility Bolles and Younger (1967) conducted a psychophysical type of experiment in which hungry and satiated animals were presented with a series of brief auditory signals of increasing intensity to determine what intensity of signal was necessary to elicit some type of startle or orienting behavior or disruption of ongoing behavior. The results indicated that the hungry animals had, on the average, a lower threshold, but Bolles and Younger also noted that what the animal was doing at the time test stimuli were presented was a much more important factor than whether the animal was deprived. For example, the threshold was very much lower when the rat was awake than when it was asleep. Moreover, when the animal's behavior at the time of testing was taken into account, there was no difference in threshold between hungry and satiated rats. Thus it appears that the overall lower average threshold of deprived animals was due to their being awake more often than the controls and not to their having intrinsically lower thresholds. Thus within the range of deprivations that were used in this study it does not appear as though deprivation facilitates the detection of external stimuli; it appears more likely that when the animal is hungry, it responds to stimulation more vigorously or more persistently. In short, the rat becomes more active when it detects an external stimulus.

The prospects of general activity being a learned reaction based on reinforcement by food rather than a direct consequence of the deprivation of food puts the subject in an entirely new light. An interesting possibility suggested by the Campbell-Sheffield studies is that activity is wholly learned. An alternative possibility, the evidence for which we will consider shortly, is that there are both learned and unlearned components in activity. But in either case the fact that general activity involves learning means that this behavior, too, is governed to some extent by associative factors, that is, by controlling stimuli and reinforcing stimuli. We will turn shortly to the question of the reinforcement mechanism, but first let us consider a special kind of associative determinant, namely, temporal cues.

Circadian cycle of activity. Even at the beginning of research with activity wheels there was reason for caution in assuming that activity was a direct index of drive level. A few experimenters (e.g., Richter, 1927; Shirley, 1928) took activity scores every hour rather than, as was the custom, every 24 hours. Their hourly records indicated that sometimes as much as one-half of the animals' total activity occurred in a few hours immediately preceding a regular feeding. Such a finding should have suggested that activity is controlled either by the time of day or by the anticipation of food rather than by any immediate consequence of deprivation itself. For many years these data were ignored, however, as the simpler energization explanation of general activity prevailed and as investigators continued to look just at total daily activity scores instead of at the distribution of activity over the 24-hour period.

Recall that Campbell and Sheffield found large increases in responsiveness to cues just prior to regular daily feeding, and much less activity (under some conditions, decreased activity) when no food was presented. One possibility is that the daily burst of activity occurs simply because the animal anticipates food when mealtime approaches. We have already seen the importance of 24-hour periodicity in the motivation of eating behavior; perhaps the same factor controls general activity. Perhaps the rat becomes active when it anticipates the regularly scheduled daily meal. Let us consider this possibility.

Bolles and de Lorge (1962b) fed rats every 19 hours or every 29 hours while the animals were confined to activity wheels, and they found no indication of anticipatory running prior to the 19- and 29-hour meals, while rats fed every 24 hours showed a large increase in running in the hours just prior to their meals. Thus anticipatory running appears to be restricted to meals presented every 24 hours. This was also the conclusion of Bolles and Stokes (1965), who tested groups of rats that had been born and reared in well-controlled environments in which lighting, noise level, feeding, and maintenance were all geared to 19-, 24-, or 29-hour cycles. Again none of the 19- or 29-hour animals showed any evidence of anticipation either in general activity or in instrumental behavior, while all of the 24-hour subjects did.

If one attempts to "stretch" the rat's normal 24-hour cyclicity by imposing gradually lengthened cycles of light and dark, it cannot be pulled very far, not more than an hour or two from the normal 24-hour period (Bolles & Ogilvie, 1966). Bolles (1970a) has shown that the anticipatory running in activity wheels that occurs when animals are fed every 24 hours is inherent in the animal; that is, it does not depend on external cues signaling that food is coming. Richter (1971) has shown that rats blinded at birth will show a good circadian cycle in activity wheels. So we have the rather peculiar conclusion that although the cycle is normally dependent upon illumination conditions (so that, e.g., most activity occurs in the dark), activity is not dependent upon such cues in order to manifest its own 24-hour periodicity. Circadian cycles have also been demonstrated with a variety of different activity measures while animals live in Skinner boxes (Evans, 1971), while they live in an elaborate maze and are fed in one part of it once a day (Hétu, 1971), or while they are monitored by other kinds of devices (e.g., Lore & Gershaw, 1966). Similar effects have been shown in thirsty rats (Bolles, 1968), although in this instance the anticipation effect is rather modest in size. On the other hand, if rats are maintained under constant illumination, their activity cycle appears to break down, and some investigators have suggested that the cyclicity of eating breaks down as well (Siegel, 1961).[11]

In conclusion, it seems that just as rats have a tendency to eat every 24 hours, so they have a tendency to run and be active

---

[11] It should be noted that what breaks down is the cyclicity of the group. Individual animals may continue to show a fairly good approximation to a 24-hour cycle, although the period may drift a little and the swing in activity during the period may not be as marked as normal. Animals usually fail to adjust to a radically new environmental periodicity imposed on them if the period is too far removed from the natural circadian rhythm (Browman, 1952; Bolles & Ogilvie, 1966). Goff and Finger (1966) have shown, however, that if the prevailing illumination is intense, it will inhibit whatever cyclicity the animal might otherwise show by virtually prohibiting all wheel running. When Goff and Finger had their animals on a 36-hour light-dark cycle, activity appeared to follow this abnormal rhythm, but when their animals were returned to constant illumination, they reverted immediately to the 24-hour periodicity, suggesting that the 36-hour illumination condition had simply suppressed the animals' natural periodicity, and not replaced it.

every 24 hours. Moreover, it appears that while these cycles can be independent, they tend to go together. The most likely explanation is that both cycles are dependent upon the same mechanism. Bolles and Duncan (1969) have shown that when an animal is fed in the middle of the day, that is, at a time when it is normally sleeping, within about a week it will come to anticipate the meal. This anticipation is shown not only by increased running in wheels but by elevation of body temperature (Bolles & Duncan, 1969). Thus the animal's whole metabolic cycle seems to have been shifted 12 hours out of phase from its normal period of greatest eating and activity. Moreover, if rats are fed regularly two meals a day separated by several hours, they quickly come to show increased activity preceding both meals (Bolles & Moot, 1973).

Reinforcement effects in general activity. If the rat is fed once a day while it is confined to an activity wheel, its activity will gradually increase over 15 days or so of testing from an initial level of something like 500 revolutions a day to perhaps 10,000 revolutions a day. The question is whether this increase in activity is due to an increase in drive over this period or due to some kind of learning mechanism. Finger et al. (1957) showed that when rats were delayed in a waiting box for an hour after coming out of an activity wheel before their daily meal, they showed significantly less increase in running than animals fed immediately after coming out of the wheel. Finger et al. suggest, therefore, that if the rat should run just prior to the regular feeding time and if this activity were then followed by feeding, running should be reinforced. By introducing a delay between the opportunity to run and the reinforcement the learning effect is minimized and much less running is obtained. Apparently, there is still some motivational effect, however, since even with an imposed delay Finger et al. found a sizable increase in activity. Finger et al. suggest that this effect may also be due to a contingency—not in the experimental situation, but in the animal's earlier life. Thus we know that under ad lib. conditions the rat shows cyclic patterns of activity and ingestion, and we know that activity tends to precede ingestion (page 116). Thus it seems entirely possible that prior to entering the activity wheel situation, the rat has created for itself a reinforcement contingency between activity and eating. To demonstrate the plausibility of this mechanism, Finger et al. (1960) maintained rats under very lenient hunger conditions (in an attempt to duplicate the short deprivations that occur when rats have food continuously available) to see whether reinforcement could be effective under these conditions. Animals had their food removed 3 hours before testing, and they were put in activity wheels for just 1 hour. Animals in the experimental group were taken directly out of the wheels and fed, whereas animals in the control group were taken from the wheels, delayed for 1 hour, and then fed. The results demonstrated convincingly the reinforcing effect of feeding upon the immediately prior running, since the control group showed no increase on subsequent test days while the experimental group increased its 1-hour activity scores about fivefold. It is important to note that these animals were under extremely low hunger conditions, equivalent to those of animals maintained ad lib., conditions under which there would ordinarily be no increase in activity (Hall & Connon, 1957; Moskowitz, 1959). Certainly, then, one factor that can control running in activity wheels is the reinforcing effect of regularly scheduled feeding. We can conclude that running in activity wheels can be learned and that this learning contributes to the high level of running characteristically seen in hungry rats.

There are other mechanisms besides the association between running and feeding that could possibly serve as reinforcement for running in activity wheels. Seward and Pereboom (1955) once suggested that wheel running may simply be enjoyable (that is, self-reinforcing) for hungry animals, and this may be as good a way as any to think of the phenomenon. But there have also been a number of specific proposals for mechanisms that would produce reinforcement. One possibility was suggested by Stevenson and Rixon (1957), who proposed that activity in general, and running in wheels in particular, may have little to do with the rat's hunger or thirst but much to do with the regulation of its body temperature. They proposed that the hungry rat runs to keep its metabolism and temperature up, even though the increased demand for energy makes the animal's nutritional condition worse. To support this argument they observed that the activity of hungry rats increases as ambient temperature decreases. Subsequent research, however, has failed to substantiate Stevenson and Rixon's hypothesis (Campbell & Lynch, 1967, 1968; Bolles et al., 1968).

Others have suggested that the rat runs to increase circulating levels of blood glucose. The level of blood glucose is supposed to drop with deprivation (see page 146), and exercise is supposed to raise it. However, the data indicate that the blood sugar level is not increased by running and that insulin injections, which should increase activity by lowering blood sugar levels further, do not do so (Jakubczak, 1969; Strutt & Stewart, 1970; Tarpy, 1971). Moreover, the blood sugar level hypothesis cannot explain the running of thirsty rats (Campbell, 1964; Bolles & Duncan, 1969).

It was noted previously that the rat may go into the activity-wheel situation with a prior history of being active when it is hungry (Finger et al., 1960). It could be argued that in the prior history of the animal it has learned to run around and look for food, that is, to be active when hungry, and that this tendency simply transfers to the activity-wheel situation even though such behavior is no longer adaptive. However, investigators who have controlled the animal's history of food-getting behavior (e.g., Campbell, 1964; Lore &

Gershaw, 1966) have found that rats are no less active if they have a history of finding food in the same place than if food is scattered about so that it must be looked for.

Collier (1970) and Collier and Hirsch (1971) propose that the rat has metabolic reasons for running when it is hungry or thirsty. Although these reasons are slightly different, the basic concept is that the animal must lose weight in order to maintain appropriate cellular balance and composition. To support this argument Collier has observed that in using wheels with different physical properties, sizes, and so on, there is an invariant in the amount of running that occurs; this invariant is the energy expended by the animal. In other words, the deprived rat runs in order to spend energy. A variant of this argument has been noted by Morrison (1968). Morrison maintained rats in metabolism cages so that oxygen consumption could be monitored; he discovered that under normal circumstances, the rat spends an appreciable amount of energy eating its food and that when deprived of food, the energy saved simply shows up in increased exploratory behavior and decreased sleep. In other words, Morrison argues that the rat has a fairly fixed level of energy output that will be allocated to feeding if food is available and to general activity in the absence of food. This is an interesting and plausible argument and perhaps it explains the modest increases in activity that occur in tilt cages, stabilimeters, and photocell cages. But this mechanism cannot account for the enormous expenditure of energy that occurs in activity wheels (a rat approximately doubles its daily caloric need when it runs 20,000 turns a day), nor does Morrison's argument explain the fact that when it has become severely deprived, the rat will run rather than eat (Routtenberg & Kuznesof, 1967).[12]

Kavanau (1967) and Collier (1970) have observed a curious feature of running: Animals like only voluntary general activity. Put in a motorized treadmill, the animal will resist running and turn off the machine if possible; but if the animal is trained to turn on the treadmill, it will do so and run for long periods of time.

One other curious phenomenon should be noted, namely, that ingestion of nonnutritive bulk depresses running in activity wheels (Hamilton, 1969). This inhibition suggests that some stimulus, such as stomach contractions, elicits wheel running. But Messing and Campbell (1971) report that this inhibition is not found if the rats are vagotomized, which suggests that it is not that the empty stomach elicits running but that the full stomach inhibits running and that if there is a stimulus that elicits running, it arises some place else.

We have seen, then, that a variety of mechanisms have been

---

[12] Although Collier (1970) calls activity wheel running a "weak" reinforcer, it is evidently reinforcing enough that the rat will literally run itself to death, shortening its life by approximately 30 percent in terminal deprivation.

proposed to account for the learning of running in activity wheels, but that none of these proposed mechanisms is very convincing. We stand about where we did at the beginning of this section with the conclusion that running in wheels is reinforcing for rats, particularly for hungry rats. But why this should be so remains uncertain.

The energization of general activity. Granting for the moment that there is a learned component to general activity and that deprivation brings this component into play, we can now examine the important question of whether activity is wholly learned or whether some part of it is generated by drive. In short, is there drive-produced energization of general activity over and above the general activity provided by associative mechanisms?

It has been known for some time that rats tested but not fed in activity wheels show increased running as a function of deprivation (Wald & Jackson, 1944; Finger & Reid, 1952; Reid & Finger, 1957; Treichler & Hall, 1962). In fact, Duda and Bolles (1963) have shown that there is a very high correlation between an animal's weight loss and its activity wheel performance even during the first 3 hours of the animal's experience in the wheel. This correlation was found regardless of the conditions under which weight was lost. That is, it made little difference whether Duda and Bolles' animals had lost weight by being on a maintenance schedule or from a single severe privation. With no food available in the wheels, the weight loss alone, rather than the conditions of deprivation that produced it, determined the activity level. This general finding has been replicated by Treichler and Collins (1965) and similar results have been reported by Wright et al. (1966) and by Connally (1968) using test sessions as short as 1 hour.

This finding suggests that there is an activation effect in the absence of learning mechanisms. But note that the learning mechanism that is excluded in this kind of experiment is the contingency between activity and eating. Whether these short tests exclude the operation of other reinforcement mechanisms is not as clear. What these short tests really exclude is the transfer to the running wheel situation of earlier learned connections between activity and eating. This exclusion was most effective in an experiment by Finger (1965), since he used very young animals with a minimal amount of prior experience and tested them for only 10 minutes. Under Finger's conditions activity still increased with deprivation. But if running in a wheel is inherently reinforcing for the rat (because it has an effect like increasing body temperature), then an appreciable amount of learning might still occur in an interval as short as 10 minutes. It might be thought that at this point we have pushed the learning hypothesis to the brink of untestability. This is a good thought. It may indeed be impossible to determine if the hungry rat runs in a wheel because it is motivated or because it is reinforced for doing so.

Another approach to the problem involves looking not at the overall level of activity obtained with deprivation, but rather at the distribution of activity. Wright (1965) gave rats good food during the day and quinine-adulterated food at night. The quinine treatment sharply reduced the amount of food consumed at night and increased running at night, so that there appeared to be a correlation between deprivation (self-imposed) and activity. But Wright went on to show that there was less running with more severe adulteration, which indicates that activity is correlated with eating rather than deprivation. Wright (1965a) also deprived some rats during the day and fed them at night; the increased running shown by these animals occurred at night, that is, during the feeding period, not during the deprivation period. A counterbalanced group fed during the day and deprived at night also tended to confine its running to the period when food was available rather than the deprivation period, so that this effect too looks more like a learning or incentive effect than a drive effect.

The specificity of general activity. More evidence against a pure energization interpretation of general activity comes from studies showing the specificity of conditions under which increased activity is found. Some of these studies are done with thirsty rats. Although water-deprived rats are known to run significantly more than satiated ones (Wald & Jackson, 1944; Finger & Reid, 1952; Hall, 1955; Campbell, 1960; Bolles, 1968), activity does not increase progressively on subsequent days but seems to stabilize almost immediately at a value that is only about twice the baseline value. Hence the progressive rise over a two-week period typically obtained with hunger (Reid & Finger, 1955) appears to be specific to hunger.[13] Campbell and Cicala (1962) report that rats under terminal water deprivation are less active than controls in stabilimeter cages.

The increase in general activity that is found with food deprivation also appears to be specific to, or at least is most pronounced in, activity wheels, although there are insufficient data with other kinds of apparatus to permit more than a tentative conclusion. Eayrs (1954) has shown that in a stabilimeter-type cage, activity scores stabilize in one day as compared to the long-term variation in individual differences typically shown by hungry rats in activity wheels. Eayrs also reported a low correlation of 0.18 between scores in wheels and scores in stabilimeter cages. Everyone who has looked for differences in functional relationships among different activity-measuring devices has found them (Weasner et al., 1960; Treichler & Hall,

[13] It also appears that if thirst is induced by means other than water deprivation, there is no energization of activity wheel running. Messing and Campbell (1971a) tested rats in activity wheels after giving them polyethylene glycol treatment or NaCl injections and found that neither cellular nor extracellular dehydration produced an increase in running (see also Wayner & Petraitis, 1967).

1962; Finger, 1961). Strong (1957) used tilt cages with different sensitivities and found that he could obtain virtually any kind of functional relationship one might imagine between deprivation conditions and activation merely by varying the sensitivity. When the recording device was made most sensitive, so that it could detect minute movements such as grooming, food deprivation produced decreased rather than increased activity. A similar result has been noted by Bolles and Sanders (1969) with ultrasonic activity-measuring devices.

The activity wheel effect also appears to be largely specific to the rat. Nicholls (1922) reported that hunger depressed activity wheel running in guinea pigs, and although Campbell et al. (1966) failed to confirm this specific finding, they did obtain striking confirmation of Nicholls' main point, which was that different species react in characteristic ways to hunger and thirst—some by becoming more active when hungry and less active when thirsty, others by showing the opposite pattern, and still others by showing no appreciable change in activity level (see also Cornish & Mrosovsky, 1965).

And so we see, perhaps to our surprise, that what was once considered to be a very general phenomenon, that is, that any kind of drive would stimulate general activity, now appears to be a very specic phenomenon. The original idea was derived from a bulk of data collected from hungry rats in activity wheels, but now we see that this phenomenon is to a large extent specific to hunger, specific to the rat, and specific to activity wheels. We can no longer accept general activity as a direct measure of drive strength. We have discovered that activity as measured by any device, but particularly as measured by activity wheels, consists of certain specific responses that are reinforceable, just like any other response might be, and that in fact much of the rise in activity that has traditionally been taken as evidence of drive now appears to be the result of a change in habit structure. The fact that different species and different activity-measuring devices yield different functional relationships presents a further predicament for any easy interpretation of general activity as an index of drive.

Two problems emerge from this conceptual reorganization. One is how to account for the apparent energizing effect of food deprivation on activity wheel running. If the effect cannot be explained in terms of increased drive, then how are we to account for it? Many psychologists have become disenchanted with the idea that general activity is a measure of the animal's need or drive (e.g., Baumeister et al., 1964), but there have been few alternative conceptions. Part of the increased running in wheels can be attributed to reinforcement, as we have seen. But there is also a component of activity wheel running that must be attributed to some kind of unlearned connection with hunger. The puzzle is that there is no obvious ulterior reason why running in an activity wheel should be more reinforcing for the hungry rat than it is for the satiated rat, but it is.

The second problem that confronts us is this: If neither the activity wheel nor the stabilimeter tilt cage can be accepted without qualification as an instrument for measuring an animal's activation, then how can general activation be measured? Or does it even make sense to try to measure the strength of behavior that bears no relation to the current drive condition?

Some new approaches to general activity

New interpretations of general activity have led to inquiries into what animals do when they are being generally active (Bindra, 1961). Bindra and Blond (1958) developed a behavior-sampling method for analyzing the rat's general activity into its various component responses. It is found that in a novel situation the animal sniffs, investigates, locomotes, grooms, and sometimes freezes. It is then natural to ask how the distribution of the animal's activities varies as a function of deprivation conditions. Using a behavior-sampling procedure, Bolles (1960) found that a single 24-hour water deprivation had the expected effect of waking up the animals and making them more active than when they were satiated but that a 2-hour food deprivation slightly depressed the level of activity. A subsequent study of the rat in its own home cage (Bolles, 1963) found that hunger had only a slight effect upon the incidence of any of the different kinds of behavior that occur in the home cage, at least during the first 2 days on the maintenance schedule. (Siegel & Steinberg, 1949, had found a more impressive increase in home-cage activity when it was measured with photobeams; it is not clear why the apparatus should make so much difference.) During the first 2 days of deprivation, the hungry animals slept and groomed and ran around about as much as they did under ad lib. conditions. However, as the maintenance schedule was continued for 12 days, the animals became somewhat more active; they slept and groomed less than normally and spent a proportionately larger part of the time exploring and walking around in their cages (Compare the first and last columns of Table 7-1.) The animals in this later study were maintained in a normal laboratory environment that provided them with numerous cues to the time of day and made it possible for them to anticipate the daily feeding. It was found that the mere approach of the observer tended to rouse the animals and make them more active.

A further study of the same type was conducted with animals maintained in isolation in order to minimize stimuli that might be cues to feeding (Bolles, unpublished). Temperature and noise were held constant, and the animals were viewed through a one-way

Theory of motivation

Table 7–1

The incidence of different kinds of activity in the home cage
as a function of deprivation conditions (in percentages of the animals'
activity over a 24-hour period)

	AD LIB	CONTINUOUS (ISOLATED)	CYCLIC (ISOLATED)	CYCLIC (NORMAL)
Sleep	61	60	58	51
Lying	4	6	4	10
Grooming	18	19	15	11
Sniffing	4	6	11	
Standing	1	2	5	[26]
Rearing	2	3	4	
Walking	1	1	2	
Eating	6	—	—	—
Drinking	3	1	1	1

window. Under these conditions some activation effects were still found (compare columns 1 and 3 in the table), but they were somewhat smaller than before. The diurnal course of activity under these conditions, clearly cyclic, suggested that the animals were using temporal cues to anticipate the regular feeding time. Another group of animals tested under the same isolation conditions but never fed in the test situation (deprived 96 hours) showed very little evidence of being more active than ad lib. animals (see column 2). When the animals did become more active, under cyclic deprivation, the only significant shift in behavior was a decrease in eating and drinking and an increase in exploration and in lying (the least active category of things the subjects did). Results with thirsty animals have been essentially the same.

The same observational technique has now been applied to female rats (Finger, 1969) to determine whether there is any indication in home-cage activity of a four- or five-day estrous cycle comparable to that often reported in activity wheels. Finger found the expected increase in activity and found that it showed up both in photocell counts as well as with the direct observational procedure. But in both cases the increase in activity was very slight, amounting on the average to only 21 percent in total activity (in the activity wheel it is common to find a tripling and quadrupling of running when the rat is in heat).

In another well-controlled study with hungry rats by Mathews and Finger (1966), observational data again confirmed that there was an increase in exploration, locomotion, and standing with corresponding decreases in the incidence of sleeping and grooming (and, of course, eating). These shifts in behavior were highly reliable but small. Mathews and Finger concluded that their data show a direct energizing effect of deprivation on home-cage behavior. That there is such an effect now seems unquestionable.

Note how our perspective on general activity has changed. Twenty years ago the prevailing concept of activity in the rat was based on the assumption that all behavior was driven by physiological needs. The developments in the intervening years have so altered our view of animal behavior that it now becomes a legitimate question to ask whether severe food deprivation has *any* direct, drive-type effect upon the rat's behavior. Perhaps it is unfortunate that we must admit that there is such an effect after all; but this admission should not obscure the major insight we have gained in the past several years: Animals do what they do because they have reasons for doing so, and the automatic, immediate activation of behavior by physiological needs turns out to be one of the minor determinants of behavior.

Exploration. To the extent that exploration has not been previously reinforced in the life history of an animal, it may be considered a form of general activity. The question naturally arises whether hunger, thirst, sexual motivation, fear, or any of the other drive-producing conditions leads to an increase in the incidence of exploration. It is plausible to suppose that the motivated animal would be more likely to explore, since a species with such a behavioral tendency would have considerable advantage in survival over a species that lacked it. Dashiell (1925) reported positive findings—hungry animals explored more than did satiated animals in his complex maze. No one questioned Dashiell's finding, nor the kind of interpretation just cited, for a quarter of a century.

But then Montgomery (1953), who was concerned with showing that exploration was an autonomous drive condition rather than subservient to other drive conditions, reported that hungry animals explored *less* than satiated animals. Dashiell's study has been repeated with equivocal results (Hall et al., 1960; Bolles & de Lorge, 1962a). Others have used complex apparatus like Dashiell's (Adlerstein & Fehrer, 1955), and simple apparatus like Montgomery's (Carr et al., 1959; Glickman & Jensen, 1961). Again the results have been contradictory. Males and females have been compared (Thompson, 1953; Zimbardo & Montgomery, 1957; Zimbardo & Miller, 1958; Lester, 1967), and different kinds of behavioral criteria have been used (Chapman & Levy, 1957; Welker, 1959; Hurwitz, 1960; Richards & Leslie, 1962; Hughes, 1965). None of these variables seems to be a crucial factor in the contradictory results.

Another approach to the problem is to give rats a choice between working for food or working for an exploratory incentive. When this is done, they sometimes appear to prefer to explore (Taylor, 1971), but sometimes, even when the results appear to come out this way, they are open to other interpretations. For example, Cohen and Stettner (1968) demonstrated that exploratory behavior may either compete with or may facilitate food-getting behavior, depending upon how the test situation is structured.

Theory of motivation

Other experimenters have tried to attribute discrepant results to early experience variables, such as prior experience with objects and with searching for food. But again, the data have tended to show that if rats are required to explore to find food in infancy, they are no more likely to explore when made hungry as adults (Woods & Bolles, 1965; Lore & Levowitz, 1966; McCall, 1967).

Curt Stern once wrote that contradictory findings indicate not that someone is wrong and someone else is right, but that the underlying principles are not generally understood. This surely must be the case here. Exploration certainly varies with some experimental parameters. It is known that young animals explore more and are generally more active than older ones (e.g., Finger, 1962) and that females characteristically explore more than males in the same situation (e.g., Lester, 1967). The trouble is that age and sex are minor determinants, and deprivation is an insignificant determinant of exploratory behavior compared with its overwhelming dependence upon the stimulus characteristics of the test situation. Psychologists have persisted is asking the wrong question about exploration. The truth is that when confronted with a novel situation, the rat spends virtually all of its time exploring, regardless of whether it is hungry or satiated.

Recently, somewhat more interesting questions have been asked about the relationship between hunger and exploration. One approach has been to use molecular observational techniques to determine whether hunger changes the rat's exploratory behavior in a novel situation. Some of this work was described previously in the section on general activity.[14]

A second approach is based upon Welker's (1957) important distinction between what he calls free and forced exploration. In most exploration studies the rat is simply put bodily into a new situation in which it must explore. The alternative to exploration is presumably freezing, since these situations typically support no other kinds of behavior. Welker proposes an alternative procedure: The rat is given sufficient time to become completely familiar with a particular situation (such as its own home cage) and then is given the opportunity to leave it for a novel situation. In free exploration the animal initiates exploration, whereas in forced exploration such behavior is virtually elicited from it. The first free-exploration study

---

[14] They walk around and sniff, rear up on their hind legs and sniff, pick up bits of dust and debris off the floor, look at objects, and look and listen to other things in the situation. If the animal is hungry and food is available, it will stop exploring to eat. If food is not available, it will take some time out from its exploring to groom. If conditions permit, it will ultimately lie down and sleep. But for the first 20 minutes or so in a novel situation the rat spends 90 percent of its time, or more, in some form of exploration.

was reported by Fehrer (1956). Her subjects were given a 24-hour familiarity or adaptation period in one chamber and then given the opportunity to explore a new adjacent chamber. Deprivation produced tremendous facilitation of free exploration. Similar findings have been reported by Bolles and de Lorge (1962) who found that hungry rats were much more likely to leave their home cages than satiated ones. Although the results do not always come out in the same manner (e.g., Lester, 1967a), this is the most often reported finding (see also Hughes, 1968, 1968a).

The third approach develops from the observation that when the rat is exploring a novel situation, it is subject to conflicting tendencies—the outgoing, exploratory tendency, on the one hand, and conservative, fear-motivated, safety-seeking tendencies, on the other. The effect of hunger can then be regarded as due either to increased exploration or to decreased fear. Some writers have suggested, to the contrary, that exploration is motivated by fear, but most investigators (e.g., Montgomery, 1955; Hayes, 1960; Baron, 1964) indicate that exploration is inhibited by fear. The balance between fear and exploration can no doubt be shifted in a number of ways, but the most important factor is probably the novelty of the test situation. A provocative study reported by Sheldon (1969) indicates that when rats are tested in a very familiar situation, they will take time off from the task at hand to explore novel stimuli; but if the test situation is itself novel, their preference is to approach familiar test stimuli.[15] These results suggest that the effect of hunger on exploration may not be so much on exploration as on the counterbalancing fear of too much novelty.

In conclusion, there is evidently a range of situations in which the hungry rat generates more behavior then the satiated rat. It is much more active in activitiy wheels and somewhat more active in tilt cages and in its home cage. It appears to leave a familiar situation sooner and may be more resistant to fear of novelty. But it is clearly not the case that hunger increases any and all "general" activity.

[15] These results provide good support for Fiske and Maddi's (1961) "optimal stimulation" hypothesis. The idea is that there is an optimum level of "effective" stimulus input, where effectiveness means something like information value and information value is a function of stimulus novelty and complexity. Fiske and Maddi maintain that if the rat is presented with familiar stimuli, arousal drops and the rat is motivated to increase stimulation. But if there is too much stimulus information coming in, the animal may withdraw and seek stimuli to which it is already adapted. This hypothesis and related versions of the optimal stimulation argument have recently been discussed by Eisenberger (1972). Eisenberger also includes in his discussion of exploratory behavior the reinforcing effects of stimulus change, a topic that we cannot pursue at this point. The evidence he cites is equivocal, but it suggests that the value of stimulus change as a reinforcer may increase with hunger.

Summary

The major effort in this chapter has not been to show that there is an energizing effect, for there was never any real question about that. The effort has been to show that energization is most readily found in some classes of behavior with some response measures and under some conditions.

Perhaps the most basic finding is that energization is most evident when there is the greatest relevance of the behavior to the animal's motivation condition. Thus the probability of eating increases continuously with weight loss. The amount eaten shows a much less orderly relationship because the amount eaten is controlled by and involved in other factors besides the animal's immediate need for food. As the connection between the rat's food deficit and its behavior is weakened, for example, as an arbitrary instrumental response requirement is imposed on the animal, it becomes problematical whether energization of that response will be found. If it is a well-learned response, then both its probability and vigor tend to increase with increased weight loss. But if the learned response is weak, then other relationships are found. If we think of general activity as behavior that bears no necessary connection with the animal's motivating condition, then we cannot conclude very much, because it turns out that much of what is called general activity is not general at all but is really instrumental behavior with weak accidental reinforcement contingencies. When we make our best efforts to eliminate or minimize these contingencies, the apparent energizing effects are much reduced or lost altogether.

Another important principle should have become apparent here, namely, that behavior is typically governed by a number of different factors and hence can be explained only by reference to a number of different factors, associative as well as motivational. The question then is, Under what conditions is the severity of the drive-producing antecedent conditions an *important* determinant of behavior? The answer seems to be: Only when the behavior in question is a necessary or instrumental part of alleviating the antecedent conditions.

8

ASSOCIATIVE ASPECTS OF MOTIVATED BEHAVIOR

*If we are to understand the behavior of adults
or even of children we need not bother
ourselves much with tissue needs. We do well
to give our attention to what the child
or adult has learned.*

E. R. Guthrie and A. L. Edwards

In Hull's theory of behavior the construct D is not itself involved in determining the direction of behavior; it merely energizes whatever habits exist in a given situation. Therefore, it is supposed to make little difference what the source of drive is. The theory implies that the source of drive can be changed without disrupting behavior. Although drive, D, is said to be a nonassociative determinant of behavior, it is implicated in two different ways in the formation of habits. Hull hypothesized, first, that drive reduction was the mechanism whereby habits are strengthened and, second, that the conditions that produce drive, such as food deprivation, have characteristic stimulus consequences, S_D, such as stomach contractions, which may enter directly into the formation of habits.

In the present chapter we will consider the experimental evidence relevant to these propositions. But before discussing these problems we will consider the evidence that has resulted from the attempts to test Hull's hypothesis that D and H are independent. The tests of all of these hypothesized properties of D have usually been undertaken in good faith, that is, in the hope of supporting Hull's theory. However, the results have not generally been very gratifying. All of these hypothetical properties of drive have turned out to have limited predictive value, and in each case there are a number of difficulties and limitations.

The present chapter will lead us to three very broad conclusions: (1) The explanation of behavior cannot be carried out as easily as we might have thought; both the motivational factors and the habit factors that determine behavior are much more complicated than had been anticipated. (2) Partly as a result of this complexity, behavior must be analyzed very carefully to determine just what stimuli and responses do, in fact, enter into association. (3) There is a growing tendency to explain the motivational components of behavior in terms of incentive rather than in terms of drive. What we will find, in short, is that Hull's propositions about the associative aspects of motivated behavior are not so much empirically wrong as they are practically inadequate.

The independence of D and H

Hull conceived of habit as a more or less permanent change in the nervous system and drive as a more or less transient motivational state. Then by hypothesizing that habit structure and motivation were functionally independent and that overt behavior was a joint function of the two, he gave a clear syntactical form to the old but imprecise distinction between learning and performance. Hull's assumption of independence involves two propositions, that $_sH_R$ is independent of drive level and that D is independent of learning. We will be concerned here with the first proposition—that what the animal learns does not depend upon its motivation during learning.[1]

There are two major lines of evidence. One involves the comparison of learning curves obtained under different drive conditions. The question then becomes whether animals under different drive conditions approach their different asymptotic performance levels at the same rate. (Recall that it was this feature of the Perin-Williams data that led Hull to postulate independence.) Quite often in studies of instrumental performance, variation in drive conditions produces little effect upon performance; but in studies in which effects are found, it is usually the case that drive conditions affect the asymptote but not the growth rate (e.g., Tolman & Honzik, 1930, errors in a complex maze; Hillman et al., 1953, speed of running in a maze; Ramond, 1954, discrimination errors; Barry, 1958, runway speed; Deese & Carpenter, 1951, latency in a runway).

---

[1] The second proposition—that D is independent of learning—would seem to be belied by the obvious fact that much of the organism's total motivation is quite apparently learned. But Hull (1943, 1952) guaranteed the correctness of this proposition by introducing secondary or acquired motivation as a separate theoretical term, keeping the unlearned part identified with D. Many recent drive theorists have tended to part with Hull on this. Brown (1961) is the most articulate member of this group; he refers to all determinants of motivation, learned and unlearned alike, as sources of D. We will consider this approach in Chapter 9.

Associative aspects of motivated behavior

Clark (1958) has reported that with a highly practiced bar-press response on fairly strenuous variable-interval reinforcement schedules, a range of from 1-hour to 23-hour food deprivation affects the rate on these three schedules proportionately (see Fig. 8-1). Hence whatever discriminative and reinforcement processes occur under these schedules of reinforcement, their effects are multiplied by the motivational effects of hours deprivation.

Davenport (1965) carried out a systematic analysis of learning curves of rats under 3-, 22-, or 41-hour food deprivation. Exponential learning curves were fitted to the trial-by-trial speed scores of each animal, and then the individual growth constants and constants describing asymptotic performance level were estimated. It was found that mean asymptotic performance increased significantly with deprivation time, but the mean growth constant did not. The slight increase found in the growth constant could probably be attributed to the failure of a few animals to perform properly in the instrumental situation under 3-hour deprivation; It would seem then

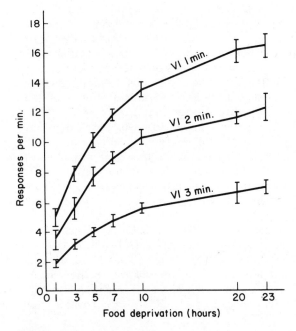

Figure 8–1

Rate of bar pressing under three different schedules of reinforcement as a function of deprivation time. The variances under each condition are indicated. (From Clark, 1958) Copyright 1958 by the Society for the Experimental Analysis of Behavior, Inc.

that in simple appetitive instrumental situations the learning curves of animals under different drive conditions approach their respective asymptotes at the same rate.

Spence (1956) has suggested that D and H may not be independent in aversive learning situations.[2] He cites two studies of instrumental-escape conditioning in which divergence of the learning curves was not found (Amsel, 1950; Campbell & Kraeling, 1953). The results of these two studies are difficult to interpret because the initial strength of the criterion response seems to depend upon the intensity of the drive-producing conditions (Campbell & Kraeling, 1953). Moreover, there is the further complication that the intensity of the drive-producing conditions is one of the things that determines the nature and strength of the responses that compete with the criterion response. Thus it seems that animals that are supposedly under different intensities of drive may also inadvertently be at different stages in the course of learning the response. In general, then, the evidence of the first sort, that is, direct comparison of acquisition performance under different drive conditions, is not conclusive; but it is at least consistent with Hull's assumption of independence.

The second line of evidence comes from those experiments in which a response is learned under one set of drive conditions and then tested under another set either during further learning or during extinction. Attention is then focused on whether performance follows the shift in drive conditions or whether there are residual carryover effects of the old drive conditions. Performance after the shift can be attributed to (1) the motivational effects of the drive state present after the shift, (2) residual effects of the prior drive state, and (3) the interaction between the two, which represents the effect of shifting per se (presumably, generalization decrements resulting from the change in that part of the total stimulus situation that depends upon the drive state). The independence hypothesis is supported to the extent that postshift performance is independent of the preshift drive condition.

Drive-shift studies of bar-pressing behavior. The first experimental attack on the problem came from Hull's own laboratory (Finan, 1940; Heathers & Arakelian, 1941). These and some of the subsequent investigations illustrate some of the methodological and interpretive complexities in this kind of research, so it will be worth our while to consider them in some detail. Finan trained four groups of

---

[2] Spence takes as a criterion of independence the divergence of the learning curves under different drive conditions. This is not quite sufficient, since curves with different rates of growth may also diverge early in training. Spence's criterian also depends upon his assumption that $_sE_R$ is related linearly to the speed of responding (Spence, 1954). Without some such assumption, of course, the question of convergence, or for that matter any question about the shapes of learning curves, becomes pointless.

rats to press a bar under 1-, 12-, 24-, or 48-hour food deprivation, after which the response was extinguished with the drive conditions equated for all groups at 24-hour deprivation. The greatest resistance to extinction was found in the 12-hour group; the 24-hour and 48-hour groups were a little lower; and the 1-hour group had the least resistance to extinction. The first inference from Finan's data would be that for a given number of reinforcements there is an optimum, moderate drive level for producing the strongest habit.

However, certain methodological features of Finan's study cast some doubt on this conclusion. For example, we are told that the time for learning under the 30 reinforcements was about the same for the four groups, approximately 24 minutes. This similarity in initial acquisition performance suggests that motivation differences were not as great as the nominal hours of deprivation would suggest, and this seems likely also in view of the fact that all groups had had six days experience with a 10 gm food ration prior to the introduction of the acquisition-drive conditions. Another problem is the possibility that animals under the different drive conditions had acquired and/or had extinguished different responses during the course of training and that differences in the subsequent extinction performance reflected these associative effects rather than residual effects of motivation. For example, it may be that during acquisition the high-drive groups attacked the bar or otherwise engaged in "excited" behavior. The reinforcements received by this behavior would not have gone into shaping the response. Moreover, this behavior would have undergone some extinction and hence would be less likely to occur in the extinction period, so the animal's extinction score might be still further depressed. Finan did not exercise sufficient control over the animal's behavior during the acquisition period to be able to offer any assurance that all animals were in fact receiving an equal number of reinforcements on the same habit.

Reynolds (1949a) attempted to improve Finan's procedure. Differential motivation was controlled by prefeeding the animals 25 percent or 100 percent of their daily ration. The instrumental response in this case was panel pushing for food pellets (presumably, the topographic details of this response are less crucial than those of bar pressing). Acquisition training occurred with well-spaced trials. But, like Finan, Reynolds found that the low-motivation group was significantly more resistant to extinction than the high-motivation group. Something unusual had evidently occurred during training, however, since a superiority of the low-motivation group had already been established (shorter latency of responding) in acquisition. Reynolds explained this anomalous finding by postulating that more inhibition had been built up under the high-motivation condition. Instead of discarding the independence hypothesis, he concluded that performance may be governed to a large degree by mechanisms other than or in addition to the simple multiplication of D and H. Thus whatever effect D may have in the determination of behavior, it may be overcome by the acquisition of inhibition effects also acquired in the learning situation.

Other experimenters (Heathers & Arakelian, 1941; Strassburger, 1950; Brown, 1956) have also worked with the resistance to extinction of a bar-press response. In these three studies the motivating conditions and acquisition performance were carefully controlled; large numbers of subjects were run; and prefeeding techniques, hours-deprivation techniques, and secondary reinforcement procedures were used as motivating conditions. In each case a pronounced effect of current deprivation was found in resistance to extinction scores, but no significant effect of prior deprivation was found. The Heathers and Arakelian study introduced an interesting variation of this design. All animals had acquired the response under identical deprivation conditions; then the high- and low-deprivation conditions were imposed for a first extinction under distributed trials. Finally, in the critical phase of the experiment, motivation conditions were equated for a second extinction. The results indicate that whether extinction is viewed as an acquisition of competing behavior, as a building up of inhibition, or as some other kind of alteration of the habit structure, it is not significantly affected by drive level.

Eisman et al. (1961) have pointed out that in the Strassburger study and in some of the others we have noted, the performance of the different groups was not reported to be sufficiently different during acquisition to give any assurance that they were under appreciably different motivation conditions. These authors point out that if the deprivation conditions have no effect on acquisition performance, we can hardly expect a valid test of the independence hypothesis. The point is not really applicable because the current motivation conditions did have a significant energizing effect on extinction performance in all the experiments that are cited. Eisman imposed weight losses of approximately 8 percent for the low-drive condition and 20 percent for the high-drive condition and obtained significant carry-over effects. The bar-press response was more resistant to extinction when it had been learned under high drive than when it had been learned under low drive. Eisman et al. were able to report that the initial bar-press training had been nearly twice as fast under the high- as under the low-drive conditions, thus "validating" their use of weight loss as the antecedent variable. Unfortunately, another variable in the study was confounded with weight loss, namely, the duration of the deprivation state; weight was brought down to the reduced value over a two- or three-week period, during which time the subjects were maintained on limited rations. Consequently, under the high-drive condition ample opportunity was provided for the acquisition of all those signs of motivation that suggest the operation of incentive motivation, and we are left with the question of whether Eisman's more-motivated animals had high drive or high incentive or high something else. A second difficulty with this study is that the rate of acquisition was not controlled (in fact, the difference in rate was used to demonstrate the energizing effect of the deprivation conditions). Therefore, we do not know for sure that the animals under the high- and low-drive conditions had acquired the same response or had received the same number of reinforcements for the same habit.[3] In summary, the bulk of the evidence from bar-pressing situations does not seem to be inconsistent with Hull's assumption of the independence of D and H but only because the evidence itself is so inconsistent.

Drive-shift studies of running behavior. In the case of running speed in a straight alley, the results have typically been quite different from those obtained with bar pressing. The indication is that when extinction is carried out under equated drive conditions, there is some carry-over of the speed of responding characteristic of acquisition-drive conditions, at least during the first few trials of extinction (Campbell & Kraeling, 1954; Lewis & Cotton, 1957; Davis, 1957; Barry, 1958; Theios, 1963). This effect is illustrated in Fig. 8-2. These results show a clear difference in running speed in acquisition as a function of drive conditions, and they also show a carry-over of these differences for 6 to 10 trials in extinction. This group of studies covers a wide range of deprivation times from 0 to 60 hours and covers acquisition under both distributed and massed trials. Hence we may place some confidence in the generality of the finding.

    The discrepancy between these results involving the speed of running and the other results involving resistance to extinction of a bar press may hinge upon the fact that running at a particular speed is one of the things that the animal learns during acquisition. We might say that the high-drive animal learns to run, whereas the low-drive animal learns to walk. Such qualitatively different responses would transfer to the extinction situation, so that running would be extinguished in the previously high-drive animals and walking would be extinguished in the previously low-drive animals. Campbell and

---

[3] The experimenter appears to have a dilemma here: If he demonstrates that current drive conditions differentially influence acquisition performance, then he cannot, in general, assume that the same response has been learned. But if he controls the learning session to guarantee topographic identity of the response under different drive conditions, then he loses the evidence that variation in those conditions has any effect. The dilemma might be escaped by taking note of more than one measure of the response, for example, by using latency scores to demonstrate the effect of variation in the drive conditions and amplitude or speed scores to demonstrate the constancy of the response.

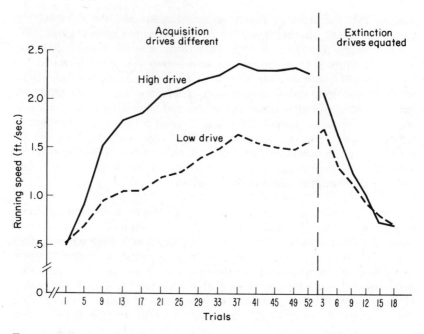

Figure 8–2

Running speed in acquisition and extinction as a function of drive condition differences in acquisition. (From Barry, 1958) Copyright (1958) by the American Psychological Association. Reprinted by permission.

Kraeling (1954) seem to have been the first to suggest this possibility. They noted that animals trained under high and low drive conditions appeared to learn qualitatively different responses. "High-drive animals, for example, learned to crouch facing the starting-box door, ready to respond immediately by dashing down the runway when the door opened. Low-drive animals, in contrast, seldom exhibited this habit . . . and never appeared to acquire the skill of running rapidly down the alley." (Campbell & Kraeling, 1954, p. 102) Then during extinction, the animals trained under low drive cannot run fast because they have not learned to do so and since reinforcement is no longer present, they do not subsequently learn to do so.

King (1959) has suggested that the carry-over effect on running speed is not actually due to the strength of the running response itself, but rather to the occurrence or nonoccurrence of competing responses that become extinguished under high drive but not under low drive. King trained rats under 12- or 60-hour food deprivation to run to food in a runway and then extinguished them with the drive conditions reversed for half of each group. King measured not only the overall running time in the usual way but also the amount of time the animals spent just running, that is, the overall running time minus the time they spent engaged in competing, nonrunning behavior. The latter measure showed that the prior acquisition-drive level had no residual effect on extinction performance. But for reasons that are not clear, King's total time measure also failed to show an effect of acquisition drive level. Because King was not able to replicate the results of the other runway studies that he was attempting to explain, we cannot assess his explanation of them.

Other investigators have also obtained negative results in this kind of situation. For example, Leach (1971) trained rats in a runway under either 10 percent or 30 percent weight-loss conditions and then tested all animals under the 10 percent condition. We should have expected a carry-over effect, that is, 30 percent animals running faster at the beginning of extinction. But this effect was not found. However, the energizing effect of greater weight loss was not found in acquisition either. Thus there was no difference to carry over. All we can conclude from King (1959) and Leach (1971) is that no matter how well intended or well designed the experiment, if there is no effect of deprivation in acquisition, there can be no test of the independence assumption. And we still do not know for certain when there is a difference in acquisition and if it does carry over into extinction, what to attribute it to.

The carry-over effect of prior drive conditions, which seems reasonably well established for response amplitude measures, might be expected in other response measures. The response with more vigor as well as the response that occurs sooner might be expected to be stronger in extinction. On the question of latency of running, however, Deese and Carpenter (1951) and Davis (1957) reported a curious asymmetrical carry-over effect. They found that animals switched from low to high hunger dropped from approximately 10-second to 2-second latencies on the first trial, but that the animals switched from high to low hunger retained a short latency of about 2 seconds (Deese & Carpenter, 1951). This pattern of performance cannot be predicted either from Campbell and Kraeling's argument or from King's analysis. The situation is confusing.

The situation is made still more confusing by the work of Mollenauer (1971, 1971a). We have been concerned here so far with the question of whether deprivation conditions contribute to what the rat learns in an instrumental learning situation. Mollenauer's data suggest that the motivating effect of deprivation is itself part of what is learned. She trained animals under either low or high deprivation conditions for various numbers of trials and then reversed the motivating conditions. The results (Mollenauer, 1971) indicate a slow, small shift in performance (in either direction) after a small amount of training and much more rapid, substantial shifts after more extended training. Evidently, while the rat is learning to run in an alley, it is also learning to appreciate its particular deprivation conditions.

Drive-shift studies of maze performance. Kendler (1945a), Teel (1952), Carper (1957), and Armus (1958) have reported similar drive-switching experiments with rats in T-mazes. In these four studies no differences in resistance to extinction or in errors were found that could be attributed to any residual effect of the acquisition drive. Unfortunately, we do not know what sort of differences to expect. In three of these studies there was no apparent effect of acquisition drive level on acquisition performance, while Kendler reported that acquisition was poorer under the higher drive condition. The difficulty here is that we do not have a very clear picture of how either acquisition or extinction performance in a T-maze depends upon either habit strength or drive; consequently, it does not make too much sense to use this situation as a test for their functional independence.

In still more complex learning situations—mazes (MacDuff, 1946; Hillman et al., 1953) and brightness discrimination (Eisman et al., 1956)—it has been found that rats that learn under different drive conditions and are then tested under equated drive conditions show no differences in error scores. In contrast to the T-maze studies noted previously, acquisition drive conditions did have a motivational effect upon acquisition performance in all of these studies. Thus even though a simple energizing effect is not always obtained in these more complex situations, when it is found it appears, usually, not to carry over when deprivation conditions are changed.

The effect of drive conditions on generalization. When an animal is tested under conditions that depart in some way from those under which it was trained, a decrement in performance is usually found. Does the animal's motivation at the time of testing have any effect upon the gradient of generalization? For example, does the animal under high drive show a broader generalization gradient than the animal under low drive? Spence (1956) has argued that since generalization is really due to altering the habit structure, the shape of the generalization gradient should be independent of D. He cites a study by Newman (1955) to support this interpretation, pointing out that the performance curve under high drive is merely a multiplication of the performance curve under low drive, as it should be on the assumption that D and H multiply. Similar results with a number of different response measures (e.g., rate of responding, heart rate, percentage occurrence) have subsequently been reported by Jenkins et al. (1958), Thomas and King (1959), Porter (1962), Golin and Bostrum (1964), Healey (1965), and Newman and Grice (1965). In each case support for the independence of D and H could be claimed.

The question would seem to be settled, but let us not be hasty. Consider an early experiment reported by Rosenbaum (1951). Rosenbaum trained rats to press a bar for food every 60 seconds.

The bar was removed and presented at regular 60-second intervals, and the latency of the bar press was recorded. After training, the bar was presented at test intervals shorter than 60 seconds. Two groups were run, and both were maintained on 24-hour food deprivation, but one, the low-drive group, was prefed a large part of its daily ration just before testing. The results are shown in Fig. 8-3.

It is clear from the figure that performance is higher under high drive than under low drive, and it is also clear that the high-drive gradient is sharper than the low-drive gradient; there is a greater decrement in response speed for the high-drive animals as test conditions depart from the 60-second training condition. An analysis of variance of the data would probably show a significant interaction between drive and stimulus conditions. We might conclude from this that Spence is wrong because D sharpens the generalization gradient. But other conclusions are possible. In his original analysis of these data Rosenbaum treated them as latency scores rather than as reciprocal latencies or speeds. Under this transformation of the data the conclusion must be reversed; Spence is still

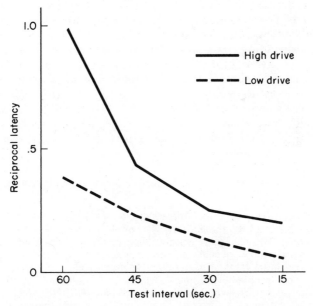

Figure 8–3

Generalization of response strength as a function of departure from training conditions (60 seconds) under high-drive and low-drive conditions. (Adapted from Rosenbaum, 1951) Copyright (1951) by the American Psychological Association. Reprinted by permission.

wrong, but because D broadens the generalization gradient! The inter-action is still significant, but it goes in the opposite direction. There is another possibility: The interaction can be eliminated, and the gradients can be given the same shape by considering the ratio of speeds or the ratio of latencies under high- and low-drive conditions.

These interesting and malleable data also permit us to look at another aspect of the problem. Our folklore tells us that under conditions of high motivation we are inclined to go off half-cocked; that is, we respond to inappropriate stimuli. Such a mechanism has also been used to explain other inappropriate behavior, such as dis-placement (see page 104). Rosenbaum's data show how this would be possible, even if increased motivation had no associative effects upon habit structure. If any arbitrary response criterion is established, such as responding within a given time interval, then it is clear from Fig. 8-3 that this criterion will be met for a broader range of stimuli under high- than under low-motivation conditions. Thus, for all prac-tical purposes, increasing deprivation will broaden the range of stimuli to which a response will generalize. Whether the generalization gradi-ent is sharper or flatter is quite a different question.[4] There is no way this second question can be answered by the results of a gen-eralization experiment until it is more firmly established how D and H and their product should be measured. If we accept as a first approximation Spence's assumption that $_sE_R$ is linearly related to speed of responding, then much of the data is consistent with the independence hypothesis. The trouble is that in Spence's analysis (1954) this first approximation is applicable only under a fairly restricted range of experimental parameters, outside of which so many other assumptions must be made that we are again left with no adequate test of the independence hypothesis (Prokasy, 1967).[5]

Corman and Miles (1966) attempted to circumvent these difficulties by looking at the *variability* of responding under different deprivation conditions. Their rats could move a bar in eight different ways to get food. Although different animals developed individual

---

[4] This distinction may help clarify a confusion that sometimes arises in understanding Jacobs' (1964) contention that as rats are made hungrier, they become increasingly choosy about what they eat. The hungrier rat of course accepts a wider range of foods, but Jacobs could still be right that its relative preference for more preferred foods increases.

[5] These problems become particularly troublesome in the human experimental literature, which will not be considered here. Most reviewers indicate that Spence's efforts to apply Hullian drive theory to human subjects (e.g., Spence, 1958) have failed to provide much support for the theory and very little support for the independence hypothesis (Bolles, 1967; Prokasy, 1967; Goulet, 1968). If this work has demonstrated any-thing, it is that human behavior is even more dependent than rat behavior upon associative factors and that so much of the human's motivation is learned that these determinants too can only be understood in associative terms.

patterns of responding, these patterns were invariant as deprivation conditions were varied.

In summary, then, a variety of evidence suggests that D and H are independent. But certain qualifications should be added to Hull's original formulation. One qualification is that independence only seems to apply to some response measures. In a simple non-competitive situation, measures of response probability such as resist-ance to extinction and latency usually support the assumption of independence, but measures of response amplitude and vigor do not. Many tests of independence rest on the assumption that habits acquired under different drive conditions will be qualitatively the same. But from a practical point of view it is now apparent that an impressive amount of experimental control must be exercised in order to guarantee that animals under different drive conditions will not learn different habits. From a theoretical point of view it now seems that behavior strength depends upon a host of factors, of which drive strength is but one. In addition, many demonstrations of inde-pendence rest on the assumption that $_sE_R$ can be directly measured as response speed, and this assumption is difficult to validate.

In complex learning situations the assumption of independ-ence is apparently justified for a wide variety of performance meas-ures. However, the evidence in this case does not provide substantial support for independence because it is not clear how D is supposed to combine with the various Hs in highly response-competitive situations to determine performance. Thus while it is not unreasonable to assume the independence of D and H, this assumption remains primarily an assumption, or a hypothesis, rather than an established fact.

The effects of irrelevant drive

One aspect of Hull's conceptualization of D is that different sources of D should be mutually interchangeable, at least as far as their contribution of D is concerned. A response established under hunger, for example, should also be energized by thirst. If the original hunger condition is still present, then there should be a *summation* of the hunger- and thirst-produced contributions to D, and the response should occur with greater strength than under the original hunger condition alone. On the other hand, if the original hunger condition is completely satisfied, the response should still occur with some strength because of the *substitution* of thirst-produced D. Hull's gen-eralized-drive concept, therefore, generated two new experimental problems: Is there, in fact, drive summation; and is there, in fact, drive substitution? Recall that Perin (1942) extinguished a bar-press response in groups of animals under 3-, 16-, and 22-hour food depri-vation (see Fig. 5-3). Hull (1943), quite reasonably, extrapolated backward from the data points and concluded that even at 0-hour deprivation the response would be maintained at something in the order of 25 percent of its maximum strength. Hull attributed this activation in the absence of hunger to the energizing of the bar-press habit by irrelevant drive conditions such as thirst, fear, exploration, and sex, which are still present in the test situation. These drives are called *irrelevant* because they remain unreduced in the hunger-food situation.

The empirical basis for Hull's assumption of activation under very low levels of hunger was examined by Koch and Daniel (1945) and Saltzman and Koch (1948). They used procedures and apparatus as much like Perin's as they could, and hence the results provide a good indication of what Perin might have obtained had he run these groups in the original study. It was found that as food deprivation was reduced below 3 hours, there is a dramatic drop in the strength of responding. Koch and Daniel found that performance at 0 hour was only 2 percent of the 24-hour level instead of the 25 percent Hull had expected from his extrapolation. These results with a resistance-to-extinction measure were nicely corroborated by Kimble (1951) and Horenstein (1951) using other response measures (compare Fig. 7-13).

The issue would seem to have been settled, but it was not. For one thing, there was other evidence besides Perin's (e.g., Elliott, 1929; Finch, 1938; Zener & McCurdy, 1939). For another, the concept of generalized drive (the idea that one source of tension might activate an activity relevant to another source of tension) was not new; it had already been given considerable emphasis in the writings of Freud and Lewin. But what probably made the generalized-drive hypothesis seem most plausible was the publication of several irrelevant-drive experiments that appeared, at least for some time, to give it empirical support. Let us look first at some of these drive summation studies.[6]

The summation of hunger and thirst. Hull's law of drive summation was first tested by Kendler (1945), who trained five groups of rats under 22-hour food deprivation to press a bar for food and then extinguished the response. Throughout the experiment the different

[6] Here and there throughout this chapter the word "drive" will be bandied about as though there were no question that there really are drives. To allay any possible confusion on this point let me say that, for example, a drive summation experiment is *not* one in which the experimenter adds drives; it is one in which he imposes simultaneously two sets of antecedent conditions. Whether in doing this he is producing two drives, two sources of drive (D), or doing something else altogether different can only be judged when the data from the experiment, and other related experiments, are analyzed. But we call such experiments drive summation experiments because (1) that is what the experimenters called them, and (2) it is verbally economical.

groups were under 0-, 3-, 6-, 12-, and 22-hour irrelevant water deprivation (water was never available in the test situation). The four lower irrelevant-drive groups gave a monotonic rise in resistance to extinction, just as Hull's combination law required. But there is a marked and statistically significant reversal with the last group. As Kendler observed, Hull's combination law appears to require some modification, at least in the case of a strong irrelevant drive state.

There might be some question here, though, whether the obtained differences in resistance to extinction reflect differences in $_sH_R$ built up in acquisition, differences in total effective drive strengths in extinction, or some combination of acquisition and extinction effects. It may well be that although all animals received the same number of reinforcements, different groups may have learned topographically different responses; and although the rate of acquisition was controlled by the experimenter, different groups may have acquired different amounts of inhibition, and so on, during the acquisition trials. Possible differences in habit structure would seem to be excluded, however, in a study by Danziger (1953) in which all animals learned to bar press for food under 22-hour food deprivation, but some had an irrelevant 17-hour water deprivation. Extinction performance was tested under either hunger, thirst, or both hunger and thirst. The response measure (reaction time during extinction) showed slightly superior performance as a result of the irrelevant drive during acquisition, but extinction performance was markedly superior under hunger alone than when it was combined with any of the irrelevant-drive conditions.

Siegel (1946) also found that animals trained while hungry to press a bar for food showed somewhat less resistance to extinction if a 22-hour irrelevant thirst was added to the 22-hour hunger. These studies, then, are in accord in showing that strong irrelevant thirst reduces the resistance to extinction of a hunger-learned response.

Kendler and Law (1950) extended these studies by considering both food and water as both the relevant- and the irrelevant-drive conditions and also by examining behavior during acquisition. It was found that whether the irrelevant condition was hunger or thirst, more errors were made in learning a maze than were made by control groups run without an irrelevant drive. The inhibition effect was highly asymmetrical, however; the thirst-relevant groups made many more errors than the hunger-relevant groups, and the thirst-with-irrelevant-hunger group made a particularly large number of errors. This general pattern of findings was corroborated by Levine (1956), who also found that both irrelevant hunger and irrelevant thirst increased errors in learning a T-maze.

While the decremental effect of a strong irrelevant drive in both acquisition and extinction seems well established, there remains some possibility of a genuine facilitory effect with relatively weak irrelevant-drive conditions such as Kendler had originally reported

Theory of motivation

(1945). To examine this possibility, Bolles and Morlock (1960) ran animals to food under 24-hour hunger and 0-, 12-, 18-, 24-, 36-, or 48-hour irrelevant thirst. To check on the generality of the summation effect, another group was run with the roles of hunger and thirst reversed. Performance was measured during the acquisition of an alley-running response; latencies and running times were recorded. The animals in the Bolles and Morlock study served as their own controls, running under the different irrelevant drive conditions in a counterbalanced order. It was found that performance under the low irrelevant-thirst conditions was significantly better (faster starting speeds and running speeds) than under hunger alone. And, as Kendler had originally found with resistance-to-extinction scores, high irrelevant thirst impaired performance. The facilitory effect was not symmetrical, however, since *all* levels of irrelevant hunger produced decrements (relative to the 0-hour irrelevant condition) for thirsty animals running to water. Thus only part of the results was consistent with the idea that low levels of irrelevant drive facilitate performance. The same asymmetry has also been found by Reynierse et al. (1970) in gerbils. This is an interesting finding because the hunger-thirst interaction phenomenon is quite different in gerbils than in rats (see page 167).

Thus whether superimposing an irrelevant-drive condition will facilitate or inhibit performance seems to depend upon what the particular relevant and irrelevant drive conditions are, as well as their severity. Bolles and Morlock's results suggest another qualification based upon the fact that

> neither the facilitory nor the decremental effects of irrelevant drives were present initially; both types of effect develop during successive testings, and even develop during the three daily trials. Hence, the animal's performance in the situation cannot be wholly determined by the deprivation conditions under which it runs. These conditions are too static to account for the dependence of performance upon the animal's prior experience, particularly its experience on the immediately prior trial. It is as if the animal does not know how fast to run under a given deprivation condition until it has (just) encountered the goal box under that particular condition. This aspect of these results suggests the operation of an incentive factor. . . . (Bolles & Morlock, 1960, p. 378.) Reprinted with permission of publisher.

Once again we find that a motivational phenomenon that seemed at first to offer the possibility of quantifying the energizing property of drive has turned out upon further analysis to be inconsistent with the hypothetical properties of the drive construct. And furthermore we find that the behavior in question seems to call for an incentive theory of motivation.

The substitution of hunger and thirst. Hull's treatment of irrelevant drive also involved the hypothesis that a response established on the basis of one drive condition would be activated by a second drive condition even when the first drive condition no longer existed. Webb (1949) was the first to test this hypothesis using a drive substitution paradigm. He trained five groups of rats under 23-hour food deprivation to press a panel for food. Four groups were then satiated for food but deprived of water for different periods of time, 0, 3, 12 and 22 hours; the fifth group was maintained under the original 23-hour food deprivation. Resistance to extinction of the food-learned panel-pushing response was measured, and the results are shown in Fig. 8-4. Webb's finding has been replicated by Brandauer (1953) and McFarland (1964). Earlier, Miller (1948a) had found that rats that had been trained to run for water, when satiated for water, ran faster under irrelevant hunger than without it. Miller interpreted this finding in terms of generalization of the drive stimuli; the animals could not, as it were, tell the difference between hunger and thirst, and so they tended to run under the inappropriate conditions.

There are other explanations, though, for Miller's results, as well as for those of Webb and Brandauer. In Miller's case, for example, the previously relevant reward was present during the testing under the irrelevant drive, suggesting a possible secondary reinforcement factor; that is, the sight and smell of food may not only be a secondary reinforcement for hungry rats but for thirsty ones as

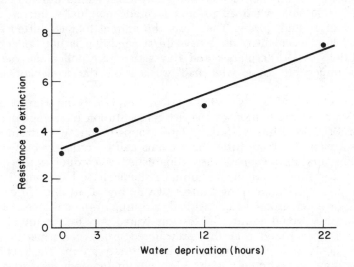

Figure 8–4

Median resistance to extinction of a hunger-learned habit as a function of hours of irrelevant thirst in rats satiated for food. (From Webb, 1949) Copyright (1949) by the American Psychological Association. Reprinted by permission.

well. Zeaman and House (1950) have pointed out two other difficulties. First, how does one define absence of the relevant drive? Should one just let the animal stop eating as Kimble (1951) did, tempt it with new food as Koch and Daniel (1945) did, induce it to overeat by social facilitation (James, 1953), or punish it for not eating (Williams & Teitelbaum, 1956)? The trouble, Zeaman and House point out, is that hunger has no natural zero point, and we have not yet arrived at any convention to define satiety operationally. The second methodological problem with the early studies of drive substitution was that they failed to take into consideration the operant level of the criterion response (i.e., the strength of the response prior to the acquisition training).

There have been several reports (Elliott, 1929; Teel, 1952; Teel & Webb, 1951) of cases in which animals after being trained to run to food were not markedly disrupted when their motivation was suddenly shifted from hunger to thirst. Such a finding lends some further support to the hypothesis that different sources of drive may be substituted for each other.

Doubt was cast over this whole set of drive-substitution studies using hunger and thirst, however, by Verplanck and Hayes' (1953) systematic investigation of the interaction of hunger and thirst. What Verplanck and Hayes discovered was that hunger and thirst could not be manipulated independently, at least not by the simple procedure of picking out food pellets or taking away water bottles a given number of hours before testing. We have noted earlier (page 166) that when an animal is made nominally thirsty, it is both hungry and thirsty. Therefore, the animal that is shifted from an old hunger condition to a new thirst condition is not under new conditions at all. Verplanck and Hayes therefore pulled the rug out from under all those who had worked on the irrelevant drive problem.

Grice and Davis (1957) tested Verplanck and Hayes' drive interaction interpretation of the drive-substitution effect against the generalized-drive interpretation. Two groups of rats were trained to press a panel for food; after the animals had been deprived of water for 22 hours the response was extinguished. According to the drive-interaction interpretation, the animals should have had considerable thirst and some interacting hunger at the time of testing. Grice and Davis gave one group water just before testing in the absence of food, so that they would go into the test motivated only by the interacting hunger. They found that this prewatered group performed significantly better than the standard 22-hour thirsty group. The fact that responding was stronger with thirst eliminated indicates that the irrelevant-thirst condition was actively suppressing the response and that responding was being maintained in thirsty animals by their interacting hunger.

So the hunger and thirst period in the history of the generalized-drive concept was brought to an end. Although there continues to be considerable interest in the interaction of hunger and thirst, the area no longer seems a proper place to investigate problems of drive summation and drive substitution.

The interaction of other drive conditions. What happens when a response is learned by hungry rats with food reinforcement and then the strength of the response is tested when the animal is no longer hungry but is motivated by some kind of aversive stimulation? The answer seems to depend on the natures of the aversive stimulation. Miles (1958a) reported that neither reducing the temperature nor injecting cocaine produced specific activation of a previously learned bar-press response. Both treatments increased the rat's general activity, but there was no disproportionate increase in bar pressing relative to the rat's other behavior in the test situation, which there should have been if (1) bar pressing is the predominant behavior in the situation, and (2) these treatments motivate behavior by increasing the level of drive.

On the other hand, it has been found that bar pressing that was previously learned with food reinforcement could be specifically activated in satiated rats by flooding the cage with water (Webb & Goodman, 1958; Siegel & Sparks, 1961). These investigators also found an increase in a variety of behaviors, but there was a greater increase in pressing the previously reinforced bar than in pressing a dummy bar used to assess the heightened level of general activity. Evidently, the drive-substitution paradigm works sometimes. But why only sometimes? Dees and Furchtgott (1964) found no evidence of intersubstitutability when they switched rats from hunger to shock escape or vice versa in a T-maze. Babb (1963) and Babb et al. (1969) found suppression going from shock escape to hunger or thirst. Perhaps the only possible conclusion is that to which Hull himself had already retreated in 1952: ". . . at least some drive conditions tend partially to motivate into action habits which have been set up on the basis of different drive conditions" (Postulate V, part D).

What happens if hunger is the irrelevant-drive condition and this motivation is added to that produced by aversive stimulation; is there summation in terms of added strength of the escape response? Again, the result seems to depend upon what the aversive stimulation is. If the stimulus to be escaped from is bright light, then there is little or no summation (Strange, 1954; Dachowski, 1964); if it is cold water, then conflicting reports can be cited (Braun et al., 1957; Rollins et al., 1965); if it is shock, then the picture is even more complicated. Dinsmoor (1958) reported that hungry rats escaped shock no better than satiated ones, and Leander (1973) found they were a little worse in avoiding it. But Franchina (1966) reported that hunger did facilitate escaping from shock when animals were given just a single escape trial. Thus Franchina was measuring the facilitation of hunger on an unlearned or unconditioned response to shock.[7] When Amsel (1950) studied the effect of hunger on a shock-escape response, he found facilitation only after a fair amount of shock-escape training had been given (and only after animals had been reassigned to groups and their performance had, for some reason, begun to deteriorate, so that it is not clear what the facilitation effect really means). Let us then leave this unsettled area and look at summation and sex.

Jarmon and Gerall (1961) failed to get any drive summation with irrelevant hunger and relevant sexual motivation in male guinea pigs. Turning this combination around, irrelevant estrous motivation in female rats has produced mixed results on hunger-motivated behavior; while there is no effect in maze performance (Ball, 1926), there is what looks like increased vigor of bar pressing (Moss, 1968). When estrous female rats are left to their own devices, they eat less than normal (Tarttelin & Gorski, 1971), which results in an appreciable weight loss, and they appear less motivated to bar press for food (Harris & Heistad, 1970). These latter inhibiting effects are impressive enough to suggest that they have a basis in the physiological state of the animal, that is, that the hormonal conditions producing estrus interact with the conditions that ordinarily regulate food intake and that the inhibition is not just due to response competition or some other behavioral mechanism.

In case the reader has at this point formulated a hypothesis that is consistent with all of the prior data, he can test it with the following relatively reliable phenomenon. Shock that is painful enough to elicit defensive behavior provides considerable facilitation of copulatory behavior in the male rat; it appears to cut short the refractory period that normally follows intromission (Barfield & Sachs, 1968; Caggiula & Eibergen, 1969).

Fortunately, the drive theorist is the only one who is obliged to treat this literature systematically. His usual approach is to say that when facilitory effects are found, they can be attributed to the contribution of irrelevant sources of drive to total D, while inhibitory

---

[7] There is an entire separate literature showing the effects of different motivation conditions on reflexive and unlearned behaviors of various kinds. This research starts with Carlson (1913), who found that the knee-jerk reflex was facilitated by hunger. This looks like a generalized-drive phenomenon; but the knee-jerk reflex is also facilitated by clenching the fist or gritting the teeth (Courts, 1939). Are these effects also to be put under the category of generalized-drive effects? This is the kind of difficult problem that the arousal theorists have tried to cope with (e.g., Duffy, 1951, 1957; Malmo, 1959). Recent developments in this area are well summarized by Bartoshuk (1971). The most significant trend is that arousal is beginning to be thought of as being like incentive rather than like drive. The reason for the shift in orientation is that when a physiological index of arousal, such as the well-studied index heart rate, is measured in an experimental situation, it increases with deprivation, as expected, but only in the presence of cues (such as the experimental situation itself) that signal reinforcement (Hahn et al., 1964; Eisman, 1966).

effects can be attributed to competing response tendencies introduced by the irrelevant motivation conditions. But this constitutes no explanation of the various kinds of behavior involved. One could just as plausibly argue that the inhibitory effects are due to motivational competition and that the facilitory effects only result from compatible response tendencies being introduced by the irrelevant-drive conditions. The fact that the generalized-drive hypothesis predicts summation gives it no advantage (since only about half of the studies have come out to support the prediction), nor does the fact that the summation hypothesis generated so much of this research add any credit to it.

The drive summation literature not only fails to provide any substantial support for the general proposition that sources of drive can summate, it also fails to reveal very much about the various kinds of behavior that have been studied. While the investigation of hunger and thirst and how they interact has gradually indicated how the physiological bases of hunger and thirst are interrelated, there have been no comparable gains in other areas. Part of the trouble has been that the research effort has been scattered over a lot of different combinations, and much of it consists of single small studies by many different researchers, so that none of the various effects, either facilitory or inhibitory, has been established with much reliability.

The situation is a little better in the case of "emotionality" and the facilitory effect it appears to have on thirst-motivated behavior. Siegel and Siegel (1949) gave control rats drinking tests after a period of deprivation. The experimental group was given a mild shock just prior to the test and drank somewhat more during the 2-hour test than the unshocked control group. This effect has been replicated using different procedures by Siegel and Brantley (1951), Amsel and Maltzman (1950), and Levine (1965), but not by Ellis (1957) or Levine (1958). It is well established that under most conditions shock will disrupt or suppress ongoing consummatory behavior.[8] Why then does emotionality have the opposite effect? Amsel and Maltzman (1950) contend that emotionality is a particular state of agitation or arousal that follows shock and persists for a period of an hour

---

[8] This is certainly the case with strong shock; with weak shock, for example, 0.2 milliamperes or less, the results are not so simple. Sterritt (1965) reported that with weak shock there may be increased eating during shock; Moyer and Baenninger (1963) and Moyer (1965) have found that even at shock intensities that suppress drinking, the suppression may only occur for a few days of testing, after which there is facilitation. Moyer suggested that the suppression phase is due to the distracting novelty of emotionality rather than its motivational effects and that the facilitation phase is due to a genuine drive summation. But a simple interaction effect seems more likely: If the shocked animal reduces its intake for a few days (Sterritt, 1965; Pare, 1965), a subsequent increase in intake may be merely a homeostatic readjustment. In any case, both of these factors, novelty of the situation and overall daily intake, must be controlled before any assessment of drive summation can be made.

or two afterward. They distinguish between emotionality on the one hand and pain and fear on the other, partly on the basis of this relatively long persistence. Thus whereas pain is an immediate and short-term reaction to aversive stimulation, fear persists longer, and emotionality longer still. A further difference is that emotionality is an internal motivational state dependent only on the animal's recent history; fear and pain are elicited by external stimulus events and are, accordingly, less dependent upon the animal's prior state. Another point of difference is that fear is a learned reaction while pain and emotionality are unlearned reactions; therefore, they constitute primary sources of drive. Moreover, Amsel and Maltzman (1950) suggest that both pain and fear are apt to introduce competing responses (unconditioned as well as previously learned defensive reactions), while emotionality does not, at least not in the naïve animal. Therefore, emotionality should be more likely to lead to summation. Some guarantee against the occurrence of emotionality-elicited behavior is obtained by testing animals in a situation that is distinct from the one in which shock is experienced; thus if an effect is found, it must be attributed to the altered state of the animal rather than to any common element of the external stimulus situations. In accordance with this interpretation Amsel and Cole (1953) found that drinking was suppressed in a situation like the shock situation, in contrast with the facilitation found by Amsel and Maltzman when they tested rats in a different situation. On the other hand, Miller (1948a) reported that rats shocked before running to food performed better than controls, whether they were shocked in the maze apparatus or in a separate apparatus. Perhaps the difference between the two studies depends upon the different responses that were being measured, drinking on the one hand and running on the other. Perhaps the different temporal factors are important. Levine et al. (1959) also obtained Miller's result when rats swam to get out of the water instead of running to get to food.

There is some evidence for an effect upon drinking of an emotionality factor that persists longer than a few hours. There are reports of captive wild rats drinking more than comparable domesticated rats, and Boice (1971) has shown that this is particularly true of the most emotionally reactive animals and the ones whose scars indicate that they had lost social status contests in the wild. The implication is that the low social status of these animals produces a stress reaction that leads them to drink excessively for many days. The variety of evidence that has been discussed suggests that there may be a genuine effect of prior aversive stimulation upon subsequent drinking behavior.[9]

[9] There is also an extensive literature reflecting attempts to validate the concept of generalized drive by showing that there are consistent individual differences in drive strength. These attempts have invariably failed. This dismal literature was reviewed by Bolles (1967) and does not need to be discussed again.

In summary, then, about the most that can be said is that some combinations of drive conditions seem to produce a facilitation of behavior, but other combinations do not. Which rule applies to any given combination of drive conditions must be determined for that particular combination because there do not seem to be any general rules. There is very little support for the idea that different sources of drive are mutually substitutable and mutually additive. There now seems little justification for the assumption that all of the different possible sources of drive contribute to the determination of behavior by the qualitatively equivalent contribution they make to D. Rather, it seems more plausible (although admittedly less parsimonious) to suppose that each source of motivation provides its own kind of motivation and its own specific response tendencies.

The reinforcing function of drive reduction

One of the fundamental propositions in Hull's drive theory is that any condition of the organism that can serve to produce drive can also serve as reinforcement when it is reduced. Certainly, this sometimes occurs. In the natural order of events the animal is hungry, it makes some instrumental response, it finds food, and it consumes the food. Subsequently, the animal has less drive and more habit strength for the instrumental response. But there are several questions here: Does the consumption of food, the stimulus consequences of consumption, or the subsequent reduction in drive constitute the critical event in reinforcement? Or, on the other hand, is it possible that the animal would have learned the instrumental response just by making it and that the presence of food merely motivates the animal to perform? These fundamental questions cannot be settled merely by observing again and again that the rat learns to work for food. It is necessary to intervene in the customary order of events, to make some unusual experimental manipulations, if we are to determine whether there is a crucial event that constitutes reinforcement, and if so, what it is.

Reinforcement as need reduction. Hull et al. (1941) trained a dog to go to one side of a T-maze to receive fistula feeding. On the other side of the maze the animal was permitted to sham eat. (This was a double-fistula preparation with one tube discharging the contents of the mouth and the other tube leading to the stomach.) In the course of eight test days the animal overcame its original preference for the sham-eating side and learned to go to the fistula-feeding side. Hull et al. interpreted these findings as evidence for the need reduction interpretation of reinforcement.

But this conclusion is perhaps a little too strong; the results indicate only that the dog learned to satisfy its need for food, not that learning occurred because the need was satisfied. There are some difficulties here. First of all, if the need reduction interpretation is taken literally, then it must be explained how learning could occur with so few or such long-delayed reinforcements. If there is some mechanism for bridging the temporal gap—whether it be an innate or an acquired cue to reinforcement (such as stomach distention, change in the circulatory system, or change in the extracellular water pool) —then the triggering of that mechanism might well be what constitutes reinforcement in the fistula-feeding situation. Specifically, perhaps under normal circumstances the taste and texture of food in the mouth reinforces instrumental behavior, and as Le Magnen (1969) has suggested these learned cues to the normal beneficial effects of eating lose their value for the sham-eating animal when the normal beneficial effects no longer occur.

Such a conceptual device solves the problem of how learning can occur with the long delay that must necessarily occur between the instrumental food-getting response and the ultimate reduction in need. The problem comes right back in a new form, however, because the cue value or the reinforcement value of food in the mouth now must be learned, so that it reflects the nutritional value of the food. How can this learning occur when the value of the food in reducing the animal's need is not known for an hour or more after eating? We will see in Chapter 9 that such learning can occur. Interestingly, the ultimate reinforcer in this scheme is still need reduction, but it is not implicated in the strengthening of instrumental behavior, only in the more limited capacity of establishing secondary reinforcers, such as the taste of food, which in turn strengthen instrumental behavior.

Another possibility is that food in the mouth loses its palatability when the dog sham eats so much. Hull noted that the dog sham ate 80 percent of its body weight before quitting.[10] Perhaps such an experience is sufficient to debilitate the mechanisms that ordinarily govern the head factors in eating. Perhaps passing this tremendous amount of food through the mouth makes it aversive. Thus Hull et al. may have been witnessing the extinction of the consummatory response and the normal incentive motivation for eating rather than the reinforcement of the instrumental response. More work should be done with sham eating.

Reinforcement without need reduction. One alternative to Hull's need reduction hypothesis of reinforcement is that reinforcement occurs when the consummatory response is permitted to occur.[11]

---

[10] It is curious that the dog would sham eat so much; it sham drinks an amount of water that closely approximates its deficit. Such findings suggest that the mouth meter is less effective in satiating the dog than stomach distention (see page 155).

[11] This idea was certainly implied by some early writers (e.g., Craig, 1918), but it did not attract much attention until it was revived by Sheffield, with whose name the idea has subsequently been associated.

Sheffield et al. (1951) found that sexually naïve male rats would learn an instrumental response when they were rewarded by being permitted to copulate with receptive females. This in itself is not surprising, but there was a gimmick in the experimental conditions —ejaculation was not permitted. Although some part of the consummatory response occurred, drive was presumably not reduced. In fact, it seems reasonable to suppose that the animal's sexual excitement, and hence drive, was increased by that part of the consummatory behavior that was permitted to occur. Nonetheless, there was learning.

This general finding has been replicated by Kaufman (1953), Kagan (1955), and Whalen (1961). In Kagan's study three groups of animals were run—one was permitted only to mount, another was permitted intromission, and the third was permitted to ejaculate. It was found that mounting alone was a relatively ineffectual reinforcement; the instrumental response was not maintained. Intromission without ejaculation led to somewhat better learning, somewhat faster running, and better maintenance of behavior; but learning was fastest for the group for which ejaculation was permitted. Thus Kagan argued that whereas the occurrence of the consummatory response, or even some components of it, can be reinforcing, greater reinforcement occurs when drive is reduced. But as we saw in the discussion of the sexual consummatory response, it is not clear that a reduction in drive can be equated with occurrence of ejaculation, since in the rat the copulatory mechanism seems to be sensitized rather than satiated by ejaculation. What does weaken with ejaculation is interest in the female, that is, the arousal mechanism. Thus we have the paradox that either the weakening of arousal (the ejaculation condition) or the increase in arousal (the intromission condition) can be reinforcing. The principal finding still stands, though, and that is that copulation without ejaculation is reinforcing even though it increases rather than decreases the animal's motivation.

According to Sheffield, then, it is not the reduction in the animal's need that matters but whether it can make a relevant consummatory response. Further evidence to support this hypothesis comes from a pair of studies (Sheffield & Roby, 1950; Sheffield et al., 1954) in which it was found that hungry rats would learn an instrumental response when reinforced by the drinking of saccharin. Sheffield found that there are marked individual differences in saccharin drinking and that these differences were highly correlated with the individual differences found in speed of running for saccharin. Saccharin is not supposed to have any nutritive value, hence the possibil-

---

The consummatory response hypothesis was briefly outlined by Sheffield et al. (1954) and described in more detail in a paper that was privately circulated in 1954 but not published until some years later (Sheffield, 1966).

ity of need reduction would seem to be ruled out.[12] Similar findings
with nonnutritive solid food have been reported by Taylor (1969).
Again Taylor found that food with the same taste and physical
characteristics was more reinforcing if it did have caloric content, but
the striking finding is that it would produce some new response learning even when it provided no calories (see also Dufour & Arnold,
1966).

Reinforcement as drive reduction. Miller (1955, 1956, 1957) has
placed a somewhat different emphasis upon the results of the sac-
charin-drinking studies and arrived at a quite different conclusion.
Miller (1957) reports that animals that had drunk saccharin solutions showed a reduction in the amount of it that was drunk immediately afterward (see also Jones, 1970). It was also found that the
prior drinking of saccharin inhibited bar pressing for saccharin,
although no such inhibition was found when it was placed directly
into the stomach through a tube. From these findings Miller concluded that saccharin is a reinforcer (since it maintained the instrumental response), but he also concluded that *drinking saccharin
reduces drive*. It is important to note that this latter conclusion
implies a definition of drive that is different from Hull's. For Hull
drive was always closely related to the animal's bodily needs, and Hull
often used "need" and "drive" interchangeably. Miller, on the other
hand, is one of those who have taken the decisive step of cutting the
usual antecedent ties of the drive construct in order to obtain a more
coherent picture of its behavioral consequences.

Although Miller has said repeatedly (e.g., Miller, 1951) that
for him drive means any strong source of stimulation, this definition
only seems to pertain to the case of aversive motivation. In the
appetitive case we have little evidence of any strong noxious stimulation that drives the animal into activity and that the animal seeks to
terminate. Recall that the Campbell and Sheffield studies of general
activity had presumably demonstrated that there were no such motivating stimuli in the case of hunger. What we find instead is that
there are certain antecedent conditions the presence of which motivate consummatory behavior and the alleviation of which reinforce
instrumental behavior. These behavioral properties define drive for
Miller in all practical cases of appetitive behavior. Thus we find that
he accepts a reduction in motivation as evidence of drive reduction.[13]

[12] Saccharin is evidently not inert, however, because it affects in
various ways the interaction of blood sugar and insulin (Jorgensen, 1950;
Smith & Capretta, 1956; Valenstein & Weber, 1965). But perhaps these are
conditioned reactions (see footnote page 146).

[13] Miller has noted that it is hazardous to rely too much on any
one behavioral criterion of drive; multiple anchoring should always be
sought. For example, Miller (1957) reported that blowing up a stomach
balloon inhibits eating in hungry animals, but he rejected the possibility

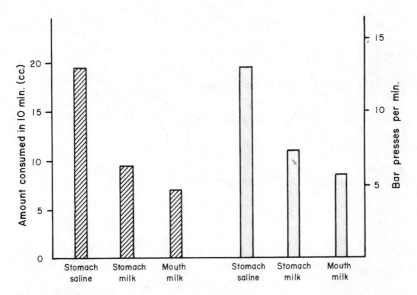

Figure 8–5

Amount of milk consumed and performance of an instrumental response after injection of saline, injection of milk, or ingestion of milk. (Adapted from Berkun et al., 1952, and Kohn, 1951) Copyright (1951 and 1952) by the American Psychological Association. Reprinted by permission.

A pair of studies from Miller's laboratory by Kohn (1951) and Berkun et al. (1952) showed that milk injected directly into the stomach inhibited eating more than did an equivalent injection of saline solution, but it failed to inhibit eating as much as an equivalent amount of milk drunk by mouth. Moreover, the same relative drive reduction under these three conditions was found for the criterion of bar pressing for food (see Fig. 8–5). Hence, Miller argued, there is evidence for two factors in drive reduction, a factor involving food in the stomach and a factor involving food in the mouth. Together they produce more drive reduction than either one alone.

An exactly parallel experiment with thirst (Miller et al., 1957) yielded parallel results. Water by stomach loading was drive reducing by a consummatory criterion but not as much so as normal drinking by mouth. Better evidence of reinforcement than the mere maintenance of behavior comes from another study (Miller & Kessen, 1952)

that this operation involves drive reduction because it failed to reinforce instrumental learning. It should also be noted that after defending it so staunchly for so many years Miller (1963) has subsequently questioned the reinforcement hypothesis. We will consider this development in Chapter 9, but here we must look at Miller's earlier defense of the hypothesis and some of the important research it has generated.

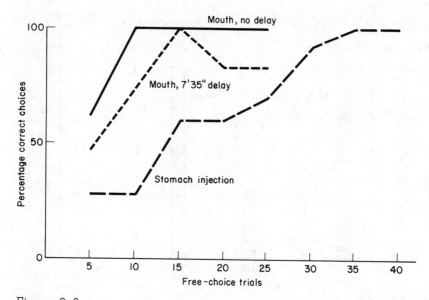

Figure 8–6

Acquisition of T-maze performance by animals previously given milk in different ways. (From Miller & Kessen, 1952) Copyright (1952) by the American Psychological Association. Reprinted by permission.

of stomach loading with milk.[14] It was found that the injection of milk directly into the stomach through a tube not only depressed subsequent consummatory behavior but also served to reinforce the acquisition of a new instrumental response. These acquisition data are shown in Fig. 8-6.

While it is evident that the stomach-injection group showed learning, its performance always lagged far behind the performance of a group that was permitted to drink milk in the usual manner. As the speed-of-running scores make clear, the mouth-drinking group always showed much more impressive motivation for their particular reinforcement than the stomach-injection group did for theirs. It would, therefore, seem extremely unlikely that food in the stomach

[14] What makes new learning a better criterion of reinforcement than the maintenance of a well-learned response is purely definitional; reinforcement *means* strengthening an S-R relationship. Maintenance of response strength can be accomplished by any number of mechanisms other than giving a reinforcer, such as increasing D, increasing the incentive, improving the situation, reducing response competition, redefining the response, and so on. By the same token, a drop in performance can indicate a failure of reinforcement (i.e., extinction), lost motivation, stimulus change, or almost anything else. For example, the best assurance we have that Miller's stomach-injection technique does not make the animals nauseous is that Miller and Kessen could get new learning with it.

is the principal source of reinforcement in normal eating. Miller and Kessen ran another group of animals that were permitted to drink, but only after a delay of several minutes (the same time it took to tube load an animal). This group (Fig. 8-6) showed performance that was approximately intermediate, both in choice of behavior and running speed, between the other two groups. Miller argued that the stomach-injection group did not perform any better than it did because it took appreciable time (7 minutes) to perform the loading. Even so, if we compare the results of Miller and Kessen with those of Kohn (1951) and Berkun et al. (1952), it appears as though the reinforcing effect of stomach loading is somewhat slower than the satiating effect. If this is the case, then it partially negates the proposition that those manipulations that reduce drive also reinforce. The temporal difference suggests that two mechanisms are involved, one for reinforcement and another, faster one, for satiation.

This impressive series of studies by Miller and his students suggests four important conclusions. First, there does seem to be a reinforcing effect of giving food or water directly through a fistula; such a procedure can be used to produce new learning. But this reinforcement is clearly far less effective than reinforcement involving the usual mode of ingestion. Hence for all practical purposes Sheffield is correct: The animal learns when it is permitted to make the consummatory response. It is probably also true that sham eating will reinforce instrumental behavior.[15]

Second, the speed with which the head factor (and perhaps also the gut factor) operates is such that reinforcement cannot be attributed to any change in the animal's nutritive condition. Miller has said: "The prompt effects produced by these two factors relieve the drive-reduction hypothesis of reinforcement . . . from the burden of trying to account for learning in terms of the long-delayed effects of the restoration of tissue needs" (Miller et al., 1957, p. 4). Hull and others who wondered whether the crucial factor in reinforcing instrumental behavior is alleviation of the animal's need have their answer—it cannot be.

A third point in connection with Miller's findings is that an antecedent anchoring of the drive condition is in terms of prior ingestion rather than in the traditional terms of deprivation or weight loss. Thus the drive that energizes the consummatory response and whose reduction reinforces instrumental behavior is not necessarily the same drive that results from deprivation. Perhaps a parametric investigation of the relationship between the prefeeding technique

[15] There is little generality across species. Sham feeding will reinforce the dog under some conditions (James, 1963) but not the rat (see page 155) or the pigeon (Sterritt & Smith, 1965). Miller and his students showed that stomach tubing will reinforce the rat, but other investigators have found no such effect for the dog or the pigeon (James, 1963; Angermeier et al., 1964; Sterritt & Smith, 1965).

and the deprivation technique for producing hunger and thirst will show that there are systematic and predictable relationships between them. But until such evidence is available, we should not assume that so much prior ingestion is functionally equivalent to so much deprivation. The comparability found, for example, by Kohn (1951), may not represent any general lawfulness but only his fortunate use of particular parametric values (viz., 24-hour deprivation and 14 cc of milk).

A fourth point is that by severing the connection between need and drive and by taking purely behavioral criteria of drive Miller has obliterated the distinction between primary and secondary drives. The two are lumped together because they affect behavior the same way. Thus we are no longer in a position to distinguish between that component of the animal's total motivation that depends solely upon the conditions of deprivation and that other component that requires prior experience with the incentive in the test situation.

Theoretically, the distinction between primary and secondary drives is made on the grounds that primary drives are innate whereas secondary ones are acquired. Secondary drives are supposed to be aroused by external stimulation, which in the past has been associated with a primary drive. Thus the sight and smell of food and oral contact with food are supposed to produce secondary motivation in the animal because they have been associated with ingestion and assimilation of food. The evidence for this conceptualization is not very compelling in the case of hunger, and it is virtually nonexistent in the case of other kinds of motivation. Sexual behavior is reinforcing for the male rat, as we have just noted, in the absence of any demonstrable prior association with sexual drive reduction. Saccharin is a reinforcer even though the laboratory animal cannot have had any opportunity to associate sweetness with nutrition since it was weaned.[16]

[16] Some animals that nurse, like cats, do not care for sweets. Some animals, like rats and men, like sweets even when they are not hungry. Some milk is not sweet. Some animals, like pigs, like saccharin before they have ever tasted milk (Foster, 1968). Still, some theorists continue to regard saccharin as a secondary reinforcer because it is sweet like milk. Another justification for regarding saccharin as a secondary reinforcer is Carper's (1957) report that it gradually loses its reinforcing power for instrumental behavior. However, Carper found that animals would continue to drink it for extended periods of time, and so did Carper and Polliard (1953) and Smith and Capretta (1956). Moreover, Sheffield and Roby (1950) and Foster (1968a) failed to obtain instrumental extinction with saccharin reinforcement. Capretta (1962) has suggested that the acceptability of saccharin decreases with hunger; this contrasts with the results of Smith and Kinney (1956) and Campbell (1958) who found that the preference for sucrose increases with hunger. Moreover, it might be argued, the palatability of nonnutritive sweets, saccharin and xylose, drops relative to sucrose as deprivation increases (Sheffield & Roby, 1950; Smith & Duffy, 1957a; Smith & Capretta, 1956). But this is probably true of Purina too, so Capretta's argument can also be discounted.

Procedurally, primary and secondary drives are distinguished by the different antecedent conditions that produce them, deprivation or intense stimulation in one case and prior experience with the reinforcer in the other. Abolishing the distinction does not imply that antecedent conditions for the newly defined drives cannot be found but only that the antecedent anchoring must be done differently. And we may also expect that it will be considerably more difficult. In any case, while Miller's strategy (see also Brown, 1961) may save the drive reduction hypothesis, it is costly; it requires a new concept of drive.

Reinforcement without sensory feedback. Another alternative to the drive reduction hypothesis of reinforcement is that the stimulus consequences of the consummatory response—food in the mouth, erotic stimulation, or whatever—is the vital factor in reinforcement rather than drive reduction or the occurrence of the consummatory response. Ordinarily, of course, the consummatory response and its stimulus feedback occur together. But there have been some attempts to effect a separation. For example, Thomson and Porter (1953) ran animals in a T-maze to a salt solution after the animals had been made sodium deficient and had been surgically deprived of their sense of taste. The animals gave some indication of learning even though, presumably, they could not sense the salt (see also Krieckhaus & Wolf, 1968).

Coppock and Chambers (1954) found that animals would learn an instrumental head-turning response in order to get an intravenous injection of glucose. A control group given injections of xylose (a nonnutritive sugar) also showed some indication of learning but not as much as the glucose group. Although these results provide evidence of reinforcement in the absence of consummatory behavior, it is not so clear that the sensory events that normally accompany ingestion have been prevented. Chambers (1956) has suggested that there may be an immediate reaction of the taste mechanism to sugar injections; this appears to be the case in human subjects. It has also been found that glucose injection leads to a slight but prompt temperature rise, which surely has some stimulus consequences and which may even be reinforcing in itself (Chambers & Fuller, 1958; see also Chambers, 1956a).

Epstein (1960) has developed a procedure with which it is possible to maintain rats without letting them drink or eat (Epstein & Teitelbaum, 1962). Whenever the rat presses a bar, food is pumped directly into the stomach. Although the learning of the response is extremely difficult to obtain under these conditions (Holman, 1969; Snowdon, 1969), once it is learned, the rat can regulate its intake over an extended period of time. Epstein and Teitelbaum were also able to show that rats would adjust their bar-pressing behavior very quickly and accurately to provide a constant daily caloric intake when the caloric payoff of a bar press was varied. If this variation in the animal's daily amount of bar pressing can be attributed to the reinforcing effect of nutritive input, then we have evidence of reinforcement in the absence not only of any consummatory behavior but also many of the usual stimulus consequences of consummatory behavior. Certain stimuli are still present, however, from among those normally resulting from ingestion; for example, there are those arising from stomach distention. Holman (1969) has reported that in order to get any reinforcement effect with this procedure it is necessary that the liquid flowing into the stomach be cold. The stomach tube in the Epstein preparation passes through the head, so Holman's results suggest that cold sensations in the head may be a necessary part of reinforcement in this situation. Both Holman and Snowdon (1969) also report behavioral anomalies such as the rat's chewing on the bar instead of pressing it. Therefore, Epstein's preparation, which promised to demonstrate reinforcement in the absence of sensory feedback, turns out to provide very little reinforcement without there being some feedback. Furthermore, it seems likely that the more substantial reinforcement effects found when food is ingested normally results from the greater feedback that normal ingestion entails. Whether any reinforcement would remain if all feedback could be completely eliminated seems to be a relatively unimportant issue.

Reinforcement by brain stimulation. A still more unusual and violent intervention in the usual consummatory behavior → need reduction → drive reduction order of events is effected in those situations in which reinforcement is produced by direct stimulation of the brain. Electrodes located in the lateral hypothalamus deliver brief, mild electrical stimulation whenever the animal presses a bar (Olds & Milner, 1954). Under these conditions animals rapidly learn to press the bar at a very high rate and will persist in doing so until overcome by sheer exhaustion. Almost simultaneously with and independent of Olds' work was the discovery by Delgado et al. (1954) of areas in the brain where electrical stimulation appeared to have negative reinforcing effects. Cats were trained to make an instrumental response to a buzzer in an ordinary avoidance situation. The buzzer was then paired with electric stimulation of several different areas of the brain. It was found that the animals made the learned response as if avoiding the brain stimulation. Subsequently, it has been found that under certain conditions direct stimulation of certain areas of the brain can produce fear reactions (Delgado et al., 1956) or can be used as an unconditioned stimulus for avoidance learning (Cohen et al., 1957). Some of these opposing effects (both positive and negative reinforcement) may result from differential electrode placement (Olds, 1956), but sometimes both rewarding and punishing effects of stimulation can be found with the same electrode placement (Roberts, 1958). Some different results may be due to the different species involved or to different durations or different electrical properties of shock (Bower & Miller, 1958). For example, it appears that when current is presented to an area that has been found to be positively reinforcing, its onset may have a positive effect, whereas its continued presentation is aversive (Stein, 1962). (See also Keesey, 1962, 1964; Poschel, 1963; and the excellent review by Olds, 1962.)

There can be very little doubt, however, that when all the conditions are right, direct brain stimulation can be used not only to reinforce bar-press behavior but also the learning of a runway and even the correct path through a maze (Olds, 1956a; Spear, 1962; Mendelson & Chorover, 1965). The vexing question here for the diehard drive reduction theorist is what is the nature of the drive that is reduced by electrical stimulations. Perhaps an appropriate drive can be invented. Perhaps it will turn out that stimulation in appropriate areas by-passes ordinary drive conditions and produces some immediate effect that is comparable to the more commonplace effect of drive reduction. Or it may be that stimulation of the "joy center" constitutes reinforcement just because it is pleasurable (Heath & Mickle, 1960, report that human subjects like it). Maybe pleasure constitutes reinforcement whether it is brought about directly by stimulation or whether it is produced naturally by the animal engaging in those kinds of behavior it enjoys.

The most interesting and promising approach to the brain stimulation phenomenon is to think of it, not as providing reinforcement, drive reduction, or joy, but rather as providing motivation. There are several variations of this idea. One is based on the discovery that reinforcing stimulation often elicits responses that resemble consummatory behaviors. It is known that some of the brain areas where stimulation is reinforcing are the same as those, for example, the lateral hypothalamus, from which feeding behavior can be elicited. Olds (1955) went further in his assertion: "All electric stimuli seem to evoke postures or automatisms that have something to do with approach to food, or attack on prey, or defense, or ingestion, or other behaviors associated with self-preservation" (p. 123). Olds has reported that an electrode placed in an area associated with hunger loses its direct reinforcing effect when the animal is satiated and gains in effectiveness when the animal is made hungrier. If androgen is injected, a treatment that should make sexual behavior particularly reinforcing, then again self-stimulation in the "hunger" area occurs at a lower rate. Similarly, it appears to be the case that when the animal is deprived of food, its rate of pressing will decrease if a high rate of pressing had been obtained under the effect of androgen. Thus there seems to be good evidence for interactions between hunger, sex, and perhaps other drives, on the one hand, and the reinforcement effects of electrical self-stimulation, on the other. These relationships suggest that one of the mechanisms underlying the reinforcing effect of electrical stimulation is the elicitation of behaviors from the lower brain centers.

After reviewing this kind of evidence, Glickman and Schiff

(1967) conclude that reinforcement, whether produced naturally by giving food to a hungry animal or produced artificially by stimulating the lateral hypothalamic area, always involves the elicitation of some species-specific behavior pattern. In effect, their hypothesis is like Sheffield's: The stimulation of the consummatory response (actually, the neural motor systems that produce it) constitutes reinforcement.

A second variation of this idea has been suggested by Deutsch and Howarth (1963) and Gallistel (1964). Their proposal is that lateral hypothalamic stimulation not only stimulates reinforcement centers of the brain but also stimulates motivation centers at the same time. Such a dual action would help account for (1) the poor resistance to extinction generally found in self-stimulation studies, (2) the poor carry-over of performance from one session to the next, (3) the breakdown of behavior on intermittent schedules and with spaced trials, and (4) the failure to find substantial secondary reinforcement based on brain stimulation. All of these effects are inconsistent with the enormously high rates of responding found when stimulation is presented on a continuous reinforcement schedule. Deutsch and Howarth (1963) propose that stimulation produces short-term motivation lasting a few seconds. Once the system is "primed" by stimulation, the animal will be motivated for more of it and simultaneously reinforced by receiving it. But following stimulation the motivation soon dissipates and the behavior collapses.[17]

A third approach is typified by Ball and Adam's (1965) hypothesis that brain stimulation is not itself reinforcing, but its short-term aftereffects are aversive. The rat pressing the bar for brain stimulation is said to be like the drunkard who does not particularly care for alcohol but drinks to get rid of his hangover. This possibility is at least consistent with a drive reduction interpretation of reinforcement.

Thus the phenomenon that was originally discovered by Olds and Milner in 1954 looked for some time as though it would permit the experimental psychologist to by-pass the normal reinforcement procedures, and would reveal the neurological basis of reinforcement and provide a direct test of the drive reduction hypothesis.

---

[17] All of these considerations are discussed in excellent reviews by Trowill et al. (1969) and Valenstein (1973). Trowill et al. attribute most of the previously cited peculiarities of brain stimulation as a reinforcer to the lack of prevailing drive rather than to failure of reinforcement. They also note that there are now contradictory reports on each of these peculiarities. They conclude that while the Deutsch and Howarth argument is generally correct, the stimulation-elicited motivation is more like incentive than like drive. This argument is supported by the remarkable discovery of Mendelson (1966, 1967) that stimulating a rat in an area that elicits eating (and presumably hunger) fails to *motivate* running in a T-maze for food or water, but when this stimulation is given in the goal where it can elicit eating or drinking, it *reinforces* the appropriate turning response.

But it has turned out to be a rather complex phenomenon, sharing with many other psychological phenomena the potential for showing us that things are not the way we thought they were. We have indeed found out something from the self-stimulation effect about reinforcement, but what we have found is a little disturbing. Reinforcement is difficult to measure (Valenstein, 1964), and the closer we come to measuring it, the more trouble we have distinguishing between reinforcement and motivation (Trowill et al., 1969). But whatever the ultimate nature of reinforcement turns out to be, it seems likely that reinforcement by electrical brain stimulation involves something other than drive reduction.

Drive induction as reinforcement. A number of writers during the 1950s invoked drives to account for learning on the grounds that learning must require drive reduction. For example, when an animal spends time in a part of the apparatus where there is no food or mate or anything else except the novelty of the apparatus itself, we may say that the animal has a tendency to explore. But when it learns a response in order to get to where it can explore, then we are tempted to talk about a drive to explore (Nissen, 1930; Montgomery, 1954; Myers & Miller, 1954). There are two difficulties here. In the first place, there is usually no evidence other than the learning at hand to indicate the existence of drive. Therefore, invoking a new drive represents the worst kind of circularity. The situation would be more secure if there were multiple anchoring of exploration; but, as we saw in Chapter 6, there do not seem to be any independently measurable antecedent conditions for exploration.

In the second place, even if there is such a drive, there is little justification for attributing learning to its reduction. By any reasonable criterion, drive would seem to be increased and not decreased when the animal explores. When the animal learns to find a situation that it can explore, it would appear as though it is the *induction* of the exploratory drive that reinforces the instrumental response. If, in fact, the drive is aroused by novelty, as Harlow (1953) insists, then what makes the animal seek it? On the other hand, while the attempts to explain exploration and spontaneous alternation by introducing the concept of a boredom drive (e.g., Myers & Miller, 1954; Brown, 1955) are not beset by these difficulties, they have others that are serious enough (see Fowler, 1967).

In considering Sheffield's work with incomplete sexual consummation we found a similar situation; it seems much more in accord with all observations of animals that the behavior that gets the animal to the goal is reinforced by the excitement, the arousal, or the increase in motivation that occurs there rather than by the quiescence that may follow some time later. It has also been argued (e.g., Maltzman, 1952; Sheffield, 1966) that in the case of hunger, too, it is the increase in excitement or the stimulation provided by food that reinforces running to food. These arguments apply equally well to the case of the alleged activity drive, thirst, and the other appetitive drives. The special problems encountered by the drive reduction theory of reinforcement in accounting for avoidance learning are so complex and so important that we will devote all of Chapter 10 to them. Suffice it to say here that these problems are so imposing that they have led most behavior theorists to abandon the drive reduction hypothesis as a universal principle of reinforcement and even to question the idea of reinforcement.

The stimulus concomitants of drive

Virtually all theories of motivation make some provision for a special class of stimuli that do more than just contribute to the associative control of behavior. Sometimes these stimuli are said to goad the animal into activity. Sometimes they are said to motivate the animal, to motivate behavior, or to motivate learning. In Hull's system this kind of stimulus is called a drive stimulus, or S_D. The stimuli that are suppose to arise from stomach contractions or from a dry mouth or from erotic stimulation or from electrical shock are not considered to provide motivation but merely to accompany the drive-producing conditions. They have no special properties other than some significance for the animal's survival; that is, these are the stimuli to which the animal must associate adaptive behavior if it is to survive.

Drive discrimination studies. In view of the functional importance of these stimuli, Hull (1933) must have been a little surprised to find that his rats required a great deal of training in order to discriminate between hunger and thirst and that discrimination was not very reliable even with extensive training. Hull had trained rats to turn one way in a T-maze to obtain water and the other way to obtain food. The animals were run alternately hungry and thirsty. It appeared as though the rat cannot easily tell when it is hungry and when it is thirsty.

Leeper (1935) reported a similar study in which considerably faster learning was found. Part of the improvement could be attributed to the fact that Leeper used two goal boxes that were spatially separated, one for hunger and one for thirst, whereas Hull had used one box and required the animals to learn different paths to it when hungry and thirsty; Fig. 8-7 diagrams the apparatus. Leeper argued that the animal does know when it is hungry and when it is thirsty but that in Hull's situation it has difficulty learning where the food and water are. Leeper's cognitive interpretation has engendered some discussion (Seeman & Williams, 1952; Deutsch, 1959) but little research, and most writers have simply concluded

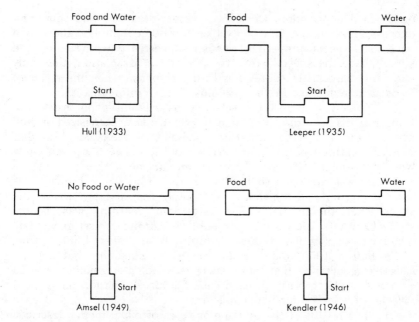

Figure 8–7

Schematic diagram of apparatus used in four drive discrimination experiments. (From Bolles, 1970b) © *Collier-Macmillan. Reprinted by permission.*

that there are discernible stimulus consequences of food deprivation and water deprivation to which the animal can associate differential responses.

Kendler (1946) reported a drive discrimination study that posed a problem for this interpretation, however. He trained rats simultaneously hungry and thirsty in a situation in which food was on one side of a T-maze and water was on the other; the animals were forced alternately to the two sides. After surprisingly few trials, the animals showed that an appropriate discrimination had been acquired. That is, when made just hungry or just thirsty on a test trial, the animals went to the appropriate side significantly more frequently than would be expected by chance. While this result is intuitively plausible (it presents no problem for Leeper's interpretation), it is somewhat embarrassing for Hullian theory. Consider the situation when the animal is, say, both hungry and thirsty, makes a turn to the left, finds food, and eats. The turning-left response should become equally conditioned to the stimuli arising from hunger and the stimuli arising from thirst. But what happens, in fact, is that the hunger-produced stimulus evidently acquires greater associative loading than the thirst stimulus. Otherwise, the animal would not have been able to make the appropriate response when tested under food deprivation. Obviously, hunger-produced and thirst-produced stimuli cannot be exactly like any other stimulus; they must have some special properties. Kendler suggested that drive-produced stimuli have the special property of selective association; they only enter into associative connection with a response when the response leads to a reduction in the stimulus (i.e., reinforcement).

One way to test the selective association hypothesis is to train animals on a discrimination in which the hypothesized stimuli arising from hunger and thirst are used as cues even though neither hunger nor thirst is a relevant drive condition. The first such study was by Amsel (1949), who trained animals on a shock avoidance task that was arranged so that when the animal was hungry, one response terminated the shock and another response terminated the shock when the animal was thirsty. Some learning was demonstrated, but only after a great amount of training. Amsel and others who have done similar studies (Winnick, 1950; Baker, 1950; Levine, 1953; Bailey, 1955; Bailey & Porter, 1955) conclude that a strict selective association hypothesis such as Kendler originally proposed cannot be correct.[18] But in each case the discrimination has proved to be an extremely difficult one to learn.

The results of the four major types of experiments described here present us with an interesting theoretical paradox. The basic experimental situations are shown in Fig. 8-7. Hull and Leeper, using very similar procedures but somewhat different apparatus, found quite different results. Hull obtained poor discrimination, whereas Leeper's animals found the problem very easy. Kendler, using conditions that should have made discrimination impossible, found rapid learning, whereas Amsel in attempting to simplify the problem by eliminating eating and drinking made it almost unsolvable for his animals. How is this pattern of results to be understood? What experimental parameter distinguishes the effective procedures from the ineffective ones?

The most obvious answer to the puzzle is that the discrimination is easy when the animal eats and drinks in different places and it is difficult under other conditions. In effect, Leeper was correct: Separation of the goal boxes is the critical parameter, but only when eating and drinking occur in them. There are two ways to explain this phenomenon. One is Leeper's original idea that in such studies the rat is not usually discriminating its internal states at all but is learning where the food and water are. If they are well

---

[18] Kendler's selective association hypothesis encountered further difficulty with irrelevant-drive experiments by Kendler and Law (1950) and Woodbury and Wilder (1954). Therefore, he gave it up (Kendler et al., 1952, 1954), attributing all of these effects—the original drive discrimination, the decrements produced with irrelevant drive (Kendler & Levine, 1951), and the asymmetrical effects of hunger and thirst—to incentive motivation mechanisms, that is, to r_G rather than to S_D.

separated, the problem is easy; if they are at the same location, as in Hull's experiment, there is confusion; if there is no eating or drinking, then the state of the organism itself can constitute a basis for solving the problem, but this is a difficult and unnatural task for the rat. The second approach to the problem is that proposed by Kendler et al. (1954) based upon the theoretical incentive motivation mechanism r_G. Like Leeper, Kendler contends that the differential S_Ds play very little part in the discrimination when differential external cues are available, but his argument is otherwise quite different. The hypothetical r_G mechanism will be discussed more fully in the next chapter. Suffice it here to say that the argument assumes that (1) during training eating becomes conditioned to environmental cues surrounding the food reward, and drinking becomes conditioned to cues surrounding the water reward; and (2) during the test the animal tends to approach those cues that have been associated with its existing motivation condition. The r_G interpretation, therefore, accounts for the rapid acquisition of drive discrimination in situations in which it is rapid (Leeper, 1935; Kendler, 1946), as well as the poor performance in Hull's situation. It also makes sense of the fact that drive-discrimination learning is always quite slow when hunger and thirst are irrelevant, for when there is no eating or drinking, there can be no conditioning of the appropriate r_Gs.[19]

It could be argued that S_D discrimination is difficult to get, not because there are no stimuli, but because S_Ds have a slow onset —they arise gradually over a long period of time. Bolles and Petrinovich (1954) attempted to overcome this handicap by means of a drive-switching procedure in which rats to be made hungry were first deprived of water for 22 hours and then offered water in the absence of food for 1 hour. Presumably the animal suddenly finds itself hungry during the course of drinking. A parallel procedure was used to produce a more rapid onset of thirst: Animals were food deprived and then given food in the absence of water. Unfortunately, while Bolles and Petrinovich obtained very rapid discrimination, they did not run the controls necessary to determine to what the rapid discrimination could be attributed. Actually, there have been few systematic studies to indicate what variables affect the ease of drive discrimination. Besch et al. (1963), using an irrelevant-drive procedure, found that the noncorrection method led to much faster learning than the correction method.

[19] The minimal drive discrimination learning found with irrelevant hunger and thirst may also depend upon r_G. There may be some generalization to the test situation from those situations in which consummatory behavior does occur. Minimal r_Gs may also occur as a direct consequence of the deprivation conditions, more or less independently of environmental conditions. Hence it may be that even when drive discrimination proceeds poorly, the acquisition that is obtained is also attributed to r_G mechanisms; this possibility should not be ruled out.

Further circumstantial evidence of drive stimuli. While some search for the locus of deprivation-produced stimuli, others invoke such stimuli for theoretical reasons whenever the behavior of animals shows some sort of associative dependence upon the conditions of deprivation. Thus S_D acquires the status of a theoretical construct. For example, Eninger (1951) found that a T-maze shock-escape response was more resistant to extinction when the animals were both trained and extinguished under the same irrelevant-drive condition (either hunger or thirst) than when they were switched from hunger to thirst or thirst to hunger. Hence it would appear that changing the irrelevant-drive conditions decreased the stability of performance in extinction, suggesting that the irrelevant-drive-produced stimuli can acquire appreciable stimulus control over the escape response. This clear-cut effect with nondiscriminative stimuli is a bit surprising in view of the aforementioned difficulty others have had in demonstrating associative control in a discrimination setting. Unfortunately, Eninger's acquisition results are not presented, so that it is not possible to determine whether, for example, there may have been some asymmetry in the acquisition results perhaps based on the interaction of thirst and susceptibility to shock.

In a similar study Wickens et al. (1949) found that reversal and relearning of a T-maze position habit occurred more quickly if the animal's relevant-drive condition (hunger or thirst) was changed so that a given position in the maze was associated with a given drive condition (and relevant consummatory response). This finding was interpreted in terms of the classical associative and retroactive inhibition paradigm, and it was taken as evidence for the reality of S_D.

Bolles (1958) replicated the overall effect found by Wickens et al. but noted that there were marked asymmetries in the pattern and number of errors made both in the reversal learning and in the relearning phases of the experiment. The superiority of the reversed-drive groups in reversal learning appeared to be largely due to the performance under one condition, namely, one in which a hunger-learned habit was reversed by thirsty animals (H-T). Animals under other conditions (T-H, H-H, and T-T) all showed comparable performance. Error scores were analyzed by distinguishing between those made prior to the first correct reversal response, pre-errors, and errors made after the first correct response, post-errors. It was observed that animals tested while hungry tended to make far fewer pre-errors but more post-errors than animals tested while thirsty. On the other hand, in reversing a hunger-learned habit there were characteristically fewer pre-errors and more post-errors than in reversing a thirst-learned habit. This pattern of results could be explained on the basis of Petrinovich and Bolles' hypothesis (1954) that hungry animals tend to be more variable in such situations than thirsty animals or on the basis of the tendency of thirsty animals to avoid a place associated with food (Kendler & Levine, 1951).

Another argument for there being discriminably different stimulus consequences of different conditions of deprivation are the demonstrations that animals can learn different responses to different intensities of deprivation conditions, that is, so-called drive-intensity discrimination. Drive-intensity discrimination has been reported by Bloomberg and Webb (1949), Jenkins and Hanratty (1949), and Bolles (1962a). Although Bolles obtained relatively rapid learning, discrimination has usually required extensive training and has not reached a high level of proficiency. The demonstration of drive-intensity discrimination opens up again, of course, all the same questions about the locus of the stimulus. Are such animals making the discrimination on the basis of stomach distention or some kind of metering of the consummatory response? Are the animals discriminating different consequences of r_G? We do not know.

Another sort of circumstantial evidence for drive stimuli comes from those studies (Rethlingshafer et al., 1951; Manning, 1956) in which animals are trained to get water on one side of a T-maze and food on the other and are then tested under a combination of different hunger and thirst conditions. Presumably, response competition will occur by virtue of associative interference of the stimuli arising from hunger and thirst. Both Rethlingshafer et al. and Manning agree in finding that with 23 hours of water deprivation, indifferent performance (50-50 on the T-maze) occurred when the irrelevant food deprivation was something like 16 hours. When the hunger and thirst roles were reversed, Rethlingshafer found again a cross-over point at about 16 hours, whereas Manning reports the value to be somewhere above 23 hours of irrelevant water deprivation. This discrepancy and, indeed, all of these results seem rather unimportant in view of the fact that the incentive variables, which play such a dominant role in hunger and thirst motivation, were not equated in value.[20]

Generalization and anticipation effects with drive stimuli. There have been a number of studies in which the motivation conditions

[20] The Manning paper has many virtues, including that of being the first (or one of the first) animal motivation studies to use estimation statistics rather than traditional inference statistics. But how can any conclusion be drawn about the relative strengths of drive prior to some assessment of incentive motivation? Manning equated the amount of time for eating and drinking, but this does not guarantee an equation of the incentive values of the food and the water. (Rethlingshafer et al. did not even describe their incentive parameters.) Hence these results would seem to have no more claim to indicating the relative strengths of hunger and thirst motivation than those of Warden et al. (1931).

of animals are shifted during the course of acquisition either once (Elliott, 1929; Hillman et al., 1953) or many times (Teel, 1952). Moreover, there are many latent-learning experiments in which the animal responds in the old way when drive conditions are shifted to a new set of conditions (Kimble, 1961). There are in addition (as we saw in discussing the independence problem) a number of studies in which drive conditions are shifted in intensity during the course of learning. Thus high-drive and low-drive groups are trained and then split in half and tested either under the same or under the shifted drive conditions. Any asymmetry in the pattern of results indicates a generalization decrement insofar as the performance of animals tested under shifted conditions is inferior on the average to the performance of animals tested under the same conditions. Although a number of such drive-shift studies have been conducted, only one gives any indication that the particular level or intensity of drive conditions had entered into the associative control of the criterion behavior. In this study (Yamaguchi, 1952) animals were trained under 3-, 12-, 24-, 48-, and 72-hour deprivation and then switched in a factorial design to 3, 24, 48, and 72 hours for testing. Although the transfer effects were all in the direction predicted by an associative interpretation, the effects were all small, and, in fact, only one comparison was significant. Once again, then, it seems that if drive stimuli enter into the associative control of behavior at all, they do so only very weakly.

A study by Birch et al. (1958) at first seemed to provide more substantial evidence of hunger-produced stimuli. Animals were maintained for 35 days in a specially constructed living cage equipped with a food trough that contained food only for 2 hours during a 24-hour period. The principal response measure was the number of food trough contacts. Early in training the number of approaches to the food trough was more or less constant over the 24 hours. But by the 35th day the animals rarely approached the food trough except in the hours immediately before the regularly scheduled meal, indicating a rather precise temporal discrimination. A striking result of the study was found when the regular feeding was omitted on the last day. As the time for eating passed, the number of approaches to the food trough again dropped back down, suggesting that the particular stimulus magnitude resulting from a 24-hour food deprivation had acquired discriminative control over the response of approaching the food trough.

It would appear that Birch et al. had found, at last, substantial evidence to demonstrate the existence of deprivation-produced stimuli. Unfortunately, however, it is entirely possible that the stimuli controlling food-trough contacts in the Birch study did not arise from the particular state of deprivation but were strictly temporal in origin. Over the course of 35 days, external cues to the time of day might acquire associative control over the criterion response, and perhaps it was such external stimuli rather than anything that can be called S_D that produced the gradient. Supporting such an alternative explanation was the fact that as the 48th hour without food drew near, there was a second increase in the number of approaches to the food trough.[21]

Bolles (1961a) attempted to test this external or appetitional hypothesis by letting rats press a bar for 1 hour for food either every 24 hours or every 29 hours. On the 24-hour cycle the time of day and the possible internal stimuli arising from deprivation were confounded, as they were on the experiments just discussed; under the 29-hour condition, though, the effects of deprivation-produced and time-of-day-produced stimuli could be isolated. Animals were maintained under the appropriate conditions for 15 deprivation cycles following which different groups received the opportunity to press the bar after the usual deprivation time or at deprivation times 5 hours longer or shorter than the training deprivation time. The 24-hour animals showed significantly shorter latency to press and greater resistance to extinction when tested at 24 hours than when tested at either 19 hours or 29 hours. These results, which are shown in Fig. 8-8, confirm those of Birch et al. However, the animals trained on a 29-hour cycle showed no such symmetrical generalization gradient. Both response measures increased continuously with deprivation time and fell uniformly below those of the 24-hour animals tested at 24 hours. Similar results have been obtained with activity wheels (Bolles & de Lorge, 1962b; Bolles & Stokes, 1965). Rats fed every 19 hours or every 29 hours in wheels failed to show any anticipation (increased running) at the regularly scheduled but adiurnal feeding time, whereas rats fed every 24 hours did, of course, show a large anticipation of the regularly scheduled diurnal feeding.

These findings indicate that deprivation time per se has little to do with either the anticipation of cyclic feeding or the maintenance of the rat's normal activity cycle. The cues that control the rat's activity and anticipation of daily feedings seem to be temporal. If the environment provides stimuli with a 24-hour periodicity, then these stimuli will control the animal's motivated behavior. But if the environmental stimuli provide no 24-hour periodicity, then the animal ignores them and shows some evidence of responding to interval stimuli that have a period near 24 hours. This conclusion suggests once more that the direct-stimulus consequences of deprivation play a very small role in the determination of behavior.

There is no more apt summary than that written some

---

[21] In a similar study Brown and Belloni (1963) failed to obtain an anticipation effect; this is one of the few failures to find anticipation when rats are fed regularly at the same time each day.

Theory of motivation

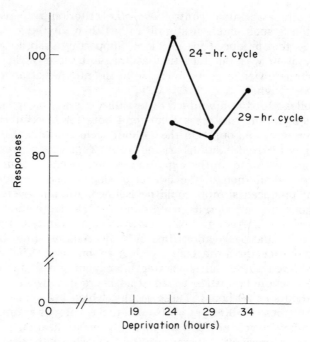

Figure 8–8

Mean number of extinction responses as a function of hours deprivation of rats trained on a 24-hour cycle or a 29-hour cycle. (From Bolles, 1961a) Reprinted with permission of the publisher of Psychological Reports.

years ago by Webb (1955) after reviewing much of the same material we have covered here:

> The data support a notion that the conditioning of responses to drive stimuli is not easy, and, where external cues are readily available, drive stimuli are likely to play only limited roles in mediating behavior. There is a trend, with increasing supportive data, to further restrict the role of the drive stimulus. There are indications that the "fractional anticipatory responses" may provide mediating stimuli in drive situations in place of the drive stimuli themselves. The situation may be quite different for drives other than hunger and thirst and in the human. From the data here reviewed, it is easy to suggest, however, that extensive theoretical use of the concept of drive states alone as cues is likely to be charming but unsupportable. (Webb, 1955, p. 296.) Reprinted with permission of author and publisher.

I would only add that 20 years later it still appears that the attempts to demonstrate S_D experimentally have succeeded instead in demonstrating the importance of r_G.

Summary

It took a long time for the drive concept to become clarified, but once the primitive notion was put into empirically testable form, primarily by Hull and his students, it did not take long for its inadequacies to be revealed. In Chapter 6 we saw that the great enthusiasm with which early researchers sought to connect motivated behavior with automatic, physiological adjustments and needs of the organism has been frustrated time and again. The idea that an animal's motivation reflects its need for this or that commodity in order to establish homeostatic equilibrium has only occasionally been demonstrated experimentally. The idea that an animal's motivation is an automatic adjustment to its state of need is attractive and appealing, but it is not justified by the facts. What the evidence seems to indicate instead is that most of the time an animal's motivation is itself learned and that if we are to explain its behavior, we must do so by using constructs other than drive.

We have seen in Chapter 7 that there is an energization effect but that it is limited. What Hull proposed for drive in general has not been demonstrated in general but is really applicable only to the case of hunger. Even with hunger, much of what Hull proposed is apparently not valid. Indeed, about all that can be said with assurance is that the rat's weight loss is directly related to the probability of eating and whatever instrumental behavior eating depends upon. As soon as the contingencies between behavior and reinforcement are removed, the evidence for any kind of motivational effect begins to collapse. It is true that the hungry rat explores and runs in an activity wheel more than nonhungry rats, but this seems more parsimoniously explained in terms of specific relationships between hunger and these kinds of behavior. All we have left, then, is the energizing of consummatory and instrumental behavior.

In the present chapter we have found that D and H are not really independent, that different sources of drive are not motivationally equivalent, that drive reduction does not constitute reinforcement, and that the stimulus concomitants of drive have no real existence. The different sources of drive are characterized more by their differences than by their common properties. And even hunger, which conforms best with theoretical requirements is more dependent upon learning, various associative factors, and incentive motivation than upon the generalized activation that Hullian drive theory required. However, the worst failure of the drive concept is that it provides little help in explaining behavior. By the time we have discovered what the associative determinants are for any particular behavior, there is very little left for D to explain.

9

MOTIVATION
AND
LEARNING

People are not born with a tendency to strive
for money, for the discovery of scientific truths, or
for symbols of social status and security. Such
motives are learned through socialization.
N. E. Miller

Probably few psychologists ever seriously entertained the idea that we are born with all of our motives. All of us, even the rat, have learned motives. The rat works for food as much because of its learned expectation of food as because of any primal thing gnawing at its stomach. Psychologists have gradually come to accept this idea, but there is as yet little agreement as how best to explain it or even to state it. In the present chapter we will consider a variety of alternative models that have been proposed to explain how some or most or perhaps all of an animal's motivation is learned. One kind of model suggests that under appropriate conditions drive itself is learned. A second type of model emphasizes incentive factors as something different from D, having different functional properties and producing different effects upon behavior. The third type of model maintains that the whole concept of motivation is expendable and that in the last analysis it is the learning of behavior that should concern us. Such models emphasize the part reinforcement plays in the regulation of behavior, while minimizing or discounting altogether the role played by any kind of motivational factor. Finally, we will look briefly at cognitive models, which maintain that reinforcement mechanisms play little or no part in the regulation of behavior. Motivational principles are of the utmost importance in cognitive models, but they are quite different from drivelike principles.

The attempt to assess these alternative models will carry us into new areas of animal motivation. It will take an extensive tour of the topics in the next several chapters to come to any decision about the usefulness of these different kinds of models in the explanation of behavior.

Acquired-drive models

From our present vantage point it seems strange that anyone would think of a homeostatic, automatic, unlearned, physiologically based motivator, such as drive, as being susceptible to learning. But remember that it was only Hull's particular drive concept that had this aspect of unlearnability, and prior to Hull's (1943) formulation there was a period of time when the word "drive" was used to describe a great variety of different motivational ideas. Some of these other motivation concepts were eminently learnable. The earliest examples were called social drives.

Acquired social drives. Tolman (1926) suggested that there are really two kinds of drives, primary or unlearned drives, which have some discernible physiological basis, and secondary or derived drives, the physiological bases of which are either lacking or unknown. He supposed that the derived drives depend in some yet to be determined manner upon the primary drives. For example, curiosity (a derived drive) might be assumed to vary according to some functional relationship with hunger (a primary drive). Later, Tolman (1932) developed the idea that the social drives develop "in the service of" the primary drives. Thus the young individual may become socially cooperative, gregarious, and so on, as a means of satisfying some more basic primary drive such as hunger or comfort.

Still later (1942, 1943), Tolman suggested a mechanism for this learning, namely, that social drives arise when primary drives are frustrated. Thus if the young organism is frustrated in its satisfaction of hunger, it might become more independent and self-assertive, thereby obtaining food, as it were, by force. Alternatively, the organism might become more dependent and self-abasing, thereby obtaining food by guile. When one or another of these modes of adjustment meets with success, it tends to become stabilized and habitual, and to the extent that it generalizes to other situations, one of these modes of adjustment could become what we call a social motive.

Thus in Tolman's thinking the social drive emerges as a well-learned habit or response tendency. Such social habits provide their own motivation without depending (except historically) upon other, extrinsic sources of motivation. In Chapter 3 we saw how, in the hands of Henry Murray, such a conception can be used to describe a great variety, perhaps almost all, of human behavior. Allport (1937) opposed the idea that human motives have anything but the most remote connection with man's physiological needs. He proposed instead that the adult's motives are self-sustaining contemporary systems that are functionally independent of the historical conditions that initially may have produced them; man's motives are "functionally autonomous." Note here that Allport did not deny the historicity of primary drives in human motivation but only their relevance to understanding the adult. The label "functional autonomy" merely reminds us, in case we should need reminding, that man's social motives have no contemporaneous connection with his physiological drives.

All of these schemes, and certainly many others as well, have considerable intrinsic interest and perhaps provide useful descriptions of behavior. But in no case do they come close to approximating an adequate explanation of social behavior. For the most part these schemes are based upon logical considerations and flourish without support from systematic empirical findings. Logic requires that if we are to have drives to explain behavior, then we must have social drives to explain social behavior. Logic tells us that since so much of man's behavior is learned, the reasons of his behavior must also be learned. But there are essentially no data on the acquisition of human social behavior, and these conceptual schemes have not been conducive to the collection of data.

Brown (1953) has emphasized that ordinarily what is referred to when speaking of a social drive or an acquired drive is simply the occurrence of some particular behavior that is relevant to a social situation. Thus we speak of a "drive for money." But Brown observes:

> In many instances, if not all, where adult human behavior has been strongly marked by money-seeking responses there appears to be little need for postulating the operation of a learned money-seeking drive. One does not learn to have a drive for money. Instead, one learns to become anxious in the presence of a variety of cues signifying the absence of money. The obtaining of money automatically terminates or drastically alters such cues, and in so doing, produces a decrease in anxiety. (Brown, 1953, p. 14)

The only so-called drive here is the anxiety that may occur in the absence of money. This is not to say that money may not be a reinforcer; it presumably is because it terminates anxiety, which is a drive-producing condition. Moreover, money may come to be a secondary positive reinforcer through its association with anxiety reduction and through its association with food and other good things in life. But to invent a drive specifically to explain money-seeking behavior is, at best, only to give the behavior a name. The same argument applies, of course, to all the social motives.

It is curious that so many writers (from Woodworth, 1918,

to Brown, 1953) who have stressed that secondary or acquired drives were only well-established response tendencies failed to see that the so-called primary drives might also be only well-established response tendencies. It would appear that primary drives were called primary as much because they had a physiological basis as because they were unlearned, and we may also suspect that the social or secondary drives were so designated, not because there was any evidence that they were learned, but because no one expected that a physiological basis for them could be found.[1]

Conditioned hunger. Dashiell (1937) suggested that the motivation characteristic of the hungry animal was only partly elicited by its internal state or nutritional condition and that the motivation to eat was also partly controlled by external stimuli, namely, those stimuli in the presence of which eating had previously occurred. In this view the whole motivational system involved in hunger was a plastic thing that could be attached to internal stimuli, such as stomach contractions, or to external stimuli, such as a familiar food dish, or to some combination of internal and external stimuli.

Seward and Seward (1937) extended this argument with the proposition that different drives occupy different positions on a continuum of internal versus external arousal (see also G. Seward, 1942). Sexual behavior was said to be relatively more dependent upon external stimulation than hunger but less so than exploration. Moreover, the Sewards suggested that through learning there is a tendency for all motivational states to shift in the direction of external arousal. We will see later that J. P. Seward and others have gone on from these assumptions to develop some very powerful theories of incentive motivation. Modern treatments of incentive motivation deal with the externally aroused component of motivation as being something other than, that is, something added to, the initial component of drive arising from the animal's physiological state. But in the early 1940s the more common assumption, and the

---

[1] This semantic problem is called to our attention perhaps most dramatically by Harlow's work on the development of affectional systems (Harlow & Zimmerman, 1959). The infant rhesus monkey has been shown by Harlow and his colleagues to require bodily comfort right from the beginning of its life, so that such a need must be unlearned. But in spite of the fact that there was nothing regulatory about the need for comfort or that anyone was likely to find any underlying cause for it in the neurological substrate, it was, nonetheless a need, as shown by the fact that animals deprived of comfort, or affection, grow up severely disturbed. Thus Harlow's work has shown the existence of needs that are real enough and give rise to motivated behavior, that are innate, but that lack the discernible physiological underpinnings of hunger and thirst. The need for bodily comfort is thus like the need to explore, and it is perhaps not just a coincidence that Harlow was instrumental in pioneering research in both areas.

assumption of Dashiell and the Sewards, was that somehow the internal state of hunger was itself aroused by external stimuli.

This concept of the external arousal of an internal state was advanced most vigorously by Anderson (1941), who also introduced the catchy phrase "externalization of drive" to describe it. In one study Anderson (1941a) trained a group of rats in a maze with food as reinforcement, then satiated them, and then ran them on a second maze without food. This group performed better on the second maze than a control group that had not had the prior experience with hunger or with the first maze. Anderson argued that because of its similarity to the first maze, the second maze had aroused hunger in the experimental group. The small difference between groups was not reliable, and the experimental and control animals differed not only in the opportunity to acquire a conditioned hunger but also in prior experience with mazes, prior experience with handling, and prior deprivation experience. Even if Anderson was correct and the experimental group had a higher drive and thus performed better, why should learning occur? Where was the reinforcement? And if there was a reinforcer, then why speak of a conditioned drive? Anderson also had replicability problems: Siegel (1943) made a careful attempt to duplicate his findings and was unable to do so.

Calvin et al. (1953) reported that they had conditioned hunger to external stimuli. Two groups of rats were placed in a distinctive box for 30 minutes a day for 24 days, one group under 22-hour food deprivation, the other under only 1-hour food deprivation. Both groups were then deprived for 12 hours and for the first time offered food in the distinctive box. The animals that had been in the box under high deprivation ate somewhat more than those that had previously been in the box under low deprivation. The difference was small, and the reliability of the difference was evidently contingent upon a covariance analysis that may not have been legitimate (Evans & Anastasio, 1968). The effect claimed by Calvin et al. has also been very difficult to replicate; Siegel and MacDonnell (1954), Scarborough and Goodson (1957), and Brozovich et al. (1963) have all reported negative results. Negative results have also been obtained when conditioned hunger has been looked for as an increment in instrumental response strength (Solomon, 1956; Dyal 1958). Negative results have also been found in comparable experiments of conditioned thirst (Novin & Miller, 1962; Pieper & Marx, 1963). However Weissman (1972) obtained both drinking and working for water in satiated animals by presenting a discriminative stimulus for water in a bar-press situation.

Myers and Miller (1954) used a still different procedure; they first trained rats in a white box to touch the door, which opened it, to get access to food in an adjoining black box. They then satiated their animals and required the performance of a new response, pressing a bar, to open the door to the black box. This response was learned, but the motivation of this new behavior could not be attributed to conditioned hunger because equally good performance was shown by control animals lacking the prior association of hunger and white box. The motivation was said, therefore, to be exploration rather than conditioned hunger. There have been reports that a distinctive box in which rats have experienced deprivation becomes aversive (Screven, 1959; Segal & Champion, 1966), but this effect too is difficult to replicate (Wike & Knutson, 1966; Swanson et al., 1966).

It might be argued that the conditioning of appetitive drives is difficult to achieve because the drive state has such a slow onset, but experimenters who have produced thirst rapidly, for example, by feeding dry food (Novin & Miller, 1962), by salt injections (Greenberg, 1954), or by hypothalamic stimulation (Andersson & Larsson, 1956) have had no better success. A more promising approach seems to be to permit animals to have differential experience with the distinctive situations and deprivation conditions, that is, to use each animal as its own control. Wright (1965) found if rats were put in one situation under high deprivation and another under low drive, they would subsequently eat more in the former (see also Trost & Homzie, 1966).

The evidence supports several conclusions. One is that satiated animals cannot readily be made hungry or thirsty by presenting them with external stimuli. Another is that if the animal is already hungry or thirsty, appropriate external stimuli may make it more so. The third conclusion is that if such an effect is genuine, it must be small, it can occur only under rather specialized conditions, and it does not markedly disturb the normal determinants of eating and drinking.

Conditioned fear. The attempts to analyze social behavior or appetitive behavior in terms of learned drives were nothing compared to the marvelous adventure that began when theorists discovered that fear could be conditioned. The story really begins back in 1916, when John Watson reported the first classical conditioning experiment to be successfully conducted in this country. Animals were restrained in an apparatus and presented with two stimuli—one, the conditioned stimulus, such as a buzzer, and the other appearing momentarily later, the unconditioned stimulus, such as an electric shock. Before conditioning, shock produced two kinds of reactions in the animals: a disruption of breathing, of heart rate, and so on, and also a reflexive movement of the foot to which the electric current was applied. After a series of presentations of both stimuli together, or pairings, both of these kinds of responses were observed to occur when the CS, which originally elicited no reaction, was presented alone. Watson had confirmed in this country the reports of numerous Russian investigators that learning could be brought about by classical conditioning.[2]

Watson did not distinguish between the two kinds of responses. For him the outcome of his experiments showed that all behavior is classically conditionable. Pairing two stimuli attaches the responses originally evoked by one of them to the other. For Watson the mere occurrence of a response in the presence of a stimulus was sufficient for a connection to be formed between them. It did not matter what the stimulus or the response was; the contiguity (occurring together) of stimulus and response was sufficient. This conception of learning was expanded by Watson and later defended at great length (e.g., Watson, 1919). A similar view of conditioning and of the universality of learning by contiguity was stated by Smith and Guthrie in 1921. We had then clearly put before us by the 1920s the idea that all behavior, including both emotional responses and instrumental responses, was learned by classical conditioning.

Meanwhile, a number of theorists more or less under the leadership of Thorndike (1911) were contending that learning occurs not as a result of the contiguous occurrence of stimulus and response but as a result of certain effects or consequences of the animal's own behavior. If the animal makes a response that leads to food, then that response will be strengthened; if an animal makes a response that terminates an aversive stimulus, then that response will be strengthened. Thorndike and his followers said very little about emotional responses because their primary concern was with adaptive, or instrumental, or operant, behavior. Thus during the 1920s we had clearly placed before us the idea that responses are learned as a result of certain consequences or reinforcements that are contingent upon their occurrence. These two conflicting conceptions of learning remained in contest for many years, and psychologists were swayed this way or that as a result of many clever experiments, but neither view was decisive. The trouble was that the evidence for emotional responses being classically conditioned became stronger and stronger while the support for the reinforcement interpretation of instrumental behavior also became more persuasive. This general pattern of results suggested a compromise that was reasonably agreeable to

[2] There were no systematic reports of Pavlov's work available in the English language until 1927, and it was not until then that Pavlovian theory and the sophistication of Pavlovian experimental procedures could be properly appreciated in this country. Bechterev's work was available in translation as early as 1913, but Bechterev's procedures were somewhat different from Pavlov's, and so was his interpretation of conditioning. Watson's interpretation was very different again, but it is primarily to his 1916 study, as well as his many theoretical writings, that we owe the tremendous enthusiasm for classical conditioning, both as a procedure and as a hypothetical learning process, in American psychology (Hilgard & Marquis, 1940).

all parties. This compromise—first proposed by Skinner (1938) and later supported by Mowrer (1947) with a host of arguments—was that classical conditioning should rule over emotional responses while reinforcement learning should reign over instrumental behavior. There were, after all, the two kinds of nervous systems, autonomic and central; and there were two kinds of behavior, emotional and instrumental (or respondent and operant), so perhaps we should expect there to be two kinds of learning.

This happy compromise soon became part of the established dogma of behavior theory. What made it dogmatic was the apparent success of Mowrer, Miller, and other drive theorists in explaining a variety of experimental results that neither the Pavlovian model nor Thorndike's model could handle alone. We will consider briefly two types of experiments; one is the avoidance learning experiment, and the other is called the acquired-drive experiment.

The avoidance learning experiment. When learning theorists first turned their attention to avoidance behavior, it was viewed as a generalized or conditioned form of escape behavior. The point is illustrated by the following hypothetical experiment. First, consider escape learning. A rat is placed in a box with a metal grid floor and given an electric shock every few minutes. Once the shock comes on, it stays on until the rat runs from one side of the box to the other. It may take several seconds for this first escape response to occur, but on successive presentations of shock the latency of the escape response gets shorter and soon comes to approach 1 or 2 seconds. This escape learning is generally rapid and durable and presents no particular problems of interpretation.[3]

Suppose now we complicate the situation slightly by programming a buzzer to go on 5 seconds before the shock and to go off when the animal runs from one side to the other. The buzzer thus serves as a signal for the forthcoming shock. As before, the rat quickly learns to escape shock, but soon a new phenomenon begins to appear. As the response occurs sooner and sooner in time, there comes a point at which the rat runs to the other side of the box before the shock comes on. Then if the situation is arranged so that these preshock responses prevent shock from occurring, they will begin to occur with increasing consistency. Thus instead of the running response being conditioned to the shock, it becomes conditioned

---

[3] Escape learning would seem to be a clear instance of learning by drive reduction, although there is a question of whether reinforcement is due to the termination of shock or to the reduction in pain or fear. However, Hullian drive theorists have been slow to study escape learning, probably because they got caught up in the explanation of avoidance learning, which they saw as a more powerful line of evidence to support the drive reduction position.

to the buzzer.[4] At this point the rat will be effectively avoiding shock. Avoidance learning data from a dog in this kind of situation are shown in Fig. 10-1 in the next chapter.

The great puzzle of avoidance behavior is to determine what reinforces it. The termination of shock, which supposedly reinforces escape behavior, cannot be effective because as the probability of avoidance behavior increases, the number of shocks is reduced. And if the animal makes a large number of consecutive responses, it removes the shock entirely. It is difficult to see how nonoccurring (avoided) shocks can reinforce avoidance behavior. Indeed, if we think of the avoidance response as simply a conditioned or generalized form of the escape response, then as soon as the animal has made a few successful avoidances, avoidance behavior should start to extinguish, that is, avoidance should be a transient phenomenon. But the fact is that avoidance behavior is often exceedingly persistent and resistant to extinction.

The way out of this theoretical difficulty was first suggested in a pair of theoretical papers by Mowrer (1938, 1939). Mowrer's approach was to assume that fear becomes classically conditioned to S+ and that it is the reduction of this fear that reinforces avoidance behavior. The role of shock is simply to condition fear to S+; it plays little direct part in establishing the avoidance response. Evidence to support this interpretation was reported by Mowrer and Lamoreaux (1946). They required rats to make one response to turn off the S+ and avoid the shock and a different response to escape the shock on those trials when they failed to avoid it. Thus any conditioning of the escape response could only interfere with the appropriate execution of the avoidance response. Nonetheless, they found good learning under these conditions—learning that appeared to be nearly as good as that of animals run under normal conditions in which the same response was effective both in escaping as well as avoiding shock. Thus the escape from shock seems to make little contribution to the strength of avoidance behavior. A further implication is that in the avoidance situation the animal is not really avoiding shock; it is escaping fear.

Further substantiation for this interpretation was obtained by Mowrer and Lamoreaux (1942). They ran three groups of rats under different conditions of S+ termination. For the experimental

---

[4] The buzzer is usually called a conditioned stimulus or CS. This usage reflects long-established custom and derives historically from an obsolete view of avoidance learning (Bolles, 1972a). It hangs on because there has been nothing better to call it. But Church (1971) has suggested that the buzzer should be called an S+. An S+ is a cue in an operant situation that the animal can do something about, whereas a CS (with or without a + sign) is a cue in a Pavlovian situation that comes on and goes off independently of the animal's behavior. I will adopt Church's designations because they will be extremely convenient later.

group S$^+$ was terminated immediately upon the occurrence of the avoidance response. For the two control groups the S$^+$ was a CS; that is, it either went off automatically after it had been on just momentarily, or else it remained on for some seconds after an avoidance response occurred. Thus for the experimental group, termination of the warning cue was contingent upon the avoidance response while for the two control groups it was not. The experimental group learned the required avoidance response more rapidly and performed it at a higher level than the two control groups. Mowrer and Lamoreaux (1942) contended that since the termination of the S$^+$ is so important in the acquisition of avoidance, the reinforcer in this situation must be reduction in the fear that is conditioned to the S$^+$. This fear is, of course, conditioned to S$^+$ on those early trials when the animal fails to avoid.

The acquired-drive experiment. The concept of fear as an acquired drive with potential motivating and reinforcing properties was given considerable support from a classic study by Miller (1948). Miller shocked rats in a white compartment and then trained them to escape to a neighboring black compartment by running through a doorway. Then in the absence of any further shock the rats were placed in the white compartment with the door to the black compartment shut; to open the door they were required to rotate a small wheel located in the wall near the door. About half of the animals did learn the new instrumental response of turning the wheel (the other half just froze). Subsequently, the wheel-turning response was extinguished, and the animals were required to press a bar in order to open the door. They learned this response too. According to the theory, the white compartment where shock was presented had come to elicit fear, and any response that got the animal out of the white chamber would be learned by the consequent reduction in fear. It should be noted that the learned responses, wheel turning and bar pressing, never occurred previously in the presence of shock, nor were they reinforced by shock termination; they were, according to Miller, new responses whose acquisition depended entirely upon the reinforcing function of fear reduction. The acquired drive interpretation was further strengthened by a pair of studies by May (1948) and Brown and Jacobs (1949) using somewhat different procedures, thereby giving the proposed acquired-drive mechanism considerable generality.

The drive theorists appeared to have a workable account of behavior in both the acquired-drive experiment and the avoidance learning experiment. In both cases the basic conception was that the acquired drive fear motivates the learned behavior and fear reduction reinforces it. In summarizing this early work of the acquired-drive theorists Miller (1951) could paint a very rosy picture; they were on the brink of being able to explain all defensive and fear-motivated behavior. In the next chapter we will see what went wrong.

The logical status of the acquired-fear drive. For the antecedent anchoring of fear there is the promise of monitoring certain reactions of the autonomic nervous system, such as increased heart rate or skin conductance, as a means of independently verifying the existence and measuring the strength of the conditioned fear. This strategy is exactly the same as trying to assess an animal's hunger in terms of blood sugar level or some other biological condition with which its motivated behavior is supposedly correlated. But an important distinction must be made between the indices of drives and the antecedent conditions that produce them. Both the indices and the antecedent conditions can serve to anchor a construct antecedently, but the logical and empirical status are quite different. For example, although we can produce hunger by depriving an animal of food, we saw in Chapter 6 that deprivation time is a poor index of hunger. We may attempt to monitor fear by measuring any of a number of possible reactions, but these reactions are not how we produce fear. Fear is produced by conditioning it to particular environmental stimuli. The experimenter's task is not so much to manipulate the state of the organism but to condition a particular kind of emotional response.

Thus on the antecedent side one difference between the acquired fear drive and a primary drive is that the latter is produced by an altered physiological state while the former is actually part of the animal's behavior. A further point of difference is that in the case of primary drive the animal's prior experience is supposed to be relatively inconsequential. Thus the argument that the animal's prior experience actually is a determinant of its eating behavior was used to argue against a primary drive interpretation of hunger in Chapter 7. By contrast, fear is supposed to be learned—it is supposed to depend upon prior experience. Without prior experience there is no fear.[5]

On the consequent side, acquired drives are just like primary drives in that they are supposed to energize behavior and their reduction is supposed to reinforce behavior. There is, however, very little direct evidence to support either of these suppositions. There is a great deal of evidence showing that animals can learn to avoid, but the reinforcing agency has been difficult to isolate experimentally, and there is no longer much reason to suppose that it is fear reduction. There is also not much reason to suppose that fear motivates avoidance behavior beyond the rather indirect and circular argument that avoidance does occur. Indeed, when we consider avoidance learning

[5] This is not to say that there are not innate fears, because of course there are (Hebb, 1946). It is true nonetheless that both in the everyday world and in the rat lab most fears depend upon the individual's experience.

in the next chapter, we will find that the whole acquired-fear-drive structure, which was specifically designed to explain avoidance behavior, is not able to do so.

Incentive motivation models

Just as the concept of drive underwent considerable conceptual evolution until put in its final form by Hull and his students, so the concept of incentive motivation has undergone considerable conceptual development, and current theory presents several alternative incentive concepts. Let us begin by looking at the classical theory of incentive as formulated by Hull.

The anticipatory goal reaction, r_G. In any trial-and-error situation the last response, the one that terminates a sequence of responses, is typically a consummatory response or goal response, which may be symbolized R_G. This R_G is elicited by the joint action of deprivation and certain specific stimuli such as the sight of food. After a number of trials we may expect that the environmental stimuli present in the goal situation will also tend to elicit R_G so that, for example, the animal will show a greater readiness to eat in a goal box where it has eaten before than in a novel box.

In the absence of an appropriate goal object, such as food, the deprivation state and the situational stimuli tend to elicit R_G, but this tendency cannot be fully realized because the stimuli arising from food are necessary for eating and also because the animal may be engaged in some other kind of activity, such as running, which is more or less incompatible with R_G. Nonetheless, Hull suggested, certain fractional components of R_G, certain parts and pieces of the total consummatory response (such as, perhaps, salivation and small incipient mouth movements) are compatible with ongoing behavior and may be elicited by stimuli to which R_G has been conditioned. Hull designated this fractional, conditionable part of the goal response r_G. We may suppose further that whenever r_G occurs, it will have certain stimulus consequences, for instance, proprioceptive feedback, which may be designated s_G. Then, if the entire experimental situation provides stimuli similar to those at the goal, r_G will tend to be elicited throughout the situation, and s_G will tend to be produced throughout the situation to provide a core of persistent stimulation that can integrate all of the animal's responses into a coherent whole.

This hypothetical r_G mechanism was proposed in a remarkable early paper by Hull (1931). As he continued to develop its implications, it became apparent that it was no longer necessary for the behavioristic psychologist to conceive of responses as being directly dependent upon external stimulation. The animal could exhibit anticipation of a goal. It could behave as though it had knowledge. It could vary its behavior in the face of obstacles (Hull, 1934); it could assemble segments of behavior into novel combinations (Hull, 1935); and its behavior could have the general appearance of adaptiveness (Hull, 1937). All these remarkably cognitive aspects of behavior could be explained, at least in principle, with the elegant assumption that the consummatory response, or some fraction of it, was elicited by environmental stimuli.

It should be emphasized that in Hull's early treatment the r_G mechanism was given only associative attributes; there was nothing motivational here—nothing like drive or incentive. And even as late as 1943, when Hull was writing the *Principles of Behavior*, the r_G-s_G mechanism was incorporated into the theory purely as an associative factor. He reasoned that when reinforcement occurs, the quantity and delay of the reinforcing agent determine the amount of reinforcement that occurs and hence the growth of habit strength. Accordingly, Hull inserted into his equations for habit strength terms involving the amount and delay of reinforcement. This then was a purely associative interpretation of incentive effects based on the r_G mechanism. A second stage of theory development, which introduced a motivational interpretation of incentive, arose as a result of the classic study by Crespi.

Crespi's study. Crespi (1942) ran different groups of rats in a straight alley one trial a day to different amounts of food. If we look at the performance of Crespi's animals during the first 20 days of running, as shown in Fig. 9-1, we can see that those fed 16 pellets on each trial performed markedly better than those fed only 1 pellet per trial and that animals receiving 256 pellets (virtually a full day's ration) performed still better. The question then is whether these differences in performance represent permanent differences in habit structure, as Hull had suggested, or merely motivational differences. To answer this question Crespi switched the conditions for his groups after 20 trials so that all animals received 16 pellets. Performance rapidly changed to levels appropriate for the new incentive values. Note particularly how rapidly, within 3 or 4 trials, the shift in running speed occurred. This change in behavior occurred more rapidly than could be reasonably attributed to a change in habit structure, that is, faster than the response was originally learned. And note finally that after the shift the animal's performance settled down to a value that corresponded to the performance of animals reinforced all along with 16 pellets; that is, there were no carry-over effects.[6] It

---

[6] Fig. 9–1 shows that animals shifted upward to 16 pellets perform better than those kept at 16 pellets. Crespi (1942) called this the *elation effect* and attributed it to a kind of emotional contrast. There is a corresponding *depression effect* in animals shifted downward. These secondary effects (secondary to the Crespi effect itself) will be discussed on page 416).

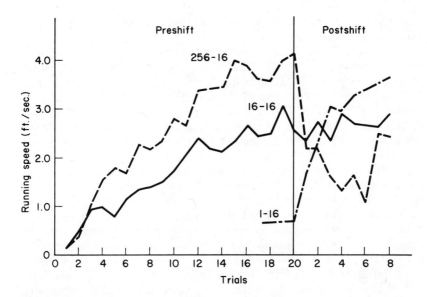

Figure 9–1

Speed of running in a long runway as a function of amount of reinforcement. For the first 19 trials different groups were given 1, 16, or 256 pellets of food (acquisition data for the 1-pellet group are not presented); after trial 20 all subjects were given 16 pellets. (Adapted from Crespi, 1942)

appears also that the different amounts of reinforcement affect the asymptote of performance but not the rate at which the asymptote is reached. All of these considerations suggest the operation of a motivational factor that multiplies the habit strength of the running response.

Hull's reaction to these findings (Hull, 1952) was to introduce a new motivational construct K and alter the old D × H equation to read K × D × H. The magnitude of K was postulated to be a function of the size or vigor of the consummatory response, R_G, which in turn presumably depends upon the amount and quality of reinforcement.

The way the r_G mechanism can be invoked to explain incentive motivation can be illustrated with some examples. In Crespi's experiment a simple runway was used. To explain Crespi's results it is only necessary to postulate (1) that animals receiving a larger number of pellets on each trial have R_G more strongly conditioned to goal-box stimuli; (2) that the stimuli present elsewhere in the apparatus are similar to those in the goal box to which R_G has been conditioned, so that these similar stimuli will elicit r_G throughout the apparatus and (3) that stronger r_G produces greater incentive motivation, K. Then, if everything else remains the same, more reinforcement will produce more motivation and faster running in the experimental situation.

For another illustration of incentive theory let us continue the analysis of Kendler's (1946) drive discrimination study, which we began on page 273. Recall that Kendler's animals were both hungry and thirsty at the time they were trained. On trials when an animal was forced to one side of the apparatus, it found water and drank; when forced to the other side, it found food and ate. Later, when tested when only hungry or only thirsty, the animals tended to choose the appropriate side. The argument is that the R_G for eating became conditioned to cues prevailing on the eating side of the apparatus, while the R_G for drinking became conditioned to cues on the drinking side. At the time of testing, an animal went to the choice point and, presumably, stopped and looked at both sides of the apparatus. The habit strengths for turning left and turning right were the same because each response had been reinforced equally often. The drive state at the time of testing gives no lead to which direction to turn; but incentive motivation does. Suppose an animal is tested hungry. When it looks to the water side, there is very little incentive motivation, but when it looks to the food side, it encounters stimuli to which eating has been conditioned. Since it is now food deprived, there will be an increment in r_G and a corresponding increment in K so that any response that occurs, such as running forward, is going to have increased motivation. The animal is more likely, therefore, to approach the food side. In other words, when the hungry rat looks to the water side, nothing happens; but when it looks to the food side, it gets excited; thus it is more likely to go to the food side.

This application of r_G theory suggests that two minor (or perhaps not so minor) qualifications must be made in the original formulation. One is that no matter how strongly r_G is conditioned to environmental stimuli, it can only be elicited when the animal is appropriately motivated to start with. Otherwise, the hungry animal looking to the water side would also be motivated by the elicitation of the r_G for drinking, and there would be no basis for the discrimination. The second qualification is that the incentive motivation produced by looking at r_G-eliciting stimuli cannot be as generalized as Hull's K × D × H formula implies. When the animal encounters these stimuli, is there really the same motivation for whatever the animal happens to be doing at that time, or is there selective facilitation of different kinds of behaviors? In a simple situation such as Crespi's runway, a selective motivation mechanism is not necessary because presumably the more motivated the animal is, the faster it will run. But in a more complex situation, for instance, in Kendler's discrimination task, some selectivity would seem to be necessary in order to ensure that the animal does something appropriate with the incentive cue, such as approaching it. This necessity is most clearly seen by contrasting the case of incentive with aversive motivation, that is, acquired fear. Suppose we feed an animal on one side of a T-maze and shock it on the other. A general, nondirective or non-selective motivational factor would make the animal likely to run when it looks to the shock side and becomes frightened, and likely to run when it looks to the food side and becomes excited. It would not do to have the animal simply become more motivated in such a situation and start running forward in which ever direction it looked. The shock cues must selectively facilitate withdrawal, and the positive cues must selectively facilitate approach. If withdrawal is selectively facilitated by fear, we may assume that other defensive behaviors, for example, freezing, are also. Further, we may suppose that if approach is selectively facilitated by incentive motivation, then other responses such as manipulatory responses and consummatory responses are also. And we must wonder just how general either kind of motivation may be.[7]

The comparison of incentive and drive. The most fundamental distinction between incentive and drive is that while drive is produced by internal events such as the physiological state of the organism, incentive is produced by external events such as environmental cues. This basic internal-external dichotomy has implications for both the practical control of behavior and its theoretical explanation. Thus the fact that incentive motivation appears to be highly dependent upon external stimulus events rather than conditions inside the organism makes it much more akin to an acquired drive than a primary source of drive. For one thing, whereas a physiological disturbance may have an immediate unlearned motivating effect, the motivating effect of external events, such as cues to food or shock, can affect the animal only after it has had some experience with these events. As we saw in Chapter 7, the fact that the rat must learn to eat in a particular situation suggests that eating is predominantly motivated by incentive rather than by drive. In effect, we attribute the innate part of the animal's total motivation to drive, and we attribute the learned part, that is, the part based upon experience with particular environmental conditions, to incentive.

A second implication of the internal-external dichotomy is that the animal's physiological state, an internal event, should contribute to drive rather than incentive. Historically, the concept of

[7] The problem of selective facilitation did not arise in Hull's formulation because for Hull r_G was primarily an associative mechanism. It provided stimuli, s_G, to which instrumental responses could be conditioned. Thus, in Kendler's situation the animals made the correct response because turning in a given direction had become conditioned to the appropriate s_G. The idea that r_G was primarily a motivator, a generalized energizer, was due to Spence (1951). It is in connection with this view of incentive motivation that the problem of selective facilitation arises. Spence had privately proposed a motivational interpretation of r_G as early as 1942, but he did not make a public statement until 1951.

drive became popular largely because of the belief that the physiological mechanisms responsible for motivated behavior would soon be discovered. While it is not clear yet what the physiological basis of, say, hunger is, presumably, there is something as measurable as blood sugar level that is causally related to food-getting behavior. But no such simple factor can be expected to underlie incentive motivation. Incentive motivation is based on external stimulation and prior experience, so it must involve much more complex neural functions than those required by the receptor signaling system that is usually assumed to underlie drive. This is not to say that lesions somewhere in the nervous system cannot affect incentive motivation; Jones and Mishkin (1972) seem to have located such a function in the pyriform area in monkeys. But there is a distinction to be made between the kinds of mechanism that underlie the two kinds of motivators because of the ultimate source of activation, namely, tissue need for food on the one hand and the perception of food objects or food-related cues on the other.

A third, practical point of difference between drive and incentive is that they are quite different in terms of antecedent conditions. For drive there is a condition of need produced prior to the time of testing, whereas for incentive there is the test situation itself; that is, there are stimuli to which the consummatory response, R_G, or some fractional part of it, r_G, has previously been conditioned. To find an index of incentive motivation, we must look not for weight loss or blood sugar level or some other internal event, but rather to the occurrence of some response from the organism that is conditioned to external stimuli.

Whether these contrasting properties of drive and incentive have any basis in reality or simply reflect conceptual conveniences for the theorist remains to be seen. But for the moment let us suppose that the distinctions can be defended; then we can conclude that whereas drive is internal, unlearned, physiological, and dependent upon antecedent conditions, incentive is externally aroused, is based on learning, is of psychological origin, and is produced by prevailing conditions.

If we assume for the moment that all of appetitive motivation is due either to drive or incentive, then the next question must be how much of the total is contributed by each. If we have a particular rat running in a particular runway, how much of its total motivation is attributable to its deprivation state, and how much of it is attributable to learned incentive factors? Unfortunately, suitable metrics elude us so that it is not possible to provide a quantitative answer to the question. Those who have dealt with it have done so at a conceptual level. The question was first put in explicit form by Seward (1942), who noted that the r_G mechanism had all of the motivational properties that we usually attribute to drive. Therefore, he proposed that incentive motivation be extended to include all 'motivation. He suggested further that what we call motivation is merely the elicitation of behavior by stimuli that have been associated with reinforcement. He noted that initially the governing stimuli might be internal, perhaps due to stomach contractions, but that after further experience external cues in the feeding situation will come to elicit motivated behavior.[8] In effect, Seward was urging that the concept of incentive has all the functional properties that drive is supposed to have and that it should, therefore, replace it.

It should be noted that drive and incentive are traditionally based upon different antecedent conditions, that is, the conditions of deprivation and the conditions (e.g., amount) of reinforcement. So if we wish to replace drive with an expanded incentive concept (or for that matter if we wish to replace incentive with an expanded drive concept), then it is necessary to make the new broadened concept be a function of both kinds of conditions. This kind of adjustment can be readily made, but the different empirical and conceptual properties of the new concept should be clearly noted.

A pair of recent experiments suggests that such a conceptual reorganization of drive and incentive is not only possible but perhaps advisable. Kurtz and Jarka (1968) trained rats in a T-maze slightly deprived on some days and very deprived on other days. On the very hungry days animals found food on one side, whereas on slightly hungry days they found food on the other side. After a series of training trials under these conditions, motivation conditions were equated at an intermediate value for all animals, and they were given a free choice in the T-maze. The preponderance of animals chose to go to the high hunger side of the apparatus. These results imply that greater deprivation gives food greater incentive value, so that, when tested, the animals would go to the side that elicited more incentive motivation. The same interpretation can be given an experiment reported by Revusky (1967) in which rats were alternately trained under high and low deprivation. On high-deprivation a given animal received one substance, for instance, milk, whereas on low-deprivation days, it received a different food, for instance, grape juice (the foods were counterbalanced across subgroups). Revusky found that after a series of such training trials his rats showed a strong preference for the food they had consumed under the high-deprivation condition.

[8] It will be recalled from our earlier discussion of Seward (page 283) that what we are calling incentive he called acquired or externalized drive. Seward's concept of over 30 years ago was quite modern, but the labels were different. Now we speak of acquired drives only in connection with aversive events; incentive motivation has gradually come to encompass all varieties of learned appetitive motivation as opposed to drive, which refers to unlearned motivation. Brown's (1961) rules are an exception; for Brown all motivation is drive whether its source is learned (what I call incentive if it is appetitive, or acquired if it is aversive) or unlearned (what I call drive).

Armed with such data and with the theoretical writings of Seward and subsequent theorists and recalling the difficulties with Hull's drive concept noted in earlier chapters, it is tempting to attribute all appetitive motivation to incentive and none of it to drive. Let us turn now to the question of whether incentive motivation concepts are powerful enough to replace other behavioral concepts.

Further extensions of incentive theory. In another provocative paper Seward (1943) suggested that the incentive motivation concept might be able to replace the concept of reinforcement. He suggested that r_G might provide enough stimulus control over an instrumental response that it could occur without having to have habit strength of its own. What appears to be the reinforcement of an instrumental response may be simply the progressive increase in incentive motivation that occurs with the continued conditioning of r_G in the goal box and the continued elicitation of r_G in the alley.[9] Seward suggested further that learning could occur in the same way in complex situations, since when the animal looks one way and then another at the choice point, the environment will provide differential elicitation of r_G, which will lead to differential motivation of the correct and incorrect responses. Thus Seward was apparently able to do away with reinforcement for instrumental behavior. In order to make the argument convincing, however, Seward had to introduce a new motivational hypothesis. He proposed that when the animal makes an incipient running response, that is, when it starts to run, r_G is aroused and provides incentive motivation for running. Incipient running thus becomes further energized until finally overt running occurs. Seward could offer no hypothesis at that early date to indicate how the mechanism actually works except "a portion of a response tends to exert a tendency to arouse the total response."[10] This mechanism was later extended to the explanation of latent learning (Seward, 1947) and several other learning phenomena (Seward, 1948). In short, the incentive motivator can act as a symbol, as an expectancy, as an incentive, and as a goad to action. Seward (1952, 1956) finally addressed himself to the question of how r_G itself is learned, and he proposed that it is learned by drive reduction.

Perhaps the most provocative and thoroughgoing statement

[9] I have taken the liberty of simplifying Seward's notation. He symbolizes incentive factors as sr_g, partly to emphasize the part they play in the associative determination of behavior, partly to indicate their mediational and intervening position between the stimulus and the response, and partly, I suspect, to indicate that we really do not know where they should be located.

[10] This is the beginning of what Seward later called tertiary motivation. The hypothesis is by no means new; we saw it first in Chapter 2 in Hobbes' concept of endeavor and again in Spencer's concept of nascent excitation.

of incentive theory is Mowrer (1960). Mowrer extends the incentive concept about as far as it can logically go. It carries the whole burden of directing and motivating behavior. According to Mowrer, the associative control of behavior, its motivation, and what appears to be its reinforcement are all consequences of the operation of hypothetical mechanisms that operate much as r_G is assumed to operate. The concept of reinforcement is not applied to instrumental behavior but only to these incentive factors. They, rather than the instrumental responses that they govern, are what is learned or extinguished by presenting or withholding reinforcement. In Mowrer's system drive is given a single limited but crucial function of reinforcing or weakening the incentive mediators. Mowrer proposes that there are four such mediators.

First, there is *fear*, which is established (or reinforced) by an increase in drive such as that produced by the onset of shock. Any stimulus present at the time of drive increase or present immediately preceding such an increase acquires ability itself to elicit fear. Such a cue presents a threat; it means that an increase in drive is impending. The behavioral effect is withdrawal from that cue. The evidence for such a mechanism comes from avoidance learning situations and is relatively substantial. It is important to note that Mowrer does not assume that the cue gains direct associative control over the avoidance response. It merely elicits the motivation for such behavior. Moreover, the cue that elicits the fear reaction may be either external or internal. If it is external, the animal will make an overt avoidance or escape response or whatever other response withdraws from or eliminates the cue. But the cue may also be internal. It may be the proprioceptive consequences of some response the animal has just made; just as we may frighten an animal by presenting stimuli that have been associated with the onset of shock, so the animal can frighten itself by making responses that have been contiguous with the onset of shock. The animal will tend to avoid or escape these internal cues, which it does by withdrawing from the stimuli, which means, in effect, that it will inhibit the response that produces them. Thus, according to Mowrer, the difference between avoidance learning and learning through punishment is simply in the locus of the cues that elicit fear in the two cases.

When a drive is reduced, for example, by the consumption of food, another motivational mediator, *hope*, is established. Hope will be subsequently elicited by any cues to the reduction in drive and will have the effect of facilitating any response that produces an approach to or retention of such cues. Evidence for such an effect is found in some of the secondary reinforcement and incentive motivation studies that we will consider later; and this evidence too is rather substantial.

Hope and fear are Mowrer's two primary mediating mechanisms, but he introduces two additional mechanisms of a secondary nature that are reinforced by the onset and termination of drive, respectively. They are elicited by cues to the onset and termination of cues rather than the onset and termination of drive. Thus *relief* is elicited by the presentation of a cue to the removal of drive. When relief occurs, it, too, produces an apparent motivating effect upon a behavior that is in the process of occurring or that produces it. Finally, Mowrer suggests that *disappointment* is produced by an increase in drive and is elicited by a cue signaling withdrawal of a cue to hope. Such a second-order cue tends to inhibit or produce withdrawal from the stimuli that elicit it.

Thus Mowrer gives us a set of incentive-type factors produced by drive induction and drive reduction, which serve to facilitate or inhibit ongoing behavior. Note that in Mowrer's system there is no direct associative control of any behavior other than the mediating or motivating responses themselves. Responses are not attached directly to or elicited by stimuli; they are simply part of an ongoing flux of behavior that is turned on or off by motivational factors.

The theoretical writings of Seward and Mowrer emphasize that there is nothing sacred in any of our basic motivational concepts. One can build a theory of behavior in which there are drives or in which there are no drives; in which there are incentives or no incentives; in which there is reinforcement for instrumental behavior or no reinforcement. One can build a theory of behavior that is based upon traditional concepts by refining or clarifying them; or one can build a theory of behavior in which the traditional concepts are put into bold new perspective.[11]

The second summarizing conclusion is that even if it is decided that some concept of incentive motivation is needed, there is nothing sacred about any of the conceptual properties it must have. We have already noted that an incentive motivational factor might be postulated to have general motivational properties, it might selectively facilitate certain classes of responses, or it might be given no motivational function at all but serve simply as an associative determinant of behavior. Similarly, the arousal of incentive motivation can be attributed to classical conditioning or to drive reduction or to some other kind of behavioral mechanism. Thirdly, the psychologist may view incentive motivation realistically; that is, he may search for its physiological or behavioral correlates, or he may view it as a central or theoretical or inferred entity. In short, we have many options in attributing functional and conceptual properties to the incentive motivational factor.

[11] There is quite a diversity of incentive theories, but since few variations have been worked out in much detail, little would be gained by citing or describing them all here. It would probably be more profitable to construct one's own variation than to scrutinize those that have gone before. The incentive theories of Seward and Mowrer are described to illustrate the inventiveness that can go into such theories.

We may summarize these different theoretical options regarding incentive motivation by means of Table 9–1. The table organizes the question of the reality status of r_G according to whether it is assumed to be an observable response, whether it has the properties of a response (e.g., it is conditionable) but is not directly observable, or whether it is something other than a response, such as a central event, with little chance of being observed. The rows of the table organize the different theoretical positions regarding the effects of incentive according to whether it is conceived as purely associative, assumed to be a generalized motivating factor, or is given the power of selectively facilitating specific classes of behavior. Over the years we have moved from the upper left part of the table toward the lower right. A third dimension might be added to the table indicating how different theorists have assumed r_G itself is learned. The idea that r_G is learned through the drive reduction reinforcement mechanism was first proposed by Hull (1943), and later accepted by Seward (1956) and Mowrer (1960). But the most widely endorsed position, first advocated by Spence (1951), is that r_G is classically conditioned. This view is probably so popular because it allows the theorist to treat incentive motivation and learned fear in the same way and attribute all learned motivation to the same kinds of processes (Rescorla & Solomon, 1967). More recently the r_G mechanism has started to be replaced by more cognitive mechanisms (Bindra, 1972; Bolles, 1972).

This discussion of incentive motivation will conclude with a further examination of these options. Specifically, we will consider whether incentive motivation can be identified as an observable classically conditioned response. The clarification of this issue should go a long way toward eliminating some of the theoretical options.

The empirical basis of r_G. In Spence's (1951) treatment of incentive motivation, it is hypothesized to depend upon the occurrence of a

Table 9–1

Different theoretical positions regarding the mechanisms of incentive motivation

BEHAVIORAL PROPERTIES	STATUS OF r_G		
	Real r_G	*Hypothetical r_G*	*No r_G*
Associative	Hull, 1930	Seward, 1942	Trapold & Overmier, 1972
Motivating	Hull, 1952	Spence, 1951 Mowrer, 1956	Mowrer, 1960 Rescorla & Solomon, 1967
Selective facilitation			Bindra, 1968 Bolles, 1972

Theory of motivation

classically conditioned fractional part of the consummatory response. The assumption originally made by Hull (1931) and subsequently endorsed by most of his followers is that, in the case of hunger, r_G can be identified as salivation. What better candidate for r_G could there be? Pavlov surely demonstrated that salivation is classically conditionable. This is an interesting and extremely important assumption because if it were supported by experimental evidence, it would confer several enormous advantages. One advantage is that if r_G could be objectively identified with some response of the autonomic nervous system, there would be a means of independently verifying the existence and the strength of incentive motivation, so that it could be assessed independently of the instrumental behavior that it is supposed to motivate. How elegant it would be to demonstrate that an animal ran more vigorously for food on those occasions when it gave bigger or more persistent salivary secretions. The whole structure of incentive motivation theory could be experimentally tested.

The second great advantage would be that we would already know how incentive motivation is learned because the entire body of knowledge that exists on classical conditioning, including Pavlov's extensive work on salivation, could be immediately incorporated into incentive theory. The third great advantage that would accrue to the psychologist who could justify the r_G assumption is that he would know how the animal's motivation could be experimentally manipulated independently of the instrumental situation itself. For example, it would be possible to classically condition r_G to certain food cues in one situation and then demonstrate the incentive motivating property of these cues when they are later introduced in a quite different instrumental situation. We will consider the results of this kind of experiment in Chapter 12. What then is the empirical status of r_G?

A few experimenters (e.g., Lewis et al., 1958; Lewis, 1959; Lewis & Kent, 1961; Kintsch & Witte, 1962; Shapiro, 1962; Miller & DeBold, 1965) have attempted to manipulate or observe r_G directly, but, unfortunately, the results have generally not been encouraging. These attempts to locate r_G have shown some of the correlations with subsequent instrumental behavior that are expected, but so far these correlations have been too low to permit anyone to say that r_G has been located or even that it has all the properties that it is supposed to have. Salivation may occur just before a rat presses a bar for food, but the rat may also salivate without pressing and it may press without salivating.

This literature has been reviewed by Rescorla and Solomon (1967) with great care and concern; they conclude that there is no justification for the belief that salivation has the properties that have been attributed to r_G. Rescorla and Solomon tell us then that if there is such an entity as r_G, that is, a classically conditioned motivator of behavior, then it must be a central event; it cannot be an observable response. This concession from Rescorla and Solomon is particularly telling because their view of motivation requires an incentive motivator.[12]

Perhaps it is not so important whether r_G is an identifiable response. Certainly the existence of r_G is not documented in most instances where it is invoked to explain a motivated behavior. It is ordinarily treated as a hypothetical construct and inferred from its functional properties. It is ordinarily assumed that r_G occurs and that it is classically conditioned to stimuli like those in the goal box. In practice, then, r_G has always been an unobserved response. The possibility that it must forever be an unobserved response need not materially affect its power to explain incentive motivation. But still, if we think of r_G purely as a construct and give it just those behavioral properties that it must have (that it is classically conditionable and that its strength determines the strength of incentive motivation), then what is the point of such a construct? The original r_G construct had a real point, but it is now largely lost. Consider again the great virtues that would have been attendant upon finding out what r_G was, namely, that we would know much about it because we already know so much about classical conditioning, that the mechanisms underlying incentive motivation would be observable, and that the motivator could be established independently of the behavioral situation in which it serves as a motivator. All of these advantages are now lost. But more than that, the fact that the salivary response is not classically conditioned according to the requirements of the theory suggests that there is something wrong with our understanding of Pavlovian conditioning itself. Thus if the mediating or motivating response does not follow the rules of classical conditioning, then it is difficult to see how classical conditioning can be cited as the mechanism for producing incentive motivation. The failure to verify independently that salivation mediates incentive motivation not only makes us question that salivation is the mediator, but it must also make us question whether classical conditioning is the responsible mechanism. We have a very serious crisis, not only concerning how we regard learned sources of motivation, but also concerning how we conceive of the learning process itself.

[12] Solomon and his students have sought long and hard to find an analogous index of fear (e.g., Black, 1971), that is, a classically conditioned emotional response, r_E, that could be directly monitored to assess the strength of the animal's fear motivation. But their search has failed to reveal any response with the appropriate properties, that is, being classically conditioned, on the one hand, and being observable and correlated with fear as inferred from the animal's instrumental behavior, on the other. So when Rescorla and Solomon (1967) concede that neither r_E nor r_G really exists as a peripheral response, that both fear and incentive motivation must be central events, we must value this judgment and take the concession seriously.

Reinforcement models

There is a peculiar complementarity between motivation and reinforcement such that if a theorist is willing to put sufficient emphasis on his motivational concepts, he can minimize the role of his reinforcement concepts (e.g., Mowrer, 1960). Conversely, if a theorist is willing to attach sufficient importance to principles of learning, then he has little need for a theory of motivation (e.g., Skinner, 1953). It is this latter type of model that we must now consider. We have already examined in Chapter 5 the basic tenet of this position, which is that the explanation of behavior can proceed better without any motivational concepts, without involving needs or drives or wants or anything else of the kind, either in the data language or among the theoretical concepts. This position is based upon the assumption that what we ordinarily call motivated behavior is neither more nor less than learned behavior. If an animal acts as though it is hungry, sexually aroused, or aroused in some other way, our evidence for this arousal is simply the occurrence of learned behaviors that have been reinforced by food, by sex, or by other types of reinforcement. This kind of explanatory model suggests that the phenomena that have been called motivational can be translated—without loss—into the phenomena of reinforcement.

One clue to the plausibility of the reinforcement model to explain motivational phenomena comes from our earlier review of the functional properties of the Hullian drive construct. Recall that of the several behavioral properties that Hull postulated for D, only the energizing property seemed to correspond, even approximately, with what has been found in the laboratory; and even the energizing property had to be amended. The energizing effect of drive conditions was seen to apply only to relevant instrumental and consummatory behaviors and not to all behaviors indiscriminately. Thus the energization principle appears applicable precisely to those responses that have had a history of reinforcement relative to the appropriate motivating conditions. If we look at the effect of deprivation on the speed of an animal running for food reward, then we find an energizing effect, but if the behavior has some other history of reinforcement or if it is in the class of general activities that are independent of prior reinforcement, then energizing effects become unpredictable and have little generality.

Another indication of the equivalence of motivational and reinforcement determinants of behavior is apparent from the consideration that even those forms of behavior that are most obviously motivated depend not so much upon the state of the organism as upon the presentation of particular cues to which particular responses have been associated in the past. Consider the following hypothetical example. A sexually mature male rat is put in a novel situation containing a female rat in heat. He will explore for a while but will soon show a fairly complex species-specific and highly predictable set of responses. The fact that we can abolish sexual behavior or at least modify it by castrating the animal or presenting a female that is not in heat or by varying a number of other experimental conditions means that the behavior is lawful, and accordingly, we can explain it in terms of this lawfulness; but it does not mean the behavior is motivated. The determinants of sexual behavior are not motivational in character because its antecedent conditions are not motivational. They are simply conditions in the presence of which fixed patterns of sexual behavior occur. Hence we are not inclined to consider this as motivated behavior, but merely as species-specific behavior released by the appropriate conditions. If we want to make the animal appear motivated, we can make the occurrence of sexual behavior contingent upon some instrumental response, such as running in an alley to get to the female. Under these conditions the animal will learn to run, and it will learn other kinds of behavior, such as climbing out of its home cage to our hand, jumping out of our hand into the start box, and scratching at the start-box door. Some of these learned responses, such as running in the alley, arise from intentional contingencies, but the others arise from accidental contingencies. Thus we do not intend that the rat should jump to our hand from its cage—that is not part of what we require it to learn— but it learns, nonetheless. This behavior indicates that the animal is more motivated, that is, more excited or aroused, after a series of training trials than it was initially. It is exactly this kind of evidence that leads us to emphasize the importance of learned motivation, in other words, incentive motivation, as the important determinant of sexually motivated behavior rather than the initial hormonal conditions, which remain constant throughout the experiment. Moreover, if we ask what particular behaviors now lead us to see the rat as motivated, we discover that they are precisely those behaviors that are learned in the situation.

The basic question is whether these two effects (learning and motivation) represent two highly correlated but different effects or merely two ways of regarding a single set of phenomena. The reinforcement model of behavior is based on the assumption that there is just a single set of phenomena to be explained and that it can be best explained as a reinforcement effect.

The semantics of reinforcement theory is equivalent to the semantics of the traditional motivational viewpoint in many respects. We can compile a list of reinforcers just as easily as we can compile a list of drives. We would expect that the two lists would correspond in a one-to-one fashion. We could break down the list of drives, as was the custom a generation ago, into primary and derived drives, but we could also break down the corresponding list of reinforcers into those that are innately reinforcing and those that have acquired reinforcing value. And again, the two analyses should correspond.

Similarly, just as we could distinguish between drives that are appetitive and due to deprivation and drives that are aversive and due to excess stimulation, so we can distinguish between positive and negative reinforcers.

There are several respects in which a reinforcement model has a more parsimonious syntax than a motivational model. Motivational concepts such as drive were used to simplify the explanation of behavior. But if we have learned anything from the evidence cited in earlier chapters, it is that the attempts to validate the drive construct have led us more and more deeply into the intricacies of behavior. Before drives can be applied to the explanation of behavior, it is necessary to determine precisely what responses are learned and what stimuli control them. A motivational theory invites us to pass over such details, whereas a reinforcement theory calls our attention immediately to them. Thus invoking motives to explain behavior is apt to keep us from finding out about behavior and to hinder our seeing what the problems are. The problems usually turn out to be associative; that is, they typically involve determining what responses are occurring and what stimuli and reinforcers are effective in controlling them. Thus a motivational theory must necessarily involve all the terms incorporated in the reinforcement theory and must include a few others in addition. If these other terms are strictly defined, then the only cost is the loss of parsimony. But history suggests there is an irresistible temptation to attach surplus meaning to motivational constructs, for example, to equate drive with need or r_G with salivation. We do not seem to be able to overcome our heritage of regarding motives as the causes of behavior.

It might be contended that many of the phenomena that have traditionally been a part of motivation theory do not lend themselves to a simple reinforcement interpretation. For example, there is no place for the phenomenon of the energization of general activity. There is no place, for example, for the fact that sexually mature rats run more in activity wheels than castrated rats. But the answer to such a charge is that rather than look for a source of drive that accounts for this difference, we should look for a source of reinforcement. What is it that reinforces activity wheel running in sexually normal animals but fails to reinforce castrated ones? The argument that animals run in wheels because they have drives is not very convincing in view of the fact that this behavior appears to be specific to rats, to hunger and sex, and largely specific to activity wheels. Indeed, the burden of explanation is really on the motivation theorist to explain why, for instance, thirsty guinea pigs do not run more in activity wheels than satiated ones (Campbell et al., 1966).

The traditional challenge for reinforcement models is to account for the apparent increase in performance that occurs when deprivation conditions are made more severe. This is a difficult question, and it turns out to be a crucial one because the energization effect is the one fundamental property of drives that appears to justify such a concept. There are several possible solutions to the problem. The oldest and still perhaps the best solution was originally suggested by Guthrie (1935), then defended by Sheffield (1948), and, more recently, revised and revitalized by Estes (1958, 1962). The essential idea is that there are important stimulus changes correlated with the conditions of deprivation; the hungry animal has sources of stimulation that are not present in the satiated animal. There are stimuli such as those arising from stomach contractions (or from other still unidentified locations), which tell the animal it is hungry. Then when appropriate instrumental responses have become conditioned to these stimuli, these responses will become more probable as deprivation stimuli loom larger in the total stimulus situation. This principle fits very nicely with the finding that the energizing effect of deprivation appears to be applicable only to responses that have been reinforced by the appropriate kind of reward.[13]

Just a few years ago, reinforcement models looked promising enough to warrant some discussion and promotion (Bolles, 1967). But now the prospects of being able to explain behavior by hypothesizing a universal reinforcement mechanism appear rather dim. In the few intervening years three important developments have become evident. One is that the concept of reinforcement has come to play a much smaller role in the explanation of human learning. To be sure, the consequences of the subject's response are still held to be important, but because they provide information about the appropriateness of his behavior or because they motivate him to perform and not because they strengthen his S-R connections. (Estes, 1971, gives a good short account of this change in orientation.)

[13] The idea that these stimuli change with deprivation conditions, becoming both more numerous and more insistent, that is, having a higher probability of being detected, provides such stimuli with an energizing function. Estes' (1958) important theoretical paper is often cited as indicating that no energization is necessary. But, to the contrary, the energization function is simply attributed to the sampling properties of stimuli rather than to a separate kind of entity such as drive. Some writers (e.g., Bolles, 1967) have been confused on this point and have further confused the issue by citing Estes' citation of a study by Cotton (1953) to attribute to Estes the belief that there is no energizing effect. Estes (1958) actually cites Cotton's experiment in this connection to illustrate a special point, namely, that there is no energizing effect when rats are trained under all different deprivation conditions and when all sources of competing behavior are removed. However, if groups of animals are trained under a single deprivation condition or if competing-response trials are counted, then an energizing effect is found (Cicala, 1961). The truth is that energizing effects are not as widespread as might be expected, and when energizing effects are found it is not necessary to have a drive type of energizer to explain them, and we are indebted to Estes (1958) for calling both points to our attention.

Theory of motivation

The second development is that reinforcement theorists themselves are becoming increasingly reluctant to attribute a direct response-strengthening function to reinforcement. The consequences of the subject's response are still held to be important, but because they permit control over his behavior and not because they strengthen his S-R connections. It is of relatively little concern how this control works, whether it is due to the discriminative, motivational, or the reinforcing function of the reinforcer; it only matters that control is achieved. Some Skinnerians will say that they have always been more concerned with controlling behavior than with postulating explanatory mechanisms; they will say that reinforcement has always meant a procedure for controlling behavior rather than a hypothetical process for strengthening it. This may be true, but it is also true that reinforcement theorists of all persuasions have emphasized the importance of certain methodological considerations that made it easy to infer that reinforcers actually reinforced. Thus the reinforcer was supposed to be *contiguous* with the response (so that it would be effective); it was supposed to be a *consequence* of the response (so that it would not elicit competing behavior); and it was supposed to be *contingent* upon the desired response (so that superstitious behavior would not be reinforced). The point is that in recent years all of these requirements have been relaxed. For example, Bloomfield (1972) proposes that contiguity itself is not necessary. Herrnstein (1969, 1970) has proposed that behavior is controlled by the relative frequency of reinforcement and that this control can be effected in the absence of any direct contact between behavior and individual reinforcing events. In effect, the animal adjusts its behavior to match the patterning of reinforcement. It is apparently the correlation rather than the contingency between response and reinforcement that permits behavior to be controlled. But if any pattern of events that can be shown to affect behavior is to be called a reinforcer, then there is no longer any reason to suppose that the effect of a reinforcer is to strengthen an S-R connection.

The third development that makes us question the utility of reinforcement models is the sudden realization that even when a reinforcer is effective under one set of circumstances, it may be quite ineffective under very similar circumstances. This realization presents the reinforcement theorist with a major crisis.

The contemporary crisis for reinforcement models. Just as recent reviewers have noted a contemporary crisis for acquired drive and incentive models of motivation because of the failure to find observable responses that mediate these kinds of motivation, so there is currently a crisis for reinforcement models. The basic difficulty is that while the laws of learning have always been assumed to be universal and to be uniformly applicable, there is a new recognition that the laws of learning are subject to a variety of constraints. The importance of such constraints was called to our attention most dramatically by the bright, noisy water experiment.

Garcia and Koelling (1966) trained a group of rats to drink bright, noisy water. This was accomplished by arranging an electronic circuit to flash a light and operate a clicker whenever an animal's tongue made contact with the fluid. Half of each group was then given a painful electric shock immediately following drinking, while the other half was subsequently made ill by administering either X-rays or lithium chloride. The next day when the animals were again offered bright, noisy water, an aversion to it, that is, less drinking, was found in animals that had been shocked but not in those animals that had become ill. In the original phase of the experiment another group had been trained to drink tasty water, that is, water containing saccharin. Then, again, half of each group was given electric shock to the feet while the other half was made ill. When tested the next day, those animals that had been ill showed an aversion to saccharin but those receiving the shock did not. If we look at the effects of the different consequences of drinking, we see that shock produced an aversion to bright, noisy water but had no effect upon the drinking of saccharin, whereas illness produced an aversion to saccharin but had no effect upon the drinking of bright, noisy water. Each half of the experiment provides a beautiful control for the other half. Thus it is not possible to argue that the illness was too long delayed after the drinking of bright, noisy water for it to have an effect because it did have an effect on the saccharin animals. In the same way, it cannot be said that the foot shock was ineffective because it did produce an aversion to bright, noisy water; it was ineffective only for inhibiting the drinking of saccharin. These results indicate that sometimes learning occurs and sometimes it does not under what would seem to be quite comparable conditions. Whether learning occurs or not appears to depend upon whether there is an appropriate relationship between the cue (the particular kind of water) and the consequence (shock or illness). Garcia and Koelling contend that one particular kind of relationship, namely, that between the taste of a food substance and the consequent illness, is particularly strong and particularly likely to lead to learning in the rat. This phenomenon, which we may call the *Garcia effect*, can be demonstrated under conditions where learning would not be expected; it can be obtained after a single experience of ingestion followed by illness, and it can be obtained even though the illness follows ingestion by several hours. On the other hand, if there is no intrinsic relationship between the cue and the consequence, as was evidently the case when the ingestion of bright, noisy water was followed by illness, then no learning may be found, even though the parameters of the experimental situation, for example, the number of trials, the time intervals, and so on, would lead us to expect learning.[14]

We will have more to say about the Garcia effect in Chapter 12 when we discuss delay of reinforcement; it is mentioned here because this experiment, together with further research on learned food aversions, has revolutionized the thinking of many theorists about what is involved in learning and about the nature of reinforcement. While it has always been recognized that some stimuli are more effective than others because they are more salient, have a higher intenstity, or are in a preferred modality, it has been assumed that once the stimulus registers in some way, it is perfectly associable and quite capable of entering into learning. In the same way, it has been known for some time that different responses differ in their baseline probability, initial strength, or operant rate, but it has been assumed that apart from their different starting points all responses were equally able to be learned. Finally, it has been acknowledged for some time that there are differences among individuals and among species in what kind of events serve to reinforce behavior. A reinforcer that is appropriate for a child may not be appropriate for an adult and vice versa, and different reinforcers may be effective with dogs and rats; but it has been assumed that if a reinforcer works, it works, and it would be as effective in strengthening one kind of behavior as another. But Garcia and Koelling demonstrate that even with stimuli that can readily enter into association, with a response (drinking) that has great strength, and with effective consequences (negative consequences in this case), some combinations of these events produce learning much more easily than others. Suddenly, we see that rather than being universally applicable the laws of learning and the materials that enter into learning have a structure of their own that must be discovered.

The critical question then is what kind of principles are needed to give structure to the pattern of what is learned. What are the organizing principles that make learning occur readily under some conditions and occur only with difficulty under other conditions? When the organizing principles are finally understood, will they prove to be themselves laws of learning or will they be better conceptualized as motivational principles? In any case, our current principles of learning no longer appear to be fundamental. The main virtue of a pure reinforcement model, as against a motivational

---

[14] It should not be thought that learning either occurs or not, because, as it turns out, it is possible for learning to occur even when there is no relationship between cue and consequence effects if we induce enough illness or run enough trials or make the cues sufficiently salient. We can also lose the Garcia effect by reversing these conditions. Thus we must think about continuously graded effects. The question is not whether learning is possible or not, but rather how rapidly and how effectively learning occurs.

reinforcement model, such as Hull's, is the greater parsimony it offers. And as long as there were few constraints on learning, such promised parsimony appeared to be a great virtue indeed. But without this promise the whole enterprise seems of dubious value—a much more optimistic approach would seem to be to search for those principles, whatever they may be, that determine when learning will occur readily and when it will not. In short, since we have discovered that learning is selective, it would seem more fruitful to look for the principles of selectivity rather than attempting to defend an approach that is based on the assumption that learning is a very general and universally applicable phenomenon.[15]

Once it is accepted that learning is selective rather than general, then, curiously, instances of its selectivity become apparent wherever we look. The phenomenon of selectivity has been with us all along, and it had even been faintly perceived from time to time. Breland and Breland (1961) described the failure of reinforcement to control behavior in some instances where reinforcement contingencies would be expected to be effective. In these cases the required response was emitted at a good rate, and reinforcment was regularly applied whenever it occurred, but the response collapsed instead of becoming stronger. Since the animals the Brelands used were not the standard laboratory animals, this peculiarity of their results could be attributed to some peculiarity of the species that they were working with, and the laws of learning could be defended against their findings. It has also been known for some time that some responses are very difficult to acquire in avoidance learning situations (Bolles, 1972a); but again, the generality of the laws of learning could be maintained if such cases were simply ascribed to some peculiarity of the avoidance learning situation. The predominant attitude until just recently was that failures of learning were anomalies, peculiarities, or laboratory curiosities, which showed, at most, that there were some exceptions to the universality of our laws of learning. Actually, it turns out that the great mass of data currently supporting the reinforcement concept comes predominantly from a very small number of highly standardized situations. Perhaps the most standardized, and certainly one of the most popular, is the pigeon pecking a key in a Skinner box for food. Here is a situation in which there could be no doubt about the efficacy of contingent reinforcement in strengthening

[15] The specificity or selectivity of learning has been at least dimly recognized for some time, but it was rarely regarded as being very important, even by those who recognized it. It is still viewed by some writers as a set of constraints upon the general laws of learning. For others (e.g., Rozin & Kalat, 1971; Seligman, 1970) there are no "general" laws of learning, only specialized kinds of learning that some animals use to solve some kinds of problems. Shettleworth (1972) describes the comparative aspects of selectivity while Hinde and Stevenson-Hinde (1973) and Seligman and Hager (1972) have edited books including a variety of papers on the selectivity of learning.

a particular response. Or so it appeared before the phenomenon of autoshaping was described by Brown and Jenkins (1968).

Autoshaping. The conventional wisdom about Skinner boxes tells us that when the animal is first put into the situation, it must be magazine trained and then reinforced for making approximations to the desired response. Initially, a bird may be reinforced for approaching or looking at the key. Then, as better approximations are made, reinforced and strengthened, the experimenter can require still closer approximations to the desired response, until eventually the animal is pecking the key and working for its food. This process of gradually shaping the desired response takes about an hour—provided the experimenter has done the magazine training appropriately, is knowledgeable about his bird, has not inadvertently reinforced inappropriate behavior, has had some prior experience with the process, and has a little luck. If the experimenter does not have everything going for him, the process may take considerably longer than an hour. Brown and Jenkins (1968) showed, however, that no magazine training, no gradual shaping of the behavior, and no intervention of the experimenter is necessary. Brown and Jenkins simply put the key-peck reinforcement contingency into effect from the beginning and from time to time lit the key and gave their birds free food not contingent upon any behavior. After an hour of this program most of their birds are busily pecking the key and obtaining their food. The birds had shaped themselves.

It would be easy for the reinforcement theorist to argue that since pecking has a high operant rate in the hungry pigeon, since the experimental situation contains little to peck at except the key, and since any accidental key pecks are reinforced, the basic contingency has a good chance of contacting the desired behavior. In short, it could be argued that autoshaping is attributable to superstitious reinforcement effects or to some lucky combination of superstitious and real reinforcement effects. But this interpretation fails to account for the critical part played in autoshaping by the key light; it also fails to account for the results of Williams and Williams (1969). Williams and Williams gave their birds free food in an autoshaping procedure, but key pecking was made ineffective; indeed, a negative contingency was introduced, so that whenever the bird pecked the key, the next scheduled presentation of free food was delayed. Thus the Williams' birds would receive more food if they did not peck the key. In spite of this negative contingency, the majority of their animals learned to peck, and some pecked the key so much that they virtually cut themselves off from all subsequent reinforcement. Here the bird pecks the key in spite of the fact that doing so delays food. Moreover, this learning occurs in the absence of anything that can reasonably be called a reinforcement contingency. How is such learning to be explained?

One possible explanation is suggested by the recent work of Moore (1971, 1973). Moore took high-speed photographs of the key-pecking response in pigeons autoshaped with food and pigeons autoshaped with water (the consummatory response is somewhat different in the two cases, being a single hard, fast peck with the open beak in the case of eating, and a series of gentler, slower movements in the case of drinking). Moore found that when the key-peck response became established by autoshaping, it bore a striking resemblance to the appropriate consummatory response. His birds appeared to be "eating" the food key and "drinking" the water key. In one experiment both behaviors were going on concurrently—the bird was both hungry and thirsty, and different key colors signaled the free presentation of food or water. Moore concludes that in this situation the key-peck response looks like a classically conditioned consummatory response rather than an operant. We are confronted with the awesome possibility that key pecking in pigeons, which has frequently been cited as the prototype of all reinforcement learning, may be acquired by an altogether different kind of learning process.

In summary, the crisis confronting the reinforcement theorist is that reinforcement models hardly seem in any position to explain learning, much less the phenomena of motivation. We know of many cases in which reinforcement theory predicts learning, yet learning does not occur. We know of other cases, like autoshaping, in which learning occurs when reinforcement theory predicts that it should not. There is the further difficulty that learning is sometimes highly particularized, as in the Garcia effect. Certain kinds of behaviors occur in the presence of very particular stimuli provided particular consequences are employed. We have discovered that the phenomenon called learning, which we had assumed to be governed by a simple set of laws universally applicable to all learned behavior, is not simple after all, or at least it is not well understood. And we must wonder whether it is meaningful to apply a process as little understood as learning to the explanation of all motivated behavior.

Cognitive models

Cognitive psychology is based upon two premises. One is that when an animal is put into a situation in which new events are programmed for it, it will incorporate information about these events. The second premise is that if the animal is then appropriately motivated, this information will be used to generate new behavior. The information typically involves goal objects or potential goal objects, that is, objects of some value to the organism. These premises are quite different from those underlying traditional S-R psychology. There are fundamental differences in both the first, or learning, premise and the second, or motivational, premise. Thus for the cognitive psychologist learning consists of the acquisition of information, whereas for the S-R psychologist learning always consists of a change in the strength of some S-R association. For the cognitive psychologist whether motivation is produced by altering the state of the animal or by providing it with external cues, the effect is to attach value to certain objects in the environment; for the S-R psychologist, on the other hand, motivation is the facilitation of whatever response has been learned. For the cognitive psychologist behavior occurs because it is a means to some end; the animal behaves because it expects some consequence. For the S-R psychologist behavior is an end in itself; it is a direct consequence of the stimuli and other factors immediately antecedent to it and is to be explained as the direct result of such factors.

Thus cognitive psychology and S-R psychology provide alternative interpretations of behavior. But it is important to recognize that although they apply quite different models to the explanation of behavior, they do not necessarily reflect different philosophies of science, differ in objectivity, or have reference to different underlying realities. Thus it is not the case that the cognitive psychologist necessarily believes in mentalism any more than the S-R psychologist must believe in mechanism. As we saw in Chapter 4 the battle lines were drawn on the mentalism-mechanism issue about 50 years ago. But the point of that chapter was to demonstrate the emergence of a new kind of psychological determinism that would provide an explanation of behavior without making any commitment to the mentalism-mechanism issue. Indeed, nearly all explanatory models in psychology avoid this issue, and they do so simply because there are psychological models designed for the explanation of behavior.

The foremost cognitive psychologist was, and perhaps always will be, Edward Tolman. The major statement of his position is the book *Purposive behavior in animals and man* (Tolman, 1932). Here Tolman continued to develop the behavioristic teleology that was outlined briefly on page 94. Although Tolman used a mentalistic language (speaking of knowledge, purpose, means-end relationships, etc.), he was clearly a behaviorist, and his mentalistic-sounding language was simply that—language chosen to contrast with the mechanistic-sounding language of the S-R psychologists of his day.[16]

For many years cognitive psychology has languished, per-

[16] Recall that the chief S-R psychologist in the early days of Tolman's theorizing was Watson. He was both a mechanist and an S-R psychologist. At that time Tolman's use of mentalistic-sounding language was perhaps a wise choice. Later, when Tolman's chief opposition was Hull and his students, Tolman's language was probably a handicap. However, the apparent differences in philosophy of science were purely verbal (Tolman, 1959).

haps because of the great hope, the heroic optimism, that characterized the Hullian effort. As it gradually became clear that Hullian theory could not explain anything like the wealth of data it was initially supposed to explain, psychology entered an atheoretical era during which, again, cognitive psychology languished. But if we are to have any behavior theory at all, then some distinct alternatives to our current concepts of incentive motivation and reinforcement could be useful, and cognitive concepts are available for this purpose.

The phenomenon that the r_G version of incentive theory was initially designed to explain was that animals often behave as though they have purposes. Even in the mechanistic era of the 1920s there was little disagreement about the fact that the rat can behave as though it knows what it is doing, as though it expects certain outcomes from its behavior, and as though it has purposes to achieve. Hull (1931) attempted to explain this phenomenon, that is, the objective purposiveness of behavior, by assuming that some fraction of the consummatory response became conditioned to environmental cues. From this assumption the events described earlier in the chapter developed. But a quite different type of explanation is possible. It is possible simply to take the rat's apparent expectancy of certain outcomes (after it has had some experience in the situation) as a behavioral datum. And by doing so we can explain the phenomenon, in the usual sense of describing it, simply by saying that under these conditions the rat has an *expectancy* of food, or shock, or whatever. In the remainder of this section I will outline briefly some of the applications and implications of this kind of approach.

Classical conditioning. Consider first what must be the simplest kind of situation, namely, one in which the animal is simply put in a particular novel apparatus and permitted to eat there. After a few such experiences the rat's behavior changes, and the cognitive psychologist is inclined to say that the rat now expects food in this situation. This is surely an inference on the part of the cognitive psychologist, but is it any greater an inference than that of the S-R psychologist who says that the consummatory response has now become classically conditioned to stimuli in the situation? Or is it merely a different inference?

The issue here is what is fundamental and what is derived. For the S-R psychologist Pavlovian conditioning is viewed as fundamental, and the expectancy phenomenon is derived from the fundamental learning process. The cognitive psychologist sees the expectancy phenomenon as fundamental and as producing the results of a Pavlovian experiment. Classical conditioning experiments are simply those in which expectancies can be developed without regard to the animal's behavior. Why did Pavlov's dog salivate? Because the CS made it expect food. Alternatively, we could say that the CS conveys information about food or that it predicts food.[17] The Pavlovian situation would appear especially effective for establishing the CS as a predictive cue because the stimulus events are, by definition, presented in a fixed relationship to each other and do not vary with the animal's behavior.

The application of cognitive theory to incentive motivation is fairly straightforward. We have the tradition of thinking of incentive motivation as mediated by a classically conditioned r_G. The conditions that are considered to condition r_G to particular environmental stimuli should be, in general, effective in making those stimuli predictors of reinforcement. In the presence of such cues the animal will have an expectancy of food, and if it is deprived, this expectancy will be manifest in several ways in its behavior: It may salivate, or it may also be motivated to give some instrumental food-getting response, either an innate reaction or one that has been previously learned. In either case we have motivation of behavior that depends upon external arousal, prior experience, and prior conditions of reinforcement. We have incentive motivation.

Instrumental learning. In most instrumental or operant learning situations there are discriminative stimuli, that is, stimuli in the presence of which responding is reinforced. These stimuli become predictive cues. The situation is thus similar to the Pavlovian situation with the important difference that the predictive value of the cues is not directly under the control of the experimenter because the animal's behavior necessarily intervenes. Consider a rat in an alley with food in the goal box. Initially, the start box does not predict food, but after the rat has made its way there the first time, the start box will be a weak predictor. On the next trial there is a little more temporal contiguity of the predictor and the consequence, and the predictive relationship will be stronger. As the animal comes to run with greater certainty and speed, the start box will become an increasingly good predictor of food.

[17] It can be argued that classical conditioning is not a label for an underlying associative process but for a procedure for demonstrating learning. In describing what happens in a learning experiment, changes in behavior may be attributed to changes in the animal itself, for example, the building up of associations, habits, or expectancies, or they may be correlated with the procedural regularities the experimenter imposes on the animal. For example, reinforcement is widely used to refer both to a hypothetical response-strengthening process within the animal that produces behavior and to an experimental procedure with which we produce behavior. It is unfortunate that one word has acquired two such different meanings. Because cognitive psychology is somewhat less developed than S-R psychology, it can avoid this semantic confusion. We will refer to *expectancy* as an underlying process, the content of what is learned, and to *predictive cues* as the predictiveness of stimuli in the experimental situation. Predictiveness is an objectively manipulable property of stimuli; expectancy is a theoretical construct.

Thus the instrumental situation as well as the Pavlovian situation provides predictive relationships among environmental events. Such a relationship can be conveniently described in terms of information, information being defined as the extent to which a prior event predicts a consequent event, in this case, a cue and a reward. Cognitive psychology assumes that the predictiveness in the environment is mirrored more or less accurately by a corresponding expectancy. If we provide information of a particular form, such as an S-S contingency, we assume that the animal learns a corresponding S-S expectancy.

Predictive cues convey information about specific consequences, for example, the amount and quality of reinforcement. Is this specific information also processed by the rat? We will see in Chapter 12 that the rat's behavior is determined in part by these parameters of reinforcement, so we may suppose that this kind of information is reflected in the rat's S-S expectancy. Since a cue for food is a cue for a particular food, therefore, we may assume that the rat learns to expect that particular food.

The next question is what other kinds of information can be assimilated and stored? Specifically, if we arrange an experiment so that reinforcement is contingent upon the animal making a particular response, can that kind of environmental information also be processed? Can the rat learn an expectancy corresponding to the experimental contingency existing between its behavior and its consequences? At this point we have two quite different options: One is to answer this question affirmatively and to postulate that in different kinds of experimental situations in which different contingencies prevail the animal is able to process the different kinds of information that correspond with these contingencies. The second approach attempts to explain behavior entirely on the basis of S-S expectancies. Let us see how this is attempted. Bindra (1969, 1972) approaches the problem in essentially the same way as Mowrer (1960) did: There is incentive but no response learning. The animal does not learn anything about the consequences of its own behavior; it simply makes more and more refined discriminations about predictive cues in this situation. Bindra assumes that predictive cues initiate a central motive state (a state that might be designated as hunger or fear, etc.) and that for each of these states there is automatic and selective facilitation of certain classes of behavior. In the case of hunger the behaviors that are facilitated by the expectancy of food depend upon the presence of certain other stimuli, which we may call *supporting stimuli*. For example, if one of the supporting stimuli in the situation is a food object, then there will be selective facilitation of some form of eating, seizing, and chewing the food. Note that the hunger state does not automatically produce a fixed consummatory response; rather, it sensitizes the animal to respond in appropriate ways to whatever supportive stimuli are available.

Theory of motivation

Thus if food is presented as a liquid diet, the rat will drink it, but if it is in solid form, the rat will chew it. This linkage between the motivational state and the class of consummatory behaviors is said to be innate, not itself subject to learning.

If the situation contains no food objects but only cues to food and if such cues are provided by objects like the bar in a Skinner box, then the motivational state will selectively facilitate manipulation. The rat presses the bar, not because it is reinforced for doing so or because it expects that doing so produces food, but simply because the bar is a predictor of food, and at the same time the bar is a manipulable object. The autoshaping phenomenon follows directly from Bindra's interpretation; the pigeon pecks the key because the key becomes a predictor of food. The fact that the animal pecks the key even when such behavior prevents food from occurring (Williams & Williams, 1969) is consistent with the idea that the animal does not learn anything about his own behavior but that all of its learning is restricted to cue-consequence relationships.[18]

The final class of behaviors that is selectively facilitated by the hunger state, according to Bindra, consists of orienting and locomotory responses. If the situation provides no support for manipulation or for eating, then the animal may just approach those cues that are better predictors of food. For example, the rat runs in the alley because while the start box may be a good predictor of food, cues within the alley are better predictors, and the goal box itself is the best predictor of food. The rat keeps approaching better predictors. In short, once the appropriate motivational state is aroused by a cue, the animal will give us certain classes of behavior; which specific response it gives us is a function of what supportive stimuli are present. It may consume, manipulate, or approach different cues according to their supportive function. A sufficiently molecular application of these concepts permits all of the animal's behavior to be explained without any response-strengthening mechanism and without any information about the animal's own behavior being processed.

Other theorists have proposed alternative accounts that may be less parsimonious than Bindra's, but that are much more flexible. Tolman himself, of course, used experimental situations that were organized spatially; the information that his animals were required to process to get food involved the location of blind alleys and through-

---

[18] A recent report by LoLordo et al. (1974) shows the importance of the stimulus-support properties of predictive cues. They found no autoshaping when they used a diffuse auditory cue to food, but they did get it when they used a localized visual cue. They also found no automaintenance of a treadle response, only of key pecking. Thus it looks as though the autoshaping effect is found only when the food cue is localized and when it supplies stimulus support for the animal's species-specific food-getting behavior.

ways in mazes. Tolman conceived of the rat in this kind of situation as learning a map of correct paths to food and then utilizing the information contained in the map to get to the food when the path was changed or the starting point was changed or the value of the goal object was changed. Over the years Tolman and his students reported a number of experiments showing that rats can process and utilize information of this form. But the force of these demonstrations was largely lost as r_G theory was developed, so that Hullian rats could do many of the tricks that Tolman's rats could do. Tolman's demonstrations lost some force, too, because many of the demonstrations appeared to have little generality. For example, latent learning could be obtained, and the existence of such a phenomenon had to be reckoned with, but in a great many experiments latent learning was not obtained, and no adequate explanation was ever given for why the processing of information failed in these cases. In general, Tolman's rat appeared to be not only cognitive but, on occasion, extremely cognitive. There seemed to be no limit to the kinds of information that it could process and subsequently utilize. But as we will see shortly, there is now good reason to suppose that there are very real constraints upon the kind of information that a particular animal can process and utilize.

The general form of expectancy in Tolman's system was S-R-S; the animal expects that in a certain situation a certain reaction will have certain consequences. The inclusion of the response term distinguishes such expectancies from the S-S expectancies previously described. Information about the animal's own behavior is very much a part of what is learned. Behavior may also be in equivalence classes, so that if an animal has learned to swim through a maze, for example, there will be immediate transfer to a task in which it must walk through the maze (Macfarlane, 1930). Perhaps such equivalence classes only require us to redefine behavior in terms of its functional properties, such as locomotion. Tolman's view was that the animal learns that if it locomotes to a particular place, there will be particular consequences. Again, we see an enormous flexibility (and inevitably a fair degree of ambiguity) in Tolman's analysis.

One recent cognitive theorist (Irwin, 1971) has suggested that in situations in which the relationship between the animal's behavior and its outcome is set either by the natural order of things or by an arbitrary experimenter, the animal learns an expectancy that corresponds specifically to that contingency. In Irwin's analysis the animal may learn an expectancy of the S-S form, but it may also learn an expectancy of the R-S form. Irwin explicitly permits an animal to process and utilize information regarding the relationship between its acts and their outcomes. A further feature of Irwin's analysis is that he sees the animal as being constantly involved in making decisions. The question for the animal is always whether to respond or not to respond or to respond in one way or another.

According to Irwin, the decision is based in a determinate manner upon the relative strengths of the different R-S expectancies and the relative values of the expected outcomes. Thus Irwin also sets no theoretical limits upon the kinds of information that the rat can process. As he quite properly points out, such limits have to be determined empirically. If we wish to know whether the rat prefers this consequence over that one, then we can arrange an experimental situation in which just these consequences are made contingent upon particular behaviors. And if the animal solves the problem, we have the needed evidence for preference. The same criterion can be introduced to provide an operational definition for discrimination of cues or discrimination of drive states or differentiation of responses. In each case if the animal solves the problem, then we have evidence for its being able to learn an expectancy of the required form, the form that corresponds to the environmental contingencies. Irwin's interpretation is, therefore, like Tolman's in that it suggests no a priori constraints upon the kind of information that can be processed by the rat. If the experimental situation imposes a contingency involving the animal's behavior, then we may anticipate that the animal's behavior will reflect its appreciation of this contingency.

A compromise position that has recently been proposed by Bolles (1972) stands somewhere between Bindra's, in which behavior is strictly determined by S-S expectancies and the selective facilitating effect of motivation, and the position of Tolman and Irwin, in which any kind of information may be represented as an expectancy. Bolles suggests that when an animal has an S-S expectancy, it may already have an innate or previously learned R-S expectancy, and if it does, then this is the behavior that will be given. For example, in the pigeon, for which pecking is a very strong food-getting response, we may suppose that the autoshaping phenomenon depends entirely upon learning an S-S expectancy. Given a cue for food, the pigeon pecks at it because it innately expects that pecking will produce food. If we give a rat a cue to shock, it is quite likely to freeze. We know from a variety of experimental evidence that freezing may effectively compete with almost any kind of behavior, so we may suppose that this is a particularly strong innate R-S expectancy in the rat. Again, we may suppose that the rat freezes because it innately expects that freezing produces safety.

On the other hand, there are many situations in which animals modify their behavior in accordance with more or less arbitrarily programmed R-S contingencies. It is necessary, therefore, to suppose that in some cases innate R-S expectancies can be replaced by learned ones that correspond to information provided by these experimental contingencies. Thus we can have it both ways. If the animal's behavior fails to be modified in our learning experiments, we can attribute this intractability to the existence of strong innate R-S expectancies. But if we can control its behavior with a reinforcement contingency, then we may suppose that it can learn an expectancy that corresponds to the imposed contingency.

Within this framework the task facing the experimental psychologist is clear. He must determine for a particular species what its innate expectancies are, what kinds of expectancies are rapidly learned, and what kinds of expectancies are difficult or impossible to learn. In short, he must discover something about the structure of the animal's information-processing abilities. As this structure becomes clear, it will be increasingly possible to predict how an animal's behavior will change with experience and how much experience it will take to produce a given change.

Summary

In the early days of behavior theory the S-R association was the only explanatory concept. All behavior was attributed to unlearned or learned S-R associations. But then, as the earlier chapters show, new kinds of experimental parameters were discovered, and new kinds of theoretical constructs were postulated to explain them. Energies, forces, instincts, and drives were postulated to be necessary to make the S-R machinery go. Hull and his followers formulated and formalized a sharp distinction between the older, associative constructs and the newer, motivational constructs. But in the preceding chapters we have seen that the distinction between habit and drive became blurred; drive did not seem to have the properties it was supposed to have, it was not independent of learning, and it failed to explain much of what was regarded as motivated behavior. When the Hullians saw this, they began to introduce new concepts, *learned* sources of motivation.

These new motivators preserved much of the old system. Although they were learned in a different way, by classical conditioning rather than by reinforcement, they made it possible to preserve the motivation-learning distinction, at least in principle, and to preserve the S-R machinery. They were themselves S-R associations, and they motivated other S-R associations. But the simplicity of the drive-habit or energy-structure distinction was gone, and, as we have seen, it was possible to formulate a variety of alternative models emphasizing either motivation or learning.

We have seen a little evidence in this chapter, and in the following chapters we will see much more indicating that the entire enterprise is in trouble. It is not clear that the new motivators are established by a classical conditioning process or even that they motivate. It is not clear that instrumental learning is established by a reinforcement process or even that it consists of strengthened S-R associations. Because of these fundamental troubles with the traditional S-R models of behavior, there has been renewed interest in alternative cognitive models. These models are based not on hypothetical S-R associations but upon expectancies as the basic unit of learning and performance. They emphasize information processing and cue utilization rather than reinforcement and motivation. We will find out more about them in the following chapters.

10

AVOIDANCE

it is by means of the emotions that we
internalize or "treasure up," as Hume has said,
a knowledge of the external world.

O. H. Mowrer

The special problems that arise in the analysis of avoidance behavior are so interesting and of such great theoretical importance that it is appropriate to devote a separate chapter to them. The early history of the problem can be cut short because it has been given in some detail elsewhere (Solomon & Brush, 1956; Bolles, 1972a). We will start with the acquired drive model that was introduced in the previous chapter, and then we will turn to the reinforcement model. We will discover that neither of these traditional ways of regarding motivated behavior can cope adequately with the complexities of avoidance behavior. The basic difficulty for both kinds of models is that it has not been possible to find any one reinforcement mechanism that explains all avoidance learning. The empirical regularities that seem to account for a given avoidance behavior appear to have little scope or generality, so that as we begin to work out an understanding of one particular avoidance response, there seems little hope that these empirical laws will explain any other avoidance response. The chapter will conclude with a brief look at some of the new developments in the avoidance area that promise to have somewhat greater power and generality.

Two-factor theory

In the preceding chapter we saw how Miller and Mowrer and other writers had proposed a promising interpretation of avoidance behavior based on the premise that avoidance is motivated by fear and reinforced by fear reduction. This account incorporated the assumption that there are two factors—one involving the learning of the avoidance response itself and the second involved with the learning of fear. The most popular interpretation of the two factors is to attribute them to separate kinds of learning processes: a drive reduc-

Theory of motivation

tion mechanism for the learning of instrumental avoidance behavior and a classical conditioning process for the learning of fear. Mowrer (1947) cited evidence from a variety of sources to support the two-factor theory, and it was widely hailed on all sides as the most acceptable account of avoidance behavior.[1]

However, almost from the outset there were some difficulties for the two-factor explanation of avoidance. One difficulty arose because of the remarkable discoveries of Solomon and his students about the extinction of avoidance. Earlier writers had noted that avoidance behavior was sometimes quite resistant to extinction, but Solomon (Solomon & Wynne, 1953; Solomon et al., 1953) reported that dogs would learn a hurdle-jumping response in a shuttle box after only a few intense shocks and that once acquired, this response was practically impossible to extinguish. Some dogs ran as many as 650 trials before the experimenters extinguished. The learning curve for a typical animal is shown in Fig. 10-1. Note that after 7 escape responses, that is, responses having latencies longer than 10 seconds, there was a sharp transition from escape to avoidance. Note that after this transition the avoidance response did not extinguish but continued to gain in strength, even though no more shocks were received.

Solomon et al. (1953) reported several other curious observations. Occasionally, a relatively long latency response (approaching 10 seconds) would occur. Typically, these trials would be followed by a series of trials having much quicker responding rather than con-

---

[1] For a number of years Miller (e.g., Miller, 1951) proposed a monolithic account of avoidance learning in which drive reduction was hypothesized to explain everything, that is, not only learning of the instrumental response but the fear learning also. Miller suggested that fear might be learned either at that moment when shock is terminated experimentally or when the pain sensation from shock habituates. Presumably, a fear response could be reinforced by its own habituation. Mowrer (1960) summarized a number of studies, done mainly under his direction, that tested the two-factor version of avoidance against Miller's one-factor version. In one such experiment Mowrer and Solomon (1954) trained rats to press a bar for food and then investigated the strength of this behavior when a stimulus was presented that had previously been paired with a shock. Experimental groups were defined by the conditions under which the cue and shock were paired. Shock was either short or long and was terminated either suddenly or gradually. It should be assumed from the drive reduction theory of reinforcement that the acquisition of fear would be poor with a long shock (because of the delay in reinforcement) or with a gradually terminated shock (because of the relative ineffectiveness of the subsequent drive reduction). Mowrer and Solomon found no difference in suppression between the groups, and they argued, therefore, that since the cue had been presented to all groups under the same conditions relative to shock onset, shock onset must be the critical factor in fear conditioning. Fear must be learned by classical conditioning. Ultimately, Miller (1963) acquiesced, at least partially, and admitted that it is the onset of shock that is critical for the learning of fear.

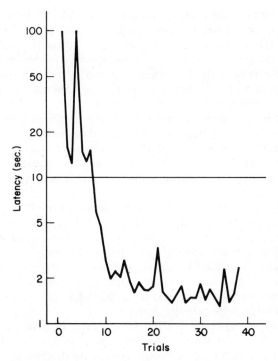

Figure 10–1

Acquisition of avoidance for a "fairly typical"
dog in a shuttle box. (From Solomon & Wynne,
1953) Copyright (1953) by the American
Psychological Association. Reprinted by
permission.

tinued deterioration of the behavior. It was as if the animal had no
inclination to test reality, but on those occasions when it almost did
so by approaching the 10-second limit, it became frightened. Another
puzzling observation was that when avoidance behavior became well
established, the hurdle-jumping response had a latency in the order of
1 or 2 seconds, which is so short that the autonomic nervous system
can hardly do more than begin reacting to the S^+. There can be little
or no fear if fear is defined as feedback from the autonomic system.
In fact, the autonomic symptoms of fear (shivering, defecation, etc.)
were observed only during the trials when a long-latency avoidance
occurred. Thus it would seem that when the avoidance response is
well established, it not only prevents shock but also to a considerable
degree prevents the fear that is supposed to motivate the behavior and
maintain the behavior by its reduction.

These phenomena pose a vexing set of facts to be explained.
Solomon and Wynne's (1954) explanation involved several assump-

tions. First, there is the familiar assumption that fear becomes classically conditioned during the nonavoidance trials and that this fear then motivates the avoidance response. The apparent failure of the fear to extinguish is explained by a new principle of *anxiety conservation*. The idea is that the latency of the well-learned response (1 or 2 seconds) is indeed too short to permit fear to occur; it is too short for the autonomic nervous system to react to the S+. Fear does not extinguish because it is "protected" by the avoidance response. In effect, fear does not extinguish because it does not occur very often. The avoidance response does not extinguish because as soon as it starts to do so, the fear reaction is given time to be reinstated, and this fear gives an extra boost to the avoidance habit to improve performance on subsequent trials.

Even with the anxiety conservation principle, avoidance should ultimately extinguish, and perhaps it does, but the extinction still seems much too slow. We have the additional problem that if short-latency responses prevent fear from occurring, that is, if well-learned avoidance behavior occurs without the animals being emotionally upset, and if fear dissipates during the course of avoidance training, then what is it that energizes the behavior? The role of fear in this situation is quite puzzling indeed.

Further complexity for the part played by fear in avoidance behavior was found by Wynne and Solomon (1955). They found that sectioning the autonomic nervous system markedly impaired the learning of a new avoidance response, but produced little disruption of a previously learned avoidance response. This finding suggests again that the full-blown fear reaction is not essential for the maintenance of avoidance. The picture we begin to get is that while fear may initially be a necessary part of the avoidance learning situation, it evidently plays much less of a role once the behavior is established. And we wonder what motivates avoidance behavior if it is not fear and what source of reinforcement maintains it if it is not a reduction in fear.

A reinforcement-model interpretation. Mowrer's two-factor, or acquired-drive, interpretation of avoidance learning was also in trouble on another side. Schoenfeld (1950) insisted that the explanation of avoidance behavior requires no assumptions about drives or fears or drive reductions or any of the other kinds of conceptual machinery that Mowrer and his followers were talking about. All of these concepts are extraneous we were told.

It is only the drive theorist's conviction that for every behavior there must be a motive—that somewhere there must be a fear or a hunger or a drive that makes behavior occur—which makes him assume that fear motivates avoidance behavior. It is only the drive theorist's other conviction, namely, that learning requires drive reduction, that makes him assume that avoidance is reinforced by a reduction in fear. Typically there is little independent evidence for fear, and indeed, as we observed briefly in the previous chapter (see page 303), the earnest efforts of many experimenters to find independent verification of emotional reactions in avoidance learning have revealed no consistent pattern. Nothing can be found that is correlated with the apparent motivation of avoidance behavior. If such evidence could be found, then Schoenfeld's argument would, of course, be largely irrelevant and the drive theorist's position would be enormously strengthened. But the fact is that these efforts have been disappointing. After carefully reviewing this literature, Rescorla and Solomon (1967) conclude that the fear that motivates avoidance behavior must be a central event—it cannot be a peripherally observable autonomic reaction. Therefore, Schoenfeld's argument about the circularity of the explanatory fear retains considerable force. Later in this chapter we will see that Solomon and his students have subsequently embarked on a series of experiments that lend much more substantial support to the drive theorist's position; but at the same time they have drastically altered the original conception of what fear is and how it is learned. Let us first examine the alternative formulation proposed by Schoenfeld.

It should be noted that Schoenfeld was not denying that the rat becomes frightened when it is shocked. His attack was directed at the a priori assumption that by being a drive, fear motivates, and at the circular argument that fear reduction reinforces. Schoenfeld suggested that the fundamental aspect of the avoidance-learning experiment is the occurrence of a stimulus (the S+), which is frequently associated with shock. Since shock is aversive, that is, a negative reinforcer, the S+ must become a conditioned negative reinforcer during the course of training. According to this position, what the animal is really doing in the learning situation is not avoiding shock and not escaping fear, but escaping the S+.

Schoenfeld's position appears to be quite different from the drive theorist's position because the reinforcing event is an experimentally manipulated event (termination of the S+) rather than an internal event (fear reduction), which is, as we have seen, basically unobservable. But in practice the difference is not all that great. Recall that when Mowrer attempted to test the fear reduction hypothesis, he assumed that the occurrence of fear was highly correlated with the occurrence of the S+; so he manipulated fear level by manipulating the S+ (see p. 288). Evidently, when theoretical statements about reinforcement are translated into experimental procedures, both the reinforcement theorist and the two-factor theorists do the same thing: They prevent S+ termination.

A second point of apparent difference also disappears if we ask either how fear is learned or how the S+ becomes aversive. It turns out that both questions have the same answer. Mowrer said that fear is classically conditioned to the S+, that is, that simply pairing the S+ with shock conditions fear to it. But Schoenfeld tells us that S+ becomes a conditioned aversive stimulus merely by being paired with shock. Thus hidden in Schoenfeld's ostensibly empirical language describing the avoidance experiment we find a second hypothetical factor called conditioned aversiveness. So again, when their theoretical statements are translated into experimental terms, the reinforcement theorist and the two-factor theorist do the same thing: They pair an originally neutral cue, the S+, with shock.[2]

Thus we see that Schoenfeld also had a two-factor theory. Although the two theorists differed in terms of their theoretical constructs, both men shared the belief that some kind of learning establishes the effectiveness of the S+ and that it is then the termination of the S+ that reinforces avoidance behavior. Mowrer would appear to be at a disadvantage because his theory refers to fear, which we have seen is very difficult to verify empirically, while Schoenfeld's account appears to be tied more closely to manipulable events such as stimuli that are paired with shock. But Schoenfeld lost this advantage because he went on to indicate that the S+ could be not only an external stimulus controlled by the experimenter, but it could also be an internal stimulus produced by the animal's behavior. For example, when the animal makes some response that is not effective in avoiding shock, and shock follows, then the proprioceptive feedback from that response will become aversive. And if the animal should then switch to some new behavior, the new behavior would be reinforced by the termination of those aversive stimuli. This mechanism was rich in explanatory power; it dealt not only with avoidance learning but with punishment (Dinsmoor, 1954, 1955) and with the different kind of avoidance learning that was soon to be reported by Sidman (1953). But, at the same time, Schoenfeld's facile extrapolation from external and experimentally controlled stimuli to internal and inferred stimuli deprived his criticism of Mowrer's position of much of its point. Does it really make much difference whether we refer to internal, unobservable fears or internal, unobservable stimuli?

[2] The argument here is that Mowrer's and Schoenfeld's theoretical interpretations of avoidance learning have the same formal structure even though the descriptive language is quite different. It should not be said, though, that the difference between them is "only semantic." Semantic differences are not only very real, they are of the utmost importance. It does make a difference whether avoidance behavior is ascribed to fear or to the aversiveness of stimuli, because as Keller and Schoenfeld (1950) have indicated, aversiveness is to be described, defined, and thought of entirely in terms of reinforcement, while fear not only conveys implications about reinforcement, it also carries even more pointed implications about motivation. The real difference, then, between how Schoenfeld and Mowrer regard avoidance behavior is that for Schoenfeld it is to be explained like any other behavior, that is, in terms of the reinforcement contingencies that control it, while for Mowrer behavior is to be explained at least as much in terms of what motivate it. This is a very real and very important conceptual difference, in spite of the logical similarity in the two men's theoretical positions.

Thus, in spite of the apparent points of difference, we can see, at least in retrospect, that the Hullian and Skinnerian positions had certain common features. In both cases there are two factors. In both cases the all-important procedure is the reinforcement provided by the termination of stimuli that are said either to have fear conditioned to them or to be aversive. And whether we think in terms of fear or in terms of aversiveness, in both cases the S^+ is given its critical powers by means of Pavlovian procedures, that is, by pairing the stimulus with shock.

These two similar explanations of avoidance behavior have become the most widely accepted interpretations of avoidance learning; one or the other has been defended and promoted by nearly every writer for over 20 years. Initially, all of the data appeared to be supportive, but more recently we have begun to see the inadequacies of both interpretations. We will see shortly how this came about, but first let us look briefly at a different kind of avoidance procedure.

Sidman avoidance. Sidman (1953) described a procedure in which the animal receives brief shocks at regular intervals, for example, every 5 seconds, if it does not make the appropriate response. The shocks are too brief for the animal to escape, but by responding appropriately during the intershock interval, the delivery of the next shock can be postponed by, say, 30 seconds. Continued pressing leads to continued postponement of shock. Under these conditions a rat eventually comes to press the bar at a fairly high rate, perhaps 500 responses per hour, which is four times the rate necessary to eliminate all shocks. Thus it gives a fairly high, even rate of responding over long periods of testing.

Another unique feature of Sidman's procedure is that, typically, there is no S^+. The only programmed events are the brief shocks. The question then is what stimuli control the response and what stimuli reinforce it? Sidman's original answer followed Schoenfeld's suggestion that the crucial stimuli are the proprioceptive consequences of the response itself. All of the responses in the animal's repertoire except bar pressing are liable to occur at the time shock comes on. Only bar pressing is safe. Thus the proprioceptive feedback from all behavior except bar pressing becomes aversive, and bar pressing must be reinforced as the animal makes behavioral transitions from freezing, biting, standing, or some other behavior to bar pressing. An alternative explanation, also discussed by Sidman (1953), is that bar pressing emerges as all other responses are suppressed by unavoided shocks. There is a punishment gradient, immediate punishment being more effective in suppressing a response than delayed shock. Although the criterion response also suffers the effect of delayed punishment, it inevitably enjoys more delayed punishment than any other response so that it is maintained while all other behaviors are more promptly punished and more strongly suppressed. Sidman (1953) observed that if the postponement time is short, so that shock can come only a few seconds after the bar press, then even this behavior is not safe, and it too deteriorates.

Sidman (1966) has discussed the fact that in well-practiced behavior the interresponse time distribution (the distribution of time intervals between successive responses) comes very close to what it would be if the animal were responding randomly in time as Fig. 10-2 shows. But he observes that some animals make systematic departures from this pattern. Some subjects tend to pace their behavior regularly at a safe rate, whereas others tend to respond in bursts. Sidman also discussed the fact that if an S+ is introduced after the behavior is well established, for instance, if a light is introduced 5 seconds before a scheduled shock, then the animal quickly learns to respond only during the light, and this improved timing persists long after the S+ is removed. This finding suggests that prior to introducing the S+ the behavior was not dependent upon time. On the other hand, the timing of behavior after the S+ is removed indicates how subtle, accurate, and persistent temporal discrimination can be.

Sidman (1962) has also pointed out that there is another potential reinforcing agency in this situation, namely, the reduction in shock frequency that results from pressing the bar. The more the rat presses, the less likely shocks become. However, Anger (1963) has observed that it is not reasonable to apply the shock reduction hypothesis to the occasional cases of rats avoiding shock successfully for many hours at a time. How can the rat discriminate such a low rate from either no shocks at all or a slightly higher rate? In short, how can such low rates be effective in shaping the animal's behavior?

Anger (1963) proposed that there are stimulus consequences of responding that persist for some time after a response so that in some sense the animal knows how long it has been since the last response. Shock never occurs in Sidman avoidance just after a response, so when the "traces" of responding are short, the animal is safe, and short traces are relatively nonaversive. But as time elapses since the last response, the probability of a shock increases, and the conditioned aversiveness of the trace increases accordingly. Early in acquisition, learning occurs because by pressing the bar the animal produces for itself new (short) traces that are much less aversive than long traces. Learning starts as soon as the animal has responded a few times, so that long traces begin to become aversive. Later in acquisition the discrimination of different lengths of traces progresses rapidly as the aversiveness of all the irrelevant stimuli dissipates. According to Anger's formulation, the effective S+ in Sidman avoidance, the stimulus whose termination reinforces avoidance, is some interoceptive consequence of not having responded recently. A similar hypothesis had been advanced by Mowrer and Keehn (1958) to explain intertrial responding in the shuttle box. They, of course, had incorporated the element of fear: Not responding produces fear, which the animal escapes by responding.

Anger's hypothesis can be said to make sense of the seeming paradox of Sidman avoidance, which is that it occurs in the absence of any demonstrable reinforcement event. It is, therefore, brought under the broad reach of the Skinnerian interpretation of behavioral control. But one may well wonder what tangible reference there could be for the hypothetical stimuli said to be *the consequence of not having responded recently.* Just what kind of stimulus is this? Does the postulation of such stimuli rescue the reinforcement interpretation of avoidance learning or make it untestable, as some critics have charged? There is some indirect evidence to support Anger's interpretation (Anger, 1963; Bolles & Popp, 1964), but the critical empirical issue is whether rats actually do show timing; that is, do they spread out their responding in time? It is clear that rats predominantly respond more or less randomly in time in bar-press Sidman avoidance, as Fig. 10-2 shows. The question is whether there is any tendency to respond at a higher-than-chance level at longer post-response times. Recent studies of this question (e.g., Hineline &

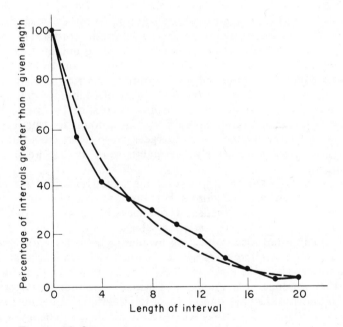

Figure 10–2

Distribution functions giving the percentage of inter-response intervals greater than a given length. The broken line is an exponential function describing events randomly distributed in time. The solid line represents the data from one well-trained subject. (From Sidman, 1954) Copyright (1954) by the American Psychological Association. Reprinted by permission.

Herrnstein, 1970) indicate that while some timing does occur, it is unstable and poorly correlated with avoidance performance.[3]

Contingencies controlling avoidance behavior. Herrnstein (1969) has noted that the customary and proper business of those involved in the experimental analysis of behavior is to discover the experimental contingencies that control behavior and not to postulate the existence of unobservable events that bring about this control. He quite properly raises the question of what experimental contingencies control Sidman avoidance behavior, since the contingencies that are typically present in the shuttle-box avoidance situation are not present in Sidman avoidance. There is no objectively defined S^+ termination, and there is not supposed to be any escape from shock. All that is left from the conventional procedure is the avoidance of shock by the appropriate response, and even this is procedurally redefined because the behavior is a free operant rather than occurring on discrete trials. If the rat responds, then shock occurs at a lower rate. In other words, the avoidance response effects a reduction in the relative frequency of shocks. To test this interpretation of avoidance behavior (specifically against Anger's timing hypothesis) Herrnstein and Hineline (1966) generalized Sidman's original procedure so that the rat always received shock randomly in time but at an average rate that depended upon its rate of responding. Thus the occurrence of an avoidance response did not guarantee freedom from immediate shock but simply reduced the probability of such an event. Herrnstein and Hineline report that learning occurs under these conditions. It is not clear that Anger's theory can account for this learning because under these conditions all traces, even short ones following the response, must be aversive, although some traces are more so than others.

But it should be emphasized the acquisition was extremely slow. Herrnstein and Hineline's best animal only began to show avoidance behavior after thousands of shocks had been received. Thus their data suggest that reduction in shock frequency is at most a sufficient condition for establishing avoidance behavior and certainly not that such a mechanism is necessary for avoidance learning. Quite the contrary, we must look elsewhere for the reinforcement mechanism that produces the much more rapid avoidance learning generally found in other avoidance learning situations. Hineline (1970) has subsequently shown that when relative shock frequency is held constant, an immediate but temporary delay of shock can serve to establish bar-press avoidance. With Hineline's procedure animals are given a series of trials in which shock occurs on every trial, but it can come either early or late in the trial depending upon whether the rat

[3] In situations other than the Skinner box, for example, the shuttle box, the rat may quickly learn extremely accurate timing (Bolles & Grossen, 1969; Riess, 1971a).

presses a bar to delay it. Bar pressing is learned under these conditions, not rapidly, but also not as slowly as reported by Herrnstein and Hineline (1966) using the procedure that permitted occasional shocks to occur immediately after a response.

The main thrust of Herrnstein's (1969) paper is still quite valid. The point is that it might be more profitable to analyze avoidance learning situations in terms of the experimental contingencies that contribute to avoidance behavior rather than attempting to account for the available data by postulating this or that reinforcing mechanism dictated by this or that theory of reinforcement. Let us see what happens when this empirical kind of approach is applied to avoidance learning in the traditional shuttle-box situation. This approach is nicely illustrated by a classic study by Kamin (1956).

Kamin (1956) ran four groups of rats in a shuttle box with a 5-second S+ preceding shock. One group was run under the conventional avoidance conditions in which the running response both terminated S+ and prevented shock. This group showed good learning and stable performance. A second group could neither terminate S+ nor prevent shock but, like all the other groups, could escape the shock by responding after its inevitable occurrence. This group showed little learning and unstable performance. The two interesting groups were those for which running either terminated S+ without preventing shock or prevented shock without terminating S+. These two groups showed approximately equal rates of acquisition that were intermediate between the two other groups. Kamin's results indicated, therefore, that S+ termination and avoidance of shock can each contribute to the acquisition of an avoidance response.

Kamin's study provided an elegant continuation of the earlier work of Mowrer and Lamoreaux (1942), which was the first to demonstrate the importance of S+ termination in shuttle-box avoidance learning. Kamin extended this finding by showing the relative importance of the two controlling contingencies, S+ termination and shock avoidance. The two contingencies appear to have about the same potential for reinforcing avoidance behavior. However, Kamin (1956) did not settle for this kind of experimental analysis; he went on to argue that S+ termination was the principal reinforcement mechanism and that the apparent efficacy of the shock avoidance contingency was an artifact.[4] But what of the other factor that Kamin found and quickly dismissed as differential punishment? What

---

[4] His argument was that animals that could only terminate S+ would have demonstrated much better performance had their running not been subject to punishment by unavoided shocks. Similarly, he argued that animals that could only prevent shock also had the possible advantage of delayed S+ termination because the S+ ultimately did go off. A follow-up study using a longer delay interval (Kamin, 1957a) tended to confirm this analysis; animals with longer-delayed S+ termination performed more poorly than the animals who could not avoid shock, whereas in the 1956 study these two groups had given comparable performances.

about the avoidance of shock? In a sense we have already discussed this issue in our brief account of Sidman avoidance, in which, of course, there is no S+ termination. We have seen that the avoidance of shock may be interpreted either as freedom from or delay of shock or as a reduction in overall shock frequency. What, too, of the escape from shock that was possible for all animals on nonavoidance trials; is it not another potential source of reinforcement? Bolles et al. (1966) attempted to replicate and extend Kamin's (1956) findings by using a factorial design in which the shock was either escapable or not, the response either produced avoidance of shock or not and produced termination of the S+ or not. The results are summarized in the left-hand column of Table 10-1. Everything appears to be in order here; the results show that the three contingencies that define the traditional shuttle-box avoidance experiment all make approximately equal contributions to the learning of the response.

But we made a major extension of this study by replicating the whole design in another apparatus, namely, a running wheel. Here the results came out quite differently, as the right-hand column of Table 10-1 shows. In the running wheel the avoidance contingency turns out to be much more important than the other two, contributing 80 percent to the total variation among groups, while both S+ termination and escape from shock make relatively minor contributions. Therefore, the relative importance of the different experimental contingencies appears to depend upon what the avoidance response is.

The contribution of the escape contingency to the acquisition of avoidance had been studied in the early research of Mowrer and Lamoreaux (1946). Recall (see page 288) that these investigators had concluded from their study that the escape contingency made a real but relatively small contribution to avoidance acquisition. What they had found was that rats that could run (or jump) to avoid and escape shock performed somewhat better than rats that were required

Table 10-1

Median percentage of avoidance responses in two different situations as a function of whether rats could avoid shock (A), escape shock (E), or terminate the S+ (T)

Available Contingencies	APPARATUS	
	Shuttle box	*Wheel*
AET	70	85
AE	40	75
AT	37	79
ET	31	38
A	15	62
E	9	26
T	10	48
None	15	28

SOURCE: Adapted from Bolles et al. (1966).

to run to avoid and jump to escape or vice versa. In other words, rats for which a particular response was effective both in avoiding shock and in escaping it learned that response only somewhat more readily than if they were required to make different responses to avoid and escape shock. However, the raw data reported by Mowrer and Lamoreaux reveal that the differences within conditions were as large as the differences between conditions. Specifically, their animals learned quite quickly to run to avoid shock, and it made little difference whether escape was accomplished by running or jumping. But jumping was acquired as an avoidance response only when escape was also accomplished by jumping. Thus, contrary to Mowrer and Lamoreaux's own conclusion, what their study really showed was that for one avoidance response (running) the escape contingency made little contribution, while for another response (jumping) it made a very substantial contribution to avoidance learning. It was only by lumping together these disparate findings that Mowrer and Lamoreaux had been able to conclude that the escape contingency made only a small contribution.

The differential contribution of escape training to the learning of different avoidance responses was further demonstrated in a study by Bolles (1969) in which three different responses were investigated: running in a wheel, turning around in the wheel (i.e., reorientation in space), and standing up on the hind legs. This was a factorial design in which each of these behaviors could be required either as an avoidance response or as an escape response, so that there were nine groups—three groups for which avoidance and escape were accomplished by the same behavior and six groups for which different responses were required to avoid and to escape. The results, shown in Fig. 10-3, reveal many kinds of different patterns. One response, standing on the hind legs, was not learned as the avoidance behavior even when the same response was effective in escaping shock. The turning-around response was learned as an avoidance response at a somewhat modest rate but only when the escape contingency was permitted to strengthen the same behavior. Finally, the running response was learned by all animals, and the escape contingency made relatively little difference in the rate of learning (see also Bolles et al., 1969). Thus for two of these responses (standing and running) the escape contingency made very little contribution, while for the third response (turning) the escape contingency appeared to be an essential part of avoidance learning.[5]

---

[5] For reasons that are not obvious this pattern of results is not always obtained. Reynierse (1972) found that running in the shuttle box was acquired as an avoidance response only if running to escape shock was also permitted, and that it made little difference whether the escape contingency was removed by delaying shock termination on escape trials or by requiring a different response, bar pressing, to escape shock. In either case immediate shock termination appeared to be an essential component in learning the shuttle-box running response.

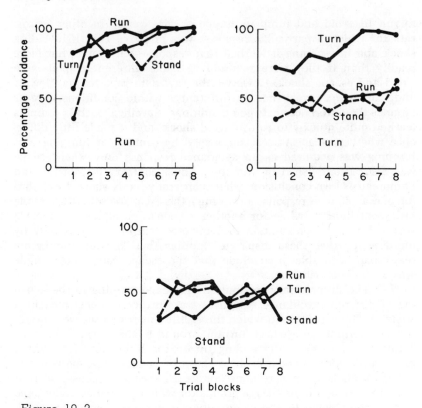

Figure 10–3

Mean percentage of avoidances on 10-trial blocks for rats required to run, turn, or stand to avoid shock and to run, turn, or stand to escape shock. The labels on individual curves refer to the escape requirement. (From Bolles, 1969) Copyright (1969) by the American Psychological Association. Reprinted by permission.

In summary, although there have been few studies specifically designed to isolate the effect of the different contingencies involved in the avoidance learning situation, the available data for the most part reveal no consistent pattern for the relative importance of the different contingencies. The general rule seems to be that there is no general rule. A particular aversive contingency, such as $S+$ termination, may be effective in controlling one avoidance response and totally ineffective in controlling another. An alternative statement of the conclusion is that while avoidance learning appears to depend upon one set of contingencies in one situation, it may require another set of contingencies in another situation. It seems fruitless, therefore, to look to any one of the experimental contingencies as constituting *the* source of reinforcement for avoidance learning. We will return to a further consideration of this curious conclusion later in a different context, and we will see further evidence for the specificity of different factors in avoidance learning. For the present, however, let us turn our attention to the S+ and examine some of its functional properties.

The properties of S+

Associative properties. If we think of the S+ as being important in avoidance because fear becomes classically conditioned to it, then we might suppose that the stimulus properties of the S+ will have an effect upon avoidance behavior. A number of studies have shown that this is the case. For example, when a light or a tone is used as the S+, the strength of avoidance behavior usually increases with the intensity of the S+ both in the shuttle box (Kessen, 1953; Schwartz, 1958; Dewson, 1965; Rohrbaugh et al., 1971) and the bar-press situation (Fantino et al., 1966; Hearst, 1969). Moreover, the onset of a light or buzzer is more effective as the S+ than its offset (Schwartz, 1958; Myers, 1960).

Studies of the effects of using different kinds of stimuli as the S+ have not yielded such a consistent picture. Sometimes (e.g., Smith et al., 1961; Freedman & Callahan, 1968) change of illumination has been found to be a poor S+, but other studies (e.g., Bolles et al., 1970) report little decrement in shuttle-box learning or performance when a light S+ is used. By contrast, an impressive and consistent difference in performance of the wheel-turning response can be attributed to the kind of auditory S+ used. Myers (1962, 1964) has found that a buzzer is much more effective than a pure tone in this situation. Myers (1962) has shown that this difference is not due merely to overall intensity but is inherent in the different qualities of stimulation. He has also reported (Myers, 1962, 1964) that sensitization control animals—that is, animals for which the cue is presented but not previously paired with shock—also give a large number of wheel-turning responses. It is as if the buzzer is intrinsically aversive for the frightened animal (see also Smith et al., 1961; Riess, 1971) in addition to being aversive because it is associated with shock. If this is the case, then different S+s can be expected to have different effects upon avoidance behavior for reasons other than their role in S+ termination. Specifically, if a particular S+ provides particularly effective control over avoidance behavior, it is not clear whether its efficacy should be attributed to its being more effective as a cue, to its termination being a more effective reinforcer, or to both of these advantages.

The cue function of the S+ is shown in those studies that have required different groups of animals to avoid shock either by approaching or withdrawing from an S+ that is localized in a particular part of the apparatus. Under these conditions the withdrawal procedure is found to be much more effective with both cats

Theory of motivation

(McAdam, 1964), and rats (Biederman et al., 1964; Whittleton et al., 1965).[6]

Perhaps the clearest evidence for the cue function of the S+, in contrast with a motivating or reinforcing function, is shown in those studies in which animals are given inevitable shocks on both sides of a choice box, but on one side shocks come on unannounced while on the other they are preceded by a cue (CS+). Rats typically show a choice for the signaled-shock side (Lockard, 1963, 1965; Brown, 1965; Perkins et al., 1966). One wonders why they prefer the CS+ side if the CS+ is aversive by virtue of being associated with shock. In the case of human subjects it is now clear that the preference for the signal results from the great aversiveness of the uncertainty of not knowing when the next shock (when it is unsignaled) is coming (Badia et al., 1966). Perhaps a similar mechanism accounts for the rat's behavior in such situations also. This situation sets the motivating or aversive function of S+ in opposition to its signal or cue value. Predominance of the cue function is shown also in situations in which shock is preceded by a series of S+s, where it is found that the rat waits for the last S+ before making an avoidance response (e.g., Levis, 1970). The same phenomenon, probably, is illustrated in the Sidman avoidance situation in which no S+ is ordinarily presented; but if shock is preceded by a 5-second S+, the rat typically delays responding until it comes on (Sidman, 1955).

The preceding studies illustrate that the S+ can serve a cue function, that is, an associative function, quite apart from whatever role it may have as a motivator of avoidance behavior or whatever reinforcing power its termination may have. We turn now to these other two functions.

Motivational properties of S+. Although it has been widely assumed for 30 years or more, there is actually very little evidence that avoidance behavior is motivated by fear conditioned to S+. This is not to say that the rat is not frightened in the avoidance situation; it undoubtedly is, particularly early in acquisition. But how much fear is evoked specifically by the S+ and how much this fear energizes avoidance behavior is quite another question.

It was previously noted (page 325) that dogs in the shuttle-box situation often show less behavioral evidence of fear as avoidance training is continued. Similar observations have been made

---

[6] It might be argued that the withdrawal of the animal from the localized S+ demonstrates that it is aversive. This use of the word "aversive" is consistent with the conventional meaning of the word but not with the technical usage the word has acquired, namely, to describe a negative reinforcer. The animal *can* terminate the S+ by approaching it, and this response might be reinforced, but the behavior is dominated by the tendency to withdraw and be rid of S+ in that manner. This dominance illustrates the cue or associative properties of the S+ as distinct from its aversiveness.

with human subjects (e.g., Bersh et al., 1956) and with rats (Kamin et al., 1963; Linden, 1969). In the latter experiments an S+ from an avoidance learning situation (hence presumably a stimulus to which fear had been conditioned) was introduced in a different situation in which the animal was working for food, and its disruptive effects upon appetitive behavior were determined. Kamin et al. and Linden reported that before the rat learned to perform effectively in the avoidance situation the S+ produced a marked suppression of feeding behavior; but as the rat acquired proficiency at the avoidance task, S+ lost its disruptive or suppressive effect.

Another approach to the problem is to see whether avoidance behavior is strengthened, or if learning occurs more readily, if a higher intensity of shock is used. In a few situations, such as one-way avoidance (see the following), shock intensity appears to have little effect on acquisition (Moyer & Korn, 1966; Theios et al., 1966). But in most situations the rat shows poorer acquisition with higher intensities of shock (Moyer & Korn, 1964; Bolles & Warren, 1965; Johnson & Church, 1965; D'Amato & Fazzaro, 1966; Theios et al., 1966; Levine, 1966; Cicala & Kremer, 1969; McAllister et al., 1971). The data of Moyer and Korn (1964), which are typical, are shown in Fig. 10-4.

It is obvious that avoidance behavior cannot be acquired or

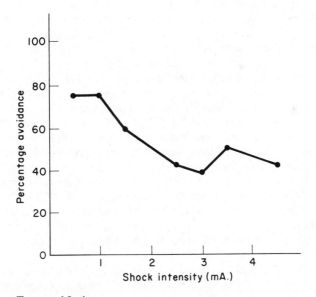

Figure 10–4

Mean percentage avoidances over the course of train-ing as a function of shock intensity. (From Moyer & Korn, 1964) Copyright (1964) by the American Psychological Association. Reprinted by permission.

maintained if shock is reduced to too low an intensity. A trivial instance would be shock so weak that it is not detected by the animal. But, apparently, once some threshold of aversiveness has been reached for all animals in the group, any further increase in shock intensity is likely to produce poorer avoidance learning. The only exception to this general rule appears to be the results of Kimble (1955), who found that the speed of a wheel-turning avoidance response increased with shock intensity. This finding may be a peculiarity of the wheel-turning response, perhaps because wheel turning is more elicited by shock than motivated by fear. It should be noted that with a previously well-established avoidance response this decreasing relationship with intensity may be reversed. It has been found that given sufficient prior training more intense shock may increase somewhat the strength of avoidance behavior and increase its resistance to extinction (D'Amato et al., 1967; Huff et al., 1967; Powell, 1970; Leander, 1973). However, much of this improved avoidance with stronger shock can be attributed to a reduction in warm-up effects rather than to higher asymptotic performance; so even these studies give little evidence for a motivational effect.

More encouraging evidence for a genuine motivational role of the S+ in avoidance is provided by a series of studies that has come out of Solomon's laboratory. The first study in this series (Solomon & Turner, 1962) illustrates the basic procedure. Solomon and Turner first trained dogs on a panel-pushing avoidance response. A light was used as the S+, and after fairly extensive avoidance training was given so that the behavior was firmly established, the dogs were removed from that situation, and the second phase or classical conditioning part of the experiment was begun. Half the animals were presented with two cues: One tone, the CS+, was invariably followed by shock, and a discriminatively different tone, the CS−, signaled the omission of shock on some trials. After each tone had been presented 50 times, the animals were returned to the avoidance situation to determine the effects of the tones on the previously learned avoidance response. A series of test trials were run in which the animals were presented with either the original S+ or the new Pavlovian CS+ or CS−. It is apparent from the reported records of the individual subjects that the response to the CS+ or danger signal (DS) was, on the average, as prompt and as persistent as the response to the original S+.[7] It looked as though fear had been classically condi-

[7] In accordance with the footnote on page 288, a cue is called a CS in a Pavlovian situation in which events occur independently of the animal's behavior, and it is called an S in an operant situation in which the animal can do something about the cue. Other distinctions are possible, however, and here it is more convenient to designate a cue predicting shock a *danger signal*, or DS, whether it is presented in a Pavlovian or an operant situation. Similarly, a cue predicting no shock will be called a *safety signal*, or SS, regardless of the situation in which it is presented.

tioned to the DS in the Pavlovian session, just as it had been conditioned to the S+ during the prior avoidance training, and that it was this fear that was motivating behavior during the subsequent test in the avoidance situation. It might be argued that in the Pavlovian situation more than fear was being learned; perhaps the animals were engaged there in some instrumental behavior that then transferred to the avoidance situation to facilitate the required avoidance response. This possibility was precluded, however, by Solomon and Turner, who conducted the Pavlovian phase of the experiment while the dogs were deeply paralyzed by d-turbocurarine (a synthetic form of curare that is free of sensory side effects).

The response of the dogs to the CS−, or safety signal, (SS), was particularly interesting. They either failed to respond to it all or if they did respond initially, this behavior extinguished rapidly during the course of testing (all testing was conducted during extinction, i.e., in the absence of further shock). It looks then as if fear is conditioned to the DS but not to the SS and that by introducing these signals as "probes" in the avoidance situation, it is possible to manipulate the fear level of the animal and hence the motivation of avoidance behavior independently of other factors controlling the avoidance response.

Further studies in this series were reported by Leaf (1964) and Overmier and Leaf (1965). The basic concept was the same in that the effects of a Pavlovian experience were assessed in subsequent avoidance behavior. Leaf used a shuttle-box response, with relatively few Pavlovian trials, and gave the Pavlovian training before avoidance training but in an apparatus different from the avoidance box. Leaf found, as had Solomon and Turner, that the latency of the avoidance response was significantly slower to the SS than it was to the original S+, and it was reliably faster to the DS than to the original S+.

An important advance in this series of studies, both in procedure and in concept, was made by Rescorla and LoLordo in 1965. Dogs were trained on a Sidman avoidance schedule in the shuttle box so that the response criterion could be the rate of responding rather than the latency of the response. The dogs were not curarized; they were simply confined to one part of the shuttle box for the Pavlovian treatment. But perhaps the most important advance over the earlier experiments was conceptual; Rescorla and LoLordo introduced the Pavlovian concept of inhibition. Pavlov (1927) had described considerable evidence to show that not only can a CS excite salivation when it is paired with food but that a different cue, a CS−, can inhibit salivation when it is explicitly paired with the withdrawal of food. One kind of evidence cited by Pavlov is that when the CS− and the CS+ are presented together, there will be less salivation than when the CS+ is presented alone. Pavlov also described several other procedures for producing inhibitory conditioning, procedures that he called conditioned inhibition, discriminative inhibition, and the method of contrast. In their study of fear conditioning Rescorla and LoLordo investigated each of these Pavlovian procedures, and in each case the results were essentially the same. There was an accelerated rate of responding during and immediately after presentation of the DS, and inhibition occurred when the SS was presented. We can think of there being some level of residual or generalized fear associated with the apparatus and other parameters of the situation. Superimposed upon this generalized fear, we can think of there being an experimentally manipulated or localized fear produced by the DS because fear was conditioned to it in the Pavlovian part of the experiment. Furthermore, we can think of the S+ in the ordinary avoidance procedure in the same way. As Mowrer had proposed years before, the S+ generates fear to motivate the avoidance response.[8] Finally, we should note that the safety signal is not just a neutral stimulus, that is, a stimulus free of fear. It must actively inhibit the generalized fear that is elicited by other cues because it suppresses avoidance behavior appreciably below the baseline rate. Rescorla and LoLordo (1965) interpreted this suppression or inhibition of avoidance behavior in Pavlovian terms, that is, as attributable to an active inhibition of conditioned fear.

Working on the assumption that there are two kinds of Pavlovian processes, Rescorla (1967) raised the following question. If a cue that is paired with shock (or food or whatever) in a Pavlovian manner produces excitation and if a cue that is explicitly associated with the absence of shock (or food, etc.) produces inhibition, then what kind of procedure must be used to establish a cue that is neutral, that is, a cue having neither an excitatory nor an inhibitory effect? Rescorla proposes that neutrality is achieved by what he calls the truly random procedure in which a cue is presented and shock is presented, but the two events bear no systematic relationship to each other. They may be scheduled randomly in time, so that on one trial the cue is associated with shock but on another trial it is associated with the absence of shock. Rescorla (1966) showed that a cue that has been presented in a truly random manner in a Pavlovian session subsequently does have no effect on ongoing avoidance behavior. That is, it does not affect the baseline rate of responding, as Fig. 10-5

[8] Note, though, that while these results suggest that avoidance behavior is motivated by the DS, they do not compel us to believe that the S+ ordinarily serves the same function. Consider that when an animal becomes extremely proficient at avoidance, responding virtually every time S+ is presented, the S+ is no longer associated with shock. Therefore, it is no longer a DS, and, in fact, it should become an SS. Consider too that the response to the DS undoubtedly occurs before any observable fear reaction could occur. These observations, originally noted by Solomon and Wynn (1953), are still very much with us, and they still present the logical dilemma of there being no obvious motivator for the avoidance response.

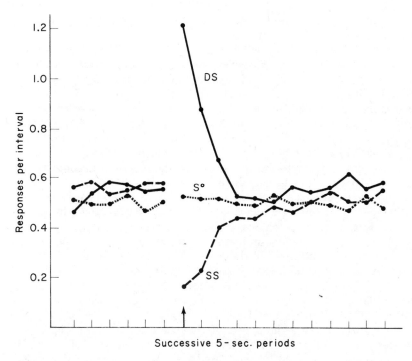

Figure 10–5

Mean number of responses per 5-second period in successive periods prior to, during, and after a 5-second cue presentation. (From Rescorla, 1966)

shows. The truly random cue (S^0) thus appears neither to excite nor to inhibit fear and hence appears to make no contribution to the motivation of avoidance behavior.[9]

    One far-reaching implication of Rescorla's analysis is that *fear becomes conditioned to a cue to the extent that the cue predicts shock.* The point is vividly demonstrated in a study (Rescorla, 1968a)

---

    [9] What these results show is that the S^0 has little or no effect on an avoidance baseline, that is, on ongoing Sidman avoidance behavior. But this may only mean that the S^0 produces no more or no less fear than is already produced by generalized apparatus cues. Generalized situational cues are also S^0s, of course, because they too are poor predictors of shock. On the other hand, when an S^0 for shock is probed on an appetitive baseline, as in a conditioned suppression experiment, it can produce some suppression (Kremer & Kamin, 1971; Benedict & Ayres, 1972). So, again, S^0 may not be neutral in an absolute sense. A further complication (Bolles & Moot, 1972; Rescorla, 1972) is that excitation is probably more rapidly conditioned than inhibition, so we might expect that an S^0 would be excitatory during the initial states of conditioning and then gradually approach neutrality as conditioning is continued.

that showed that if rats encounter a certain probability of shock in the presence of a cue and the same probability of shock in the absence of the cue, then little fear or safety or anything else appears to be conditioned to the cue. Neutrality is achieved here in spite of the fact that a great deal of fear undoubtedly occurs in the conditioning situation and in spite of the fact that there may be several occasions on which the cue is actually paired with shock. Thus it appears that classical conditioning of either fear or safety depends upon the predictive relationship between the cue and shock rather than, as had always been assumed, the "pairing" of cue and consequence. This interpretation provides a fresh view of fear conditioning and the part it plays in defensive behavior. It also provides a means of comprehending a variety of data that have heretofore been inexplicable. For example, Badia and Culbertson (1972) have been able to show that the rat's choice for signaled versus unsignaled shocks (surely one of the anachronisms in the literature) is due to the period of safety marked by the absence of the signal. In effect, the rat can relax as long as the signal is off. In the case of unsignaled shocks, however, there are no predictors of danger, but there are also no predictors of safety; therefore, the rat can never relax. And this latter state of affairs is aversive.

In discussing the status of these developments at that time, Rescorla and Solomon (1967) suggest several conclusions. One is that avoidance behavior is motivated by fear, as two-factor theorists had maintained all along. But this conclusion was made much more convincing by those studies that had (1) manipulated fear in a Pavlovian situation independently of the motivated response itself and that had (2) shown inhibition of fear. The second conclusion is that while fear is acquired by Pavlovian conditioning, Pavlovian conditioning must be reconceptualized. It involves not contiguity of CS and UCS, that is, pairing, but establishing a predictive relationship between CS and UCS. It also involves not the attachment of a response to the CS but the learning of the predictive relationship between CS and UCS. What survives from Pavlov is a set of procedures for arranging environmental contingencies independently of the animal's behavior. Third, fear is not primarily an autonomic response but is a central event, some kind of central representation of the relationship between the cue and shock.

It would seem to be a very short step from Rescorla and Solomon's position—that is, that avoidance behavior is motivated by a central event representing the prediction of shock—to the cognitive position that avoidance behavior occurs because the animal "expects" shock. It is difficult to see what a central event representing the prediction of shock might be called if it is not called an expectancy. But whereas some writers (e.g., Bolles, 1972) have taken that short step, Rescorla and Solomon (1967) resist doing so; nor has Rescorla taken it more recently (e.g., Rescorla, 1972). Rescorla, equipped with his new view of conditioning, seems to occupy a middle ground between the traditional two-factor theory and an explicitly cognitive theory: Avoidance is motivated by fear, and fear is a central event that can be either excited or inhibited by Pavlovian procedures.

Reinforcing properties of S+ termination. We turn next to the major theoretical question of whether S+ termination constitutes reinforcement for avoidance behavior. The S+ has been cast in this role by virtually all theorists in the Hullian and Skinnerian traditions. We have seen that this role is justified by several lines of evidence, one of which is simply that avoidance is learned. The argument is that if learning occurs, there must be a reinforcer, and it is not obvious what else it could be if it is not S+ termination. We have already noted the early study of Mowrer and Lamoreaux (1942) in which groups of rats were run in the shuttle box with an S+ that could not be terminated, because it was either too short (the so-called trace procedure) or too long (continuing for some seconds after the avoidance response). Both procedures produced severe decrements in avoidance learning. In addition, Kamin (1957) demonstrated that the more S+ termination is delayed following the occurrence of the avoidance response, the greater is the decrement in learning. These data are shown in Fig. 10-6. Bower et al. (1965) showed that permitting an avoidance response to produce a greater change in S+ intensity led to better learning. All of these considerations appear to justify the common assumption that avoidance is reinforced by S+ termination.

In an interesting variation of the usual avoidance experiment, Dinsmoor (1962) presented rats with a series of unavoidable and inescapable shocks in the presence of a discriminative stimulus, an S+. Although his animals could do nothing about individual shocks, they could press a bar to terminate the S+ and cut off the series of shocks that were associated with it. The response was learned, and it is tempting to attribute the learning to S+ termination, especially since none of the other scheduled events were in contact with the animal's behavior. But this argument is not consistent with the results of an elaboration of this procedure (Dinsmoor & Clayton, 1963) in which animals were trained, as before, to make a response to terminate an S+ and a series of shocks but then were trained to make another response, bar pressing, to produce the S+ so that they could terminate it and the shocks. If Dinsmoor's original study showed that the S+ is a negative reinforcer, then the Dinsmoor and Clayton study must show that S+ is also a positive reinforcer!

There is a further logical difficulty with the S+ termination hypothesis. We saw in the previous section that the behavioral evidence of fear tends to dissipate during avoidance training so that ultimately the avoidance response occurs before any appreciable fear can be elicited by S+. (Alternatively, we could say that the S+ must

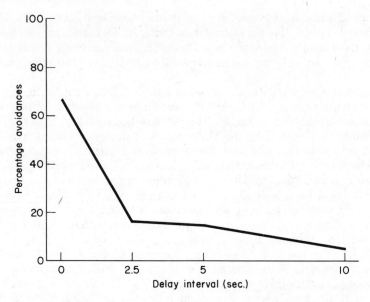

Figure 10–6

Median percentage of avoidances in 100 trials as a function of the delay of CS termination after a response. (Data from Kamin, 1957) Copyright (1957) by the American Psychological Association. Reprinted by permission.

ultimately stop being aversive because it is no longer paired with, or predicts, shock.) And if there is no fear, or aversiveness, there can be no reduction in fear, or aversiveness. The role of S+ termination in avoidance behavior is evidently more complicated than earlier writers had anticipated. Some insight into this complexity is found in studies of avoidance extinction. Katzev (1967) showed that the S+ termination contingency can help maintain avoidance behavior in extinction. However, subsequent investigators (Hartley, 1968; Bolles et al., 1971; Dillow et al., 1972) demonstrated that this apparent reinforcing effect of S+ is obtained only under conditions in which extinction is produced by simply withdrawing all shock. With an extinction procedure like that advocated by Davenport and Olson (1968), in which shocks still occur but the avoidance response is no longer effective in avoiding them, the S+ termination contingency no longer contributes to the maintenance of behavior (Bolles et al., 1971). The S+ termination hypothesis is, therefore, considerably weakened as a general explanation of avoidance behavior.

Perhaps the most serious limitation upon the S+ termination reinforcement mechanism is illustrated by the report of Bolles et al. (1966) that while S+ termination was effective in the shuttle box, it appeared to make little contribution to running-wheel avoidance (see

Table 10-1, page 334). Mogenson et al. (1965), as well as unpublished results from our own laboratory, indicate that S$^+$ termination has virtually no effect on bar-press avoidance. The rat can learn to press the bar to avoid shock just as well (which is not very well) with or without S$^+$ termination. Similarly, Theios et al. (1966) have shown that S$^+$ makes no discernible contribution to avoidance learning in the one-way avoidance situation. Thus the effectiveness of the S$^+$ termination contingency found in the shuttle box may be unique to the shuttle box. We must look elsewhere for a more general reinforcement mechanism.

S$^+$ termination as response feedback. In most instrumental or operant learning situations there is some clearly denotable event that is made contingent upon the appropriate response. In the appetitive case this event is often food, and the reinforcing effect of food is readily demonstrated by the loss of behavior when food is delayed or withheld. But consider what happens when the animal makes the appropriate response in the avoidance situation. By definition, the important event, shock, does not occur. We cannot attribute reinforcement to the nonoccurrence of shock because there is no way a nonoccurring event can have contact with the behavior. If S$^+$ termination is incorporated into the experiment, then it can be pointed to as a possible reinforcer. And sure enough if S$^+$ termination is delayed or withheld, there is a loss of behavior, at least in the shuttle box. But what is really the effect of delaying or withholding S$^+$ termination? Is it to remove reinforcement or to remove all feedback, that is, all stimulus consequences of responding? The reinforcement theorist may say that these two kinds of consequences are the same, but they are logically and empirically separable. It is only necessary to introduce a new kind of cue, a feedback stimulus (FS), whenever the avoidance response occurs and then to manipulate this contingency independently of S$^+$ termination. If there is a response contingent FS, then perhaps the S$^+$ termination contingency can be abandoned without losing avoidance behavior. That this is indeed the case was shown first by Keehn and Nakkash (1959) in the running-wheel situation, and subsequently by D'Amato et al. (1968) with bar-press avoidance and by Bower et al. (1965) and Bolles and Grossen (1969) with the shuttle box. In all of these situations the use of a brief FS virtually eliminated the decremental effects of withdrawing S$^+$ termination. Furthermore, Bolles and Grossen (1969) found that it did not matter whether S$^+$ termination was prevented by using a trace procedure or by prolonging the S$^+$ after the response had occurred. In both cases using the FS eliminated the decrement (see Fig. 10-7).

These findings suggest, first, that a response-contingent cue or FS facilitates avoidance learning, but, more importantly, the results suggest that in situations in which S$^+$ termination is effective

Theory of motivation

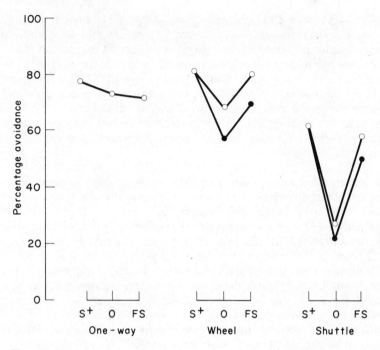

Figure 10–7

*Mean percentage of avoidances for rats trained with either S⁺
termination, FS presentation, or neither. The solid points are for
groups with the S⁺ termination contingency removed by using a
trace procedure. The rats were trained 20 trials in the one-way
situation, 40 trials in the running wheel, or 80 trials in the
shuttle box. (Data from Bolles & Grossen, 1969; figure reproduced
from Bolles, 1970) Copyright (1970) by the American Psychological Association. Reprinted by permission.*

(primarily in the shuttle box), it too may operate by being a feedback
stimulus. The importance of the S⁺ termination contingency may
not be that the S⁺ is aversive but that the absence of the S⁺ is a
positively reinforcing FS. How can the termination of S⁺ and the
onset of the FS or the non-S⁺ be empirically distinguished? Dinsmoor
and Sears (1973) have described a clever technique for making this
distinction. They used a tone as the FS and varied its frequency in
a series of generalization tests. They obtained a sharp generalization
gradient (at least in one animal) indicating that maintenance of avoidance behavior can be more dependent upon the FS than upon the S⁺.

Let us pursue the argument a little further by asking why the
FS should be a reinforcing event. The most obvious answer is suggested by Rescorla's analysis of the motivation of avoidance behavior
(see page 343). Just as the S⁺ has been hypothesized to be an aversive
event because it predicts shock and just as the presentation of an

S$^+$ has been assumed to motivate avoidance behavior, so we can hypothesize that the presentation of an FS will be a positive event because it predicts safety, and its presentation will demotivate or inhibit avoidance behavior. The significant aspect of the FS is thus hypothesized to be that, because it occurs only after an avoidance response, it predicts a period of safety: The animal receives no more shock until the next trial. The main difference between an FS and an SS is that the FS is necessarily established as a safety signal during the conduct of an avoidance learning experiment, whereas an SS is usually established using a noncontingent Pavlovian procedure, such as that used by Rescorla and LoLordo. In short, the FS is by definition established with a procedure in which it is contingent upon the animal's behavior, whereas the SS can be established using Pavlovian procedures. But this difference in the establishment of the different kinds of cues should not obscure the possibility that they may have the same behavioral effects by virtue of both predicting safety.[10]

The behavioral equivalence of the FS and the SS has been shown in a pair of studies by Rescorla. In one study (Rescorla, 1968) dogs were trained on a Sidman avoidance schedule in a shuttle box. There was no S$^+$ but a response produced a brief FS. After this training the FS contingency was discontinued, and the FS was presented as a noncontingent probe on the avoidance baseline. It had a clearly depressing effect. Thus the previously established FS was acting as an SS to inhibit avoidance. Rescorla argued that because the FS predicted safety in avoidance training, it had become an SS and, therefore, an inhibitor of fear.

In another study (Rescorla, 1969) dogs were trained to avoid shock by pressing either of two panels. Training was conducted to equalize pressing on the two panels. The dogs were then subjected to a series of Pavlovian trials in which an SS was associated with absence of shock. Then they were returned to the panel-pressing avoidance situation and the previously established SS introduced as a consequence of pressing one of the panels. The animals quickly showed a learned preference for the panel that produced the SS. Thus, apparently, a noncontingent or classically conditioned SS can serve in a reinforcing capacity when it is subsequently introduced as FS. A similar demonstration with rats, using a wheel-turning response, has been reported by Weisman and Litner (1969). These experimenters established an SS noncontingently and then introduced

[10] The idea that avoidance behavior is reinforced by a positive consequence of responding rather than by the termination of a negative antecedent of responding has been defended by Denny and his students. Denny's position assumes that there is, in effect, a consummatory response, which is not readily observable but is readily inferred from the outcome of various experiments. The consummatory response is relaxation. Denny (1971) has summarized the theory and has surveyed a variety of evidence to support it.

it as a consequence of responding whenever the animals responsed at a high rate (DRH training) and at a low rate of responding (DRL training). In both cases it was possible to produce clear changes in the rate of responding by means of the apparently reinforcing effect of the cue.[11]

The properties of the response

One of the greatest difficulties besetting the behavior theorist is that when he applies the usual experimental procedures to the training of avoidance behavior, he discovers that they are much more effective with some avoidance responses than with others. Let us look at the literature on the learning of different avoidance responses. We will start with one of the easiest responses to learn, running in the one-way situation.

One-way avoidance. What is now called one-way avoidance evolved from the earlier acquired-drive experiment. May (1948) trained rats to escape shock by running from one compartment to another. After a series of such trials the response was extinguished in the sense that the shock was discontinued; but presumably because the start box continued to elicit fear, the rat continued to run to the safe compartment when given the opportunity to do so. Thus there was first a series of escape trials with no possibility of avoidance, and then there was a series of trials in which the rat could and did run from the place where it had been shocked. Sheffield and Temmer (1950) were the first to introduce a brief interval before shock onset during which animals actually could avoid shock by running out of the shock compartment. The acquisition of the avoidance response in this experiment was not described in detail, but it evidently proceeded rapidly.

Subsequent investigators have found that the two procedures, that is, those of May and of Sheffield and Temmer, produce essentially the same level of running and the same resistance to extinction. In all cases learning is very rapid, requiring typically only three or

---

[11] It is unfortunate that the reinforcing effects reported by both Rescorla (1969) and Weisman and Litner (1969) indicate only a new form, or patterning, of the old response rather than the acquisition of a new avoidance response. Thus both studies used a relatively weak criterion of reinforcement. Perhaps a somewhat more direct and impressive demonstration of the reinforcing function of an FS is that obtained by Moot (1973). Moot first established avoidance behavior in a shuttle box, using an FS, and then transferred rats to bar-press avoidance. Experimental animals that obtained the previously established FS as a consequence of bar pressing learned the new response much more rapidly and performed at a much higher level than animals in various control groups, which showed the typically slow and uncertain acquisition.

four shocks (Radlow, 1958; Santos, 1960). Thus it seems to make little difference whether the rat is shocked following a failure to run or whether it is shocked while running is prevented. The total number of shocks received seems to dictate how aversive the shock box becomes, and this in turn dictates how likely the animal is to leave it (see also Blanchard & Blanchard, 1968). Moyer and Korn (1966) report that the speed of one-way avoidance learning is also unaffected by the intensity of shock, and, even more remarkably, McGinnis and Theios (1972) report that when rats are shocked on only a proportion of the trials on which they fail to avoid, the governing factor in the rate of learning is the number of shocks received rather than the number of trials. The picture we get of one-way avoidance is that after receiving about four shocks under almost any conditions, the rat will run from the shock compartment to the safe compartment. Once this behavior is established, it is executed with approximately 100 percent proficiency and requires approximately 100 trials to extinguish (McGinnis & Theios, 1972).

There are other situations in which avoidance learning proceeds with tremendous rapidity. For example, Maatsch (1959) shocked rats in a box from which they could leap onto a surrounding ledge. He found that this avoidance response was sometimes established after a single shock trial.

Part of the rapid learning that occurs in the one-way situation can be attributed to the fact that the animal is always moving in the same direction through space (Olton & Isaacson, 1968). Some of it can be attributed to the fact that the animals are handled between trials in order to initiate the next trial (Wahlsten & Sharp, 1969). The handling of frightened animals is, of course, a hazard and a nuisance, so it is perhaps understandable that a number of investigators have attempted to design automated apparatus that will permit animals to run to a safe box or to jump up onto a safe ledge (Baum, 1965; Tenen, 1966; Wedeking, 1967; Davis et al., 1967; Kruger et al., 1969). However, none of these devices appears to lead to the extremely rapid acquisition that is found in the old-fashioned apparatus in which the experimenter must initiate each trial.

Skinner-box avoidance. The Skinner box, which is such a convenient and customary part of appetitive learning, poses a number of challenges to the experimenter who tries to study avoidance in it. Rats have peculiar difficulty in learning the bar-press response. Sidman had obtained bar-press avoidance using his procedure in 1953, but nothing was reported using the standard shuttle-box type of procedures until much later (Myers, 1959). Even then, the early reports all emphasized the difficulty of the task (Meyer et al., 1960; Hoffman et al., 1961; D'Amato & Schiff, 1964). Some investigators have facilitated learning by shaping approximations to appropriate bar-press behavior (Feldman & Bremner, 1963; Keehn & Webster, 1968). Others have facilitated it to some extent by using a weak shock (Bolles & Warren, 1965; D'Amato & Fazzaro, 1966), by using a long interstimulus interval (Bolles et al., 1966a), by using an intense S^+ (Fantino et al., 1966), and by handling their animals between trials (Wahlsten et al., 1968).

But it has become clear that although all of these procedures can help establish bar-press avoidance, none of them really solves the problem. Many animals still fail to learn, and most animals that do learn perform poorly. The rat is also relatively poor at learning the wheel-turning manipulandum response (Smith et al., 1961), and even when such learning occurs, it is often subject to a poop-out effect; that is, a partially learned response begins to disintegrate after a few hundred trials (Anderson & Nakamura, 1964; Coons et al., 1960).

The situation with avoidance learning in pigeons is even more remarkable in that it was not until 1969, by which time immense flocks of pigeons had learned to peck keys for food, that Hineline and Rachlin were able to report key-peck avoidance in these birds. When their report appeared, it was impressive not so much because it showed that this behavior had finally been brought under operant control but, to the contrary, because it showed that key-peck avoidance was extremely fragile and its acquisition depended upon a great amount of prior shaping, various kinds of preliminary training, and some highly specialized techniques. In effect, Hineline and Rachlin showed that it is quite impractical to train key-peck avoidance. Pigeons do somewhat better in other situations—the shuttle box (MacPhail, 1968) and a treadle-pressing situation (Smith & Keller, 1970). There is a well-known but unpublished report by Bedford and Anger (1968) of pigeons quickly learning to hop from one perch to another in a shuttle type of situation.

In summary, responses such as key pecking, bar pressing, and turning a wheel are learned only gradually if at all. Responses such as running in the shuttle box are learned in a modest number of trials, and performance usually becomes relatively proficient. Other responses, such as running in a wheel, are learned even more quickly and are performed more consistently (Bolles et al., 1966). Finally, some responses are learned with extreme rapidity and are performed at a level approaching 100 percent. A serious indictment of our major theories of learning is that they give us little reason to expect such enormous differences in learning. The prevailing accounts of avoidance learning, for example, that it is reinforced by S^+ termination, have had to be augmented by special ad hoc hypotheses to explain why some avoidance responses appear to be readily reinforced but others do not. Let us consider some of these special hypotheses.

The freezing hypothesis. One of the earliest suggestions (Meyer et al., 1960) was that the rat freezes in the Skinner box, and freezing competes with bar pressing. The argument is not entirely convincing. For one thing the bar-press response often has a reasonably high operant rate; it occurs on perhaps 15 percent of the trials (and, of course, it occurs on the remaining 85 percent of the trials as an escape response). But in spite of the fact that the animal ultimately makes the response on every trial, there is frequently no learning. A number of treatments are known to improve shuttle-box performance, for instance, hunger, amphetamine injections, and limbic lesions, but these effects are not always attributable to freezing (Liss, 1968). Comparable effects have not generally been shown in the Skinner box, where freezing is supposed to be a more serious problem. It has been found that stimulant drugs will produce temporary improvement in bar-press avoidance (Hearst & Whalen, 1963; Pearl et al., 1968), and it has been shown that previously establishing bar pressing with food reinforcement can facilitate its performance in the avoidance situation (Cicero & Myers, 1968; Kulkarni & Job, 1970), but none of these effects appears to involve immediate positive transfer, which the freezing hypothesis would predict. The improvement only becomes apparent with continued training, that is, after the response has acquired some strength. Moreover, in the case of stimulants it has been found that the beneficial effect is reversible so that the behavior collapses when the drug is withdrawn. This finding raises the question of why freezing fails to dissipate in the Skinner box— what mechanism maintains it?

A variant of the freezing hypothesis is that the rat fails to learn bar pressing because it learns instead to hold the bar down. But although techniques that reduce bar holding, for example, continuing shock for a brief interval after the bar is pressed (Bolles & Warren, 1965a), may make the rat release the bar, they produce little improvement in avoidance learning. Similarly, Grigg (1970) reports that while different kinds of shock produce different amounts of bar holding, these differences are not correlated with avoidance performance. It seems unlikely, therefore, that holding the bar is the immediate cause of poor avoidance acquisition. Holding the bar and, short of that, touching the bar during the intertrial interval are clearly of considerable advantage to the rat. Doing so puts the rat in an excellent position to terminate shock quickly on the next trial (Migler, 1963). Bolles and McGillis (1968) reported that within only a few trials the rat terminates shock in about 0.05 seconds. The discovery of such extremely rapid escape responses has a number of implica-nitions; one is that the rat can only make responses with such a short latency if it is well situated to do so. Typically, this involves touching the bar, perhaps holding it down with minimal pressure, so that when shock comes on, there can be a reflexive lurch that quickly cuts it off. It is also apparent that a response with such a short latency cannot properly be considered an operant. It must be a reflex, a respondent, a reaction immediately elicited by shock. Apparently, only by holding the bar or by touching it during the intertrial interval can the animal generate such short-latency responses. With this mode of responding the rat achieves a relatively good solution to the Skinner-box problem, and although the optimum solution would be to avoid shock, the animal may be trapped by the relative efficacy of this reflexive behavior into not making avoidance responses. Thus if the rat were to let go of the bar and give genuine operant avoidance responses, it might avoid shock on 80 percent of the trials, but it might also receive more total shock on the remaining 20 percent of the trials than it would by adopting the freezing-holding mode of responding.

Meyer et al. (1960) suggested another variant of the freezing hypothesis, namely, that bar pressing is difficult to train because (1) it is topographically similar to freezing and (2) freezing is initially very strong. Hence freezing may gain enough strength through generalization every time bar pressing is reinforced so that it can always stay stronger than bar pressing. This hypothesis implies that good learning requires the avoidance response to be incompatible with freezing. But when this implication has been tested by permitting the rat to avoid shock by making any kind of response, that is, by selecting any alternative to freezing, very little learning has been found (Graf & Bitterman, 1963; Greene & Peacock, 1965; Brener & Goesling, 1970). Masterson et al. (1972) tested the hypothesis by requiring rats to jump, a vigorous avoidance response quite different from freezing, and found little learning.

As attractive as the freezing hypothesis appears at first glance, it fails to provide a convincing account of bar-press avoidance. Specifically, it fails to tell us why freezing persists to such an extent in the Skinner box and dissipates with continued training in other types of situations. It is almost as if freezing is not a cause of the failure to learn but results from it. It is as if the rat freezes in the Skinner box because it fails to learn the bar-press response.

The reflexiveness hypothesis. Turner and Solomon (1962) studied avoidance learning of toe flexion in human subjects. Their subjects had considerable difficulty learning the particular form of toe movement that was elicited by shock but little trouble learning a voluntary toe movement. These results led Turner and Solomon to conclude that a reflexive response could not be readily acquired in the avoidance situation. Further evidence supporting this hypothesis was reported by Warren and Bolles (1967). Rats were trained in a running wheel to avoid shock by running forward, but different groups were shocked either in the front feet or in the hind feet following a failure to avoid shock. Shock applied to the hind feet causes rats to lurch forward, and it might be supposed that since this behavior is compatible with the avoidance response, it would facilitate learning to run forward to avoid shock. It might be supposed that rats shocked in the front feet, which makes them recoil, would have trouble learning to run forward. But our results were just the opposite: The animals for which the elicited response was compatible with running forward actually showed poorer learning.

The implication for bar-press avoidance should be clear. If the animal is freezing or at least remaining motionless while holding on to the bar and if shock elicits short-latency or reflexive responses, then these circumstances may make it more difficult for the rat to learn an operant or voluntary bar-press response. In effect, the desired behavior may be too similar topographically to the undesired behavior for it to be acquired.

The discrimination hypothesis. Successful avoidance learning requires that the behavior be restricted to appropriate temporal and spatial cues. Perhaps the frightened rat is poor at discriminating appropriate from inappropriate cues. A number of experimenters have attempted to train rats to go, say, to the white side of a T-maze to avoid shock. It is generally found that either the animal fails to discriminate white from black or else it fails to make the discrimination in time to avoid shock. (One of the rare reports of successful discrimination learning, Horel et al., 1966, provides so little data on acquisition that the animals' success in learning the discrimination cannot be assessed.) Flakus (1961) tried to train rats to make one avoidance response in the presence of one S+ and another response in the presence of another S+. His attempts to establish this discrimination proved futile.

It could be argued that the difficulty in the Skinner box is that the rat becomes overwhelmed by the overall undesirability of being there so that the small stimulus change that occurs when it does press the bar is difficult to discriminate from the mass of other aversive cues. We might suppose that any alteration of the traditional experimental procedure that makes the consequences of responding more salient would facilitate bar-press avoidance. There is a variety of suggestive evidence indicating that this is the case. For example, Jones and Swanson (1966) showed that bar-press learning proceeds more rapidly if intertrial responses (i.e., responses in the absence of the S+) are punished by shock. Cole and Fantino (1966) and Christophersen and Denny (1967) have shown that withdrawing the bar after a response and presenting it again as part of the S+ also helps. It is not yet clear whether these procedures are effective because they facilitate discrimination between S+ and S− conditions in the Skinner box or because they prevent holding the bar.

D'Amato et al. (1964) reported that bar-press avoidance proceeds somewhat better if the shock is discontinuous, for example, presented in 0.2-second bursts every 2 seconds. This facilitation was attributed to a discrimination effect. It was proposed that escape behavior (responses occurring during the series of brief shock pulses) is more likely to generalize to avoidance behavior (behavior occurring prior to the onset of the shock series) because the situations are more nearly alike than is typically the case with continuous shock. In other words, the absence of shock during much of the time when escape behavior occurs makes the escape situation more like the avoidance situation than is typically the case; thus the avoidance response should gain more strength from this source. There is, however, no indication that bar-press avoidance gains much strength from the escape contingency. Moreover, D'Amato reports that his rats do terminate the shock on most trials even though they have only 0.2 seconds to do so. Recall that Bolles and McGillis (1968) also found escape responses occurring very rapidly in the bar-press situation. If these short-latency responses are reflexive, they should not be expected to be subject to reinforcement. So whether or not an escape contingency is programmed, once the rat starts freezing on the bar and making short-latency escape responses, there can be no effective escape contingency. These considerations argue against D'Amato's interpretation of the discontinuous shock effect (see also Hess & Shafer, 1968; Bintz et al., 1970). Discontinuous shock also facilitates shuttle-box avoidance (Moyer & Chapman, 1966). It seems most probable that discontinuous shock is merely shock of low average intensity as D'Amato's own data suggest (D'Amato & Fazzaro, 1966).

Thus while the discrimination hypothesis is attractive and is supported by several lines of evidence, it is apparent that it alone cannot account for the great difficulty the rat has in learning bar-press avoidance, nor does it alone seem able to exlpain why certain other responses are so easy to learn.

The inadequate reinforcement hypothesis. Related to the discrimination hypothesis is the idea that in the bar-press situation nearly all stimuli are aversive and remain aversive after the avoidance response has occurred. Perhaps termination of the $S+$ does not produce enough reduction in the total aversiveness to provide adequate reinforcement. The speed of learning and the level of performance attained in different situations are clearly related to the amount of stimulus change produced by the response or, as Bolles and Grossen (1969) describe it, to the amount of feedback intrinsic in the different responses. The trouble with bar pressing may be that it is a response that requires little effort, and hence it provides little proprioceptive feedback; and it does little to change the animal's immediate environment, and hence it provides little external feedback. The main stimulus change is the extrinsic feedback provided by $S+$ termination, and perhaps this is simply not enough of a change to constitute adequate reinforcement.

The earlier discussion of the different properties of $S+$ tends to support such an argument. There is the important question, though, of whether the critical consideration is the amount of stimulus change or the kind of stimulus change the avoidance response produces. There is abundant evidence that fear (or aversiveness) is especially well associated with environmental or place cues, such as those provided by the apparatus in which shock is given. The importance of the rat's getting out of the shock situation has been shown in both avoidance and acquired-drive experiments (Bolles, 1971), and the importance of place cues in a variety of fear conditioning experiments has been reviewed by McAllister and McAllister (1971). Thus we must question whether running out of the shock situation is so effectively learned because it has the general effect of producing a lot of stimulus change or because it has the specific effect of getting the rat to a new location.

Consider the following experiment by Masterson (1970). For one group of rats, pressing the bar avoided shock and terminated the $S+$ and had the additional effect of opening a door through which the animal could run out of the Skinner box. These animals showed impressive learning compared with controls trained under the normal bar-press conditions in which they were confined to the box. It is not certain whether the good learning reported by Masterson is attributable to the large amount of stimulation made contingent upon pressing the bar or is more properly attributed to the fact that the animals were actually permitted to get away. But recall (page 354) that when Masterson et al. (1972) tried to train a jumping response, that is, a response providing a great deal of feedback but not involving flight, they found poor learning. Consider too the curious case of freezing as an avoidance response. The whole point of freezing from a biological point of view is that it minimizes response feedback, keeps the animal in the same place, and does nothing to alter external stimulation. Freezing should, therefore, be difficult to learn, but the results tell a different story. It is rapidly learned and is performed at a very high level (Bolles & Riley, 1973). We may suppose that it is not the amount of stimulus change but the *nature* of the stimulus change that is important in avoidance learning. It seems to be the kind of consequence the response produces that makes some avoidance responses much more readily learned than others.

Although the various ad hoc hypotheses that have been advanced to account for poor bar-press avoidance all have considerable merit and much intrinsic interest, none of them adequately explains why some responses are so very much more readily acquired than others in the avoidance situation. We must seek a new approach to the problem.

Species-specific defense reactions

It is clear that nature provides little opportunity for an animal to learn about predators or other kinds of natural hazards. The conditions that might make such learning possible are rarely met in nature.

We may suppose, therefore, that an animal must have a repertoire of innate species-specific defense reactions that occur when it is frightened. We may suppose further that such responses will interact with arbitrarily required instrumental responses so as to produce either facilitation of or competition with the response to be learned. Thus if we require a rat to freeze to avoid shock, it readily learns to do so because freezing is one of its species-specific defense reactions (SSDR). If we require a rat to run in a one-way situation, it readily learns to do so because running away is an SSDR. Bar pressing is not readily learned because it is not an SSDR and it is in competition with freezing and flight attempts, which are SSDRs.[12]

When stated in the form of a competing-response principle, the SSDR hypothesis is plausible and innocuous; it simply states that some avoidance responses are easier to learn than others because they are compatible with the animal's innate defensive reactions. But several considerations indicate that a competing-response interpretation of the SSDR hypothesis is much too weak. Consider again the avoidance learning data shown in Fig. 10-3. There we had three different responses that differed greatly in learnability. One was not learned at all; one was learned with great rapidity; and the third was learned at a relatively modest rate. Note that in each case the response had a strong operant level, occurring on nearly half of the initial trials. Any kind of competing response interpretation can account for a response not occurring and not being learned for that reason. But the difficulty here is much more profound. It is that a particular response may not be learned even though it has a substantial rate of occurrence. The difficulty is evidently not in the failure of the response to occur but in its failure to be reinforced by the experimental contingencies.

A second difficulty with the competing-response version of the SSDR hypothesis is that the topography of an avoidance response appears to be much less important than its functional properties. The

[12] What kinds of behaviors the animal uses to defend itself can be best determined by putting it in a natural kind of environment and then frightening it to determine what it does. Some animals, but by no means all, will run or fly away. Some animals will freeze; some will turn and fight. Many animals have their own unique defensive reactions; for example, the chameleon changes color, the opossum plays dead, many snakes release odorous substances, and the turtle retreats into its shell. These and many other kinds of behavior can be verified to be SSDRs. The situation is somewhat more complicated because an animal's defensive behavior is typically adjusted to cope specifically with the perceived threat. Thus the animal may attack one predator and run from another. When we use shock as the frightening stimulus, we tend to hold this factor constant; but on the other hand, it is not clear how electric shock is perceived. Another complication is that an animal's defensive behavior is typically adjusted to cope specifically with the perceived environment. It may run away when under cover and freeze when out in the open. In the laboratory we vary this factor with other aspects of the situation but not very systematically.

evidence for this point is merely suggestive and needs much more careful documentation, but the point can be made this way: One-way avoidance is learned much faster than shuttle-box avoidance, although the same running movements occur in the two cases. The fundamental consideration seems to be, therefore, that in the one-way situation the animal runs away, whereas in the shuttle box it merely runs. The point is further illustrated in an unpublished study done by Perry Duncan at the University of Washington. Duncan attempted to train rats to run a distance of 6 inches or more in any direction. The animals could run back or forth, in circles, or in any other manner, as long as they ran 6 inches. Duncan found that in spite of the fact that the running responses occurred on approximately 80 percent of all trials, running per se was not learned as an avoidance response; that is, the incidence of running declined gradually over the course of training. Apparently, running is effectively learned in the one-way situation because it permits the animal to get away; running is somewhat effective in the shuttle box because it permits the animal to get away in some relativistic sense; and running is not learned in the open situation Duncan used because there was no sense in which running gets the animal out of the situation. Simply putting in a barrier to divide the space into two parts so that the rat can go from one side to the other makes the problem solvable. We can conclude that it is not running that is learned as an avoidance response but running away. It is the function that the behavior serves that matters and not its topography.[13]

Another way to regard the functional property of an SSDR is in terms of the kind of stimulus consequences it produces. Getting to a new situation is an important consequence, as we have just seen, but there are other consequences. Thus freezing minimizes all stimulus change. Grossen and Kelley (1972) have shown that the frightened rat has a strong thigmotaxic tendency; that is, it tends to stay close to walls and away from open areas. Allison et al. (1967) have shown that the frightened rat has a strong tendency to approach dark areas and stay away from light areas. The Allison et al. study was conducted in the context of the acquired-drive experiment, and the results raise a serious question about the early experiment of Miller (1948). Recall that Miller required rats to perform a new response to get from a white shock compartment to a black safe compartment. The learning of this new response was cited as evidence

---

[13] Let us do a thought experiment. Recall again from Fig. 10–3 the results of the group that failed to learn to stand up to avoid shock. Suppose that the experimental situation was altered slightly so that by standing up the rat could reach a door through which it could climb out of the apparatus. Can there be any doubt that this response, including the standing-up topography, would have been very rapidly learned? If we grant the outcome of the experiment, it seems again that it is what the response accomplishes that matters and not what movements are involved in it.

that fear reduction was reinforcing, and this argument did much to popularize the two-factor theory of avoidance behavior (see page 289). But the study by Allison et al. indicates that Miller's results are obtained only when the animals can go from white to black. The best that can be said for the acquired-drive experiment is that the learning that occurs is severely restricted to a narrow class of responses. A recent review of the acquired-drive literature (Bolles, 1971) concludes that no learning is obtained unless the response is an SSDR.

The SSDR hypothesis must be strengthened to state that some responses are much more reinforceable than others and that reinforceability is dependent upon the functional properties of the behavior (Bolles, 1970). This stronger version of the SSDR idea was originally based on the argument that in most avoidance situations the rat has only two kinds of functionally different defensive behaviors, fleeing and freezing. We can get the rat to flee by punishing freezing, which is what happens in the shuttle box because freezing fails to avoid shock. Running is, therefore, simply behavior that remains after freezing is suppressed. On the other hand, we can think of freezing as what remains if we punish all attempts at flight, which is what happens in the bar-press situation. The rat might freeze in the back of the box, but such behavior cannot persist because shock disrupts it. The only place the animal can freeze is poised delicately in front of the bar so that shock can be quickly terminated before it disrupts the freezing. It was suggested that the rat is only able to learn bar-press avoidance by starting from a stage in which it freezes while holding the bar (Bolles, 1970).

The simplicity of this scheme was that it required no reinforcement mechanism to account for avoidance learning that occurs with fair rapidity, that is, within 50 or fewer trials. This hypothetical mechanism was augmented by a second mechanism to account for instances of avoidance learning that occur more slowly. This second mechanism was the reinforcement of behavior by response-produced feedback stimuli. Presumably, it takes some number of trials, perhaps 50 or more, for the safety-signal value of the FS to be established, and the FS cannot be effective before it is established as a predictor of safety. So learning that occurs rapidly, for instance, in the one-way situation, cannot be based on reinforcement from this source but must be dependent upon differential punishment of SSDRs. Thus the 1970 version of the SSDR hypothesis proposed that there are two mechanisms in avoidance learning, a fast-acting one involving just selection among SSDRs and a slower-acting one based on reinforcement by the FS which can modify the animal's original SSDRs. This proposal seemed quite attractive—until we looked at freezing as an avoidance response.

The freezing experiment. Freezing is ordinarily unwanted behavior. It is the behavior that is ordinarily assumed to interfere with running or bar pressing. But the punishment version of the SSDR hypothesis asserted that running is acquired only to the extent that freezing is suppressed by punishment. To test this idea Bolles and Riley (1973) investigated whether freezing is subject to direct experimental control. One group of rats was trained on a Sidman avoidance schedule; as long as an animal was active, it was shocked every 5 seconds, but the series of shocks was withheld as soon as freezing occurred. The shock series was reinstated when an animal stopped freezing and was active for a period of 15 seconds. For this group freezing avoided shock. There was a complementary punishment group; the contingencies were reversed so that animals were shocked 15 seconds after freezing began and for as long as freezing continued. The results for these two experimental groups, together with the results for an extinction group, are shown in Fig. 10-8. Two yoked control groups were also run; they were scheduled to receive shock, regardless of their behavior, at the same average rate as the animals in the respective experimental groups.

Freezing was rapidly acquired. The incidence of freezing went to a level of approximately 97 percent within 20 minutes and

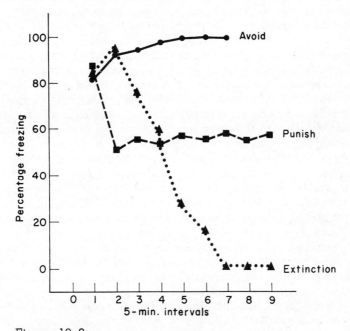

Figure 10–8

The proportion of time freezing occurred in successive 5-minute intervals when freezing avoided shock, was punished by shock, or when shock was discontinued. All animals received avoidance training for the first 5 minutes. (From Bolles & Riley, 1973)

remained there for an extended period of time. Similarly, the animals that were punished for freezing showed a sharp drop in freezing and remained at this lower level, as the figure shows. The levels of freezing in the two yoked control groups were 58 percent and 77 percent, which suggests that there is a large elicited or respondent component to freezing—not an unexpected finding. However, there appeared to be appreciable and highly reliable effects of both the punishment and the avoidance contingencies in addition to the respondent component of freezing. One would be tempted to conclude that in addition to being elicited by shock, freezing is also subject to control by the consequences that are programmed for it. Therefore, freezing appears to be in part respondent and in part operant. And the discovery that freezing can be rapidly learned or suppressed would seem to confirm the 1970 version of the SSDR hypothesis.

However, this conclusion would be hasty. We are not quite through analyzing the data. Note that the punishment animals gave no evidence of a learning curve; the incidence of freezing was found to be unchanged from the first minute of the punishment condition to the end of training. The behavior is too independent of time for it to be properly considered the result of learning. There is the further problem, originally noted by Church (1964), that in this type of situation, in which there is great respondent-operant overlap (i.e., in which the behavior can be controlled by both respondent and operant procedures), a serious statistical artifact biases any comparison between animals given contingent and noncontingent treatment. The argument is this: The animals in the avoidance group gave long bouts of freezing, but ultimately they stopped freezing and received a shock. However, the avoidance contingency severely limited the amount of movement that could occur among each of the experimental animals. On the other hand, the control procedure permitted an occasional animal to accumulate an appreciable amount of time moving. Thus the comparison between control and experimental animals is seriously biased in favor of showing less overall freezing in the experimental group. Church's argument can also be applied to the animals under the punishment conditions. The argument here is that for the experimental animals the punishment contingency permitted little freezing to occur in any animal, while the control conditions permitted an occasional animal to accumulate several seconds of freezing before the next noncontingent shock was likely to be presented. Again, the comparison of the two groups must necessarily show less freezing in the experimental group.

Freezing in this situation can be described most aptly by the diagram in Fig. 10-9. The fact is that at the intensities used by Bolles and Riley shock invariably disrupted freezing and produced movement for a period of a few seconds (10 seconds on the average). Then freezing continued for 15 minutes on the average before movement resumed. The best way to determine whether the experimental contingencies had any reinforcing or punishing effect upon freezing

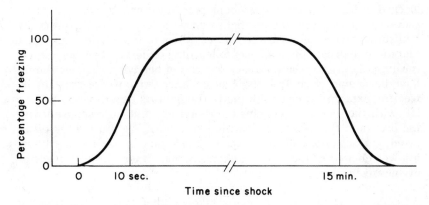

Figure 10–9

Schematic diagram showing the incidence of freezing occurring as a function of the time since the last shock.

is to determine whether the type of function shown in Fig. 10-9 is different for the different groups. In other words, does the animal that is punished for freezing resume freezing more slowly after the last shock than the animal that avoids shock by freezing? In the Bolles and Riley experiment the answer to this question was clearly no; there was no difference. We were led to conclude, therefore, that freezing was not actually strengthened by the avoidance procedure nor weakened by the punishment procedure. All that the supposed learning curves in Fig. 10-8 show is that when rats are shocked occasionally, as under the avoidance conditions, they freeze more than when they are shocked frequently, as under the punishment conditions. So in spite of the fact that the level of freezing can be manipulated by imposing various kinds of consequences upon its occurrence (which makes it an operant by definition), its occurrence is totally dictated by the temporal distribution of shocks (which makes it a respondent by definition). Put another way, although freezing appears to be controlled by its programmed consequences, this control can be attributed entirely to elicitation by shock without regard to the punishing effect of shock or the reinforcing effect of withholding shock.

Our attempts to establish aggressive behavior as an avoidance response have been no more successful. Unpublished studies of rats avoiding shock by attacking or threatening other rats suggest that although these behaviors have a high operant level, they too are not subject to reinforcement.[14] Aggressive behavior does not seem to be

[14] One reason, perhaps, is that the target animal, the one that is to be the object of aggression, tends to give appeasement behavior, so that even if the subject's aggression might be strengthened by the avoidance of shock, it is effectively inhibited by the appeasement behavior of the target animal.

learned either with the punishment procedure or the avoidance procedure. If neither freezing nor fighting is subject to learning, either by punishment or avoidance procedures, then it follows logically that flight attempts cannot be subject to learning either. If they were and if the animal only has these three categories of behavior, then we should have been able to control flight as an alternative to freezing in the freezing experiment or to fighting in the fighting experiments. We are left with the incredible conclusion, therefore, that no response learning occurs in the avoidance learning situation! We must think of all avoidance behavior as being respondent in the same sense that freezing was elicited in the freezing experiments, either by shock itself or by cues to shock.

A cognitive interpretation. Let us take another look at the freezing function shown in Fig. 10-9. There are two parts of the function. The first part following immediately after shock is straightforward enough; shock elicits a variety of unconditioned responses such as leaping around, running, and vocalizing. Since these behaviors are what we ordinarily think of as unconditioned responses to shock, they present no problem of interpretation. But what about the other part of the function—the high incidence of freezing that persists for several minutes. Is it too elicited by shock? Is it due to a long-lasting hormonal reaction to shock? Is it due to reverberation within the autonomic nervous system? The answer seems to be no or at least not primarily. If the animal is removed from the shock situation a few seconds after shock and put in a new environment where shock has not been experienced, the level of freezing is very much reduced and it is much less persistent (e.g., Blanchard & Blanchard, 1969). How then are we to explain the prolonged bouts of freezing seen in the shock situation? The simplest answer seems to be that the animal freezes because it expects shock to occur. After just a few shocks, perhaps three or four, environmental cues become S^+s for shock, and in the kind of apparatus used in the freezing experiment the animal's principal SSDR is freezing. Therefore, the rat freezes because it expects shock.

The SSDR hypothesis can now be restated in a new and much stronger form. When an animal is shocked in a given experimental context, certain stimulus events are programmed to precede shock and others are programmed to precede safety. After some experience with these conditions an animal learns expectancies that correspond to the experimental contingencies: It learns what S^+s predict shock and what S^-s predict safety. With this kind of orientation the new SSDR hypothesis (Bolles, 1972) proposes that the animal's behavior consists entirely of SSDRs, the topography of which is determined in part by the animal's expectancies of danger and safety and in part by the structure of environmental supporting stimuli.

The argument can be illustrated by citing the freezing experiment once more. There were no distinctive events or places that were easily discriminated as safety signals, nor were the animals trained long enough for the consequences of their own behavior to be discriminated as safety signals. Hence there was no learning about safety. But the experimental chamber was quickly perceived as a predictor of shock, and for 15 minutes or so the entire situation remained a mass of undifferentiated danger signals. The test box also provided little stimulus support for any SSDR besides freezing. The importance of supporting stimuli is suggested by considering what we might have found had our animals been trained and tested in a running wheel or in a long, slender tube. Little freezing would be expected because the rat's prime SSDR would have been running. Roughly, we may suppose that when the test situation looks like a place to freeze, the animal will freeze if it expects shock; when the situation looks like a place to run, the animal will run in it. The repertoire of SSDRs is governed by environmental stimuli that support one or another kind of defensive reaction.

More specifically, we may suppose that the rat freezes in the Skinner box when it expects shock because the Skinner box does not seem like a place to run. Evidently, the shuttle box is not initially seen as a place to run either. But after a few trials, after the S^+s for shock have been learned, that is, after the temporal and spatial cues have become established as danger signals, the rat begins to discriminate the safety signals. The feedback from its own behavior, the termination of the S^+, and, most importantly, the "other end" of the shuttle box all gradually become perceived as safety signals. The reason the other end of the box is so important is that this is the one safe cue to which the rat can direct specific behaviors; it can approach such an S^-. The other S^-s in the situation do not call for or support any particular behavior; they only make the animal less frightened. To the extent that the animal can direct its innate defensive behavior to a specific safety signal in the situation such a cue will appear to have a reinforcing effect on the animal's behavior.[15]

The cognitive theorist has little trouble accounting for the vast differences that are found in the rates of learning different kinds of avoidance behaviors. For example, the one-way situation is structured at the outset so that one location is seen as dangerous and another as safe, and if the situation is also structured so that it provides stimuli for running, that is, if the situation supports running,

[15] We may note one important point of difference between a cognitive theory and a reinforcement theory. For the reinforcement theorist, getting to the other end of the apparatus terminates the S^+, which reinforces the running response. To the cognitive theorist the other end is a safety signal that the animal approaches. The animal responds as it does because it is motivated to do so rather than because it is reinforced for doing so.

then running will occur and the rat will solve the problem in three or four trials. In the bar-press situation environmental cues provide little support for any behavior other than freezing. Moreover, bar-press avoidance is ordinarily programmed so that freezing produces a tolerable if not optimum solution to the problem, so that a very high incidence of freezing is found. There are safety signals, such as the stimulus consequences of pressing the bar, but these are evidently difficult for the rat to discriminate from the overwhelming mass of danger cues. Furthermore, the rat has relatively little specific defensive behavior to direct at the bar because manipulatory behavior is not part of its innate defensive repertoire. But even though the necessary discrimination is difficult, an occasional rat will learn it and ultimately demonstrate effective bar-press avoidance. This discrimination can be facilitated by a variety of techniques that direct attention to the S$^-$, such as previously establishing the S$^-$ in another situation (Moot, 1973).

Summary

The prevailing interpretation of avoidance behavior is that it is motivated by fear and reinforced by fear reduction. But the attempts to confirm this interpretation by monitoring fear have not been successful. An alternative interpretation, that avoidance behavior is strengthened and maintained by conditioned aversive stimuli, has had little more success. It is now apparent that whatever importance these fear-arousing or aversive stimuli have, they have it because they predict shock rather than because they are paired with shock. It is also apparent that avoidance is as much dependent upon the situational predictors of safety as upon the predictors of shock.

The major defect with the prevailing interpretations, however, is that while they may be able to account for avoidance learning in some situations, most notably the shuttle box, they cannot explain the learning, or lack of it, found in other situations. In some cases learning can be shown after a single trial; in other cases there may be no learning after 1000 trials. To explain this immense range of learning capabilities it is necessary to focus upon the animal rather than on the experimental contingencies and to consider its species-specific defensive behaviors. When this is done, a new kind of explanatory model is discovered. This model is cognitive in that it attributes the animal's behavior largely to its innate reaction to expected danger and safety. Most of the variance in the results of avoidance learning experiments can be accounted for by assuming that the rat withdraws from or freezes in the presence of danger cues and approaches or in other ways produces safety cues.

11
PUNISHMENT
AND
FRUSTRATION

the strengthening of a connection by satisfying
consequences seems, in view of our experiments
and of certain general considerations, to be
more universal, inevitable, and direct than the
weakening of a connection by annoying
consequences. The latter seems more specialized,
contingent upon what the annoyer in question
makes the animal do, and indirect.

E. L. Thorndike

People have probably always used punishment in attempting to control the behavior of other people. Punishment is certainly an important part of our culture. Parents are supposed to punish their children when they are naughty; the clergy punishes its parishioners when they are sinful; the defenders of law and order punish those whose acts are judged to be illegal or dangerous. And although there has always been a tendency to use punishment regardless of what its consequences may be (that is, in retribution), this usage has probably always been tempered with the idea that punishment served a corrective measure, that is, that it served somehow to improve the behavior of the punished person. In effect, there has always been some belief in the idea that punishment is an effective way to minimize undesired behavior.

It must have seemed quite natural, therefore, that when our first learning theorist, Thorndike, began to formulate explicit laws of learning, his laws would include not only a principle of response strengthening or reinforcement but also a symmetrical principle of response weakening or punishment. Thorndike (1911) asserted that the future strength of an S-R connection is governed by its effect. If the effect is a positive reward, the S-R connection will be strengthened, and if the effect is a negative punishment or an annoying state of affairs, the S-R connection that preceded it will be weakened. And although Thorndike had many critics, there seems to have been no criticism of the negative part of the law of effect; for who could doubt that contingent punishment would weaken behavior?

The present discussion of punishment will start at the point where Thorndike himself questioned the punishment part of the law of effect (Thorndike, 1932) and will proceed through a variety of different theoretical developments. We will consider the possibility that Thorndike's original formulation was correct (that is, that punishment is effective), the possibility that punishment has no response-weakening effect, and the other possibility that punishment has varied and indeterminate effects. Writers will be cited who maintain that punishment is a good and effective way to reduce behavior; others will be cited who contend that punishment is both ineffective and morally wrong. We will see attempts to explain the results of punishment experiments in purely associative terms, in motivational terms, and in cognitive terms.

Varied effects of punishment

Punishment in verbal learning. Thorndike (1932) presented evidence from a series of studies, which, he said, left him no alternative but to reject the idea that punishment can weaken an S-R connection. In a typical experiment a subject would be presented with a long list of words and required to guess numbers from one to ten to associate with each word of the list. Responses might be either ignored, rewarded by the verbal statement "right," or punished by the verbal statement "wrong." The subject was instructed to learn which numbers went with which words, so that on a test trial he could repeat those that were said to be right and to vary those that were said to be wrong. Thorndike found that subjects tended to repeat the correct responses. They also showed an above-chance tendency to repeat those responses that elicited no response from the experimenter (demonstrating, he assumed, the law of exercise— learning through mere repetition without an aftereffect). But the important finding was that subjects also tended to repeat at an above-chance level responses that they had been told were wrong.

Thorndike's asymmetrical law of effect was not universally accepted. Critics were quick to point out certain basic methodological flaws. For one thing, it is gratuitous to assume that the numbers from one to ten have equal probabilities of occurrence. Subjects tend to use numbers in systematic ways; they come into the experimental situation with well-established verbal habits for using numbers. Subsequent investigation has demonstrated that the expected repetition rate for numbers given in guessing sequences is closer to 15 percent than to 10 percent. Another difficulty here is in the possible generalization effects, such as the spread-of-effect phenomenon, which is the tendency for associations near a reinforced association to be repeated.

A great deal of research effort has gone into teasing out the different variables and effects that influence performance in this sort of verbal learning situation. Sometimes Thorndike is confirmed, and sometimes he is repudiated. But Stone (1953), with the wisdom from some 20 years of such research to draw on, conducted an experiment that seems to control the relevant factors and provide a real test of the asymmetrical law of effect. Stone made lavish use of subjects (160 in a group), precision presentation apparatus, a carefully counterbalanced design, and a control group to establish the zero reinforcement baseline. He found that under these conditions telling a subject "wrong" strengthens that response more than telling him nothing. It appears, then, that verbal punishment is a slightly positive reinforcer.

The definition of punishment. Dinsmoor (1954) has dismissed this whole line of research on the grounds that according to the empirical law of effect, a punisher is an event that stamps out; thus if "wrong" fails to do this, it is not a punisher. All we have discovered, Dinsmoor implies, from this research is that "wrong" is not a punisher in this situation; we have discovered nothing about the experimental treatments that are punishers. Stone was evidently aware of this possible interpretation, however, and accordingly culminated his work on this problem with a study of the same sort as before, in which an electric shock was used (Stone & Walter, 1951). The findings were the same as before; an electric shock is a weak positive reinforcer in this situation.

Certainly, we know that electric shock can be used as an effective punisher in other situations and that "wrong" can be used effectively also.[1] If we take Dinsmoor's charge seriously, then it seems likely that there may be no punishers for human subjects in Thorndike's situation. No matter how correct that possibility may be empirically, it seems somehow intuitively wrong. The problem here is that there are two alternative definitions of punishment. If we center our definition about the aversive stimulus, or "annoyer," to use Thorndike's term, punishment can be defined as a *procedure* in which such a stimulus is made contingent upon some response. We can then proceed to determine whether this or that behavior is weakened when it is punished. This strategy, which is the one Thorndike adopted, is consistent with everyday usage. If we slap a child for stealing cookies

---

[1] There are a number of studies (e.g., Brackbill & O'Hara, 1958) showing that verbal punishment, saying "wrong," can be effective in more complex situations than those that Thorndike used, for example, in concept formation problems. Perhaps this is because the subject attacks such problems with relatively long-term verbal hypotheses rather than the arbitrary short-term associations Thorndike studied.

from the cookie jar, we do so with the intent of weakening that behavior, and the use of this procedure with this intent makes it punishment whether or not the procedure reduces cookie stealing.

A quite different definition of punishment, suggested by Dinsmoor's remark, and subsequently made quite explicit by Azrin and Holz (1966), centers the definition on a change in behavior. Azrin and Holz define punishment as the weakening of behavior rather than as the procedure that weakens it. To distinguish punishment from other reductions in behavior, it must be produced by a contingent stimulus event, which we may call a punishing stimulus if it is effective. With this definition there can be no such thing as ineffective punishment or an ineffective punishing stimulus, because if there is no weakening of behavior, there is no punishment.

In this chapter Thorndike's strategy will be adopted. Punishment will be a procedure in which an aversive stimulus is presented when a particular response occurs. This procedure will be called the punishment procedure, and the consequent weakening of behavior will be called either a punishing effect or, when a more theoretically neutral term is required, suppression. Thus suppression will be used in essentially the same way that Azrin and Holz use punishment, namely, to describe the fact that behavior has been weakened because of the use of a contingent aversive stimulus.[2]

Spatially localized punishment. Punishment is sometimes tremendously effective in weakening behavior. Consider the following hypothetical situation. A hungry rat is put into a novel environment and allowed to explore for a few moments until it finds food. The animal is allowed to eat for a few seconds, and then the shock is turned on. If the shock is brief, intense, and localized in the vicinity of the food, then the animal will quickly withdraw as far as possible from the food, crouch, and show signs of emotional disturbance. After a few moments it may approach the food again. But when it is shocked once more, the tendency to approach will be reduced to near zero strength. The animal learns not to approach the food. The rapidity and effectiveness of this kind of learning is illustrated by Masserman's

---

[2] This point regarding the definition of punishment was also raised by Church (1963) in his important review of the punishment literature. Church also observed that there is some danger in the definition of aversive stimulus. Aversive was defined here (page 185) on the basis of whether it will support escape learning. The reason for this definition is not that escape learning has any prior claim but simply that escape training is more likely to be effective over the conceivable range of aversive stimuli than the avoidance procedure (see Chapter 10), a punishment procedure (see this chapter), or a classical conditioning procedure. In practice, of course, there is little difficulty determining which stimuli are aversive and which are not, and there is no real ambiguity in asking whether a particular aversive stimulus will be effective as a punisher.

(1943) report that under these conditions a cat may starve rather than eat the dangerous food again.[3]

Paradoxical effects of punishment. To add to the confusion, a variety of situations have been discovered in which the application of a punishing stimulus can *increase* the strength of the punished response (according to Azrin and Holz's analysis, shock must be a positive reinforcer in these cases). These different situations reveal the fundamental fact that when electric shock is used as a punishing stimulus, it can have a variety of effects upon behavior besides weakening the particular response upon which it is made contingent, and that sometimes these other effects can predominate over the response-suppressing effect of shock. In the next section we will look briefly at the experimental evidence that illustrates the response-eliciting effect, the motivating and reinforcing effects, the discriminative function, and the attention-getting value that electric shock can have.

Behavioral effects of shock

Response-eliciting effect. Recall Thorndike's (1932) assertion that the effect of punishment depends at least in part upon what the punishing stimulus makes the subject do. At the time Thorndike made this assertion there was no direct experimental support for it. But a much later experiment by Fowler and Miller (1963) does support Thorndike's conjecture. Fowler and Miller trained rats to run in an alley for food. At the goal some animals were shocked in the hind paws, and some were shocked in the forepaws. During the course of training, the forepaw subjects ran progressively slower than a control group that received no shock. Here then was the customary suppressing effect from punishing the running response. But animals shocked in the hind paws ran progressively faster than the control group, thus defying not only the traditional utilitarian conception of punishment but also much of the experimental data showing suppressive effects. This paradoxical facilitation of the running response might be expected, however, if we think of hind paw shock as eliciting a lurching-forward reaction, whereas forepaw shock elicits a startle or recoil reaction. It is only necessary to assume that part of what Fowler and Miller's animals learned was a tendency to make that response that was elicited by the punishing stimulus. In the case of the animals shocked in the hind paws, they should run faster because

---

[3] Instances of one-trial learning through punishment have been reported (e.g., Hudson, 1950; Jarvik & Essman, 1960; Pearlman et al., 1961). Morgan (1894) reported perhaps the first such case—chicks learn, sometimes in one trial to avoid bitter-tasting caterpillars. Morgan had a hypothesis very close to the one that will be developed here to explain it.

shock elicits lurching forward, which adds an increment to the speed of going forward. On the other hand, animals shocked in the forepaws are reinforced for running but also learn the competing recoil reaction and hence should have trouble running forward.

The poor performance of the forepaw animals might be explained on the basis of a response-competition mechanism. The fast running of the hind paw animals might be explained on the basis of additional motivation provided by conditioned fear, that is, increased drive level. But it is not clear how the difference between the two groups can be explained without invoking at some point the argument that part of what the animal learns in the situation is the specific response elicited by the punishing stimulus.

Although some writers, most recently Denny (1971), have used a similar type of elicitation mechanism to explain a variety of phenomena in avoidance learning, the discussion of avoidance in the previous chapter (page 354) indicates that there is very little evidence that the response elicited by shock is likely to be learned as an avoidance response. The Fowler and Miller experiment, therefore, remains one of the few convincing demonstrations that rats can learn the response elicited by shock.[4]

Reinforcing and motivating effects—the vicious circle phenomenon.
Gwinn (1949) trained rats to escape shock by running in a circular kind of apparatus. He then punished running in one part of the apparatus by shocking the rats whenever they ran through it. Gwinn found that this punishment produced faster running rather than suppression of running. Indeed, his animals continued accelerating until they became so frightened that their reaction was no longer running but freezing. Mowrer (1947), who first considered this type of phenomenon and predicted its occurrence, labeled it the vicious circle effect. As might be expected, Mowrer's interpretation of the phenomenon involved the two mechanisms of motivation and reinforce-

[4] It might be thought that the classical conditioning literature provides a mass of evidence for the acquisition of elicited responses. But, on the contrary, direct comparisons of classically conditioned defensive reactions and operant avoidance learning show that there is very little direct transfer (e.g., Bolles, 1972a; Wahlsten & Cole, 1972). Wahlsten and Cole showed that in the case of the response that seems most likely to be classically conditionable as an avoidance response, that is, leg flexion in the dog, the topography of the response, its temporal properties—all of its attributes—were different in the conditioned form and in the operant form. They conclude that there is no reason to suppose classical conditioning contributes to the acquisition of the avoidance reaction. In addition, Wahlsten (1972) has shown that while shock elicits different kinds of behaviors from different strains of mice, there is no correlation across strains between the ease of eliciting a response and the ease with which topographically similar responses are learned as avoidance behaviors. Thus as attractive as the elicitation hypothesis is in terms of its parsimony, there is very little direct evidence to support it.

ment. On the one hand, shock in the alley continues to provide fear motivation for running, and running through the shock continues to provide strong reinforcement of running. The vicious circle phenomenon illustrates, therefore, that in addition to whatever behavior-suppressing properties shock may have when used as a punishing stimulus, it can also supply both fear motivation and a potent source of reinforcement. The persistence of behavior when it is properly motivated and properly reinforced is, of course, not surprising. Nonetheless, it is possible to think of continued running in this situation as paradoxical in the sense that the animal could eliminate the need for any further running and prevent all subsequent shock simply by remaining quietly in the start box. Apparently, the animal chooses to subject itself to further shock by continuing to run.[5]

Brown and his students have made much ado about the vicious circle phenomenon. In their original experiment (Brown et al., 1964) rats were first trained to escape shock in an alley by running out of the electrified start box, through the electrified alley, and into a safe goal box. Then shock was removed from the start box and presented in only a portion of the alley. Brown et al. report that the resistance to extinction of the escape response was much greater under these conditions than under control conditions in which no more shock was presented. In their paper Brown et al. propose that vicious circle running can be best demonstrated by (1) making a gradual transition from the escape-acquisition to the punishment-

[5] Because the animal appears to choose to receive continued punishment in this situation, the behavior has sometimes been called masochistic or self-punitive. Both labels are inappropriate. In clinical and especially in subclinical cases of masochism, the individual is in no real sense choosing to be hurt. Rather, he is seeking relief from other more intense stimulation such as fear or guilt, or he is seeking aversive stimulation as a means of obtaining more positive kinds of gratification, such as attention or sexual arousal. Until closer parallels have been developed between the compulsions shown by masochistic individuals and the persistence of escape behavior by rats in runways, it is a disservice to all concerned to attach a common label to the two phenomena. Nor is the rat in any real sense choosing to punish itself. Given a real choice the rat will, of course, avoid the vicious circle situation entirely. Once in the start box, however, it may very well be making the best of a bad situation. O'Neil et al. (1970) reported that confining the rat to the start box in the absence of further shock abolished vicious circle running. O'Neil et al. attribute this result to the dissipation of fear in the start box. But it could be attributed to the acquisition of other defensive behaviors, such as freezing. The loss of a learned response certainly does not necessarily mean the loss of motivation (cf. Page, 1955; Coulter et al., 1971). I suspect that O'Neil et al. could have obtained the same result by confining their animals to the start box and shocking them there! Such a treatment would maintain fear level but would lead to the acquisition of other behaviors such as freezing. The point is that the rat may have many reasons for running or not running in the alley, and the existence of shock in the alley is only one of these many considerations.

extinction phases of the study, (2) using moderate levels of punishment, (3) originally establishing a very strong escape response, and (4) using a distinctive goal box. Subsequent investigations (reviewed by Brown, 1969) have indicated, however, that the vicious circle effect does not depend upon any one of these four methodological factors. Thus no one of them can be said to provide the magic ingredient for obtaining vicious circle behavior. Although it is not necessary to fade shock out of the start box gradually or to fade it into the alley gradually, the transition does have to be made with some care because if the rat should recoil or retreat when it encounters shock under the novel conditions instead of running forward, the running behavior will be promptly lost. In other words, in addition to the motivating and the reinforcing effects of shock in the alley, the response-eliciting effects of shock must be considered; if it elicits too much behavior other than the vicious circle behavior, then the latter will not be found.

The need for originally establishing running with escape training has also fallen by the wayside. Thus Brown (1969) has discussed a number of studies in which previously learned avoidance running persists when it is punished. Although there are few studies using procedures comparable enough to permit a direct comparison of avoidance and escape training, there is some indication (e.g., Beecroft & Brown, 1967; Babb & Hom, 1971) that it is not avoidance versus escape training per se that matters, but rather how quickly the running response is initiated at the beginning of a trial that governs resistance to extinction. Subsequently, it has been found (Melvin & Stenmark, 1968; Galvani, 1969) that confining rats to the start box, giving them either shock or a cue previously associated with shock, and only then giving them the opportunity to run, produces running that can then be maintained by shock in the alley. In addition, Brown (1969, p. 500) was able to obtain a vicious circle effect with previously established running for food. Brown suggests that it is necessary to have a very strong response that will survive the initial shock trials. But, as we will see, even this requirement does not seem to be necessary.

There is an old series of closely related studies, beginning with Yerkes and Dodson (1908), in which mice were put in a choice situation where if they approached one cue they would be shocked, and if they approached another cue nothing would happen. The animals were not hungry, there was no food, and there was no shock except after an incorrect response. Since the original behavior had no apparent motivation, we might wonder why the animal would venture forth with the risk of being shocked when it might just stay put and avoid all shock. Some subjects did refuse to run, perhaps as many as a third of the group, but the median animal ran even though it had no particular reason for doing so and even though it was punished on a large number of trials for doing so. What was the source of motivation for this behavior? Exploration is a possibility, but it seems unlikely that any exploratory behavior would survive the many shocks or the many trials that were commonly needed to obtain discrimination learning in the Yerkes box. The only reasonable explanation of the behavior is that the animals ran because they were frightened. Comparable results have been reported by Cole (1911) with chicks, Dodson (1915) with kittens, Vaughn and Diserens (1930) with human subjects, as well as by Hoge and Stocking (1912), Dodson (1917) and Warden and Aylesworth (1927) with rats. All of these results suggest that once an animal becomes frightened, its fear can provide enough motivation to keep behavior going in the absence of any specific response training.

The fourth factor that Brown et al. proposed as an important ingredient of the vicious circle phenomenon is that the goal box should be distinctive. The argument is that the goal box should be as different from the start box as possible to minimize unwanted response generalization and as different from the alley as possible to provide substantial reinforcement when the animal enters it. But Babb and Hom (1971) have shown that this requirement is also not a necessary part of the vicious circle phenomenon. They shocked animals in the goal box after either avoidance or escape training and found substantial vicious circle effects in both cases.

Thus we see that none of the four procedural suggestions of Brown et al. (1964) as to how to facilitate vicious circle behavior proves to be an essential ingredient for obtaining the effect. The effect has been reported with each of the four factors missing. Apparently, what this means is that vicious circle running is multiply determined or overdetermined by the experimental conditions.

The usual explanation of vicious circle behavior, originally proposed by Mowrer (1947) and subsequently endorsed by Brown (1969), provides a multiplicity of mechanisms, any one of which could account for this paradoxical effect. There is powerful reinforcement (according to the reinforcement theorist) in the initial escape training. There is also continued reinforcement from running out of the punishing region of the alley. Moreover, there are the danger-signal aspects of the start box and the safety-signal aspects of the goal box to provide further reinforcement for running. The running response also has a great deal of motivation. Fear is conditioned to the entire apparatus except, presumably, the goal box. Certainly, the start box is a cue to shock, and it is clear that running is initially a very strong response in the apparatus used in most of these studies. That is, in addition to the generalized motivational effect of fear and the specific reinforcement provided for the running response, there is the additional factor that the shock elicits running and that the entire apparatus provides stimulus support for running. Thus there is

Theory of motivation

a third mechanism, a purely associative mechanism for promoting the running response and for maintaining it once it is established. In short, shock not only contributes to the overall drive level and should therefore be expected to strengthen the running response, it should also selectively facilitate running because running is an SSDR in this kind of apparatus.

Much of the research effort of Brown and his students has been addressed to questions such as where in the alley to locate the shock, what intensity of shock to use, whether to punish all responses or only some proportion of them, and so on. It is unfortunate that so much effort has gone into these parametric questions rather than into a clarification of the underlying mechanisms. How much of the vicious circle effect is due just to the maintenance of fear? For example, would the same effects be obtained if animals were simply shocked either in the same or a different apparatus? How much of the behavior is due to purely associative or elicitation factors? Bender (1969) has shown that presenting a buzzer that has been paired with shock is nearly as effective in maintaining running as shock itself when presented in the alley (see also Hallenborg & Fallon, 1971). Does such a procedure eliminate the elicitation effect of shock or does it merely provide cues to which the animal is already prepared to give its dominant SSDR, that is, running?

It should be emphasized that there are some severe limitations on the generality of the vicious circle phenomenon. For example, most of the results that have been reported have only demonstrated greater resistance to extinction of a previously established running response. Typically, the effect of punishing a previously learned escape response is to extend extinction from about 25 trials to about 75 trials. Brown has given no indication of why the running response should ever extinguish when it has so many devices to support it. If fear is constantly being maintained, and the presumed sources of reinforcement continue to operate, why does the animal ultimately stop running? Is it because it finally learns that the start box is a safe place, a nonpredictor of shock?

Mowrer's motivation-reinforcement interpretation of the vicious circle phenomenon requires not only the maintenance of responding but also a greater probability of responding. For example, there should be a shorter latency of leaving the start box when running is punished. However, when this effect has been sought, it has not been found (Delude, 1969). In some cases those who have claimed to demonstrate it (e.g., Siegel et al., 1971) report no such effect (perhaps because their rats were already running as fast as they could), but, again, only better maintenance of speed during the course of extinction.

One of the greatest limitations upon the phenomenon is that it has only been reported with running behavior. Comparable procedures with animals trained, say, to escape shock by pressing a bar usually produce suppression when the response is punished.[6] In an apparent exception, Fitzgerald and Walloch (1969) claim to have shown a vicious circle effect with a wheel-turning escape response. However, facilitation of the response was found only under one condition, namely, when punishment was so long delayed on a given trial that it occurred just before the next trial, at which point it might be expected to facilitate the previously learned escape response.

Discriminative properties of shock. In addition to the other properties it may have, shock can also serve to signal other important experimental events in an experimental situation. Consider, for example, the following experiment by Dinsmoor (1952). Animals were run on a mixed schedule in which there were randomly scheduled periods of partial reinforcement and extinction with no signals to indicate which was in effect at any given time. Dinsmoor then added a punishment contingency to the extinction component, so that the shock could serve to signal that extinction was in effect. Responding occurred at a high rate until a shock was received; it then proceeded at a low rate until a response was not shocked; it then returned immediately to the high rate. Under these conditions, then, the rat was evidently using the shock given as punishment as an S^Δ for responding for food. Thus rather than simply suppressing the behavior, contingent shock served to provide discriminative control over it.

In an interesting extension of this procedure, Holz and Azrin (1961) trained animals on a mixed schedule involving partial reinforcement and extinction, but punishment was added to the reinforcement component. Here the animal's choice was between receiving food and shock or nothing, and under these conditions the response rate was higher in the punished (and reinforced) component than in the extinction component. Thus the information provided by punishment can be used by an animal either to respond more or to respond less depending upon what information is conveyed about positive reinforcement. Azrin and Holz (1966) discuss further implications of punishment serving a discriminative function to control behavior.

The attention-getting property of shock. It has been known for a number of years that under appropriate conditions electric shock can facilitate discrimination learning, even though it is used as though it were punishing the correct response. Muenzinger (1934) showed that rats would learn a discrimination problem in a T-maze some-

---

[6] There is a variety of experimental situations using operant rather than discrete trial or instrumental techniques in which either contingent or noncontingent shock paradoxically helps maintain or elicit the ongoing behavior. Some of this literature has been reviewed by Stretch (1972).

what better if in addition to obtaining food the correct response also produced a mild shock. Muenzinger's original interpretation of this finding was that the shock produces a mild state of conflict—it slowed the animal down so that the appropriate stimuli were more likely to be attended to. Muenzinger's interpretation seemed reasonable enough, but it has been replaced by a somewhat better one on the basis of a series of experiments conducted by Fowler and Wischner (1969). Their work indicates that because shock itself is such a salient stimulus it tends to attach salience (i.e., discriminability) to other stimuli associated with it. Apparently, giving shock for the correct response not only slows the animal down but also enriches the number of possible associations or mediations that accrue to the stimulus by virtue of being associated with shock. Consider the use of verbal labels by human subjects. In many human learning situations performance is much better if verbal labels, or mediators, can be attached to the stimuli to be discriminated. The shock for the rat is like the verbal label for the human. Evidence for this argument comes from a variety of studies such as those that show that the facilitating effect of punishing the correct response is greatest with difficult tasks where the discriminanda are inherently not very salient (Fowler & Wischner, 1969).

Like all of the paradoxical effects of punishment, these results indicate that electric shock has a variety of different effects upon behavior. It can be used to elicit behavior; it can be used to motivate or reinforce behavior; it can also be used to gain discriminative control or attentional control over behavior. All of these effects are to be expected from shock used in different ways; what is perhaps surprising is that they can all be obtained when shock is used as a punisher. What have been called the paradoxical effects of punishment are thus simply instances where the experimental situation has been arranged so that one or another or some combination of these other effects of shock are more prominant than the punishing or response-weakening effect that we expect punishment to have.

The paradoxical effects of punishment are potentially quite instructive about the mechanisms involved specifically in punishment and more generally in other applications of shock. Certainly, any theory of punishment must not only be able to account for the expected suppressing effect of punishment, it must also be flexible enough to explain these paradoxical effects. It should be emphasized, though, that the bulk of the research done with punishment has yielded rather consistent, often systematic, and really quite unremarkable behavioral effects. Let us consider some of the data.

Suppressing effect of punishment. It has been shown that in the runway the suppression of a previously established running response depends upon the intensity of shock (Karsh, 1962, 1964; Appel, 1963; Baron, 1965; Misanin et al., 1966), how close the animal is to where

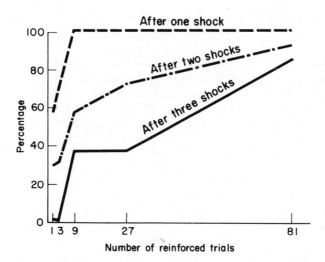

Figure 11–1

*Percentage of animals that reach the goal after they
have been shocked there as a function of the number
of previous training trials reinforced by food. (From
Kaufman & Miller, 1949) Copyright (1949) by the
American Psychological Association. Reprinted by
permission.*

shock is received (Brown, 1948; Karsh, 1962), and how strong the
original running response is (Karsh, 1962). There is also abundant
evidence showing that immediate punishment is more effective than
delayed punishment (e.g., Kamin, 1959; Baron, 1965; Misanin et al.,
1966). It might be expected that these different experimental variables could be played off against each other; for example, we might
expect the effectiveness of punishment to increase with the number
of times punishment is applied and to decrease with the number of
times that the response has been previously reinforced. The interaction of these particular variables has been studied by Kaufman
and Miller (1949) in one of the early conflict studies, which Fig. 11-1
illustrates.[7]

Reference to the overall "effectiveness" of punishment may
be a little too global, because there are a number of different ways in
which the effectiveness of punishment can be assessed. Suppose we
have some behavior that, prior to the introduction of punishment,
has some stable initial strength as measured either by its rate in an

[7] This conception was one source of the brilliant work done by
Miller and his co-workers on conflict. We will not consider this work here
because it lends itself directly to an associationistic interpretation without
involving any new facts or concepts about motivation. The best review is
Miller (1959).

operant situation or its latency in an instrumental situation. Suppose then that at some point this behavior is punished. We may anticipate that there will be rapid suppression, that is, weakening of the response, when the punishment procedure is instituted, as diagrammed in Fig. 11-2. We may suppose further that if the punishment procedure is continued, there will be some partial recovery so that during the course of the punishment training the behavior will not be as suppressed as it was initially. Finally, we may suppose that when punishment is discontinued, there will be further recovery in the strength of the response as the effects of punishment extinguish. In speaking about the effectiveness of punishment, then, it is relevant to ask how rapid and profound the initial suppression is when punishment is instituted, to what extent and how rapidly the animal will adapt to or recover from this initial suppression, how long following the termination of the punishment treatment it takes the behavior to recover to its final strength, or whether there is some permanent loss of behavior strength.

In recent years a great deal of punishment research has been conducted in the Skinner box, and it is only for this situation that even tentative answers can be given to the various questions just raised about the effectiveness of punishment. It has been shown by a number of investigators that the level of responding at which the animal stabilizes during punishment training depends in a critical manner on shock intensity (Azrin, 1960; Boe, 1966; Camp et al., 1967). Boe (1971) reports the interesting finding that shocks that vary in intensity suppress more effectively than shocks that are fixed at the mean intensity. Miller (1960) had observed earlier that the suppressive effect of shock could be reduced by bringing it up to final

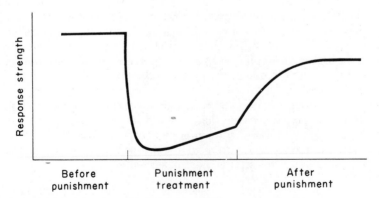

Figure 11-2

Schematic diagram showing the weakening (suppression) and recovery of behavior during and after punishment.

intensity gradually over a series of trials. It has also been found that there may be relatively rapid recovery from low-intensity shock and that the recovery may be total, that is, leaving no permanent effect (Estes, 1944; Azrin, 1960; Rachlin, 1966; Tellish & Dunstone, 1971). On the other hand, with intense shock there tends to be more profound initial suppression, slower recovery, and the final level of response strength may be much lower than the initial level; in other words, there do seem to be some permanent effects (Azrin, 1960; Boe & Church, 1967). Boe (1971a) has shown that the rate of recovery is a sensitive function of the number of shocks received in the punishment treatment.

In addition to increasing the intensity of shock comparable effects can be produced by giving shocks of longer duration. The results of Storms et al. (1963), Boe (1966), Smith et al. (1966), and Church et al. (1967) suggest that what matters is the total amount of shock received and that it makes little difference whether longer-duration shock or higher-intensity shock is used.

The situation is actually a little more complicated than it appears because most of the work on punishment in a Skinner box has been done with behavior maintained by a variable-interval reinforcement schedule. The VI schedule has the virtue of producing stable, smooth rates of responding, and the primary effect of punishment is to reduce the rate and sometimes to reduce the regularity of behavior. But quite different effects may be found with other maintenance schedules. Azrin (1960) found that on behavior maintained by an FI schedule, punishment had relatively little effect on the terminal end of the scallop but markedly suppressed behavior in the first part of the interval when the rate of responding was already low. Azrin (1959) has reported that punishment of FR behavior had the similar effect of increasing the postreinforcement pause but had little effect on the final ratio run. In this connection Lyon and Felton (1966) observed that the effect of a CS for shock was found almost exclusively when it occurred during the postreinforcement pause where it prolonged the pause. If the suppression cue was presented during the ratio run, it had little effect. So although the behavior is suppressed on the average, the effect of shock is quite dependent upon the local rate of responding. Thus we may begin to suspect that even in situations in which punishment is alleged to have systematic suppressive effects on behavior, these effects may also prove on further analysis to be quite varied.

Theories of punishment

The original theory of punishment, that given us by our cultural tradition, is that punishment is bad and to be avoided; because we are rational and have free will we do avoid it. This theory (or, more properly, pretheory) can be dismissed on the grounds discussed in Chapter 2, that is, that it provides no explanatory mechanisms. Similarly, we may dismiss the behavioristic utilitarianism of Hernstein (Hernstein, 1969; Rachlin & Hernstein, 1969), which asserts that certain classes of events, such as shock, do enable us to control behavior. The effect of this control is that subjects minimize the amount of bad things, like shock, and maximize the amount of good things, like food, by changing the rate of responding as a consequence of the good things and bad things that are contingent upon their behavior. What Herrnstein asserts is true enough, but it too provides no explanatory mechanisms; it simply gives a guideline for how we can control behavior.

The first explanatory principle to account for the effects of punishment was, as we have already discussed, that proposed by Thorndike (1911). Punishment was said to weaken whatever S-R connection preceded it. We have already seen that Thorndike abandoned this proposal because he found that it was not universal. He found that there were situations in which the effects of punishment appeared to be indirect and unpredictable. Thorndike never developed a more systematic account of punishment, but he noted that the effectiveness of punishment depended upon the availability of other kinds of behaviors and the kinds of behavior elicited by the punishing stimulus.

The elicitation hypothesis. Among the major learning theorists, Guthrie (1934, 1935) was the first to deal systematically with punishment. For Guthrie there was no reinforcement principle. A response became attached to a configuration of stimuli simply because it occurred in their presence. The effect of a reinforcer was to produce behaviors that could be conditioned to the other stimuli present at the time of reinforcement. The effect of punishment was, similarly, to produce behavior such as withdrawal reactions that could become conditioned to stimuli present at the time of punishment. Thus for Guthrie the only behavior that could be learned on the basis of punishment was the particular response that was elicited by the punishing stimulus, that is, withdrawal, cowering, or the fear reaction itself. If the conditions of punishment were arranged so that punishment produced withdrawal, then the organism would learn to withdraw. If punishment produced freezing or cowering, then the organism would learn to freeze or cower. But if the rat was punished for running in a situation in which the reaction to punishment was running, then punishment could only generate more running. Thus Guthrie had a ready account of the vicious circle phenomena.

Guthrie's elicitation interpretation of punishment never attracted much of a following because, like the other aspects of his theory, there has never been much direct evidence to test it against alternative formulations. The experiment by Fowler and Miller

(1963) described previously provided the kind of data Guthrie needed.

More support for Guthrie's theory was provided by Adelman and Maatsch (1955), who trained rats to run into a box for food and then extinguished running under different conditions. One group was permitted to jump out through the top of the box to escape the frustrating situation, while another group was required to back up out of the box. The back-up group quit running to the box almost immediately, whereas the jump-out group continued to run to the box and jump out of it for many trials. Again, all animals did what the punishment (frustration, in this case) made them do—jump out, which was compatible with the running response, or retreat, which effectively interfered with running. Unfortunately, these results are not easy to replicate (e.g. Theios & Bower, 1964). Guthrie's interpretation also makes sense of Thorndike's failure to find punishing effects in the verbal learning situation because being told "wrong," should not produce any reaction that would compete with a verbal utterance. (But at the same time, it is not clear how Guthrie could explain the learning of verbal responses that occur when they produce a positive effect.) More data consistent with an elicitation interpretation of punishment was reported by Bolles and Seelbach (1964). We studied the punishing effect of loud noise on different responses in the rat's repertoire; we found that some responses were suppressed but others were not. Our explanation was that the onset of loud noise elicits a reflexive head movement that interferes with the learning of a head movement (which was suppressed by punishment) but fails to compete with standing up or grooming (which were not suppressed by punishment). Partly on the strength of such results, Guthrie's interpretation of punishment was advocated in the first edition of this book (Bolles, 1967).

The escape hypothesis. While contiguity theorists seem to have been primarily interested in the failures of punishment and the paradoxical effects of punishment, drive theorists have tended to emphasize the customary suppressive effect of punishment. In one of the first statements of the drive reduction position Miller and Dollard (1941) maintained that punishment could produce learning because the punishing stimulus presents a source of drive and its termination constitutes drive reduction. Therefore, they proposed that an animal will learn any response that immediately precedes the termination of the punishing stimulus. This learned response then interferes with the performance of the original punished response. As they describe it:

> A child touches a hot radiator. The pain elicits a (withdrawal) response, and the escape from pain rewards this response. Since the sight and muscular feel of the hand approaching the radiator are similar in certain respects to the sight and muscular feel of the hand touching the radiator, the strongly rewarded response

of withdrawal will be expected to generalize from the latter situation to the former. After one or more trials, the child will reach out its hand toward the radiator and withdraw it before touching the radiator. The withdrawal response will become anticipatory; it will occur before that of actually touching the radiator. This is obviously adaptive, since it enables the child to avoid getting burned. (Miller & Dollard, 1941, pp. 49–50)

What is proposed here is that the stimuli that initially control approach responses come to elicit withdrawal because of the very rapid learning (escape learning) of withdrawal in the presence of stimuli like those that initially controlled the approach.

The escape hypothesis has an elegant simplicity, but there are two considerations suggesting that it may be overly simple, that is, too simple to account for much of the data. One consideration is that punishment effects can be found quite readily when shock is presented in very brief bursts, such as 0.1 seconds. It would seem to be impossible for the rat to make, or even to begin, an escape response in so short an interval. Moreover, it is possible to separate experimentally the onset from the termination of shock. Both Leitenberg (1965) and Bolles and Warren (1966) have found that delaying the termination of a punishing stimulus does little to reduce its effectiveness as a punishing stimulus but that delaying its onset has a much more profound effect. It appears, therefore, that it is the onset of the punishing stimulus rather than its termination that, at least in those situations that were studied, makes it effective.

The second major problem is that the animal in the punishment study is obviously frightened. Whether we look at autonomic reactions, suppression of ongoing behavior, or the restriction of the animal's behavioral repertoire to a limited set of SSDRs—however we define fear—the punished animal is obviously frightened, particularly during the early stages of punishment training when suppression is most profound. The escape hypothesis makes no provision for any effects of fear. Accordingly, the escape hypothesis cannot give a complete picture of what is going on in the punishment situation.

The avoidance hypothesis. In 1947 Mowrer proposed that the punishment procedure is simply a variation of the avoidance procedure and that the mechanisms controlling the subject's behavior are essentially identical in the two cases. This idea was subsequently elaborated by Mowrer in 1950 and 1960. According to Mowrer, the fear response becomes classically conditioned to stimuli that are associated with shock. In the avoidance situation the fear stimulus may be an external warning signal, or it may be the part of the apparatus in which the shock is presented, or it may be the response feedback from the animal's own behavior. This last class of stimuli plays an important role for Mowrer in the punishment situation. The argument is that when a response is punished, its proprioceptive feedback is associated with shock, and so fear is classically conditioned to these stimuli. When the animal subsequently begins to make this response, it will experience the conditioned fear. If it then makes some alternative response, this other behavior will be reinforced by the resulting reduction in fear. Thus for Mowrer the explanation of punishment is precisely the same as the explanation for avoidance, the only difference being that in the avoidance situation a particular response occurs because all alternatives to it have fear-arousing consequences. In the punishment situation, however, one particular response does not occur because it has fear-arousing consequences.

Presumably, one can explain anything with Mowrer's avoidance hypothesis that one can with the escape hypothesis, and a bit more. In both cases punishment is effective when some behavior other than the punished response is learned. The difference is that for the escape paradigm learning is attributed to a primary negative reinforcer, whereas for Mowrer's avoidance paradigm learning is due to a conditioned negative reinforcer, that is, fear reduction. It should be apparent that just as Mowrer's fear reduction view of avoidance was readily translated into Skinnerian terms by redefining the critical stimulus as aversive rather than as fear inducing, so his account of punishment can be translated into Skinnerian terms, as Dinsmoor (1954, 1955) has done. The punishment procedure is said to be effective when, and to the extent that, the feedback from the animal's own behavior becomes aversive. These two versions of the punishment phenomenon are today the accepted interpretations. They have become, in effect, the official and standard explanations of punishment.

The viability of the avoidance hypothesis hinges on the empirical question of whether the specific fear produced by punishing a particular response has any different effects upon behavior than the generalized fear produced by shocking an animal without regard to its behavior. We will discuss this difficult question shortly. But before we do so, it is necessary to look at some alternative interpretations of punishment.

The conditioned-suppression hypothesis. Even if we accept the proposition that punishment can work indirectly by strengthening behavior that competes with the punished response, there is still a question of whether punishment has any direct effect on the punished response itself. Estes (1944) investigated this question in what has become one of the most famous and important of all papers on punishment. Estes reported a number of studies in this paper, but the basic procedure was this: Rats were trained to press a bar for food, and then this response was extinguished. In the control group the response was simply extinguished, and the animals gave about 200 responses in extinction. In the experimental group the response was also extinguished, but first the animals were punished several times for pressing the bar. And they too gave about 200 responses in extinction. The punished animals did take longer to extinguish in the sense that suppression persisted for some time after the punishment phase, but as soon as the animals began pressing the bar again, they resumed at the normal rate (or at an even higher, compensatory rate), and from that point they generated as much behavior in extinction as the control animals. Estes concluded that punishing bar pressing does not weaken it but only produces a temporary decrement in responding, as if the animals had been physically restrained from pressing the bar for a period of time. In terms of the scheme illustrated in Fig. 11-2, Estes had found that while shock produced suppression, there was complete recovery to the level of responding characteristic of nonpunished controls.

Furthermore, Estes (1944) reported that it made little difference whether shocks in his situation were correlated with bar pressing (the punishment procedure) or presented independently of the animal's behavior. Hence, he argued (as Estes & Skinner, 1941, had earlier), that the effect of shock was to produce a diffuse generalized emotional state, anxiety. The animal's behavior while in this state consists primarily of freezing and crouching and, of course, withdrawal from the situation. It was this emotional state, together with its immobilizing effect upon behavior, that competed with and thus suppressed bar pressing.

We may suppose that if fear is conditioned to any particular part of the environment, the animal will withdraw from it. A gradient of withdrawal behavior can be derived from the fact that stimuli anywhere in the test situation are likely to be similar to the stimuli near the source of shock, so that fear will occur everywhere in the situation but in an amount that depends upon stimulus generalization. The animal can minimize its fear by minimizing the similarity between where it is and where shock is. Fear should ultimately extinguish, and there should be a corresponding recovery of the original behavior.

Estes' study and his interpretation of it have generated an enormous amount of discussion. Estes promoted the idea (or legend, as Solomon, 1964, calls it) that punishment is an ineffective way of controlling behavior. Skinner has argued further that because punishment is ineffective, its use in controlling human behavior is indefensible. He observes that it would be morally indefensible even if it were effective (Skinner, 1948a), but that it is all the more so because it is not effective, has undesired side effects, and frequently has unpredictable effects (Skinner, 1953).[8]

[8] Of course, punishment will continue to be used in attempting to control behavior whether it is effective or not. One reason is that as tough as punishment may be on the punishee, using it is reinforcing to the punisher because it can usually be counted on to produce prompt suppression of behavior that the punisher finds aversive. Skinner's moral

Azrin and Holz (1966) have advanced the interesting argument that it is inappropriate to compare the effectiveness of punishment with that of positive reinforcement in controlling behavior. Rather, they suggest, the effectiveness of punishment should be judged relative to other procedures for weakening behavior. On this score, they conclude, punishment compares more than favorably with satiation, with stimulus change, with physical restraint, and with conditioned suppression as alternative techniques for reducing response strength. They contend that punishment, especially when used in conjunction with other response-weakening techniques, can be enormously effective in weakening behavior. Azrin and Holz maintain that effective punishment procedures include the use of intense, immediate punishment, reinstating punishment training from time to time, giving the organism alternative forms of available behavior, and not permitting the subject to escape or avoid punishment by making unauthorized, that is, sneaky, responses. As sound as Azrin and Holz's conclusions may be for the practical purpose of weakening behavior, their extended analysis of the punishment experiment leaves the basic theoretical issues unresolved. We do not know why punishment is sometimes very effective, sometimes ineffective, and sometimes has paradoxical effects. The assurance that high intensities of shock are more likely to suppress ongoing behavior may be true, but we would like to know why this is so. Does more shock simply produce more fear and hence more profound and long-lasting suppression, as Estes (1944) might contend, or does it introduce other kinds of response-weakening mechanisms? The assurance that response-contingent shock produces more suppression than response-independent shock may also be true, under some conditions, but again we would like to know why. Does contingent shock actively weaken the response in some way, or, as Estes might contend, does it merely ensure that fear will become conditioned specifically to the bar, so the rat will be more likely to stay away from it? In support of this idea Dunham et al. (1969) found that when their pigeons were punished for pecking a key, they continued to peck, but they pecked off the key!

The virtue of Estes' conditioned-suppression hypothesis is that it provides a clear and systematic account of a mechanism that

---

argument can be countered on other grounds, however. One is that there is a segment of our society that believes that if a rule is right, then enforcing the rule by punishment is right. In other words, retributive punishment may be fair and just even when it has no corrective effect upon the behavior of the punishee. My own moral principles are most consistent with those of Ginott (1965) when he argues that the punishment of children is perfectly defensible provided that it is made explicitly clear to the child that he is not being punished because he is a worthless person, but rather that the punisher is attempting to alter his behavior because *it* is offensive. In effect, the child should be enlisted as an ally in changing his behavior rather than being made an enemy.

we know can produce decrements in behavior and that can explain much of the punishment literature without having to make the assumption that when punishment does produce a decrement, it must be because some alternative response is learned or because the punished response itself is weakened. How far the conditioned-suppression hypothesis can go toward explaining all of the punishment literature still remains to be determined. We still do not know if there is any response learning with the punishment procedure. We know only that much of what appears to be response learning (or suppression) must ultimately be attributed to the animal's altered motivation rather than to associative processes per se.

The motivation competition hypothesis. After reviewing a quarter century of work and discussion generated by his earlier conditioned-suppression hypothesis of punishment, Estes (1969) abandoned it in favor of a new hypothesis. All of the prior theories of punishment had involved competition, and Estes continued this tradition of thinking in terms of competition.[9] But his new theory involved a new type of competition. When punishment is effective, it is because it causes competition at a motivational level rather than response competition. Estes' old model suggested that the rat was too busy freezing to press the bar. The new model requires us to think of the animal as too busy being frightened to be hungry. Fear not only produces its own behaviors, such as freezing, but it also inhibits the hunger system that gives rise to food-getting behavior.

This interpretation leads to predictions that are remarkably consistent with those generated by common sense, as well as with certain biological considerations. For example, the need to defend one's self should have priority over feeding, at least on a short-term basis. Thus we should expect the inhibitory effects of different motivational systems to be arranged hierarchically, so that fear would inhibit food-getting behavior much more rapidly and effectively than hunger would inhibit defensive behavior. (Although that can happen, too; see, e.g., Wilson & Dinsmoor, 1970.)

It is clear from Estes' discussion that the motivational systems he has in mind for producing different kinds of behavior are more incentive-like than drivelike. They are triggered and "amplified" by external cues to food, or danger, or whatever. We may summarize

[9] Curiously, Estes' conditioned-suppression hypothesis, as well as the avoidance, the escape, and the elicitation hypotheses, all attribute the effects of punishment to the occurrence of some behavior that competes with the punished response; none of these hypotheses attributes any direct response-weakening effect to punishment. The punished response only appears weaker because the animal is engaged in some other behavior, either instrumental withdrawal (Mowrer) or anxiety-induced freezing (Estes), which competes with the punished response.

Estes' new position by saying that cues to shock reduce the incentive motivation that maintains hunger-motivated behavior. Millenson and de Villiers (1972) have analyzed a variety of evidence that supports Estes' new interpretation. This support, however, depends upon one additional assumption, which is that strength of appetitive behavior is a negatively accelerated, increasing function of incentive motivation. Such a function is shown in Fig. 11-3. The curvature of the function results in a given increment of incentive motivation having a large effect on behavior when incentive motivation is low and a smaller effect when it is already high. This appears to be an eminently reasonable assumption, even though it is not clear how one would actually determine the precise shape of the incentive function. Then granting such a functional relationship and granting that a given amount of fear will produce a fixed decrement in the amount of incentive motivation, this amount of fear will have less effect on behavior when behavior is strongly motivated than when incentive motivation is low. Millenson and de Villiers present a surprising range of evidence that is at least qualitatively consistent with this model. For example, we have already noted that Azrin (1959) and Lyon and Felton (1966) found suppression to be much greater in those parts of fixed-ratio behavior where the animal is pausing than when the animal is making the terminal run. If we can assume that the temporal pattern-

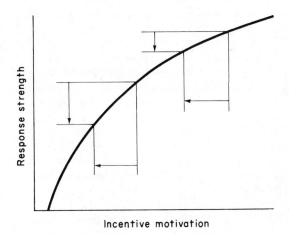

Figure 11–3

Hypothetical function relating response strength to the strength of incentive motivation. Loss in response strength corresponding to a unit loss in incentive motivation at two levels of incentive is indicated. (From Millenson & de Villiers, 1972)

ing of FR behavior reflects variation in momentary incentive, that is, that it is controlled by temporal and other kinds of cues to food, then this otherwise inexplicable effect begins to make sense.

Predictive-cue hypothesis. So far little has been said about any cognitive interpretation of punishment. However, a good case for this type of explanatory model can be made simply by describing an experiment reported some years ago by Azrin (1956). In some ways this study, when properly interpreted, is the definitive experiment on punishment. Azrin initially trained pigeons to peck a key for food on a VI-3 schedule. The key was alternately blue and orange for 2-minute periods. Shock never occurred during the blue condition, but when the key was orange, shock was programmed according to one of four sets of experimental conditions. Under two of these conditions shock was contingent on a key peck, while under the other two shock was presented noncontingently. Orthogonal to this arrangement was the scheduling of shock either at a fixed time, 1 minute into the orange light, or at random times, on the average of once during the orange light. Each pigeon was run as its own control and rotated through the different experimental conditions on enough sessions so that behavior stabilized under each condition.

The results diagrammed in Fig. 11-4 indicate that each set of conditions for programming shock produced its own characteristic pattern of responding. Consider first the behavior of animals under the fixed-time, noncontingent condition. Behavior occurred at the high rate characteristic of a VI-3 reinforcement schedule as long as the blue light was on (this was true under all four of the conditions). A high rate of responding was also obtained both early and late in the orange light, but pecking was suppressed during the mid-portion of the orange light presentation, that is, at that time when the noncontingent shock was scheduled to occur. Second, under the fixed-time, contingent condition there was a high rate of responding up to the time when the shock was possible, that is, midway through the orange light. But there was virtually total suppression after that point until the orange light went off. Third, under the variable-time, noncontingent condition there was a moderate degree of suppression throughout the orange light (the rate of responding was highly variable under this condition). Finally, under conditions of variable-time and contingent shock there was nearly total suppression during the entire interval marked by the orange light, that is, when pecking might be punished.

Azrin's (1956) own conclusions from these results were perhaps appropriate at the time they were formulated, but they now seem needlessly conservative. He concluded that shock on a variable schedule leads to more stable rates of responding than shock programmed on a fixed schedule, and he noted that this difference was analogous to the effects produced by positive reinforcement on varia-

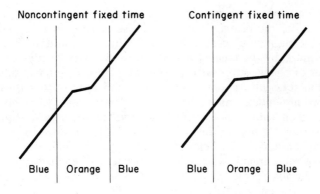

Noncontingent fixed time   Contingent fixed time

Blue | Orange | Blue   Blue | Orange | Blue

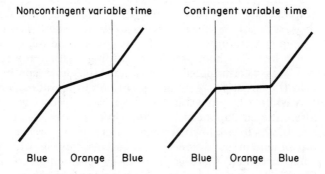

Noncontingent variable time   Contingent variable time

Blue | Orange | Blue   Blue | Orange | Blue

Figure 11–4

*Composite cumulative records of pigeons pecking for
food while receiving either contingent or noncontingent shock scheduled either at a fixed time or
at varied times into the orange light. (From Azrin,
1956)*

ble and fixed schedules. His second conclusion was that less overall
responding was found when shock was contingent on responding than
when it was programmed noncontingently. This conclusion has been
widely cited in support of the proposition that the response contingency contributes to the suppressive effects of punishment.

But Azrin's results can be given a much more simple, elegant,
and unifying interpretation. What they show is that behavior is
suppressed in the presence of stimulus conditions that predict shock
and proceeds at the baseline rate in the presence of stimulus conditions that predict no shock. There is apparently considerable generality in the kind of predictive cue that can suppress behavior. First the
external stimulation provided by the orange light is an effective sup-

pressor; no suppression was found, at least in steady-state responding, except during the orange light. The lapse of time in the presence of the orange light is a second kind of stimulus condition that can be discriminated by the pigeon, and when the passage of time becomes a predictor of shock, suppression is found. Note particularly that in the fixed-time schedules suppression was found only during those intervals in which shock was liable to occur. Under the variable-time conditions, when time was not itself a predictor of shock, suppression occurred more or less uniformly throughout the orange light. Finally, when the animal's own behavior became a predictor of shock, that predictive relationship was also incorporated. We can say that whatever conditions predict shock—either internal or external stimuli or even a contingency involving the animal's own behavior—whatever these conditions may be, they will suppress ongoing appetitive behavior.

Why did Azrin find the response contingency to be a factor when other experimenters (e.g., Estes, 1944) have failed to find such an effect? Azrin's own answer appears to be sufficient. He gave his animals prolonged training under the different conditions. We may presume that he gave them sufficient training so that the response contingency was discriminated from among the other contingencies operating in the situation. Why did Azrin obtain stimulus control of suppression while other investigators often find diffuse, generalized, and undifferentiated suppression? The same answer can be given: extended training. It is known from a variety of research that when either punishment or conditioned-suppression training with intense shock is first instituted, there is likely to be total suppression. Then behavior begins to recover during the intervals or in the presence of stimuli that predict no shock (Carman, 1972). Although Azrin does not describe the course of this recovery in his 1956 study, we may suppose that there was initially generalized suppression, that his animals first recovered in the presence of the blue light, then recovered during the safe portions of the orange light, and finally (under the variable-time, noncontingent condition) recovered at least partially through all parts of the orange light.[10]

---

[10] Note that it is not logically necessary for the animal to discriminate the contingency between its behavior and shock. Consider, for instance, the animal under variable-time, contingent conditions. We can assume that early in training these conditions produce almost total suppression, that is, a very low rate of responding. It then follows that shock is very likely to be primed when the animal makes its first tentative responses in the orange light. Under these conditions the orange light continues to be a strong danger signal, and the low rate of responding in its presence may be due to this alone. By contrast, under the variable-time, noncontingent condition, the orange light is sometimes associated with shock and sometimes not; it is, therefore, a relatively poor danger signal. Thus we do not know whether the response contingency is really discriminated or whether it merely programs stronger S-S contingencies.

A cognitive or predictive cue theorist can argue that the results of a punishment experiment can be explained on the basis of two simple hypotheses. The first is that the rat very rapidly learns about danger signals as predictors of shock so that they produce rapid suppression of appetitive behavior. Estes' (1944) famous experiments illustrate the generalized suppression that is found. But then, as the animal continues to experience the situation, it gradually begins to discriminate safety signals, that is, predictors of nonshock, and its behavior recovers from suppression in the presence of these safety signals, whatever form they may take (as Azrin's experiment illustrates). Some safety signals are simply more readily discriminated than others, and recovery proceeds faster in their presence.

The response contingency problem

Although it is now well established that a response can be weakened by making electric shock contingent upon its occurrence, there is little agreement about why the weakening occurs, nor is there much agreement about why the weakening sometimes does not occur. We still do not know whether Thorndike was correct 60 years ago when he said that punishment weakens an S-R connection or whether he was correct 20 years later when he said that punishment does not weaken S-R connections but has only indirect effects on behavior. We still do not know whether Estes was correct in 1944 when he suggested that all the response-weakening effects of punishment could be attributed to conditioned emotional reactions or whether the truth lies with those (e.g., Solomon, 1964; Azrin & Holz, 1966) who contend that the fundamental reality of punishment is that it weakens responses on which it is made contingent.

There are two fundamental issues here. One is whether the suppressive effects of punishment are due to generalized motivational effects of the punishing stimulus (Estes) or to some associative mechanism that operates specifically on a particular behavior. The second issue is that even if response-specific effects of punishment can be found, how are they to be interpreted? Are they due to the weakening of S-R connections? As we saw in Chapter 9, the S-R connection is currently being replaced by a variety of alternative motivational and cognitive devices. Perhaps these new explanatory models can clarify what occurs in the punishment situation. Let us look first at the question of whether, in addition to its diffuse and generalized suppression effect, punishment has a specific effect upon the punished response.

Conditioned suppression. There is an experimental procedure that produces effective suppression of ongoing behavior without there being any contingency between the response and the aversive stimulus. When originally described by Estes and Skinner (1941), it was called the conditioned emotional response (CER) procedure, but more recently it is called the conditioned-suppression procedure. Estes and Skinner started with rats pressing a bar for food. The animals were then presented with a CS followed by shock. The first shocks produced marked suppression of bar pressing. But then after only a few pairings of the CS with shocks there was anticipatory suppression; that is, the response was suppressed by the buzzer alone prior to shock coming on. This suppression was found even though the bar-press response itself was never immediately punished (shock was postponed briefly if a bar press occurred immediately before it was scheduled). The suppressing effect of the CS was attributed to a conditioned emotional reaction. Estes and Skinner suggested, therefore, that in a punishment situation, in which shock is contingent on bar pressing, the suppression found could also be due to a conditioned emotional reaction. Recall that Estes (1944) found no more suppression with contingent shock than with noncontingent shock. Estes' comparison of contingent and noncontingent procedures provides an obvious means of testing the importance of the response contingency. His own results, to state them again, indicates that the response contingency itself is of little consequence in the amount of suppression that is produced. But the issue has been considered important enough to generate further investigation, as we shall see.

Discriminative punishment. It should be noted that besides the contingency relationship there is another difference between the conditioned-suppression experiment and the traditional punishment experiment. In the former there is usually a CS that signals when shock will occur (typically, it is scheduled for the end of the CS), whereas in the punishment situation there is usually no such cue (because, typically, all responses are punished as long as the punishment contingency is in effect). Hunt and Brady (1955) made the two procedures more comparable by introducing a discriminative cue into the punishment situation. They thus invented what has been called the discriminative-punishment procedure. With this procedure there is a CS during which responses are punished on some kind of schedule that, in the ideal case, distributes shocks throughout the CS to match those received by a comparable conditioned-suppression group. No shocks are given in the absence of the CS.

Hunt and Brady (1955) established bar pressing in two groups of rats and then tested them under these two sets of conditions. During successive 3-minute intervals the CS was either presented or not in a random order as shown in Fig. 11-5. It is apparent from the bottom part of the figure that after a single CS-shock pairing, the CS produced nearly total suppression. It is also apparent from the top part of the figure that there was considerable suppression in

Punishment and frustration

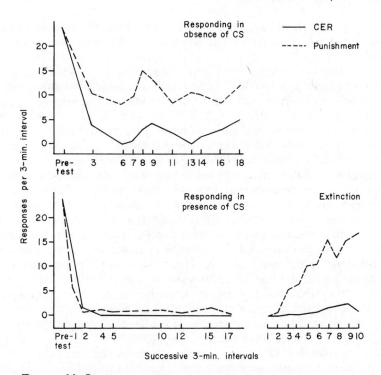

Figure 11–5

*Rate of bar pressing prior to introduction of shock, during
3-minute intervals of aversive stimulation, during interspersed
3-minute intervals, and in extinction for animals either
shocked for bar pressing (punishment) or shocked independently of bar pressing (CER) in the aversive stimulation
intervals. (From Hunt & Brady, 1955) Copyright (1955) by
the American Psychological Association. Reprinted by
permission.*

the absence of the CS, particularly under the noncontingent condition. Thus we might conclude that a great deal of fear was conditioned to generalized apparatus cues under the conditioned suppression condition and somewhat less fear was conditioned to such cues
under the punishment condition. In both cases a great deal of fear
was conditioned to the CS. There is the additional important conclusion that in all cases suppression can be attributed to the amount of
fear conditioned to the various cues in the situation and that none of
it has been attributed to a direct weakening effect of contingent
shock. Certainly, there is no evidence in these data for a response
contingency effect. This study, therefore, supports the Estes-Skinner
argument that all suppressive effects, whether due to contingent or

Theory of motivation

noncontingent shock, are attributable to conditioned emotional reactions (or, if we prefer, the predictive value of different stimuli in the situation).

These results contrast with those found by Azrin (1956), which were discussed earlier. Azrin had found more total suppression with punishment than with noncontingent shock. The principal point of difference is that Hunt and Brady's animals, like Estes', were tested in only one session, whereas Azrin gave his animals extensive training. Thus while Azrin has shown that shock as a response consequence *can* be an important behavior determinant, it seems that such an effect may play a small role in the great bulk of suppression that is found in other experiments, particularly those in which less extensive training is given. The point is that it is one thing to show that a rat's behavior or a pigeon's behavior is subject to a particular kind of experimental control, and it is quite another thing to conclude that this control is an immediate or effective or important determinant of its behavior. If the Estes and the Hunt and Brady findings describe the situation for the first 10 or 20 sessions, and if Azrin's results only emerge after that point, then we should conclude that contingent punishment is not an efficient mechanism for weakening behavior, at least not when compared with the generalized suppressive effect of noncontingent aversive stimulation.

A great deal of research has been done in the past decade with the conditioned-suppression procedure, but relatively little of it provides a direct comparison with comparable punishment procedures.[11] For further investigation of the importance of the response contingency, we are indebted primarily to the work of Church and his students. Our discussion of punishment will close with a brief account of their findings.

Church's experiments. Church (1969) describes an unpublished experiment in which three groups of rats were trained to press a bar for food on a VI-1 schedule. One group was an unshocked control, and one group was shocked noncontingently on a VI-2 schedule. For the third group, shocks were set up or primed on a VI-2 schedule and then delivered upon the occurrence of the next response. Instead of an explicit CS signaling the periods of shock, an entire 30-minute session constituted the test period; shock was signaled, therefore, by the whole experimental situation rather than by a discrete CS. Suppression was judged relative to the rate of responding in the session prior to the introduction of shock by the ratio $A/(A + B)$, where

[11] We cannot examine this literature here, but there are excellent discussions by Church (1969) and Myer (1971). We can note the report by Schuster and Rachlin (1968) that animals given a choice between punishment and comparable noncontingent shock show no clear preference.

A represents the rate of responding during the punishment phase and B the rate of responding prior to punishment.[12] The results indicate greater suppression under the contingent condition.

Granting for the moment that this is so, we may ask if a contingency effect necessarily means that the specific contingency between the response and shock is the determining factor. An alternative mechanism is suggested by the fact that with the punishment procedure there is greater contiguity, that is, closeness in time, of response and shock. To test this possibility Camp et al. (1967) gave rats contingent shock but delayed its presentation for 30 seconds after the response occurred. They maintained the contingency, therefore, but removed the contiguity between response and shock. Camp et al. found that suppression was identical to that of noncontingently shocked animals. We may suppose that even though the contingency was there, the animals did not discriminate it, since their behavior was like that of animals shocked noncontingently. Thus these results show the importance of contiguity.[13] And they suggest that if the contingency dimension is a real one, it is not the real contingency that matters as much as whether the contingency is discriminated by the animal.[14]

Consider a further set of experiments reported by Church

[12] Church (1969) has shown that on statistical grounds this is the optimum index for measuring suppression. It results in a ratio (the so-called suppression ratio) of 0.5 when there is no suppression and values approaching 0 as suppression becomes more severe. As useful as the suppression ratio is for summarizing the results of a suppression experiment, it is a poor substitute for describing both the A and B quantities. Suppression ratios may be relatively high, approaching 0.5, even when the animals' behavior is severely suppressed by situational cues. Suppression ratios can suggest that a punishment procedure produces more suppression than a noncontingent procedure simply because with the latter there may be very little behavior either during the CS or between the CSs. Millenson and deVilliers (1972) give further reasons for describing the levels of behavior rather than just a summary suppression ratio.

[13] The importance of contiguity is also shown by other studies that have systematically delayed punishment. Such studies typically find a gradient; sometimes it is relatively flat (Kamin, 1959), and sometimes it is relatively steep. The shape of the gradient undoubtedly depends upon what the animal does during the delay interval. In the case of Camp et al.'s animals a substantial amount of bar pressing occurred during the interval so that it could be said that the relationship between the response and shock really was noncontingent.

[14] Church (1969) has suggested that the failure to find response contingency effects may sometimes be due to the fact that the learning of this contingency is blocked or "overshadowed" by the learning of other contingencies, for example, between environmental cues or the CS and shock. In other words, if the rat initially attributes shock to the Skinner box, a considerable amount of training may be required if the attribution to its own behavior is to be learned.

et al. (1970). In one experiment a direct comparison between discriminative punishment and noncontingent procedures yielded higher suppression ratios (and hence less suppression) for the noncontingent procedure. In a second experiment animals were trained for two responses, bar pressing and chain pulling. After these responses had been established and then were totally suppressed, either by punishment or by conditioned suppression, all shocks were discontinued, and the course of recovery was determined while the animals were free to make either the response that had been made during the shock treatment or the other response. The animals under the punishment condition showed somewhat more rapid recovery on the nonpunished than on the punished response. But this apparent difference was not supported by statistical analysis; nor is it clear to what extent the more rapid recovery might be due to the change in the stimulus situation provided by offering the animal a different manipulandum or to the fact that more fear was undoubtedly conditioned to the specific manipulandum. Thus the results of this experiment are inconclusive. Also inconclusive are the results of a third experiment on the recovery of animals trained concurrently on both responses and then punished for one or the other. The trouble here was that there was little recovery under any condition. Thus while this set of experiments suggests that the response contingency may be an important factor in suppression, the evidence is far from convincing.

Further doubt about the importance of the response contingency is expressed by Church et al. (1970a) in another discriminative-punishment study. They asked whether a shock cue suppresses behavior because it signifies an increase in shock frequency (that is, it is a predictor of shock) or because it signifies that the response contingency is in effect (that is, it signals that the animal's behavior will become a predictor of shock). To answer this question Church et al. tested groups of animals under conditions in which the cue did not indicate an increase in shock frequency. This was accomplished by making shock contingent on responding in the presence of a cue and presenting shock noncontingently in the absence of the cue. The situation was arranged so that the cue signified no increase in shock but only that shock would be contingent on the response. The experimental question is whether the rat will suppress when a cue signals the response contingency, even when the cue signifies nothing about the frequency of shock.

Several groups run under these conditions showed greater suppression to the cue. It might be assumed, therefore, that Church and his co-workers had finally isolated the critical factor and shown that the response contingency has an immediate and direct suppressing effect. But further analysis of their data led them to just the opposite conclusion. First they discovered that under these conditions most bar presses occurred shortly after a shock had been delivered. Therefore, we have the peculiar situation that the immediate effect of shock was to increase responding.[15] Next, Church et al. observed that as the average time for priming the next shock approached, the rate of responding was extremely low—so low that an appreciable amount of time elapsed for the punishment animals between the time when shock was primed and when the next response occurred, and was punished. One complication, then, is that the contingent animals received shock less often than the noncontingent animals. Now while this result might lead us to think that with fewer shocks there would be less suppression, we should recall that the shock was eliciting the behavior; so with fewer shocks fewer responses were elicited. A mathematical calculation of the rates of responding and temporal distributions of shocks showed that this difference in the rate of shock was able to account precisely for the difference in rate of responding.

What this complicated analysis means is this. While it is apparently true that imposing a response-shock contingency on the animal led to greater response suppression, this effect was not attributable to response weakening per se but to the fact that in this situation shock elicited or acted as a discriminative stimulus for a particular pattern of responding. This state of affairs is like that discovered by Bolles and Riley (1973), that is, that it was possible to control freezing with a punishment contingency but that this contingency had no response-weakening effect (see page 363). The punishment contingency simply prevented much freezing from occurring; in Church's situation the punishment contingency prevented much bar pressing from occurring. In summary, none of Church's extensive work on the problem requires us to believe that punishment acts specifically to weaken the response that precedes it.

We are left with a rather strange picture of punishment in which all parties to the controversy seem to be correct. Thorndike and Estes were correct when they suggested that punishment has no direct response-weakening effect. They were correct again when they suggested that the effect of punishment is determined primarily by the kind of behaviors that are elicited either by the punishing stimulus itself or by cues to punishment. On the other hand, the operant conditioners (and parents and others) who would use the punishment procedure to weaken behavior are justified in trying it, because it does often suppress behavior. Extrapolating beyond our present data, I would guess that Estes (1969) is correct in asserting that the

---

[15] It is not clear whether Church's rats were subject to something like the gambler's fallacy (once shocked, they responded as though they were not likely to be shocked again), whether shock simply increased the activity level so that more bar presses were generated, or whether because they responded at such a low rate and had little chance of collecting reinforcement prior to shock, the postshock burst was a kind of contrast effect. Whatever the cause, the rate of responding was high immediately after shock and then declined.

reason punishment suppresses is that the punished animal is not as hungry in the presence of cues to shock. I would guess further that once this is firmly established and once we know how readily different danger signals and safety signals are discriminated, there would be little more that we would need to know about punishment.

Frustration

It has been known for some time that an animal may respond more vigorously when reinforcement is suddenly withdrawn than it does when reinforcement is given (e.g., Miller & Stevenson, 1936; Marzocco, 1951). Marzocco found that when the force exerted on the bar had stabilized at about 30 g, it increased sharply to nearly 50 g when reinforcement was withheld. This effect, the momentary increase in the vigor of an instrumental response as a consequence of withholding (or delaying) reinforcement, is called the frustration effect. Although the frustration effect is frequently interpreted as evidence for an increase in drive, this interpretation is not always compelling. A frustration effect can be a simple artifact. Thus if the rate of bar pressing is measured instead of the vigor of the response, it too is likely to rise momentarily at the beginning of extinction. But this increase may be due to the fact that in the absence of reinforcement, bar pressing is no longer interrupted by eating.

It is also possible that the effects of thwarting are genuine but due to associative rather than motivational factors (we will refer to the procedure as thwarting and to the hypothetical or observed consequences of thwarting as frustration). Thus we may think of thwarting as eliciting particular responses or particular modes of responding. The early book by Dollard et al. (1939), *Frustration and aggression*, set forth the hypothesis that frustration is a necessary and sufficient condition for aggression. The argument was basically associative; frustration is an emotional state of the organism, but aggressive behavior is not so much motivated by frustration as elicited by it. Here, then, one effect of thwarting was hypothesized to be a specific innate reaction. Grooming is another reaction presumably given by frustrated animals (see page 104). There are also, no doubt, learned reactions and modes of responding that occur when reinforcement is not obtained. Consider again Marzocco's animals in the Skinner box. There were surely many times in acquisition when they pressed with less than 30 g force, failed to get reinforcement, then pressed with more force and got it. Thus we can be sure that the animals were differentially reinforced specifically for "trying harder" and we may suppose that this occurred in extinction because the conditions controlling such behavior (that is, nonreinforcement) were present. Another associative aspect of frustration is that when rats are thwarted, their behavior typically becomes more variable and comes to include components such as biting the bar. These effects can also be most cogently viewed as specific associative reactions to the failure of reinforcement.[16]

Thus the history of the problem shows that prior to systematic experimental investigation, the frustration effect was variously attributed to the associative effects of thwarting (Dollard et al., 1939; Lawson & Marx, 1958), to the motivational effects of thwarting (Rohrer, 1949), or to some combination of the two (Brown & Farber, 1951). In what follows we will see that frustration has been viewed as a drive phenomenon, as an incentive phenomenon, as a reinforcement phenomenon, and as a cognitive phenomenon. The history of the subject is instructive because it nicely parallels the history of motivation theory in general. It tells the story of animal motivation theory in miniature.

Frustration as an acquired drive. Experimental work on frustration has been largely dominated by Amsel and his co-workers. Amsel and Roussel (1952) devised the prototype double-alley apparatus that has been the model for much subsequent work. Rats ran in the first alley to the first goal box and ate, and then they moved on through the second alley to the second goal box and ate again. After the running response had been acquired, food was withheld from the first goal box on half of the trials. On the other half of the trials food was given in both the first and the second goal boxes as in acquisition. Thus each animal served as its own control to indicate the effect of presenting versus withholding reinforcement in the first goal box. Both the speed of entering the second runway and the speed of running in the second alley were significantly faster on those trials in which food was withheld, as Fig. 11-6 shows. Amsel argued that this effect provided a clearer demonstration of frustration than the usual frustration effect because it was manifest in a response other than the one that was thwarted. Running in the two alleys is similar, of course, but the temporal order of events suggests that the increment in running in the second alley is due to increased motivation. Tacker and Way (1968) used an interesting variation of the double-alley apparatus; their second alley led not to more food but to an open field where activity level could be measured. Activity increased on the first few nonfood trials.

A quite different interpretation has been proposed by Staddon (1970) in a critical examination of the frustration effect. Staddon observes that in many experimental situations there is a characteristic

---

[16] In recent years even the assumed intrinsic linkage between frustration and aggression has been questioned (e.g., Feshbach, 1964; Buss, 1966). Perhaps this too is learned. Certainly, instrumental aggression pays off, not only in the animal colony but among civilized people. For programmatic applications to human motivational problems and a good historical treatment of frustration see Lawson (1965).

Theory of motivation

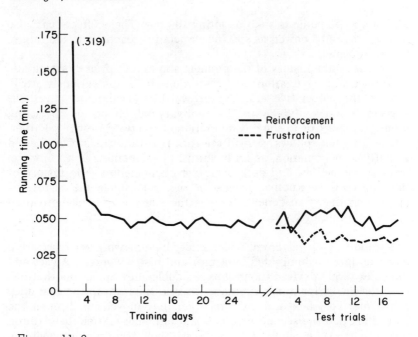

Figure 11–6

Running time on the second part of a runway in acquisition and on subsequent test trials when reinforcement is either presented or withheld at the end of the first part of the runway. (From Amsel & Roussel, 1952) Copyright (1952) by the American Psychological Association. Reprinted by permission.

pause in performance following reinforcement. The pause may occur because the animal is swallowing its food, washing its face, looking for more food, or simply getting back to the stimulus conditions that control the instrumental response and that were disrupted by the presentation of food. But whatever its cause, there is frequently a post-reinforcement pause.[17] Staddon suggests that the omission of reinforcement in the first goal box of the double-alley runway produces faster running in the second alley simply by eliminating this pause.

Staddon discusses a number of parallels between bar-press effects and alley-running effects. Many of the same phenomena that have been studied by Amsel and his followers are also well known to the students of reinforcement schedules. For example, both the fixed-

[17] Incidentally, a recent study of Griffiths and Thompson (1973) suggests that what is commonly called the postreinforcement pause might more properly be considered to be a prework pause. It depends upon the upcoming response requirement on a ratio schedule rather than the just-completed run of responses.

interval scallop and the fixed-ratio pause may be, at least in part, illustrations of animals' tendency to pause in their work following the ingestion of food. To test his reinforcement inhibition hypothesis against the more familiar frustration effect hypothesis, Staddon trained pigeons to key peck for food under a reinforcement schedule that produced an inverted scallop, that is, a high rate of responding following reinforcement and then a tailing off in response rate. (The inverted scallop was produced by reinforcing the animals on a VI schedule during the first 60 seconds of which pecking was reinforced; but after this point food was obtained by not pecking for a 10-second interval.) When the inverted-scallop behavior was established, some scheduled reinforcements were omitted and replaced by a time-out. Staddon found that the effect of omission was reduced responding. That is, he found an inverted frustration effect.

These results suggest that the postreinforcement pause is not a necessary part of key-pecking behavior and that it can be replaced by other modes of responding. But more to the point of frustration theory, they suggest that the failure of reinforcement produces more of whatever behavior reinforcement was correlated with. In the typical key-peck experiment the pigeon pauses immediately after reinforcement, and omitting reinforcement leads to increased responding. McMillan (1971) has shown that on a VI schedule that produces uniform rates of responding throughout the interreinforcement interval there is no frustration effect. Kello (1972) has reported that when events, such as a time-out, are substituted for food, the size of the frustration effect depends upon how different the event is from the stimulus conditions accompanying food. Whether Staddon's mechanism can explain the variety of frustration effects that have been reported is not yet clear. But it is clear that we have no reason to postulate a new source of drive to facilitate performance in the frustration situation if associative mechanisms of the sort that Staddon has proposed can account for it.

Frustration as a negative incentive. Almost from the beginning of his work on frustration, Amsel has interpreted frustration as an incentive phenomenon rather than, or as well as, a drive phenomenon. The reason was in part that the frustration effect appeared to be under stimulus control, that is, to depend upon environmental cues (Amsel & Hancock, 1957), and in part because during the 1950s many phenomena originally conceived in terms of drive became translated into incentive terms (e.g., the Kendler et al., 1954, interpretation of latent learning). To some extent this translation is simply semantic. The question hinges upon whether drive is regarded as a feature of motivated behavior or as an antecedent of motivated behavior. To put it another way, the issue is whether incentive motivation is regarded as something contributing to drive (Brown, 1961) or as something relatively independent of drive (Spence, 1956). In any case it is clear that frustration appears only after experience in the situation, that frustration effects can be elicited by presenting stimuli that have been paired with thwarting, and that under these conditions the effect can move forward in a chain of responses so that the animal appears to anticipate frustration. Such considerations led Amsel (1958, 1962) to propose that frustration is more incentive-like like than drivelike.

Amsel assumes that the withdrawal of reinforcement produces some innate and immediate frustration reaction, R_F, the exact nature of which is never specified. This reaction is said to be an emotional source of generalized drive, just as the fear reaction, R_E, is assumed to be an emotional source of drive. A peculiarity of the hypothetical R_F is that its occurrence is assumed to depend upon the prior occurrence of r_G. If there is no incentive motivation there can be no frustration; if there is strong evocation of r_G, there will be a strong R_F when food is withheld. These propositions can be tested by determining whether the frustration effect varies in magnitude in the appropriate manner as the incentive-producing conditions of reinforcement are varied. For example, a greater amount of reinforcement in the first goal box should produce more frustration than a small amount when it is withdrawn. Such enhanced frustration effects are usually found (e.g., Peckham & Amsel, 1967; Barrett et al., 1965; Krippner et al., 1967; Daly, 1968) but not always (Seward et al., 1957). Seward et al. suggest that a possible explanation of the frustration effect, where it is found, and particularly when large amounts of reinforcement are used, is that food eaten in the first goal box may reduce the animal's hunger motivation. They showed that prefeeding animals does produce slower running (see also Kemble & Clayton, 1967).

A further complication arises when the attempt is made to control for this effect by running a group of animals that is never fed in the first goal box until the intermittent-reinforcement phase of the experiment is reached. When such controls are used, animals typically show the frustration effect immediately upon experiencing the intermittent reinforcement (Wagner, 1959; Ison et al., 1967; McCain & McVean, 1967). How can the animal be frustrated if it has not been previously reinforced? Amsel's interpretation requires that r_G be well established before R_F can occur. To add to the puzzle consider again the Amsel and Roussel data shown in Fig. 11-6. Note that the frustration effect appears to develop after several trials. It is not clear why frustration should increase during testing, especially since r_G should begin to extinguish on no-food trials. Note too that the difference between conditions also appears to be due nearly as much to slower running after reinforcement as to faster running after nonreinforcement. It is apparent that whether or not frustration plays a part in producing these effects, there must be a number of other mechanisms governing the speed of running.

If the withdrawal of reinforcement produces frustration, it might be anticipated that any experimental treatment that worsens the conditions of reinforcement would also produce frustration. For example, reinforcement in the first goal box might be delayed on some trials. But the frustration effect has not been found under these conditions (e.g., McHose, 1966; Sgro et al., 1969, 1970). McHose (1968) obtained a delay effect but only by using a complex design in which both delay and amount of reinforcement were varied.

A frustration effect might also be expected if the reinforcement provided in the first goal is reduced in amount rather than omitted entirely. McHose and Ludvigson (1965) trained rats to run to 10 pellets and then gave them only 2 pellets on some trials. They report no enhanced running in the second alley on these trials. On the other hand, Daly (1968) found a slight enhancement of second-alley running speed in a similar kind of design. One of the differences in Daly's study was that her animals were subjected to a larger shift in incentive, that is, from 15 pellets to 1 pellet. There is the further problem in these studies (see also Karabenick, 1969) in that the performance of the shifted animals was the same, rather than better as frustration theory requires, as that of controls maintained all along on the small amount of reinforcement.

Another complication arises at this point. When the amount of reinforcement in the first goal box is suddenly reduced, we not only have conditions for producing frustration, we also have conditions for producing a contrast effect, specifically, a depression effect (see Chapter 12). If there is no effect of reducing the amount of reinforcement, it may be because of offsetting tendencies to run faster because of frustration and to run slower because of depression. McHose and his students have reported a series of studies attempting to separate these effects, for example, by using within- and between-subject designs (e.g., Barrett et al., 1965; McHewitt et al., 1969; McHose & Gavelek, 1969). Their results, which are complicated, appear to demonstrate a variety of contrast effects and not much of a frustration effect.

In spite of all the various discrepancies between theoretical predictions and the empirical results of frustration studies, the theory has received widespread attention. Part of its success is no doubt due to its extension to other kinds of phenomena. These applications are based on some further assumptions (Amsel, 1958, 1962). One assumption in Amsel's theory is that while R_F itself occurs only when reinforcement is withdrawn, there is a classically conditionable fraction of the response (r_F), and this incentive motivator is assumed to have behavioral effects that are parallel to those of r_G. Thus the rat is assumed to withdraw from and to make other competing responses to those stimuli to which r_F has been conditioned, just as it is assumed to approach or make other instrumental responses to stimuli to which r_G has been conditioned. The resulting depression of behavior accounts for extinction and a variety of discrimination learning effects. Food cues get r_G classically conditioned to them and hence motivate and provide associative control for approach behavior. Similarly, cues for the withdrawal of food get r_F conditioned to them and hence motivate and control withdrawal behavior.

One of the major achievements of Amsel's theory is that it provides a hypothetical explanation of the partial-reinforcement extinction effect (i.e., the prominent and well-known effect that behavior is more resistant to extinction after partial reinforcement than after continuous reinforcement). The partial-reinforcement effect is explained by another assumption that completes the parallel between r_F and r_G. There are hypothesized to be stimulus consequences of r_F that can enter into the associative control of behavior. The situation is again analogous to the case of r_G in which the internal consequences of, or feedback from, the incentive motivator are assumed to play a part in the control of instrumental behavior. If an instrumental response is not reinforced, so that r_F becomes conditioned to the cues that control it, and if the response is reinforced on the subsequent trial, the inherent aversiveness of r_F can be overcome. Ultimately, the feedback from r_F can be a source of associative strength for the response. In other words, the animal learns to respond after it has been frustrated because such persistence is ultimately reinforced. Although the partial-reinforcement effect had previously been described in these colloquial terms, there has been no formal S-R machinery to explain it.

Amsel's interpretation of the partial-reinforcement effect has generated a large amount of research, and much of it is consistent with his analysis (Amsel, 1967). But the theory is beset by two terrible difficulties. One is that Amsel requires the partial-reinforcement effect to appear only after a substantial amount of training. There must be enough training to condition R_G so that R_F can occur, then for r_F to be conditioned, then for there to be a phase in which r_F is aversive, and then for a final phase in which the stimulus consequences of r_F gain positive control over behavior. Amsel's own determinations suggest that about 60 trials are necessary for the rat to get through these various stages.[18] But McCain (1966) has discovered that the partial-reinforcement effect can be obtained with a very small number of acquisition trials. We will turn shortly to those data; here we merely note that they indicate that Amsel's analysis appears to be unnecessarily complex.

---

[18] The development of these stages can be monitored in various ways, for instance, by correlating performance on the discrimination task with the existence of the frustration effect (e.g., Hug, 1970).

The second serious problem for Amsel's theory is that it is based upon conceptual machinery that at one time was the accepted machinery for explaining incentive motivation. But today that type of machinery, involving r_G, r_F, and r_E, appears unnecessarily complicated. In addition there now seems to be little chance of directly verifying the existence of classically conditioned emotional mediators (Rescorla & Solomon, 1967). The postulation of an r_F mechanism as an analog of the r_G mechanism seemed reasonable as long as there was good hope of confirming, verifying, and making use of the latter. But as our hope fades for justifying the assumption of r_G, the postulation of an analogous r_F seems rather pointless.

Frustration as negative reinforcement. Reinforcement theorists in the operant tradition have shown relatively little interest in frustration effects or in developing an appropriate theory to deal with these effects. For one thing, the partial-reinforcement effect is typically taken as a basic fact of behavior, not derivable from other more basic principles. It does not need to be explained—it simply is. However, there has been some interest in the question of whether or not frustration is aversive. In Amsel's account there must be aversiveness at some stage to provide a basis for discrimination learning. But, curiously, in spite of the widespread belief that frustration must be aversive and the central importance of this belief in many accounts of behavior, there has been surprisingly little experimental evidence to support it.

Wagner (1963) asked whether animals would learn a new response to terminate stimuli in one situation that had been paired with nonreinforcement in another situation. His results revealed no learning of the new response, only that it was maintained at its initial operant level better in the experimental animals than in controls that did not have the "reinforcing" stimulus previously paired with nonreinforcement. Subsequently, Brown and Wagner (1964) showed that a punishing stimulus and a frustrating stimulus could be intersubstituted without disrupting behavior in either case, and they argued that since punishment is aversive, the frustrating stimulus must also be aversive. This evidence is also rather weak. In reviewing a number of such studies, including his own, Wagner (1969) admitted that although there was a fair amount of circumstantial evidence for the aversiveness of frustration, the evidence was not as compelling as it should be.

The issue was further clouded by Leitenberg's (1965a) question of whether an animal prefers not to be frustrated. When such a preference is suggested, the animal may simply be showing a preference for positive reinforcement. Other things being equal, an animal prefers to have food available rather than having it withdrawn, and this preference does not necessarily mean that the withdrawal of food is aversive or that cues associated with it are aversive.

This curious situation was remedied by Daly (1969), who reported a study much like Wagner's (1963), in which rats were trained to run for 15 pellets and then shifted to either 1 or 0 pellets. A distinctive box was used or a light cue was presented on those trials when reward was reduced or omitted. The animals were then trained on a new response, a hurdle jump, to turn off the light, or to get out of the box. Clear escape learning was found with both kinds of conditions. Daly (1969a) then duplicated these findings using a noncontingent procedure in which animals were simply placed in the goal box and not fed. Again, a new response to get out of the box was learned. Thus we finally see that both the withdrawal of food and cues predicting the withdrawal of food are aversive in the strict sense that their termination is reinforcing. How far the multitude of phenomena that have been attributed to frustration can be accounted for purely by its negative reinforcing properties remains to be determined.

A cognitive interpretation. We have seen in earlier chapters that there is a resurgence of interest in cognitive models, as against S-R reinforcement models in general and incentive motivation models in particular. The transition has not yet occurred in the area of frustration, but there are indications that it is about to occur. Two things are needed first: There must be data that clearly show the inadequacy of existing models, and there must be a demonstration of the power of alternative formulations—formulations with a more cognitive flavor. The first step was accomplished largely by McCain's discovery that the partial-reinforcement effect could be obtained after a single reinforced trial (McCain, 1966; McCain & Brown, 1967; McCain, 1968). In the basic experimental paradigm animals are given two acquisition trials. On the first trial the experimental group receives no reinforcement while the control group does. On the second trial all animals are reinforced, and then extinction is begun. Extinction proceeds rapidly, of course, because of the small number of reinforcements. But in spite of the fact that the control animals have twice as many reinforced trials in acquisition, they extinguish more rapidly than the experimental group, which was frustrated on one trial. There appears to be no way in which Amsel's theory, assuming as it does a multistage development, can handle McCain's results. Nor can it handle similar findings recently reported by Capaldi and Waters (1970) and Capaldi et al. (1970), again using a very small number of acquisition trials.[19]

[19] Amsel et al. (1968) suggest that when a substantial amount of food is used, as it frequently is in McCain's studies, the animal may make a number of approach responses to it, thereby multiplying the effective number of times r_G can become conditioned. Traupman (1971) found that rats do learn more quickly to run to a multipellet reward than an equivalent single large one, but the extinction data after five acquisition trials do not support Amsel's conjecture.

The second step, that is, the formulation of an alternative interpretation of the partial-reinforcement effect, has been taken by Capaldi (1967, 1970). Capaldi's hypothesis is, in effect, that animals remember what happened on the preceding trial. If the preceeding trial was not rewarded, then that information is available in some form at the time of the next trial. If the subsequent trial is rewarded, then the memory of the earlier nonreinforcement can become a predictor of food. Then in extinction, when all trials are unreinforced, the predictive value of nonreinforcement on the earlier trial will persist long enough to produce the partial-reinforcement effect. According to Capaldi's analysis, the various factors that had been a part of traditional incentive theory—such as intertrial interval, the goal gradient, where a reward is given, the number of trials—in fact virtually all the parameters that had been implicated in Amsel's analysis of frustration, become irrelevant. The only important consideration is the number of times in training that nonreward is followed by reward. Considerable recent research both from Capaldi's own lab as well as from other labs (reviewed by Capaldi, 1970) support his account.

Capaldi's interpretation, so far, is not explicitly cognitive, but it does emphasize those elements that characterize cognitive theories, namely, the retention and retrieval of information. Perhaps, most importantly, Capaldi emphasizes that the "frustrated" animal is learning about stimulus events rather than strengthening the connection of a response to a stimulus.

It would be easy to take the next step, to assert simply that the animal runs in the partial-reinforcement situation because, and to the extent that, prior nonreinforcement becomes a predictor of food. The question then is whether it is reasonable to believe that the rat can learn such an expectancy after experiencing the relevant stimulus contingencies only once.

Summary

Shock appears to have many of the same functions in the punishment situation that it was seen to have in the avoidance situation. It elicits certain behaviors; it can serve a discriminative function; it can facilitate some behaviors and interrupt others. But perhaps the most important function of shock is that it establishes situational stimuli as predictors of danger and predictors of safety. Danger cues appear to inhibit the motivation for appetitive behavior and, at the same time, to release defensive behaviors, such as withdrawal and freezing. There is no more indication that punishment by shock weakens S-R connections than there is that the avoidance of shock, or escape from an S+, strengthens them.

The history of research on frustration, like that on punishment and avoidance, shows the inadequacy of earlier explanatory models. A great multitude of behavioral effects have been attributed to frustration as a drive state, as a kind of negative incentive, and as an aversive condition. Whether it will prove more profitable to attribute some or all of these effects to cognitive factors remains to be seen.

12
THE
CONDITIONS
OF
REINFORCEMENT

Increase in response strength does not necessarily
mean increase in strength of S-R connections; it
may mean simply that when a situation is
repeated the response is more likely to occur.
As we shall see, there are other ways than learning
by which the probability of a response may
be increased.
J. P. Seward

One of experimental psychology's major achievements is the demonstration of how important the programmed consequences of a response are in determining its strength. If the consequences are made more favorable, for example, if more food, more probable food, or better food is given, then the response increases in strength. If the consequences are made less favorable, for example, if food is withdrawn, then the response gets weaker. The present chapter will consider these kinds of effects and some possible interpretations of them.

It is customary and proper to refer to those consequences that strengthen behavior as reinforcers. But it can no longer be taken for granted that improved conditions of reinforcement produce more learning. Hull could make that assumption in 1943 (we saw in Chapter 9 that Hull made the amount of food received one of the parameters of habit strength). Subsequently, Hull, and most other theorists, took the position that the amount of reinforcement made contingent upon a response did not actually produce more reinforcement, it only produced more incentive motivation. The phrase "amount of reinforcement," therefore, became a description of the experimental treatment, for example, describing the amount of food given in the goal box, rather than a hypothetical statement about the underlying learning process, such as hypothesizing how strongly the response has been motivated. The distinction is difficult to clarify, partly because the historical tradition of thinking of a reinforcer as a strengthener of S-R connections interferes with the contemporary custom of thinking of a reinforcer as a procedural event. The distinction is also difficult to maintain because the conditions of reinforcement not only produce incentive motivation, they may also produce learning. Few psychologists are ready to attribute all changes in behavior to changed patterns of incentive motivation, that is, to dismiss entirely the S-R connection-strengthening function of reinforcement. But times are changing. The preceding two chapters dealing with the aversive case suggest that there is very little actual response strengthening going on in most avoidance learning situations and very little actual response weakening going on in most punishment situations. The next chapter, on secondary reinforcement, will show that not much reinforcement in the literal sense occurs in secondary reinforcement experiments either. One of our tasks in the present chapter will be to try to separate the instrumental learning effects from the incentive motivation effects to determine to what extent reinforcing events do literally reinforce. Another task will be more empirical; we will try to see how instrumental behavior is correlated with varied conditions of reinforcement. In addition, we will discuss some of the incentive motivation mechanisms that have been proposed to explain how behavior depends upon the conditions of reinforcement.

Amount of reinforcement

The classic experiment that established the basic concept of incentive motivation was Crespi's (1942). Crespi trained different groups of rats in a runway with very different amounts of reinforcement and found that the groups reached very different levels of performance. The speed of running was positively correlated with the amount of reinforcement (AOR). This is the basic AOR effect. The discussion of Crespi's experiment in Chapter 9 (see page 292) emphasized that the effect was motivational, or was so interpreted, because when Crespi equated the AOR parameter for all groups after 20 trials, the performance levels quickly converged. Thus the original differences defining the AOR effect were not permanent but reflected the contemporary AOR conditions. We also noted in Chapter 9 how these results were formalized by Spence (1951) and Hull (1952) into a theoretical structure in which the AOR was hypothesized to control the strength of r_G and, hence, incentive motivation, K.

The main features of Crespi's study have been replicated by Zeaman (1949), Metzger et al. (1957) and a number of other investigators cited by Spence (1956). The AOR effect is found in alley-running speed even when trials on which there is competing behavior are discounted (Pereboom & Crawford, 1958; Kintsch, 1962; Marx & Brownstein, 1963). Thus the AOR effect is found both in the probability of running and in the vigor of running.

Incentive effects in different situations. AOR effects, of one kind or another, have been reported in almost all imaginable kinds of situations. Bar-pressing rate increases with AOR on a variety of schedules (Hodos & Kalman, 1963; Meltzer & Brahlek, 1968; Powell, 1969). Powell has apparently localized the AOR effect on the postreinforcement pause. Pressing decreases with AOR on a DRL schedule (Beer & Trumble, 1965). DiLollo et al. (1965) report that the force of bar pressing varies inversely with AOR, which is a little surprising. Improved maze performance is sometimes obtained (e.g., Cross et al., 1964) but not usually (e.g., Furchtgott & Rubin, 1953; Maher & Wickens, 1954; McKelvey, 1956).

The AOR parameter has been frequently reported to have no effect in discrimination learning problems. Rats frequently do not learn a black-white discrimination any faster with a large AOR than with a small AOR (e.g., Reynolds, 1949; Hopkins, 1955; Schrier, 1956). Most of these researchers have reported that rats run faster for a large incentive but that they do not learn the discrimination any sooner. On the other hand, incentive effects have usually been demonstrated with primates in discrimination problems (several studies are cited by Schrier, 1958). Superficially, this looks like a species difference, but a better solution of the dilemma was proposed by both Lawson (1957) and Schrier (1958). It seems that in primate studies experimenters are economical of animals and tend to use the same ones over again under different conditions, thereby permitting each subject eventually to find out about large and small AORs. In rat studies, however, different subjects are usually used under the different conditions, each under a fixed AOR. This difference in methodology can be characterized as absolute versus differential training, but it is more frequently described as variation between- versus within-subjects. It has proved to be an important variable, not only in these studies but in the investigation of AOR effects generally. Using the two procedures produces clearly different AOR effects both for rats (Lawson, 1957) and monkeys (Schrier, 1958). It seems safe to conclude that the training method is an important variable here and that animals trained under differing AOR conditions show much clearer incentive effects in selective learning situations than animals trained under a constant AOR.[1]

[1] It has been suggested that the absolute or between-subjects method works when the absolute AORs are low, near the threshold of reinforcement (Schrier, 1956; Pubols, 1961). This may only mean that some animals in the small AOR group do not learn. If their mean performance is down just for this reason, then this is not very informative.

Most topics in incentive motivation initially seem relatively simple but end up looking far more complex, and the AOR effect in discrimination learning is no exception. While between-subjects designs sometimes produce no AOR effect there are also reports of substantial AOR effects using the between-subjects method in both brightness and spatial discrimination situations (Reynolds, 1950; Lawson et al., 1959; Clayton & Koplin, 1964; Waller, 1968; Weisinger et al., 1973). In some cases the effects are so clear that the failure of other experimenters to find them has been attributed to various inadvertent methodological flaws. For example, Waller (1968) points out that positive instances of AOR effects have only been obtained when the ratio of high to low AOR was 4 to 1 or more. Such a restriction would make sense in a within-subjects experiment, but why it should apply in a between-subjects experiment is not clear. Weisinger et al. (1973) report that not only does the between-subjects design produce an AOR effect in discrimination learning, but the effect is not increased by giving animals experience with differential AORs, that is, by approximating a within-subjects design. If this is confusing, consider the case of extinction.

AOR effects in extinction. Another approach to the question of whether AOR affects just incentive motivation or has permanent effects on the strength of behavior is to look at performance in extinction after a response has been acquired under different AOR conditions. Recall that the motivational effect of deprivation has been consistently revealed in extinction data (see Chapter 7); the same approach might be expected to clarify the functional properties of AOR.

Lawrence and Miller (1947), Reynolds (1950), Fehrer (1956a) and Metzger et al. (1957) reported that although the rat tends to take into extinction the level of performance attained in acquisition, the AOR experienced in acquisition had inconsistent effects upon the ultimate resistance to extinction. In part, the trouble was that no one was sure of how to analyze the data. For example, Metzger et al. (1957) found substantial performance differences in extinction but found that when acquisition differences were removed by an analysis of covariance, the extinction differences disappeared.[2]

Then the picture began to change dramatically. Two large-scale, well-controlled studies by Hulse (1958) and by Wagner (1961) showed a clear *inverse* relationship between AOR in acquisition and resistance to extinction, as Fig. 12-1 shows. The more reinforcement

[2] The issue here is whether the differences found in extinction can be attributed to motivational differences or whether they are also dependent upon learning. The trouble is that the incentive motivation factor is assumed to be learned. Hence the differences removed by covariance may include the differences we are looking for (Evans & Anastasio, 1968).

animals receive, the sooner they stop running in extinction. This inverse relationship argues against the view that the AOR parameter makes a contribution to habit strength, but it also argues against any simple motivational interpretation. If a greater AOR simply increases incentive motivation, then behavior should be more persistent in extinction rather than less. Amsel (1962) has suggested that larger AORs produce a bigger r_G and, therefore, there will be a greater r_F when reinforcement is suddenly withdrawn. Accordingly, the inverse relationship should not appear in animals trained under partial reinforcement because, according to Amsel, r_F is not aversive or disruptive following partial reinforcement. Both Hulse's (1958) and Wagner's (1961) results indicate that this is the case.

On the other hand, Capaldi and Sparling (1971) tested Amsel's interpretation by conducting the extinction test under amobarbital (a drug that appears to minimize frustration effects in rats). They found the inverse relationship to be just as strong in drugged rats as in normal controls. Further evidence against Amsel's proposal is that while the inverse relationship has been found under a considerable range of experimental conditions, it seems to be most evident when rats are severely deprived (Zaretsky, 1965; Marx, 1967) and when they are given extended training (Hill & Spear, 1962; Ison, 1962; Theios & Brelsford, 1964). The frustration interpretation

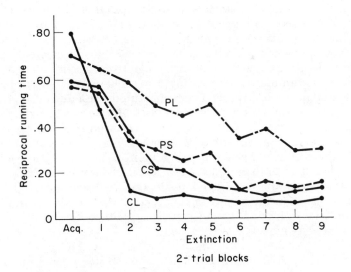

Figure 12-1

Running speed in extinction after partial (P) or continuous (C) reinforcement with a large (L) or small (S) AOR. (From Hulse, 1958) Copyright (1958) by the American Psychological Association. Reprinted by permission.

requires that the inverse relationship be more pronounced with large AORs. But a large-scale study by Hill and Wallace (1967) revealed no such interaction between AOR and resistance to extinction. However, they also found a direct relationship between AOR and resistance to extinction, and in further contrast with other experimenters they found no interaction between the amount of training and the direction of the AOR effect. Since all of these studies used a running response, it is not clear how the different patterns of results should be explained. Perhaps the Hill and Wallace data are different because they gave their animals many pseudotrials in which they were placed in the apparatus but not permitted to run; that is, they may have introduced some sort of partial-reinforcement parameter.

The only other proposal, besides Amsel's, to account for the inverse relationship between AOR and extinction performance is Capaldi's (1967) suggestion that the zero AOR received in extinction is more discriminably different from a large AOR than it is from a small AOR. This appears to be a relatively innocent proposal; it asserts only that performance declines during extinction because of a generalization decrement, that is, a change from the conditions prevailing in acquisition. No one could take offense at invoking such a well-established associative mechanism. On the other hand, Capaldi's argument puts a new light on the incentive motivation issue. It suggests that the AOR-extinction effect may be associative and does not require the r_G-r_F mechanisms that Spence and his students have become so dependent upon. More specifically, it does not require a separate motivational mechanism, a mechanism other than that which makes the animal run in the first place. Furthermore, Capaldi's analysis lends itself to a much more cognitive interpretation. We can think of the animal's experiencing a particular AOR, discriminating it from other AORs, and later remembering it. In effect, the generalization decrement argument permits the AOR effect to be explained by quite different mechanisms from those involved in the conventional r_G interpretation of incentive motivation. We are beginning to discover that the Hull-Spence interpretation of incentive motivation is irrevocably tied to their general S-R reinforcement model of behavior and that even the traditional distinction between motivation and learning is an intrinsic part of that model. We are also beginning to see that incentive motivation can be accounted for by other kinds of explanatory models.

Contrast effects. Recall that when Crespi shifted AOR from 256 to 16 pellets, his animals performed more poorly than controls receiving 16 pellets all along. This undershooting of the control's performance is called *negative contrast*. It has been found by virtually everyone who has looked for it. But apparently the effect can be abolished by treating rats with amobarbital at the time of testing (Rosen et al., 1967; Ison & Northman, 1968) or by imposing a long time interval between preshift and postshift trials (Gleitman & Steinman, 1964). The first effect is consistent with Crespi's original idea that contrast is due to some kind of emotional reaction; the Gleitman and Steinman effect is consistent with the idea that rats usually remember AOR conditions, but given a long enough retention interval they forget. In addition, Mikulka et al. (1967) report that negative contrast is not found following partial reinforcement with the original AOR. This finding, together with the results with tranquilized rats (amobarbital acts like a tranquilizer), suggests that negative contrast may be a frustration effect, but it is not clear why the inhibitory or aversive aspect of frustration should predominate over the hypothetical drive-inducing aspect to produce slower running rather than faster running when food is withheld.

The negative contrast effect can also be readily interpreted as a generalization decrement phenomenon. A change in the conditions of reinforcement produces decrements in performance (Capaldi, 1972). Capaldi does not deny the importance of frustration, but he argues that rather than being a motivation factor, frustration introduces new stimuli into the situation at the time the animal is tested. The negative contrast effect can be reduced by giving rats prior experience with reductions in AOR so that the stimuli arising from this treatment are not new at the time of testing. The negative contrast effect is also reduced by using a long intertrial interval so that the immediate or unconditioned or emotional component of frustration can dissipate, leaving behind only the long-term, or conditioned component of frustration to be present at the time of testing (Capaldi, 1972).

The story on positive contrast is quite different. Crespi found that rats shifted from 1 to 16 pellets overshot the performance of controls receiving 16 pellets all along. Thus Crespi found a *positive contrast* effect, and Spear and Spitzner (1968) also found it, but most investigators have not. Weinstock (1971) finds it when he lets his animals explore the apparatus first. Dunham (1968), after a careful review of the contrast literature, concluded that positive contrast does not exist.[3]

But it has been argued (e.g., Pereboom, 1957) that the failure to observe positive contrast might be due to a ceiling effect; the controls, running for the large AOR, may be going at the maximum possible speed, so that the animals shifted up to the large AOR could not run any faster. The argument is not entirely compelling because it is not supported by any evidence of leveling off at a maximum speed as AOR increases. Nonetheless, the ceiling hypothesis suggests

---

[3] When positive contrast is claimed, Dunham points out, it may be due to the fact that all animals may continue to show increased performance with continued training. Hence it is necessary to have a control group that shows this increase and compare the experimental group with them.

that if some device could be found to slow the animals, a positive contrast might be obtained. Shanab et al. (1969), Shanab and Biller (1972), and Mellgren et al. (1972) report that when reinforcement is delayed to produce an overall deficit in running, rats do show a positive contrast effect.

Bower (1961) introduced a new procedure for studying contrast effects. With Crespi's design, animals receive a series of trials with one AOR and another series with another AOR; the contrast results from a shift across successive events, so that the procedure has come to be called *successive contrast.* With Bower's procedure there are discriminative cues in the runway, for example, a particular rat might receive 8 pellets when the alley is white and only 1 pellet when it is black. The contrast develops over a series of trials as the cues are discriminated. This procedure is called (with some license) *simultaneous contrast.* Again, negative contrast is nearly always found and positive contrast only rarely (e.g., Ludvigson & Gay, 1967). Spear has devised a further elaboration of this procedure, which presents the animal with a choice between the white and black runways. With this procedure both positive and negative contrast effects can be found, but once again negative contrast is more common (Hill & Spear, 1963; Spear & Hill, 1965; Spear & Spitzner, 1966, Spear & Pavlik, 1966).[4]

The pattern is a relatively simple one so far. The bulk of the research shows that positive contrast effects are not found unless some special arrangements, such as delaying reinforcement for all animals, are made to produce it. On the other hand, negative contrast effects are found unless some special arrangements, such as drugging all animals, are made to prevent it. But the situation is really much more complicated than this, and certainly the explanation of even this oversimplified summary cannot be simple. One complication is that while contrast effects tend to be transient, lasting only a few trials with the successive contrast procedure, much of Spear's data indicates that they are much more persistent with the simultaneous contrast procedure, which Fig. 12-2 illustrates.

A second complication is that additional second-order effects are found when rats are subjected to repeated shifts in AOR condition. Consider an experiment by Spear and Spitzner (1966) in which there were three stages. In stage 1 experimental animals received a large AOR and controls a small AOR. In stage 2 all animals received a small AOR (and those shifted down showed a good negative contrast effect). In stage 3 all animals received a large AOR. The question is whether in stage 3 the experimental animals encountering the

---

[4] As we will see shortly, animals very quickly learn the discrimination; hence very little data can be obtained unless forced trials are used. Typically, the animal is given a free-choice trial and is forced the opposite way on the next trial, and the data of interest are speeds of running on large and small AOR trials.

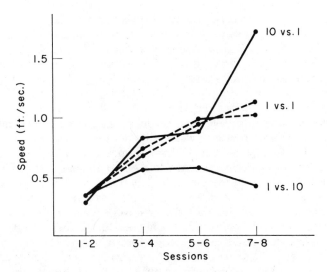

Figure 12–2

Speed of running to a large and a small AOR in an AOR discrimination task. (Adapted from Spear & Hill, 1965) Copyright (1965) by the American Psychological Association. Reprinted by permission.

large AOR for the second time behave differently from the controls encountering it for the first time. The answer is that they do, at least under some conditions. The experimental animals behave as though they remember and recognize the large AOR, even though ample opportunity was given in stage 2 for the original r_G to be replaced by a new one. Spear (1967) has reviewed a number of contrast studies, many done in his own laboratory, which argue for a memory interpretation of AOR effects.

Discrimination of AOR. Learning under different AORs is not the same thing as learning to discriminate different AORs. Festinger (1943), Denny and King (1955), Pereboom (1957), Reynolds and Anderson (1961), Davenport (1963), and Clayton (1964) have all demonstrated that rats in a simple two-choice situation rapidly learn to go to the side that offers the greater AOR. Denny and King, Pereboom, and Davenport also did reversal training with the large- and small-AOR sides reversed. Their rats were able to learn both the original discrimination and the reversal; but it is of some interest that reversal required 10 trials or so, in contrast with the 1 or 2 trials necessary to obtain shifted performance in a noncompetitive runway, and that performance on successive reversals became worse instead of better (Davenport, 1963). The discrimination of AOR is a particularly interesting procedure because it appears to produce faster learning than most other kinds of discrimination training. Even learning to go to one side of a T-maze is a more difficult problem because rats tend to have strong initial side preferences. Why such preferences do not interfere with differential AOR learning is not clear, but the procedure clearly warrants further use and study.

The interaction of drive and incentive. Hull (1952) had proposed that drive, D, and incentive motivation, K, multiply to determine the organism's total motivation. Primarily on the basis of a study by Ramond (1954), Spence (1956) has proposed that the proper combination law is additive; D and K should add together and jointly multiply habit strength to determine behavior. At one time it seemed terribly important to test these alternative formulations, and a number of ingenious experimental designs were used in an attempt to perform the crucial experiment.[5] The results of these studies have supported Spence's additive law, Hull's multiplicative law, and various combinations of the two. The conclusion in all cases, however, rests upon some a priori assumption about how $_sE_R$ is linearly related to response speed and response probability. But as we noted in Chapter 8, quite different conclusions can be obtained if one makes other assumptions. The point is that any quantitative analysis of performance curves presupposes a quantitative scaling of performance.

Reynolds and Anderson (1961) avoided this problem by running animals in an AOR discrimination in a T-maze. Two groups were run, one under high drive and one under low drive. It can be shown algebraically that if D and K multiply, then the high-drive group should learn the discrimination faster than the low-drive group. According to Spence's additive hypothesis, there should be no difference between groups, provided the competing habits can be assumed to be equal. Since an equal number of reinforcements was given on both sides (by using forced trials), discrimination would have to be based solely upon the differential K factors involved and hence be independent of drive. Identical acquisition was found for the two groups, thereby nicely supporting Spence's additive hypothesis.

There is the problem, however, that incentive motivation seems to require some minimum amount of prior deprivation; Seward and Procter (1960) and Seward et al. (1960) found that if there is no deprivation, then no amount of food will maintain behavior. Thus the additive formula appears to fail in the area near zero drive. Black (1965) has proposed a solution to this problem. He suggests that K be reconceptualized so that it becomes a function of deprivation time (or weight loss). Then, as the deprivation condition disappears, both

---

[5] This literature is described by Hall (1966). Typically, there are four groups, high and low drive combined factorially with high and low incentive. An analysis of variance is then carried out, and a significant interaction is taken as evidence that D and K interact.

D and K would approach zero; and the additive relationship could be retained. Black's proposal is good as far as it goes. But it should be emphasized that in his proposal D and K have come to stand for procedural manipulations (deprivation and AOR) and not the explanatory mechanisms defined by the hypothetical properties Hull gave them. Thus the proper conclusion is not that D and K add but that deprivation and AOR have additive effects upon behavior, provided that there is some minimal amount of deprivation.[6]

The relationship between deprivation and incentive is evidently a little more complicated than this, however. Recall that when deprivation conditions are shifted, performance does not reveal a contrast effect, but rather a carry-over effect (see page 241). That is, the performance of the shifted animals changes over several trials to the level of controls without overshooting the new asymptote. But Gragg and Black (1967) have discovered that if AOR conditions are shifted at the same time—either up or down, it does not seem to matter which—the shift in deprivation conditions produces a contrast effect rather than the customary carry-over effect. This puzzling phenomenon has also been reported by Capaldi (1971); it suggests that altered AOR conditions sensitize the rat to the alterations of other parameter conditions, including deprivation conditions.

Further complications. One implication of the r_G model of incentive motivation is that both incentive effects and frustration effects should be more evident in the strength of behavior near the goal box where r_G is more strongly elicited than near the start box. Goodrich (1959) was apparently the first to test this implication in a study that did not involve the AOR parameter, but the method was soon used by many of Spence's other students who were concerned with AOR. The method involves a series of photocells and electric clocks so that independent measures can be obtained for (1) the speed with which the rat leaves the start box and traverses the first few inches of the runway, (2) running speed in the middle of the runway, and (3) the speed in the last part of the runway. Wagner (1961) used this method to study the interactive effects of percentage of reinforcement, amount of training, and AOR. A portion of Wagner's data is shown in Fig. 12-3.

Experimental psychology had entered the technological era; here were data that could not have been collected by an ordinary graduate student with an ordinary stopwatch. We had also entered

[6] This conclusion needs a further qualification, because an animal satiated for one food may be eager to eat another food, especially if it is highly palatable. The trouble is that both deprivation and AOR are arbitrary dimensions, defined for the convenience of the experimenter. We need a concept, such as value, which is closer to the animal. Then we could determine how deprivation, amount, and palatability of a food jointly determine value.

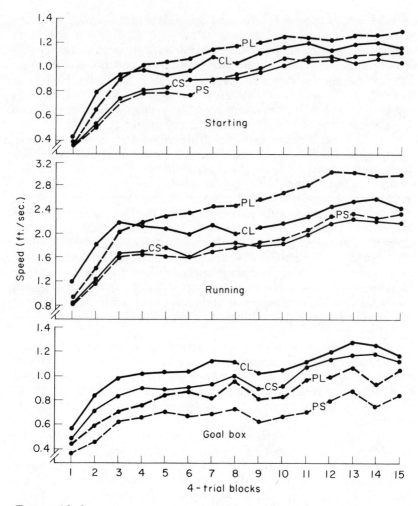

Figure 12–3

*Speed of running in different parts of an alley during partial (P) or
continuous (C) reinforcement with a large (L) or small (S) AOR.
(From Wagner, 1961) Copyright (1961) by the American Psychological
Association. Reprinted by permission.*

the era of sophisticated experimental designs; here are meaningful
third-order interactions to watch for. Note that animals receiving
a large AOR ran faster than those receiving a small AOR, and that
while this difference is not most evident near the goal box (as predicted), it is least evident in the start area. Note that animals on 50
percent reinforcement ran faster than the 100 percent animals in the
start area, but more slowly near the goal (as predicted), and that it

took several trials for this interaction to develop (as predicted). Note too that this cross-over effect was more evident in animals receiving a large AOR than in those receiving a small AOR and that this effect also took several trials to develop (this is the third-order interaction, which suggests, as predicted, that with more r_G there will be more r_F, which ultimately provides more stimulus support for the partially reinforced response). Wagner's data provide a great deal of support for Amsel's frustration interpretation of various partial reinforcement effects and AOR effects. But, at the same time, they introduce a degree of complexity into the analysis of the problem that must raise some doubt about the point of the entire enterprise.

Almost since the time when Crespi reported the first AOR experiment, it has been assumed (partly because of Crespi's data) that the AOR variable affected performance rather than learning per se. Although Spence (1956, p. 139) raised a question about this assumption, neither he nor anyone else appears to have seriously doubted that different AORs affect performance through motivational effects upon instrumental behavior rather than through an associative effect upon the instrumental behavior. However, in none of the early studies was there any reason to suppose that asymptotic levels of performance had been reached. Crespi's animals were obviously showing increased running speed at the time AOR conditions were shifted (see page 290), and subsequent researchers have rarely given very many preshift trials. A series of experiments has now been reported by McCain et al. (1971) in which animals are maintained on different AORs for 100 trials or more. These studies show that the differences between different AOR groups all disappear with continued training!

The McCain experiments were conducted under a variety of conditions, so that we may assume that the results have some generality. Whether performance curves under different AOR conditions must always converge to the same asymptote remains to be seen. But in any case, there is clearly some range of experimental conditions under which different AORs produce different rates of learning rather than different asymptotes of performance. We suddenly see that the mass of research that has been done to discover something about motivational processes may have been trying to tell us something about learning processes. And we see also that we are much in need of a fresh new interpretation of incentive motivation.

Quality of reinforcement

Some of the earliest research on incentive motivation compared the effectiveness of different kinds of reinforcement. For example, Simmons (1924) reported that rats would not perform as well in a maze when they were rewarded with sunflower seeds as when they were rewarded with their usual food, which was bread and milk. Tolman (1932) summarized a number of studies done under his direction that vividly demonstrated the importance of incentive factors in animal performance. For example, Elliott (1928) demonstrated that when animals were shifted from a less-preferred to a more-preferred reinforcer, their maze performance improved; and when they were shifted to a less-preferred reinforcer, their performance worsened. The change in performance in both cases was immediate (and there were no contrast effects). When improved performance followed a shift from no reward to some reward, we had the latent-learning effect (Blodgett, 1929). Elliott (1929) demonstrated that a complete shift in the quality of reinforcement—from water to food—failed to disrupt behavior seriously if deprivation conditions were shifted from thirst to hunger at the same time. Perhaps the most interesting and dramatic of these studies was the one reported by Tinklepaugh (1928). He found that when monkeys were suddenly shifted from a highly preferred to a less-preferred food (from banana to lettuce), they became quite emotional, disturbed, and upset. Tolman (1932) concluded from such results that behavior is determined not by the reinforcing effect of reward but by the animal's anticipation of reward.

Interest in the effects of different kinds or qualities of reinforcement was revived by a methodological problem that arose in the AOR research. In the typical AOR experiment there are several interrelated factors that must necessarily be somewhat confounded, such as the amount of time in the goal box, the amount consumed, the rate of consumption, the amount of consummatory behavior, and the amount of stimulation resulting from this consummatory behavior. Wike and Barrientos (1957) reported that drinking from a small-bore water tube has more incentive value than drinking from a large-bore tube (rats learned to go to the one rather than the other in a T-maze). This finding argues for the importance of the amount of consummatory activity as against the amount consumed or the amount of drive reduction involved, since Wike and Barrientos had equated consumption under the two conditions. This conclusion has been supported by Hall and Kling (1960) and by Goodrich (1960) using sucrose. On the other hand, Kling (1956) reported incentive effects positively correlated with rate of consumption. Perhaps all these dimensions are relevant.

One way out of the dilemma is to train rats to press a bar for a sucrose solution and then test them with different concentrations of sucrose, so that the amount of consummatory behavior can be operationally distinguished from the amount of reinforcement. When Guttman (1953) first did this, he found that when the amount of drinking was held constant, the rate of bar pressing generally increased with concentration, although there was a reversal with the highest concentration of sucrose. Similar findings have been reported by Young and Shuford (1955) and Dufort and Kimble (1956). Different concentrations of sucrose, therefore, provide a new dimension of reinforcement, the quality of reinforcement (QOR), although they are often described as amounts of reinforcement.[7]

There are a number of close parallels, as well as some differences, between the effects of the QOR and the AOR parameters. With high concentrations of sucrose there is usually a drop-off in consummatory and instrumental behavior. This drop-off occurs even when the animal does not ingest enough sucrose to affect its caloric need nor enough to create an appreciable osmotic pressure. But in preference tests (Young & Greene, 1953) or when consumption is measured just in the first few minutes (Collier & Siskel, 1959) or on partial reinforcement schedules (Collier & Myers, 1961) performance is monotonically related to concentration.[8] Operating within these constraints performance increases consistently with improved QOR conditions. This is the basic QOR effect.

The QOR effect is found in runways (Collier & Marx, 1959; Goodrich, 1959; Brush et al., 1961; Kraeling, 1961), in the Skinner box (e.g., Collier et al., 1959), in a T-maze (Ison, 1964), and where the animal simply has to drink (Hulse et al., 1960). The QOR effect sometimes carries over into extinction (Collier & Marx, 1959; Marx et al., 1963). And when QOR and AOR are both varied, it usually turns out that quality is the more important variable (Goodrich, 1960; Kraeling, 1961; Schaeffer & Hanna, 1966). Rats quickly learn to discriminate different QORs (Black, 1965a).

When QOR conditions are shifted, in a Crespi type of experiment, appropriate shifts in performance are usually found (e.g., Guttman, 1953; Homzie & Ross, 1962; Rosen & Ison, 1965; Panksepp & Trowill, 1971), but not always (Spear, 1965; Rosen, 1966). So far, the effects of the QOR parameter look very much like those of

---

[7] The mistake probably stems from the idea that since the animals are hungry and need calories, they receive a bigger reward with a higher concentration. But many of the same incentive effects have been demonstrated in satiated animals. And probably all of the effects that have been obtained with sucrose can be demonstrated with saccharin (Collier, 1962). Guttman (1954) determined equal reinforcing values for sucrose and glucose and found that it is not concentration (and hence calories) that produces equivalent reinforcement values but judged sweetness. Guttman also determined the reinforcement threshold for concentration and found that it lies very close to the sensory detection threshold. Further evidence, both behavioral and physiological, has been summarized by Pfaffmann (1960). The conclusion seems inescapable that the reinforcing effect of sugars is the sensory stimulation they provide. To put it plainly, it is the sweetness that counts.

[8] Collier et al. (1961) call this drop-off a postingestion effect, even though it is not what is ordinarily conceived of as satiety. According to Collier and Myers (1961), performance with sucrose reinforcement depends upon three factors, sweetness, hunger, and this postingestion factor.

the AOR parameter. But there are some interesting differences. Reduction in QOR fails to produce a frustration effect in the double-runway apparatus (Prytula & Braud, 1969). (And so does complete removal of a sugar tablet, Dunlap & Frates, 1970.) And the shifts in performance when QOR conditions are shifted are not like those found by Crespi. They tend to develop quite slowly, sometimes appearing only after animals have been shifted for several sessions.

Collier and Marx (1959) reported another difference in post-shift performance between QOR and AOR. They found large contrast effects, both positive and negative. These contrast effects were peculiar, too, in that they developed slowly and were quite persistent. They did not appear to be attributable to momentary emotional reactions to the changed QOR conditions. Other research from Marx's laboratory shows similar big, slow, persistent contrast effects in different experimental contexts (Pieper & Marx, 1963; Marx et al., 1963). Dunham and Kilps (1969) contended that Marx's contrast effects result from confounded changes in drive; specifically, they argue that his animals gained weight when shifted to high sucrose concentrations, and they found no contrast when body weights were held constant. The point is a good one methodologically, but the conclusion is not decisive, since when weights are controlled it is still possible to get both positive contrast (Marx, 1969) and negative contrast (Vogel et al., 1968; Weinstein, 1970) or both (Panksepp & Trowill, 1971). But this time the effects are very brief, lasting only a minute or so. When contrast effects are not found, it is probably because the test is too brief (e.g., Ison & Glass, 1968) or too long (Dunham & Kilps, 1969); the demonstration appears to require an appropriate analysis across time.

Meanwhile, although it had begun to appear that contrast effects were not found when saccharin concentrations were shifted, Weinstein (1970) has shown that if saccharin concentrations are chosen to produce responding comparable to sucrose responding, contrast effects just like those found with sucrose are obtained. Weinstein also found that the time course of the effect was the same; there must be a suitable analysis of responding across time.

Delay of reinforcement

One of the most consistent phenomena in the literature of animal motivation is that if a delay is imposed between the execution of an instrumental response and its reinforcing consequence, there will be a decrement in the strength of the response. Early experimenters demonstrated this decremental effect in the Columbia obstruction box (Hamilton, 1929), in problem boxes (Roberts, 1930), in various kinds of bar-press apparatus (Perin, 1943; Logan, 1952), in a variety of mazes (Warden & Haas, 1927; Wolfe, 1934; Cooper, 1938), and in runways (Peterson, 1956; Holder et al., 1957). Decrements have been found mostly in hungry animals, but they have been found as well in animals that are thirsty (Fehrer, 1956a), escaping from shock (Fowler & Trapold, 1962), and working for electrical brain stimulation (Keesey, 1964; Culbertson, 1970).[9]

One of the earliest studies, which became a classic because it apparently refuted the law of effect, was that of Watson (1917). Watson did not run a control group with no delay, but the fact that his experimental animals showed any learning of the response to get to the goal box when there was a long delay before food was given, was interpreted as a fatal finding for Thorndike's law of reinforcement. According to Thorndike (according to Watson), the animals should have learned to do what they did during the delay interval, that is, sit and wait, rather than learn the response that got them into the goal box, that is, digging their way into it. Although Watson's experiment is not very impressive by today's standards, nonetheless, it focuses our attention on several important issues that are still of considerable concern. One issue is whether the animal's behavior during the delay interval is learned to some extent, perhaps enough to interfere with the instrumental response or enough to explain the decrements usually found with delay. A second issue is the empirical question of how the effectiveness of reinforcement declines with increasing delays. The most pointed question arising from Watson's study is why learning occurs at all with a delay. Granting that decrements are found and are to be expected, why does any learning occur? One obvious answer is that primary reinforcement still has some effectiveness even when it is delayed. That is, there may be some empirically determinable gradient of delay. But another obvious answer is that since food is ultimately presented in the goal box, the goal box should become a secondary reinforcer. Entering the goal box should provide, therefore, immediate secondary reinforcement for the instrumental behavior that gets the animal there. Let us pursue this argument in more detail.

The secondary-reinforcement hypothesis. Some of the early studies had indicated that a delay of reinforcement (DOR) produced more serious decrements in performance when the delay was imposed in a special delay chamber preceding the goal than when it was imposed in the goal box itself. Then Perkins (1947) showed that the decrement was particularly severe when the delay was imposed in a box physically distinctive from the goal box. Perkins had attempted to

---

[9] Renner (1964) gives a good account of the history of this early research; he also relates it to the work of Tolman and others on the principle of least effort. Rats are lazy and quickly learn the quickest way to get to food, that is, to minimize the delay of reinforcement. Renner also struggles with Hull's rather confusing treatment of the problem, which we will not examine here.

eliminate secondary reinforcement by making the delay box dissimilar enough from the goal box that it would have little secondary reinforcing power; but he was evidently not entirely successful because, it was argued, he still obtained some learning.

The study that was apparently most successful in eliminating the effects of secondary reinforcement was that by Grice (1948). He required animals to learn a black-white discrimination; different groups were delayed for different periods of time in a gray delay chamber prior to running into the goal box, which was also gray. Thus in Grice's situation the secondary reinforcing stimuli occurred immediately following both correct and incorrect responses; thus secondary reinforcement could provide no differential strengthening of responding to black and white. Grice's results are shown in Fig. 12-4.

In contrast with earlier experiments Grice had found that there was virtually no reinforcement, that is, no discrimination learning, when the delay was longer than just a few seconds. Spence (for whom Grice worked at the time) parlayed these results into a major theoretical point (Spence, 1947). He maintained that the gradient of delay was extremely short, so that for all practical purposes reinforcement had to be delivered almost immediately following a response if there was to be any learning. The corollary is that if any learning occurs when food is delayed more than a few seconds,

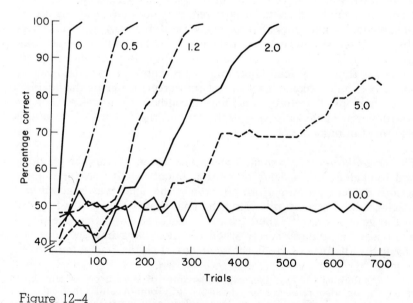

Figure 12–4

Acquisition of a black-white discrimination as a function of the delay, in seconds, of primary reinforcement. (From Grice, 1948) Copyright (1948) by the American Psychological Association. Reprinted by permission.

such learning must be attributed to secondary reinforcement. Since secondary reinforcers are generally encountered immediately after the response occurs, Spence (1947) was able to draw the elegant unifying conclusion that all learning must be attributed to immediate reinforcement, either primary or secondary. This supposition, soon supported by Jenkin's (1950) claim that secondary reinforcement also had a very short temporal gradient, appeared to settle the question. Prior studies of the DOR effect that had found long gradients and small decrements became mere exercises in manipulating secondary reinforcement; the concept of secondary reinforcement itself was considerably strengthened (see page 461); and the basic hypothetical mechanisms of habit formation became considerably simplified. But like most "settled" questions it became unstuck.

For one thing, Grice's data can no longer be taken at face value. Although he obviously found a sharp gradient for the DOR parameter, it is doubtful that the effect can be attributed specifically to the delay of reinforcement. Lawrence and Hommel (1961) trained rats in a situation like Grice's but with the important difference that running to the white cue led, after the delay, to a black goal box and running to the black cue led to a white goal box. Lawrence and Hommel found reasonably good discrimination learning under these conditions even with fairly long delays. Here the secondary reinforcing property of goal stimuli could not have facilitated the discrimination, and the associative property of the goal stimuli (the animal's tendency to approach them) could only interfere with the discrimination, but it was learned, nevertheless.

The key consideration in interpreting Grice's study is that the delay of reinforcement is just one of several factors that could have prevented learning from occurring. One factor noted by Lawrence and Hommel is that the correct and incorrect end boxes were not discriminable in Grice's situation. Making them discriminable makes learning possible even in the face of the competing tendencies introduced by Lawrence and Hommel's procedure. Evidently, the distinctiveness of the goal box is much more important than its similarity to the delay box. Another factor is that when Grice's animals failed to learn the discrimination, they showed strong position habits. This behavior was then reinforced on 50 percent of the trials, and this inadvertent schedule of reinforcing the wrong behavior may have precluded learning the right behavior. Put in cognitive terms, the animals did not have the expectancy of 100 percent payoff. A recent study by Michael Wilson at the University of Washington has shown that when rats are given a short series of forced trials to the correct cue, so that they learn to expect reward 100 percent of the time, they then have little trouble solving Grice's discrimination problem.

The other problem with Spence's secondary-reinforcement hypothesis of the DOR effect is that there are now a number of different lines of evidence supporting alternative hypotheses. Let us consider some of these.

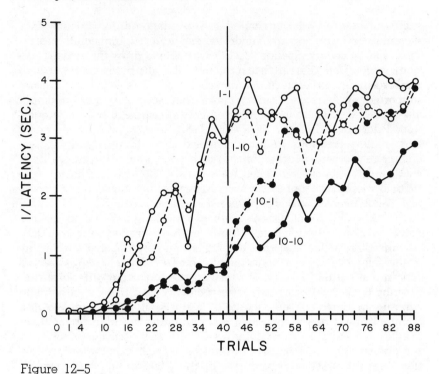

Figure 12–5

Response latency of rats with a 1-second or a 10-second DOR or switched after 40 trials. (From Harker, 1956) Copyright (1956) by the American Psychological Association. Reprinted by permission.

The incentive motivation hypothesis. Some theorists (e.g., Hull, 1952; Logan, 1960; Renner, 1964) have tried to incorporate DOR into incentive motivation. The more immediate reinforcement is, the more strongly r_G becomes conditioned to situational cues, and the more incentive motivation is produced.[10] The immediate question then is whether the DOR effect (i.e., the deficit in performance with delay) is due to a loss of motivation or to a partial failure of learning. The way to answer this question is by means of a Crespi type of study in which DOR is shifted. Harker (1956) conducted such a study; he used a bar-press response and delayed food presentation 1 second or 10 seconds for different groups. The results are shown in Fig. 12-5.

First note that Harker obtained unequal rates of acquisition under the different DOR conditions. It looks as though the 10-second

[10] Logan (1960) has contrasted the implications of this assumption with the implications of assuming that *different* r_Gs are conditioned. He describes several experiments suggesting that the latter assumption is the proper one for the AOR parameter.

animals would eventually catch up. Similar differences in the rates of acquisition (as opposed to differences in the asymptotes of performance that a motivational interpretation requires) have been reported by other experimenters (e.g., Sgro & Weinstock, 1963; Sgro et al., 1967; Wike & McWilliams, 1967). When Harker shifted his animals up in incentive (i.e., reduced the delay), they showed a corresponding improvement in performance, but the improvement occurred rather gradually. Indeed, the improvement occurred just as slowly as the original acquisition of animals with the short DOR. When animals were shifted down in incentive (i.e., increased delay), there was no apparent loss in performance. Thus Harker's data are different on several counts from Crespi's (see Fig. 9-2), and on each count Crespi's AOR effect looks like a motivational effect while Harker's DOR effect looks like impaired learning. It should be noted, however, that different effects have been reported, so that sometimes fairly rapid changes in performance are found when DOR conditions are changed (e.g., Logan, 1952; Wike et al., 1968), but sometimes not (Myers, 1958; Lawrence & Hommel, 1961). The critical conditions for obtaining shifts or not obtaining them are unclear.

Sgro and Weinstock (1963) reported a positive contrast effect when DOR conditions were improved, but the effect appears to result from some anomaly in the control group. More substantial-looking negative contrast effects have been reported by Beery (1968) and by Gavelek and McHose (1970). But there is, in general, little direct evidence that DOR effects are attributable to incentive motivation.[11]

The frustration hypothesis. There is some evidence that DOR can produce frustration effects, even though delays introduced in the double-alley apparatus fail to produce consistent effects (see Chapter 11). If animals are delayed part way through a chain of behavior, for instance in the middle of a runway, then only that portion of the run that precedes the delay is adversely affected (Gilhousen, 1938; Cooper, 1938; Holder et al., 1957). The behavior after the delay may show facilitory effects (Holder et al., 1957). But sometimes no postdelay effect is reported (Wist, 1962). It may be important that Wist's experiment was run in an extremely well-insulated runway so that external cues were minimal and, consequently, so was the opportunity for the elicitation of r_G. This facilitory effect upon postdelay behavior can be taken as evidence of frustration-produced drive,

---

[11] There are a number of studies apparently conducted to support a utilitarian kind of motivational model. A large AOR is good, but a large DOR is bad. These goods and bads can be balanced off against each other in various ways and in various situations (e.g., Logan, 1965; Renner, 1966; McDiarmid & Rilling, 1965), but what does this mean? To be tall is good and to have only one eye is bad. If we discover that a one-eyed six-footer is as attractive as a man 5 feet 8 inches with two eyes, what does this mean?

and the predelay decrement as evidence of aversive conditioned frustration, r_F. It also seems to make some difference whether delay is incurred early in the apparatus, near the start box, or near the other end, in the vicinity of the goal box (Brown & Gentry, 1948). (Logan, 1960, running one trial a day, failed to see this effect.) Also, when a number of trials are run in a session, the delay decrement materializes only on the later trials (e.g., Holder et al., 1957). Such effects suggest the operation of an r_G mechanism and possibly the closely related r_F mechanism.

Another phenomenon that is consistent with the frustration hypothesis is that while DOR may impair performance in acquisition, it can also increase resistance to extinction (Crum et al., 1951; Fehrer, 1956a; Pubols, 1958; Sgro & Weinstock, 1963; Marx et al., 1965). But under some conditions there is no greater persistence; when it is found, it may not necessarily be due to a frustration mechanism, because McCain and Bowen (1967) found it after a single acquisition trial. Further trouble for the frustration explanation of the extinction effect has been discovered by Tombaugh (1966). Tombaugh raised the question of whether superior resistance to extinction with DOR is due to differences established in acquisition, such as competing responses, or due to shifts in procedure between acquisition and extinction. Extinction necessarily implies delay of reinforcement (infinite delay), and hence going into extinction may be merely more familiar to animals that have previously experienced delay. Tombaugh introduced different delays (i.e., confinements in acquisition and extinction) and had several groups shifted in different ways, such as from long delay in acquisition to short delay in extinction. Three effects were found. First, everything else being equal, delays in acquisition retarded extinction. Second, everything else being equal, delays in extinction facilitated extinction. Third, and most interesting, a change in DOR conditions produced contrast effects, both positive and negative. The overshifts were large but occurred relatively slowly. These effects have been confirmed by Wike and McWilliams (1967) and Wike et al. (1968). All of these findings depend, however, on the assumption that confinement *after* reinforcement is functionally comparable to delay *before* reinforcement. Some evidence is available to justify this assumption (e.g., Fehrer, 1956a; McCain & Bowen, 1967; Mikulka et al., 1967). These results suggest, therefore, that there is a motivational, or at least an emotional, basis to the DOR effect after all.

The competing response hypothesis. Spence (1956) offered a basically associative explanation of Harker's findings based upon the incidental observation that animals under the 10-second delay condition seemed unable to wait at the food cup during the delay interval, whereas animals under shorter delays could. Thus the problem was evidently a more difficult one for the long-delay animals. We may think of the difficulty either in terms of uncontrolled variation in the response to be acquired, or we may think of it as requiring the learning of a chain of responses to bridge the gap between pressing the bar and obtaining reinforcement. Carlton (1954) attempted to test the hypothesis that the activity occurring in the goal box during the delay interval is a crucial variable in the effects of delayed reinforcement. He ran animals in a situation similar to Harker's, but one group was tested in a very narrow apparatus to restrict the animal's behavior, while another group was tested in a more open box where competing behavior could occur. The results (see Spence, 1956, p. 162) of restricting the animal's repertoire tended to confirm the competing-response prediction. Bradley and Wong (1969) have also shown that a larger goal box produces greater resistance to extinction, especially for partially reinforced animals. It is unfortunate, though, that no one has observed their animals during the delay interval to determine what these responses are, to demonstrate that they actually compete, and that the competition can explain the decrement.[12]

Learning with very long delays. It should be apparent that underlying all of the theory and research discussed so far there is the assumption that learning takes place when a reinforcing event occurs at the same time that a stimulus and a response occur. If reinforcement is delayed so that only some lingering neural consequence of the stimulus remains (the hypothetical stimulus trace), there must be less reinforcement. The less the fading trace resembles the original stimulus, the less learning there can be. This was Watson's argument in 1917, and it was Spence's argument in 1947. The fact that learning occurs meant to Watson that the law of reinforcement was invalid; it meant to Spence that a new source of reinforcement, secondary reinforcers, had to be postulated. Secondary reinforcement makes learning possible, and the delayed occurrence of primary reinforcement strengthens a variety of other competing behaviors so that the overall effect is a decrement in performance. This is the customary behavioristic account, but it is obviously applicable, at best, to a limited range of experimental situations.

It has been known for a long time that learning can occur in situations in which reinforcement is long delayed and in which there is no possible opportunity for the operation of secondary reinforcement. Munn (1950) summarizes a variety of different delayed-response situations in which a cue is presented momentarily and then withdrawn, and the animal is restrained for some period of time before it can respond. As Munn indicates, a lively debate arose because many theorists could not accept the possibility of learning

---

[12] Longstreth (1964) observed several behaviors in the goal box, but he did not find their occurrence correlated with instrumental performance.

under such conditions. Subsequently, Petrinovich and Bolles (1957) showed that rats could learn to alternate in a T-maze when an interval of several hours intervened between trials. Here the only cue on a given trial was an event that had occurred hours before on the previous trial. The only conclusion we could reach was that the animal "remembered where it went last time." Capaldi (1970) has described some studies showing that rats can learn a temporal alternation (food, no food, on alternate trials) when an interval of 24 hours intervened between trials. Again, the only cue on a given trial was an event that had occurred the day before. And, again, Capaldi reached the conclusion that the animal remembered what happened last time. It is curious that psychologists have been so reluctant to concede that rats can remember. This reluctance is an intrinsic part of the S-R reinforcement doctrine. And the evidence that animals can remember certain classes of events and respond accordingly is a serious challenge to that doctrine.

But there is a delay phenomenon that presents an even greater challenge. In the experiments just cited, only the stimulus had to be remembered. Reinforcement could, supposedly, connect the response to the memory of the stimulus by acting immediately upon the contiguous stimulus-memory and response. But what if the stimulus and the response occur at about the same time and the consequence only occurs much later? In this paradigm both the stimulus and the response must be remembered, and they must already be linked or associated in some way (so that they will be remembered together) at the time reinforcement finally occurs. Learning is inconceivable under these bizarre conditions; but Garcia has shown that such learning not only occurs but that it occurs in very few trials. The animal drinks a novel substance, such as saccharin (the taste is the stimulus and drinking is the response), and perhaps an hour later the animal, having been injected with poison in the interim, becomes ill. The next day it drinks much less saccharin than controls that did not become ill or other controls that did not drink saccharin the day before. The animal has learned to avoid saccharin in one trial and with the consequences of its behavior delayed one hour.[13]

Such rapid and efficient learning under these conditions shatters all of our preconceived ideas about the necessary conditions for learning. It seems absurd to suppose that the stimulus and response are simultaneously remembered and connected (actually, disconnected) by the aversive consequence acting on the memories of them. A much simpler and more plausible account is based upon a different kind of association: It is the cue (taste) and consequence

[13] Revusky and Garcia (1970) have reviewed a number of experiments on the Garcia effect. Learned food aversions are found under a great variety of conditions, one of the most important of which is that the food be novel.

(illness) that are associated rather than the cue and the response. Once the taste becomes a predictor of illness, explaining the change in response strength is no problem. It is controlled by the motivating or predictive properties of the cue. The animal does not refrain from drinking because that behavior has been punished but more simply because the substance has become a predictor of illness; it tastes bad.

Thus there are two reasons why the explanation of the Garcia effect forces us to abandon conventional associationism. One is that the learning that occurs in the food aversion experiment does not seem to be S-R learning; it is much more plausible to regard it as S-S* learning, where S is the taste of the food and S* is illness. The second reason is that the events, S and S*, which are "associated," do not occur together but are well separated in time so that it is much more plausible to regard the Garcia effect as a memory phenomenon. But there is a third consideration, which indicates that the learning in this situation is not associative learning but a memory phenomenon. The existence of learned aversions to food demonstrates that at the time the animal becomes ill it does remember what it ate.[14] The interesting issue, however, is not *whether* it remembers what it ate at this time but *why* it remembers this particular event. Why does it not remember something else, or why does it not associate its illness with where it is at the time it gets ill or with what it has just been doing? The rat's memory evidently has a structure that makes the retrieval of taste memories particularly probable when it is ill.[15] Earlier writers have proposed that there are specific predispositions to learn particular associations, but these predispositions have been treated as special relationships between responses and reinforcers (e.g., Thorndike's belongingness and Seligman's, 1970, preparedness) or between stimulus events (e.g., Revusky & Garcia's, 1970, stimulus relevance). Now it is clear we need a comparable concept to apply to the retrieval of specific memories. Such a concept is Tulving's (1972) episodic memory.

[14] Further evidence of such memories is the learning-to-eat effect (see page 258). This latter effect might be regarded as simple S-R reinforcement learning: Eating new food in a new situation is reinforced by the immediate sensory consequences of eating it. This interpretation is not entirely convincing, however, because it is not clear how such learning could be undone if the animal were to become ill later or were to gain no calories. Nevertheless, we ought to determine whether eating new food in a new place is immediately reinforcing before concluding that the learning-to-eat effect is a memory phenomenon.

[15] Alternatively, we might suppose that the association is not made at the time of illness but later when the animal again encounters the test food. Thus it may be that at the time of tasting the novel food the second time the animal remembers its illness. This possibility does not change the force of the argument, however, because in either case the animal must remember one event when it experiences the other.

Tulving observes that the materials used in human learning studies are often very familiar words, words that obviously are permanently stored in long-term memory. If a subject cannot remember "apple" in an experiment, it is not because it is lost from the general or semantic memory but only that it is not retrieved within the context of the experiment. The experimental situation provides a set of cues that together define an episode. The subject is not learning a mass of S-R associations but is segregating those semantic items that define the episode, so that the presentation of some episodic items will produce retrieval of the others, such as "apple." Within this framework we can say that the usual episode we arbitrarily define for the rat is so poorly organized (in relation to the structure of the rat's semantic memory) that learning is only found when the arbitrary events occur together in time. Grice's (1948) experiment is a good illustration. But if the episode is organized in accordance with the inherent structure of the animal's semantic memory, then DOR becomes almost irrelevant, as shown by Garcia's bright-noisy water experiment (Garcia & Koelling, 1966).

Percentage of reinforcement

An enormous experimental literature has grown up in the past several years concerning the behavioral effects of reinforcing behavior on some kind of partial-reinforcement schedule, as against reinforcing every response. Even the part of this literature that compares 50 percent and 100 percent payoffs in a runway has become quite extensive. Fortunately, there are two excellent reviews of the runway literature (Bitterman & Schoel, 1970; Robbins, 1971). Both reviews indicate that a variety of POR effects have been reported, but many of these have already been mentioned here in discussing other topics. Note, for example, that Hulse's data, shown in Fig. 12-1, reveal an interaction between AOR and POR in extinction performance and that Wagner's data, shown in Fig. 12-3, reveal interactions between AOR and POR and interactions between both of these parameters and the amount of training on the instrumental task. The general rule seems to be that the POR variable alters, sometimes dramatically, the effects of other conditions of reinforcement.

The main theoretical issue to which much of the current research is addressed is whether Capaldi's (1967, 1970) memory-of-aftereffects interpretation is better able to generate and explain the data than Amsel's (1962, 1967) frustration interpretation. Robbins (1971) concludes that Capaldi's interpretation has the advantage at several points while Bitterman and Schoel suggest, as I have here, that any motivational system based upon the r_G mechanism needs to be reconceptualized. But the data are diverse and complex, and it will take some time to resolve the issue.

The response contingency problem

Just as the basic question in punishment theory is whether the negative consequence weakens the specific response, so the basic question in incentive theory is whether the positive consequence strengthens the specific response. Just as the punishment procedure has motivational and other effects that can affect response strength indirectly, so the reinforcement procedure motivates the animal and produces indirect effects upon response strength. In both cases there are noncontingent procedures that produce effects so like those produced by contingent consequences that we must wonder whether the contingency relationship really contributes to the determination of behavior. That is, the results of noncontingent shock are so much like the results of punishment that the response-weakening effect of punishment can be called into question. Similarly, the results of incentive motivation experiments so closely resemble the results of a reinforcement experiment that the response-strengthening effects of reinforcement can be doubted. Perhaps all of the effects of both positive and negative consequences can be explained by means of the assumption that consequences merely establish predictive cues that, in turn, govern the animal's behavior. We will not be able to settle this issue here, but we will consider it and examine some of the experimental literature that raises the issue.

Transfer of control experiments. One type of incentive motivation experiment introduces a cue for food into one situation after the cue has been established in a different situation. In the first such study Walker (1942) trained rats to bar press for food, then trained them in an alley to run for food in the presence of a discriminative cue. When the S+ for food had gained discriminative control of running, the animals were returned to Skinner box for testing and the S+ was introduced as a probe during the extinction of bar pressing. It produced a sharp increment in responding. Walker concluded that when a cue has become a discriminative stimulus for one response, it can serve the same function for any other response.[16] This was the prototype for all subsequent transfer of control studies.

    The basic paradigm was used again by Estes (1943, 1948), the difference being that he used a Pavlovian procedure within the Skinner box itself; that is, between the initial bar-press training and

    [16] At least, Walker added, it can serve the same function for all responses that vary together with the same drive. We might substitute the proviso at least for all responses controlled by the same reinforcer (Estes, 1948). Estes (1949) and Hyde and Trapold (1967) have suggested that no such proviso is needed because they demonstrated transfer of control across deprivation conditions, that is, from hunger to thirst. But this suggestion can be discounted in view of the interaction between hunger and thirst (see page 166). Probably some such proviso is necessary.

the extinction test his animals were confined to the box and a cue was paired a number of times with free food. Estes also found a sharp rise in extinction performance when the cue was introduced as a probe. Then, curiously, this kind of experiment was forgotten for some years until it was revived by Morse and Skinner (1958). (Walker and Estes had both been students of Skinner's.) Pigeons were trained to key peck and were then given a number of differential conditioning sessions in which one key color signaled noncontingent food (i.e., free food) and another key color signaled no food. When the key peck response was extinguished, the food cue helped maintain responding.

Bower and Grusec (1964) introduced a further development of the procedure. They trained thirsty rats on an auditory discrimination after the discriminative cues had previously been associated in a Pavlovian session either with food or the absence of food. The results, shown in Fig. 12-6, indicate that the discrimination was learned much more rapidly by a group for which the S^D had previously predicted food (the consistent group) than by a group for which the S^D had previously predicted no food (the reversed group). These data indicate that there was little immediate transfer; the main advantage of the consistent group was that it was able to learn the discrimination faster. Note that the effect of the prior discrimination experience was manifest about equally in greater responding to the consistently positive cue and less responding to the consistently negative cue. That is, Bower and Grusec's animals appeared to have learned as much about, and to have been affected as much by, the negative cue and the positive cue. Subsequent experiments have sometimes shown the same kind of symmetry (Trapold & Winokur, 1967; Mellgren & Ost, 1969), but not always (Trapold et al., 1968, 1969).

These studies, taken together, show transfer of control in rats and pigeons, with hunger and thirst motivation, and in both acquisition (where faster learning is found in the appropriate consistent groups) and extinction (where faster extinction is found in reversed groups). Trapold has reported a series of studies that add further generality to the transfer-of-control phenomenon. One study employed a special Skinner box in which one bar moved up and down and the other moved back and forth. When responding on one bar was brought under discriminative control, this control was found to transfer immediately to the other bar (Trapold & Odom, 1965; Trapold & Fairlie, 1965). This transfer was evidently not just response generalization because there was little savings in the original learning of the second response before discrimination training was begun. In another study Trapold (1966) brought bar pressing under discriminative control and then reversed it. The comparison was between two groups, one that went immediately into reversal training and another group that received an interposed Pavlovian session in which

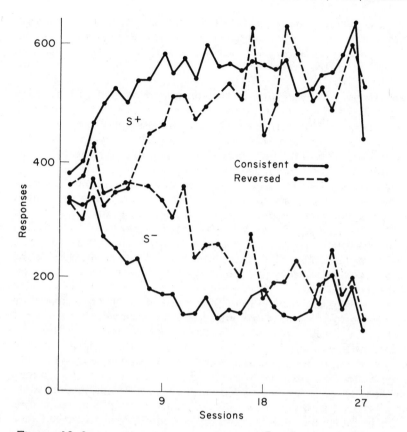

Figure 12–6

Mean responses per session to the positive and negative discriminative stimuli following noncontingent experience with consistent or reversed cues. (From Bower & Grusec, 1964) Copyright 1964 by the Society for the Experimental Analysis of Behavior, Inc.

the predictive value of the cues was reversed. This noncontingent experience was found to hasten reversal learning. One of the most intriguing studies reported by Trapold and his students demonstrated transfer of temporal control. Rats were trained to bar press on a FI-2 schedule after one group had received noncontingent food every 2 minutes and the control group had received noncontingent food on a random schedule that averaged 2 minutes. The noncontingent FI experience led to much faster development of the FI scallop (Trapold et al., 1965).

All of these studies demonstrate that the discriminative control of an instrumental response can be affected by previously established positive or negative food cues and that these cues can be established either noncontingently or in a prior instrumental situation. The results can be interpreted either in terms of a classical conditioning model of incentive motivation (for example, the r_G becomes conditioned to the positive cue) or in terms of a more cognitive predictive-cue model.

Direct-placement experiments. Two things are alleged to happen in the goal box: The response is supposed to be reinforced by food consumed there, and incentive motivation is supposed to be created. If the animal were simply placed directly in the goal box instead of being required to run into it, then there should be no reinforcement of any particular response, but incentive motivation should still be created. It ought to be possible to get a rat to run in an alley simply by giving it a series of direct placements in the goal box. Although there have been no reports of such an effect in the simple runway, Seward (1949) obtained a comparable effect in a T-maze. After exploring the maze, rats were directly placed in one end box and fed; on a subsequent test trial a significant proportion of the group went to the positive box. However, this effect is evidently difficult to obtain (Seward et al. 1952).

Seward and Levy (1949) described an alternative procedure that proved to be much more effective. They reasoned that just as it ought to be possible to establish incentive motivation by giving noncontingent food, so it should be possible to reduce incentive motivation by withdrawing food. Seward and Levy trained animals to run to food and then gave a number of direct placements in the empty goal box; these animals stopped running considerably sooner than controls receiving no nonreinforced placements. This technique, which is called the *latent-extinction* procedure, has been used in a number of studies. After reviewing many of these studies Moltz (1957) was able to conclude that all of the data were consistent with an r_G interpretation of incentive motivation.[17]

Subsequent research has not always provided such consistent support, however. For example, Hughes et al. (1960) and Koppman and Grice (1963) found that the magnitude of the latent-extinction effect bore no systematic relationship to the similarity of runway stimuli to those present in the goal box. The results of Dyal (1962) and Clifford (1964) suggest that the latent-extinction effect can be quite transient, that its strength depends upon where in the alley running speed is measured, and that these parameters have interactive effects with the number of direct placements that are

---

[17] Moltz observed that the theoretical conditions for establishing incentive motivation are essentially the same as those that establish a secondary reinforcer, namely, pairing some cue with primary reinforcement. In this connection Moltz and Maddi (1956) found that direct placement in the empty box not only produced an apparent loss of incentive motivation but a corresponding loss of the secondary reinforcing effectiveness of the goal box.

given. In short, Dyal and Clifford had discovered a number of effects that have been implicated in a frustration interpretation of nonreward. Further research has revealed a number of such effects, both with negative (extinction) placements and positive (with food) placements. Too many positive placements can impair performance and hasten extinction (Theios & Brelsford, 1964; North & Carl, 1968; Porter & Madison, 1971); a large AOR given in direct placement can reduce resistance to extinction (Davenport & Mueller, 1968); and a small number of negative placements can produce a partial-reinforcement effect in extinction (Trapold & Doren, 1966; Homzie & Rudy, 1971). It appears then that the direct-placement procedure not only introduces a number of incentive motivation effects but it can also bring about a number of frustration effects.

Further evidence for the equivalence of noncontingent procedures and the customary reinforcement procedure is that noncontingent cues can be established that signal different AORs, and these cues may then have the expected effects on the strength of behavior in a subsequent test (Campbell et al., 1969; Flaherty & Davenport, 1969). Although Hyde et al. (1969) failed to obtain such an effect in the speed of bar pressing (they did obtain a contingent AOR effect), Trapold and Bell (1964) obtained something like an AOR contrast effect in a direct-placement experiment.

A serious problem in interpreting the direct-placement literature is that while this procedure does not require the animal to make any particular response, the animal may respond anyway. In other words, the direct-placement procedure may not eliminate all instrumental behavior, even though it requires no specific behavior. Particularly troublesome is the possibility that the rat in the goal box may make small approach and going-forward responses that are learned (reinforced) and that then facilitate or generalize to running in the test situation. Trapold and Doren (1966) gave two groups of rats negative direct placements; one group was placed with its face in the food cup while the other was placed 8 inches from it. When the running response was subsequently extinguished, it was expected that the direct-placement animals would show a partial-reinforcement effect, that is, greater resistance to extinction than control animals without the placement experience. This effect was found, but only in the group that had run 8 inches. It could be argued that the partial-reinforcement effect depended upon running becoming conditioned to S_F, and the face-in-the-dish animals had no opportunity for this conditioning to occur. The argument is a little tenuous, but it is consistent with subsequent findings (e.g., Patten & Rudy, 1966, 1967; Porter et al., 1971). If it should turn out that the animal must engage in some minimal amount of approach behavior before frustration effects and incentive effects can be found with the direct-placement procedure, then, of course, there would be little point in using it. Such a conclusion would also be rather damaging to a cognitive interpretation of these effects, since it would indicate that the basic effect of reinforcement is, after all, to strengthen responses.

Other noncontingent experiments. One approach to the question of whether the animal's response is an important part of incentive motivation learning is to look for generalized energizing effects of predictive cues. Trapold (1962) posed the question of whether a cue for food would potentiate, or facilitate a wholly unrelated reaction, namely, the startle reflex. He found that it did not.[18] Suppose a food cue is suddenly introduced into a situation in which there are few other cues to food, and no particular behavior is likely to produce food. The answer in this case is clear: There is a sharp increase in general activity (Bindra & Palfai, 1967; Zamble, 1967). Bindra and Palfai watched their animals and found various kinds of exploratory behavior; Zamble uses automatic recording devices and calls the increased activity "conditioned excitement." He also reports interesting changes in excitement when moderately long cues are used (Zamble, 1968, 1969; see also Williams, 1970; Mikulka et al., 1972).

Suppose that, in contrast with these situations, a food cue is presented when the animal already has abundant cues to food and is already performing a well-learned instrumental response. Under these conditions the additional cue appears to have little effect either upon starting speed or running speed (Bolles et al., 1970).[19] However, when the cue (a buzzer that had been paired with food in the goal box) is presented in extinction, it increases performance and prolongs extinction (Marx & Murphy, 1961; Bolles et al., 1970). Perhaps in acquisition the additional cue is masked by those that have already gained control of the running response. Perhaps in extinction the contextual cues convey conflicting messages, some still predicting food while others are predicting the withdrawal of food. In such a situation an additional cue could be decisive, at least at a certain point in extinction.

It is apparent that we know relatively little about extinction, about why the animal persists as long as it does, or why it ultimately quits. It is curious that many of the noncontingent effects that have been described here appear to be stronger and more persistent in extinction than during acquisition. Perhaps the appropriate comparisons of contingent and noncontingent procedures can help

[18] Trapold evidently assumed that a drive type of motivator would potentiate startle. Brown (1961) cites an unpublished study by Merryman to argue for this effect, but it is a myth (Fechter & Ison, 1972). Apparently, the startle reflex is not potentiated by either drives or incentives, so that it can provide no answer to the question Trapold was asking.

[19] LoLordo et al. (1974) found that when a pigeon key was lighted to signal free food, it disrupted the ongoing behavior, which was stepping on a treadle for food. The pigeons started pecking the key.

provide a clearer picture of extinction as well as learning. Rescorla and Skucy (1969) reported an interesting experiment in which extinction was accomplished, not by removing food from the situation altogether but by removing the contingency between bar pressing and food. Food was still presented, but its delivery was not contingent upon the response. Rescorla and Skucy found much more responding under these conditions. They concluded, therefore, that the customary extinction procedure must involve conditioned inhibition (the consequences of responding come to predict no food). Alternatively, we might conclude that the continued presentation of food maintains incentive motivation; it continues to maintain some of the contextual stimuli as predictors of food, whereas with the customary procedure all stimuli in the situation become predictors of no food. However that may be, the procedure deserves further study.

This section began with a question: What contribution does the contingency between response and consequence make to the strength of the response? It would have been desirable to compare response strengths in contingent and noncontingent situations so that the common part, incentive motivation, could be separated from the distinctive part, the reinforcement effect. Unfortunately, there do not seem to be any direct quantitative comparisons of the two procedures in the experimental literature. While there have been several comparisons of punishment and conditioned-suppression procedures (see Chapter 11), there seem to be no corresponding comparisons between positive reinforcement and noncontingent procedures. Hence we have had to settle for the much weaker and less efficient strategy of showing that a great number of effects found with reinforcement procedures can be duplicated with noncontingent procedures. In nearly every case the comparison must be made across different experiments, and that is a hazardous business. In nearly every case the comparison is merely qualitative; the direct placement technique, for example, produces the same kind of behavioral effects that reinforcement produces, but we do not know whether the effects are quantitatively the same. It would have been desirable, for example, to compare how quickly behavior changes when AOR conditions are changed with comparable contingent and noncontingent procedures.

We may be a little suspicious that the contingent and noncontingent effects are not quantitatively the same. The data reported by Trapold et al. (1969) suggest that reversing discriminative control of bar pressing requires about ten times as many trials when it is done noncontingently. Recall that asymptotic performance in a noncompetitive learning situation is typically reached in about 40 trials. Recall also that in a Crespi type of experiment performance level may stabilize in 3 or 4 trials. The incentive effects that we must explain can occur quite rapidly. Yet in most noncontingent experiments, behavior changes much more slowly, and the establishment of a food cue with noncontingent procedures is apparently quite slow. Experimenters typically use 100 or 200 or even 300 pairings. In other words, it looks as though the various noncontingent effects merely mimic the effects found when there is a response contingency; the two kinds of effects may not be the same thing.

But perhaps the animal attends to stimuli better when it can produce them and when it can orient toward and direct its behavior toward them. Perhaps the animal in the noncontingent situation is engaged in various behaviors that later interfere with the index response. Perhaps the animal can discriminate the noncontingent training situation from the subsequent test situation so that cues established in the former are out of context in the latter. Perhaps, in short, noncontingent and contingent effects are the same, and we simply have not yet been clever enough to show it.

Summary

Because it is by manipulating the conditions of reinforcement that we control and regulate behavior, the study of these conditions is of considerable interest in its own right. It has been found that increasing AOR increases performance in acquisition but may impair performance later in extinction. When the AOR is changed, behavior changes too but in different ways depending upon the circumstances. It is clear that the effects of a given AOR are relative; behavior depends not only on current AOR conditions but on the animal's experience with other AOR conditions. The effects of QOR are similar in most respects to those of AOR, but there are some differences. The effects of DOR are different again, and these effects are further complicated by the fact that delays may be imposed midway in a response chain or at the end of it. In the first case behavior following the delay may be facilitated rather than weakened. All of these parameters appear to interact with each other and with the schedule of reinforcement. So although it can be said that performance generally improves when the conditions of reinforcement are improved, there appears at present to be no simple way to describe how much performance will increase.

The major theoretical issue remains unresolved. The question is whether, or to what extent, the increased performance found with improved conditions of reinforcement is due to better learning, that is, more reinforcement of the behavior. Much of the research that has been considered, especially the research with noncontingent procedures, suggests that different conditions of reinforcement simply create more or less incentive motivation to produce more or less behavior without affecting the strength of the underlying S-R association. But the disappearance of both AOR and DOR effects with extended training, the existence of persistent contrast effects, and the relative inefficiency of the noncontingent procedures all argue strongly for the view that the conditions of reinforcement do affect learning as well as motivation. Perhaps the issue itself is a false one; perhaps it only arises within the framework of a theory that attributes learning to the strengthening of S-R associations and motivation to the occurrence of r_G. And perhaps the issue will resolve itself when we have a better explanatory model.

13

SECONDARY

REINFORCEMENT

*To select out the click and glamorize it into a
"secondary reinforcer" is totally unnecessary,
gratuitous, and theoretically harmful.*
B. R. Bugelski

No concept in all of psychology is in such a state of theoretical disarray as the concept of secondary reinforcement. We know that there are secondary reinforcers because we know that the bulk of human behavior is learned by means of socially instilled rewards and punishments. But we know essentially nothing about how this instilling is done. The attempts to conduct systematic laboratory investigations to disclose how secondary reinforcers are established have as often as not failed to obtain any effects at all, much less show how they depend upon experimental parameters. A number of recent writers have suggested that there may not even be such a phenomenon as secondary reinforcement; or if there is such a thing, that it has properties that make it quite different from what we had expected.

On the other hand, some theorists seem to have been so eager to find laboratory evidence of secondary reinforcement that they have been willing to accept purported claims that simply were not substantiated by the data. We will have occasion in the present chapter to look at some of these amazing discrepancies between data and interpretation; we will find that they have arisen mainly because there has been relatively little agreement about either (1) what effects secondary reinforcers are supposed to have on behavior or (2) what conditions are supposed to be necessary to establish them. In the present chapter we will consider a number of specific proposals pertaining both to the functional properties of secondary reinforcers and to their establishment.

Early experiments on secondary reinforcement

The first experimental investigation of secondary reinforcement appears to have been Frolov's study of higher order conditioning, which is briefly described by Pavlov (1927). Frolov first obtained classical conditioning of salivation in dogs, using an auditory stimulus as the CS. Then, in the crucial second phase of the experiment, a new visual CS was paired with the auditory stimulus, which now supposedly had reinforcing powers. Pavlov reports that salivation did become conditioned to the visual stimulus, although he admitted that the effect was quite fragile. But Frolov's results do fit the paradigm of secondary reinforcement; a once neutral stimulus (the auditory one) is paired with a reinforcer (food), and then when subsequently tested, it appears itself to have the power to produce new learning.

Williams (1929) reported an experiment in which animals were taught a black-white discrimination in one apparatus using food reinforcement; then this apparatus, without food, was placed at the end of a maze in lieu of a goal box. The animals performed better, although not significantly so, under these conditions than when a plain empty box was placed at the end of the maze. In the somewhat mixed terminology of that era, Williams claimed that the conditioned stimulus in the discrimination problem had acquired the power of reinforcing learning in a new task.

A third early experiment was described by Grindley (1929). Grindley ran chicks down an alley to food that was behind a glass partition so that it could be seen but not eaten. Grindley's chicks showed an increase in running speed for a few trials and then they slowed down again, presumably indicating the extinction of the secondary reinforcing power of the sight of food.

Another early experiment, important because it served as a prototype for many subsequent secondary-reinforcement studies, was reported by Skinner (1938). Skinner first magazine trained rats (what this consists of is training the rat to approach a food cup and eat when the food delivery mechanism makes a characteristic click in presenting the food pellet). After magazine training the bar was presented for the first time but, in contrast to the usual custom, bar presses resulted in no food, only the operation of the empty food magazine, that is, the click. What Skinner found was that during a half hour of bar-press testing, there was a substantial number of responses (about 50); Skinner attributed this behavior to the secondary reinforcing effect of the click. The cumulative record indicates that the rate of responding was highest initially and that it gradually weakened over the half hour of testing, as though the behavior was being extinguished. Skinner attributed this extinction to the loss of the secondary reinforcing powers of the click.

Theory of motivation

None of these early experiments furnished convincing evidence of secondary reinforcement. In each case the alleged learning was transient and disappeared in a few trials. Frolov had no controls to assess the possibility that the higher-order conditioning might be just pseudoconditioning or sensitization. Pavlov himself cautioned that the effect could only be obtained under very special conditions. Razran (1955), after surveying a mass of Russian and American literature, concluded that Frolov's results are not generally replicable. Higher-order conditioning is at best a laboratory curiosity; it is surely not the sort of thing that can explain social learning and motivation.[1]

In the studies by Williams, Grindley, and Skinner there were no control groups to indicate that the secondary reinforcer was actually producing any new learning. Only Grindley gave any evidence of a learning curve, that is, an improvement in performance over the course of testing, and Skinner's data look like extinction. None of these experimenters excluded the possibility that there may have been weak primary reinforcers operating in the situation, for example, the handling Williams gave her animals at the goal or sensory reinforcing effects in Skinner's situation. None of these experimenters took the trouble to demonstrate that the secondary-reinforcement effects depended upon the prior association of the click or goal box or whatever with food.[2] Furthermore, we can place little confidence in the generality of the reported effects because of the small number of animals that were run in these early studies and the failure of these experimenters to test for the reliability of their results. Even so, many writers (e.g., Hull, 1943) accepted all these results without question.

The behavioral effects of secondary reinforcers

The uncertain status of secondary-reinforcement results largely from the peculiar circumstance that the term has never been firmly anchored on the behavioral side. The second word in the term "secondary reinforcer" would seem to imply an event that has acquired the power to reinforce, that is, to produce new learning. This meaning was evidently intended in each of the experiments that have just been described. In each case the investigator associated an originally

[1] Pairing the second CS with the first CS in the absence of food should make it a conditioned inhibitor of salivation, and it does, Pavlov reports, unless there is an unusually long interstimulus interval. These delicate parametric considerations are apparently much less troublesome with fear conditioning. Razran (1961) indicates that higher-order conditioning has been more frequently found using aversive stimuli.

[2] Unpublished results from our own laboratory indicate that in a situation similar to Skinner's the same amount of behavior is generated by animals that have been magazine trained but with a click different from that used in testing and by animals fed in the Skinner box but not magazine trained there.

neutral stimulus with food and then made its occurrence contingent on some new response. The trouble with this straightforward strategy is that it does not work; the evidence for new learning has never been convincing. Accordingly, the concept of secondary reinforcement has been broadened so that it has a host of other behavioral properties besides producing learning. Secondary reinforcers are alleged to have, and are widely cited to explain, a mass of different behavioral effects other than reinforcement. This diversification of the secondary-reinforcement concept is illustrated by a remarkable paper by Wolfe (1936).

Wolfe trained chimpanzees to insert tokens (poker chips) into a vending machine to obtain grapes. After this behavior had been established, a new task was introduced so that the chimps had to earn tokens. Wolfe used a work machine in which the animal had to lift a weight in order to obtain a visible incentive, which was either food (a grape) or a token that could be exchanged for food. Wolfe was not concerned with new learning; his subjects had many sessions in which working the machine was immediately reinforced with food. His interest was in other behavioral properties of the tokens. Let us look at the specific experimental situations that Wolfe used.

In Experiment 1 and 2 it was found that some chimpanzees would work as hard and as fast for the tokens as for the grapes that were visible in the apparatus. Wolfe concluded from this that the tokens had incentive value. But let us examine the behavior more carefully. Were the tokens acting as a motivator, that is, exciting the animal or causing it to give more of a previously learned response? Or were they eliciting behavior; that is, was the visible token simply part of the total stimulus situation? Or were the tokens reinforcing responding on the work machine in the same way grapes were reinforcing it? The results of Experiments 1 and 2 show that the token had an important effect upon behavior, but they do not clarify whether this effect was motivational, associative, or attributable to reinforcement.[3]

In Experiment 3 a delay was introduced between working the machine and obtaining food. The delay was imposed under a variety of different conditions, including one in which the animals could obtain and hold on to a token during the delay interval. It was found that this condition led to much more substantial maintenance of behavior than any other delay condition. Here we have a wholly new function for a secondary reinforcer to perform. Having the

[3] It should be noted that at the time Wolfe's study was conducted, the conceptual distinction between food as an incentive, that is, a motivator of behavior, and food as a reinforcer of behavior was not generally recognized, nor was the distinction between learning and performance explicitly made, except by Tolman (1932) and his students. Even though Wolfe's work was done at Yale, it was done before Hull and his group began to think in terms of the learning-performance dichotomy.

token in hand permits the animal to manage a delay. This is not clearly a motivational, discriminative, or reinforcing function; it is a different property of the token that results from its association with food. In Experiment 4 animals were required to work for several tokens before food could be obtained. Wolfe found that responding extinguished in all his animals, but for one of them holding tokens retarded extinction relative to a no-token condition. Here we have still a different function of the token. It maintains behavior. Such a function might be attributed to an increment in motivation, to reinstatement of better stimulus conditions, or to reinforcement. As we will see shortly, subsequent writers have attributed all of these different properties to secondary reinforcers. But the fact is that it is clearly a different function from the acquisition of a new response. Similar procedures were used in Experiment 5, but extinction was so rapid that the results could not be interpreted.

In Experiments 6 and 7 Wolfe trained his animals to discriminate among tokens of different colors, which could be exchanged for one or two pieces of food or water or playing with Wolfe or leaving the situation. No new behavior was required in any of these cases, and most of the testing required a good deal of sophisticated communication between the experimenter and the subject. But it is clear that the various discriminations were made and that the subjects could use the various tokens for their different purposes. Perhaps Wolfe's most interesting observations were of subjects caged in pairs when they were simply given poker chips. A variety of dominance, begging, and stealing behaviors were observed. It was clear that, speaking loosely, the tokens had acquired some kind of value, which initially depended upon their exchange value but which became a property of the tokens themselves. The evidence of these diverse behaviors indicates, again, the appropriateness of saying that the tokens were incentives, but it is not so evident how such behavior (behavior remarkably like the kinds of human social learning and motivation for which the idea of secondary reinforcement was originally invented) falls into our analytical categories. We cannot say whether the incentive value of the tokens demonstrates motivational, associative, or reinforcement processes.

In his conclusion Wolfe (1936) said that the token might be assumed to be (1) a thing that because of learned associations now has intrinsic value, (2) a sign or signal of something to come, or (3) an instrument, a means to an end. At the time Wolfe did his research, it was fashionable and appropriate to regard all of the effects he had demonstrated as incentive effects. In later years we have become more analytical about what we mean by incentive, and hence we have to be more analytical about the diverse effects reported by Wolfe. But, at the same time, we have become quite uncritical about using the term "secondary reinforcement," that is, using it to explain almost any behavior that is not immediately attributable to primary reinforcement. And, as we will see, all of the phenomena reported by Wolfe have been cited by subsequent writers to support their concept of secondary reinforcement.

Our task in this chapter is to consider the different kinds of behavioral phenomena—the acquisition of new responses, the maintenance of old responses, the motivating and discriminating function of stimuli—which are attributed to secondary reinforcement, to see what the properties of this concept really are.[4]

The reinforcement of new responses. In the strictest sense, we should not speak of secondary reinforcement unless we have evidence of new learning that can be attributed to the reinforcing effect of a previously neutral stimulus. Cowles (1937) observed that Wolfe's token-reward studies had not demonstrated new learning, and he set about remedying this deficiency. He first trained chimpanzees (the same ones Wolfe had used) to take a token from one of two covered boxes in a series of two-choice, left-right discriminations. He required them to accumulate a number of tokens (10 or 20 for different subjects) before exchanging them for raisins. The discrimination and a series of reversals were learned by most of the subjects. The task was then expanded to a five-alternative situation in which one of the five positions yielded a token. Again, a number of tokens had to be accumulated before they could be exchanged. Then Cowles moved on (with the same subjects) to a visual discrimination between large and small circles and further discriminations among different colors. In each of these situations some subjects learned the discriminations and the reversals. In all cases the tokens were enclosed in boxes, so that seeing them was a consequence of, rather than an antecedent of, responding. But we may ask whether the learning that occurred was S-R learning or S-S learning. Putting the question a different way, is it not true that Cowles' animals simply had to learn which discriminandum yielded the poker chip?

As reinforcement theory became more popular, it became increasingly important to accept whatever evidence there was for secondary reinforcement. Not only were Cowles' data, which were substantial, accepted, but so were the results of Frolov, Williams, and Grindley, which showed little learning, and so were the data of many other experimenters, which clearly indicated that no learning

---

[4] One of the strangest corruptions of the secondary-reinforcement concept is the claim that token-reward effects have been demonstrated in dogs (Ellson, 1937), cats (Smith, 1939), and rats (Malagodi, 1967). In each case the animal was given an object, like a ball, that had to be dropped into a hole to obtain food. Because the ball was "exchanged" for food, it was called a token. But these studies demonstrate neither new response learning reinforced by the ball nor any of the interesting incentive effects seen in the poker-chip studies. The ball is simply an object that must be responded to in a specific way to obtain food. It is like the bar in that respect; should we call the bar a token too?

Theory of motivation

had occurred. For example, D'Amato (1955) fed rats in a distinctive box and then put this box and a neutral one, both empty, on opposite sides of a T-maze. He asked whether the animals would learn to go to the distinctive secondary reinforcing box where they had previously eaten. The trial-by-trial performance of the group is shown in Fig. 13-1. Note that there is no rise in the learning curve. D'Amato acknowledged this, but he pointed to the fact that the whole curve averaged significantly above 50 percent and took this as evidence of secondary reinforcement. D'Amato was not the only good experimenter to draw such a strange conclusion from such date; it had been done before, for example, by Hall (1951) and Lawson (1953).

A somewhat more convincing demonstration of new response learning had been reported by Saltzman (1949). Saltzman's animals were trained to run a straight alley to a distinctive box for food, and then this box was placed in one side of a T-maze (the nonpreferred side for each subject). On the opposite side was a box that was novel for one group (the continuous-reinforcement group) and that for another group (the differential-reinforcement group) had been used in the straight alley on trials when food had been withheld. A control group was run with primary reinforcement in the T-maze. The learning of the T-maze habit for these three groups is shown in Fig. 13-2.

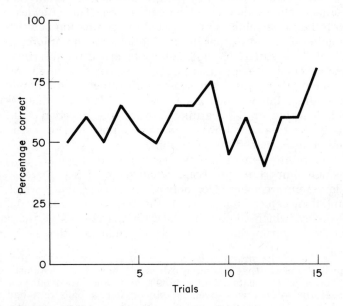

Figure 13-1

Alleged learning on the basis of secondary reinforcement. (Data from D'Amato, 1955) Copyright (1955) by the American Psychological Association. Reprinted by permission.

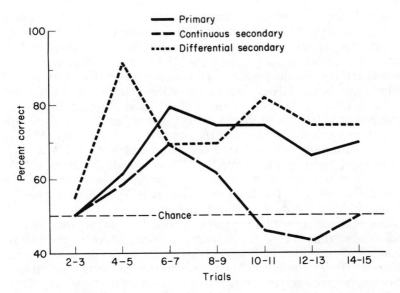

Figure 13–2

A comparison of T-maze performance reinforced by food or by going to a box previously associated with food. Previously, all subjects had run an alley and eaten in the box. For the continuous group alley running had always been reinforced, but for the differential group running had been reinforced in this box but not reinforced in a box of a different color that was later put on the incorrect side of the T-maze. (Adapted from Saltzman, 1949) Copyright (1949) by the American Psychological Association. Reprinted by permission.

(Saltzman ran other groups whose results are not indicated in the figure.)

Several features of Saltzman's experiment should be noted. One is that the rats could not see the goal boxes at the choice point; hence it cannot be said that they were merely making approach responses to stimuli they had learned to approach in the alley. Second, the secondary-reinforcement effect was considerably more durable for the animals in the differential-reinforcement group than for the continuous group; for the latter the secondary reinforcing effect was quite short-lived. It has been suggested that the poor showing of the continuous group was due to frustration that occurred when the empty box was encountered for the first time or to exploratory effects produced by the novelty of the situation. In this connection Reynolds et al. (1963) had some success controlling these competing tendencies, and they report somewhat more stable performance with continuous prior training than Saltzman found. On the other hand, Lieberman (1967) was unable to replicate the Saltzman study.

Even granting that Saltzman had obtained new response

learning, there are two qualifications that must be noted. One is that no one has yet run the controls necessary to demonstrate that learning in this situation depends upon approaching the positive box rather than avoiding the negative one. The second point is that it has been found that it is not differential training per se that matters, but rather that the animals receive the secondary reinforcing stimulus on only a portion of the trials. Klein (1959) gave different degrees of intermittent pairing for different groups, and although he reported no data on acquisition, he did find the greatest preference for the secondary reinforcing box in those animals for which the box had been the most intermittently associated with food (see also Wallace, 1970).

The importance of partial reinforcement in establishing a secondary reinforcer has been emphasized by Zimmerman (1957). Zimmerman's procedure involved a double intermittency. First, a buzzer was paired with primary reinforcement on an intermittent schedule, so that during the magazine-training phase of the experiment the animals obtained food only a fraction of the times the buzzer sounded. Under these conditions the buzzer acquires very strong stimulus control over the response of turning to the food cup. Then in the test for the secondary reinforcing effects of the buzzer only a fraction of the bar presses produced the buzzer. Zimmerman obtained a lot of bar pressing, but he did not run the appropriate control groups to assure us that all the behavior was attributable to the secondary reinforcing effects of the buzzer. He had no group that got the buzzer in the absence of prior pairing with food, nor did he have a group that had secondary-reinforcement training on a continuous schedule. The evidence for secondary reinforcement in Zimmerman's study is presumptive—he found many more bar-press responses than earlier experimenters had observed. Indeed, Zimmerman found somewhat too much behavior; there was no extinction apparent in his cumulative records.

Zimmerman (1959) attempted to extend these procedures to a running situation in which pressing a bar opened a door to where food had been. Extremely durable behavior was again found, but the appropriate controls were still lacking. Subsequent investigators (e.g., McNamara & Paige, 1962; Wike et al., 1962) have run the necessary control animals and found that Zimmerman's results probably were not due to secondary reinforcement. Apparently, the bar-press situation was aversive, and getting out of it was inherently reinforcing (Keehn, 1962; Wike & Platt, 1962; McNamara, 1963; Wike et al., 1963).

There are a number of other studies indicating that secondary-reinforcement effects are more substantial when the secondary reinforcer is established by intermittent pairing with food (e.g., D'Amato et al., 1958; Fox & King, 1961). The Fox and King study supports Zimmerman's argument that double intermittency is an important procedural detail in producing substantial amounts of new response learning with secondary reinforcers; either intermittency alone was much less effective. (Davenport & Sardello's, 1966, test of Zimmerman's hypothesis can be dismissed because they obtained only about 30 responses per session.)

None of the results we have considered can give much comfort to those who would like to believe that secondary reinforcers actually reinforce. Virtually everyone who has claimed to have found learning of a new response is subject to some serious criticism; they did not use the appropriate controls; they did not demonstrate improvement over time; they did not eliminate all primary reinforcement; or they obtained only a few responses. When the learning of new responses is specifically sought, it typically is not found. And when a secondary reinforcer can be shown to have a dramatic effect on the animal's behavior (Wolfe, 1936; Cowles, 1937), the effect cannot be unequivocally atttributed to the learning of new responses. We must conclude that, whatever other properties a secondary reinforcer may have, it is not capable of producing a significant amount of new learning.[5]

The maintenance of previously learned responses. Bugelski (1938) trained two groups of rats to press a bar for food, and when the behavior was well established, he extinguished it. One group still produced the click in extinction and the other group did not (food was withheld from both groups). Bugelski reported that subjects undergoing extinction without the click quit responding more quickly than those with the click. Presumably, the click helped to maintain the learned bar-press response and for this reason can be called a secondary reinforcer.

These results suggest alternative explanations, however. Bitterman et al. (1953) have pointed out that Bugelski's findings and much of the other evidence often cited to support the concept of secondary reinforcement could be interpreted simply on the basis of what is called the discrimination hypothesis. Bitterman et al. argue that, of course, Bugelski's animals responded more with the click than without it, because the click had been present in acquisition; the subjects without the click in extinction were under conditions that differed from the acquisition conditions. The difference can be discriminated and, accordingly, behavior decrements occur.

A similar but somewhat more pointed alternative was later

---

[5] One other reviewer (Longstreth, 1971) has come to the same conclusion. Others suggest that new learning could be shown if only the appropriate experiment could be devised (Wike, 1966; Hendry, 1969). Wike (1969) suggests that new learning occurs, but it is fragile and short-lived if the secondary reinforcer is not backed up by primary reinforcement. Still others (Kelleher & Gollub, 1962) tell us they have devised the appropriate experiment, and that it involves chain schedules of primary reinforcement.

suggested by Bugelski himself (1956). He contended that the click has no special properties; it is simply one of the stimuli that elicit one of the responses in the chain of behavior leading to food. He says:

> it would appear that rather than talking about secondary reinforcement we might more logically conceive the click to be a stimulus which happens to become associated with one segment of a chain of responses, namely, that part of the pattern which we can label "going to the food cup." . . . When it is dropped out of the picture, the pattern is to that extent weakened or altered so that the behavior is less likely to occur and will be eliminated more rapidly as the rest of the pattern gets extinguished. [p. 93][6]

Bugelski's argument differs from that of Bitterman et al. in that he attributes the difference in extinction performance to the fact that a chain of behavior is broken for one group but not for the other. White (1953), a student of Bugelski's, trained several groups of rats to press a bar and observed the behavior chain during the course of acquisition and extinction. As Bugelski describes it:

> When all the rats were trained they were given different *pre-extinction* training. Some rats were placed in a box without a bar present and were presented with the click at an average of 30 seconds. The click was followed ordinarily by an approach to the food cup, now empty. As the clicks continued the fruitless trips began to decline until they stopped altogether (usually within a period of 30 clicks). It would appear that the food-cup approach was extinguished as far as the click was concerned. The next day the rats were replaced in the box with the bar present and underwent ordinary extinction (that is, no food was dropped to them after the bar-presses). Allowing for "spontaneous recovery" and for the probable short-circuiting of the behavior so that the click might not be particularly important if food was present, we could expect the rats to make some food-cup approaches, which they did. However, an interesting chain of events began to unfold. The rats began to cut down on the number of trips to the food cup after bar-pressing, compared with the normal (non-pre-extinguish) group. Their behavior toward the food cup became less regular, frequently they failed to reach it at all, and frequently they failed to "search" it for food. As the food-cup behavior began to break down, the entire pattern of return to the bar also weakened and broke down. Now the rat did not get to the bar and consequently could not press it. When it did get around to the bar and pressed, it failed to go to the cup, and consequently spent more time in the bar area. Spending more time in the bar area permitted a few more bar-presses than might be ordinary, but even that behavior

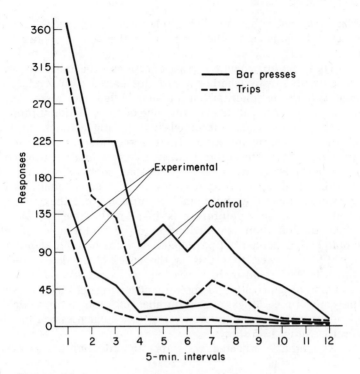

Figure 13–3

Extinction performance of bar pressing and trips to the food cup in successive 5-minute intervals in a 1-hour extinction session. The experimental group had a 30-minute pre-extinction session with the click presented irregularly but without the bar being present. The control group also had 30-minute preextinction experience but without the click. Note how the prior extinction of going to the food cup depressed bar pressing for the experimental group. (Data from White, 1953; figure reproduced from The Psychology of Learning *by B. R. Bugelski. Copyright © 1956 by Holt, Rinehart and Winston, Inc. Reprinted by permission of Holt, Rinehart and Winston, Inc.*

began to weaken. The pre-extinguished rats met an extinction criterion sooner than did the control animals. [pp. 91–93][7]

The results from White's study are shown in Fig. 13-3. One of the great virtues of these data, and of Bugelski's description of the animals' behavior, is that they suggest how the strength of the

[7] From *The Psychology of Learning* by B. R. Bugelski. Copyright © 1956 by Holt, Rinehart and Winston, Inc. Reprinted by permission of Holt, Rinehart and Winston, Inc.

criterion response, the one being maintained by secondary reinforcement, depends upon the strength of the next response in the
chain.

These findings point to two questions. The question we are
concerned with here is whether a stimulus paired with primary reinforcement helps to maintain a previously learned response. The
answer is clearly yes; this is evidently one of the functional properties
of secondary reinforcers. But Bugelski is raising a much more profound and interesting question: Does a secondary reinforcer have
any functional properties other than its ability to maintain behavior?
More particularly, if we can assume that such stimuli maintain
behavior by eliciting the next response in a response chain, is there
any reason to make the additional assumptions that they reinforce?

If a secondary reinforcer is just another part of the total
stimulus situation, then its contribution to the maintenance of behavior should be independent of parameters such as hours of deprivation.
Miles (1956) showed that this is the case. Miles determined the
resistance to extinction of bar pressing, with and without the click,
as a function of deprivation at the time of testing, as Fig. 13-4 shows.
At the same time, Miles ran a number of groups for which the
independent variable was the number of times bar pressing had been
reinforced, as Fig. 13-5 shows.

As might be expected, resistance to extinction increased with

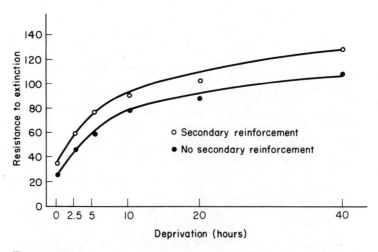

Figure 13–4

*Median resistance to extinction of a bar-press response as a
function of hours food deprivation in extinction. The secondary
reinforcement groups received light and click in extinction,
and the other groups did not. (From Miles, 1956) Copyright
(1956) by the American Psychological Association. Reprinted
by permission.*

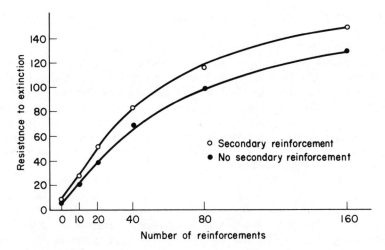

Figure 13–5

Median resistance to extinction of a bar-press response as a function of the number of reinforcements in acquisition. The secondary reinforcement groups received light and click in extinction and the other groups did not. (From Miles, 1956) Copyright (1956) by the American Psychological Association. Reprinted by permission.

both the number of reinforcements and the severity of deprivation state, and in both cases there was an increasing contribution of the secondary reinforcer to the total number of responses. These elegant data could be presented in a number of ways. Consider that if the differences between curves were plotted to show how many additional responses could be attributed to the click, the resulting monotonic curves could be cited to show that the strength of a secondary reinforcer depends on how strongly it is conditioned and upon how motivated the animal is. Alternatively, the data could be presented as they are here to convey the impression that secondary reinforcement is a relatively minor factor in extinction performance. The data could also be plotted as ratios showing what proportion of the extinction performance can be attributed to the click. Miles (1956) himself emphasized that this ratio is very nearly constant over the entire range of drive and habit-strength parameters. Regardless of the particular values under which it is tested, the secondary reinforcer accounts for about 15 percent of the animal's performance. Miles drew the elegant conclusion, therefore, that the associative and motivating aspects of the secondary reinforcer are no different from those of any other stimulus. The click is no more or no less than one of the many stimuli controlling the behavior in the situation. To remove it is simply to lessen the stimulus support for the established behavior.

The motivating function. One effect that is rarely adequately allowed for in studies of secondary reinforcement is that the click excites the animal; it increases energy output and activity level. Wolfe (1936) reported a variety of observations indicating that his animals became excited upon seeing or receiving a token. In the Skinner box perhaps the click makes the animal cling to or attack the bar, thereby boosting its response score. Bar pressing tends to include bursts of responses, particularly early in acquisition, and perhaps this is why. An appropriately micro analysis of bar-press acquisition in the secondary-reinforcement situation might show how important such an effect is.

Excitement could occur simply because excited behavior typically precedes feeding. Food cues could selectively facilitate excited behavior in hungry animals. So we may wonder whether incentive stimuli in general act as secondary reinforcers because they produce excitement. Recall that Hull and Spence attributed both secondary reinforcement and incentive motivation to the same response mechanism, r_G. Hence, according to the Hull-Spence model, a number of intimate relationships between incentive motivation and secondary reinforcement would have to be expected.

The facilitation effect. Even if the click does not markedly excite the animal, it should, as a consequence of magazine training, increase the probability of pressing the bar, if only because it elicits approach to the food cup, which keeps the animal near the front of the box and consequently near the bar (Wyckoff et al., 1958; Myers, 1958). Crowder et al. (1959) attempted to control for this facilitation effect and obtain secondary-reinforcement effects over and beyond it. Their control for facilitation was accomplished by using a yoked control procedure in which a pair of animals was given secondary-reinforcement training and then tested together in two boxes arranged so that one of the pair produced the click for both animals. Thus both animals had the advantage of whatever facilitation the click produced, but only the experimental animal had it contingent on responding. It is unfortunate that Crowder and his colleagues did not run other controls to determine, for example, whether the yoked controls did in fact have a higher rate of responding than animals with no click, as the facilitation hypothesis requires. It is also unfortunate that they presented no learning curves, that the yoked control procedure cannot guarantee a separation of elicitation and reinforcement effects, and that, in general, they failed to test their interesting hypothesis. We cannot tell how much of the responding was because of the click and how much was for the click.

The impairment of discrimination learning. Denny (1948) found that rats would learn a simple position habit in a T-maze more quickly if the correct goal box and the incorrect one were different colors than if they were the same color. Denny argued that the color of the positive box becomes a secondary reinforcer by being associated with food and that if this stimulus was also present in the incorrect end box, it would tend to produce an increment in the strength of the incorrect response by virtue of its secondary reinforcing power. This would hinder discrimination learning. Denny's findings have been confirmed by Saltzman (1950), Ehrenfreund (1949, 1954), Webb and Nolan (1953), Bauer and Lawrence (1953), and Grice and Goldman (1955).

The mediation of delays. Wolfe (1936) found that his chimps performed better when food was delayed if they were able to hold on to their tokens during the delay interval. Perkins (1947) found that his rats performed better when food was delayed if they were able to stay in a box similar to the goal box during the delay interval. In both cases the improved performance was attributed to secondary reinforcement. The tokens, because they could be exchanged for food, and the goal box, because it was associated with food, were said to be secondary reinforcers that maintain or strengthen behavior in the temporary absence of primary reinforcement. We saw (page 429) the importance Spence (1947) attached to this phenomenon, that is, how he used it to infer a very short temporal gradient of reinforcement. The bridging of delays together with the impairing of discrimination learning do not necessarily represent a different kind of hypothetical function for secondary reinforcers to perform; both effects can be attributed to reinforcement. But they do introduce new lines of presumptive or indirect evidence for the existence of and the importance of secondary reinforcers. The general argument is that there must be secondary reinforcers (and they must have the power to reinforce) because there must be some mechanism to explain the learning that occurs in situations where primary reinforcement cannot explain it.

Behavior chaining. Even when the experimenter looks just at a single response, the animal is typically engaged in a chain of responses that ultimately lead to primary reinforcement. In some cases the chain is obvious. In the token-reward studies the animals were explicitly required to obtain the poker chips and then to exchange them for food. In the bar-press situation only bar pressing is usually recorded, but the rat obviously must engage in a series of different responses: approaching the bar, contacting it, pressing it, going to the food hopper, finding food, eating it, and so on. A sufficiently micro analysis of behavior will show that in most situations animals perform a sequence of different responses.

Skinner (1938) has proposed that in all such cases each response in the sequence produces a distinctive new stimulus, either interoceptive or exceroceptive, which marks off and separates the different responses. Each of these stimuli, then, becomes a discriminative stimulus for the next response in the sequence. Skinner argues further that each of these stimuli also acts as a secondary reinforcer to strengthen the preceding response, that is, the behavior that produced it.

But rather than speculate about the existence and properties of stimuli that effect the transition from one response to another in a chain, it is better to provide an explicit exceroceptive stimulus that serves this function and to use it to mark a change in the schedule of reinforcement. Such a procedure constitutes either a multiple or a chain schedule, depending upon the circumstances. Consider the case reported by Ferster and Skinner (1957, p. 667) of a bird trained to peck a key for food in the presence of one stimulus, S_1, and not in the presence of another stimulus, S_2. The two stimuli marked random fixed periods of pecking for food and extinction. Under this multiple schedule the bird's behavior eventually stabilized in a pattern of very low rates during the extinction cue and high rates in the presence of the food cue. At this point Ferster and Skinner switched their animals from a multiple to a chain schedule; the difference here is that on the chain schedule the negative component was no longer of fixed duration but could be terminated by responding on some kind of schedule and replaced by the positive component. In other words, the animal could now work to get into the second component in which it could work for food. When the conditions were switched to a chain schedule, Ferster and Skinner found there was a substantial increase of pecking in the presence of the negative cue. Note that the consequence of responding to the negative cue in a chain schedule is to produce the positive cue, and since introducing this consequence increases the rate of responding in much the same way that introducing food as a consequence would, it could be concluded that the positive cue is a secondary reinforcer.[8] Looked at another way, when the cue for food was scheduled by the experimenters to occur independently of the animal's behavior, there was little behavior preceding it; but when it was made contingent upon responding, the animal worked to produce it.

Now in the Ferster and Skinner experiment the change in each component was scheduled on a VI-1 schedule so that the first response after 1 minute in the negative cue produced the positive stimulus, and then the first response after 1 minute produced food and put the animal back on to the negative cue. We might ask whether the animal's behavior under these conditions is any different than it would be if the animal were simply on a schedule such as a VI-2 that produced the same overall rate of food reinforcement. Kelleher and Gollub (1962) go to some trouble to convince us that

---

[8] Kelleher and Gollub (1962) tell us, apparently in all seriousness, that secondary reinforcers should be called conditioned reinforcers, first, so that we will remember that they are established by conditioning (whatever that is), and second, so that we will not be confused by tertiary and quaternary reinforcers (whatever they are).

this is not the case. For one thing, on a VI-2 schedule there should be just a single, long scallop, whereas on the VI-1, VI-1 chain schedule there is typically a scallop in each component.

Consider the following experiment by Ferster and Skinner (1957, page 690). Pigeons were first trained on a tandem schedule (which is like a chain schedule in that the animal gets from one component to the next by responding on some schedule, but there are no cues to mark the different components). In this case the two components were FR-120 and DRL 6 seconds (after 120 responses the first response after a 6-second pause was reinforced). Thus the two components of the tandem schedule were quite different, one calling for a high rate of responding and the other one calling for a low rate. Since there were no cues to signal which component was in effect at any time, the birds gave intermediate and rather unstable rates of responding. But when they were switched to a chain schedule, that is, when there were differential cues to indicate the two components, these cues quickly gained control over fast responding during the FR component and slow responding during the DRL component. The argument is again that just as the form the behavior took on the second (DRL) component can be attributed to food as a reinforcer, so the form of responding in the first (FR) component can be attributed to the presentation of the positive cue as a secondary reinforcer. If the control of behavior by food can be attributed to its primary reinforcing value, then the control of behavior by the cue to food makes it a secondary reinforcer. Kelleher and Gollub (1962) discuss these and a variety of similar experiments in which a considerable range of different reinforcement schedules are programmed for the first and second components of chain schedules. In each case, they contend, the behavior is found to be characteristic of the immediate consequence for each component, that is, food on the one hand and the cue to food on the other hand. And in each case the behavior is said to be governed by the schedule in effect in each component and to be relatively independent of the schedule operating in the other component.

This kind of evidence from chain and multiple schedule experiments has been widely cited as demonstrating the viability, indeed, the necessity, of a secondary-reinforcement concept. But there are some difficulties with the argument. First, one gets a vague feeling that the discriminative function and the reinforcing function of the secondary reinforcer are redundant. Certainly the use of a chain or multiple schedule breaks the total chain of behavior into discernible parts, and the stimulus in question is programmed in discernibly different ways in each part. But the question is whether the different kinds of control exercised by programming a stimulus as a discriminative stimulus or as a reinforcer really represent different kinds of psychological mechanisms; or are they merely different ways of programming a stimulus? We are urged by Kelleher and Gollub (1962) to think of the behavior in the second component as being under the discriminative control of the secondary reinforcer. But can we not think of the behavior in the first component as also being under discriminative control, namely, by the *absence* of the secondary reinforcer? And if we can, is it not superfluous to view the behavior as also being controlled by its consequence, the secondary reinforcer? Alternatively, if we prefer to explain behavior in terms of its consequences, is it necessary to cite also the discriminative conditions that control it? The animal on a chain schedule may simply be doing one thing in the presence of one cue and something else in the presence of another cue because that is how it gets food. It seems unnecessary to assume that each part of the behavior is controlled both by its antecedents and by its consequences.

A second aspect of the problem is that the operant behavior-controller has a severely limited set of explanatory mechanisms. If some piece of behavior is found to be correlated with antecedent conditions then they must be exerting discriminative control, because that is half of the weapons in the operant-man's explanatory arsenal. The other half is that if the behavior is found to be correlated with its consequences, then they must be reinforcers, because there is no other way to account for it.

A third difficulty is that because the Skinnerian is primarily interested in the rate of responding and because he typically uses schedules that generate high rates, the animal's behavior is seen as a continuous stream of ever-recurring responses. It is difficult, therefore, to tell which events are antecedent to responding and which are consequences of responding. When an appropriate analysis is made, it often leads to surprising results. For example, in Staddon's (1970) analysis of the frustration effect he studied the effect of omitting food, which surely must be interpreted as altering the consequences of responding. Yet his results (see also Kello, 1972) indicate that omitting food produces its effect by changing the discriminative control of the ongoing stream of behavior. The point is that an established piece of behavior, an organized chain of responses, has its own integrity; it is gratuitous to invoke a secondary reinforcer to explain its integrity.

To summarize our review of the behavioral properties that have been attributed to secondary reinforcers, it should be emphasized that there is very little evidence that they can be used to produce new learning. The naïve idea that secondary reinforcers should reinforce has had to be replaced with a multitude of more sophisticated ideas about how they at least help maintain behavior, and how they motivate and facilitate behavior. They also have hypothetical interactions with other reinforcement mechanisms so that, for example, they impair learning in some situations and facilitate it in others. In short, if a theorist attributes learning to reinforcement, as many theorists do, then secondary reinforcers are handy devices to explain all the learning that occurs in the apparent absence of reinforcement.

Other kinds of secondary reinforcers. A fundamental assumption in Mowrer's (1960) theory of learning is that stimuli that signal the termination of aversive stimulation should acquire positive reinforcing value; they should come to elicit relief. Barlow (1952) first put the question in empirical terms: Will an animal learn a new response that produces a stimulus that has previously been associated with the termination of shock? Barlow gave rats 10-second shocks, near the end of which a light was presented. The next day they were put in a situation in which for half of them touching a bar turned the light on and for the other half touching the bar turned the light off. Barlow did not report any learning curves, but he did report that the animals tended to have the light on more than off. A possible artifact from using this kind of response measure is that the light might elicit fear rather than relief, and Barlow's rats froze on the bar whenever they produced the light.

Beck (1961) describes several variations on this theme, most of which have failed to support Barlow and Mowrer's position. Smith and Buchanan (1954) and Buchanan (1958) have found some supporting evidence in a somewhat different situation. In these studies hungry rats were trained to approach one box to get food and terminate shock and to approach another box to get food (no shock). Later they were given a preference test between the two boxes (no shock). Comparison with control animals indicated stronger approach behavior for the box that had been associated with shock termination. It should be noted, however, that this situation provided no real test of learning. Therefore, the results cannot be taken to indicate a reinforcement effect of secondary reinforcement. Beck (1961) reviewed the problems here with considerable care and insight and concluded that at that time there was little evidence that stimuli contiguous with shock termination become secondary reinforcers.

Since Beck's review more support for Barlow's hypothesis has been found (Evans, 1962; Wagman & Allen, 1964; Lawler, 1965); but the demonstrated effects remain small and rather fragile, and still no learning curves have appeared. In a more recent review Siegel and Milby (1969) point out that none of the purported claims for the relief effect have adequately separated potential reinforcing effects from the confounding elicitation and discriminative effects. Another reviewer (LoLordo, 1969) also dismissed the existing claims on various methodological grounds. LoLordo also calls attention to the anomaly that the conditions for establishing a relief secondary reinforcer are precisely those that establish a safety signal. It is curious that there is a fair amount of evidence for a reinforcing effect of the latter (see Chapter 10) and so little for a reinforcing effect of the former.

There is also little evidence for what are called generalized conditioned reinforcers. Commenting upon the fact that the efficacy of social reinforcement in people appears to be independent of current deprivation conditions, Skinner (1953) suggested that their generality was due to their having been associated with a number of different primary reinforcers. Somehow Skinner came to the conclusion that if a stimulus was associated with enough different kinds of motivation-reinforcement procedures, it would remain effective in the absence of any motivation condition. Experimental support for this conception has been sought by running animals alternately hungry and thirsty, or both hungry and thirsty, and showing that the resulting behavior is more durable than it is when animals are run under only a single drive condition. It is not clear what implications such findings have in view of the known interactions of hunger and thirst (see Chapter 6) and the fact that any variability in acquisition conditions can be expected to lead to more durable behavior.

The establishment of secondary reinforcers

Virtually all theorists subscribe to the principle that an originally neutral cue becomes a secondary reinforcer when it bears some kind of relationship to food or other primary reinforcer. The question is what is the nature of this relationship? We turn now to a discussion of some of the different relationships that have been suggested as being critical.

The contiguity hypothesis. One of the simplest hypotheses about secondary reinforcement is that a neutral stimulus acquires reinforcing properties merely by being contiguous with the events constituting primary reinforcement. Pavlov made the contiguity principle the basis of his explanation of higher-order conditioning. Hull (1943) accepted contiguity as a general working hypothesis, probably because he accepted the case Pavlov made for higher-order conditioning, and although Hull supplemented the contiguity hypothesis with other, more specific proposals, he never abandoned it. In 1951 Spence postulated that r_G provided the basis for both incentive motivation (Spence, 1951) and secondary reinforcement (Spence, 1951a). But, while Hull accepted both of these propositions, he clung to the idea that contiguity was the basic condition for establishing r_G. His final statement was that a stimulus "which occurs repeatedly and consistently in close conjunction with a reinforcing state of affairs, . . . will itself acquire the power to act as a reinforcing agent" (Hull, 1952, p. 6).[9]

[9] Learning by contiguity does not necessarily mean learning by classical conditioning, even though in the Hullian system the two are virtually synonymous because Hull recognized only two kinds of learning, Thorndikian reinforcement learning and Pavlovian contiguity learning. But Watson, Guthrie, and even Tolman and Mowrer (1960) subscribed to the general empirical law of contiguity (that is, more is learned when events occur closer in time) without endorsing Pavlovian conditioning mechanisms.

A study by Bersh (1951) showed that if a delay of just a few seconds was introduced between a light signaling food and the presentation of food in magazine training, subsequent bar pressing for the light was sharply reduced. He found the best performance when the magazine-training interval had been 0.5 seconds to 1 second. Similar results, as shown in Fig. 13-6, were also reported by Jenkins (1950). A number of writers have noted the similarity between this short optimum interval and the short optimum interval for obtaining classical conditioning, and they have suggested that the classical conditioning of r_G provides the mechanism for establishing a secondary reinforcer.

Although contiguity is an important, and perhaps necessary, part of establishing a secondary reinforcer, contiguity alone is apparently not sufficient. Schoenfeld et al. (1950) trained two groups of rats to press a bar for food. For the experimental group a light of 1-second duration was turned on at the onset of eating. Considerable care was taken to make this stimulus accompany rather than precede

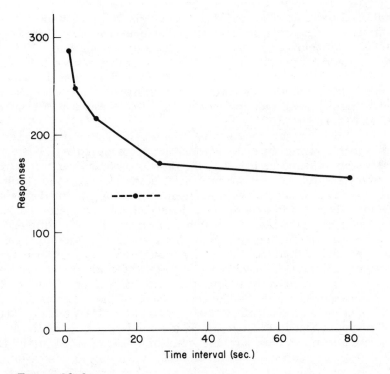

Figure 13–6

Mean number of bar presses for a buzzer in 6 hours of testing as a function of the interval between buzzer and food during acquisition. The isolated point indicates the performance of animals with no buzzer. (From Jenkins, 1950)

the consummatory response as it does in most secondary reinforcement situations. The control group received no light stimulus. After acquisition the response was extinguished under conditions such that a bar press no longer produced food but did present the 1-second light. No difference in performance between the groups was found. Schoenfeld et al. did not run a group for which the light preceded the consummatory response by a short interval—such as is the case when the click of the feeding mechanism is used as a secondary reinforcer—to show that a group trained with the light would have greater resistance to extinction than the control group. But they could cite the studies by Bersh and Jenkins to make the point. These results support the argument that secondary reinforcement is based upon a classical conditioning process. But Schoenfeld et al. argued instead for a different kind of process, which we must now consider.

The discriminative-stimulus hypothesis. Skinner had suggested as early as 1938 that a necessary condition for establishing a stimulus as a secondary reinforcer is that it be a discriminative stimulus. What this means in Skinnerian terminology is that responding is reinforced on some schedule when the discriminative stimulus (S^D) is present, but never in its absence. What happens under these conditions is, of course, that the animal learns to respond more or less exclusively in the presence of S^D. After this learning has occurred, the stimulus is said to set the occasion for responding or to be a discriminative stimulus or, according to this hypothesis, to be a secondary reinforcer. Direct evidence for this hypothesis comes from a study by Dinsmoor (1950).

Dinsmoor gave two groups of animals discrimination training on bar pressing. In extinction one group produced the S^D for 3 seconds by pressing the bar (i.e., the S^D was used as though it were a reinforcer—following the response). For the second group extinction conditions were similar to those in acquisition in that the light was on except for 3 seconds immediately after a response (i.e., it was still being presented as though it were an S^D). No difference in extinction responding was found between the two groups. Dinsmoor concluded that there is no functional difference between the discriminative and the reinforcing functions of a stimulus as far as the organism is concerned; any difference is merely a matter of temporal relationship to suit the convenience of the experimenter.

Keller and Schoenfeld (1950) tied all of this work together and proposed that in order to act as a secondary reinforcer for any response a stimulus must have the status of a discriminative stimulus for a response, either the same one, as in Dinsmoor's study, or a different one. In a chain schedule the same response is usually required, but the pattern of responding is typically different prior to and in the presence of the stimulus in question. Therefore, it is easy to attribute its effect on responding in the first component to its reinforcing function and its effect on responding in the second component to its discriminative function.

Although much of the data generated by chain and multiple schedules is consistent with this kind of analysis, the argument is not entirely convincing (page 463). In a chain schedule the stimulus that is called a secondary reinforcer is necessarily a discriminative stimulus, but we should recall that the chain schedule was designed specifically to make this the case. It is possible to construct a schedule in which this is not the case. Consider a procedure developed by Zimmerman (1963). Key pecking was maintained by food on a VI schedule, but concurrently pecking occasionally produced what Zimmerman called a brief stimulus, which was also presented immediately prior to food. Thus Zimmerman's procedure associates the stimulus with food, but it is not a discriminative stimulus because it is not present at the time pecking for food is reinforced. It is a concurrent schedule in which the animal is producing two kinds of consequences at once on different reinforcement schedules. Zimmerman reports that after the behavior is stabilized it is possible to withdraw the food reinforcement and sustain key pecking for long periods of time simply by presenting the brief stimulus intermittently as a consequence (Zimmerman, 1969). This and similar procedures have now been used by a number of investigators to show secondary reinforcing effects (e.g., de Lorge, 1969; Thomas, 1969).

A complication in these studies has been noted by de Lorge (1969). He observes that a comparable brief stimulus *not* associated with food sometimes maintains behavior when made contingent on key pecking in much the same way that the food-associated stimulus does. He suggests that the stimulus may act as a counter (cf. Ferster & Skinner, 1957) as much as a secondary reinforcer.

On the other hand, it should be noted that in these studies the brief stimulus may not be just a brief stimulus but a rather special stimulus; typically, it is the presentation of the food hopper with the food covered or illumination of the food hopper for 0.5 seconds. We may suppose that while such a stimulus is not a discriminative stimulus for key pecking, it does have discriminative control over the next response in the chain, that is, going to the food hopper.

The basic trouble with the discriminative-stimulus hypothesis of secondary reinforcement is that the concept of a discriminative stimulus itself is conceptually barren. It is hard to believe that a stimulus that simply sets the occasion for reinforcement becomes a reinforcer or that if it does become a reinforcer, it is because it sets the occasion. Such an account may be an objective description of how the situation is programmed, but it seems to miss the point of what the animal is doing in the Skinner box. More to the point would be to ask what the discriminative stimulus makes the animal do. Let us consider the possibility that it makes the animal give a particular response.

The elicitation hypothesis. Hull (1943) conjectured that a stimulus acquires secondary reinforcing properties to the extent that it comes to elicit a response. He proposed further that a stimulus acquires secondary reinforcing properties to the extent that it elicits r_G. The principal use Hull and his followers made of this hypothesis, as we have observed, was to explain incentive motivation. It was often called secondary reinforcement, but the explanatory emphasis was usually upon the motivating aspects of r_G rather than upon its possible reinforcing powers.

Much of the subsequent research suggests that the elicited response may be another overt response in a chain of instrumental responses.[10] The study by Zimmerman (1963) illustrates the point; lighting the food hopper undoubtedly made his birds leave the key and go to the hopper (see also Kelleher, 1961). An explicit test of the elicitation hypothesis was reported by Wyckoff et al. (1958). They trained rats to approach and lick a water dipper in response to the sound of a buzzer. The rats were then tested in a situation in which lever pressing produced the buzzer but no water. The data showed that the buzzer did come to elicit approach to the water dipper and that the animal did learn to press the bar for the buzzer. However, the acquisition of bar pressing was not significantly better for these subjects than for subjects for which pressing the bar turned the buzzer off! Wyckoff et al. suggest that a large part of the literature that appears to support the concept of secondary reinforcement may be more readily interpreted in terms of the response-eliciting effects of the alleged secondary reinforcer.

Weiss and Lawson (1962) have observed that Wyckoff's animals were run on a variable-interval schedule in which considerable pausing after the buzzer might be expected. An analysis of their own data, also obtained under VI conditions, showed that this was the case. This does not alter the force of the argument; the data still suggest that the function of the buzzer was not primarily that of reinforcing the response that preceded it, but rather to produce the behavior that had previously been conditioned to it. Whether the eliciting effect produces an increase or a decrease in the strength of the response that is supposedly being reinforced would seem to depend entirely upon whether the elicited response carries the animal back into or further away from the situation in which the reinforced response is likely to occur. Thus the buzzer in Wyckoff's situation took the animals away from the bar and, therefore, depressed

---

[10] "Elicited" is not quite the right word. It was appropriate for r_G, insofar as r_G was hypothetically a classically conditioned respondent. But the word implies a kind of causation that is not usually deemed appropriate for operant or instrumental behaviors. However, other words, for instance, "evoked," "engendered," "instigated," lack any consensus of usage, so we will use "elicited" with the understanding that it does not convey exactly what we mean.

bar pressing; but if the animal has learned to get excited or to attack the apparatus when the buzzer sounds, then it may get excited or attack the bar and show a large increase in bar pressing.

Consider the following results reported by Bolles (1961b). Rats were trained in a two-bar situation in which each bar paid off in food equally often—on the average every 15 seconds. The animals were trained until they were pressing approximately 50 percent of the time on each bar. However, they were trained under two different conditions. Under one condition the phasing of reinforcement on the two bars was adjusted so that receiving reinforcement on one bar made the next reinforcement more likely on the second bar. For the other group the situation was reversed so that perseverating on the same bar was more likely to produce the next reinforcement. In extinction animals in the second group gave the preponderance of their responses to the click-producing bar, while those in the first group gave the preponderance of their responses to the nonclick bar. When the two sets of results were averaged together, no overall preference was found for the click; the click in no sense served in lieu of food to maintain behavior. What the results suggest is that the effect of the click, indeed, the effect of any secondary reinforcer, is to instruct the animal what to do next, specifically, how to obtain the next piece of food. It serves to identify where the animal is in a chain of behavior and to specify what the next link should be. Such results, like those of White (1953), Miles (1956), and Hulicka and Capeheart (1960), suggest that when the response-eliciting properties of the secondary reinforcer have been fully accounted for, there may be nothing left for a hypothetical reinforcing property to explain.

In one study (Ratner, 1956) approaching the food cup (or water dipper) was extinguished prior to testing for the reinforcing effects of the click. In other studies (Ratner, 1956a; Morrow et al., 1965), although no explicit extinction was given, the goal-approach response was found to extinguish during testing. In either case it would be expected that as the click lost the ability to elicit approaching the goal, it would lose the ability to reinforce the new bar-press response. The writers argued against a discriminative control interpretation, but in both cases only small, transient effects were found. The studies do not constitute a test of the hypothesis because in none of them is it clear that approaching the goal, or any other response, had come under strong discriminative control of the click.

Nakamura et al. (1963) showed in another way the importance of attaching a vigorous approach response to a stimulus that is to become a secondary reinforcer. They ran pairs of rats in a competitive situation in which, upon presentation of the stimulus, only the animal that ran faster to the food received any food. After this differential reinforcement of vigorous running the cue for such running was found to be a relatively durable discriminative stimulus.

An important question about the elicitation hypothesis is

whether the response elicited during the test of a secondary reinforcer must be the same response the stimulus elicited when it was being established as a secondary reinforcer. Keehn (1962) seems to have shown that it must be the same. Subjects required to make a new response to a secondary reinforcer failed to show acquisition of a new response that produced it, whereas subjects that could make the old response to the secondary reinforcer did show acquisition. This not only provides an ingenious confirmation of the elicitation hypothesis, it also shows that secondary reinforcers are not autonomous; we cannot consider the secondary reinforcer as the end point of a segment of behavior, we must also consider the following response.

The elicitation hypothesis looks rather attractive at this point. Like the other hypotheses that were discussed previously, it seems to come close to getting at the central issue in secondary reinforcement. But like them, it is not entirely satisfactory. The essence of the thing still eludes us.

The information hypothesis. Miller (1963) has proposed a hypothesis of secondary reinforcement that is like the discriminative-stimulus and elicitation hypotheses in some respects but that emphasizes a slightly different aspect of the situation and leads to a much less mechanistic view of secondary reinforcement. According to Miller, a primary reinforcer ordinarily follows a series of other stimulus events. The question he raises is whether all of the stimuli preceding primary reinforcement have secondary reinforcing powers or whether this is reserved just for those that have some special function. Miller suggests that there is a special function involved, namely, the informational value of the stimulus. There is ordinarily considerable redundancy in the sequence of stimuli arising from seeing food, approaching it, having food in the mouth, swallowing it, and so on. There is no new information, no gain in predictive power, in these subsequent stimuli; once the animal sees the food, primary reinforcement (whatever its ultimate basis) will follow. The sight of food in this case is the last information-conveying stimulus, and as such it is the reinforcer for prior instrumental responses. We might change the information value of seeing food by means of a fistula procedure, in which case we ought to find, as Hull et al. (1951) found, that seeing food and even the stimuli arising from food in the mouth lose their reinforcing effect. In other words, Miller is saying that the last informative or nonredundant stimulus preceding primary reinforcement acquires secondary reinforcing powers; subsequent stimuli have no reinforcing power because they convey no new information. Note that this hypothesis makes sense out of the findings of Schoenfeld et al. that stimuli concurrent with eating fail to acquire secondary reinforcing powers; they are redundant.

Egger and Miller (1962) tested the informational hypothesis. Basically, what they did was to train two groups of rats to press a bar for food; extinguish this response (in order to get rid of some of the variability found in the resistance to extinction measure); and then test the resistance to extinction in a second session in which pressing the bar produced a stimulus, S_2, that had been associated in various ways with reinforcement during training. For both groups, S_2 had been regularly presented 1.5 seconds prior to reinforcement, so it was technically a discriminative stimulus. But for one group it had been redundant, because it had been regularly preceded by another stimulus, S_1. For the second group S_2 had also been preceded by S_1, but in this case S_1 was not itself a good predictor of food because it had also been presented alone. Thus for the one group S_2 was a reliable but uninformative predictor of food, while for the second group S_2 was both reliable and informative. The opposite relationship held for S_1; that is, in the first group S_1 was informative and in the second group it was not. When the groups were tested by making either S_1 or S_2 contingent upon bar pressing, it was found that in both cases the informative condition produced more responding. The first group worked more for S_1, and the second group worked more for S_2. This interaction was highly reliable. Unfortunately, we cannot tell whether the uninformative stimulus in each case had any secondary reinforcing value, nor do we know if the same result would have been obtained using other measures of secondary reinforcement, such as the acquisition of new behavior. But the results indicate that, other things being equal, the more informative of two stimuli better sustains behavior as a secondary reinforcer.

In a second study (Egger & Miller, 1963) the nature of the cues was different, but the concept was the same. The animals received three food pellets from time to time, which were signaled for one group by a single pellet and a light or tone cue. The cue here was redundant because the single pellet preceded it. In a second group the cue was not preceded by a food pellet, so that it was informative about the three pellets. In a third group the cue was informative about food even though it was preceded by a food pellet because single pellets were given at other times not followed by the cue and not followed by more food. Finally, there was a group to control for pseudoconditioning in which pellets and cues were presented but uncorrelated in time. The results came out as in the first experiment; that is, when the cue was made contingent upon bar pressing during extinction, there was more responding for it by the group for which it was informative. The loss of information or the introduction of redundancy in the experimental conditions produced a loss of secondary reinforcing effect.

Egger and Miller's work has generated much discussion, and some research. The basic paradigm, but with various parametric changes, has been used by McCausland et al. (1967) and Thomas et al. (1968), and both studies support the information hypothesis.

However, McCausland et al. report that this confirmation requires there to be neither too few nor too many training trials. McKeever and Forrin (1966) attempted to test the information hypothesis against the contiguity hypothesis in a spatial discrimination situation. Animals were initially trained on a black-white discrimination. For two groups the correct response was approaching white to get to a black goal box or approaching black to get to a white goal box. When this discrimination had been learned, all animals were then retrained on a position habit in which one side was gray and the other side was black or white; there was no food in the second situation, only the boxes that had been approached (i.e., informative) in the prior training or that had been contiguous with the reward in the prior training. McKeever and Forrin found that under the various conditions all animals showed about the same preference for black and white. There was no indication that the informative cue was any more reinforcing than the contiguous cue. Actually, there was little indication of secondary reinforcement in any group, since no learning curves were presented. (None of these studies shows new response acquisition.) But if the preference can be attributed to secondary reinforcement, then it was influenced by contiguity as much as by the prediction of reinforcement. One problem with the design of this study, pointed out by Seligman (1966a), is that all of the white and black boxes may have been redundant, since the important predictor of food may have been visible to the animals in the start box.

There have also been applications of the Egger and Miller hypothesis to the aversive case. Seligman (1966) asked whether a cue that is informative about shock will be more punishing when made contingent upon a response than a cue that is a reliable but redundant predictor of shock. He found that the more predictive cue appeared to produce somewhat more suppression, but, on the other hand, even the unreliable or redundant predictor of shock produced appreciable suppression. He concluded, therefore, that a predictor of shock is effective partly because it conveys information about shock and partly simply because it is contiguous with shock. Ayres (1966) posed the same question in a conditioned-suppression situation and found that contiguity was the all-important factor. Redundant predictors of shock produced just as much suppression as informative ones.

Long before the recent interest in the informational property of cues had developed, Wyckoff (1952) reported a highly innovative experiment that was based on a similar view of secondary reinforcement. Wyckoff trained pigeons on a mixed schedule in which one component was an FI-30 and the other component was extinction. The two components were presented in random order with no signals to indicate which component was in effect at a given time. While the animals were pecking a key for food on this schedule, they also demonstrated learning of a different response, stepping on a treadle, which had the effect of momentarily converting the mixed schedule into a multiple schedule. That is, responding on the treadle produced key lights that signaled which component was operative at the moment, red for the FI component and green for extinction. The treadle response had no effect on delivery of food; all it did, presumably, was to present discriminative stimuli for pecking the key. Wyckoff ran control procedures that showed that if the red and green key lights were not correlated with the components of the schedule, that is, with the food payoff, then responding dropped out. In short, Wyckoff's animals learned a new response in order to convert a mixed schedule to a multiple schedule, that is, to add discriminative stimuli to the schedule. Wyckoff called this new response an observing response, since it produced information about reinforcement without affecting reinforcement itself. Information about primary reinforcement, he suggested (Wyckoff, 1959), is what comprises secondary reinforcement.

Variations of Wyckoff's procedure have generally produced comparable results (Prokasy, 1956; Bower et al., 1966). In both of these studies animals were required to respond in one of two ways, both of which produced food on the same partial-reinforcement schedule, but one of which provided information as to whether food would be available on that trial. With this type of procedure information about reinforcement was found to be reinforcing, since the animal's choice between the two equally good options was evidently determined by the fact that information plus food was preferred over food alone. This result can be contrasted with that reported by Schuster (1969), who found that pigeons showed no preference for food plus a cue contiguous with food over food alone.

Wyckoff's original experiment has been subjected to critical examination by Hirota (1972). Hirota asked whether the treadle response was maintained by the aversiveness of the neutral key (when Wyckoff's key was not displaying the red and green cues, it was white), the information value of the positive cue, the information value of both cues, or some other aspect of the situation. Hirota found, much to the distress of information theorists, that the observing response was not independent of the key-pecking response. His animals apparently found it more convenient to peck the key while standing on the treadle. He found, in effect, that when the rate of key pecking was partialed out of the treadle response rate, no correlation remained between standing on the treadle and the consequent key colors. Evidently the Wyckoff experiment requires further careful examination.

Wilton and Clement (1971) have reported results with a somewhat improved version of the Wyckoff experiment. In their procedure food was presented independently of the animal's behavior 50 seconds after the start of the trial. The animal could only wait

for its noncontingent food; superstitious pecking was actually discouraged by a 5-second hold; that is, the delivery of food was delayed
for 5 seconds after the last response. Noncontingent food was presented on half the trials, and on the other half there was a time-out,
which took the animal into the next trial. During all this, the animal
could, of course, peck the key. If it did so 15 seconds after the start
of the trial, the key was converted either to red or to green. Under
correlated conditions the red and green meant food and no food on
that particular trial. Under uncorrelated conditions the occurrence
of food was not correlated with the key light. Under the uncorrelated
condition the rate of key pecking dropped, not to zero, but to a low
rate (the persistence of behavior suggests that there was still adven-
titious reinforcement even with the 5-second hold). Under the
informative, or correlated-key, condition, there was a high rate of
responding in the first 15 seconds of the trial. We do not know what
happened after 15 seconds, but in a similar study Hendry and Coulbourn (1967) found a high rate of pecking almost all the time.[11]

In a further study Wilton and Clement (1971a) varied the
probability that food would be presented on a given trial. Their argument was that if food occurs on most trials, then the cue signaling
food is relatively uninformative compared, say, to the condition in
which food occurs on only 20 percent of the trials, and there should
be correspondingly less responding on the white key to produce the
cue. In his theoretical summary of these studies Wilton (1972) was
able to make a good case that it is the information about reinforcement that governs the extent to which the animal will work for this
information. Dinsmoor et al. (1969) have raised the interesting question of whether all information is reinforcing, that is, bad news as
well as good news. They conclude that, in spite of some evidence to
the contrary, no news is preferable to bad news.

The Sign-Post Hypothesis. The information hypothesis, as just
described, is provocative, is in keeping with the changing thought of
the times, and carries a variety of cognitive implications. But, at the
same time, it does not seem to provide exactly the interpretation of
secondary reinforcement that we need. This is apparent in the fact

---

[11] One aspect of the behavior in this situation that has not been
examined is the extent to which the differential cues lead to differential
behavior. It is conceivable that the animal is simply displaying a chain in
which pressing the treadle leads to a discriminative stimulus in the presence of which it pecks and is reinforced. The animal may not be choosing
between information and no information, but rather running off a chain
of responses, all of which are reinforced by the occurrence of food at the
end of the chain. That is, we do not know to what extent the observing
response is concurrent behavior and to what extent it is part of a chain of
behavior. Similarly, we do not know, when the light is on the key itself,
if it is properly regarded as information about reinforcement or as a discriminative cue for responding for reinforcement.

that the results of the information experiments have not been consistent among themselves. In many cases the results have been rather weak and are subject to alternative interpretations. The question is whether there is some aspect of the secondary reinforcing stimulus, which is similar to the information concept, that can do a better job of ordering the diverse findings that have been considered.

One possibility was suggested by Wolfe (1936). Recall he had suggested that the token reward might acquire intrinsic value. But he also suggested that the token might be a sign or signal of something else to come; it might be an instrument or a means to an end. We have seen that apart from some unsystematic observations in Wolfe's original report there has been no data to indicate that the secondary reinforcer is a thing that has value in and of itself, that it can serve to strengthen behavior *in lieu of* primary reinforcement.[12] The other possibility suggested by Wolfe has been largely ignored, but the evidence is remarkably consistent with it. The idea is that what we call a secondary reinforcer is a means to an end, or a sign-post for primary reinforcement. The clearest evidence for this argument is the ease with which a chain of behavior can be built, as long as the food is at the end of the chain, and the contrasting difficulty of sustaining any kind of behavior, particularly in developing new behavior, when the terminal reinforcer is removed. When the cue for food is no longer a cue for food or a sign post or a means to an end, it is very difficult to reinforce behavior with it.

What we may call the sign-post theory has been recently revitalized by Longstreth (1971). He presents the case for this interpretation with the following loose but dramatic example.

> Johnny comes in promptly from play when called by his mother, washes his hands, sits down quietly at the dinner table, and exhibits good manners and proper etiquette throughout the meal. Occasionally his mother or father indicates approval with a smile, a verbalization such as "good," and otherwise exhibits signs of social approval. Suppose a psychologist has been invited to dinner. The question occurs to him, why is this child so well-behaved? If he is of the S[r] [secondary reinforcement] persuasion, he would probably reason that social approval, having been paired with established reinforcers many times in the child's past, and now presented systematically after episodes of good behavior, secondarily reinforces such behavior and maintains it at a high level of frequency.
>
> We say no. The reason Johnny behaved so well was because he had a plan. The plan was that he intended to ask his

[12] Recall that it was this in-lieu-of function that originally inspired Tolman and other early behavior theorists to talk about acquired drives and secondary reinforcers. But the research that has been discussed in this chapter, starting with Skinner's (1938) report of extinction when bar pressing produced only the click, reveals no case in which a stimulus used in lieu of primary reinforcement substantially reinforces new responses.

parents if he could stay up late and watch a special program on TV. His strategy was that, if his parents were in a "good mood" after dinner, they would be much more likely to grant his request. He therefore behaved in a way calculated to instill the good mood. Social approval from his parents was merely an index of mood state; the greater the frequency of social approval, the better their mood. Thus he behaved in such a way as to maximize the frequency of social approval from his parents. [p. 56]

We can see from the illustration of little Johnny's behavior that the sign-post aspect of a cue must necessarily be highly correlated with other aspects that have been emphasized in previous interpretations of secondary reinforcement. Secondary reinforcement by social approval has clear information value because it has in the past been a predictor of different kinds of permission. Social approval is also evidently a discriminative stimulus for continuing whatever behavior Johnny is engaged in, just as withdrawal of approval would be a cue for altering his ongoing behavior. It is also apparent that social approval has elicitation properties. If we observe it in isolation at any one time, we see that it helps to maintain ongoing behavior, and there should be little question that it could also serve to produce the learning of innovative behaviors on Johnny's part, as long as approval is what he is looking for. But even though these different behavioral properties of approval can be identified in this situation, they should not obscure the fact that the essence of what little Johnny is doing is using approval as a sign-post, as a means to an end.

One final experiment: Albert and Mah (1972) placed satiated rats in a box where they could investigate a small chamber containing a water spout (the animals had a history of drinking from such a spout). The next day the spout was removed, and the animals were made thirsty and returned to the test box. It was found that they spent a large part of their time investigating the chamber that had contained the spout. The possibility that the spout had intrinsic interest was controlled by the use of other metal objects and by the use of sated control animals. How else can these results be interpreted except by saying that the thirsty rats were looking for the water spout? And how else are we to explain the strengthened behavior in this situation, except by saying that the water spout was a sign-post, a means to a desired end?

REFERENCES

Where two dates are given, the first is the date of original publication, and this is the date cited in the text. The second date, given at the end, is the date of the English translation or of the particular edition that has been quoted.

Abrams, R., & Hammel, H. T. (1964) Hypothalamic temperature in unanesthetized albino rats during feeding and sleeping. *Amer. J. Physiol.*, 206: 641–646.

Ach, N. (1905) *Ueber die Willenstaetigheit und das Denken.* Goettingen: Vandenhoeck und Ruprecht.

Adelman, H. M., & Maatsch, J. L. (1955) Resistance to extinction as a function of the type of response elicited by shock. *J. exp. Psychol.*, 50: 61–65.

Adler, N. T. (1969) Effects of the male's copulatory behavior on successful pregnancy of the female rat. *J. comp. physiol. Psychol.*, 69: 613–622.

Adler, N. T., & Bermant, G. (1966) Sexual behavior of male rats: Effects of reduced sensory feedback. *J. comp. physiol. Psychol.*, 61: 240–243.

Adler, N. T., & Zoloth, S. R. (1970) Copulatory behavior can inhibit pregnancy in female rats. *Science*, 168: 1480–1482.

Adlerstein, A., & Fehrer, E. (1955) The effect of food deprivation on exploratory behavior in a complex maze. *J. comp. physiol. Psychol.*, 48: 250–254.

Adolph, E. F. (1939) Measurements of water drinking in dogs. *Amer. J. Physiol.*, 125: 75–86.

Adolph, E. F. (1943) *Physiological regulations.* Tempe, Ariz.: J. Cattell.

Adolph, E. F. (1947) Urges to eat and drink in rats. *Amer. J. Physiol.*, 151: 110–125.

Adolph, E. F. (1947a) *Physiology of man in the desert.* New York: Wiley.

Adolph, E. F. (1950) Thirst and its inhibition in the stomach. *Amer. J. Physiol.*, 161: 374–386.

Adolph, E. F. (1964) Regulation of body water content through water ingestion. In M. J. Wayner (Ed.), *Thirst.* Elmsford, N.Y.: Pergamon.

Adolph, E. F., Barker, J. F., & Hoy, P. A. (1954) Multiple factors in thirst. *Amer. J. Physiol.*, 178: 538–562.

Albert, D. J., & Mah, C. J. (1972) An examination of conditioned reinforcement using a one-trial learning procedure. *Learn. Motiv.*, 3: 369–388.

Allison, J. (1964) Strength of preference for food, magnitude of food reward, and performance in instrumental conditioning. *J. comp. physiol. Psychol.*, 57: 217–223.

Allison, J. (1971) Microbehavioral features of nutritive and nonnutritive drinking in rats. *J. comp. physiol. Psychol.*, 76: 408–417.

Allison, J., Larson, D., & Jensen, D. D. (1967) Acquired fear, brightness preference, and one-way shuttle box performance. *Psychon. Sci.*, 8: 269–270.

Allison, J., & Rocha, S. M. (1965) Time spent with food and nonfood incentives as a function of food deprivation. *Psychon. Sci.*, 2: 63–64.

Allport, G. W. (1937) Functional autonomy of motives. *Amer. J. Psychol.*, 50: 141–156.

Allport, G. W. (1937a) *Personality: A psychological interpretation.* New York: Holt, Rinehart & Winston.

Allport, G. W. (1943) The ego in contemporary psychology. *Psychol. Rev.*, 50: 451–476.

Allport, G. W. (1947) Scientific models and human morals. *Psychol. Rev.*, 54: 182–192.

Almli, C. R. (1970) Hyperosmolarity accompanies hypovolemia: A simple explanation of additivity of stimuli for drinking. *Physiol. Behav.*, 5: 1021–1028.

Almli, C. R. (1971) Hypervolemia at the polyethylene glycol induced onset of drinking. *Physiol. Behav.*, 7: 369–373.

Amsel, A. (1949) Selective association and the anticipatory goal response mechanism as explanatory concepts in learning theory. *J. exp. Psychol.*, 39: 785–799.

Amsel, A. (1950) The combination of a primary appetitional need with primary and secondary emotionally derived needs. *J. exp. Psychol.*, 40: 1–14.

Amsel, A. (1958) The role of frustrative nonreward in noncontinuous situations. *Psychol. Bull.*, 55: 102–119.

Amsel, A. (1962) Frustrative nonreward in partial reinforcement and discrimination learning: Some recent history and a theoretical extension. *Psychol. Rev.*, 69: 306–328.

Amsel, A. (1967) Partial reinforcement effects on vigor and persistence: Advances in frustration theory derived from a variety of within-subjects experiments. In K. W. Spence and J. T. Spence (Eds.), *The psychology of learning and motivation, I.* New York: Academic.

Amsel, A., & Cole, K. F. (1953) Generalization of fear motivated interference with water intake. *J. exp. Psychol.*, 46: 243–247.

Amsel, A., & Hancock, W. (1957) Motivational properties of frustration: III. Relation of frustration effect to antedating goal factors. *J. exp. Psychol.*, 53: 126–131.

Amsel, A., Hug, J., & Surridge, C. (1968) Goal approaches and the partial reinforcement effect after minimal acquisition. *J. exp. Psychol.*, 77: 530–534.

Amsel, A., & Maltzman, I. (1950) The effect upon generalized drive strength of emotionality as inferred from the level of consummatory response. *J. exp. Psychol.*, 40: 563–569.

Amsel, A., & Roussel, J. (1952) Motivational properties of frustration: I. Effect of a running response of the addition of frustration to the motivational complex. *J. exp. Psychol.*, 43: 363–368.

Amsel, A., & Work, M. S. (1961) The role of learned factors in "spontaneous" activity. *J. comp. physiol. Psychol.*, 54: 527–532.

Amsel, A., Work, M. S., & Penick, E. C. (1962) Activity during and between periods of stimulus change related to feeding. *J. comp. physiol. Psychol.*, 55: 1114–1117.

Anand, B. K., & Brobeck, J. R. (1951) Localization of a "feeding center" in the hypothalamus of the rat. *Proc. Soc. exp. Biol. Med.*, 77: 323–324.

Anderson, E. E. (1941) Externalization of drive: I. Theoretical considerations. *Psychol. Rev.*, 48: 204–224.

Anderson, E. E. (1941a) Externalization of drive: II. Maze learning by non-rewarded and by satiated rats. *J. genet. Psychol.*, 59: 397–426.

Anderson, E. E. (1941b) Externalization of drive: IV. The effect of prefeeding on the maze performance of hungry non-rewarded rats. *J. comp. physiol. Psychol.*, 31: 349–352.

Anderson, N. H., & Nakamura, C. Y. (1964) Avoidance decrement in avoidance conditioning. *J. comp. physiol. Psychol.*, 57: 196–204.

Andersson, B. (1951) The effect and localization of electrical stimulation of certains parts of the brain stem in sheep and goats. *Acta Physiol. Scand.*, 23: 1–16.

Andersson, B. (1953) The effects of injections of hypertonic NaCl-solutions into different parts of the hypothalamus of goats. *Acta Physiol. Scand.*, 28: 188–201.

Andersson, B., & Larsson, S. (1956) An attempt to condition hypothalamic polydipsia. *Acta physiol. Scand.*, 36: 377–382.

Andrew, R. J. (1956) Normal and irrelevant toilet behavior in *Emberiza spp. Brit. J. anim. Behav.*, 4: 85–91.

Anger, D. (1963) The role of temporal discrimination in the reinforcement of Sidman avoidance behavior. *J. exp. anal. Behav.*, 6: 477–506.

Angermeier, W. F., Locke, D., & Harris, A. (1964) Direct stomach feeding in the pigeon. *Psychol. Rep.*, 15: 771–774.

Appel, J. B. (1963) Punishment and shock intensity. *Science*, 141: 528–529.

Armstrong, E. A. (1947) *Bird display and behaviour*. London: Cambridge University Press.

Armstrong, E. A. (1950) The nature and function of displacement activities. *Symp. Soc. exp. Biol.*, 4: 361–386.

Armus, H. L. (1958) Drive level and habit reversal. *Psychol. Rep.*, 4: 31–34.

Arnold, M. (Ed.) (1970) *Feelings and emotions*. New York: Academic.

Atkinson, J. W. (1964) *An introduction to motivation*. New York: Van Nostrand Reinhold.

Ayres, C. E. (1921) Instinct and capacity: I. The instinct of belief-in instincts. *J. Philos.*, 18: 561–566.

Ayres, J. J. B. (1966) Conditioned suppression and the information hypothesis. *J. comp. physiol. Psychol.*, 62: 21–25.

Azrin, N. H. (1956) Some effects of two intermittent schedules of immediate and non-immediate punishment. *J. Psychol.*, 42: 3–21.

Azrin, N. H. (1959) Punishment and recovery during fixed-ratio performance. *J. exp. anal. Behav.*, 2: 301–305.

Azrin, N. H. (1960) Effects of punishment intensity during variable-interval reinforcement. *J. exp. anal. Behav.*, 3: 123–142.

Azrin, N. H., & Holz, W. C. (1966) Punishment. In W. K. Honig (Ed.), *Operant behavior: Areas of research and application.* New York: Academic.

Babb, H. (1963) Transfer between habits based upon shock and thirst. *J. comp. physiol. Psychol.,* 56: 318–323.

Babb, H., Bulgatz, M. G., & Matthews, L. J. (1969) Transfer from shock-escape to thirst- or hunger-motivated responding. *J. comp. physiol. Psychol.,* 67: 129–133.

Babb, H., & Hom, H. L., Jr. (1971) Self-punitive responding by goal-shocked rats. *J. comp. physiol. Psychol.,* 77: 482–488.

Badia, P., & Culbertson, S. (1972) The relative aversiveness of signalled vs unsignalled escapable and inescapable shock. *J. exp. anal. Behav.,* 17: 463–471.

Badia, P., McBane, B., Suter, S., & Lewis, P. (1966) Preference behavior in an immediate vs variably delayed shock situation with and without a warning signal. *J. exp. Psychol.,* 72: 847–852.

Bailey, C. (1928) *The Greek atomists and Epicurus.* Oxford: Clarendon.

Bailey, C. J. (1955) The effectiveness of drives as cues. *J. comp. physiol. Psychol.,* 48: 183–187.

Bailey, C. J., & Porter, L. W. (1955) Relevant cues in drive discrimination in cats. *J. comp. physiol. Psychol.,* 48: 180–182.

Bain, A. (1864) *The senses and the intellect,* 2nd ed.

Baker, R. A. (1950) Establishment of a nonpositional drive discrimination. *J. comp. physiol. Psychol.,* 43: 409–415.

Baker, R. A. (1953) Aperiodic feeding behavior in the albino rat. *J. comp. physiol. Psychol.,* 46: 422–426.

Baker, R. A. (1955) The effects of repeated deprivation experience on feeding behavior. *J. comp. physiol. Psychol.,* 48: 37–42.

Balagura, S. (1968) Influence of osmotic and caloric loads upon lateral hypothalamic self-stimulation. *J. comp. physiol. Psychol.,* 66: 325–328.

Baldwin, J. M. (1913) *History of psychology.* New York: Putnam.

Ball, G. G., & Adams, D. W. (1965) Intracranial stimulation as an avoidance or escape response. *Psychon. Sci.,* 3: 39–40.

Ball, J. (1926) The female sex cycle as a factor in learning in the rat. *Amer. J. Physiol.,* 78: 533–536.

Barclay, J. R. (1959) Franz Brentano and Sigmund Freud. Ph.D. dissertation, University of Michigan.

Bard, P. (1935) The effects of denervation of the genitalia on the oestrual behavior of cats. *Amer. J. Physiol.,* 113: 5.

Bard, P. (1936) Oestrual behavior in surviving decorticate cats. *Amer. J. Physiol.,* 116: 4–5.

Bard, P. (1939) Central nervous mechanisms for emotional behavior patterns in animals. *Res. Publ. Ass. nerv. ment. Dis.,* 19: 190–218.

Bard, P. (1940) The hypothalamus and sexual behavior. *Res. Publ. Ass. nerv. ment. Dis.,* 20: 551–579.

Bare, J. K. (1959) Hunger, deprivation, and the day-night cycle. *J. comp. physiol. Psychol.,* 52: 129–131.

Bare, J. K., & Cicala, G. (1960) Deprivation and time of testing as determinants of food intake. *J. comp. physiol. Psychol.,* 53: 151–154.

Barfield, R. J., & Geyer, L. A. (1972) Sexual behavior: Ultrasonic post-ejaculatory song of the male rat. *Science,* 76: 1349–1350.

Barlow, J. A. (1952) Secondary motivation through classical conditioning:

One trial nonmotor learning in the white rat. *Amer. Psychologist*, 7: 273.

Baron, A. (1964) Suppression of exploratory behavior by aversive stimulation. *J. comp. physiol. Psychol.*, 57: 299–301.

Baron, A. (1965) Delayed punishment of a runway response. *J. comp. physiol. Psychol.*, 60: 131–134.

Barrett, R. J., Peyser, C. S., & McHose, J. H. (1965) Effects of complete and incomplete reward reduction on a subsequent response. *Psychon. Sci.*, 3: 277–278.

Barry, H., III (1958) Effects of strength of drive on learning and on extinction. *J. exp. Psychol.*, 55: 473–481.

Barry, H. (1967) Effects of drive strength on extinction and spontaneous recovery. *J. exp. Psychol.*, 73: 419–421.

Bartoshuk, A. K. (1971) Motivation. In J. W. Kling and L. A. Riggs (Eds.), *Experimental psychology*. New York: Holt, Rinehart & Winston.

Bash, K. W. (1939) An investigation into a possible organic basis for the hunger drive. *J. comp. Psychol.*, 28: 109–134.

Bastock, M. (1967) *Courtship*. Chicago: Aldine.

Bateson, P. P. G. (1966) The characteristics and context of imprinting. *Biol. Rev.*, 41: 177–220.

Bauer, F. J., & Lawrence, D. H. (1953) Influence of similarity of choice-point and goal cues on discrimination learning. *J. comp. physiol. Psychol.*, 46: 241–248.

Baum, M. (1965) An automatic apparatus for the avoidance training of rats. *Psychol. Rep.*, 16: 1205–1211.

Baumeister, A., Hawkins, W. F., & Cromwell, R. L. (1964) Need state and activity level. *Psychol. Bull.*, 61: 438–453.

Bayer, E. (1929) Beitraege zur Zweikomponententheorie des Hungres. *Z. Psychol.*, 112: 1–54.

Beach, F. A. (1942) Analysis of factors involved in the arousal, maintenance and manifestation of sexual excitement in male animals. *Psychosom. Med.*, 4:173–198.

Beach, F. A. (1942a) Analysis of the stimuli adequate to elicit mating behavior in the sexually-inexperienced male rat. *J. comp. Psychol.*, 33: 163–207.

Beach, F. A. (1947) A review of physiological and psychological studies of sexual behavior in mammals. *Physiol. Rev.*, 27: 240–307.

Beach, F. A. (1948) *Hormones and behavior*. New York: Harper & Row.

Beach, F. A. (1956) Characteristics of masculine "sex drive." In M. R. Jones (Ed.), *Nebraska symposium on motivation*. Lincoln, Neb.: University of Nebraska Press.

Beach, F. A. (1958) Neural and chemical regulation of behavior. In H. F. Harlow and C. N. Woolsey (Eds.), *Biological and biochemical bases of behavior*. Madison, Wis.: University of Wisconsin Press.

Beach, F. A. (1965) (Ed.), *Sex and behavior*. New York: Wiley.

Beach, F. A. (1970) Coital behavior in dogs. VI. Long-term effects of castration upon mating in the male. *J. comp. physiol. Psychol. Monogr.*, 70: 1–32.

Beach, F. A., & Fowler, H. (1959) Individual differences in the response of male rats to androgen. *J. comp. physiol. Psychol.*, 52: 50–52.

Beach, F. A., & Jordan, L. (1956) Sexual exhaustion and recovery in the male rat. *Quart. J. exp. Psychol.*, 8: 121–133.

Beach, F. A., & Jordan, L. (1956a) Effects of sexual reinforcement upon the performance of male rats in a straight runway. *J. comp. physiol. Psychol.*, 49: 105–110.

Beach, F. A., & Ransom, T. W. (1967) Effects of environmental variation on ejaculatory frequency in male rats. *J. comp. physiol. Psychol.*, 64: 384–387.

Beaton, R. D. (1969) Blood pH as a possible hunger cue: Negative evidence. *Psychon. Sci.*, 15: 247–248.

Bechterev, V. M. (1904) *La psychologie objective.* Paris: Alcan, 1913.

Beck, R. C. (1961) On secondary reinforcement and shock termination. *Psychol. Bull.*, 58: 28–45.

Beck, R. C. (1962) The rat's adaptation to a 23.5-hour water-deprivation schedule. *J. comp. physiol. Psychol.*, 55: 646–648.

Beck, R. C. (1964) Some effects of restricted water intake on consummatory behavior in the rat. In M. J. Wayner (Ed.), *Thirst.* Elmsford, N.Y.: Pergamon.

Beck, R. C., & Horne, M. (1964) Some effects of two thirst-control procedures on eating, drinking, and body weight of the rat. *J. gen. Psychol.*, 71: 93–101.

Bedford, J., & Anger, D. (1968) Flight as an avoidance response in pigeons. Paper presented at Psychonomic Society, St. Louis, 1968.

Beebe-Center, J. G. (1951) Feeling and emotion. In H. Nelson (Ed.), *Theoretical foundations of psychology.* New York: Van Nostrand Reinhold.

Beecroft, R. S., & Brown, J. S. (1967) Punishment following escape and avoidance training. *Psychon. Sci.*, 8: 349–350.

Beer, B., & Trumble, G. (1965) Timing behavior as a function of amount of reinforcement. *Psychon. Sci.*, 2: 71–72.

Beer, C. G., (1963–1964) Ethology—the zoologist's approach to behaviour. *Tuatara*, 11: 170–177; 12: 16–39. Reprinted in P. H. Klopfer and J. P. Hailman (Eds.), *Control and development of behavior.* Reading, Mass.: Addison-Wesley.

Beery, R. G. (1968) A negative contrast effect of reward delay in differential conditioning. *J. exp. Psychol.*, 77: 429–434.

Bellows, R. T. (1939) Time factors in water drinking in dogs. *Amer. J. Physiol.*, 125: 87–97.

Bender, L. (1969) Secondary punishment and self-punitive avoidance behavior in the rat. *J. comp. physiol. Psychol.*, 69: 261–266.

Benedict, J. O., & Ayres, J. J. B. (1972) Factors affecting conditioning in the truly random control procedure in the rat. *J. comp. physiol. Psychol.*, 78: 323–330.

Berkun, M. M., Kessen, M. L., & Miller, N. E. (1952) Hunger-reducing effects of food by stomach fistula versus food by mouth measured by a consummatory response. *J. comp. physiol. Psychol.*, 45: 550–554.

Berlyne, D. E. (1950) Novelty and curiosity as determinants of exploratory behavior. *Brit. J. Psychol.*, 41: 68–80.

Berlyne, D. E. (1960) *Conflict, arousal, and curiosity.* New York: McGraw-Hill.

Berlyne, D. E. (1963) Motivational problems raised by exploratory and epistemic behavior. In S. Koch (Ed.), *Psychology: A study of a science*, Vol. V. New York: McGraw-Hill.

Berlyne, D. E., & Slater, J. (1957) Perceptual curiosity, exploratory behavior, and maze learning. *J. comp. physiol. Psychol.*, 50: 228–232.

Bermant, G. (1961) Response latencies of female rats during sexual intercourse. *Science*, 133: 1771–1773.

Bermant, G. (1964) Effects of single and multiple enforced intercopulatory intervals on the sexual behavior of male rats. *J. comp. physiol. Psychol.*, 57: 398–403.

Bermant, G., & Davidson, J. M. (1974) *Biological bases of sexual behavior.* New York: Harper & Row.

Bermant, G., Lott, D. F., & Anderson, L. (1968) Temporal characteristics of the Coolidge effect in male rat copulatory behavior. *J. comp. physiol. Psychol.*, 65: 447–452.

Bermant, G., & Westbrook, W. H. (1966) Peripheral factors in the regulation of sexual contact by female rats. *J. comp. physiol. Psychol.*, 61: 244–250.

Bernard, C. (1878) *Lecons sur les phenomenes de la vie en communs aux animaux et aux vegetaux.*

Bernfeld, S. (1944) Freud's earliest theories and the school of Helmholtz. *Psychoanal. Quart.*, 13: 341–362.

Bersh, P. J. (1951) The influence of two variables upon the establishment of a secondary reinforcer for operant responses. *J. exp. Psychol.*, 41: 62–73.

Bersh, P. J., Notterman, J. M., & Schoenfeld, W. N. (1956) Extinction of a human cardiac-response during avoidance-conditioning. *Amer. J. Psychol.*, 69: 244–251.

Besch, N. F., Morris, H., & Levine, S. (1963) A comparison between correction and noncorrection methods in drive discrimination. *J. exp. Psychol.*, 65: 414–419.

Biederman, G. B., D'Amato, M. R., & Keller, D. M. (1964) Facilitation of discriminated avoidance learning by dissociation of CS and manipulandum. *Psychon. Sci.*, 1: 229–230.

Bindra, D. (1961) Components of general activity and the analysis of behavior. *Psychol. Rev.*, 68: 205–215.

Bindra, D. (1968) Neuropsychological interpretation of the effects of drive and incentive motivation on general activity and instrumental behavior. *Psychol. Rev.*, 75: 1–22.

Bindra, D. (1969) The interrelated mechanisms of reinforcement and motivation, and the nature of their influence on response. In W. J. Arnold and D. Levine (Eds.), *Nebraska symposium on motivation*. Lincoln, Neb.: University of Nebraska Press.

Bindra, D. (1972) A unified account of classical conditioning and operant training. In W. F. Prokasy and A. H. Black (Eds.), *Classical conditioning*. New York: Appleton.

Bindra, D., & Blond, J. (1958) A time-sample method for measuring general activity and its components. *Canad. J. Psychol.*, 12: 74–76.

Bindra, D., & Palfai, T. (1967) Nature of positive and negative incentive-motivational effects on general activity. *J. comp. physiol. Psychol.*, 69: 288–297.

Bing, F. C., & Mendel, L. B. (1931) The relationship between food and water intakes in mice. *Amer. J. Physiol.*, 98: 169–179.

Bintz, J., Kellicutt, M., & Peacock, K. (1970) Avoidance conditioning and movement-contingent US presentation. *J. comp. physiol. Psychol.*, 72: 250–256.

Birch, D. (1955) Discrimination as a function of the ratio of nonreinforced to reinforced trials. *J. comp. physiol. Psychol.*, 48: 371–374.

Birch, D., Burnstein, E., & Clark, R. A. (1958) Response strength as a function of hours of food deprivation under a controlled maintenance schedule. *J. comp. physiol. Psychol.*, 51: 350–354.

Bitterman, M. E., Fedderson, W. F., & Tyler, D. W. (1953) Secondary reinforcement and the discrimination hypothesis. *Amer. J. Psychol.*, 66: 456–464.

Bitterman, M. E., & Schoel, W. M. (1970) Instrumental learning in animals: Parameters of reinforcement. *Ann. Rev. Psychol.*, 21: 367–436.

Black, A. H. (1971) Autonomic aversive conditioning in infrahuman subjects. In F. R. Brush (Ed.), *Aversive conditioning and learning.* New York: Academic.

Black, R. W. (1965) On the combination of drive and incentive motivation. *Psychol. Rev.*, 72: 310–317.

Black, R. W. (1965a) Discrimination learning as a function of varying pairs of sucrose rewards. *J. exp. Psychol.*, 70: 452–458.

Blanchard, R. J., & Blanchard, D. C. (1968) Escape and avoidance responses to a fear eliciting situation. *Psychon. Sci.*, 13: 19–20.

Blanchard, R. J., & Blanchard, D. C. (1969) Crouching as an index of fear. *J. comp. physiol. Psychol.*, 67: 370–375.

Blass, E. M. (1968) Separation of cellular from extracellular controls of drinking in rats by frontal brain damage. *Science*, 162: 1501–1503.

Blass, E. M., & Fitzsimons, J. T. (1970) Additivity of effect and interaction of a cellular and an extracellular stimulus of drinking. *J. comp. physiol. Psychol.*, 70: 200–205.

Blodgett, H. C. (1929) The effect of the introduction of reward upon the maze performance of rats. *Univ. Calif. Publ. Psychol.*, 4: 113–134.

Bloomberg, R., & Webb, W. B. (1949) Various degrees within a single drive as cues for spatial response learning in the white rat. *J. exp. Psychol.*, 39: 628–636.

Bloomfield, T. M. (1972) Reinforcement schedules: Contingency or contiguity? In R. M. Gilbert and J. R. Millenson (Eds.), *Reinforcement, behavioral analyses.* New York: Academic.

Boe, E. E. (1966) Effect of punishment duration and intensity on the extinction of an instrumental response. *J. exp. Psychol.*, 72: 125–131.

Boe, E. E. (1971) Variable punishment. *J. comp. physiol. Psychol.*, 75: 73–76.

Boe, E. E. (1971a) Recovery from signalled shock as a function of response contingency in rats. *J. comp. physiol. Psychol.*, 77: 122–130.

Boe, E. E., & Church, R. M. (1967) Permanent effects of punishment during extinction. *J. comp. physiol. Psychol.*, 63: 486–492.

Boice, R. (1967) Lick rates and topographies as taxonomic criteria in Southwestern rodents. *Psychon. Sci.*, 9: 431–432.

Boice, R. (1971) Excessive water intake in captive Norway rats with scar-markings. *Physiol. Behav.*, 7: 723–725.

Bolles, R. C. (1958) A replication and further analysis of a study on position reversal learning in hungry and thirsty rats. *J. comp. physiol. Psychol.*, 51: 349.

Bolles, R. C. (1960) Grooming behavior in the rat. *J. comp. physiol. Psychol.*, 53: 306–310.

Bolles, R. C. (1961) The interaction of hunger and thirst in the rat. *J. comp. physiol. Psychol.*, 54: 580–584.

Bolles, R. C. (1961a) The generalization of deprivation-produced stimuli. *Psychol. Rep.*, 9: 623–626.

Bolles, R. C. (1961b) Is the "click" a token reward? *Psychol. Rec.*, 11: 163–168.

Bolles, R. C. (1962) The readiness to eat and drink: The effect of deprivation conditions. *J. comp. physiol. Psychol.*, 55: 230–234.

Bolles, R. C. (1962a) A psychophysical study of hunger in the rat. *J. exp. Psychol.*, 63: 387–390.

Bolles, R. C. (1963) Effect of food deprivation upon the rat's behavior in its homecage. *J. comp. physiol. Psychol.*, 56: 456–460.

Bolles, R. C. (1963a) Psychological determinism and the problem of morality. *J. sci. study Relig.*, 2: 182–189.

Bolles, R. C. (1965) Readiness to eat: Effects of age, sex, and weight loss. *J. comp. physiol. Psychol.*, 60: 88–92.

Bolles, R. C. (1965a) Consummatory behavior in rats maintained a-periodically. *J. comp. physiol. Psychol.*, 60: 239–243.

Bolles, R. C. (1967) *Theory of motivation.* New York: Harper & Row.

Bolles, R. C. (1968) Anticipatory general activity in thirsty rats. *J. comp. physiol. Psychol.*, 65: 511–513.

Bolles, R. C. (1969) Avoidance and escape learning: Simultaneous acquisition of different responses. *J. comp. physiol. Psychol.*, 68: 355–358.

Bolles, R. C. (1970) Species-specific defense reactions and avoidance learning. *Psychol. Rev.*, 71: 32–48.

Bolles, R. C. (1970a) The cue value of illumination change in anticipatory general activity. *Learn. Motiv.*, 1: 177–185.

Bolles, R. C. (1970b) Interactions with motivation. In M. H. Marx (Ed.), *Learning: Interactions.* London: Collier-Macmillan.

Bolles, R. C. (1971) Species-specific defense reactions. In F. R. Brush (Ed.), *Aversive conditioning and learning.* New York: Academic.

Bolles, R. C. (1972) Reinforcement, expectancy, and learning. *Psychol. Rev.*, 79: 394–409.

Bolles, R. C. (1972a) The avoidance learning problem. In G. H. Bower (Ed.), *The psychology of learning and motivation,* Vol. 6. New York: Academic.

Bolles, R. C., & de Lorge, J. (1962) Effect of hunger on exploration in a familiar locale. *Psychol. Rep.*, 10: 54.

Bolles, R. C., & de Lorge, J. (1962a) Exploration in a Dashiell maze as a function of prior deprivation, current deprivation, and sex. *Canad. J. Psychol.*, 16: 221–227.

Bolles, R. C., & de Lorge, J. (1962b) The rat's adjustment to a-diurnal feeding cycles. *J. comp. physiol. Psychol.*, 55: 760–762.

Bolles, R. C., & Duncan, P. M. (1969) Daily course of activity and subcutaneous body temperature in hungry and thirsty rats. *Physiol. & Behav.*, 4: 87–89.

Bolles, R. C., Duncan, P. M., Grossen, N. E., & Matter, C. F. (1968) Relationship between activity level and body temperature in the rat. *Psychol. Rep.*, 23: 991–994.

Bolles, R. C., & Grossen, N. E. (1969) Effects of an informational stimulus on the acquisition of avoidance behavior in rats. *J. comp. physiol. Psychol.*, 68: 90–99.

Bolles, R. C., Grossen, N. E., & Hargrave, G. E. (1969) The effects of an escape contingency upon running wheel and one-way avoidance learning. *Psychon. Sci.*, 16: 33–34.

Bolles, R. C., Grossen, N. E., Hargrave, G. E., & Duncan, P. M. (1970) Effects of conditioned appetitive stimuli on the acquisition and extinction of a runway response. *J. exp. Psychol.*, 85: 138–140.

Bolles, R. C., & McGillis, D. B. (1968) The non-operant nature of the bar-press escape response. *Psychon. Sci.*, 11: 261–262.

Bolles, R. C., & Moot, S. A. (1972) Derived motives. *Ann. Rev. Psychol.*, 23: 51–72.

Bolles, R. C., & Moot, S. A. (1973) The rat's anticipation of two meals a day. *J. comp. physiol. Psychol.*, 83: 510–514.

Bolles, R. C., Moot, S. A., & Grossen, N. E. (1971) The extinction of shuttlebox avoidance. *Learn. Motiv.*, 2: 324–333.

Bolles, R. C., & Morlock, H. (1960) Some asymmetrical drive summation phenomena. *Psychol. Rep.*, 6: 373–378.

Bolles, R. C., & Ogilvie, R. D. (1966) Effects of adiurnal lighting and feeding on the rat's diurnal activity cycle. *J. comp. physiol. Psychol.*, 62: 141–143.

Bolles, R., & Petrinovich, L. (1954) A technique for obtaining rapid drive discrimination in the rat. *J. comp. physiol. Psychol.*, 47: 378–380.

Bolles, R., & Petrinovich, L. (1956) Body weight changes and behavioral attributes. *J. comp. physiol. Psychol.*, 49: 177–180.

Bolles, R. C., & Popp, R. J. (1964) Parameters affecting the acquisition of Sidman avoidance. *J. exp. anal. Behav.*, 7: 315–321.

Bolles, R. C., & Rapp, H. M. (1965) Readiness to eat and drink: Effect of stimulus conditions. *J. comp. physiol. Psychol.*, 60: 93–97.

Bolles, R. C., Rapp, H. M., & White, G. C. (1968a) Failure of sexual activity to reinforce female rats. *J. comp. physiol. Psychol.*, 65: 311–313.

Bolles, R. C., & Riley, A. L. (1973) Freezing as an avoidance response: Another look at the operant-respondent distinction. *Learn. Motiv.*, 4: 268–275.

Bolles, R. C., & Sanders, G. H. (1969) What does the ultrasonic activity recording device measure? *Behav. Res. Meth. & Instru.*, 1: 180–182.

Bolles, R. C., & Seelbach, S. E. (1964) Punishing and reinforcing effects of noise onset and termination for different responses. *J. comp. physiol. Psychol.*, 58: 127–131.

Bolles, R. C., & Stokes, L. W. (1965) Rat's anticipation of diurnal and a-diurnal feeding. *J. comp. physiol. Psychol.*, 60: 290–294.

Bolles, R. C., Stokes, L. W., & Younger, M. S. (1966) Does CS termination reinforce avoidance behavior? *J. comp. physiol. Psychol.*, 62 201–207.

Bolles, R. C., Sulzbacher, S. I., & Arant, H. (1964) Innateness of the adrenalectomized rat's acceptance of salt. *Psychon. Sci.*, 1: 21–22.

Bolles, R. C., & Warren, J. A., Jr. (1965) The acquisition of bar press avoidance as a function of shock intensity. *Psychon. Sci.*, 3: 297–298.

Bolles, R. C., & Warren, J. A., Jr. (1965a) Effects of delayed UCS termination on classical avoidance learning of the bar-press response. *Psychol. Rep.*, 17: 687–690.

Bolles, R. C., & Warren, J. A., Jr. (1966) Effects of delay on the punishing and reinforcing effects of noise onset and termination. *J. comp. physiol. Psychol.*, 61: 475–477.

Bolles, R. C., Warren, J. A., Jr., & Ostrov, N. (1966a) The role of the CS-US interval in bar-press avoidance learning. *Psychon. Sci.*, 6: 113–114.

Bolles, R. C., & Younger, M. S. (1967) The effect of hunger on the threshold of behavioral arousal. *Psychon. Sci.*, 7: 243–244.

Booth, D. A. (1970) An expression of body weight regulation in feeding behavior. *Psychon. Sci.*, 21: 293.

Booth, D. A. (1972) Conditioned satiety in the rat. *J. comp. physiol. Psychol.*, 81: 457–471.

Booth, D. A., & Brookover, T. (1968) Hunger elicited in the rat by a single injection of bovine crystalline insulin. *Physiol. Behav.*, 3: 447–453.

Booth, D. A., & Pain, J. F. (1970) Effects of a single insulin injection on approaches to food and on the temporal pattern of feeding. *Psychon. Sci.*, 21: 17–19.

Boring, E. G. (1950) *A history of experimental psychology*, 2nd ed. New York: Appleton.

Boring, E. G., & Luce, A. (1917) The psychological basis of appetite. *Amer. J. Psychol.*, 28: 443–453.

Bousfield, W. A., & Elliott, M. H. (1934) The effect of fasting on the eating behavior of rats. *J. genet. Psychol.*, 1934, 45: 227–237.

Bousfield, W. A., & Sherif, M. (1932) Hunger as a factor in learning. *Amer. J. Psychol.*, 44: 552–554.

Bousfield, W. A., & Spear, E. (1935) Influence of hunger on the pecking responses of chickens. *Amer. J. Psychol.*, 47: 482–484.

Bower, G. H. (1961) Correlated delay of reinforcement. *J. comp. physiol. Psychol.*, 54: 196–203.

Bower, G. H., & Grusec, T. (1964) Effect of prior Pavlovian discrimination training upon learning an operant discrimination. *J. exp. anal. Behav.*, 7: 401–404.

Bower, G. H., McLean, J., & Meacham, J. (1966) Value of knowing when reinforcement is due. *J. comp. physiol. Psychol.*, 62: 183–192.

Bower, G. H., & Miller, N. E. (1958) Rewarding and punishing effects from stimulating the same place in the rat's brain. *J. comp. physiol. Psychol.*, 51: 669–674.

Bower, G. H., Starr, R., & Lazarovitz, L. (1965) Amount of response-produced change in the CS and avoidance learning. *J. comp. physiol. Psychol.*, 59: 13–17.

Brackbill, Y., & O'Hara, J. (1958) The relative effectiveness of reward and punishment for discrimination learning in children. *J. comp. physiol. Psychol.*, 51: 747–751.

Bradley, H. W., & Wong, R. (1969) Extinction as a function of size of goal box, reinforcement schedule, and competing responses. *Psychon. Sci.*, 17: 189–191.

Brandauer, C. M. (1953) A confirmation of Webb's data concerning the action of irrelevant drives. *J. exp. Psychol.*, 45: 150–152.

Braun, H. W., Wedekind, C. E., & Smudski, J. F. (1957) The effect of an irrelevant drive on maze learning in the rat. *J. exp. Psychol.*, 54: 148–152.

Breland, K., & Breland, M. (1961) The misbehavior of organisms. *Amer. Psychologist,* 16: 681–684.

Brener, J., & Goesling, W. J. (1970) Avoidance conditioning of activity and immobility in rats. *J. comp. physiol. Psychol.,* 70: 276–280.

Bridgman, P. (1932) *The logic of modern physics,* 2nd ed. New York: Macmillan.

Broadhurst, P. L. (1957) Determinants of emotionality in the rat: I. Situational factors. *Brit. J. Psychol.,* 48: 1–12.

Brobeck, J. R. (1960) Food and temperature. In *Recent progress in hormone research.* New York: Academic.

Brody, S. (1945) *Bioenergetics and growth.* New York: Reinhold.

Browman, L. G. (1952) Artificial 16 hr. day activity rhythms in the white rat. *Amer. J. Physiol.,* 168: 694–697.

Brown, J. F. (1932) Ueber die dynamismchen Eigenschaften der Realitaet und Irrealitaet. *Psychol. Forsch.,* 14: 46–61.

Brown, J. L. (1956) The effect of drive on learning with secondary reinforcement. *J. comp. physiol. Psychol.,* 49: 254–260.

Brown, J. S. (1948) Gradients of approach and avoidance responses and their relation to level of motivation. *J. comp. physiol. Psychol.,* 41: 450–465.

Brown, J. S. (1953) Problems presented by the concept of acquired drives. In *Current theory and research in motivation: A symposium.* Lincoln, Neb.: University of Nebraska Press.

Brown, J. S. (1955) Pleasure-seeking behavior and the drive reduction hypothesis. *Psychol. Rev.,* 62: 169–179.

Brown, J. S. (1961) *The motivation of behavior.* New York: McGraw-Hill.

Brown, J. S. (1969) Factors affecting self-punitive locomotor behavior. In B. A. Campbell and R. M. Church (Eds.), *Punishment and aversive behavior.* New York: Appleton.

Brown, J. S., & Belloni, M. (1963) Performance as a function of deprivation time following periodic feeding in an isolated environment. *J. comp. physiol. Psychol.,* 56: 105–110.

Brown, J. S., & Farber, I. E. (1951) Emotions conceptualized as intervening variables—with suggestions toward a theory of frustration. *Psychol. Bull.,* 48: 465–495.

Brown, J. S., & Jacobs, A. (1949) Role of fear in motivation and acquisition of responses. *J. exp. Psychol.,* 39: 747–759.

Brown, J. S., Martin, R. C., & Morrow, M. W. (1964) Self-punitive behavior in the rat: Facilitative effects of punishment on resistance to extinction. *J. comp. physiol. Psychol.,* 57: 127–133.

Brown, P. L., & Jenkins, H. M. (1968) Auto-shaping of the pigeon's keypeck. *J. exp. anal. Behav.,* 11: 1–8.

Brown, R. (1965) Discrimination of avoidable and unavoidable shock. *Brit. J. Psychol.,* 56: 275–283.

Brown, R. T., & Wagner, A. R. (1964) Resistance to punishment and extinction following training with shock or nonreinforcement. *J. exp. Psychol.,* 68: 503–507.

Brown, T. (1820) *Lectures on the philosophy of the human mind.*

Brown, W. L., & Gentry, G. (1948) The effect of intra-maze delay: II. Various intervals of delay. *J. comp. physiol. Psychol.,* 41: 403–407.

Brownstein, A. J., & Hillix, W. A. (1960) Drive accommodation and learning. *Psychol. Rec.,* 10: 21–24.

Brozovich, R., Malony, N., & Wright, L. (1963) An attempt to establish a secondary drive based upon a primary appetitional drive. *Psychol. Rep.*, 13: 283–288.

Bruce, R. H. (1938) The effect of lessening the drive upon performance by white rats in a maze. *J. comp. Psychol.*, 25: 225–248.

Bruner, J. S., Matter, J., & Papanek, M. L. (1955) Breadth of learning as a function of drive level and mechanization. *Psychol. Rev.*, 62: 1–10.

Brunswick, E. (1952) The conceptual framework of psychology. In R. Carnap and C. Morris (Eds.), *Int. Encycl. Unif. Sci.*, Vol. I, No. 10. Chicago: University of Chicago Press, 1955.

Brush, F. R., Goodrich, K. P., Teghtsoonian, R., & Eisman, E. H. (1961) Running speed as a function of deprivation condition and concentration of sucrose incentive. *Psychol. Rep.*, 9: 627–634.

Buchanan, G. N. (1958) The effects of various punishment-escape events upon subsequent choice behavior of rats. *J. comp. physiol. Psychol.*, 51: 355–362.

Budgell, P. (1970) The effect of changes in ambient temperature on water intake and evaporative water loss. *Psychon. Sci.*, 20: 275–276.

Bugelski, B. R. (1938) Extinction with and without sub-goal reinforcement. *J. comp. Psychol.*, 26: 121–133.

Bugelski, B. R. (1956) *The psychology of learning*. New York: Holt, Rinehart & Winston.

Bulatao, E., & Carlson, A. J. (1924) Contributions to the physiology of the stomach: Influence of experimental changes in blood sugar level on the gastric hunger contraction. *Amer. J. Physiol.*, 69: 107–115.

Bunge, M. (1959) *Causality*. Cambridge, Mass.: Harvard University Press.

Burke, G. H., Mook, D. G., & Blass, E. M. (1972) Hyperreactivity to quinine associated with osmotic thirst in the rat. *J. comp. physiol. Psychol.*, 78: 32–39.

Bury, J. B. (1913) *A history of freedom of thought*. New York: Holt, Rinehart & Winston.

Buss, A. H. (1966) Instrumentality of aggression, feedback, and frustration as determinants of physical aggression. *J. Pers. Soc. Psychol.*, 3: 153–162.

Butler, R. A. (1953) Discrimination learning by rhesus moneksy to visual-exploration motivation. *J. comp. physiol. Psychol.*, 46: 95–98.

Butler, R. A., & Harlow, H. F. (1954) Persistence of visual exploration in monkeys. *J. comp. physiol. Psychol.*, 47: 258–263.

Butter, C. M., & Campbell, B. A. (1960) Running speed as a function of successive reversals in hunger drive level. *J. comp. physiol. Psychol.*, 53: 52–54.

Caggiula, A. R., & Eibergen, R. (1969) Copulation of virgin male rats evoked by painful peripheral stimulation. *J. comp. physiol. Psychol.*, 69: 414–419.

Calvin, J. S., Bicknell, E., & Sperling, D. S. (1953) Establishment of a conditioned drive based upon the hunger drive. *J. comp. physiol. Psychol.*, 46: 173–175.

Camp, D. S., Raymond, G. A., & Church, R. M. (1967) Temporal relationship between response and punishment. *J. exp. Psychol.*, 74: 114–123.

Campbell, B. A. (1955) The fractional reduction in noxious stimulation required to produce "just noticeable" learning. *J. comp. physiol. Psychol.*, 48: 141–148.

Campbell, B. A. (1958) Absolute and relative sucrose preference thresholds for hungry and satiated rats. *J. comp. physiol. Psychol.*, 51: 795–800.

Campbell, B. A. (1960) Effects of water deprivation on random activity. *J. comp. physiol. Psychol.*, 53: 240–241.

Campbell, B. A. (1964) Theory and research on the effects of water deprivation on random activity in the rat. In M. J. Wayner (Ed.), *Thirst.* Elmsford, N.Y.: Pergamon.

Campbell, B. A., & Cicala, G. A. (1962) Studies of water deprivation in rats as a function of age. *J. comp. physiol. Psychol.*, 55: 763–768.

Campbell, B. A., & Fibiger, H. C. (1970) Effects of insulin on spontaneous activity during food deprivation. *J. comp. physiol. Psychol.*, 71: 341–346.

Campbell, B. A., & Kraeling, D. (1953) Response strength as a function of drive level and amount of drive reduction. *J. exp. Psychol.*, 45: 97–101.

Campbell, B. A., & Kraeling, D. (1954) Response strength as a function of drive level during training and extinction. *J. comp. physiol. Psychol.*, 47: 101–103.

Campbell, B. A., & Lynch, G. S. (1967) Activity and thermoregulation during food deprivation in the rat. *Physiol. Behav.*, 2: 311–313.

Campbell, B. A., & Lynch, G. S. (1968) Influence of hunger and thirst on the relationship between spontaneous activity and body temperature. *J. comp. physiol. Psychol.*, 65: 492–498.

Campbell, B. A., & Masterson, F. A. (1969) Phychophysics of punishment. In B. A. Campbell and R. M. Church (Eds.), *Punishment and aversive behavior.* New York: Appleton.

Campbell, B. A., & Sheffield, F. D. (1953) Relation of random activity to food deprivation. *J. comp. physiol. Psychol.*, 46: 320–322.

Campbell, B. A., Smith, N. F., Misanin, J. R., & Jaynes, J. (1966) Species differences in activity during hunger and thirst. *J. comp. physiol. Psychol.*, 61: 123–127.

Campbell, B. A., Teghtsoonian, R., & Williams, R. A. (1961) Activity, weight loss, and survival time of food-deprived rats as a function of age. *J. comp. physiol. Psychol.*, 54: 216–219.

Campbell, P. E., Fixsen, D. L., & Phillips, E. (1969) The reinstatement effect: Amount of noncontingent reward in the runway. *Psychon. Sci.*, 14: 228–229.

Candland, D. K., & Culbertson, J. L. (1963) Age, type and duration of deprivation, and consummatory preference in the rat. *J. comp. physiol. Psychol.*, 56: 565–568.

Cannon, W. B. (1918) The physiological basis of thirst. *Proc. Roy. Soc. Lond.*, 90B: 283–301.

Cannon, W. B. (1929) *Bodily changes in pain, hunger, fear and rage*, 2nd ed. New York: Appleton.

Cannon, W. B. (1934) Hunger and thirst. In C. Murchison (Ed.), *Handbook of general experimental psychology.* Worcester, Mass.: Clark University Press.

Cannon, W. B., & Washburn, A. L. (1912) An explanation of hunger. *Amer. J. Physiol.*, 29: 441–454.

Capaldi, E. D. (1971) Simultaneous shifts in reward magnitude and level of food deprivation. *Psychon. Sci.*, 23: 357–360.

Capaldi, E. D. (1972) Effect on rats' straight alley performance of shifts in body weight as a function of method of weight maintenance. *Psychon. Sci.*, 28: 44–46.

Capaldi, E. J. (1967) A sequential hypothesis of instrumental learning. In K. W. Spence and J. T. Spence (Eds.), *The psychology of learning and motivation.* New York: Academic.

Capaldi, E. J., (1970) An analysis of the role of reward and reward magnitude in instrumental learning. In J. H. Reynierse (Ed.), *Current issues in animal learning.* Lincoln, Neb.: University of Nebraska Press.

Capaldi, E. J. (1972) Successive negative contrast: Intertrial interval, type of shift, and four sources of generalization decrement. *J. exp. Psychol.*, 96: 433–438.

Capaldi, E. J., Capaldi, E. D., & Kassover, K. (1970) An instrumental partial reinforcement effect in the absence of any overt instrumental acquisition training. *Psychon. Sci.*, 21: 145–147.

Capaldi, E. J., & Sparling, D. L. (1971) Amobarbital vs saline extinction following different magnitudes of consistent reinforcement. *Psychon. Sci.*, 23: 215–217.

Capaldi, E. J., & Waters, R. W. (1970) Conditioning and nonconditioning interpretations of small-trial phenomena. *J. exp. Psychol.*, 84: 518–522.

Capretta, P. J. (1962) Saccharin consumption under varied conditions of hunger drive. *J. comp. physiol. Psychol.*, 55: 656–660.

Carlisle, H. J., & Stellar, E. (1969) Caloric regulation and food preference in normal, hyperphagic, and aphagic rats. *J. comp. physiol. Psychol.*, 69: 107–114.

Carlson, A. J. (1912) The relation between the contractions of the empty stomach and the sensation of hunger. *Amer. J. Physiol.*, 31: 175–192.

Carlson, A. J. (1913) The influence of the contractions of the empty stomach in man on the vaso-motor center, on the rate of heartbeat, and on the reflex excitability of the spinal cord. *Amer. J. Physiol.*, 31, 318–327.

Carlson, A. J. (1916) *The control of hunger in health and disease.* Chicago: University of Chicago Press.

Carlsson, S., & Larsson, K. (1964) Mating in male rats after local anesthetization of the glans penis. *Z. Tierpsychol.*, 21: 854–856.

Carlton, P. L. (1954) Response strength as a function of delay of reward and physical confinement. Unpublished M.A. thesis, State University of Iowa. Cited by Spence (1956).

Carlton, P. L. (1955) The effect of time of food deprivation on selective learning. Unpublished Ph.D. dissertation, State University of Iowa.

Carlton, P. L., & Marks, R. A. (1958) Cold exposure and heat reinforced operant behavior. *Science*, 128: 1344.

Carman, J. B. (1972) Generalization of activity following discriminative punishment training. *Psychon. Sci.*, 28: 19–21.

Carmichael, L. (1926) The development of behavior in vertebrates experimentally removed from the influence of external stimulation. *Psychol. Rev.*, 33: 51–58.

Carnap, R. (1936) Testability and meaning. *Philos. Sci.*, 3: 419–471.

Carper, J. W. (1957) A comparison of the reinforcing value of a nutritive and a non-nutritive substance under conditions of specific and general hunger. *Amer. J. Psychol.*, 60: 270–277.

Carper, J. W., & Polliard, F. (1953) A comparison of the intake of glucose and saccharin solutions under conditions of caloric need. *Amer. J. Psychol.*, 66: 479–482.

Carr, R. M., Overall, J. E., White, R. K., & Brown, W. L. (1959) The effects of food deprivation and restricted activity upon exploratory behavior of the rat. *J. genet. Psychol.*, 95: 321–328.

Cartwright, D. (1959) Lewinian theory as a contemporary systematic framework. In S. Koch (Ed.), *Psychology: A study of a science*, Vol. II. New York: McGraw-Hill.

Carus, C. G. (1866) *Psychologie oder Seele in der Reinhenfolge der Tierwelt.*

Chambers, R. M. (1956) Some physiological bases for reinforcing properties of reward injections. *J. comp. physiol. Psychol.*, 49: 565–568.

Chambers, R. M. (1956a) Effects of intravenous glucose injections on learning, general activity, and hunger drive. *J. comp. physiol. Psychol.*, 49: 558–564.

Chambers, R. M., & Fuller, J. L. (1958) Conditioning of skin temperature changes in dogs. *J. comp. physiol. Psychol.*, 51: 223–226.

Champion, R. A. (1954) Drive-strength and competing response tendencies. Unpublished M.A. thesis, State University of Iowa.

Chapman, H. W., & Epstein, A. N. (1970) Prandial drinking induced by atropine. *Physiol. Behav.*, 5: 549–554.

Chapman, R. M., & Levy, N. (1957) Hunger drive and reinforcing effect of novel stimuli. *J. comp. physiol. Psychol.*, 50: 233–238.

Charlesworth, W. R., & Thompson, W. R. (1957) Effect of lack of visual stimulus variation on exploratory behavior in the adult white rat. *Psychol. Rep.*, 3: 509–512.

Christophersen, E. R., & Denny, M. R. (1967) Retractable-bar avoidance. *Psychon. Sci.*, 9: 579–580.

Church, R. M. (1963) The varied effects of punishment on behavior. *Psychol. Rev.*, 70: 369–402.

Church, R. M. (1964) Systematic effect of random error in the yoked control design. *Psychol. Bull.*, 62: 122–131.

Church, R. M. (1969) Response suppression. In B. A. Campbell and R. M. Church (Eds.), *Punishment and aversive behavior*. New York: Appleton.

Church, R. M. (1971) Aversive behavior. In J. W. Kling and L. A. Riggs (Eds.), *Experimental psychology*. New York: Holt, Rinehart & Winston.

Church, R. M., Raymond, G. A., & Beauchamp, R. D. (1967) Response suppression as a function of intensity and duration of a punishment. *J. comp. physiol. Psychol.*, 63: 39–44.

Church, R. M., Wooten, C. L., & Matthews, T. J. (1970) Discriminative punishment and the conditioned emotional response. *Learn. Motiv.*, 1: 1–17.

Church, R. M., Wooten, C. L., & Matthews, T. J. (1970a) Contingency between response and an aversive event in the rat. *J. comp. physiol. Psychol.*, 72: 476–485.

Cicala, G. A. (1961) Running speed in rats as a function of drive level and presence or absence of competing response trials. *J. exp. Psychol.*, 62: 329–334.

Cicala, G. A., & Kremer, E. (1969) The effects of shock intensity and d-amphetamine on avoidance learning. *Psychon. Sci.*, 14: 41–42.

Cicero, T. J., & Myers, R. D. (1968) Facilitation of discriminated avoidance learning by prior operant training. *Psychol. Rep.*, 22: 1273–1276.

Cizek, L. J. (1959) Long-term observations on relationship between food and water ingestion in the dog. *Amer. J. Physiol.*, 197: 342–346.

Cizek, L. J. (1961) Relationship between food and water ingestion in the rabbit. *Amer. J. Physiol.*, 201: 557–566.

Clark, F. C. (1958) The effect of deprivation and frequency of reinforcement on variable-interval responding. *J. exp. anal. Behav.*, 1: 221–228.

Clayton, K. N. (1964) T-maze choice learning as a joint function of the reward magnitudes for the alternatives. *J. comp. physiol. Psychol.*, 58: 333–338.

Clayton, K. N., & Koplin, S. T. (1964) T-maze learning as a joint function of probability and magnitude of reward. *Psychon. Sci.*, 1: 381–382.

Clifford, T. (1964) Extinction following continuous reward and latent extinction. *J. exp. Psychol.*, 68: 456–465.

Coate, W. B. (1964) Effect of deprivation on postdiscrimination stimulus generalization in the rat. *J. comp. physiol. Psychol.*, 57: 134–138.

Cofer, C. N., & Appley, M. H. (1964) *Motivation: Theory and research.* New York: Wiley.

Cohen, B. D., Brown, G. W., & Brown, M. L. (1957) Avoidance learning motivated by hypothalamic stimulation. *J. exp. Psychol.*, 53: 228–233.

Cohen, J. S., & Stettner, L. J. (1968) Effect of deprivation level on responses to novel alleys in albino rats. *Psychon. Sci.*, 11: 103–104.

Cohen, J. S., & Telegdy, G. A. (1970) Effect of a drive level on habit strength in a discrimination task. *Psychon. Sci.*, 19: 27–29.

Cole, L. W. (1911) The relation of strength of stimulus to rate of learning in the chick. *J. anim. Behav.*, 1: 111–124.

Cole, M., & Fantino, E. (1966) Temporal variables and trial discreteness in lever-press avoidance. *Psychon. Sci.*, 6: 217–218.

Collier, G. (1962) Some properties of saccharin as a reinforcer. *J. exp. Psychol.*, 64: 184–191.

Collier, G. (1962a) Consummatory and instrumental responding as functions of deprivation. *J. exp. Psychol.*, 64: 410–414.

Collier, G. (1964) Thirst as a determinant of reinforcement. In M. J. Wayner (Ed.), *Thirst.* Elmsford, N.Y.: Pergamon.

Collier, G. (1969) Body weight loss as a measure of motivation in hunger and thirst. *Ann. N.Y. Acad. Sci.*, 157: 594–609.

Collier, G. (1970) Work: A weak reinforcer. *Trans. N.Y. Acad. Sci.*, 32: 557–576.

Collier, G., & Bolles, R. (1968) Some determinants of intake of sucrose solutions. *J. comp. physiol. Psychol.*, 65: 379–383.

Collier, G., & Bolles, R. C. (1968a) Hunger, thirst, and their interaction as determinants of sucrose consumption. *J. comp. physiol. Psychol.*, 66: 633–641.

Collier, G., & Hirsch, E. (1971) Reinforcing properties of spontaneous activity in the rat. *J. comp. physiol. Psychol.*, 77: 155–160.

Collier, G. H., Hirsch, E., & Hamlin, P. H. (1972) The ecological determinants of reinforcement. *Physiol. Behav.*, 9: 705–716.

Collier, G., & Knarr, F. (1966) Defense of water balance in the rat. *J. comp. physiol. Psychol.*, 61: 5–10.

Collier, G., Knarr, F. A., & Marx, M. H. (1961) Some relations between the intensive properties of the consummatory response and reinforcement. *J. exp. Psychol.*, 62: 484–495.

Collier, G., & Levitsky, D. (1967) Defense of water balance in rats: Behavioral and physiological responses to depletion. *J. comp. physiol. Psychol.*, 64: 59–67.

Collier, G., Levitsky, D., & Squibb, R. L. (1967) Instrumental performance as a function of the energy content of the diet. *J. comp. physiol. Psychol.*, 64: 68–72.

Collier, G., Levitsky, D., & Weinberg, C. (1968) Body weight loss as a measure of motivation in thirsty guinea pigs. *Psychon. Sci.*, 10: 27–28.

Collier, G., & Marx, M. H. (1959) Changes in performance as a function of shifts in the magnitude of reinforcement. *J. exp. Psychol.*, 57: 305–309.

Collier, G., & Myers, L. (1961) The loci of reinforcement. *J. exp. Psychol.* 61: 57–66.

Collier, G., & Siskel, M., Jr. (1959) Performance as a joint function of amount of reinforcement and inter-reinforcement interval. *J. exp. Psychol.*, 57: 115–120.

Connally, R. E. (1968) Drive and habit components of running activity in the rat follow food deprivation. *Psychon. Sci.*, 12: 9–10.

Coons, E. E., Anderson, N. H., & Myers, A. K. (1960) Disappearance of avoidance responding during continued training. *J. comp. physiol. Psychol.*, 53: 290–292.

Cooper, J. B. (1938) The effect upon performance of introduction and removal of a delay within the maze. *J. comp. Psychol.*, 25: 457–462.

Cooper, L. M. (1963) Operant behavior as a function of stimulus complexity. *J. comp. physiol. Psychol.*, 56: 857–862.

Copeland, M. A. (1926) Desire, choice, and purpose from a natural-evolutionary standpoint. *Psychol. Rev.*, 33: 245–267.

Coppock, H. W., & Chambers, R. M. (1954) Reinforcement of position preference by automatic intravenous injections of glucose. *J. comp. physiol. Psychol.*, 47: 355–358.

Corbit, J. D. (1965) Effect of intravenous sodium chloride on drinking in the rat. *J. comp. physiol. Psychol.*, 60: 397–406.

Corbit, J. D. (1967) Effect of hypervolemia on drinking in the rat. *J. comp. physiol. Psychol.*, 64: 250–255.

Corbit, J. D. (1968) Cellular dehydration and hypovolaemia are additive in producing thirst. *Nature*, 218: 886–887.

Corbit, J. D. (1969) Osmotic thirst: Theoretical and experimental analysis. *J. comp. physiol. Psychol.*, 67: 3–14.

Corbit, J. D., & Luschei, E. S. (1969) Invariance of the rat's rate of drinking. *J. comp. physiol. Psychol.*, 69: 119–125.

Corbit, J. D., & Stellar, E. (1964) Palatibility, food intake, and obesity in normal and hyperphagic rats. *J. comp. physiol. Psychol.*, 58: 63–67.

Corbit, J. D., & Tuchapsky, S. (1968) Gross hypervolemia: Stimulation of diuresis without effect upon drinking. *J. comp. physiol. Psychol.*, 65: 38–41.

Corman, C. D., & Miles, R. C. (1966) Invariance of operant topography throughout changes in motivational conditions. *J. comp. physiol. Psychol.*, 62: 60–64.

Cornish, E. R., & Mrosovsky, N. (1965) Activity during food deprivation and satiation of six species of rodent. *Anim. Behav.*, 13: 242–248.

Cotton, J. W. (1953) Running time as a function of amount of food deprivation. *J. exp. Psychol.*, 46: 188–198.

Cotton, J. W., Hill, W. F., & Shanab, M. E. (1969) Extinction under nine food deprivation levels. *Psychon. Sci.*, 14: 37–38.

Coulter, X., Riccio, D. C., & Page, H. A. (1969) Effects of blocking on instrumental avoidance response: Facilitated extinction but persistence of "fear." *J. comp. physiol. Psychol.*, 68: 377–381.

Courts, F. A. (1939) The knee-jerk as a measure of muscular tension. *J. exp. Psychol.*, 24: 520–529.

Cowgill, G. R. (1928) The energy factor in relation to food intake: Experiments on the dog. *Amer. J. Physiol.*, 85: 45–64.

Cowles, J. T. (1937) Food tokens as incentives for learning by chimpanzees. *Comp. Psychol. Monogr.*, 14 (Serial No. 71).

Craig, W. (1918) Appetites and aversions as constituents of instincts. *Biol. Bull.*, 34: 91–107.

Crawford, M. L. J. (1970) Shock-avoidance and shock-escape drinking in rats: Rate of licking. *Psychon. Sci.*, 21: 304–305.

Crespi, L. P. (1942) Quantitative variation of incentive and performance in the white rat. *Amer. J. Psychol.*, 55: 467–517.

Crombie, A. C. (1959) *Medieval and early modern science*. Garden City, N.Y.: Doubleday.

Cross, H. A., Rankin, R. J., & Wilson, J. (1964) Influence of amount of reward on maze learning in hooded and albino rats. *Psychon. Sci.*, 1: 275–276.

Crowder, W. F., Gill, K., Hodge, C. C., & Nash, F. A. (1959) Secondary reinforcement or response facilitation?: II. Response acquisition. *J. Psychol.*, 48: 303–306.

Crum, J., Brown, W. L., & Bitterman, M. E. (1951) The effect of partial and delayed reinforcement on resistance to extinction. *Amer. J. Psychol.*, 64: 228–237.

Culbertson, J. L. (1970) Effects of brief reinforcement delays on acquisition and extinction of brightness discrimination in rats. *J. comp. physiol. Psychol.*, 70: 317–325.

Dachowski, L. (1964) Irrelevant thirst drives and light aversion. *Psychol. Rep.*, 14: 899–904.

Daly, H. B. (1968) Excitatory and inhibitory effects of complete and incomplete reward reduction in the double runway. *J. exp. Psychol.*, 76: 430–438.

Daly, H. B. (1969) Learning of a hurdle-jump response to escape cues paired with reduced reward or frustrative nonreward. *J. exp. Psychol.*, 79: 146–157.

Daly, H. B. (1969a) Is instrumental responding necessary for nonreward following reward to be frustrating? *J. exp. Psychol.*, 80: 186–187.

D'Amato, M. R. (1955) Transfer of secondary reinforcement across the hunger and thirst drives. *J. exp. Psychol.*, 49: 352–356.

D'Amato, M. R., & Fazzaro, J. (1966) Discriminated lever-press avoidance learning as a function of type and intensity of shock. *J. comp. physiol. Psychol.*, 61: 313–315.

D'Amato, M. R., Fazzaro, J., & Etkin, M. (1967) Discriminated bar-press avoidance maintenance and extinction in rats as a function of shock intensity. *J. comp. physiol. Psychol.*, 63: 351–354.

D'Amato, M. R., Fazzaro, J., & Etkin, M. (1968) Anticipatory responding and avoidance discrimination as factors in avoidance conditioning. *J. exp. Psychol.*, 77: 41–47.

D'Amato, M. R., Keller, D., & DiCara, L. (1964) Facilitation of discriminated avoidance learning by discontinuous shock. *J. comp. physiol. Psychol.*, 58: 344–349.

D'Amato, M. R., Lachman, R., & Kivy, P. (1958) Secondary reinforcement as affected by reward schedule and the testing situation. *J. comp. physiol. Psychol.*, 51: 734–741.

D'Amato, M. R., & Schiff, D. (1964) Long-term discriminated avoidance performance in the rat. *J. comp. physiol. Psychol.*, 57: 123–126.

Danziger, K. (1953) The interaction of hunger and thirst in the rat. *Quart. J. exp. Psychol.*, 5: 10–21.

Darwin, C. A. (1859) *The origin of species by means of natural selection.*

Darwin, C. A. (1872) *The expression of the emotions in man and animals.*

Dashiell, J. F. (1925) A quantitative demonstration of animal drive. *J. comp. Psychol.*, 5: 205–208.

Dashiell, J. F. (1937) *Fundamentals of general psychology*, 2nd ed. Boston: Houghton Mifflin.

Davenport, D. G., & Goulet, L. R. (1964) Motivational artifacts in standard food-deprivation schedules. *J. comp. physiol. Psychol.*, 57: 237–240.

Davenport, D. G., & Mueller, J. H. (1968) Resistance to extinction as a function of nonresponse incentive shift. *Psychon. Sci.*, 10: 243–244.

Davenport, D. G., & Olson, R. D. (1968) A reinterpretation of extinction in discriminated avoidance. *Psychon. Sci.*, 13: 5–6.

Davenport, D. G., & Sardello, R. J. (1966) Double intermittent reward scheduling and secondary reinforcer strength. *Psychon. Sci.*, 6: 417–418.

Davenport, J. W. (1963) Spatial discrimination and reversal learning involving magnitude of reinforcement. *Psychol. Rep.*, 12: 655–665.

Davenport, J. W. (1965) Distribution of M and i parameters for rats trained under varying hunger drive levels. *J. genet. Psychol.*, 106: 113–121.

Davis, C. M. (1928) Self-selection of diet by newly weaned infants. *Amer. J. Dis. Children*, 36: 651–679.

Davis, J. D., Gallagher, R. J., Ladove, R. F., & Turausky, A. J. (1969) Inhibition of food intake by a hormonal factor. *J. comp. physiol. Psychol.*, 67: 407–414.

Davis, J. D., & Keehn, J. D. (1959) Magnitude of reinforcement and consummatory behavior. *Science*, 130: 269–270.

Davis, R. C., Garafolo, L., & Kveim, K. (1959) Conditions associated with gastrointestinal activity. *J. comp. physiol. Psychol.*, 52: 466–475.

Davis, R. H. (1957) The effect of drive reversal on latency, amplitude, and activity level. *J. exp. Psychol.*, 53: 310–315.

Davis, R. T., Settlage, P. H., & Harlow, H. F. (1950) Performance of nor-

mal and brain-operated monkeys on mechanical puzzles with and
without food incentive. *J. genet. Psychol.*, 77: 305–311.

Davis, W. M., Babbini, M., & Huneycutt, B. D. (1967) A new apparatus
for one-way locomotor avoidance without handling. *Psychon. Sci.*,
8: 185–186.

Deaux, E., Sato, E., & Kakolewski, J. W. (1970) Emergence of systemic
cues evoking food-associated drinking. *Physiol. Behav.*, 5: 1177–
1179.

Dees, J. W., & Furchtgott, E. (1964) Drive generalization. *Psychol. Rep.*
15: 807–810.

Deese, J., & Carpenter, J. A. (1951) Drive level and reinforcement. *J. exp.
Psychol.*, 42: 236–238.

Delgado, J. M. R., Roberts, W. W., & Miller, N. E. (1954) Learning motivated by electrical stimulation of the brain. *Amer. J. Physiol.*, 179:
587–593.

Delgado, J. M. R., Rosvold, H. E., & Looney, E. (1956) Evoking conditioned fear by electrical stimulation of subcortical structures in
the monkey brain. *J. comp. physiol. Psychol.*, 49: 373–380.

de Lorge, J. (1969) The influence of pairing with primary reinforcement
on the maintenance of conditioned reinforcement in second-order
schedules. In D. P. Hendry (Ed.), *Conditioned reinforcement.*
Homewood, Ill.: Dorsey Press.

Delude, L. A. (1969) The vicious circle phenomenon: A result of measurement artifact. *J. comp. physiol. Psychol.*, 69: 246–252.

Denniston, R. H. (1954) Quantification and comparison of sex drives
under various conditions in terms of a learned response. *J. comp.
physiol. Psychol.*, 47: 437–440.

Denny, M. R. (1948) The effect of using differential end boxes in a simple
T-maze learning situation. *J. exp. Psychol.*, 38: 245–249.

Denny, M. R. (1971) Relaxation theory and experiments. In F. R. Brush
(Ed.), *Aversive conditioning and learning.* New York: Academic.

Denny, M. R., & King, G. F. (1955) Differential response learning on the
basis of differential size of reward. *J. genet. Psychol.*, 87: 317–321.

Descartes, R. (1649) *Passions of the soul.* In E. S. Haldane and G. R. T.
Ross, *The philosophical works of Descartes.* Cambridge, Mass.:
Harvard University Press, 1911. (Reprinted by Dover, 1955).

Descartes, R. (1677) *Tractatus de homine.*

Deutsch, J. A. (1959) The Hull-Leeper drive discrimination situation—a
control experiment. *Quart. J. exp. Psychol.*, 11: 155–163.

Deutsch, J. A., & Howarth, C. I. (1963) Some tests of a theory of intracranial self-stimulation. *Psychol. Rev.*, 70: 444–460.

Dewson, J. H., III. (1965) Avoidance responses to pure tones in the rat.
Psychon. Sci., 2: 113–114.

Dillow, P. V., Myerson, J., Slaughter, L., & Hurwitz, H. M. B. (1972)
Safety signals and the acquisition and extinction of lever-press
discriminated avoidance in rats. *Brit. J. Psychol.*, 63: 583–591.

DiLollo, V., Ensminger, W. D., & Notterman, J. M. (1965) Response force
as a function of amount of reinforcement. *J. exp. Psychol.*, 70:
27–31.

Dinsmoor, J. A. (1950) A quantitative comparison of the discriminative
and reinforcing functions of a stimulus. *J. exp. Psychol.*, 40:
458–472.

Dinsmoor, J. A. (1952) A discrimination based on punishment. *Quart. J. exp. Psychol.*, 4: 27–45.

Dinsmoor, J. A. (1952a) The effect of hunger on discriminated responding. *J. abnorm. soc. Psychol.*, 47: 67–72.

Dinsmoor, J. A. (1954) Punishment: I. The avoidance hypothesis. *Psychol. Rev.*, 61: 34–46.

Dinsmoor, J. A. (1955) Punishment: II. An interpretation of empirical findings. *Psychol. Rev.*, 62: 96–105.

Dinsmoor, J. A. (1958) Pulse duration and food deprivation in escape-from-shock training. *Psychol. Rep.*, 4: 531–534.

Dinsmoor, J. A. (1962) Variable-interval escape from stimuli accompanied by shocks. *J. exp. anal. Behav.*, 5: 41–47.

Dinsmoor, J. A., & Clayton, M. H. (1963) Chaining and secondary reinforcement based on escape from shock. *J. exp. anal. Behav.*, 6: 75–80.

Dinsmoor, J. A., Flint, G. A., Smith, R. F., & Viemeister, N. F. (1969) Differential reinforcing effects of stimuli associated with the presence or absence of a schedule of punishment. In D. P. Hendry (Ed.), *Conditioned reinforcement*. Homewood, Ill.: Dorsey.

Dinsmoor, J. A., & Sears, G. W. (1973) Control of avoidance by a response-produced stimulus. *Learn. Motiv.*, 4: 284–293.

Dodson, J. D. (1915) The relation of strength of stimulus to rapidity of habit-formation. *J. anim. Behav.*, 5: 330–336.

Dodson, J. D. (1917) Relative values of reward and punishment in habit formation. *Psychobiology*, 1: 231–276.

Dollard, J., Doob, L. W., Miller, N. E., Mowrer, O. H., & Sears, R. R. (1939) *Frustration and aggression*. New Haven, Conn.: Yale University Press.

Doty, R. L. (1974) A cry for the liberation of the female rodent: Courtship and copulation in *rodentia. Psychol. Bull.*, 81: 159–172.

Drever, J. (1917) *Instinct in man*. Cambridge: Cambridge University Press.

Duda, J. J., & Bolles, R. C. (1963) Effects of prior deprivation, current deprivation, and weight loss on the activity of the hungry rat. *J. comp. physiol. Psychol.*, 56: 569–571.

Duffy, E. (1951) The concept of energy mobilization. *Psychol. Rev.*, 58: 30–40.

Duffy, E. (1957) The psychological significance of the concept of "arousal" or "activation." *Psychol. Rev.*, 64: 265–275.

Dufort, R. H. (1963) Weight loss in rats continuously deprived of food, water, and both food and water. *Psychol. Rep.*, 12: 307–312.

Dufort, R. H., & Blick, K. A. (1962) Adjustment of the rat to a 23-hour water-deprivation schedule. *J. comp. physiol. Psychol.*, 55: 649–651.

Dufort, R. H., Funderburk, A. J., & Rollins, H. A. (1966) The rat's adjustment to the 23-hour water-deprivation schedule under two conditions of food availability. *Psychon. Sci.*, 4: 365–366.

Dufort, R. H., & Kimble, G. A. (1956) Changes in response strength with changes in the amount of reinforcement. *J. exp. Psychol.*, 51: 185–191.

Dufort, R. H., & Wright, J. H. (1962) Food intake as a function of duration of food deprivation. *J. Psychol.*, 53: 465–468.

Dufour, V. L., & Arnold, M. B. (1966) Taste of saccharin as sufficient reward for performance. *Psychol. Rep.*, 19: 1293–1294.

Dunham, P. J. (1968) Contrasted conditions of reinforcement: A selective critique. *Psychol. Bull.*, 69: 295–315.

Dunham, P. J., Mariner, A., & Adams, H. (1969) Enhancement of off-key pecking by on-key punishment. *J. exp. anal. Behav.*, 12: 789–797.

Dunham, P. J., & Kilps, B. (1969) Shifts in magnitude of reinforcement: Confounded factors or contrast effects? *J. exp. Psychol.*, 79: 373–374.

Dunlap, K. (1919) Are there any instincts? *J. abnorm. soc. Psychol.*, 14: 307–311.

Dunlap, K. (1922) *Elements of scientific psychology.* St. Louis, Mo.: Mosby.

Dunlap, K. (1923) The foundations of social psychology. *Psychol. Rev.*, 30: 81–102.

Dunlap, W. P., & Frates, S. B. (1970) Influence of deprivation on the frustration effect. *Psychon. Sci.*, 21: 1–2.

Dyal, J. A. (1958) Secondary-motivation based on appetites and aversions. *Psychol. Rep.*, 4: 698.

Dyal, J. A. (1962) Latent extinction as a function of number and duration of pre-extinction exposures. *J. exp. Psychol.*, 63: 98–104.

Eayrs, J. T. (1954) Spontaneous activity in the rat. *Brit. J. anim. Behav.*, 11: 25–30.

Egger, M. D., & Miller, N. E. (1962) Secondary reinforcement in rats as a function of information value and reliability of the stimulus. *J. exp. Psychol.*, 64: 97–104.

Egger, M. D., & Miller, N. E. (1963) When is a reward reinforcing?: An experimental study of the information hypothesis. *J. comp. physiol. Psychol.*, 56: 132–137.

Ehrenfreund, D. (1949) The effect of a secondary reinforcing agent in black-white discrimination. *J. comp. physiol. Psychol.*, 42: 1–5.

Ehrenfreund, D. (1954) Generalization of secondary reinforcement in discrimination learning. *J. comp. physiol. Psychol.*, 47: 311–314.

Ehrenfreund, D. (1960) The motivational effect of a continuous weight loss schedule. *Psychol. Rep.*, 6: 339–345.

Ehrlich, A. (1959) Effects of past experience on exploratory behaviour in rats. *Canad. J. Psychol.*, 13: 248–254.

Eibl-Eibesfeldt, I. (1970) *Ethology.* New York: Holt, Rinehart & Winston.

Eiseley, L. (1958) *Darwin's century.* Garden City, N.Y.: Doubleday.

Eisenberger, R. (1972) Explanation of rewards that do not reduce tissue needs. *Psychol. Bull.*, 77: 319–339.

Eisman, E. (1956) An investigation of the parameters defining drive (D). *J. exp. Psychol.*, 52: 85–89.

Eisman, E. (1966) Effects of deprivation and consummatory activity on heart rate. *J. comp. physiol. Psychol.*, 62: 71–75.

Eisman, E., Asimow, A., & Maltzman, I. (1956) Habit strength as a function of drive in a brightness discrimination problem. *J. exp. Psychol.*, 52: 58–64.

Eisman, E., Linton, M., & Theios, J. (1960) The relationship between response strength and one parameter of the hunger drive. *J. comp. physiol. Psychol.*, 53: 356–363.

Eisman, E., Theios, J., & Linton, M. (1961) Habit strength as a function of drive in a bar-pressing situation. *Psychol. Rep.*, 9: 583–590.

Elliott, M. H. (1928) The effect of change of reward on the maze performance of rats. *Univ. Calif. Publ. Psychol.*, 4: 19–30.

Elliott, M. H. (1929) The effect of change of "drive" on maze performance. *Univ. Calif. Publ. Psychol.*, 4: 185–188.

Ellis, N. R. (1957) The immediate effect of emotionality upon behavior strength. *J. exp. Psychol.*, 54: 339–344.

Ellson, D. G. (1937) The acquisition of a token-reward habit in dogs. *J. comp. Psychol.*, 24: 505–522.

Eninger, M. U. (1951) The role of irrelevant drive stimuli in learning theory. *J. exp. Psychol.*, 41: 446–449.

Epstein, A. N. (1960) Water intake without the act of drinking. *Science*, 131: 497–498.

Epstein, A. N., & Teitelbaum, P. (1962) Regulation of food intake in the absence of taste, smell, and other oropharyngeal sensations. *J. comp. physiol. Psychol.*, 55: 753–759.

Epstein, A. N., & Teitelbaum, P. (1964) Severe and persistent deficits in thirst in rats with lateral hypothalamic damage. In M. J. Wayner (Ed.), *Thirst*. Elmsford, N.Y.: Pergamon.

Estes, W. K. (1943) Discriminative conditioning: I. A. discriminative property of conditioned anticipation. *J. exp. Psychol.*, 32: 150–155.

Estes, W. K. (1944) An experimental study of punishment. *Psychol. Monogr.*, 57 (Whole No. 263).

Estes, W. K. (1948) Discriminative conditioning: II. Effects of a Pavlovian conditioned stimulus upon a subsequently established operant response. *J. exp. Psychol.*, 38: 173–177.

Estes, W. K. (1949) Generalization of secondary reinforcement from the primary drive. *J. comp. physiol. Psychol.*, 42: 286–295.

Estes, W. K. (1954) Kurt Lewin. In W. K. Estes et al., *Modern learning theory*. New York: Appleton.

Estes, W. K. (1958) Stimulus-response theory of drive. In M. R. Jones (Ed.), *Nebraska symposium on motivation*. Lincoln, Neb.: University of Nebraska Press.

Estes, W. K. (1962) Learning theory. *Ann. Rev. Psychol.*, 13: 107–144.

Estes, W. K. (1969) Outline of a theory of punishment. In B. A. Campbell and R. M. Church (Eds.), *Punishment and aversive behavior*. New York: Appleton.

Estes, W. K. (1971) Reward in human learning: Theoretical issues and strategic choice points. In R. Glaser (Ed.), *The nature of reinforcement*. New York: Academic.

Estes, W. K., & Skinner, B. F. (1941) Some quantitative properties of anxiety. *J. exp. Psychol.*, 29: 390–400.

Evans, H. L. (1971) Rats' activity: Influence of light-dark cycle, food presentation and deprivation. *Physiol. Behav.*, 7: 455–459.

Evans, S. H., & Anastasio, E. J. (1968) Misuse of analysis of covariance when treatment effect and covariate are confounded. *Psychol. Bull.*, 69: 225–234.

Evans, W. O. (1962) Producing either positive or negative tendencies to a stimulus associated with shock. *J. exp. anal. Behav.*, 5: 335–337.

Everett, J. W. (1961) The mammalian female reproductive cycle and its controlling mechanisms. In W. C. Young (Ed.), *Sex and internal secretions*. Baltimore, Md.: Williams & Wilkins.

Evvard, J. M. (1916) In the appetite of swine a reliable indication of physiological needs? *Proc. Iowa Acad. Sci.*, 4: 91–98.

Falk, J. L. (1961) Production of polydipsia in normal rats by an intermittent food schedule. *Science*, 133: 195–196.

Falk, J. L., (1965) Water intake and NaCl appetite in sodium depletion. *Psychol. Rep.*, 16: 315–325.

Falk, J. L. (1969) Conditions producing psychogenic polydipsia in animals. *Ann. N.Y. Acad. Sci.*, 157: 569–593.

Fallon, D. (1965) Effects of cyclic deprivation upon consummatory behavior: The role of deprivation history. *J. comp. physiol. Psychol.*, 60: 283–287.

Fantino, E., Sharp, D., & Cole, M. (1966) Factors facilitating lever-press avoidance. *J. comp. physiol. Psychol.*, 66: 214–217.

Farrer, A. M. (1959) *The freedom of the will.* London: Black.

Fay, J. W. (1939) *American psychology before William James.* New Brunswick, N.J.: Rutgers University Press.

Fearing, F. (1930) *Reflex action: A study in the history of physiological psychology.* Baltimore, Md.: Williams & Wilkins.

Fechter, L. D., & Ison, J. R. (1972) The inhibition of the acoustic startle reaction in rats by food and water deprivation. *Learn. Motiv.*, 3: 109–124.

Fehrer, E. (1956) The effects of hunger and familiarity of locale on exploration. *J. comp. physiol. Psychol.*, 49: 549–552.

Fehrer, E. (1956a) Effect of amount of reinforcement and of pre- and postreinforcement delays on learning and extinction. *J. exp. Psychol.*, 52: 167–176.

Feldman, R. S., & Bremner, F. J. (1963) A method for rapid conditioning of stable avoidance bar pressing behavior. *J. exp. anal. Behav.*, 6: 393–394.

Fenichel, O. (1934) On the psychology of boredom. In D. Rapaport, *Organization and pathology of thought.* New York: Columbia University Press, 1951.

Ferster, C. B., & Skinner, B. F. (1957) *Schedules of reinforcement.* New York. Appleton.

Feshbach, S. (1964) The function of aggression and the regulation of aggressive drive. *Psychol. Rev.*, 71: 257–272.

Festinger, L. (1943) Development of differential appetite in the rat. *J. exp. Psychol.*, 32: 226–234.

Finan, J. L. (1940) Quantitative studies in motivation: I. Strength of conditioning under varying degrees of hunger. *J. comp. Psychol.*, 29: 119–134.

Finch, G. (1938) Hunger as a determinant of conditional and unconditional salivary response magnitude. *Amer. J. Physiol.*, 123: 379–382.

Finger, F. W. (1961) Estrous activity as a function of measuring device. *J. comp. physiol. Psychol.*, 54: 524–526.

Finger, F. W. (1962) Activity change under deprivation as a function of age. *J. comp. physiol. Psychol.*, 55: 100–102.

Finger, F. W. (1965) Effect of food deprivation on running-wheel activity in naïve rats. *Psychol. Rep.*, 16: 753–757.

Finger, F. W. (1969) Estrus and general activity in the rat. *J. comp. physiol. Psychol.*, 68: 461–466.

Finger, F. W. & Reid, L. S. (1952) The effect of water deprivation and subsequent satiation upon general activity in the rat. *J. comp. physiol. Psychol.*, 45: 368–372.

Finger, F. W., Reid, L. S., & Weasner, M. H. (1957) The effect of reinforcement upon activity during cyclic food deprivation. *J. comp. physiol. Psychol.*, 50: 495–498.

Finger, F. W., Reid, L. S., & Weasner, M. H. (1960) Activity changes as a function of reinforcement under low drive. *J. comp. physiol. Psychol.*, 53: 385–387.

Fink, J. B., & Patton, R. M. (1953) Decrement of a learned drinking response accompanying changes in several stimulus characteristics. *J. comp. physiol. Psychol.*, 46: 23–27.

Fisher, A. E. (1962) Effects of stimulus variation on sexual satiation in the male rat. *J. comp. physiol. Psychol.*, 55: 614–620.

Fiske, D. W., & Maddi, S. R. (1961) A conceptual framework. In D. W. Fiske and S. R. Maddi (Eds.), *Functions of varied experience.* Homewood, Ill.: Dorsey.

Fitzgerald, R. D., & Walloch, R. A. (1969) Resistance to extinction of a punished wheel-turning escape response in rats. *J. comp. physiol. Psychol.*, 68: 254–261.

Fitzsimons, J. T. (1957) Normal drinking in rats. *J. Physiol.* (London), 136, 139.

Fitzsimons, J. T. (1961) Drinking by nephrectomized rats injected with various substances. *J. Physiol.* (London), 155: 563–579.

Fitzsimons, J. T. (1961a) Drinking by rats depleted of body fluid without increase in osmotic pressure. *J. Physiol.* (London), 159: 297–309.

Fitzsimons, J. T. (1969) Effect of nephrectomy on the additivity of certain stimuli on drinking in the rat. *J. comp. physiol. Psychol.*, 68: 308–314.

Fitzsimons, J. T. (1971) The physiology of thirst: A review of the extraneural aspects of the mechanisms of drinking. *Progr. Physiol. Psychol.*, 4: 119–201.

Fitzsimons, J. T. (1972) Thirst. *Physiol. Rev.*, 52: 468–561.

Fitzsimons, J. T., & Le Magnen, J. (1969) Eating as a regulatory control of drinking in the rat. *J. comp. physiol. Psychol.*, 67: 273–283.

Fitzsimons, J. T., & Oatley, K. (1968) Additivity of stimuli for drinking in rats. *J. comp. physiol. Psychol.*, 66: 450–455.

Flaherty, C. F., & Davenport, J. W. (1969) Effect of instrumental response pretraining in classical-to-instrumental transfer of a differential reward magnitude discrimination. *Psychon. Sci.*, 15: 235–237.

Flakus, W. J. (1961) The acquisition of two different shock-avoidance responses to two different initially neutral stimuli. Ph.D. dissertation, University of Buffalo.

Ford, C. S., & Beach, F. A. *Patterns of sexual behavior.* New York: Harper & Row.

Foster, R. (1968) The reward value of saccharin solution prior to eating experience. *Psychon. Sci.*, 10: 83–84.

Foster, R. (1968a) Extinction of the consummatory response to a saccharin solution. *Psychon. Sci.*, 10: 81–82.

Fowler, H. (1963) Exploratory motivation and animal handling: The effect on runway performance of start-box exposure time. *J. comp. physiol. Psychol.*, 56: 866–871.

Fowler, H. (1965) *Curiosity and exploratory behavior.* New York: Macmillan.

Fowler, H. (1967) Satiation and curiosity. In K. W. Spence and J. T. Spence (Eds.), *Psychology of learning and motivation.* New York: Academic.

Fowler, H., & Miller, N. E. (1963) Facilitation and inhibition of runway performance by hind- and forepaw shock of various intensities. *J. comp. physiol. Psychol.,* 56: 801–805.

Fowler, H., & Trapold, M. A. (1962) Escape performance as a function of delay of reinforcement. *J. exp. Psychol.,* 63: 464–467.

Fowler, H., & Whalen, R. E. (1961) Variation in incentive stimulus and sexual behavior in the male rat. *J. comp. physiol. Psychol.,* 54: 68–71.

Fowler, H., & Wischner, G. J. (1969) The varied effects of punishment in discrimination learning. In B. A. Campbell and R. M. Church (Eds.), *Punishment and aversive behavior.* New York: Appleton.

Fox, R. E., & King, R. A. (1961) The effects of reinforcement scheduling on the strength of a secondary reinforcer. *J. comp. physiol. Psychol.,* 54: 266–269.

Fox, S. S. (1962) Self-maintained sensory input and sensory deprivation in monkeys: A behavioral and neuropharmacological study. *J. comp. physiol. Psychol.,* 55: 438–444.

Franchina, J. J. (1966) Combined sources of motivation and escape responding. *Psychon. Sci.,* 6: 221–222.

Freedman, P. E., & Callahan, B. S. (1968) Discriminative compartmental CSs in shuttlebox avoidance acquisition. *Psychon. Sci.,* 12: 341–342.

French, D., Fitzpatrick, D., & Law, O. T. (1972) Operant investigation of mating preference in female rats. *J. comp. physiol. Psychol.,* 81: 226–232.

Freud, A. (1936) *The ego and the mechanisms of defence.* London: Hogarth, 1937.

Freud, S. (1895) Project for a scientific psychology. Published posthumously in *The origins of psycho-analysis.* New York: Basic Books, 1954.

Freud, S. (1900) The interpretation of dreams. In A. A. Brill (Ed.), *The basic writings of Sigmund Freud.* New York: Modern Library, 1938.

Freud, S. (1915) Instincts and their vicissitudes. In *Collected papers,* Vol. IV. New York: Basic Books, 1959.

Freud, S. (1917) One of the difficulties of psycho-analysis. In *Collected paper,* Vol. IV. New York: Basic Books, 1959.

Freud, S. (1920) *Beyond the pleasure principle.* London: Hogarth (1948).

Freud, S. (1922) Psycho-analysis. In *Collected papers,* Vol. V. New York: Basic Books, 1959.

Freud, S. (1925) The resistances to psycho-analysis. In *Collected papers,* Vol. V. New York: Basic Books, 1959.

Freud, S. (1926) Inhibitions, symptoms and anxiety. In *Collected works,* Vol. XX. London: Hogarth, 1959.

Freud, S. (1940) *An outline of psychoanalysis.* New York: Norton, 1949.

Freud, S., & Breuer, J. (1892) On the theory of hysterical attacks. In *Collected papers,* Vol. V. New York: Basic Books, 1959.

Theory of motivation

Fuller, J. L., & Thompson, W. R. (1960) *Behavior genetics*. New York: Wiley.

Furchtgott, E., & Rubin, R. D. (1953) The effect of magnitude of reward on maze learning in the white rat. *J. comp. physiol. Psychol.*, 46: 9–12.

Gallistel, C. R. (1964) Electrical self-stimulation and its theoretical implications. *Psychol. Bull.*, 61: 23–34.

Galvani, P. F. (1969) Self-punitive behavior as a function of number of prior fear-conditioning trials. *J. comp. physiol. Psychol.*, 68: 359–363.

Gamble, J. L. (1953) *Chemical anatomy physiology and pathology of extracellular fluid*. Cambridge, Mass.: Harvard University Press.

Garcia, J., & Koelling, R. A. (1966) Relation of cue to consequence in avoidance learning. *Psychon. Sci.*, 4: 123–124.

Gavelek, J. R., & McHose, J. H. (1970) Contrast effects in differential delay of reward conditioning. *J. exp. Psychol.*, 86: 454–457.

Gentile, R. L. (1970) The role of taste preference in the eating behavior of the albino rat. *Physiol. Behav.*, 5: 311–316.

Gerall, A. A. (1958) Effect of interruption of copulation on male guinea pig sexual behavior. *Psychol. Rep.*, 4: 215–221.

Ghent, L. (1951) The relation of experience to the development of hunger. *Canad. J. Psychol.*, 5: 77–81.

Ghent, L. (1957) Some effects of deprivation on eating and drinking behavior. *J. comp. physiol. Psychol.*, 50: 172–176.

Gibbs, J., Young, R. C., & Smith, G. P. (1973) Cholecystokinin decreases food intake in rats. *J. comp. physiol. Psychol.*, 84: 488–495.

Gibson, J. J. (1941) A critical review of the concept of set in contemporary experimental psychology. *Psychol. Bull.*, 38: 781–871.

Gilbert, T. F., & James, W. T. (1956) The dependency of cyclic feeding behavior on internal and external cues. *J. comp. physiol. Psychol.*, 49: 342–344.

Gilhousen, H. C. (1938) Temporal relations in anticipatory reactions of the white rat. *J. comp. Psychol.*, 26: 163–175.

Gilman, A. (1937) The relation between blood osmotic pressure, fluid intake, and voluntary water intake of thirsty rats. *Amer. J. Physiol.*, 120: 323–328.

Gilson, E. (1956) *The Christian philosophy of Thomas Aquinas*. New York: Random House.

Ginott, H. G. (1965) *Between parent and child*. New York: Macmillan.

Glanzer, M. (1953) Stimulus satiation: A construct to explain spontaneous alternation, variability, and exploratory behavior. *Psych. Rev.*, 60: 257–268.

Glanzer, M. (1958) Curiosity, exploratory drive, and stimulus satiation. *Psychol. Bull.*, 55: 302–315.

Gleitman, H., & Steinman, F. (1964) Depression effect as a function of retention interval before and after shift in reward magnitude. *J. comp. physiol. Psychol.*, 57: 158–160.

Glickman, S. E., & Jensen, G. D. (1961) The effects of hunger and thirst on Y-maze exploration. *J. comp. physiol. Psychol.*, 54: 83–85.

Glickman, S. E., & Schiff, B. B. (1967) A biological theory of reinforcement. *Psychol. Rev.*, 74: 81–109.

Goff, M. L., & Finger, F. W. (1966) Activity rhythms and adiurnal light-dark control. *Science*, 154: 1346–1348.

Golin, S., & Bostrum, B. (1964) Stimulus generalization as a function of drive and strength of competing responses to generalized stimuli. *Psychol. Rep.*, 14: 611–619.

Goodrich, K. P. (1959) Performance in different segments of an instrumental response chain as a function of reinforcement schedule. *J. exp. Psychol.*, 57: 57–63.

Goodrich, K. P. (1960) Running speed and drinking rate as functions of sucrose concentration and amount of consummatory activity. *J. comp. physiol. Psychol.*, 53: 245–250.

Goulet, L. R. (1968) Anxiety (drive) and verbal learning: Implications for research and some methodological consideration. *Psychol. Bull.*, 69: 235–247.

Graf, V., & Bitterman, M. E. (1963) General activity as instrumental: Application to avoidance training. *J. exp. anal. Behav.*, 6: 301–305.

Gragg, L., & Black, R. W. (1967) Runway performance following shifts in drive and reward magnitude. *Psychon. Sci.*, 8: 177–178.

Graham, C. H. (1950) Behavior, perception and the psychophysical methods. *Psychol. Rev.*, 57: 108–120.

Green, H. H. (1925) Perverted appetites. *Physiol. Rev.*, 5: 336–348.

Greenberg, I. (1954) The acquisition of a thirst drive. Unpublished Ph.D. dissertation, University of Pennsylvania.

Greene, J. T., & Peacock, L. J. (1965) Response competition in conditioned avoidance. *Psychon. Sci.*, 3: 125–126.

Gregersen, M. I. (1932) Studies on the regulation of water intake: II. Conditions affecting the daily water intake of dogs as registered continuously by a potometer. *Amer. J. Physiol.*, 102: 344–349.

Grice, G. R. (1948) The relation of secondary reinforcement to delayed reward in visual discrimination learning. *J. exp. Psychol.*, 38: 1–16.

Grice, G. R., & Davis, J. D. (1957) Effect on irrelevant thirst motivation on a response learned with food reward. *J. exp. Psychol.*, 53: 347–352.

Grice, G. R., & Goldman, H. M. (1955) Generalized extinction and secondary reinforcement in visual discrimination learning with delayed reward. *J. exp. Psychol.*, 50: 197–200.

Griffiths, R. R., & Thompson, T. (1973) The post-reinforcement pause: A misnomer. *Psychol. Rec.*, 23: 229–235.

Grigg, P. (1970) Lever holding and avoidance in the rat, with constant current and constant voltage UCS. *Psychon. Sci.*, 20: 133–134.

Grindley, G. C. (1929) Experiments on the influence of the amount of reward on learning in young chickens. *Brit. J. Psychol.*, 30: 173–180.

Grossen, N. E., & Kelley, M. J. (1972) Species-specific behavior and acquisition of avoidance behavior in rats. *J. comp. physiol. Psychol.*, 81: 307–310.

Grossman, S. P. (1966) The VMH: A center for affective reactions, satiety, or both? *Physiol. Behav.*, 1: 1–10.

Grunt, J. A., & Young, W. C. (1952) Differential reactivity of individuals and the response of the male guinea pig to testosterone propionate. *Endocrinology*, 51: 237–248.

Grunt, J. A., & Young, W. C. (1953) Consistency of sexual behavior patterns in individual male guinea pigs following castration and androgen therapy. *J. comp. physiol. Psychol.*, 46: 138–144.

Guthrie, E. R. (1934) Reward and punishment. *Psychol. Rev.*, 41: 450–460.

Guthrie, E. R. (1935) *The psychology of learning.* New York: Harper & Row (2nd ed., 1952).

Gutman, Y., & Krausz, M. (1969) Regulation of food and water intake in rats as related to plasma osmolarity and volume. *Physiol. Behav.*, 4: 311–315.

Guttman, N. (1953) Operant conditioning, extinction, and periodic reinforcement in relation to concentration of sucrose used as reinforcing agent. *J. exp. Psychol.*, 46: 213–224.

Guttman, N. (1954) Equal-reinforcement values for sucrose and glucose solutions compared with equal-sweetness values. *J. comp. physiol. Psychol.*, 47: 358–361.

Gwinn, G. T. (1949) Effect of punishment on acts motivated by fear. *J. exp. Psychol.*, 39: 260–269.

Hahn, W. W., Stern, J. A., & Fehr, F. S. (1964) Generalizability of heart rate as a measure of drive state. *J. comp. physiol. Psychol.*, 58: 305–309.

Hainsworth, F. R., Stricker, E. M., & Epstein, A. N. (1968) Water metabolism in the heat: Dehydration and drinking. *Amer. J. Physiol.*, 214: 983–989.

Hall, C. S., & Lindzey, G. (1957) *Theories of personality.* New York: Wiley.

Hall, J. F. (1951) Studies in secondary reinforcement: I. Secondary reinforcement as a function of the frequency of primary reinforcement. *J. comp. physiol. Psychol.*, 44: 246–251.

Hall, J. F. (1955) Activity as a function of a restricted drinking schedule. *J. comp. physiol. Psychol.*, 48: 265–266.

Hall, J. F. (1956) The relationship between external stimulation, food deprivation, and activity. *J. comp. physiol. Psychol.*, 49: 339–341.

Hall, J. F. (1958) The influence of learning in activity wheel behavior. *J. genet. Psychol.*, 92: 121–125.

Hall, J. F. (1966) *The psychology of learning.* Philadelphia: Lippincott.

Hall, J. F., & Connon, H. E. (1957) Activity under low motivational levels as a function of the method of manipulating the deprivation. *J. genet. Psychol.*, 91: 137–142.

Hall, J. F., Low, L., & Hanford, P. V. (1960) A comparison of the activity of hungry, thirsty, and satiated rats in the Dashiell checkerboard maze. *J. comp. physiol. Psychol.*, 53: 155–158.

Hall, J. F., Smith, K., Schnitzer, S. B., & Hanford, P. V. (1953) Elevation of activity level in the rat following transition from ad libitum to restricted feeding. *J. comp. physiol. Psychol.*, 46: 429–433.

Hall, R. D., & Kling, J. W. (1960) Amount of consummatory activity and performance in a modified T maze. *J. comp. physiol. Psychol.*, 53: 165–168.

Hallenborg, B. P., & Fallon, D. (1971) Influence of fear and frustration on the motivation of self-punitive behavior. *Learn. Motiv.*, 2: 26–39.

Hamilton, C. L. (1963) Interaction of food intake and temperature regulation in the rat. *J. comp. physiol. Psychol.*, 56: 476–488.

Hamilton, C. L. (1969) Ingestion of nonnutritive bulk and wheel running in the rat. *J. comp. physiol. Psychol.*, 69: 481–484.

Hamilton, E. L. (1929) The effect of delayed incentive on the hunger drive in the white rat. *Genet. Psychol. Monogr.*, 5: 133–207.

Hamilton, L. W., & Flaherty, C. F. (1973) Interactive effects of deprivation in the albino rat. *Learn. Motiv.*, 4: 148–162.

Hamilton, W. (1858) *Metaphysics.*

Härd, E., & Larsson, K. (1968) Visual stimulation and mating behavior in male rats. *J. comp. physiol. Psychol.*, 66: 805–807.

Härd, E., & Larsson, K. (1970) Effects of delaying intromissions on the male rat's mating behavior. *J. comp. physiol. Psychol.*, 70: 413–419.

Harker, G. S. (1956) Delay of reward and performance of an instrumental response. *J. exp. Psychol.*, 51: 303–310.

Harlow, H. F. (1950) Learning and satiation of response in intrinsically motivated complex puzzle performance by monkeys. *J. comp. physiol. Psychol.*, 43: 289–294.

Harlow, H. F. (1953) Motivation as a factor in the acquisition of new responses. In *Current theory and research in motivation: A symposium.* Lincoln, Neb.: University of Nebraska Press.

Harlow, H. F., Harlow, M. K., & Meyer, D. R. (1950) Learning motivated by a manipulation drive. *J. exp. Psychol.*, 40: 228–234.

Harlow, H. F., & Zimmerman, R. R. (1959) Affectional responses in the infant monkey. *Science*, 130: 421–432.

Harmon, F. L. (1951) *Principles of psychology*, Rev. ed. Milwaukee, Wis.: Bruce.

Harper, A. E., & Spivey, H. E. (1958) Relationship between food intake and osmotic effect of dietary carbohydrate. *Amer. J. Physiol.*, 193: 483–487.

Harriman, A. E., & MacLeod, R. B. (1953) Discriminative thresholds of salt for normal and adrenalectomized rats. *Amer. J. Psychol.*, 66: 465–471.

Harris, W. C., & Heistad, G. T. (1970) Food-reinforced responding in rats during estrus. *J. comp. physiol. Psychol.*, 70: 206–212.

Hart, B. L. (1967) Sexual reflexes and mating behavior in the male dog. *J. comp. physiol. Psychol.*, 64: 388–399.

Harte, R. A., Travers, J. A., & Sarich, P. (1948) Voluntary caloric intake of the growing rat. *J. Nutrition*, 36: 667–679.

Hartley, D. L. (1968) Sources of reinforcement in learned avoidance. *J. comp. physiol. Psychol.*, 66: 12–16.

Hartmann, H. (1958) *Ego psychology and the problem of adaptation.* New York: International Universities.

Hatton, G. I., & Almli, C. R. (1969) Plasma osmotic pressure and volume changes as determinants of drinking thresholds. *Physiol. Behav.*, 4: 207–214.

Hatton, G. I., & Bennett, C. T. (1970) Satiation of thirst and termination of drinking: Roles of plasma osmolarity and absorption. *Physiol. Behav.*, 5: 479–487.

Hatton, G. I., & O'Kelley, L. I. (1966) Water regulation in the rat: Consummatory and excretory responses to short-term osmotic stress. *J. comp. physiol. Psychol.*, 61: 477–479.

Hatton, G. I., & Thornton, L. W. (1968) Hypertonic injections, blood changes, and initiation of drinking. *J. comp. physiol. Psychol.*, 66: 503–506.

Hausmann, M. F. (1932) The behavior of albino rats in choosing food and stimulants. *J. comp. Psychol.*, 13: 279–309.

Hayes, K. J. (1960) Exploration and fear. *Psychol. Rep.*, 6: 91–93.

Healey, A. F., (1965) Compound stimuli, drive strength, and primary stimulus generalization. *J. exp. Psychol.*, 69: 536–538.

Hearst, E. (1969) Stimulus intensity dynamism and auditory generalization for approach and avoidance behavior in rats. *J. comp. physiol. Psychol.*, 68: 111–117.

Hearst, E., & Whalen, R. E. (1963) Facilitating effects of d-amphetamine on discriminated-avoidance performance. *J. comp. physiol. Psychol.*, 56: 124–128.

Heath, R. G., & Mickle, W. A. (1960) Evaluation of seven years' experience with depth electrode studies in human patients. In E. R. Ramey and D. S. O'Doherty (Eds.), *Electrical studies on the unanesthetized brain.* New York: Harper & Row.

Heathers, G. L., & Arakelian, P. (1941) The relationship between strength of drive and rate of extinction of a bar-pressing reaction in the rat. *J. gen. Psychol.*, 24: 243–258.

Hebb, D. O. (1946) On the nature of fear. *Psychol. Rev.*, 53: 259–276.

Hebb, D. O. (1949) *The organization of behavior.* New York: Wiley.

Hebb, D. O. (1955) Drives and the C.N.S. (Conceptual nervous system). *Psychol. Rev.*, 62: 243–254.

Heider, F. (1960) The Gestalt theory of motivation. In M. R. Jones (Ed.), *Nebraska symposium on motivation.* Lincoln, Neb.: University of Nebraska Press.

Heinroth, O. (1911) Beitrage zur Biologie, namentlich Ethologie und Psychologie der Anatiden. *Verh. V. Int. Ornithol. Kongr. Berlin*, 589–702.

Heller, H. (1949) Effects of dehydration on adult and newborn rats. *J. Physiol.*, 108: 303–314.

Hempel, C. G., & Oppenheim, P. (1948) Studies in the logic of explanation. *Philos. Sci.*, 15: 135–175.

Hendricks, S. E. (1969) Influence of neonatally administered hormones and early gonadectomy on rats' sexual behavior. *J. comp. physiol. Psychol.*, 69: 408–413.

Hendry, D. P. (Ed.) (1969) *Conditioned reinforcement.* Homewood, Ill.: Dorsey.

Hendry, D. P., & Coulbourn, J. N. (1967) Reinforcing effect of an informative stimulus that is not a positive discriminative stimulus. *Psychon. Sci.*, 7: 241–242.

Hendry, D. P., & Rasche, R. H. (1961) Analysis of a new nonnutritive positive reinforcer based on thirst. *J. comp. physiol. Psychol.*, 54: 477–483.

Heron, W. T., & Skinner, B. F. (1937) Changes in hunger during starvation. *Psychol. Rec.*, 1: 51–60.

Herrnstein, R. J. (1969) Method and theory in the study of avoidance. *Psychol. Rev.*, 76: 49–69.

Herrnstein, R. J. (1970) On the law of effect. *J. exp. anal. Behav.*, 13: 243–266.

Herrnstein, R. J., & Hineline, P. N. (1966) Negative reinforcement as shock-frequency reduction. *J. exp. anal. Behav.*, 9: 421–430.

Hervey, G. R. (1959) The effects of lesions in the hypothalamus in parabiotic rats. *J. Physiol.* (London), 145: 336–352.

Hess, J. H., & Shafer, J. N. (1968) Discontinuous shock and generalization to the preshock period in discriminated avoidance learning. *Psychon. Sci.*, 10: 175–176.

Hetherington, A. W., & Ranson, S. W. (1940) Hypothalamic lesions and adiposity in the rat. *Anat. Rec.*, 78: 149–172.

Hétu, R. (1971) Deprivation-feeding cycle and locomotor activity of the albino rat in a complex maze. *Psychol. Rec.*, 21: 125–130.

Hilgard, E. R., & Marquis, D. G. (1940) *Conditioning and learning.* New York: Appleton.

Hill, W. F. (1956) Activity as an autonomous drive. *J. comp. physiol. Psychol.*, 49: 15–19.

Hill, W. F., & Spear, N. E. (1962) Resistance to extinction as a joint function of reward magnitude and the spacing of extinction trials. *J. exp. Psychol.*, 64: 636–639.

Hill, W. F., & Spear, N. E. (1963) Choice between magnitudes of reward in a T maze. *J. comp. physiol. Psychol.*, 56: 723–726.

Hill, W. F., & Wallace, W. P. (1967) Reward magnitude and number of training trials as joint factors in extinction. *Psychon. Sci.*, 7: 267–268.

Hillman, B., Hunter, W. S., & Kimble, G. A. (1953) The effect of drive level on the maze performance of the white rat. *J. comp. physiol. Psychol.*, 46: 87–89.

Hinde, R. A. (1954) Changes in responsiveness to a constant stimulus. *Brit. J. anim. Behav.*, 2: 41–55.

Hinde, R. A. (1956) Ethological models and the concept of 'drive.' *Brit. J. Philos. Sci.*, 6: 321–331.

Hinde, R. A. (1959) Unitary drives. *Anim. Behav.*, 7: 130–141.

Hinde, R. A. (1960) Energy models of motivation. *Symp. Soc. exp. Biol.*, 14: 199–213.

Hinde, R. A. (1965) Interaction of internal and external factors in integrations of canary reproduction. In F. A. Beach, (Ed.), *Sex and behavior.* New York: Wiley.

Hinde, R. A. (1970) *Animal behaviour*, 2nd ed. New York: McGraw-Hill.

Hinde, R. A., & Stevenson-Hinde, J. (Eds.) (1973) *Constraints on learning.* New York: Academic.

Hineline, P. N. (1970) Negative reinforcement without shock reduction. *J. exp. anal. Behav.*, 14: 259–268.

Hineline, P. N., & Herrnstein, R. J. (1970) Timing in free-operant and discrete-trial avoidance. *J. exp. anal. Behav.*, 13: 113–126.

Hineline, P. N., & Rachlin, H. (1969) Escape and avoidance of shock by pigeons pecking a key. *J. exp. anal. Behav.*, 12: 533–538.

Hirota, T. T. (1972) The Wyckoff observing response—a reappraisal. *J. exp. anal. Behav.*, 18: 263–280.

Hitchcock, F. A. (1928) The effect of low protein and protein-free diets and starvation on the voluntary activity of the albino rat. *Amer. J. Physiol.*, 84: 410–416.

Hobbes, T. (1651) *Leviathan.*

Hobhouse, L. T. (1901) *Mind in evolution.* New York: Macmillan.

Hodos, W., & Kalman, G. (1963) Effects of increment size and reinforcer volume on progressive ratio performance. *J. exp. anal. Behav.*, 6: 387–392.

Hoebel, B. G., & Teitelbaum, P. (1966) Weight regulation in normal and hypothalamic hyperphagic rats. *J. comp. physiol. Psychol.*, 61: 189–193.

Hoelzel, F. (1927) Central factors in hunger. *Amer. J. Physiol.*, 82: 665–671.

Hoelzel, F. (1957) Dr. A. J. Carlson and the concept of hunger. *Amer. J. clin. Nutr.*, 5: 659–662.

Hoelzel, F., & Carlson, A. J. (1952) The alleged disappearance of hunger during starvation. *Science*, 115: 526–527.

Hoffman, H. S., & Fleshler, M. (1962) The course of emotionality in the development of avoidance. *J. exp. Psychol.*, 64: 288–294.

Hoffman, H. S., Fleshler, M., & Chorny, H. (1961) Discriminated bar-press avoidance. *J. exp. anal. Behav.*, 4: 309–316.

Hoge, M. A., & Stocking, R. L. (1912) A note on the relative value of punishment and reward as motives. *J. anim. Behav.*, 2: 43–50.

Holder, W. B., Marx, M. H., Holder, E. E., & Collier, G. (1957) Response strength as a function of delay in a runway. *J. exp. Psychol.*, 53: 316–323.

Hollingworth, H. L. (1931) Effect and affect in learning. *Psychol. Rev.*, 38: 153–159.

Holman, G. L. (1969) Intragastric reinforcement effect. *J. comp. physiol. Psychol.*, 69: 432–441.

Holmes, J. H., & Gregersen, M. I. (1950) Observations on drinking induced by hypertonic solution. *Amer. J. Physiol.*, 162: 326–337.

Holmes, S. J. (1911) *The evolution of animal intelligence.* New York: Holt, Rinehart & Winston.

Holt, E. B. (1915) *The Freudian wish and its place in ethics.* New York: Holt, Rinehart & Winston.

Holz, W. C., & Azrin, N. H. (1961) Discriminative properties of punishment. *J. exp. anal. Behav.*, 4: 225–232.

Homzie, M. J., & Ross, L. E. (1962) Runway performance following a reduction in the concentration of a liquid reward. *J. comp. physiol. Psychol.*, 55: 1029–1033.

Homzie, M. J., & Rudy, J. W. (1971) Effect of runway performance of reinforcement contingencies established to empty goal-box placements. *Learn. Motiv.*, 2: 95–101.

Hopkins, C. O. (1955) Effectiveness of secondary reinforcing stimuli as a function of the quantity and quality of food reinforcement. *J. exp. Psychol.*, 50: 339–342.

Horel, J. A., Bettinger, L. A., Royce, G. J., & Meyer, D. R. (1966) Role of neocortex in the learning and relearning of two visual habits by the rat. *J. comp. physiol. Psychol.*, 61: 66–78.

Horenstein, B. R. (1951) Performance of conditioned responses as a function of strength of hunger drive. *J. comp. physiol. Psychol.*, 44: 210–224.

Hoskins, R. G. (1925) Studies on vigor: II. The effects of castration on voluntary activity. *Amer. J. Physiol.*, 72: 324–330.

Hsiao, S. (1967) Saline drinking effects on food and water intake in rats. *Psychol. Rep.*, 21: 1025–1028.

Hsiao, S. (1970) Feeding-drinking interaction: Intake of salted food and saline solutions by rats. *Canad. J. Psychol.*, 24: 8–14.

Hsiao, S. (1970a) Reciprocal and additive effects of hyperoncotic and hypertonic treatments on feeding and drinking in rats. *Psychon. Sci.*, 19: 303–304.

Hsiao, S., & Pertsulakes, W. (1970) Feeding-drinking interaction: Food rationing and intake of liquids varying in taste, caloric and osmotic properties. *Physiol. Behav.*, 5: 1495–1497.

Hsiao, S., & Trankina, F. (1969) Thirst-hunger interaction: I. Effects of body-fluid restoration on food and water intake in water-deprived rats. *J. comp. physiol. Psychol.*, 69: 448–453.

Hudson, B. B. (1950) One-trial learning in the domestic rat. *Genet. Psychol., Monogr.*, 41, No. 1.

Huff, F. W., Piantanida, T. P., & Morris, G. L. (1967) Free operant avoidance responding as a function of serially presented variations of UCS intensity. *Psychon. Sci.*, 8: 111–112.

Hug, J. J. (1970) Frustration effect after development of patterned responding to single-alternation responding. *Psychon. Sci.*, 21: 61–62.

Hughes, D., Davis, J. D., & Grice, G. R. (1960) Goal box and alley similarity as a factor in latent extinction. *J. comp. physiol. Psychol.*, 53: 612–614.

Hughes, R. N. (1965) Food deprivation and locomotor exploration in the white rat. *Anim. Behav.*, 13: 30–32.

Hughes, R. N. (1968) Effects of food deprivation, deprivation experience and sex on exploration in rats. *Brit. J. Psychol.*, 59: 47–53.

Hughes, R. N. (1968a) Behaviour of male and female rats with free choice of two environments differing in novelty. *Anim. Behav.*, 16: 92–96.

Hulicka, I. M., & Capeheart, J. (1960) Is the "click" a secondary reinforcer? *Psychol. Rec.*, 10: 29–37.

Hull, C. L. (1931) Goal attraction and directing ideas conceived as habit phenomena. *Psychol. Rev.*, 38: 487–506.

Hull, C. L. (1933) Differential habituation to internal stimuli in the albino rat. *J. comp. Psychol.*, 16: 255–273.

Hull, C. L. (1934) The concept of the habit-family hierarchy and maze learning. *Psychol. Rev.*, 41: 33–54, 134–152.

Hull, C. L. (1935) The mechanism of the assembly of behavior segments in novel combinations suitable for problem solution. *Psychol. Rev.*, 42: 219–245.

Hull, C. L. (1937) Mind, mechanism, and adaptive behavior. *Psychol. Rev.*, 44: 1–32.

Hull, C. L. (1943) *Principles of behavior.* New York: Appleton.

Hull, C. L. (1952) *A behavior system.* New Haven, Conn.: Yale University Press.

Hull, C. L., Hovland, C. I., Ross, R. T., Hall, M., Perkins, D. T., & Fitch, F. B. (1940) *Mathematico-deductive theory of rote learning.* New Haven, Conn.: Yale University Press.

Hull, C. L., Livingston, J. R., Rouse, R. O., & Barker, A. N. (1951) True, sham, and esophageal feeding as reinforcements. *J. comp. physiol. Psychol.*, 44: 236–245.

Hulse, S. H. (1958) Amount and percentage of reinforcement and duration of goal confinement in conditioning and extinction. *J. exp. Psychol.*, 56: 48–57.

Hulse, S. H., Snyder, H. L., & Bacon, W. E. (1960) Instrumental licking behavior as a function of schedule, volume, and concentration of a saccharine reinforcer. *J. exp. Psychol.*, 60: 359–364.

Hulse, S. H., & Suter, S. (1968) One-drop licking in rats. *J. comp. physiol. Psychol.*, 66: 536–539.

Hume, D. (1739) *Treatise of human nature.*

Hume, D. (1779) *Dialogues on natural religion.*

Humphrey, G. (1951) *Thinking.* London: Methuen.

Hunt, H. F., & Brady, J. V. (1955) Some effects of punishment and intercurrent "anxiety" on a simple operant. *J. comp. physiol. Psychol.*, 48: 305–310.

Hurwitz, H. M. B. (1960) Light onset and food as concurrent reinforcers. *Psychol. Rep.*, 6: 359–362.

Hutcheson, F. (1728) *Essay on the nature and conduct of the passions and affections.*

Hyde, T. S., & Trapold, M. A. (1967) Enhanced stimulus generalization of a food reinforced response to a CS for water. *Psychon. Sci.*, 9: 513–514.

Hyde, T. S., Trapold, M. A., & Gross, D. M. (1969) The facilitative effect of a CS for reinforcement upon instrumental responding as a function of reinforcement magnitude: A test of incentive motivation theory. *J. exp. Psychol.*, 78: 423–428.

Imada, H. (1964) "Vigor" of water drinking behavior of rats as a function of thirst drive. *Jap. psychol. Res.*, 6: 108–114.

Irwin, F. W. (1971) *Intentional behavior and motivation.* Philadelphia: Lippincott.

Ison, J. R. (1962) Experimental extinction as a function of number of reinforcement. *J. exp. Psychol.*, 64: 314–317.

Ison, J. R., (1964) Acquisition and reversal of a spatial response as a function of sucrose concentration. *J. exp. Psychol.*, 67: 495–496.

Ison, J. R., Daly, H. B., & Glass, D. H. (1967) Amobarbitol sodium and the effects of reward and nonreward in the Amsel double runway. *Psychol. Rep.*, 20: 491–496.

Ison, J. R., & Glass, D. H. (1968) Consummatory training and subsequent instrumental behavior: A long term consequence of differential reinforcement magnitudes. *J. comp. physiol. Psychol.*, 65: 524–525.

Ison, J. R., & Northman, J. (1968) Amobarbitol sodium and instrumental performance changes following an increase in reward magnitude. *Psychon. Sci.*, 12: 185–186.

Jacobs, H. L. (1964) Evaluation of the osmotic effects of glucose loads in food satiation. *J. comp. physiol. Psychol.*, 57: 309–310.

Jakubczak, L. F. (1969) Effects of blood-glucose levels on wheel-running activity of food-deprived rats. *Psychon. Sci.*, 16: 157–158.

James, W. (1890) *Principles of psychology.* (2 vols.)

James, W. (1914) *The varieties of religious experience.* New York: McKay.

James, W. T. (1953) Social facilitation of eating behavior in puppies after satiation. *J. comp. physiol. Psychol.,* 48: 427–428.

James, W. T. (1963) An analysis of esophageal feeding as a form of operant reinforcement in the dog. *Psychol. Rep.,* 12: 31–39.

James, W. T., & Gilbert, T. F. (1957) Elimination of eating behavior by food injection in weaned puppies. *Psychol. Rep.,* 3: 167–168.

Jammer, M. (1957) *Concepts of force.* Cambridge, Mass.: Harvard University Press.

Janis, I. L. (1958) The psychoanalytic interview as an observational method. In G. Lindzey (Ed.), *Assessment of human motives.* New York: Holt, Rinehart & Winston.

Janowitz, H. D., & Grossman, M. I. (1948) Effect of parenteral administration of glucose and protein hydrolysate on food intake in the rat. *Amer. J. Physiol.,* 155: 28–32.

Janowitz, H. D., & Grossman, M. I. (1949) Effect of variations in nutritive density on intake of food of dogs and rats. *Amer. J. Physiol.,* 158: 184–193.

Janowitz, H. D., & Grossman, M. I. (1949a) Some factors affecting the food intake of normal dogs and dogs with esophagostomy and gastric fistula. *Amer. J. Physiol.,* 159: 143–148.

Janowitz, H. D., & Grossman, M. I. (1951) Effect of prefeeding, alcohol and bitters on food intake of dogs. *Amer. J. Physiol.,* 164: 182–186.

Janowitz, H. D., & Hollander, F. (1955) The time factor in the adjustment of food intake to varied caloric requirement in the dog: A study of the precision of appetite. *Ann. N.Y. Acad. Sci.,* 63: 56–67.

Janowitz, H. D., & Ivy, A. C. (1949) Role of blood sugar levels in spontaneous and insulin-induced hunger in man. *J. appl. Physiol.,* 1: 643–645.

Jarmon, H., & Gerall, A. A. (1961) The effect of food deprivation upon the sexual performance of male guinea pigs. *J. comp. physiol. Psychol.,* 54: 306–309.

Jarvik, M. E., & Essman, W. B. (1960) A simple one-trial learning situation for mice. *Psych. Rep.,* 6: 290.

Jenkins, J. J., & Hanratty, J. A. (1949) Drive intensity discrimination in the white rat. *J. comp. physiol. Psychol.,* 42: 228–232.

Jenkins, M. (1928) The effect of segregation on the sex behavior of the white rat as measured by the obstruction method. *Genet. Psychol. Monogr.,* 3: 455–571.

Jenkins, T. N., Warner, L. H., & Warden, C. J. (1926) Standard apparatus for the study of animal motivation. *J. comp. Psychol.,* 6: 361–382.

Jenkins, W. O. (1950) A temporal gradient of derived reinforcement. *Amer. J. Psychol.,* 63: 237–243.

Jenkins, W. O., Pascal, G. R., & Walker, R. W., Jr. (1958) Deprivation and generalization. *J. exp. Psychol.,* 56: 274–277.

Jennings, H. S. (1906) *The behavior of lower organisms.* New York: Columbia University Press.

Jensen, G. D. (1960) Learning and performance as functions of ration size, hours of privation, and effort requirement. *J. exp. Psychol.,* 59: 261–268.

Johnson, J. L., & Church, R. M. (1965) Effect of shock intensity on non-discriminative avoidance learning of rats in a shuttlebox. *Psychon. Sci.*, 3: 497–498.

Jones, B., & Mishkin, M. (1972) Limbic lesions and the problem of stimulus-reinforcement associations. *J. exp. Neurol.*, 36: 362–377.

Jones, E. (1953) *The life and work of Sigmund Freud.* New York: Basic Books.

Jones, E. C. (1970) Effects of ingesting nonnutritive sweet substances on subsequent sucrose consumption. *Psychon. Sci.*, 21: 23–24.

Jones, E. C., & Swanson, A. M. (1966) Discriminated lever-press avoidance. *Psychon. Sci.*, 6: 351–352.

Jørgensen, H. (1950) The influence of saccharine on the blood sugar. *Acta Physiol. Scand.*, 20: 37.

Kagan, J. (1955) Differential reward value of incomplete and complete sexual behavior. *J. comp. physiol. Psychol.*, 48: 59–64.

Kagan, J., & Berkun, M. M. (1954) The reward value of running activity. *J. comp. physiol. Psychol.*, 47: 108.

Kamin, L. J. (1956) The effects of termination of the CS and avoidance of the US on avoidance learning. *J. comp. physiol. Psychol.*, 49: 420–424.

Kamin, L. J. (1957) The gradient of delay of secondary reward in avoidance learning. *J. comp. physiol. Psychol.*, 50: 445–449.

Kamin, L. J. (1957a) The effects of termination of the CS and avoidance of the US on avoidance learning: An extension. *Canad. J. Psychol.*, 11: 48–56.

Kamin, L. J. (1959) The delay-of-punishment gradient. *J. comp. physiol. Psychol.*, 52: 434–437.

Kamin, L. J., Brimer, C. J., & Black, A. H. (1963) Conditioned suppression as a monitor of fear of the CS in the course of avoidance training. *J. comp. physiol. Psychol.*, 56: 497–501.

Kantor, J. R. (1947) *Problems of physiological psychology.* Bloomington, Ind.: Principia Press.

Kaplan, M. (1952) The effect of noxious stimulus intensity and duration during intermittent reinforcement of escape behavior. *J. comp. physiol. Psychol.*, 45: 538–549.

Karabenick, S. A. (1969) Effects of reward increase and reduction in the double runway. *J. exp. Psychol.*, 82: 79–87.

Karsh, E. B. (1962) Effects of number of rewarded trials and intensity of punishment on running speed. *J. comp. physiol. Psychol.*, 55: 44–51.

Karsh, E. B. (1964) Punishment: Trial spacing and shock intensity as determinants of behavior in a discrete operant situation. *J. comp. physiol. Psychol.*, 58: 299–302.

Katzev, R. (1967) Extinguishing avoidance responses as a function of delayed warning signal termination. *J. exp. Psychol.*, 75: 339–344.

Kaufman, E. L., & Miller, N. E. (1949) Effect of number of reinforcements on strength of approach in an approach-avoidance conflict. *J. comp. physiol. Psychol.*, 42: 65–74.

Kaufman, R. S. (1953) Effects of preventing intromission upon sexual behavior in rats. *J. comp. physiol. Psychol.*, 46: 209–211.

Kavanau, J. L. (1967) Behavior of captive white-footed mice. *Science*, 155: 1623–1639.

Keehn, J. D. (1962) The effect of post-stimulus conditions on the secondary reinforcing power of a stimulus. *J. comp. physiol. Psychol.*, 55: 22–26.

Keehn, J. D., & Arnold, E. M. M. (1960) Licking rates of albino rats. *Science*, 132: 739–741.

Keehn, J. D., & Barakat, H. (1964) Local response rates as affected by reinforcement quality. *Psychol. Rep.*, 15: 519–524.

Keehn, J. D., & Nakkash, S. (1959) Effect of a signal contingent upon an avoidance response. *Nature*, 184: 566–568.

Keehn, J. D., & Webster, C. D. (1968) Rapid discriminated bar-press avoidance through avoidance shaping. *Psychon. Sci.*, 10: 21–22.

Keesey, R. E. (1962) The relationship between pulse frequency, intensity, and duration and the rate of responding for intracranial stimulation. *J. comp. physiol. Psychol.*, 55: 671–678.

Keesey, R. E. (1964) Duration of stimulation and the reward properties of hypothalamic stimulation. *J. comp. physiol. Psychol.*, 58: 201–207.

Keesey, R. E. (1964a) Intracranial reward delay and the acquisition rate of a brightness discrimination. *Science*, 143: 702–703.

Kelleher, R. T. (1961) Schedules of conditioned reinforcement during experimental extinction. *J. exp. anal. Behav.*, 4: 1–5.

Kelleher, R. T., & Gollub, L. R. (1962) A review of positive conditioned reinforcement. *J. exp. anal. Behav.*, 5: 543–597.

Keller, F. S. (1937) *The definition of psychology.* New York: Appleton.

Keller, F. S., & Schoenfeld, W. N. (1950) *Principles of psychology.* New York: Appleton.

Keller, J. V. (1966) Delayed escape from light by the albino rat. *J. exp. anal. Behav.*, 9: 655–658.

Kello, J. E. (1972) The reinforcement-omission effect on fixed-interval schedules: Frustration or inhibition? *Learn. Motiv.*, 3: 138–147.

Kelly, G. A. (1958) Man's construction of his alternatives. In G. Lindzey (Ed.), *Assessment of human motives.* New York: Holt, Rinehart & Winston.

Kemble, E. D., & Clayton, K. N. (1967) Prefeeding and the apparent frustration effect. *Psychon. Sci.*, 9: 491–492.

Kendler, H. H. (1945) Drive interaction: I. Learning as a function of the simultaneous presence of the hunger and thirst drives. *J. exp. Psychol.*, 35: 96–109.

Kendler, H. H. (1945a) Drive interaction: II. Experimental analysis of the role of drive in learning theory. *J. exp. Psychol.*, 35: 188–198.

Kendler, H. H. (1946) The influence of simultaneous hunger and thirst drives upon the learning of two opposed spatial responses of the white rat. *J. exp. Psychol.*, 36: 212–220.

Kendler, H. H., Karasik, A. D., & Schrier, A. M. (1954) Studies of the effect of change of drive: III. Amounts of switching produced by shifting drive from thirst to hunger and from hunger to thirst. *J. exp. Psychol.*, 47: 179–182.

Kendler, H. H., & Law, F. E. (1950) An experimental test of the selective principle of association of drive stimuli. *J. exp. Psychol.*, 40: 299–304.

Kendler, H. H., & Levine, S. (1951) Studies of the effect of change of drive: I. From hunger to thirst in a T-maze. *J. exp. Psychol.*, 41: 429–436.

Kendler, H. H., Levine, S., Altchek, E., & Peters, H. (1952) Studies of the effect of change of drive: II. From hunger to different intensities of a thirst drive in a T-maze. *J. exp. Psychol.*, 44: 1–4.

Kennedy, G. C. (1953) The role of depot fat in the hypothalamic control of food intake in the rat. *Proc. Roy. Soc.*, 140B: 578–592.

Kessen, W. (1953) Response strength and continued stimulus intensity. *J. exp. Psychol.*, 45: 82–86.

Kessen, W., Kimble, G. A., & Hillman, B. M. (1960) Effects of deprivation and scheduling on water intake in the white rat. *Science*, 131: 1735–1736.

Kimble, G. A. (1951) Behavior strength as a function of the intensity of the hunger drive. *J. exp. Psychol.*, 41: 341–348.

Kimble, G. A. (1955) Shock intensity and avoidance learning. *J. comp. physiol. Psychol.*, 48: 281–284.

Kimble, G. A. (1961) *Hilgard and Marquis' conditioning and learning.* New York: Appleton.

King, R. A. (1959) The effects of training and motivation on the components of a learned instrumental response. Unpublished Ph.D. dissertation, Duke University. Cited by Kimble (1961).

Kintsch, W. (1962) Runway performance as a function of drive strength and magnitude of reinforcement. *J. comp. physiol. Psychol.*, 55: 882–887.

Kintsch, W., & Witte, R. S. (1962) Concurrent conditioning of bar press and salivation responses. *J. comp. physiol. Psychol.*, 55: 963–968.

Kissileff, H. R. (1969) Food-associated drinking in the rat. *J. comp. physiol. Psychol.*, 67: 284–300.

Kissileff, H. R. (1969a) Oropharyngeal control of prandial drinking. *J. comp. physiol. Psychol.*, 67: 309–319.

Kleiber, M. (1961) *The fire of life.* New York: Wiley.

Klein, R. M. (1959) Intermittent primary reinforcement as a parameter of secondary reinforcement. *J. exp. Psychol.*, 58: 423–427.

Kleitman, N. (1927) The effect of starvation on the daily consumption of water by the dog. *Amer. J. Physiol.*, 81: 336–340.

Kleitman, N. (1963) *Sleep and wakefulness*, 2nd ed. Chicago: University of Chicago Press.

Kling, J. W. (1956) Speed of running as a function of goal-box behavior. *J. comp. physiol. Psychol.*, 49: 474–476.

Koch, S. (1941) The logical character of the motivation concept. *Psychol. Rev.*, 48: 15–38, 127–154.

Koch, S., & Daniel, W. J. (1945) The effect of satiation on the behavior mediated by a habit of maximum strength. *J. exp. Psychol.*, 35: 167–187.

Kohn, M. (1951) Satiation of hunger from food injected directly into the stomach versus food ingested by mouth. *J. comp. physiol. Psychol.*, 44: 412–422.

Koppman, J. W., & Grice, G. R. (1963) Goal-box and alley similarity in latent extinction. *J. exp. Psychol.*, 66: 611–612.

Kraeling, D. (1961) Analysis of amount of reward as a variable in learning. *J. comp. physiol. Psychol.*, 54: 560–564.

Krasne, F. B. (1962) General disruption resulting from electrical stimulus of ventromedial hypothalamus. *Science*, 138: 822–823.

Kremer, E. F., & Kamin, L. J. (1971) The truly random control procedure: Associative or nonassociative effects in rats. *J. comp. physiol. Psychol.*, 74: 203–210.

Krieckhaus, E. E., & Wolf, G. (1968) Acquisition of sodium by rats: Interaction of innate mechanisms and latent learning. *J. comp. physiol. Psychol.*, 65: 197–201.

Krippner, R. A., Endsley, R. C., & Tacker, R. S. (1967) Magnitude of G_1 reward and the frustration effect in a between subjects design. *Psychon. Sci.*, 9: 385–386.

Kruger, B. M., Galvani, P. F., & Brown, J. S. (1969) A comparison of simulated one-way and shuttle avoidance in an automated apparatus. *Behav. Res. Meth. & Instru.*, 1: 143–147.

Krutch, J. W. (1956) *The great chain of life.* Boston: Houghton Mifflin.

Kuehn, R. E., & Zucker, I. (1968) Reproductive behavior of the Mongolian gerbil (*Meriones ungutculatus*). *J. comp. physiol. Psychol.*, 66: 747–752.

Kulkarni, A. S., & Job, W. M. (1970) Instrumental response pretraining and avoidance acquisition in rats. *J. comp. physiol. Psychol.*, 70: 254–257.

Kuo, Z. Y. (1924) A psychology without heredity. *Psychol. Rev.*, 31: 427–448.

Kuo, Z. Y. (1928) The fundamental error of the concept of purpose and the trial and error fallacy. *Psychol. Rev.*, 35: 414–433.

Kuo, Z. Y. (1929) The net result of the anti-heredity movement in psychology. *Psychol. Rev.*, 36: 191–199.

Kurtz, K. H. (1970) Food deprivation and effort expended for food. *Learn. Motiv.*, 1: 281–296.

Kurtz, K. H., & Jarka, R. G. (1968) Position preference based on differential food privation. *J. comp. physiol. Psychol.*, 66: 518–521.

Kutscher, C. L. (1966) Adaptation to three types of water-deprivation schedules in the hooded rat. *Psychon. Sci.*, 6: 37–38.

Kutscher, C. L. (1969) Species differences in the interaction of feeding and drinking. *Ann. N.Y. Acad. Sci.*, 157: 539–551.

Lachman, R. (1961) The influence of thirst and schedules of reinforcement-nonreinforcement ratios upon brightness discrimination. *J. exp. Psychol.*, 62: 80–87.

Lamarck, J. B. (1809) *Philosophie zoologique.*

Lange, A. (1873) *The history of materialism,* 3rd ed. Trans. by E. C. Thomas. New York: Harcourt Brace Jovanovich, 1925.

Larsson, K. (1956) *Conditioning and sexual behavior in the male albino rat.* Stockholm: Almquist & Wiksell.

Larsson, K. (1959) The effect of restraint upon copulatory behavior in the rat. *Anim. Behav.*, 7: 23–25.

Larsson, K. (1966) Individual differences in reactivity to androgen in male rats. *Physiol. Behav.*, 1: 255–258.

Larsson, K. (1967) Testicular hormone and developmental changes in mating behavior of the male rat. *J. comp. physiol. Psychol.*, 63: 223–230.

Larsson, K. (1969) Failure of gonadal and gonadotrophic hormones to compensate for an impaired sexual function in anosmic male rats. *Physiol. Behav.*, 4: 733–737.

Lashley, K. S. (1938) Experimental analysis of instinctual behavior. *Psychol. Rev.*, 45: 445–471.

Lawler, E. E., III. (1965) Secondary reinforcement value of stimuli associated with shock reduction. *Quart. J. exp. Psychol.*, 17: 57–62.

Lawrence, D. H., & Hommel, L. (1961) The influence of differential goal boxes on discrimination learning involving delay of reinforcement. *J. comp. physiol. Psychol.*, 54: 552–555.

Lawrence, D. H., & Mason, W. A. (1955) Intake and weight adjustment in rats to changes in feeding schedule. *J. comp. physiol. Psychol.*, 48: 43–46.

Lawrence, D. H., & Mason, W. A. (1955a) Food intake in the rat as a function of deprivation intervals and feeding rhythms. *J. comp. physiol. Psychol.*, 48: 267–271.

Lawrence, D. H., & Miller, N. E. (1947) A positive relationship between reinforcement and resistance to extinction produced by removing a source of confusion from a technique that had produced opposite results. *J. exp. Psychol.*, 37: 494–509.

Lawson, R. (1953) Amount of primary reward and strength of secondary reward. *J. exp. Psychol.*, 46: 183–187.

Lawson, R. (1957) Brightness discrimination performance and secondary reward strength as a function of primary reward amount. *J. comp. physiol. Psychol.*, 50: 35–39.

Lawson, R. (1965) *Frustration: The development of a scientific concept.* New York: Macmillan.

Lawson, R., Cross, H. A., & Tambe, J. T. (1959) Effects of large and small rewards on maze performance after different prior experiences with reward amounts. *J. comp. physiol. Psychol.*, 52: 717–720.

Lawson, R., & Marx, M. H. (1958) Frustration: Theory and experiment. *Genet. Psychol. Monogr.*, 57: 393–464.

Leach, D. A. (1971) Rat's extinction performance as a function of deprivation level during training and partial reinforcement. *J. comp. physiol. Psychol.*, 75: 317–323.

Leaf, R. C. (1964) Avoidance response evocation as a function of prior discriminative fear conditioning under curare. *J. comp. physiol. Psychol.*, 58: 446–449.

Leander, J. D. (1973) Effects of food deprivation on free-operant avoidance behavior. *J. exp. anal. Behav.*, 19: 17–24.

Leeper, R. (1935) The role of motivation in learning: A study of the phenomenon of differential motivational control of the utilization of habits. *J. genet. Psychol.*, 46: 3–40.

Leeper, R. W. (1943) *Lewin's topological and vector psychology.* Eugene, Ore.: University of Oregon Press.

Lehrman, D. S. (1962) Interaction of hormonal and experiential influences on development of behavior. In E. L. Bliss (Ed.), *Roots of behavior.* New York: Harper & Row.

Lehrman, D. S. (1970) Semantic and conceptual issues in the nature-nurture problem. In L. R. Aronson, E. Tobach, D. S. Lehrman, and J. S. Rosenblatt (Eds.), *Development and evolution of behavior.* San Francisco: Freeman.

Leitenberg, H. (1965) Response initiation and response termination: Analysis of effects of punishment and escape contingencies. *Psychol. Rep.*, 16: 569–575.

Leitenberg, H. (1965a) Is time-out from positive reinforcement an aversive event? A review of the experimental literature. *Psychol. Rev.*, 64: 428–441.

Le Magnen, J. (1959) Etude d'un phenomene d'appetit provisionnel. *Compte Rendus Acad. Sci.*, 249: 2400–2402.

Le Magnen, J. (1969) Peripheral and systemic actions of food in the caloric regulation of intake. *Ann. N.Y. Acad. Sci.*, 57: 1126–1156.

Le Magnen, J., Devos, M., Gaudilliere, J., Louis-Sylvestrie, J., & Tallon, S. (1973) Role of a lipostatic mechanism in regulation by feeding of energy balance in rats. *J. comp. physiol. Psychol.*, 84: 1–23.

Le Magnen, J., & Tallon, S. (1963) Enregistrement et analyse preliminaire de la periodicité alimentaire spontanée chez le rat blanc. *J. Physiol., Paris*, II: 286–287.

Lepkovsky, S., Lyman, R., Fleming, D., Nagumo, M., & Dimick, M. M. (1957) Gastrointestinal regulation of water and its effect on food intake and rate of digestion. *Amer. J. Physiol.*, 188: 327–331.

Lester, D. (1967) Sex differences in exploration: Toward a theory of exploration. *Psychol. Rec.*, 17: 55–62.

Lester, D. (1967a) Sex differences in exploration of a familiar locale. *Psych. Rec.*, 17: 63–64.

Levine, S. (1953) The role of irrelevant drive stimuli in learning. *J. exp. Psychol.*, 45: 410–416.

Levine, S. (1956) The effects of a strong irrelevant drive on learning. *Psychol. Rep.*, 2: 29–33.

Levine, S. (1957) Infantile experience and consummatory behavior in adulthood. *J. comp. physiol. Psychol.*, 50: 609–612.

Levine, S. (1958) Noxious stimulation in adult rats and consummatory behavior. *J. comp. physiol. Psychol.*, 51: 230–233.

Levine, S. (1965) Water consumption: Emotionally produced facilitation or suppression. *Psychron. Sci.*, 3: 105–106.

Levine, S. (1966) UCS intensity and avoidance learning. *J. exp. Psychol.*, 71: 163–164.

Levine, S., Staats, S. R., & Frommer, G. (1959) Drive summation in a water maze. *Psychol. Rep.*, 5: 301–304.

Levis, D. J. (1970) Serial CS presentation and shuttlebox avoidance conditioning: A further look at the tendency to delay responding. *Psychon. Sci.*, 20: 145–147.

Levitsky, D. A. (1970) Feeding patterns of rats in response to fasts and changes in environmental conditions. *Physiol. Behav.*, 5: 291–300.

Levitsky, D. A., & Collier, G. (1968) Effects of diet and deprivation on meal eating behavior in rats. *Physiol. Behav.*, 3: 137–140.

Lewin, K. (1917) Kriegslandschaft. *Z. Psychol.*, 12: 212–247.

Lewin, K. (1922) Das Problem der Willenmessung der Assoziation. *Psychol. Forsch.*, 1: 191–302; 2: 65–140.

Lewin, K. (1926) Vorsatz, Wille und Beduerfnis. In D. Rapaport (Ed.), *Organization and pathology of thought*. New York: Columbia University Press, 1951.

Lewin, K. (1926a) Vorbemerkungen ueber die psychischen Kraefte und Energien und ueber die Struktur der Seele. *Psychol. Forsch.*, 7: 294–329.

Lewin, K. (1927) Gesetz und Experiment in der Psychologie. *Symposium*, 1: 375–421.

Lewin, K. (1936) *Principles of topological psychology*. New York: McGraw-Hill.

Lewin, K. (1938) *The conceptual representation and the measurement of psychological forces*. Durham, N.C.: Duke University Press.

Lewis, D. J. (1959) A control for the direct manipulation of the fractional anticipatory goal response. *Psychol. Rep.*, 5: 753–756.

Lewis, D. J., Butler, D., & Diamond, A. L. (1958) Direct manipulation of the fractional anticipatory goal response. *Psychol. Rep.*, 4: 575–578.

Lewis, D. J., & Cotton, J. W. (1957) Learning and performance as a function of drive strength during acquisition and extinction. *J. comp. physiol. Psychol.*, 50: 189–194.

Lewis, D. J., & Cotton, J. W. (1960) Effect of runway size and drive strength on acquisition and extinction. *J. exp. Psychol.*, 59: 402–408.

Lewis, D. J., & Kent, N. D. (1961) Attempted direct activation and deactivation of the fractional anticipatory goal response. *Psychol. Rep.*, 8: 107–110.

Lieberman, S. M. (1967) A study of secondary reinforcement. Unpublished Master's thesis, University of Southern California. Cited by Longstreth, 1971.

Linden, D. R. (1969) Attenuation and reestablishment of the CER by discriminated avoidance conditioning. *J. comp. physiol. Psychol.*, 69: 573–578.

Liss, P. (1968) Avoidance and freezing behavior following damage to the hippocampus or fornix. *J. comp. physiol. Psychol.*, 66: 193–197.

Littman, R. A. (1958) Motives, history and causes. In M. R. Jones (Ed.), *Nebraska symposium on motivation*. Lincoln, Neb.: University of Nebraska Press.

Lockard, J. S. (1963) Choice of a warning signal or no warning signal in an unavoidable shock situation. *J. comp. physiol. Psychol.*, 56: 526–530.

Lockard, J. S. (1965) Choice of a warning stimulus or none in several unavoidable-shock situations. *Psychon. Sci.*, 3: 5–6.

Locke, J. (1960) *An essay concerning human understanding.*

Logan, F. A. (1952) The role of delay of reinforcement in determining reaction potential. *J. exp. Psychol.*, 43: 393–399.

Logan, F. A. (1952a) Three estimates of differential excitatory tendency. *Psychol. Rev.*, 59: 300–307.

Logan, F. A. (1960) *Incentive.* New Haven, Conn.: Yale University Press.

Logan, F. A. (1965) Decision making by rats: Delay versus amount of reward. *J. comp. physiol. Psychol.*, 59: 1–12.

LoLordo, V. M. (1969) Positive conditioned reinforcement from aversive situations. *Psychol. Bull.*, 72: 193–203.

LoLordo, V. M., McMillan, J. C., & Riley, A. L. (1974) The effects of auditory and visual signals for response-independent food upon food-reinforced pecking and treadle-pressing. *Learn. Motiv.*, 5: 24–41.

Longstreth, L. E. (1964) Extinction as a function of goal box behavior. *Psychon. Sci.*, 1: 379–380.

Longstreth, L. E. (1971) A cognitive interpretation of secondary reinforcement. In J. K. Cole (Ed.), *Nebraska symposium on motivation*. Lincoln, Neb.: University of Nebraska Press.

Lorber, S. H., Komarov, S. A., & Shay, H. (1950) Effect of sham feeding on gastric motor activity of the dog. *Amer. J. Physiol.*, 162: 447–451.

Lore, R. K. (1968) Effect of confinement upon subsequent activity. *J. comp. physiol. Psychol.*, 65: 372–374.

Lore, R. K., & Gershaw, N. J. (1966) The effect of differential feeding histories on the distribution of home cage activity. *Psychon. Sci.*, 6: 213–214.

Lore, R. K., & Levowitz, A. (1966) Differential rearing and free versus forced exploration. *Psychon. Sci.*, 5: 421–422.

Lorenz, K. (1935) Der Kumpans in der Umwelt des Vogels. *J. Ornithol.*, 83: 137–213. In C. Schiller (Ed.), *Instinctive behavior*. New York: International Universities, 1957.

Lorenz, K. (1937) Uber die Bildung Instinktbegriffes. *Die Naturwissenschaften*, 25: 289–300, 307–318, 324–331. In C. Schiller (Ed.), *Instinctive behavior*. New York: International Universities, 1957.

Lorenz, K. (1950) The comparative method in studying innate behavior patterns. *Symp. Soc. exp. Biol.*, 4: 221–268.

Lotter, E. C., Woods, S. C., & Vasselli, J. R. (1973) Schedule-induced polydipsia: An artifact. *J. comp. physiol. Psychol.*, 83: 478–484.

Lubbock, J. (1882) *Ants, bees, and wasps.*

Luckhardt, A. B., & Carlson, A. J. (1915) Contributions to the physiology of the stomach. XVII: On the chemical control of the gastric hunger mechanism. *Amer. J. Physiol.*, 36: 37–46.

Ludvigson, H. W., & Gay, R. A. (1967) An investigation of conditions determining contrast effects in differential reward conditioning. *J. exp. Psychol.*, 75: 37–42.

Lyon, D. O., & Felton, M. (1966) Conditioned suppression and fixed ratio schedules of reinforcement. *Psychol. Rec.*, 16: 433–440.

Maatsch, J. L. (1959) Learning and fixation after a single shock trial. *J. comp. physiol. Psychol.*, 52: 408–410.

MacDuff, M. (1946) The effect on retention of varying degrees of motivation during learning in rats. *J. comp. Psychol.*, 39: 207–240.

Macfarlane, D. A. (1930) The role of kinesthesis in maze learning. *Univ. Calif. Publ. Psychol.*, 4: 277–305.

Mach, E. (1900) *Analyse der Empfindungen*, 2nd ed.

MacPhail, E. M. (1968) Avoidance responding in pigeons. *J. exp. anal. Behav.*, 11: 629–632.

Magendie, F. (1831) *Precis elementaire de physiologie*, 4th ed.

Maher, W. B., & Wickens, D. D. (1954) Effect of differential quantity of reward on acquisition and performance of a maze habit. *J. comp. physiol. Psychol.*, 47: 44–46.

Malagodi, E. F. (1967) Variable-interval schedules of token reinforcement. *Psychon. Sci.*, 8: 471–472.

Malmo, R. B. (1959) Activation: A neuropsychological dimension. *Psychol. Rev.*, 66: 367–386.

Maltzman, I. (1952) The process need. *Psychol. Rev.*, 59: 40–48.

Mandler, J. M. (1958) Effect of early food deprivation on adult behavior in the rat. *J. comp. physiol. Psychol.*, 51: 513–517.

Manning, H. M. (1956) The effect of varying conditions of hunger and thirst on two responses learned to hunger or thirst alone. *J. comp. physiol. Psychol.*, 49: 249–253.

Margenau, H. (1950) *The nature of physical reality*. New York: McGraw-Hill.

Margules, D. L. (1970) Alpha-adrenergic receptors in hypothalamus for the suppression of feeding behavior by satiety. *J. comp. physiol. Psychol.*, 73: 1–12.

Marshall, J. F., Turner, B. H., & Teitelbaum, P. (1971) Sensory neglect produced by lateral hypothalamic damage. *Science*, 174: 523–525.

Marwine, A. G., & Collier, G. (1971) Instrumental and consummatory behavior as a function of rate of weight loss and weight maintenance schedule. *J. comp. physiol. Psychol.*, 74: 441–447.

Marx, M. H. (1952) Infantile deprivation and adult behavior in the rat: Retention of increased rate of eating. *J. comp. physiol. Psychol.*, 45: 43–49.

Marx, M. H. (1967) Interaction of drive and reward as a determiner of resistance to extinction. *J. comp. physiol. Psychol.*, 64: 488–489.

Marx, M. H. (1969) Positive contrast in instrumental learning from qualitative shift in incentive. *Psychon. Sci.*, 16: 254–255.

Marx, M. H., & Brownstein, A. J. (1963) Effects of incentive magnitude on running speeds without competing responses in acquisition and extinction. *J. exp. Psychol.*, 65: 182–189.

Marx, M. H., McCoy, D. F., & Tombaugh, J. W. (1965) Resistance to extinction as a function of constant delay of reinforcement. *Psychon. Sci.*, 2: 333–334.

Marx, M. H., & Murphy, W. W. (1961) Resistance to extinction as a function of the presentation of a motivating cue in the startbox. *J. comp. physiol. Psychol.*, 54: 207–210.

Marx, M. H., Tombaugh, J. W., Cole, C., & Dougherty, D. (1963) Persistence of nonreinforced responding as a function of the direction of a prior-ordered incentive shift. *J. exp. Psychol.*, 66: 542–546.

Marzocco, F. N. (1951) Frustration effect as a function of drive level, habit strength, and distribution of trials during extinction. Unpublished Ph.D. dissertation, State University of Iowa. Cited by Brown (1961).

Masserman, J. H. (1943) *Behavior and neurosis.* Chicago: University of Chicago Press.

Masterson, F. A. (1970) Is termination of a warning signal an effective reward for the rat? *J. comp. physiol. Psychol.*, 72: 471–475.

Masterson, F. A., Whipple, M. C., & Benner, S. (1972) The role of proprioceptive stimulus change in the rat's avoidance learning. *Psychon. Sci.*, 27: 260–262.

Mathews, S. R., Jr., & Finger, F. W. (1966) Direct observation of the rat's activity during food deprivation. *Physiol. Behav.*, 1: 85–88.

Matthews, T. J. (1971) Thermal motivation in the rat. *J. comp. physiol. Psychol.*, 74: 240–247.

May, M. A. (1948) Experimentally acquired drives. *J. exp. Psychol.*, 38: 66–77.

McAdam, D. (1964) Effects of positional relations between subject, CS, and US on shuttle-box avoidance learning in cats. *J. comp. physiol. Psychol.*, 58: 302–304.

McAllister, W. R., & McAllister, D. E. (1971) Behavioral measurement of conditioned fear. In F. R. Brush (Ed.), *Aversive conditioning and learning.* New York: Academic.

McAllister, W. R., McAllister, D. E., & Douglass, W. K. (1971) The inverse relationship between shock intensity and shuttle-box avoidance learning in rats: A reinforcement explanation. *J. comp. physiol. Psychol.*, 74: 426–433.

McCain, G. (1966) Partial reinforcement effects following a small number of acquisition trials. *Psychon. Monogr. Suppl.*, 1: 251–270.

McCain, G. (1968) The partial reinforcement effect after minimal acquisition: single pellet reward. *Psychon. Sci.*, 13: 151–152.

McCain, G., & Bowen, J. (1967) Pre- and postreinforcement delay with a small number of acquisition trials. *Psychon. Sci.*, 7: 121–122.

McCain, G., & Brown, E. R. (1967) Partial reinforcement with a small number of trials: Two acquisition trials. *Psychon. Sci.*, 7: 265–266.

McCain, G., Dyleski, D., & McElvain, G. (1971) Reward magnitude and instrumental responses: Consistent reward. *Psychon. Monogr. Suppl.*, 3: 249–256.

McCain, G., & McVean, G. (1967) Effects of prior reinforcement or non-reinforcement on later performance in a double alley. *J. exp. Psychol.*, 73: 620–627.

McCall, R. B. (1967) Movable and immovable object experience and exploratory behavior. *Psychon. Sci.*, 8: 473–474.

McCausland, D. F., Menzer, G. W., Demsey, T. K., & Birkimer, J. C. (1967) Response-contingent and non-contingent informative and redundant secondary reinformers. *Psychon. Sci.*, 8: 293–294.

McCleary, R. A. (1953) Taste and post-ingestion factors in specific-hunger behavior. *J. comp. physiol. Psychol.*, 46: 411–421.

McCosh, J. (1874) *The Scottish philosophy.*

McDiarmid, C. G., & Rilling, M. E. (1965) Reinforcement delay and reinforcement rate as determinants of schedule preference. *Psychon. Sci.*, 2: 195–196.

McDougall, W. (1908) *An introduction to social psychology*, 8th ed. Boston: Luce, 1914.

McDougall, W. (1932) *The energies of men.* London: Methuen.

McFarland, D. J. (1964) Interaction of hunger and thirst in the Barbary dove. *J. comp. physiol. Psychol.*, 58: 174–179.

McFarland, D. (1969) Separation of satiating and rewarding consequences of drinking. *Physiol. Behav.*, 4: 987–989.

McFarland, D. J., & L'Angellier, A. B. (1966) Disinhibition of drinking during satiation of feeding behaviour in the Barbary dove. *Anim. Behav.*, 14: 463–467.

McGill, T. E. (1965) Studies of the sexual behavior of male laboratory mice: Effects of genotype, recovery of sex drive, and theory. In F. A. Beach (Ed.), *Sex and behavior.* New York: Wiley.

McGill, T. E., & Blight, W. C. (1963) The sexual behavior of hybrid male mice compared with the behavior of males of the inbred parent strain. *Anim. Behav.*, 11: 480–483.

McGinnis, R. W., & Theios, J. (1972) Effect of probabilistic shock schedules on acquisition, asymptotic responding, and extinction of an avoidance response. *Learn. Motiv.*, 3: 403–419.

McHewitt, E. R., Calef, R. S., Maxwell, F. R., Jr., Meyer, P. A., & McHose, J. H. (1969) Synthesis of double alley and discrimination phenomena: Apparent positive S⁺ contrast in differential conditioning. *Psychon. Sci.*, 16: 137–139.

McHose, J. H. (1966) Incentive reduction: Delay increase and subsequent responding. *Psychon. Sci.*, 5: 213–214.

McHose, J. H. (1968) Incentive reduction: Varied simultaneous reductions and subsequent responding. *Psychon. Sci.*, 11: 313–314.

McHose, J. H., & Gavelek, J. R. (1969) The frustration effect as a function of training magnitude: Within- and between-Ss designs. *Psychon. Sci.*, 17: 261–262.

McHose, J. H., & Ludvigson, H. W. (1965) The role of reward magnitude and incomplete reduction in reward magnitude in the frustration effect. *J. exp. Psychol.*, 70: 490–495.

McKeever, B., & Forrin, B. (1966) Secondary reinforcing properties of informative and non-informative stimuli. *Psychon. Sci.*, 4: 115–116.

McKelvey, R. K. (1956) The relationship between training methods and reward variables in brightness discrimination learning. *J. comp. physiol. Psychol.*, 49: 485–491.

McMahon, R. R., & Games, P. A. (1964) Adaptation to cyclic food deprivation in the acquisition of an instrumental running response. *Psychol. Rep.*, 14: 755–758.

McMillan, J. C. (1971) Percentage reinforcement of fixed-ratio and variable interval performances. *J. exp. anal. Behav.*, 15: 297–302.

McNamara, H. J. (1963) Effects of drive, discrimination training and response disruption on response strength in the absence of primary reinforcement. *Psychol. Rep.*, 12: 683–690.

McNamara, H. J., & Paige, A. B. (1962) An elaboration of Zimmerman's procedure for demonstrating durable secondary reinforcement. *Psychol. Rep.*, 11: 801–803.

Megibow, M., & Zeigler, H. P. (1968) Readiness to eat in the pigeon. *Psychon. Sci.*, 12: 17–18.

Mellgren, R. L., & Ost, J. W. P. (1969) Transfer of Pavlovian differential conditioning to an operant discrimination. *J. comp. physiol. Psychol.*, 67: 390–394.

Mellgren, R. L., Wrather, D. M., & Dyck, D. G. (1972) Differential conditioning and contrast effects in rats. *J. comp. physiol. Psychol.*, 80: 478–483.

Meltzer, D., & Brahlek, J. A. (1968) Quantity of reinforcement and fixed-interval performance. *Psychon. Sci.*, 12: 207–208.

Melvin, K. B., & Stenmark, D. (1968) Facilitative effects of punishment on establishment of a fear motivated response. *J. comp. physiol. Psychol.*, 65: 517–519.

Mendelson, J. (1966) Role of hunger in T-maze learning for food in rats. *J. comp. physiol. Psychol.*, 62: 341–349.

Mendelson, J. (1967) Lateral hypothalamic stimulation in satiated rats: The rewarding effects of self-induced drinking. *Science*, 157: 1077–1079.

Mendelson, J., & Chorover, S. L. (1965) Lateral hypothalamic stimulation in satiated rats: T-maze learning for food. *Science*, 149: 559–561.

Merlan, P. (1945) Brentano and Freud. *J. Hist. Ideas*, 6: 375–377.

Messer, K. (1906) Experimentell-psychologische Untersuchungen über das Denken. *Arch. Psychol.*, 8: 1–224.

Messing, R. B., & Campbell, B. A. (1971) Effect of nonnutritive bulk and food deprivation on wheel-running activity of vagotomized rats. *J. comp. physiol. Psychol.*, 77: 403–405.

Messing, R. B., & Campbell, B. A. (1971a) Dissociation of arousal and regulatory behaviors induced by hypertonic and hypovolemic thirst. *J. comp. physiol. Psychol.*, 76: 305–310.

Metzger, R., Cotton, J. W., & Lewis, D. J. (1957) Effect of reinforcement magnitude and of order of presentation of different magnitudes on runway behavior. *J. comp. physiol. Psychol.*, 50: 184–188.

Meyer, D. R. (1951) Food deprivation and discrimination learning by monkeys. *J. exp. Psychol.*, 41: 10–16.

Meyer, D. R., Cho, C., & Wesemann, A. F. (1960) On problems of conditioned discriminated lever-press avoidance responses. *Psychol. Rev.*, 67: 224–228.

Migler, B. (1963) Bar holding during escape conditioning. *J. exp. anal. Behav.*, 6: 65–72.

Mikulka, P. J., Kendall, P., Constantine, J., & Porterfield, L. (1972) The effect of Pavlovian CS⁺ and CS⁻ on exploratory behavior. *Psychon. Sci.*, 27: 308–310.

Mikulka, P. J., Vogel, J. R., & Spear, N. E. (1967) Postconsummatory delay and goal box confinement. *Psychon. Sci.*, 9: 381–382.

Miles, R. C. (1956) The relative effectiveness of secondary reinforcers throughout deprivation and habit-strength parameters. *J. comp. physiol. Psychol.*, 49: 126–130.

Miles, R. C. (1958) Learning in kittens with manipulatory, exploratory and food incentives. *J. comp. physiol. Psychol.*, 51: 39–42.

Miles, R. C. (1958a) The effect of an irrelevant motive on learning. *J. comp. physiol. Psychol.*, 51: 258–261.

Miles, R. C. (1959) Discrimination in the squirrel monkey as a function of deprivation and problem difficulty. *J. exp. Psychol.*, 52: 15–19.

Millenson, J. R., & de Villiers, P. (1972) Motivational properties of conditioned anxiety. In R. M. Gilbert and J. R. Millenson (Eds.), *Reinforcement, behavioral analyses*. New York: Academic.

Miller, N. E. (1948) Studies in fear as an acquirable drive: I. Fear as motivation and fear-reduction as reinforcement in the learning of new responses. *J. exp. Psychol.*, 38: 89–101.

Miller, N. E. (1948a) Theory and experiment relating psychoanalytic displacement to stimulus-response generalization. *J. abnorm. soc. Psychol.*, 43: 155–178.

Miller, N. E. (1951) Learnable drives and rewards. In S. S. Stevens (Ed.), *Handbook of experimental psychology*. New York: Wiley.

Miller, N. E. (1955) Shortcomings of food consumption as a measure of hunger: Results from other behavioral techniques. *Ann. N.Y. Acad. Sci.*, 68: 141–143.

Miller, N. E. (1956) Effects of drugs on motivation: The value of using a variety of measures. *Ann. N.Y. Acad. Sci.*, 65: 318–333.

Miller, N. E. (1957) Experiments on motivation. *Science*, 126: 1271–1278.

Miller, N. E. (1959) Liberalization of basic S-R concepts: Extensions to conflict behavior, motivation, and social learning. In S. Koch (Ed.), *Psychology, a study of a science*, Vol. 2. New York: McGraw-Hill.

Miller, N. E. (1960) Learning resistance to pain and fear: Effects of overlearning, exposure, and rewarded exposure in context. *J. exp. Psychol.*, 60: 137–145.

Miller, N. E. (1963) Some reflections on the law of effect produce a new alternative to drive reduction. In M. R. Jones (Ed.) *Nebraska symposium on motivation*, Lincoln, Neb.: University of Nebraska Press.

Miller, N. E., Bailey, C. J., & Stevenson, J. A. F. (1950) Decreased "hunger" but increased food intake resulting from hypothalamic lesions. *Science*, 112: 256–259.

Miller, N. E., & DeBold, R. C. (1965) Classically conditioned tongue-licking and operant bar pressing recorded simultaneously in the rat. *J. comp. physiol. Psychol.*, 59: 109–111.

Miller, N. E., & Dollard, J. (1941) *Social learning and imitation.* New Haven, Conn.: Yale University Press.

Miller, N. E., & Kessen, M. L. (1952) Reward effects of food via stomach fistula compared with those of food via mouth. *J. comp. physiol. Psychol.*, 45: 555–564.

Miller, N. E., Sampliner, R. I., & Woodrow, P. (1957) Thirst-reducing effects of water by stomach fistula vs. water by mouth measured by both a consummatory and an instrumental response. *J. comp. physiol. Psychol.*, 50: 1–5.

Miller, N. E., & Stevenson, S. S. (1936) Agitated behavior of rats during experimental extinction and a curve of spontaneous recovery. *J. comp. Psychol.*, 21: 205–231.

Misanin, J. R., Campbell, B. A., & Smith, N. F. (1966) Duration of punishment and the delay of punishment gradient. *Canad. J. Psychol.*, 20: 407–412.

Misiak, H., & Staudt, V. M. (1954) *Catholics in psychology.* New York: McGraw-Hill.

Mogenson, G. J., Mullin, A. D., & Clark, E. A. (1965) Effects of delayed secondary reinforcement and response requirements on avoidance learning. *Canad. J. Psychol.*, 19: 61–73.

Moll, R. P. (1959) The effect of drive level on acquisition of the consummatory response. *J. comp. physiol. Psychol.*, 52: 116–119.

Moll, R. P. (1964) Drive and maturation effects in the development of consummatory behavior. *Psychol. Rep.*, 15: 295–302.

Moll, R. P. (1964a) Effect of drive and drive stabilization on performance and extinction of bar pressing. *J. comp. physiol. Psychol.*, 57: 459–461.

Mollenauer, S. O. (1971) Repeated variations in deprivation level: Different effects depending on amount of training. *J. comp. physiol. Psychol.*, 77: 318–322.

Mollenauer, S. O. (1971a) Shifts in deprivation level: Different effects depending on amount of preshift training. *Learn. Motiv.*, 2: 58–66.

Moltz, H. (1957) Latent extinction and the fractional anticipatory response mechanism. *Psychol. Rev.*, 64: 229–241.

Moltz, H., & Maddi, S. R. (1956) Reduction of secondary reward value as a function of drive strength during latent extinction. *J. exp. Psychol.*, 52: 71–76.

Montgomery, K. C. (1953) The effect of the hunger and thirst drives upon exploratory behavior. *J. comp. physiol. Psychol.*, 46: 315–319.

Montgomery, K. C. (1953a) The effect of activity deprivation on exploratory behavior. *J. comp. physiol. Psychol.*, 46: 438–441.

Montgomery, K. C. (1954) The role of the exploratory drive in learning. *J. comp. physiol. Psychol.*, 47: 60–64.

Montgomery, K. C. (1955) The relation between fear induced by novel stimulation and exploratory behavior. *J. comp. physiol. Psychol.*, 48: 254–260.

Montgomery, K. C., & Monkman, J. A. (1955) The relation between fear and exploratory behavior. *J. comp. physiol. Psychol.*, 48: 132–136.

Montgomery, K. C., & Segall, M. (1955) Discrimination learning based upon the exploratory drive. *J. comp. physiol. Psychol.*, 48: 225–228.

Montgomery, K. C., & Zimbardo, P. G. (1957) Effect of sensory and behavioral deprivation upon exploratory behavior in the rat. *Percept. mot. Skills*, 7: 223–229.

Montgomery, M. F. (1931) The role of the salivary glands in the thirst mechanism. *Amer. J. Physiol.*, 96: 221–227.

Monti, P. M. (1971) Consummatory behavior as a function of deprivation level of the rat. *Psychon. Sci.*, 25: 23–25.

Mook, D. G. (1963) Oral and postingestional determinants of the intake of various solutions in rats with esophageal fistulas. *J. comp. physiol. Psychol.*, 56: 645–659.

Moore, B. R. (1971) On directed respondents. Unpublished Ph.D. dissertation, Stanford University.

Moore, B. R. (1973) The role of directed Pavlovian reactions in simple instrumental learning in the pigeon. In R. A. Hinde and J. Stevenson-Hinde (Eds.), *Constraints on learning*. New York: Academic.

Moot, S. A. (1973) The function of feedback stimuli in avoidance behavior. Unpublished research, University of Washington.

Morgan, C. L. (1894) *Introduction to comparative psychology.*

Morgan, C. T. (1943) *Physiological psychology.* New York: McGraw-Hill.

Morgan, C. T., & Fields, P. E. (1938) The effect of variable preliminary feeding upon the rat's speed of locomotion. *J. comp. Psychol.*, 26: 331–348.

Morgan, C. T., & Morgan, J. D. (1940) Studies in hunger: II. The relation of gastric denervation and dietary sugar to the effects of insulin upon food intake in the rat. *J. genet. Psychol.*, 57: 153–163.

Morgan, J. J. B. (1916) The overcoming of distractions and other resistances. *Arch. Psychol.*, 35: 1–84.

Morgan, J. J. B. (1923) The measurement of instincts. *Psychol. Bull.*, 20: 94.

Morgane, P. J., & Jacobs, H. L. (1969) Hunger and satiety. In G. H. Bourne (Ed.), *World review of nutrition and dietetics*. Basel: Karger.

Morrison, S. D. (1968) The constancy of the energy expended by rats on spontaneous activity and the distribution of activity between feeding and non-feeding. *J. Physiol.*, 197: 305–323.

Morrison, S. D., Lin, H. J., Eckel, H. E., van Itallie, T. B., & Mayer, J. (1958) Gastric contractions in the rat. *Amer. J. Physiol.*, 193: 4–8.

Morrow, J. E., Sachs, L. B., & Belair, R. R. (1965) Further evidence on the dependence between reinforcing and discriminative functions of a stimulus. *Psychon. Sci.*, 2: 61–62.

Morse, W. H., & Skinner, B. F. (1958) Some factors involved in the stimulus control of behavior. *J. exp. anal. Behav.*, 1: 103–107.

Moskowitz, M. J. (1959) Running-wheel activity in the white rat as a function of combined food and water deprivation. *J. comp. physiol. Psychol.*, 52: 621–625.

Moss, F. A. (1924) Study of animal drives. *J. exp. Psychol.*, 7: 165–185.

Moss, R. L. (1968) Changes in bar-press duration accompanying the estrous cycle. *J. comp. physiol. Psychol.*, 66: 460–466.

Mowrer, O. H. (1938) Preparatory set (expectancy)—a determinant in motivation and learning. *Psychol. Rev.*, 45: 62–91.

Mowrer, O. H. (1939) A stimulus-response analysis of anxiety and its role as a reinforcing agent. *Psychol. Rev.*, 46: 553–564.

Mowrer, O. H. (1947) On the dual nature of learning: A reinterpretation of "conditioning" and "problem-solving." *Harv. educ. Rev.*, 17: 102–148.

Mowrer, O. H. (1950) *Learning theory and personality dynamics.* New York: Ronald.

Mowrer, O. H. (1956) Two-factor learning theory reconsidered, with special reference to secondary reinforcement and the concept of habit. *Psychol. Rev.*, 63: 114–128.

Mowrer, O. H. (1960) *Learning theory and behavior.* New York: Wiley.

Mowrer, O. H., & Keehn, J. D. (1958) How are inter-trial 'avoidance' responses reinforced? *Psychol. Rev.*, 65: 209–221.

Mowrer, O. H., & Lamoreaux, R. R. (1942) Avoidance conditioning and signal duration: A study of secondary motivation and reward. *Psychol. Monogr.*, 54 (No. 247).

Mowrer, O. H., & Lamoreaux, R. R. (1946) Fear as an intervening variable in avoidance conditioning. *J. comp. Psychol.*, 39: 29–50.

Mowrer, O. H., & Solomon, L. N. (1954) Contiguity versus drive-reduction in conditioned fear: The proximity and abruptness of drive-reduction. *Amer. J. Psychol.*, 67: 15–25.

Moyer, K. E. (1965) Effect of experience with emotion provoking stimuli on water consumption in the rat. *Psychon. Sci.*, 2: 251–252.

Moyer, K. E., & Baenninger, R. (1963) Effect of environmental change and electric shock on water consumption in the rat. *Psychol. Rep.*, 13: 179–185.

Moyer, K. E., & Bunnell, B. N. (1962) Effect of stomach distention caused by water on food and water consumption in the rat. *J. comp. physiol. Psychol.*, 55: 652–655.

Moyer, K. E., & Chapman, J. A. (1966) Effect of continuous vs. discontinuous shock on shuttle box avoidance of the rat. *Psychon. Sci.*, 4: 197–198.

Moyer, K. E., & Korn, J. H. (1964) Effect of USC intensity on the acquisition and extinction of an avoidance response. *J. exp. Psychol.*, 67: 352–359.

Moyer, K. E., & Korn, J. H. (1966) Effect of UCS intensity on the acquisition and extinction of a one-way avoidance response. *Psychon. Sci.*, 4: 121–122.

Muenzinger, K. F. (1934) Motivation in learning: I. Electric shock for correct response in the visual discrimination habit. *J. comp. Psychol.*, 17: 267–277.

Munn, N. L. (1950) *Handbook of psychological research on the rat.* Boston: Houghton Mifflin.

Murphy, M. R., & Schneider, G. E. (1970) Olfactory bulb removal eliminates mating behavior in the male golden hamster. *Science*, 167: 302–304.

Murray, H. A. (1938) *Explorations in personality.* New York: Oxford University Press.

Myer, J. S. (1971) Some effects of noncontingent aversive stimulation. In F. R. Brush (Ed.), *Aversive conditioning and learning.* New York: Academic.

Myer, J. S., & Kowell, A. P. (1970) Eating patterns and body weight changes of snakes when eating and when food deprived. *Physiol. Behav.,* 6: 71–74.

Myer, J. S., & Kowell, A. P. (1971) Loss and subsequent recovery of body weight in water-deprived snakes (*Elaphe obsoleta obsoleta*). *J. comp. physiol. Psychol.,* 75: 5–9.

Myers, A. K. (1959) Avoidance learning as a function of several training conditions and strain differences in rats. *J. comp. physiol. Psychol.,* 52: 381–386.

Myers, A. K. (1960) Onset vs. termination of stimulus energy as the CS in avoidance conditioning and pseudoconditioning. *J. comp. physiol. Psychol.,* 53: 72–78.

Myers, A. K. (1962) Effects of CS intensity and quality in avoidance conditioning. *J. comp. physiol. Psychol.,* 55: 57–61.

Myers, A. K. (1964) Discriminated operant avoidance learning in Wistar and G-4 rats as a function of type of warning stimulus. *J. comp. physiol. Psychol.,* 58: 453–455.

Myers, A. K., & Miller, N. E. (1954) Failure to find a learned drive based on hunger; evidence for learning motivated by "exploration." *J. comp. physiol. Psychol.,* 47: 428–436.

Myers, J. L. (1958) The effects of delay of reinforcement upon an operant discrimination in the pigeon. *J. exp. Psychol.,* 55: 363–368.

Nakamura, C. Y., Smith, J. C., & Schwartz, F. W. (1963) Establishment of a lasting discriminative stimulus in rats by competition training. *J. comp. physiol. Psychol.,* 56: 852–856.

Newman, J. R. (1955) Stimulus generalization of an instrumental response under high and low levels of drive. *Amer. Psychologist,* 10: 459–461.

Newman, J. R., & Grice, G. R. (1965) Stimulus generalization as a function of drive level, and the relation between two measures of response strength. *J. exp. Psychol.,* 69: 357–362.

Newton, I. (1687) *Principia.* . . . See F. Cajori, *Sir Isaac Newton's Mathematical principles of natural philosophy and his system of the world.* Berkeley, Calif.: University of California Press, 1934.

Nicholls, E. E. (1922) A study of the spontaneous activity of the guinea pig. *J. comp. Psychol.,* 2: 303–330.

Nissen, H. W. (1930) A study of exploratory behavior in the white rat by means of the obstruction method. *J. genet. Psychol.,* 37: 361–376.

North, A. J., & Carl, D. F. (1968) Acquisition and extinction with rewarded goal box placements interpolated among training trials. *Psychon. Sci.,* 13: 7–8.

Notterman, J. M., & Mintz, D. E. (1965) *Dynamics of response.* New York: Wiley.

Novin, D., & Miller, N. E. (1962) Failure to condition thirst induced by feeding dry food to hungry rats. *J. comp. physiol. Psychol.,* 55: 373–374.

Oatley, K. (1964) Changes of blood volume and osmotic pressure in the production of thirst. *Nature,* 202: 1341–1342.

O'Kelly, L. I., & Beck, R. C. (1960) Water regulation in the rat: III. The artificial control of thirst with stomach loads of water and sodium chloride. *Psychol. Monogr.*, 74 (No. 500).

Olds, J. (1955) Physiological mechanisms of reward. In M. R. Jones (Ed.), *Nebraska symposium on motivation*. Lincoln, Neb.: University of Nebraska Press.

Olds, J. (1956) A preliminary mapping of the electrical reinforcing effects in the rat brain. *J. comp. physiol. Psychol.*, 49: 281–285.

Olds, J. (1956a) Runway and maze behavior controlled by baso-medial forebrain stimulation in the rat. *J. comp. physiol. Psychol.*, 49: 507–512.

Olds, J. (1962) Hypothalamic substrates of reward. *Physiol. Rev.*, 42: 554–604.

Olds, J., & Milner, P. (1954) Positive reinforcement produced by electrical stimulation of septal area and other regions of the rat brain. *J. comp. physiol. Psychol.*, 47: 419–427.

Olton, D. S., & Isaacson, R. L. (1968) Importance of spatial location in active avoidance tasks. *J. comp. physiol. Psychol.*, 65: 535–539.

O'Neil, H. F., Jr., Skeen, L. C., & Ryan, F. J. (1970) Prevention of vicious circle behavior. *J. comp. physiol. Psychol.*, 70: 281–285.

Overmier, J. B., & Leaf, R. C. (1965) Effects of discriminated Pavlovian fear conditioning upon previously or subsequently acquired avoidance responding. *J. comp. physiol. Psychol.*, 60: 213–217.

Ovsiankina, M. (1928) Die Wiederaufnahme unterbrochener Handlungen. *Psychol. Forsch.*, 11: 302–379.

Page, H. A. (1955) The facilitation of experimental extinction by response prevention as a function of the acquisition of a new response. *J. comp. physiol. Psychol.*, 48: 14–16.

Panksepp, J. (1971) A re-examination of the role of the ventromedial hypothalamus in feeding behavior. *Physiol. Behav.*, 7: 385–394.

Panksepp, J. (1973) Reanalysis of feeding patterns in the rat. *J. comp. physiol. Psychol.*, 82: 78–94.

Panksepp, J., & Trowill, J. A. (1971) Positive and negative contrast in licking with shifts in sucrose concentration as a function of food deprivation. *Learn. Motiv.*, 2: 49–57.

Pare, W. P. (1965) Stress and consummatory behavior in the albino rat. *Psychol. Rep.*, 16: 399–405.

Patten, R. L., & Rudy, J. W. (1966) The effect on choice behavior of cues paired with noncontingent reward. *Psychon. Sci.*, 6: 121–122.

Patten, R. L., & Rudy, J. W. (1967) Orienting during classical conditioning: Acquired versus unconditioned responding. *Psychon. Sci.*, 7: 27–28.

Pavlik, W. B., & Reynolds, W. F. (1963) Effects of deprivation schedule and reward magnitude on acquisition and extinction performance. *J. comp. physiol. Psychol.*, 56: 452–455.

Pavlov, I. P. (1902) *The work of the digestive glands*. London: Griffin.

Pavlov, I. P. (1927) *Conditioned reflexes*. Trans. by G. V. Anrep. New York: Oxford University Press.

Pearl, J., Aceto, M. D., & Fitzgerald, J. J. (1968) Stimulant drugs and temporary increases in avoidance responding. *J. comp. physiol. Psychol.*, 65: 50–54.

Pearl, R., & Fairchild, T. E. (1921) Studies in the physiology of reproduction in the domestic fowl: XIX. On the influence of free choice of food materials in winter egg production and body weight. *Amer. J. Hygiene*, 1: 253–277.

Pearlman, C. A., Sharpless, S. K., & Jarvik, M. E. (1961) Retrograde amnesia produced by anesthetic and convulsant agents. *J. comp. physiol. Psychol.*, 54: 109–112.

Pearson, K. (1911) *The grammar of science*, 3rd ed. London: Black.

Peck, J. W., & Novin, D. (1971) Evidence that osmoreceptors mediating drinking in rabbits are in the lateral preoptic area. *J. comp. physiol. Psychol.*, 74: 134–147.

Peckham, R. H., Jr., & Amsel, A. (1967) Within-subject demonstration of a relationship between frustration and magnitude of reward in a differential magnitude of reward discrimination. *J. exp. Psychol.*, 73: 187–195.

Peirce, J. T., & Nuttall, R. L. (1961) Self-paced sexual behavior in the female rat. *J. comp. physiol. Psychol.*, 54: 310–313.

Penick, S. B., Smith, G. P., Wieneke, K., Jr., & Hinkle, L. E., Jr. (1963) An experimental evaluation of the relationship between hunger and gastric motility. *Amer. J. Physiol.*, 205: 421–426.

Pereboom, A. C. (1957) An analysis and revision of Hull's Theorem 30. *J. exp. Psychol.*, 53: 234–238.

Pereboom, A. C., & Crawford, B. M. (1958) Instrumental and competing behavior as a function of trials and reward magnitude. *J. exp. Psychol.*, 56: 82–85.

Perin, C. T. (1942) Behavioral potentiality as a joint function of the amount of training and the degree of hunger at the time of extinction. *J. exp. Psychol.*, 30: 93–113.

Perin, C. T. (1943) The effect of delayed reinforcement upon the differentiation of bar responses in white rats. *J. exp. Psychol.*, 32: 95–109.

Perkins, C. C., Jr. (1947) The relation of secondary reward to gradients of reinforcement. *J. exp. Psychol.*, 37: 377–392.

Perkins, C. C., Jr., Seymann, R. G., Levis, D. J., & Spencer, H. R., Jr. (1966) Factors affecting preference for signal-shock over shock-signal. *J. exp. Psychol.*, 72: 190–196.

Pernice, B., & Scagliosi, G. (1895) Ueber die Wirkung der Wasserentziehung auf Thiere. *Arch. path. Anat.*, 139: 155–184.

Perrin, F. A. C. (1923) The psychology of motivation. *Psychol. Rev.*, 30: 176–191.

Perry, R. B. (1918) Docility and purposiveness. *Psychol. Rev.*, 25: 1–21.

Peters, R. H., & Kent, M. A. (1970) Preoptic temperature during oral and intragastric feeding. *Psychon. Sci.*, 20: 135–136.

Peters, R. S. (1956) *Thomas Hobbes*. Harmondsworth, Middlesex: Penguin.

Peters, R. S. (1958) *The concept of motivation*. New York: Humanities.

Peterson, L. R. (1956) Variable delayed reinforcement. *J. comp. physiol. Psychol.*, 49: 232–234.

Petrinovich, L., & Bolles, R. C. (1957) Delayed alternation: Evidence for symbolic processes in the rat. *J. comp. physiol. Psychol.*, 50: 363–365.

Pfaff, D. (1970) Nature of sex hormone effects on rat sex behavior: Specificity of effects and individual patterns of response. *J. comp. physiol. Psychol.*, 73: 349–358.

Pfaffman, C. (1960) The pleasures of sensation. *Psychol. Rev.*, 67: 253–268.

Pieper, W. A., & Marx, M. H. (1963) Conditioning of a previously neutral cue to the onset of a metabolic drive: Two instances of negative results. *Psychol. Rec.*, 13: 191–195.

Pieper, W. A., & Marx, M. H. (1963a) Effects of within-session incentive contrast on instrumental acquisition and performance. *J. exp. Psychol.*, 65: 568–571.

Pliskoff, S., & Tolliver, G. (1960) Water-deprivation-produced sign reversal of a conditioned reinforcer based upon dry food. *J. exp. anal. Behav.*, 3: 323–329.

Porter, J. J. (1962) Stimulus generalization as a function of UCS intensity in eyelid conditioning. *J. exp. Psychol.*, 64: 311–313.

Porter, J. J., Madison, H. L., & Swatek, A. J. (1971) Incentive and frustration effect of direct goal placements. *Psychon. Sci.*, 22: 314–316.

Poschel, B. P. H. (1963) Is centrally-elicited positive reinforcement associated with onset or termination of stimulation? *J. comp. physiol. Psychol.*, 56: 604–607.

Powell, R. W. (1969) The effect of reinforcement magnitude upon responding under fixed-ratio schedules. *J. exp. anal. Behav.*, 12: 605–608.

Powell, R. W. (1970) The effect of shock intensity upon responding under a multiple-avoidance schedule. *J. exp. anal. Behav.*, 14: 321–329.

Powell, R. W. (1971) Effects of deprivation and prefeeding on variable interval responding. *Psychon. Sci.*, 25: 141–142.

Powelson, M. H. (1925) Gastric transplantation. *Science*, 62: 247–248.

Powley, T. L., & Keesey, R. E. (1969) Relationship of body weight to the lateral hypothalamic feeding syndrome. *J. comp. physiol. Psychol.*, 70: 25–36.

Pratt, C. C. (1939) *The logic of modern psychology.* New York: Macmillan.

Premack, D. (1962) Reversibility of the reinforcement relation. *Science*, 136: 255–257.

Premack, D., & Kintsch, W. (1970) A description of free responding in the rat. *Learn. Motiv.*, 1: 321–336.

Prokasy, W. F., Jr. (1956) The acquisition of observing responses in the absence of differential external reinforcement. *J. comp. physiol. Psychol.*, 49: 131–134.

Prokasy, W. F. (1967) Do D and H multiply to determine performance in human conditioning? *Psychol. Bull.*, 67: 368–377.

Prytula, R. E., & Braud, W. G. (1969) Absolute sucrose incentive reduction: Frustration or demotivation. *Psychon. Sci.*, 15: 249–250.

Pubols, B. H., Jr. (1958) Delay of reinforcement, response perseveration, and discrimination reversal. *J. exp. Psychol.*, 56: 32–40.

Pubols, B. H., Jr. (1961) The acquisition and reversal of a position habit as a function of incentive magnitude, *J. comp. physiol. Psychol.*, 54: 94–97.

Rabe, E. F., & Corbit, J. D. (1973) Postingestional control of sodium chloride solution drinking in the rat. *J. comp. physiol. Psychol.*, 84: 268–274.

Rachlin, H. (1966) Recovery of responses during mild punishment. *J. exp. anal. Behav.*, 9: 251–263.

Rachlin, H., & Herrnstein, R. J. (1969) Hedonism revisited: On the negative law of effect. In B. A. Campbell and R. M. Church (Eds.), *Punishment and aversive behavior.* New York: Appleton.

Radlow, R. (1958) Some factors affecting habit strength in aversive training. *J. comp. physiol. Psychol.*, 51: 630–636.

Ramond, C. K. (1954) Performance in selective learning as a function of hunger. *J. exp. Psychol.*, 48: 265–270.

Ramond, C. K. (1954a) Performance in instrumental learning as a joint function of delay of reinforcement and time of deprivation. *J. exp. Psychol.*, 47: 248–250.

Ramond, C. K., Carlton, P. L., & McAllister, W. R. (1955) Feeding method, body weight, and performance in instrumental learning. *J. comp. physiol. Psychol.*, 48: 294–298.

Rampone, A. J., & Shirasu, M. E. (1964) Temperature changes in the rat in response to feeding. *Science*, 144: 317–319.

Ranson, S. W. (1939) Somnolence caused by hypothalamic lesions in the monkey. *Arch. neurol. Psychiat.*, 41: 1–23.

Rapaport, D. (1960) On the psychoanalytic theory of motivation. In M. R. Jones (Ed.), *Nebraska symposium on motivation.* Lincoln, Neb.: University of Nebraska Press.

Ratner, S. C. (1956) Effect of extinction of dipper-approaching on subsequent extinction of bar-pressing and dipper-approaching. *J. comp. physiol. Psychol.*, 49: 576–581.

Ratner, S. C. (1956a) Reinforcing and discriminative properties of the click in a Skinner box. *Psychol. Rep.*, 2: 332.

Ray, A. J., Jr. (1966) Shuttle avoidance: Rapid acquisition by rats to a pressurized air unconditioned stimulus. *Psychon. Sci.*, 5: 29–30.

Razran, G. (1955) A note on second-order conditioning—and secondary reinforcement. *Psychol. Rev.*, 62: 327–332.

Razran, G. (1961) The observable unconscious and the inferable conscious in current Soviet psychophysiology: Interoceptive conditioning, semantic conditioning, and the orienting reflex. *Psychol. Rev.*, 68: 81–147.

Reed, J. D. (1947) Spontaneous activity of animals. *Psychol. Bull.*, 44: 393–412.

Reid, L. S., & Finger, F. W. (1955) The rat's adjustment to 23-hour food deprivation cycles. *J. comp. physiol. Psychol.*, 48: 110–113.

Reid, L. S., & Finger, F. W. (1957) The effect of activity restriction upon adjustment to cyclic food deprivation. *J. comp. physiol. Psychol.*, 50: 491–494.

Reid, T. (1785) *Essays on the intellectual powers of man.*

Reid, T. (1788) *Essays on the active powers of the human mind.*

Renner, K. E. (1964) Delay of reinforcement: A historical review. *Psychol. Bull.*, 61: 341–361.

Renner, K. E. (1966) Temporal integration: The relative utility of immediate versus delayed reward and punishment. *J. exp. Psychol.*, 72: 901–903.

Rescorla, R. A. (1966) Predictability and number of pairings in Pavlovian fear conditioning. *Psychon. Sci.*, 4: 383–384.

Rescorla, R. A. (1967) Pavlovian conditioning and its proper control procedure. *Psychol. Rev.*, 74: 71–80.

Rescorla, R. A. (1968) Pavlovian conditioned fear in Sidman avoidance learning. *J. comp. physiol. Psychol.*, 65: 55–60.

Rescorla, R. A. (1968a) Probability of shock in the presence and absence of CS in fear conditioning. *J. comp. physiol. Psychol.*, 66: 1–5.

Rescorla, R. A. (1969) Establishment of a positive reinforcer through contrast with shock. *J. comp. physiol. Psychol.*, 67: 260–263.

Rescorla, R. A. (1972) Informational variables in Pavlovian conditioning. In G. H. Bower (Ed.), *The psychology of learning and motivation*, Vol. 6. New York: Academic.

Rescorla, R. A., & LoLordo, V. M. (1965) Inhibition of avoidance behavior. *J. comp. physiol. Psychol.*, 59: 406–412.

Rescorla, R. A., & Skucy, J. C. (1969) Effect of response-independent reinforcers during extinction. *J. comp. physiol. Psychol.*, 67: 381–389.

Rescorla, R. A., & Solomon, R. L. (1967) Two-process learning theory: Relationships between Pavlovian conditioning and instrumental learning. *Psychol. Rev.*, 74: 151–182.

Rethlingshafer, D., Eschenbach, A., & Stone, J. T. (1951) Combined drives in learning. *J. exp. Psychol.*, 41: 226–231.

Revusky, B. T. (1970) Failure to support the hypothesis that eating is anticipatory of need. *Psychol. Rep.*, 27: 199–205.

Revusky, S. H. (1967) Hunger level during food consumption: Effects on subsequent preferences. *Psychon. Sci.*, 7: 109–110.

Revusky, S. H., & Garcia, J. (1970) Learned associations over long delays. In G. H. Bower (Ed.), *The psychology of learning and motivation*, Vol. 4. New York: Academic.

Rexroad, C. N. (1933) Goal-objects, purposes, and behavior. *Psychol. Rev.*, 40: 271–281.

Reynierse, J. H. (1972) Differentiation of escape and avoidance responding in rats. *J. comp. physiol. Psychol.*, 79: 165–170.

Reynierse, J. H., Scavio, M. J., Jr., & Spanier, D. (1970) Interaction of hunger and thirst in Mongolian gerbils. *J. comp. physiol. Psychol.*, 70: 126–135.

Reynolds, B. (1949) The acquisition of a black-white discrimination habit under two levels of reinforcement. *J. exp. Psychol.*, 39: 760–769.

Reynolds, B. (1949a) The relationship between the strength of a habit and the degree of drive present during acquisition. *J. exp. Psychol.*, 39: 296–306.

Reynolds, B. (1950) Acquisition of a simple spatial discrimination as a function of the amount of reinforcement. *J. exp. Psychol.*, 40: 152–160.

Reynolds, W. F., & Anderson, J. E. (1961) Choice behavior in a T-maze as a function of deprivation period and magnitude of reward. *Psychol. Rep.*, 8: 131–134.

Reynolds, W. F., Pavlik, W. B., Schwartz, M. M., & Besch, N. F. (1963) Maze learning by secondary reinforcement without discrimination training. *Psychol. Rep.*, 12: 775–781.

Riccio, D. C., & Thach, J. S., Jr. (1966) Rotation as an aversive stimulus for rats. *Psychon. Sci.*, 5: 267–268.

Richards, T. W. (1936) The importance of hunger in the bodily activity of the neonate. *Psychol. Bull.*, 33: 817–835.

Richards, W. J., & Leslie, G. R. (1962) Food and water deprivation as influences on exploration. *J. comp. physiol. Psychol.*, 55: 834–837.

Richter, C. P. (1922) A behavioristic study of the activity of the rat. *Comp. Psychol. Monogr.*, 1 (Serial No. 2).

Richter, C. P. (1927) Animal behavior and internal drives. *Quart. Rev. Biol.*, 2: 307–343.

Richter, C. P. (1936) Increased salt appetite in adrenalectomized rats. *Amer. J. Physiol.*, 115: 155–161.

Richter, C. P. (1939) Salt taste thresholds of normal and adrenalectomized rats. *Endocrinology*, 24: 367–371.

Richter, C. P. (1942–1943) Total self-regulatory functions in animals and human beings. *Harvey Lectures*, 38: 63–103.

Richter, C. P. (1971) Inborn nature of the rat's 24-hour clock. *J. comp. physiol. Psychol.*, 75: 1–4.

Richter, C. P., Holt, L. E., & Barelare, B. (1938) Nutritional requirements for normal growth and reproduction in rats studied by the self-selection method. *Amer. J. Physiol.*, 122: 734–744.

Riess, D. (1971) The buzzer as a primary aversive stimulus: III. Unconditioned and conditioned suppression of barpress avoidance. *Psychon. Sci.*, 25: 212–214.

Riess, D. (1971a) Shuttleboxes, Skinner boxes, and Sidman avoidance in rats: Acquisition and terminal performance as a function of response topography. *Psychon. Sci.*, 25: 283–286.

Robbins, D. (1971) Partial reinforcement: A selective review of the alleyway literature since 1960. *Psychol. Bull.*, 76: 415–431.

Roberts, W. H. (1930) The effect of delayed feeding of white rats in a problem cage. *J. genet. Psychol.*, 37: 35–58.

Roberts, W. W. (1958) Both rewarding and punishing effects from stimulation of posterior hypothalamus of cats with same electrode at same intensity. *J. comp. physiol. Psychol.*, 51: 400–407.

Robertson, J. M. (1930) *A history of free thought in the 19th century.* New York: Putnam.

Robinson, E. A., & Adolph, E. F. (1943) Patterns of normal water drinking in dogs. *Amer. J. Physiol.*, 139: 39–44.

Rodgers, W., & Rozin, P. (1966) Novel food preferences in thiamine-deficient rats. *J. comp. physiol. Psychol.*, 61: 1–4.

Rogers, F. T., & Martin, C. L. (1926) X-ray observations of hunger contractions in man. *Amer. J. Physiol.*, 76: 349–353.

Rohrbaugh, M., Brennan, J. F., & Riccio, D. C. (1971) Control of two-way shuttle avoidance in rats by auditory frequency and intensity. *J. comp. physiol. Psychol.*, 75: 324–330.

Rohrer, J. H. (1949) A motivational state resulting from non-reward. *J. comp. physiol. Psychol.*, 42: 476–485.

Rollins, J. B., Thomas, R. K., & Remley, N. R. (1965) An investigation of drive summation in a water runway. *Psychon. Sci.*, 3: 183–184.

Romanes, G. J. (1882) *Animal intelligence.*

Root, W. S., & Bard, P. (1937) Erection in the cat following removal of lumbo-sacral segments. *Amer. J. Physiol.*, 119: 392–393.

Rosen, A. J. (1966) Incentive-shift performance as a function of magnitude and number of sucrose rewards. *J. comp. physiol. Psychol.*, 62: 487–490.

Rosen, A. J., Glass, D. H., & Ison, J. R. (1967) Amobarbital sodium and instrumental performance changes following reward reduction. *Psychon. Sci.*, 9: 129–130.

Rosen, A. J., & Ison, J. R. (1965) Runway performance following changes in sucrose rewards. *Psychon. Sci.*, 2: 335–336.

Rosenbaum, G. (1951) Temporal gradients of response strength with two levels of motivation. *J. exp. Psychol.*, 41: 261–267.

Rosenzweig, M. R. (1962) The mechanisms of hunger and thirst. In L. Postman (Ed.), *Psychology in the making.* New York: Knopf.

Routtenberg, A., & Kuznesof, A. Y. (1967) Self-starvation of rats living in activity wheels on a restricted feeding schedule. *J. comp. physiol. Psychol.*, 64: 414–421.

Rowell, C. H. F. (1961) Displacement grooming in the chaffinch. *Anim. Behav.*, 9: 38–63.

Rozin, P. (1964) Comparative biology of feeding patterns and mechanisms. *Fed. Proc.*, 23: 60–65.

Rozin, P. (1965) Specific hunger for thiamine: Recovery from deficiency and thiamine preference. *J. comp. physiol. Psychol.*, 59: 98–101.

Rozin, P. (1968) Are carbohydrate and protein intakes separately regulated? *J. comp. physiol. Psychol.*, 65: 23–29.

Rozin, P., & Kalat, J. W. (1971) Specific hungers and poison avoidance as adaptive specializations of learning. *Psychol. Rev.*, 78: 459–486.

Russell, E. S. (1916) *Form and function.* London: Murray.

Sachs, B. D., & Barfield, R. J. (1970) Temporal patterning of sexual behavior in the male rat. *J. comp. physiol. Psychol.*, 73: 359–364.

Sackett, R. S. (1939) The effect of strength of drive at the time of extinction upon resistance to extinction in rats. *J. comp. Psychol.*, 27: 411–431.

Saltzman, I. J. (1949) Maze learning in the absence of primary reinforcement: A study of secondary reinforcement. *J. comp. physiol. Psychol.*, 42: 161–173.

Saltzman, I. J. (1950) Generalization of secondary reinforcement. *J. exp. Psychol.*, 40: 189–193.

Saltzman, I. J., & Koch, S. (1948) The effect of low intensities of hunger on the behavior mediated by a habit of maximum strength. *J. exp. Psychol.*, 38: 347–370.

Santos, J. R. (1960) The influence of amount and kind of training on the acquisition and extinction of escape and avoidance responses. *J. comp. physiol. Psychol.*, 53: 284–289.

Scarborough, B. B., & Goodson, F. E. (1957) Properties of stimuli associated with strong and weak hunger drive in the rat. *J. genet. Psychol.*, 91: 257–261.

Schachter, S., & Singer, J. E. (1962) Cognitive, social, and physiological determinants of emotional state. *Psychol. Rev.*, 69: 379–399.

Schaeffer, R. W., & Hanna, B. (1966) Effects of quality and quantity of reinforcement upon response rate in acquisition and extinction. *Psychol. Rep.*, 18: 819–829.

Schaeffer, R. W., & Huff, R. (1965) Lick rates in cats. *Psychon. Sci.*, 3: 377–378.

Schaeffer, R. W., & Premack, D. (1961) Licking rates in infant albino rats. *Science*, 134: 1980–1981.

Schaeffer, R. W., & Salzberg, C. L. (1973) Licking response distributions associated with the acquisition of schedule-induced polydipsia. *Bull. Psychon. Soc.*, 2: 205–207.

Schmidt-Nielsen, B., Schmidt-Nielsen, K., Brokaw, A., & Schneiderman, H. (1948) Water conservation in desert rodents. *J. cell. comp. Physiol.*, 32: 331–360.

Schmidt-Nielsen, B., Schmidt-Nielsen, K., Houpt, T. R., & Jarnum, S. A. (1956) Water balance of the camel. *Amer. J. Physiol.*, 185: 185–194.

Schoenfeld, W. N. (1950) An experimental approach to anxiety, escape, and avoidance behavior. In P. H. Hoch and J. Zubin (Eds.), *Anxiety*. New York: Grune & Stratton.

Schoenfeld, W. N., Antonitis, J. J., & Bersh, P. J. (1950) A preliminary study of training conditions necessary for secondary reinforcement. *J. exp. Psychol.*, 40: 40–45.

Schrier, A. M. (1956) Amount of incentive and performance on a black-white discrimination problem. *J. comp. physiol. Psychol.*, 49: 123–125.

Schrier, A. M. (1958) Comparison of two methods of investigating the effect of amount of reward on performance. *J. comp. physiol. Psychol.*, 51: 725–731.

Schuster, R. H. (1969) A functional analysis of conditioned reinforcement. In D. P. Hendry (Ed.), *Conditioned reinforcement*. Homewood, Ill.: Dorsey.

Schuster, R. H., & Rachlin, H. (1968) Indifference between punishment and free shock: Evidence for the negative law of effect. *J. exp. anal. Behav.*, 11: 777–786.

Schwartz, M. (1956) Instrumental and consummatory measures of sexual capacity in the male rat. *J. comp. physiol. Psychol.*, 49: 328–333.

Schwartz, M. (1958) Conditioned-stimulus variables in avoidance learning. *J. exp. Psychol.*, 55: 347–351.

Schwartzbaum, J. S., & Ward, H. P. (1958) An osmotic factor in the regulation of food intake in the rat. *J. comp. physiol. Psychol.*, 51: 555–560.

Sclafani, A. (1972) The effects of food deprivation and palatability on the latency to eat of normal and hyperphagic rats. *Physiol. Behav.*, 8: 977–979.

Sclafani, A., & Grossman, S. P. (1969) Hyperphagia produced by knife cuts between the medial and lateral hypothalamus in the rat. *Physiol. Behav.*, 4: 533–538.

Scott, E. M., & Verney, E. L. (1949) Self-selection of diet: VI. The nature of appetites for B vitamins. *J. Nutrition*, 34: 471–480.

Scott, W. W., Scott, C. C., & Luckhardt, A. B. (1938) Observations on the blood-sugar level before, during and after hunger periods in humans. *Amer. J. Physiol.*, 123: 243–247.

Screven, C. G. (1959) Conditioned-hunger drive as indicated by avoidance of a situation previously associated with hunger. *Psychol. Rec.*, 9: 109–114.

Seeman, W., & Williams, H. (1952) An experimental note on a Hull-Leeper difference. *J. exp. Psychol.*, 44: 40–43.

Segal, B., & Champion, R. A. (1966) The acquisition of activating and reinforcing properties by stimuli associated with food deprivation. *Austral. J. Psychol.*, 18: 57–62.

Seligman, M. E. P. (1966) CS redundancy and secondary punishment. *J. exp. Psychol.*, 72: 546–550.

Seligman, M. E. P. (1966a) Comment on McKeever and Forrin. *Psychon. Sci.*, 5: 299.

Seligman, M. E. P. (1970) On the generality of the laws of learning. *Psychol. Rev.*, 77: 406–418.

Seligman, M. E. P., & Hager, J. (Eds.) (1972) *Biological boundaries of learning.* New York: Appleton.

Seward, G. (1942) The "validation" of drives. *Psychol. Rev.*, 49: 88–95.

Seward, J. P. (1942) Note on the externalization of drive. *Psychol. Rev.*, 49: 197–199.

Seward, J. P. (1943) Reinforcement in terms of association. *Psychol. Rev.*, 50: 187–202.

Seward, J. P. (1947) A theoretical derivation of latent learning. *Psychol. Rev.*, 54: 83–98.

Seward, J. P. (1948) The sign of a symbol: A reply to Professor Allport. *Psychol. Rev.*, 55: 277–296.

Seward, J. P. (1949) An experimental analysis of latent learning. *J. exp. Psychol.*, 39: 177–186.

Seward, J. P., (1952) Introduction to a theory of motivation in learning. *Psychol., Rev.*, 59: 405–413.

Seward, J. P. (1956) Drive, incentive, and reinforcement. *Psychol. Rev.*, 63: 195–203.

Seward, J. P., Datel, W. E., & Levy, N. (1952) Tests of two hypotheses of latent learning. *J. exp. Psychol.*, 43: 274–280.

Seward, J. P., & Levy, N. (1949) Sign learning as a factor in extinction. *J. exp. Psychol.*, 39: 660–668.

Seward, J. P., & Pereboom, A. C. (1955) A note on the learning of "spontaneous" activity. *Amer. J. Psychol.*, 68: 139–142.

Seward, J. P., Pereboom, A. C., Butler, B., & Jones, R. B. (1957) The role of prefeeding in an apparent frustration effect. *J. exp. Psychol.*, 54: 445–450.

Seward, J. P., & Procter, D. M. (1960) Performance as a function of drive, reward, and habit strength. *Amer. J. Psychol.*, 73: 448–453.

Seward, J. P., & Seward, G. H. (1937) Internal and external determinants of drives. *Psychol. Rev.*, 44: 349–363.

Seward, J. P., & Seward, G. H. (1940) Studies on the reproductive activities of the guinea pig: I. Factors in maternal behavior. *J. comp. Psychol.*, 29: 1–24.

Seward, J. P., Shea, R. A., & Davenport, R. H. (1960) Further evidence for the interaction of drive and reward. *Amer. J. Psychol.*, 73: 370–379.

Sgro, J. A., Dyal, J. A., & Anastasio, E. J. (1967) Effects of constant delay of reinforcement on acquisition asymptote and resistance to extinction. *J. exp. Psychol.*, 73: 634–636.

Sgro, J. A., Glotfelty, R. A., & Moore, B. D. (1970) Delay of reward in the double alleyway: A within-subjects versus between-groups comparison. *J. exp. Psychol.*, 84: 82–87.

Sgro, J. A., Glotfelty, R. A., & Podlesni, J. A. (1969) Contrast effects and delay of reward in the double alleyway. *Psychon. Sci.*, 16, 29–31.

Sgro, J. A., & Weinstock, S. (1963) Effects of delay on subsequent running under immediate reinforcement. *J. exp. Psychol.*, 66: 260–263.

Shanab, M. E., & Biller, J. D. (1972) Positive contrast in the runway obtained following a shift in both delay and magnitude of reward. *Learn. Motiv.*, 3: 179–184.

Shanab, M. E., Sanders, R., & Premack, D. (1969) Positive contrast in the runway obtained with delay of reward. *Science*, 164: 724–725.

Shapiro, M. M. (1962) Temporal relationship between salivation and lever pressing with differential reinforcement of low rates. *J. comp. physiol. Psychol.*, 55: 567–571.

Share, I., Martyniuk, E., & Grossman, M. I. (1952) Effect of prolonged intragastric feeding on oral food intake in dogs. *Amer. J. Physiol.*, 169: 229–235.

Sheffield, F. D. (1948) Avoidance training and the contiguity principle. *J. comp. physiol. Psychol.*, 41: 165–177.

Sheffield, F. D. (1966) New evidence on the drive-induction theory of reinforcement. In R. N. Haber (Ed.), *Current research in motivation*. New York: Holt, Rinehart & Winston.

Sheffield, F. D., & Campbell, B. A. (1954) The role of experience in the "spontaneous" activity of hungry rats. *J. comp. physiol. Psychol.*, 47: 97–100.

Sheffield, F. D., & Roby, T. B. (1950) Reward value of a non-nutritive sweet taste. *J. comp. physiol. Psychol.*, 43: 471–481.

Sheffield, F. D., & Temmer, H. (1950) Relative resistance to extinction of escape training and avoidance training. *J. exp. Psychol.*, 40: 287–298.

Sheffield, F. D., Wulff, J. J., & Backer, R. (1951) Reward value of copulation without sex drive reduction. *J. comp. physiol. Psychol.*, 44: 3–8.

Sheldon, A. B. (1969) Preference for familiar versus novel stimuli as a function of the familiarity of the environment. *J. comp. physiol. Psychol.*, 67: 516–521.

Sherrington, C. S. (1906) *The integrative action of the nervous system.* New Haven, Conn.: Yale University Press.

Shettleworth, S. J. (1972) Constraints on learning. In D. S. Lehrman, R. A. Hinde, and E. Shaw (Eds.), *Advances in the study of behavior*, Vol. 4. New York: Academic.

Shirley, M. (1928) Studies in activity: II. Activity rhythms; age and activity; activity after rest. *J. comp. Psychol.*, 8: 159–186.

Shirley, M. (1929) Spontaneous activity. *Psychol. Bull.*, 26: 341–365.

Sidman, M. (1953) Two temporal parameters of the maintenance of avoidance behavior by the white rat. *J. comp. physiol. Psychol.*, 46: 253–261.

Sidman, M. (1954) The temporal distribution of avoidance responses. *J. comp. physiol. Psychol.*, 47: 399–402.

Sidman, M. (1955) Some properties of the warning stimulus in avoidance behavior. *J. comp. physiol. Psychol.*, 48: 444–450.

Sidman, M. (1962) Reduction of shock frequency as reinforcement for avoidance behavior. *J. exp. anal. Behav.*, 5: 247–257.

Sidman, M. (1966) Avoidance behavior. In W. K. Honig (Ed.), *Operant behavior: Areas of research and application.* New York: Appleton.

Siegel, P. S. (1943) Drive shift, a conceptual and experimental analysis. *J. comp. Psychol.*, 35: 139–148.

Siegel, P. S. (1946) Alien drive, habit strength, and resistance to extinction. *J. comp. Psychol.*, 39: 307–317.

Siegel, P. S. (1947) The relationship between voluntary water intake, body weight loss, and number of hours of water privation in the rat. *J. comp. physiol. Psychol.*, 40: 231–238.

Siegel, P. S. (1961) Food intake in the rat in relation to the dark-light cycle. *J. comp. physiol. Psychol.*, 54: 294–301.

Siegel, P. S., & Brantley, J. J. (1951) The relationship of emotionality to the consummatory response of eating. *J. exp. Psychol.*, 42: 304–306.

Siegel, P. S., & Correia, M. J. (1963) Speed of resumption of eating following distraction in relation to number of hours food-deprivation. *Psychol. Rec.*, 13: 39–44.

Siegel, P. S., & MacDonnell, M. F. (1954) A repetition of the Calvin-Bicknell-Sperling study of conditioned drive. *J. comp. physiol. Psychol.*, 47: 250–252.

Siegel, P. S., Melvin, K. B., & Wagner, J. D. (1971) Vicious circle behavior in the rat: Measurement problems visited again. *J. comp. physiol. Psychol.*, 76: 311–315.

Siegel, P. S., & Milby, J. B. (1969) Secondary reinforcement in relation to shock termination. *Psychol. Bull.*, 72: 146–156.

Siegel, P. S., & Siegel, H. S. (1949) The effect of emotionality on the water intake of the rat. *J. comp. physiol. Psychol.*, 42: 12–16.

Siegel, P. S., & Sparks, D. L. (1961) Irrelevant aversive stimulation as an activator of an appetitional response: A replication. *Psychol. Rep.*, 9: 700.

Siegel, P. S., & Steinberg, M. (1949) Activity level as a function of hunger. *J. comp. physiol. Psychol.*, 42: 413–416.

Siegel, P. S., & Stuckey, H. L. (1947) The diurnal course of water and food intake in the normal mature rat. *J. comp. physiol. Psychol.*, 40: 365–370.

Siegel, S. (1972) Conditioning of insulin-induced glycemia. *J. comp. physiol. Psychol.*, 78: 233–241.

Siegel, S., & Nettleton, N. (1970) Conditioning of insulin-induced hyperphagia. *J. comp. physiol. Psychol.*, 72: 390–393.

Simmons, R. (1924) The relative effectiveness of certain incentives in animal learning. *Comp. Psychol. Monogr.*, 2 (Serial No. 7).

Singer, C. (1959) *A short history of scientific ideas to 1900*. New York: Oxford University Press.

Skinner, B. F. (1936) Conditioning and extinction and their relation to drive. *J. gen. Psychol.*, 14: 296–317.

Skinner, B. F. (1938) *The behavior of organisms*. New York: Appleton.

Skinner, B. F. (1948) *Walden Two*. New York: Macmillan.

Skinner, B. F. (1950) Are theories of learning necessary? *Psychol. Rev.*, 57: 193–216.

Skinner, B. F. (1953) *Science and human behavior*. New York: Macmillan.

Skinner, B. F. (1959) *Cumulative record*. New York: Appleton.

Slonaker, J. R. (1924) The effects of pubescence, oestration, and menopause on the voluntary activity of the albino rat. *Amer. J. Physiol.*, 68: 294–315.

Smith, F. V. (1960) *The explanation of human behavior*, 2nd ed. London: Constable.

Smith, M. F. (1939) The establishment and extinction of the token-reward habit in the cat. *J. gen. Psychol.*, 20: 475–486.

Smith, M. F., & Smith, K. U. (1939) Thirst-motivated activity and its extinction in the cat. *J. gen. Psychol.*, 21: 89–98.

Smith, M. H., Jr. (1966) Effects of intravenous injections on eating. *J. comp. physiol. Psychol.*, 61: 11–14.

Smith, M. H., Jr. (1966a) Effect of hypertonic preloads on concurrent eating and drinking. *J. comp. physiol. Psychol.*, 61: 398–401.

Smith, M. H., Jr. (1972) Evidence for a learning component of sodium hunger in rats. *J. comp. physiol. Psychol.*, 78: 242–247.

Smith, M. H., Jr., & Duffy, M. (1957) Some physiological factors that regulate eating behavior. *J. comp. physiol. Psychol.*, 50: 601–609.

Smith, M. H., Jr., & Duffy, M. (1957a) Consumption of sucrose and saccharine by hungry and satiated rats. *J. comp. physiol. Psychol.*, 50: 65–69.

Smith, M. H., Jr., & Kinney, G. C. (1956) Sugar as a reward for hungry and nonhungry rats. *J. exp. Psychol.*, 51: 348–352.

Smith, M. H., Jr., Pool, R., & Weinberg, H. (1958) Evidence for a learning theory of specific hunger. *J. comp. physiol. Psychol.*, 51: 758–763.

Smith, M. H., Jr., Pool, R., & Weinberg, H. (1959) The effect of peripherally induced shifts in water balance on eating. *J. comp. physiol. Psychol.*, 52: 289–293.

Smith, M. H., Jr., Pool, R., & Weinberg, M. (1962) The role of bulk in the control of eating. *J. comp. physiol. Psychol.*, 55: 115–120.

Smith, M. H., Jr., Salisbury, R., & Weinberg, H. (1961) The reaction of hyperthalamic-hyperphagic rats to stomach preloads. *J. comp. physiol. Psychol.*, 54: 660–664.

Smith, M. P., & Buchanan, G. (1954) Acquisition of secondary reward by cues associated with shock reduction. *J. exp. Psychol.*, 48: 123–126.

Smith, M. P., & Capretta, P. J. (1956) Effects of drive level and experience on the reward value of saccharine solutions. *J. comp. physiol. Psychol.*, 49: 553–557.

Smith, N. F., Misanin, J. R., & Campbell, B. A. (1966) Effect of punishment of an avoidance response: Facilitation or inhibition? *Psychon. Sci.*, 4: 271–272.

Smith, O. A., Jr., McFarland, W. L., & Taylor, E. (1961) Performance in a shock-avoidance conditioning situation interpreted as pseudo-conditioning. *J. comp. physiol. Psychol.*, 54: 154–157.

Smith, R. F., & Keller, F. R. (1970) Free-operant avoidance in the pigeon using a treadle response. *J. exp. anal. Behav.*, 13: 211–214.

Smith, S., & Guthrie, E. R. (1921) *General psychology in terms of behavior*. New York: Appleton.

Snowdon, C. T. (1969) Motivation, regulation, and the control of meal parameters with oral and intragastric feeding. *J. comp. physiol. Psychol.*, 69: 91–100.

Solomon, R. L. (1956) The externalization of hunger and frustration drive. *J. comp. physiol. Psychol.*, 49: 145–148.

Solomon, R. L. (1964) Punishment. *Amer. Psychologist*, 19: 239–253.

Solomon, R. L., & Brush, E. S. (1956) Experimentally derived conceptions of anxiety and aversion. In M. R. Jones (Ed.), *Nebraska sym-*

posium on motivation. Lincoln, Neb.: University of Nebraska Press.

Solomon, R. L., Kamin, L. J., & Wynne, L. C. (1953) Traumatic avoidance learning: The outcomes of several extinction procedures with dogs. *J. abnorm. soc. Psychol.,* 48: 291–302.

Solomon, R. L., & Turner, L. H. (1962) Discriminative classical conditioning in dogs paralyzed by curare can later control discriminative avoidance responses in the normal state. *Psychol. Rev.,* 69: 202–219.

Solomon, R. L., & Wynne, L. C. (1953) Traumatic avoidance learning: Acquisition in normal dogs. *Psychol. Monogr.,* 67 (No. 354).

Solomon, R. L., & Wynne, L. C. (1954) Traumatic avoidance learning: The principles of anxiety conservation and partial irreversibility. *Psychol. Rev.,* 61: 353–385.

Soulairac, A. (1952) La signification physiologique de la période réfractaire dans le comportement sexuel du rat male. *J. Physiol.,* 44: 99–113.

Spear, N. E. (1962) Comparison of the reinforcing effect of brain stimulation on Skinner box, runway, and maze performance. *J. comp. physiol. Psychol.,* 55: 679–684.

Spear, N. E. (1965) Replication report: Absence of a successive contrast effect on instrumental running behavior after a shift in sucrose concentration. *Psychol. Rep.,* 16: 393–394.

Spear, N. E. (1967) Retention of reinforcement magnitude. *Psychol. Rev.,* 74: 216–234.

Spear, N. E., & Hill, W. F. (1965) Adjustment to new reward: Simultaneous and successive-contrast effects. *J. exp. Psychol.,* 70: 510–519.

Spear, N. E., & Pavlik, W. B. (1966) Percentage of reinforcement and reward magnitude effects in a T maze: Between and within subjects. *J. comp. physiol. Psychol.,* 71: 521–528.

Spear, N. E., & Spitzner, J. H. (1966) Simultaneous and successive contrast effects of reward magnitude in selective learning. *Psychol. Monogr.,* 80 (No. 618).

Spear, N. E., & Spitzner, J. H. (1968) Residual effects of reinforcement magnitude. *J. exp. Psychol.,* 77: 135–139.

Spence, K. W. (1944) The nature of theory construction in contemporary psychology. *Psychol. Rev.,* 51: 47–68.

Spence, K. W. (1947) The role of secondary reinforcement in delayed reward learning. *Psychol. Rev.,* 54: 1–8.

Spence, K. W. (1951) Theoretical interpretations of learning. In S. S. Stevens (Ed.), *Handbook of experimental psychology.* New York: Wiley.

Spence, K. W. (1951a) Theoretical interpretations of learning. In C. P. Stone (Ed.), *Comparative psychology,* 3rd ed. Englewood Cliffs, N.J.: Prentice-Hall.

Spence, K. W. (1954) The relation of response latency and speed to the intervening variables and N in S-R theory. *Psychol. Rev.,* 61: 209–216.

Spence, K. W. (1956) *Behavior theory and conditioning.* New Haven, Conn.: Yale University Press.

Spence, K. W., Goodrich, K. P., & Ross, L. E. (1959) Performance in differential conditioning and discrimination learning as a function of hunger and relative response frequency. *J. exp. Psychol.*, 58: 8–16.

Spencer, H. (1880) *Principles of psychology*, 3rd ed.

Staddon, J. E. R. (1970) Temporal effects of reinforcement: A negative "frustration" effect. *Learn. Motiv.*, 1: 227–247.

Stein, L. (1962) An analysis of stimulus-duration preference in self-stimulation of the brain. *J. comp. physiol. Psychol.*, 55: 405–414.

Stellar, E., & Hill, J. H. (1952) The rat's rate of drinking as a function of water deprivation. *J. comp. physiol. Psychol.*, 45: 96–102.

Sterritt, G. M. (1965) Inhibition and facilitation of eating by electric shock: III. A further study of the role of strain and of shock level. *Psychon. Sci.*, 2: 319–320.

Sterritt, G. M., & Smith, M. P. (1965) Reinforcing effects of specific components of feeding in young leghorn chicks. *J. comp. physiol. Psychol.*, 59: 171–175.

Stevens, S. S. (1935) Operational definitions of psychological concepts. *Psychol. Rev.*, 42: 517–527.

Stevens, S. S., Carton, A. S., & Shickman, G. M. (1958) A scale of apparent intensity of electric shock. *J. exp. Psychol.*, 56: 328–334.

Stevenson, J. A. F., & Rixon, R. H. (1957) Environmental temperature and deprivation of food and water on the spontaneous activity of rats. *Yale J. Biol. Med.*, 29: 575–584.

Stewart, C. C. (1898) Variations in daily activity produced by alcohol and by changes in barometric pressure and diet, with a description of recording method. *Amer. J. Physiol.*, 1: 40–56.

Stewart, D. (1792–1827) *Elements of the philosophy of the human mind.*

Stolurow, L. M. (1951) Rodent behavior in the presence of barriers: II. The metabolic maintenance method; a technique for caloric drive control and manipulation. *J. genet. Psychol.*, 79: 289–335.

Stone, C. P. (1926) The initial copulatory response of female rats reared in isolation from the age of 20 days to puberty. *J. comp. Psychol.*, 6: 73–83.

Stone, C. P. (1927) Retention of copulatory ability in male rats following castration. *J. comp. Psychol.*, 7: 369–387.

Stone, C. P. (1929) The age factor in animal learning: I. Rats in the problem box and the maze. *Genet. Psychol. Monogr.*, 5: 8–130.

Stone, C. P. (1939) Copulatory activity in adult male rats following castration and injections of testosterone proprionate. *Endocrinology*, 24: 165–174.

Stone, C. P., Barker, R. G., & Tomilin, M. I. (1935) Sexual drive in potent and impotent male rats as measured by the Columbia obstruction apparatus. *J. genet. Psychol.*, 47: 33–48.

Stone, C. P., & Ferguson, L. (1938) Preferential responses of male albino rats to food and to receptive females. *J. comp. Psychol.*, 26: 237–253.

Stone, C. P., & Sturman-Huble, M. (1927) Food vs. sex as incentives for male rats on the maze learning problem. *Amer. J. Psychol.*, 38: 403–408.

Stone, G. R. (1953) The effect of negative incentives in serial learning: VII. Theory of punishment. *J. gen. Psychol.*, 48: 133–161.

Stone, G. R., & Walter, N. (1951) The effect of negative incentives in serial learning: VI. Response repetition as a function of an isolated electric shock punishment. *J. exp. Psychol.*, 41: 411–418.

Storms, L. H., Boroczi, G., & Broen, W. E., Jr. (1963) Effects of punishment as a function of strain of rat and duration of shock. *J. comp. physiol. Psychol.*, 56: 1022–1026.

Stout, G. F. (1903) *The groundwork of psychology.* New York: Hinds, Noble, & Eldredge.

Strange, J. R. (1954) The effect of an irrelevant drive on the reaction tendency specific to another drive. *J. gen. Psychol.*, 51: 31–40.

Strassburger, R. C. (1950) Resistance to extinction of a conditioned operant as related to drive level at reinforcement. *J. exp. Psychol.*, 49: 473–487.

Stretch, R. (1972) Development and maintenance of responding under schedules of electric-shock presentation. In R. M. Gilbert and J. R. Millenson (Eds.), *Reinforcement, behavioral analyses.* New York: Academic.

Stricker, E. M. (1966) Extracellular fluid volume and thirst. *Amer. J. Physiol.*, 211: 232–238.

Stricker, E. M. (1968) Some physiological and motivational properties of the hypovolemic stimulus of thirst. *Physiol. Behav.*, 3: 379–385.

Stricker, E. M. (1971) Inhibition of thirst in rats following hypovolemia and/or caval ligation. *Physiol. Behav.*, 6: 293–298.

Strominger, J. L. (1946–1947). The relation between water intake and food intake in normal rats and in rats with hypothalamic hyperphagia. *Yale J. Biol. Med.*, 19: 279–287.

Strong, T. N., Jr. (1957) Activity in the white rat as a function of apparatus and hunger. *J. comp. physiol. Psychol.*, 50: 596–600.

Strutt, G. F., & Stewart, C. N. (1970) The role of blood glucose in activity related self-starvation. *Psychon. Sci.*, 18: 287–289.

Swanson, A. M., Brackmann, J. F., Jr., Dublirer, E. M., & Moss, D. J. (1966) Effect of thirst drive conditioning on shuttle performance by satiated rats. *Psychol. Rec.*, 16: 25–31.

Szymanski, J. S. (1914) Eine Methode zur Untersuchung der Ruhe und Aqtivitaetsperioden bei Tieren. *Arch. ges. Physiol.*, 158: 343–385.

Szymanski, J. S. (1918) Abhandlungen zum Aufbau der Lehre von den Handlungen der Tiere. *Arch. ges. Physiol.*, 170: 220–237.

Tacker, R. S., & Way, J. (1968) Motivational properties of nonreward. *Psychon. Sci.*, 10: 103–104.

Tang, M., & Collier, G. (1971) Effect of successive deprivations and recoveries on the level of instrumental performance in the rat. *J. comp. physiol. Psychol.*, 74: 108–114.

Tarpy, R. M. (1971) Effects of food deprivation on spontaneous activity and blood glucose. *Psychol. Rep.*, 28: 463–469.

Tarttelin, M. F., & Gorski, R. A. (1971) Variations in food and water intake in the normal and acyclic female rat. *Physiol. Behav.*, 7: 847–852.

Taylor, C. J. (1969) Effects of palatable nonnutritive bulk as a reinforcer. *J. comp. physiol. Psychol.*, 69: 286–290.

Taylor, C. J., & Bruning, J. L. (1967) Effects of nonnutritive bulk on eating behavior. *J. comp. physiol. Psychol.*, 64: 353–355.

Taylor, G. T. (1971) The incentive value of complexity. *Psychon. Sci.*, 22: 143–144.

Teel, K. S. (1952) Habit strength as a function of motivation during learning. *J. comp. physiol. Psychol.*, 45: 188–191.

Teel, K. S., & Webb, W. B. (1951) Response evocation on satiated trials in the T-maze. *J. exp. Psychol.*, 41: 148–152.

Teghtsoonian, R., & Campbell, B. A. (1960) Random activity of the rat during food deprivation as a function of environment. *J. comp. physiol. Psychol.*, 53: 242–244.

Teitelbaum, P. (1955) Sensory control of hypothalamic hyperphagia. *J. comp. physiol. Psychol.*, 48: 156–163.

Teitelbaum, P. (1957) Random and food-directed activity in hyperphagic and normal rats. *J. comp. physiol. Psychol.*, 50: 486–490.

Teitelbaum, P., & Campbell, B. A. (1958) Ingestion patterns in hyperphagic and normal rats. *J. comp. physiol. Psychol.*, 51: 135–141.

Teitelbaum, P., & Epstein, A. N. (1962) The lateral hypothalamic syndrome: Recovery of feeding and drinking after lateral hypothalamic lesions. *Psychol. Rev.*, 69: 74–90.

Telegdy, G. A., & Cohen, J. S. (1971) Cue utilization and drive level in albino rats. *J. comp. physiol. Psychol.*, 75: 248–253.

Tellish, J. A., & Dunstone, J. J. (1971) Punishment of variable ratio maintained behavior. *Psychol. Rec.*, 21: 49–52.

Tenen, S. S. (1966) An automated one-way avoidance box for the rat. *Psychon. Sci.*, 6: 407–408.

Theios, J. (1963) Drive stimulus generalization increments. *J. comp. physiol. Psychol.*, 56: 691–695.

Theios, J., & Bower, G. H. (1964) A test of the competing response-interference hypothesis of extinction. *Psychon. Sci.*, 1: 395–396.

Theios, J., & Brelsford, J. (1964) Overlearning-extinction effect as an incentive effect. *J. exp. Psychol.*, 67: 463–467.

Theios, J., Lynch, A. D., & Lowe, W. F., Jr. (1966) Differential effects of shock intensity on one-way and shuttle avoidance conditioning. *J. exp. Psychol.*, 72: 294–299.

Thilly, F. (1957) *History of philosophy*, 3rd ed. Revised by L. Wood. New York: Holt, Rinehart & Winston.

Thomas, D. R., Berman, D. L., & Serednesky, G. E., & Lyons, J. (1968) Information value and stimulus configuring as factors in conditioned reinforcement. *J. exp. Psychol.*, 76: 181–189.

Thomas, D. R., & King, R. A. (1959) Stimulus generalization as a function of level of motivation. *J. exp. Psychol.*, 57: 323–328.

Thomas, D. W., & Mayer, J. (1968) Meal taking and regulation of food intake by normal and hypothalamic hyperphagic rats. *J. comp. physiol. Psychol.*, 66: 642–653.

Thomas, J. R. (1969) Maintenance of behavior by conditioned reinforcement in the signaled absence of primary reinforcement. In D. P. Hendry (Ed.), *Conditioned reinforcement*. Homewood, Ill.: Dorsey.

Thompson, W. R. (1953) Exploratory behavior as a function of hunger in "bright" and "dull" rats. *J. comp. physiol. Psychol.*, 46: 323–326.

Thomson, C. W., & Porter, P. B. (1953) Need reduction and primary reinforcement: Maze learning by sodium-deprived rats for a subthreshold saline reward. *J. comp. physiol. Psychol.*, 46: 281–287.

Thorndike, E. L. (1911) *Animal intelligence.* New York: Macmillan.

Thorndike, E. L. (1932) *The fundamentals of learning.* New York: Columbia University Press.

Thurstone, L. L. (1923) The stimulus-response fallacy in psychology. *Psychol. Rev.*, 30: 354–369.

Timberlake, W. D., & Birch, D. (1967) Complexity, novelty, and food deprivation as determinants of speed of shift of behavior. *J. comp. physiol. Psychol.*, 63: 545–548.

Tinbergen, N. (1940) Die Ubersprungbewegung. *Z. Tierpsychol.*, 4: 1–40.

Tinbergen, N. (1951) *The study of instinct.* New York: Oxford University Press.

Tinklepaugh, O. L. (1928) An experimental study of representative factors in monkeys. *J. comp. Psychol.*, 8: 197–236.

Tolman, E. C. (1920) Instinct and purpose. *Psychol. Rev.*, 27: 218–233.

Tolman, E. C. (1923) The nature of instinct. *Psychol. Bull.*, 20: 200–218.

Tolman, E. C. (1923a) A behavioristic account of the emotions. *Psychol. Rev.*, 30: 217–227.

Tolman, E. C. (1926) The nature of fundamental drives. *J. abnorm. soc. Psychol.*, 5: 349–358.

Tolman, E. C. (1932) Purposive behavior in animals and men. New York: Appleton.

Tolman, E. C. (1936) Operational behaviorism and current trends in psychology. In E. C. Tolman, *Collected papers in psychology.* Berkeley, Calif.: University of California Press, 1951.

Tolman, E. C. (1942) *Drives toward war.* New York: Appleton.

Tolman, E. C. (1943) A drive-conversion diagram. *Psychol. Rev.*, 50: 503–513.

Tolman, E. C. (1959) Principles of purposive behavior. In S. Koch (Ed.), *Psychology: A study of a science, Vol. 2.* New York: McGraw-Hill.

Tolman, E. C., & Gleitman, H. (1949) Studies in spatial learning: VII. Place and response learning under different degrees of motivation. *J. exp. Psychol.*, 39: 653–659.

Tolman, E. C., & Honzik, C. H. (1930) Degrees of hunger; reward and nonreward; and maze learning in rats. *Univ. Calif. Publ. Psychol.*, 4: 241–256.

Tombaugh, T. N. (1966) Resistance to extinction as a function of the interaction between training and extinction delays. *Psychol. Rep.*, 19: 791–798.

Towbin, E. J. (1949) Gastric distention as a factor in the satiation of thirst in esophagostomized dogs. *Amer. J. Physiol.*, 159: 533–541.

Trapold, M. A. (1962) The effect of incentive motivation on an unrelated reflex response. *J. comp. physiol. Psychol.*, 55: 1034–1039.

Trapold, M. A. (1966) Reversal of an operant discrimination by noncontingent discrimination reversal training. *Psychon. Sci.*, 4: 247–248.

Trapold, M. A., & Bell, J. E. (1964) Effect of noncontingent exposure to shifts in reward magnitude on subsequent instrumental runway performance. *Psychol. Rep.*, 15: 679–684.

Trapold, M. A., Carlson, J. G., & Myers, W. A. (1965) The effect of noncontingent fixed- and variable-interval reinforcement upon subsequent acquisition of the fixed-interval scallop. *Psychon. Sci.*, 2: 261–262.

Trapold, M. A., & Doren, D. G. (1966) Effect of noncontingent partial reinforcement on the resistance to extinction of a runway response. *J. exp. Psychol.*, 71: 429–431.

Trapold, M. A., & Fairlie, J. (1965) Transfer of discrimination learning based upon contingent and noncontingent training procedures. *Psychol. Rep.*, 17: 239–246.

Trapold, M. A., & Fowler, H. (1960) Instrumental escape performance as a function of the intensity of noxious stimulation. *J. exp. Psychol.*, 60: 323–326.

Trapold, M. A., Gross, D. M., & Lawton, G. W. (1969) Reversal of an instrumental discrimination by classical discriminative conditioning. *J. exp. Psychol.*, 78: 686–689.

Trapold, M. A., Lawton, G. W., Dick, R. A., & Gross, D. M. (1968) Transfer of training from differential classical to differential instrumental conditioning. *J. exp. Psychol.*, 76: 568–573.

Trapold, M. A., & Odom, P. B. (1965) Transfer of an operant discrimination and a discrimination reversal between two manipulandum-defined responses. *Psychol. Rep.*, 16: 1213–1221.

Trapold, M. A., & Overmier, J. B. (1972) The second learning process in instrumental learning. In A. H. Black and W. F. Prokasy (Eds.), *Classical conditioning II: Current theory and research.* New York: Appleton.

Trapold, M. A., & Winokur, S. (1967) Transfer from classical conditioning and extinction to acquisition, extinction, and stimulus generalization of a positively reinforced instrumental response. *J. exp. Psychol.*, 73: 517–525.

Traupman, K. L. (1971) Acquisition and extinction of an instrumental running response with single- or multiple-pellet reward. *Psychon. Sci.*, 22: 61–63.

Treichler, F. R., & Collins, R. W. (1965) Comparison of cyclic and continuous deprivation on wheel running. *J. comp. physiol. Psychol.*, 60: 447–448.

Treichler, F. R., & Hall, J. F. (1962) The relationship between deprivation, weight loss, and several measures of activity. *J. comp. physiol. Psychol.*, 55: 346–349.

Treichler, F. R., & Hamilton, D. M. (1967) Relationships between deprivation and air-drinking behavior. *J. comp. physiol. Psychol.*, 63: 541–544.

Troland, L. T. (1928) *The fundamentals of human motivation.* New York: Van Nostrand Reinhold.

Trost, R. C., & Homzie, M. J. (1966) A further investigation of conditioned hunger. *Psychon. Sci.*, 5: 355–356.

Trowill, J. A., Panksepp, J., & Gandelman, R. (1969) An incentive model of rewarding brain stimulation. *Psychol. Rev.*, 76: 264–281.

Tsai, C. (1925) The relative strength of sex and hunger motives in the albino rat. *J. comp. Psychol.*, 5: 407–415.

Tsang, Y. C. (1938) Hunger motivation in gastrectomized rats. *J. comp. Psychol.*, 26: 1–17.

Tulving, E. (1972) Episodic and semantic memory. In E. Tulving and W. Donaldson (Eds.), *Organization of memory.* New York: Academic.

Turner, L. H., & Solomon, R. L. (1962) Human traumatic avoidance learning: Theory and experiments on the operant-respondent distinction and failures to learn. *Psychol. Monogr.*, 76 (No. 559).

Uexkull, J. von (1909) *Umwelt und Innerwelt der Tiere.* Berlin, Vienna: Springer.

Valenstein, E. S. (1964) Problems of measurement and interpretation with reinforcing brain stimulation. *Psychol. Rev.*, 71: 415–437.

Valenstein, E. S. (1973) *Brain stimulation and motivation.* Glenview, Ill.: Scott, Foresman.

Valenstein, E. S., & Weber, M. L. (1965) Potentiation of insulin shock by saccharin. *J. comp. physiol. Psychol.*, 60: 443–446.

Vaughn, J., & Diserens, C. M. (1930) The relative effects of various intensities of punishment on learning and efficiency. *J. comp. Psychol.*, 10: 55–66.

Verplanck, W. S. (1955) Since learned behavior is innate, and vice versa, what now? *Psychol. Rev.*, 62: 139–144.

Verplanck, W. S., & Hayes, J. R. (1953) Eating and drinking as a function of maintenance schedule. *J. comp. physiol. Psychol.*, 46: 327–333.

Verworn, M. (1889) *Psycho-physiologische Protistenstudien.*

Vogel, J. R., Mikulka, P. J., & Spear, N. E. (1968) Effects of shifts in sucrose and saccharine concentrations on licking behavior in the rat. *J. comp. physiol. Psychol.*, 66: 661–666.

Wada, T. (1922) An experimental study of hunger in its relation to activity. *Arch. Psychol.*, 8 (Serial No. 57).

Wagman, W., & Allen, J. D. (1964) The development of a conditioned positive reinforcer based upon the termination of shock. *Psychon. Sci.*, 1: 363–364.

Wagner, A. R. (1959) The role of reinforcement and nonreinforcement in an "apparent frustration effect." *J. exp. Psychol.*, 57: 130–136.

Wagner, A. R. (1961) Effects of amount and percentage of reinforcement and number of acquisition trials on conditioning and extinction. *J. exp. Psychol.*, 62: 234–242.

Wagner, A. R. (1963) Conditioned frustration as a learned drive. *J. exp. Psychol.*, 66: 142–148.

Wagner, A. R. (1969) Frustrative nonreward: A variety of punishment. In B. A. Campbell and M. R. Church (Eds.), *Punishment and aversive behavior.* New York: Appleton.

Wahlsten, D. (1972) Phenotypic and genetic relations between initial response to electric shock and rate of avoidance learning in mice. *Behav. Genet.*, 2: 211–240.

Wahlsten, D. L., & Cole, M. (1972) Classical and avoidance training of leg flexion in the dog. In A. H. Black and W. F. Prokasy (Eds.), *Classical conditioning II: Current theory and research.* New York: Appleton.

Wahlsten, D., Cole, M., Sharp, D., & Fantino, E. (1968) Facilitation of bar-press avoidance by handling during the intertrial interval. *J. comp. physiol. Psychol.*, 65: 170–175.

Wahlsten, D., & Sharp, D. (1969) Improvement of shuttle avoidance by handling during the intertrial interval. *J. comp. physiol. Psychol.*, 67: 252–259.

Wald, G., & Jackson, B. (1944) Activity and nutritional deprivation. *Proc. Nat. Acad. Sci.*, 30: 255–263.

Walike, B. C., & Smith, O. A. (1972) Regulation of food intake during intermittent and continuous cross circulation in monkeys (*Macaca mulatta*). *J. comp. physiol. Psychol.*, 80: 372–381.

Walker, D. W., & Remley, N. R. (1970) The relationships among percentage body weight loss, free fatty acids and consummatory behavior in rats. *Physiol. Behav.*, 5: 301–309.

Walker, K. C. (1942) Effects of a discriminative stimulus transferred to a previously unassociated response. *J. exp. Psychol.*, 31: 312–321.

Wallace, R. B. (1970) Comparison of two techniques for the assessment of conditioned reinforcement in the runway. *J. gen. Psychol.*, 83: 87–96.

Waller, T. G. (1968) Effects of magnitude of reward in spatial and brightness discrimination tasks. *J. comp. physiol. Psychol.*, 66: 122–127.

Wampler, R. S. (1973) Increased motivation in rats with ventromedical hypothalamic lesions. *J. comp. physiol. Psychol.*, 84: 275–285.

Wang, G. H. (1923) Relation between "spontaneous" activity and oestrus cycle in the white rat. *Comp. Psychol. Monogr.*, 2 (Serial No. 6).

Wang, G. H., Richter, C. P., & Guttmacher, A. F. (1925) Activity studies of male castrated rats with ovarian transplants, and correlation of the activity with the histology of the grafts. *Amer. J. Physiol.*, 73: 581–598.

Wangensteen, O. H., & Carlson, A. J. (1931) Hunger sensations in a patient after total gastrectomy. *Proc. Soc. exp. Biol.*, 28: 545–547.

Warden, C. J., et al. (1931) *Animal motivation: Experimental studies on the albino rat.* New York: Columbia University Press.

Warden, C. J., & Aylesworth, M. (1927) The relative value of reward and punishment in the formation of a visual discrimination habit in the white rat. *J. comp. Psychol.*, 7: 117–127.

Warden, C. J., & Haas, E. L. (1927) The effect of short intervals of delay in feeding upon speed of maze learning. *J. comp. Psychol.*, 7: 107–116.

Warden, C. J., Jenkins, T. N., & Warner, L. H. (1936) *Comparative psychology.* New York: Ronald.

Warner, L. H. (1927) A study of sex drive in the white rat by means of the obstruction method. *Comp. Psychol. Monogr.*, 4 (Serial No. 22).

Warren, H. C. (1921) *A history of the association psychology.* New York: Scribner.

Warren, J. A., Jr., & Bolles, R. C. (1967) A reevaluation of a simple contiguity interpretation of avoidance learning. *J. comp. physiol. Psychol.*, 64: 179–182.

Washburn, M. F. (1908) *The animal mind.* New York: Macmillan.

Watson, J. (1895) *Hedonistic theories from Aristippus to Spencer.*

Watson, J. B. (1916) The place of the conditioned reflex in psychology. *Psychol. Rev.*, 23: 89–116.

Watson, J. B. (1917) The effect of delayed feeding upon learning. *Psychobiol.*, 1: 51–59.

Watson, J. B. (1919) *Psychology from the standpoint of a behaviorist.* Philadelphia: Lippincott.

Watt, H. (1905) Experimentelle Beitgaege zu einer Theorie des Denkens. *Arch. Psychol.*, 4: 289–436.

Wayner, M. S., & Petraitis, J. (1967) Effects of water deprivation and salt arousal of drinking on wheel turning activity of rats. *Physiol. Behav.*, 2: 273–275.

Weasner, M. H., Finger, F. W., & Reid, L. S. (1960) Activity changes under food deprivation as a function of recording device. *J. comp. physiol. Psychol.*, 53: 470–474.

Webb, W. B. (1949) The motivational aspect of an irrelevant drive in the behavior of the white rat. *J. exp. Psychol.*, 39: 1–14.

Webb, W. B. (1955) Drive stimuli as cues. *Psychol. Rep.*, 1: 287–298.

Webb, W. B. (1957) Antecedents of sleep. *J. exp. Psychol.*, 53: 162–166.

Webb, W. B., & Goodman, I. J. (1958) Activating role of an irrelevant drive in absence of the relevant drive. *Psychol. Rep.*, 4: 235–238.

Webb, W. B., & Nolan, C. Y. (1953) Cues for discrimination as secondary reinforcing agents: A confirmation. *J. comp. physiol. Psychol.*, 46: 180–181.

Wedeking, P. W. (1967) Rat avoidance in a dual, one-way shuttle apparatus. *Psychon. Sci.*, 8: 33–34.

Weijnen, J. A. W. M. (1972) *Lick-contingent electrical stimulation of the tongue.* Utrecht: Drukkerij Elinkwijk.

Weiner, B. (1972) *Theories of motivation.* Chicago: Markham.

Weinstein, L. (1970) Negative incentive contrast effects with saccharin vs sucrose and partial reinforcement. *Psychon. Sci.*, 21: 276–278.

Weinstock, R. B. (1971) Preacquisition exploration of the runway in the determination of contrast effects in the rat. *J. comp. physiol. Psychol.*, 75: 107–115.

Weinstock, R. B. (1972) Maintenance schedules and hunger drive: An examination of the rat literature. *Psychol. Bull.*, 78: 311–320.

Weir, L. G., Larson, E. E., & Roundtree, L. G. (1922) Studies in diabetes insipidus, water balance, and water intoxication. *Arch. int. Med.*, 29: 306–330.

Weisinger, R. S., Parker, L. F., & Bolles, R. C. (1973) Effects of amount of reward on acquisition of a black-white discrimination. *Bull. Psychon. Soc.*, 2: 27–28.

Weisman, R. G., & Litner, J. S. (1969) Positive conditioned reinforcement of Sidman avoidance behavior in rats. *J. comp. physiol. Psychol.*, 68: 597–603.

Weiss, B., & Moore, E. W. (1956) Drive level as a factor in distribution of responses in fixed-interval reinforcement. *J. exp. Psychol.*, 52: 82–84.

Weiss, S. J., & Lawson, R. (1962) Secondary reinforcement as a suppressor of rate of responding in the free operant situation. *J. comp. physiol. Psychol.*, 55: 1016–1019.

Weissman, A. (1972) Elicitation by a discriminative stimulus of water-reinforced behavior and drinking in water-satiated rats. *Psychon. Sci.*, 28: 155–156.

Welker, W. I. (1957) "Free" versus "forced" exploration of a novel situation. *Psych. Rep.*, 3: 95–108.

Welker, W. I. (1959) Escape, exploratory, and food-seeking responses of rats in a novel situation. *J. comp. physiol. Psychol.*, 52: 106–111.

Wells, W. R. (1923) The anti-instinct fallacy. *Psychol. Rev.*, 30: 228–234.

Wetzel, R. J. (1959) The effect of experience with a taste reward. *J. comp. physiol. Psychol.*, 52: 267–271.

Whalen, R. E. (1961) Effects of mounting without intromission and intromission without ejaculation on sexual behavior and maze learning. *J. comp. physiol. Psychol.*, 54: 409–415.

Whalen, R. E. (1963) Sexual behavior of cats. *Anim. Behav.*, 20: 321–342.

White, R. T. (1953) Analysis of the function of a secondary reinforcing stimulus in a serial learning situation. Unpublished Ph.D. disservation. University of Buffalo. Cited by Bugelski (1956).

Whittleton, J. D., Kostanek, D. J., & Sawrey, J. M. (1965) CS directionality and intensity in avoidance learning and extinction. *Psychon. Sci.*, 3: 415–416.

Wickens, D. D., Hall, J., & Reid, L. S. (1949) Associative and retroactive inhibition as a function of the drive stimulus. *J. comp. physiol. Psychol.*, 42: 398–403.

Wike, E. L. (1966) *Secondary reinforcement: Selected experiments.* New York: Harper & Row.

Wike, E. L. (1969) Secondary reinforcement: Some research and theoretical issues. In W. J. Arnold & D. Levine (Eds.), *Nebraska symposium on motivation.* Lincoln, Neb.: University of Nebraska Press.

Wike, E. L., & Barrientos, G. (1957) Selective learning as a function of differential consummatory activity. *Psychol. Rep.*, 3: 255–258.

Wike, E. L., & Knutson, D. L. (1966) Learned drives based on hunger. *Psychol. Rec.*, 16: 297–303.

Wike, E. L., & McWilliams, J. (1967) The effects of long-term training with delayed reward and delay-box confinement on instrumental performance. *Psychon. Sci.*, 9: 389–390.

Wike, E. L., & Platt, J. R. (1962) Reinforcement schedules and bar pressing: Some extensions of Zimmerman's work. *Psychol. Rec.*, 12: 273–278.

Wike, E. L., Platt, J. R., & Knowles, J. M. (1962) The reward value of getting out of a starting box: Further extensions of Zimmerman's work. *Psychol. Rec.*, 12: 397–400.

Wike, E. L., Platt, J. R., & Scott, D. (1963) Drive and secondary reinforcement: Further extensions of Zimmerman's work. *Psychol. Rec.*, 13: 45–50.

Wike, E. L., Sheldon, S. S., & Cour, C. A. (1968) Instrumental performance as a function of increasing and decreasing delays of reinforcement. *Psychol. Rec.*, 18: 19–24.

Wike, E. L., & Wike, S. S. (1972) Escape conditioning and low frequency whole-body vibration: The effects of frequency, amplitude, and controls for noise and activation. *Psychon. Sci.*, 27: 161–164.

Williams, D. R., & Teitelbaum, P. (1956) Control of drinking behavior by means of an operant-conditioning technique. *Science*, 124: 1294–1296.

Williams, D. R., & Williams, H. (1969) Auto-maintenance in the pigeon: Sustained pecking despite contingent non-reinforcement. *J. exp. anal. Behav.*, 12: 511–520.

Williams, J. L. (1970) Effects of the duration of a secondary reinforcer on subsequent instrumental responses. *J. exp. Psychol.*, 83: 348–351.

Williams, K. A. (1929) The reward value of a conditioned stimulus. *Univ. Calif. Publ. Psychol.*, 4: 31–55.

Williams, R. A. (1968) Effects of repeated food deprivations and repeated feeding tests on feeding behavior. *J. comp. physiol. Psychol.*, 65: 222–226.

Williams, R. A., & Campbell, B. A. (1961) Weight loss and quinine-milk ingestion as measures of "hunger" in infant and adult rats. *J. comp. physiol. Psychol.*, 54: 220–222.

Williams, S. B. (1938) Resistance to extinction as a function of the number of reinforcements. *J. exp. Psychol.*, 23: 506–521.

Wilm, E. C. (1925) *The theories of instinct.* New Haven, Conn.: Yale University Press.

Wilson, E. H., & Dinsmoor, J. A. (1970) Effect of feeding on "fear" as measured by passive avoidance in rats. *J. comp. physiol. Psychol.*, 70: 431–439.

Wilton, R. N. (1972) The role of information in the emission of observing responses and partial reinforcement acquisition phenomena. *Learn. Motiv.*, 3: 479–499.

Wilton, R. N., & Clement, R. O. (1971) Observing responses and informative stimuli. *J. exp. anal. Behav.*, 115: 199–204.

Wilton, R. N., & Clement, R. O. (1971a) The role of information in the emission of observing responses: A test of two hypotheses. *J. exp. anal. Behav.*, 16: 161–166.

Winnick, W. A. (1950) The discriminative functions of drive-stimuli independent of the action of the drive as motivation. *Amer. J. Psychol.*, 63: 196–205.

Wist, E. R. (1962) Amount, delay, and position of delay of reinforcement as parameters of runway performance. *J. exp. Psychol.*, 63: 160–166.

Wolf, S., & Wolff, H. G. (1943) *Human gastric function.* New York: Oxford University Press.

Wolfe, J. B. (1934) The effect of delayed reward upon learning in the white rat. *J. comp. Psychol.*, 17: 1–21.

Wolfe, J. B. (1936) Effectiveness of token rewards for chimpanzees. *Comp. Psychol. Monogr.*, 12 (Serial No. 60).

Wolpe, J. (1950) Need-reduction, drive-reduction, and reinforcement: A neurophysiological view. *Psychol. Rev.*, 57: 19–26.

Woodbury, C. B., & Wilder, D. H. (1954) The principle of selective association of drive stimuli. *J. exp. Psychol.*, 47: 301–302.

Woods, P. J., & Bolles, R. C. (1965) Effects of current hunger and prior eating habits on exploratory behavior. *J. comp. physiol. Psychol.*, 60: 141–143.

Woods, P. J., Davidson, E. H., & Peters, R. J., Jr. (1964) Instrumental escape conditioning in a water tank: Effects of variations in drive stimulus intensity and reinforcement magnitude. *J. comp. physiol. Psychol.*, 57: 466–470.

Woods, S. C., Makous, W., & Hutton, R. A. (1969) Temporal parameters of conditioned hypoglycemia. *J. comp. physiol. Psychol.*, 69: 301–307.

Woods, S. C., & Porte, D., Jr. (1975) The regulation of metabolism by the central nervous system. In R. Levine and R. Luft (Eds.), *Progress in metabolic disorders.* New York: Academic.

Woodworth, R. S. (1918) *Dynamic psychology.* New York: Columbia University Press.

Woodworth, R. S. (1924) Four varieties of behaviorism. *Psychol. Rev.*, 31: 257–264.

Wright, D. H. (1965) Modifications in the rat's diurnal activity pattern as a function of opportunity for reinforcement by ingestion. *J. comp. physiol. Psychol.*, 59: 463–465.

Wright, J. H. (1965) Test for a learned drive based on the hunger drive. *J. exp. Psychol.*, 70: 580–584.

Wright, J. H., Gescheider, G. A., & Johnson, M. L. (1966) Energizing effects of combined food and water deprivation upon general activity. *Psychon. Sci.*, 5: 415–416.

Wyckoff, L. B. (1952) The role of observing responses in discrimination learning. *Psychol. Rev.*, 59: 431–442.

Wyckoff, L. B. (1959) Toward a quantitative theory of secondary reinforcement. *Psychol. Rev.*, 66: 68–79.

Wyckoff, L. B., Sidowski, J., & Chambliss, D. J. (1958) An experimental study of the relationship between secondary reinforcing and cue effects of a stimulus. *J. comp. physiol. Psychol.*, 51: 103–109.

Wynne, L. C., & Solomon, R. L. (1955) Traumatic avoidance learning: Acquisition and extinction in dogs deprived of normal peripheral autonomic functioning. *Genet. Psychol. Monogr.*, 52: 241–284.

Yamaguchi, H. G. (1951) Drive (D) as a function of hours of hunger (h). *J. exp. Psychol.*, 42: 108–117.

Yamaguchi, H. G. (1952) Gradients of drive stimulus (S_D) intensity generalization. *J. exp. Psychol.*, 43: 298–304.

Yerkes, R. M., & Dodson, J. D. (1908) The relation of strength of stimulus to rapidity of habit-formation. *J. comp. neurol. Psychol.*, 18: 459–482.

Young, P. T. (1936) *Motivation of behavior.* New York: Wiley.

Young, P. T. (1941) The experimental analysis of appetite. *Psychol. Bull.*, 38: 129–164.

Young, P. T. (1948) Appetite, palatability and feeding habit: A critical review. *Psychol. Bull.*, 45: 289–320.

Young, P. T. (1949) Food-seeking drive, affective process, and learning. *Psychol. Rev.*, 56: 98–121.

Young, P. T. (1959) The role of affective processes in learning and motivation. *Psychol. Rev.*, 66: 104–125.

Young, P. T., & Greene, J. T. (1953) Quantity of food ingested as a measure of relative acceptability. *J. comp. physiol. Psychol.*, 46: 288–294.

Young, P. T., & Shuford, E. H., Jr. (1955) Quantitative control of motivation through sucrose solutions of different concentrations. *J. comp. physiol. Psychol.*, 48: 114–118.

Young, W. C. (1961) The hormones and mating behavior. In W. C. Young (Ed.), *Sex and internal secretions*, 3rd ed. Baltimore, Md.: Williams & Wilkins.

Zamble, E. (1967) Classical conditioning of excitement anticipatory to food reward. *J. comp. physiol. Psychol.*, 63: 526–529.

Zamble, E. (1969) Classical conditioning of excitement anticipatory to food reward: Partial reinforcement. *Psychon. Sci.*, 10: 115–116.

Zamble, E. (1969) Conditioned motivational patterns in instrumental responding of rats. *J. comp. physiol. Psychol.*, 69: 536–543.

Zaretsky, H. H. (1965) Runway performance during extinction as a function of drive and incentive. *J. comp. physiol. Psychol.*, 60: 463–464.

Zeaman, D. (1949) Response latency as a function of the amount of reinforcement. *J. exp. Psychol.*, 39: 466–483.

Zeaman, D., & House, B. (1950) Response latency at zero drive after varying numbers of reinforcements. *J. exp. Psychol.*, 40: 570–583.

Zeigarnik, B. (1927) Ueber das Behalten von erledigten und unerledigten Handlungen. *Psychol. Forsch.*, 9: 1–85.

Zeigler, H. P. (1964) Displacement activity and motivational theory: A case study in the history of ethology. *Psychol. Bull.*, 61: 362–376.

Zeigler, H. P., Green, H. L., & Lehrer, R. (1971) Patterns of feeding behavior in the pigeon. *J. comp. physiol. Psychol.*, 76: 468–477.

Zeller, E. (1883) *Outlines of the history of Greek philosophy*, 13th ed. Trans. by L. R. Palmer. New York: Meridian, 1957.

Zener, K. E., & McCurdy, H. G. (1939) Analysis of motivational factors in conditioned behavior: I. The differential effect of changes in hunger upon conditioned, unconditioned and spontaneous salivary secretion. *J. Psychol.*, 8: 321–350.

Zigler, M. J. (1923) Instinct and the psychological viewpoint. *Psychol. Rev.*, 29: 447–460.

Zilboorg, G. (1951) *Sigmund Freud.* New York: Scribner.

Zilboorg, G., & Henry, G. W. (1941) *A history of medical psychology.* New York: Norton.

Zimbardo, P. G., & Miller, N. E. (1958) Facilitation of exploration by hunger in rats. *J. comp. physiol. Psychol.*, 51: 43–46.

Zimbardo, P. G., & Montgomery, K. C. (1957) The relative strengths of consummatory responses in hunger, thirst, and exploratory drive. *J. comp. physiol. Psychol.*, 50: 504–508.

Zimmerman, D. W. (1957) Durable secondary reinforcement: Method and theory. *Psychol. Rev.*, 64: 373–383.

Zimmerman, D. W. (1959) Sustained performance in rats based on secondary reinforcement. *J. comp. physiol. Psychol.*, 52: 353–358.

Zimmerman, J. (1963) Technique for sustaining behavior with conditioned reinforcement. *Science*, 142: 682–684.

Zimmerman, J. (1969) Meanwhile . . . back at the key. In D. P. Hendry (Ed.), *Conditioned reinforcement.* Homewood, Ill.: Dorsey.

Zweig, S. (1932) *Mental healers.* New York: Garden City Books.

INDEX
OF NAMES

Abrams, R., 156
Ach, N., 69
Adams, D. W., 268
Adelman, H. M., 383
Adler, N. T., 177, 179
Adlerstein, A., 231
Adolph, E. F., 113, 115,
    137–139, 153, 154, 158,
    162, 165, 192, 205, 206
Albert, D. J., 478
Allen, J. D., 465
Allison, J., 201, 203, 356
Allport, G. W., 40, 62, 281
Almli, C. R., 160–162, 167,
    205
Amsel, A., 220, 238, 254–
    256, 272, 401, 403–407,
    415, 436
Anand, B. K., 149
Anastasio, E. J., 284, 414
Anderson, E. E., 284
Anderson, J. E., 419, 420
Anderson, N. H., 352
Andersson, B., 150, 161,
    285
Andrew, R. J., 106
Anger, D., 330, 331, 352
Angermeier, W. F., 263
Appel, J. B., 378
Appley, M. H., 55
Aquinas, T., 23, 27, 59
Arakelian, P., 238, 240
Aristotle, 3
Armstrong, E. A., 104
Armus, H. L., 216, 244
Arnold, E. M. M., 203
Arnold, M., 94
Arnold, M. B., 260
Atkinson, J. W., 89, 212
Aylesworth, M., 375
Ayres, C. E., 91
Ayres, J. J. B., 343, 474
Azrin, N. H., 370, 377,
    381, 387, 389, 390–393

Babb, H., 253, 374, 375
Badia, P., 338, 344
Baenninger, R., 255
Bailey, C., 24

Bailey, C. J., 272
Bain, A., 43
Baker, R. A., 117, 141, 194,
    195
Balagura, S., 153
Ball, G. G., 268
Ball, J., 254
Barakat, H., 203
Barclay, J. R., 59
Bard, P., 114, 177
Bare, J. K., 193
Barfield, R. J., 173, 174,
    254
Barlow, J. A., 465
Baron, A., 233, 378, 379
Barrett, R. J., 404, 405
Barrientos, G., 424
Barry, H., 212, 214, 236,
    241, 242
Bartoshuk, A. K., 254
Bash, K. W., 113, 117,
    147, 196
Bastock, M., 171
Bateson, P. P. G., 104
Bauer, F. J., 461
Baum, M., 351
Baumeister, A., 228
Bayer, E., 201
Beach, F. A., 114, 170,
    174, 176, 177–179, 208,
    214
Beaton, R. D., 148
Bechterev, V. M., 286
Beck, R. C., 193, 207, 465
Bedford, J., 352
Beebe-Center, J. G., 94
Beecroft, R. S., 374
Beer, B., 413
Beer, C. G., 105
Beery, R. G., 431
Bell, J. E., 441
Belloni, M., 277
Bellows, R. T., 113, 165
Bender, L., 376
Benedict, J. O., 343
Bennett, C. T., 165, 205
Berkun, M. M., 152, 183,
    261,
Berlyne, D. E., 180–182

Bermant, G., 170, 174–176,
    179
Bernard, C., 111
Bernfeld, S., 55
Bersh, P. J., 467
Besch, N. F., 273
Biederman, G. B., 338
Biller, J. D., 418
Bindra, D., 229, 301, 317,
    442
Bing, F. C., 153
Bintz, J., 356
Birch, D., 201, 216, 276
Bitterman, M. E., 354, 436,
    455
Black, A. H., 303
Black, R. W., 420, 421, 425
Blanchard, D. C., 351, 364
Blanchard, R. J., 351, 364
Blass, E. M., 161
Blick, K. A., 205
Blight, W. C., 178
Blodgett, H. C., 424
Blond, J., 229
Bloomberg, R., 275
Bloomfield, T. M., 308
Boe, E. E., 380, 381
Boice, R., 204, 256
Bolles, R. C., 24, 116, 118,
    139, 141, 143, 145, 165,
    167, 176, 185, 186, 193,
    195, 200–202, 204–207,
    220–224, 226–229, 231–
    233, 250, 273–275, 277,
    278, 301, 307, 320, 323,
    331, 334–336, 343, 344,
    346–348, 352–354, 356,
    357, 360, 361, 383, 434,
    442, 471
Booth, D. A., 139, 146,
    197
Boring, E. G., 34, 55, 60,
    69, 111
Bostrum, B., 244
Bousfield, W. A., 141, 201
Bowen, J., 432
Bower, G. H., 266, 345,
    347, 383, 418, 438, 439,
    475

Brackbill, Y., 369
Bradley, H. W., 433
Brady, J. V., 394, 395
Brahlek, J. A., 413
Brandauer, C. M., 251
Brantley, J. J., 254
Braud, W. G., 426
Braun, H. W., 253
Breland, K., 311
Breland, M., 311
Brelsford, J., 415, 441
Bremner, F. J., 351
Brener, J., 354
Brentano, F., 59
Breuer, J., 56
Bridgman, P., 9
Broadhurst, P. L., 184
Brobeck, J. R., 149, 156
Brody, S., 138
Brookover, T., 146
Browman, L. G., 222
Brown, E. R., 408
Brown, J. F., 74
Brown, J. L., 240
Brown, J. S., 128, 129, 181,
  236, 269, 277, 282, 289,
  373–375, 379, 401, 442
Brown, P. L., 312
Brown, R., 338
Brown, R. T., 407
Brown, T., 33
Brown, W. L., 432
Brownstein, A. J., 141, 413
Brozovich, R., 284
Bruce, R. H., 113
Brücke, E., 55
Bruner, J. S., 216
Bruning, J. L., 157
Brunswik, E., 78
Brush, E. S., 323
Brush, F. R., 425
Buchanan, G. N., 465
Budgell, P., 154
Bugelski, B. R., 455–458
Bulatao, E., 147
Bunge, M., 7
Bunnell, B. N., 164
Burke, G. H., 161
Bury, J. B., 32, 33
Buss, A. H., 401
Butler, R. A., 182
Butter, C. M., 214

Caggiula, A. R., 254
Callahan, B. S., 337
Calvin, J. S., 284
Camp, D. S., 380, 397
Campbell, B. A., 142, 143,
  146, 149, 163, 185, 186,
  195, 214, 218–221, 224,
  225, 227, 228, 238, 241,
  242, 264, 306
Campbell, P. E., 441

Candland, D. K., 200
Cannon, W. B., 110–113,
  145
Capaldi, E. D., 142, 421
Capaldi, E. J., 408, 409,
  415–417, 434, 436
Capeheart, J., 471
Capretta, P. J., 260, 264
Carl, D. F., 441
Carlisle, H. J., 151
Carlson, A. J., 110–113,
  147, 254
Carlsson, S., 179
Carlton, P. L., 185, 216,
  433
Carman, J. B., 392
Carmichael, L., 99
Carnap, R., 14
Carpenter, J. A., 211, 236,
  243
Carper, J. W., 216, 244,
  264
Carr, R. M., 231
Cartwright, D., 72
Carus, C. G., 40
Chambers, R. M., 265
Champion, R. A., 216
Chapman, H. W., 168
Chapman, J. A., 356
Chapman, R. M., 181, 231
Charlesworth, W. R., 182
Chorover, S. L., 267
Church, R. M., 288, 339,
  362, 370, 381, 396–398
Cicala, G. A., 163, 193,
  227, 307
Cicero, T. J., 353
Cizek, L. J., 154, 167, 168
Clark, F. C., 212, 237
Clayton, K. N., 404, 414,
  419
Clayton, M. H., 345
Clement, R. O., 475, 476
Clifford, T., 440
Coate, W. B., 217
Cofer, C. N., 55
Cohen, B. D., 266
Cohen, J. S., 216, 231
Cole, K. F., 256
Cole, M., 355, 372, 375
Collier, G., 139, 141, 142,
  153, 154, 162, 164, 166,
  167, 193, 195, 197–200,
  204–206, 212, 213, 225,
  425, 426
Collins, R. W., 226
Connally, R. E., 226
Connon, H. E., 224
Coons, E. E., 352
Cooper, J. B., 426, 431
Cooper, L. M., 185
Copeland, M. A., 128
Coppock, H. W., 265
Corbit, J. D., 139, 152,

158, 159–161, 164, 203,
  207
Corman, C. D., 246
Cornish, E. R., 228
Correia, M. J., 201
Cotton, J. W., 212, 214,
  241, 307
Coulbourn, J. N., 476
Coulter, X., 373
Courts, F. A., 254
Cowgill, G. R., 139
Cowles, J. T., 451, 455
Craig, W., 95, 96
Crawford, B. M., 413
Crawford, M. L. J., 169,
  203
Crespi, L. P., 292, 293,
  412, 431
Crombie, A. C., 24
Cross, H. A., 413
Crowder, W. F., 460
Crum, J., 432
Culbertson, J. L., 200, 427
Culbertson, S., 344

Dachowski, L., 253
Daly, H. B., 404, 405, 408
D'Amato, M. R., 340, 351,
  352, 355, 356, 452, 455
Daniel, W. J., 212, 248,
  252
Danziger, K., 249
Darwin, C. A., 37–41, 89
Dashiell, J. F., 120, 126,
  231, 283
Davenport, D. G., 142,
  346, 441, 455
Davenport, J. M., 441
Davenport, J. W., 237, 419
Davidson, J. M., 170
Davis, C. M., 118
Davis, J. D., 147, 203, 252
Davis, R. C., 110
Davis, R. H., 241, 243
Davis, R. T., 180
Davis, W. M., 351
Deaux, E., 205
DeBold, R. C., 302
Dees, J. W., 253
Deese, J., 211, 236, 243
Delgado, J. M. R., 266
de Lorge, J., 221, 231, 233,
  277, 469
Delude, L. A., 376
Denniston, R. H., 179
Denny, M. R., 349, 355,
  372, 419, 460
Descartes, R., 25, 26
Deutsch, J. A., 268, 270
de Villiers, P., 389, 397
Dewson, J. H., 337
Dillow, P. W., 346
DiLollo, V., 413

Dinsmoor, J. A., 217, 253, 328, 345, 348, 369, 377, 385, 388, 468, 476
Diserens, C. M., 375
Dodson, J. D., 215, 374, 375
Dollard, J., 128, 383, 400, 401
Doren, D. G., 441
Doty, R. L., 176
Drever, J., 35, 41
Duda, J. J., 141, 226
Duffy, E., 254
Duffy, M., 152, 154
Dufort, R. H., 163, 164, 191, 205, 425
Dufour, V. L., 260
Duncan, P. M., 223, 224, 359
Dunham, P. J., 417, 426
Dunlap, K., 92, 98
Dunlap, W. P., 425
Dunstone, J. J., 381
Dyal, J. A., 284, 440

Eayrs, J. T., 227
Egger, M. D., 472, 473
Ehrenfreund, D., 141, 142, 461
Ehrlich, A., 182
Eibergen, R., 254
Eibl-Eibesfeldt, I., 107
Eiseley, L., 35
Eisenberger, R., 233
Eisman, E., 140, 215, 240, 244, 254
Elliott, M. H., 141, 248, 252, 276, 424
Ellis, N. R., 255
Ellson, D. G., 451
Eninger, M. U., 274
Epstein, A. N., 150, 155, 168, 265
Essman, W. B., 371
Estes, W. K., 13, 72, 128, 307, 381, 385, 386, 388, 392, 394, 399, 437
Evans, H. L., 222
Evans, S. H., 284, 414
Evans, W. O., 465
Everett, J. W., 177
Evvard, J. M., 117

Fairlie, J., 438
Falk, J. L., 161, 169
Fallon, D., 192, 376
Fantino, E., 337, 352, 355
Farber, I. E., 401
Farrer, A. M., 30
Fay, J. W., 34
Fazzaro, J., 339, 352, 356
Fearing, F., 25

Fechter, L. D., 442
Fehrer, E., 231, 233, 414, 427, 432
Feldman, R. S., 351
Felton, M., 381, 389
Fenichel, O., 58
Ferguson, L., 121
Ferster, C. B., 462, 463
Feshbach, S., 401
Festinger, L., 419
Fibiger, H. C., 146
Fields, P. E., 113
Finan, J. L., 212, 238, 239
Finch, G., 248
Finger, F. W., 140, 141, 153, 192, 222, 223, 224, 226–228, 230, 232
Fink, J. B., 205
Fisher, A. E., 174
Fiske, D. W., 233
Fitzgerald, R. D., 377
Fitzsimons, J. T., 111, 139, 159–161, 164, 165, 167, 170, 195
Flaherty, C. F., 167, 441
Flakus, W. J., 355
Ford, C. S., 170
Forrin, B., 474
Foster, R., 264
Fowler, H., 174, 178, 181–183, 208, 211, 214, 269, 371, 378, 427
Fox, R. E., 454
Fox, S. S., 182
Franchina, J. J., 253
Frates, S. B., 425
Freedman, P. E., 337
French, D., 176
Freud, A., 63
Freud, S., 12, 50, 54–68
Frolov, G. P., 447
Fuller, J. L., 105, 265
Furchtgott, E., 253, 413

Gallistel, C. R., 268
Galvani, P. F., 374
Gamble, J. L., 158
Games, P. A., 142
Garcia, J., 309, 434, 436
Gavelek, J. R., 405, 431
Gay, R. A., 418
Gentile, R. L., 195
Gentry, G., 432
Gerall, A. A., 174, 254
Gershaw, N. J., 222, 225
Geyer, L. A., 173
Ghent, L., 192, 204
Gibbs, J., 148
Gibson, J. J., 69
Gilbert, T. F., 153, 154
Gilhousen, H. C., 431
Gilman, A., 158
Gilson, E., 23

Ginott, H. G., 387
Glanzer, M., 181
Glass, D. H., 426
Gleitman, H., 215, 417
Glickman, S. E., 231, 267
Goesling, W. J., 354
Goff, M. L., 222
Goldman, H. M., 461
Golin, S., 244
Gollub, L. R., 455, 462, 463
Goodman, I. J., 253
Goodrich, K. P., 421, 424, 425
Goodson, F. E., 284
Gorski, R. A., 254
Goulet, L. R., 142, 246
Graf, V., 354
Gragg, L., 421
Graham, C. H., 69
Green, H. H., 118
Greenberg, I., 285
Greene, J. T., 354, 425
Gregersen, M. I., 158, 164–167
Grice, G. R., 244, 252, 428, 436, 440, 461
Griffiths, R. R., 402
Grigg, P., 353
Grindley, G. C., 446
Grossen, N. E., 332, 347, 356, 359
Grossman, M. I., 139, 146, 152, 154
Grossman, S. P., 150, 151
Grunt, J. A., 178
Grusec, T., 438, 439
Guthrie, E. R., 128, 286, 307, 382, 383
Gutman, Y., 153, 165
Guttman, N., 424, 425
Gwinn, G. T., 372

Haas, E. L., 426
Hager, J., 311
Hahn, W. W., 254
Hainsworth, F. R., 154
Hall, C. S., 62, 81
Hall, J. F., 140, 141, 220, 226, 227, 420, 452
Hall, R. D., 424
Hallenborg, B. P., 376
Hamilton, C. L., 154, 167
Hamilton, D. M., 169
Hamilton, E. L., 122, 426
Hamilton, L. W., 167
Hamilton, W., 33
Hammel, H. T., 156
Hancock, W., 403
Hanna, B., 425
Hanratty, J. A., 275
Hard, E., 174, 179
Harker, G. S., 430, 431

Harlow, H. F., 180, 182, 269, 283
Harmon, F. L., 23
Harper, A. E., 153, 154
Harriman, A. E., 118
Harris, W. C., 254
Hart, B. L., 177
Harte, R. A., 139
Hartley, D. L., 346
Hartmann, H., 62
Hatton, G. I., 158, 159, 165, 167, 205
Hausmann, M. F., 139
Hayes, J. R., 153, 165, 252
Hayes, K. J., 233
Healey, A. F., 244
Hearst, E., 337, 353
Heath, R. G., 267
Heathers, G. L., 238, 240
Hebb, D. O., 49, 105, 290
Heider, F., 72, 73
Heinroth, O., 103
Heistad, G. T., 254
Heller, H., 159
Hempel, C. G., 8
Hendricks, S. E., 176
Hendry, D. P., 169, 455, 476
Heron, W. T., 212
Herrnstein, R. J., 308, 332, 333, 382
Hervey, G. R., 147
Hess, J. H., 356
Hetherington, A. W., 114, 149
Hetu, R., 222
Hilgard, E. R., 286
Hill, J. H., 203, 204
Hill, W. F., 183, 415, 418, 419
Hillix, W. A., 141
Hillman, B., 215, 236, 244, 276
Hinde, R. A., 105, 107, 171, 311
Hineline, P. N., 331–333, 352
Hirota, T. T., 475
Hirsch, E., 225
Hitchcock, F. A., 117
Hobbes, T., 27–29, 298
Hobhouse, L. T., 41
Hodos, W., 413
Hoebel, B. G., 146, 151
Hoelzel, F., 111, 112
Hoffman, H. S., 351
Hoge, M. A., 375
Holder, W. B., 427, 431, 432
Hollander, F., 154
Hollingworth, H. L., 128
Holman, G. L., 156, 265, 266
Holmes, J. H., 158, 164

Holmes, S. J., 41
Holt, E. B., 95
Holz, W. C., 370, 377, 387, 393
Hom, H. L., Jr., 374, 375
Hommel, L., 429, 431
Homzie, M. J., 285, 425, 441
Honzik, C. H., 215, 236
Hopkins, C. O., 413
Horel, J. A., 355
Horenstein, B. R., 211, 212, 248
Horne, M., 193
Hoskins, R. G., 117
House, B., 252
Howarth, C. I., 268
Hsiao, S., 153, 160, 161, 162
Hudson, B. B., 371
Huff, F. W., 340
Huff, R., 203
Hug, J. J., 406
Hughes, D., 440
Hughes, R. N., 231, 233
Hulicka, I. M., 471
Hull, C. L., 11, 126, 129–133, 137, 155, 215, 235, 236, 247, 253, 257, 270, 271, 291–293, 301, 315, 411, 412, 420, 466, 470, 472
Hulse, S. H., 414, 415, 425
Hume, D., 4, 7, 32
Humphrey, G., 69, 70
Hunt, H. F., 394, 395
Hurwitz, H. M. B., 231
Hutcheson, F., 31
Hyde, T. S., 437, 441

Imada, H., 204
Irwin, F. W., 319
Isaacson, R. L., 351
Ison, J. R., 404, 415, 416, 425, 426, 442
Ivy, A. C., 146

Jackson, B., 117, 226, 227
Jacobs, H. L., 147, 153, 246, 289
Jakubczak, L. F., 224
James, W., 23, 33, 35, 87–89
James, W. T., 153–155, 252, 260
Jammer, M., 48
Janis, I. L., 67
Janowitz, H. D., 139, 146, 152, 154
Jarka, R. G., 297
Jarmon, H., 254
Jarvik, M. E., 371
Jenkins, H. M., 312
Jenkins, J. J., 275

Jenkins, M., 175
Jenkins, T. N., 120
Jenkins, W. O., 244, 429, 467
Jennings, H. S., 110
Jensen, G. D., 216, 231
Job, W. M., 353
Johnson, J. L., 339
Jones, B., 296
Jones, E., 55, 60
Jones, E. C., 260, 355
Jordan, L., 176, 208, 210, 214
Jorgensen, H., 260

Kagan, J., 183, 259
Kalat, J. W., 118, 119, 311
Kalman, G., 413
Kamin, L. J., 333, 338, 343, 345, 346, 379, 397
Kantor, J. R., 47
Kaplan, M., 185
Karabenick, S. A., 405
Karsh, E. B., 378, 379
Katzev, R., 346
Kaufman, E. L., 379
Kaufman, R. S., 259
Kavanau, J. L., 225
Keehn, J. D., 203, 330, 347, 351, 454
Keesey, R. E., 151, 267, 427
Kelleher, R. T., 455, 462, 463, 470
Keller, F. R., 352
Keller, F. S., 40, 328, 468
Keller, J. V., 185
Kelley, M. J., 359
Kello, J. E., 403, 464
Kelly, G. A., 49
Kemble, E. D., 404
Kendler, H. H., 244, 248, 249, 271–273, 275, 294
Kennedy, G. C., 148
Kent, M. A., 156
Kent, N. D., 302
Kessen, M. L., 261, 262
Kessen, W., 205, 337
Kilps, B., 426
Kimble, G. A., 211, 248, 252, 276, 340, 425
King, G. F., 419
King, R. A., 242, 244, 454
Kinney, G. C., 264
Kintsch, W., 302, 413
Kissileff, H. R., 168
Kleiber, M., 138
Klein, R. M., 454
Kleitman, N., 165, 184
Kling, J. W., 424
Knarr, F. A., 162
Knutson, D. L., 285
Koch, S., 19, 212, 248, 252
Koelling, R. A., 309, 436

Kohn, M., 154, 261
Koplin, S. T., 414
Koppman, J. W., 440
Korn, J. H., 339, 351
Kowell, A. P., 144, 200
Kraeling, D., 238, 241, 242, 425
Krasne, F. B., 150
Krausz, M., 153, 165
Kremer, E. F., 343
Krieckhaus, E. E., 118, 265
Krippner, R. A., 404
Kruger, B. M., 351
Krutch, J. W., 30
Kuehn, R. E., 177
Kulkarni, A. S., 353
Kuo, Z. Y., 99, 128
Kurtz, K. H., 215, 297
Kutscher, C. L., 163, 167, 168
Kuznesof, A. Y., 225

Lachman, R., 216
Lamarck, J. B., 37, 89
Lamoreaux, R. R., 288, 289, 334, 345
Lange, A., 22
L'Angellier, A. B., 153
Larsson, K., 174, 178, 179, 285
Lashley, K. S., 58, 100
Law, F. E., 249
Lawler, E. E., 465
Lawrence, D. H., 46, 140, 192–194, 205, 414, 429, 431
Lawson, R., 401, 413, 414, 452, 470
Leach, D. A., 243
Leaf, R. C., 341
Leander, J. D., 253, 340
Leeper, R. W., 72, 270, 271
Lehrman, D. S., 105, 172
Leitenberg, H., 384, 407
Le Magnen, J., 139, 155, 165, 167, 193, 195–197, 258
Lepkovsky, S., 159, 166
Leslie, G. R., 231
Lester, D., 231, 232
Levine, S., 193, 249, 255, 256, 272, 275, 336
Levis, D. J., 338
Levitsky, D. A., 153, 154, 162, 164, 192, 193, 195, 201, 212
Levowitz, A., 232
Levy, N., 181, 231, 440
Lewin, K., 70–80
Lewis, D. J., 214, 241, 302
Lieberman, S. M., 453
Linden, D. R., 339

Lindzey, G., 62, 81
Liss, P., 353
Litner, J. S., 349, 350
Littman, R. A., 49
Lockard, J. S., 338
Locke, J., 30, 31
Logan, F. A., 211, 426, 430, 431, 432
LoLordo, V. M., 318, 341, 442, 465
Longstreth, L. E., 433, 455, 477, 478
Lorber, S. H., 113
Lore, R. K., 183, 222, 224, 232
Lorenz, K., 58, 101–104
Lotter, E. C., 169
Lubbock, J., 120
Luce, A., 111
Luckhardt, A. B., 147
Ludvigson, H. W., 405, 418
Lynch, G. S., 224
Lyon, D. O., 381, 389

Maatsch, J. L., 351, 383
McAdam, D., 338
McAllister, D. E., 356
McAllister, W. R., 339, 356
McCain, G., 404, 406, 408, 423, 432
McCall, R. B., 232
McCausland, D. F., 473, 474
McCleary, R. A., 152
McCosh, J., 33
McCurdy, H. G., 214, 248
McDiarmid, C. G., 431
MacDonnell, M. F., 284
McDougall, W., 89–91, 93, 97, 99
MacDuff, M., 244
McFarland, D. J., 153, 154, 165, 251
Macfarlane, D. A., 319
McGill, T. E., 177, 178
McGillis, D. B., 353
McGinnis, R. W., 351
Mach, E., 46
McHewitt, E. R., 405
McHose, J. H., 405, 431
McKeever, B., 474
McKelvey, R. K., 413
MacLeod, R. B., 118
McMahon, R. R., 142
McMillan, J. C., 403
McNamara, H. J., 454
MacPhail, E. M., 352
McVean, G., 404
McWilliams, J., 431, 432
Maddi, S. R., 233, 440
Madison, H. L., 441
Magendie, F., 35
Mah, C. J., 478

Maher, W. B., 413
Malagodi, E. F., 451
Malmo, R. B., 254
Maltzman, I., 225, 256, 269
Mandler, J. M., 193
Manning, H. M., 275
Margenau, H., 13
Margules, D. L., 161
Marks, R. A., 185
Marquis, D. G., 286
Marshall, J. F., 150
Martin, C. L., 110
Marwine, A. G., 142
Marx, M. H., 193, 284, 401, 415, 425, 426, 432, 442
Marzocco, F. N., 400
Mason, W. A., 140, 192, 193, 194, 205
Masserman, J. H., 370
Masterson, F. A., 186, 354, 357
Mathews, S. R., 230
Matthews, T. J., 184
May, M. A., 289, 350
Mayer, J., 195, 196
Megibow, M., 200
Mellgren, R. L., 418, 438
Meltzer, D., 413
Melvin, K. B., 374
Mendel, L. B., 153
Mendelson, J., 267, 268
Merlan, P., 60
Messer, K., 69
Messing, R. B., 225, 227
Metzger, R., 412, 414
Meyer, D. R., 216, 352, 354
Mickle, W. A., 267
Migler, B., 353
Mikulka, P. J., 417, 432, 442
Milby, J. B., 465
Miles, R. C., 181, 216, 246, 253, 458, 459, 471
Millenson, J. R., 389, 397
Miller, N. E., 128, 149, 164, 165, 181, 189, 190, 231, 251, 256, 260–264, 266, 269, 284, 289, 302, 324, 359, 371, 379, 380, 383, 400, 414, 472, 473
Milner, P., 266
Mintz, D. E., 214
Misanin, J. R., 378, 379
Mishkin, M., 296
Misiak, H., 23
Mogenson, G. J., 347
Moll, R. P., 141, 192, 201
Mollenauer, S. O., 243
Moltz, H., 440
Monkman, J. A., 181
Montgomery, K. C., 181, 182, 200, 231, 233, 269

Montgomery, M. F., 113
Monti, P. M., 195
Mook, D. G., 152, 154, 165
Moore, B. R., 313
Moore, E. W., 212
Moot, S. A., 223, 343, 350
Morgan, C. L., 41, 110, 371
Morgan, C. T., 113, 114, 127
Morgan, J. D., 113
Morgan, J. J. B., 120
Morgane, P. J., 147
Morlock, H., 250
Morrison, S. D., 146, 225
Morrow, J. E., 471
Morse, W. H., 438
Moskowitz, M. J., 141, 224
Moss, F. A., 120
Moss, R. F., 254
Mowrer, O. H., 287–289, 299–301, 324, 330, 334, 345, 372, 375, 384, 465
Moyer, K. E., 164, 255, 339, 351, 356
Mrosovsky, N., 228
Mueller, J. H., 441
Muenzinger, K. F., 377
Munn, N. L., 115, 218, 433
Murphy, M. R., 179
Murphy, W. W., 442
Murray, H. A., 80–84
Myer, J. S., 144, 200, 396
Myers, A. K., 181, 269, 284, 337, 351
Myers, J. L., 431, 460
Myers, L., 425
Myers, R. D., 353

Nakamura, C. Y., 352, 471
Nakkash, S., 347
Nettleton, N., 146
Newman, J. R., 244
Newton, I., 45
Nicholls, E. E., 228
Nissen, H. W., 269
North, A. J., 441
Northman, J., 416
Notterman, J. M., 214
Novin, D., 161, 284, 285
Nuttall, R. L., 176

Oatley, K., 159, 161
Odom, P. B., 438
Ogilvie, R. D., 222
O'Hara, J., 369
O'Kelly, L. I., 159, 207
Olds, J., 266–268
Olson, R. D., 346
Olton, D. S., 351
O'Neil, H. F., 373
Oppenheim, P., 8

Ost, J. W. P., 438
Overmier, J. B., 301, 341
Ovsiankina, M., 74

Page, H. A., 373
Paige, A. B., 454
Pain, J. F., 146
Palfai, T., 442
Panksepp, J., 151, 196, 197, 425, 426
Pare, W. P., 255
Patten, R. L., 441
Patton, R. M., 205
Pavlik, W. B., 212, 418
Pavlov, I. P., 155, 286, 341, 447
Peacock, L. J., 354
Pearl, J., 353
Pearl, R., 118
Pearlman, C. A., 371
Pearson, K., 45
Peck, J. W., 161
Peckham, R. H., 404
Peirce, J. T., 176
Penick, S. B., 110
Pereboom, A. C., 224, 413, 417, 419
Perin, C. T., 130–133, 212, 426
Perkins, C. C., 427, 461
Pernice, B., 154
Perrin, F. A. C., 99
Perry, R. B., 95
Pertsulakes, W., 167
Peters, R. S., 27, 35, 64, 156
Peterson, L. R., 427
Petraitis, J., 227
Petrinovich, L., 141, 273, 274, 434
Pfaff, D., 176
Pfaffman, C., 425
Pieper, W. A., 284, 426
Plato, 22
Platt, J. R., 454
Pliskoff, S., 166
Polliard, F., 264
Popp, R. J., 331
Porte, D., Jr., 148, 198
Porter, J. J., 244, 441
Porter, L. W., 272
Porter, P. B., 265
Poschel, B. P. H., 267
Powell, R. W., 213, 340, 413
Powelson, M. H., 116
Powley, T. L., 151
Pratt, C. C., 68
Premack, D., 183, 203
Procter, D. M., 420
Prokasy, W. F., 246, 475
Prytula, R. E., 426
Pubols, B. H., 413, 432

Rabe, E. F., 152
Rachlin, H., 352, 381, 382, 396
Radlow, R., 351
Ramond, C. K., 211, 215, 236, 420
Rampone, A. J., 156
Ransom, T. W., 174
Ranson, S. W., 114, 149
Rapaport, D., 61, 64
Rapp, H. M., 200
Rasche, R. H., 169
Ratner, S. C., 471
Ray, A. J., 185
Razran, G., 448
Reed, J. D., 218
Reid, L. S., 140, 141, 153, 192, 226, 227
Reid, T., 33
Remley, N. R., 148
Renner, K. E., 427, 431
Rescorla, R. A., 301–303, 327, 341–344, 349, 350, 407, 443
Rethlingshafer, D., 275
Revusky, B. T., 193
Revusky, S. H., 297, 434
Rexroad, C. N., 128
Reynierse, J. H., 167, 250, 335
Reynolds, B., 211, 239, 413, 414
Reynolds, W. F., 212, 419, 420, 453
Riccio, D. C., 185
Richards, T. W., 116
Richards, W. J., 231
Richter, C. P., 116–118, 195, 198, 221, 222
Riess, D., 332, 337
Riley, A. L., 357, 361
Rilling, M. E., 431
Rixon, R. H., 224
Robbins, D., 436
Roberts, W. H., 426
Roberts, W. W., 266
Robertson, J. M., 33
Robinson, E. A., 165, 205
Roby, T. B., 259, 264
Rocha, S. M., 201
Rodgers, W., 119
Rogers, F. T., 110
Rohrbaugh, M., 337
Rohrer, J. H., 401
Rollins, J. B., 253
Romanes, G. J., 40
Root, W. S., 114
Rosen, A. J., 416, 425
Rosenbaum, G., 244, 245
Rosenzweig, M. R., 110
Ross, L. E., 425
Roussel, J., 401
Routtenberg, A., 225
Rowell, C. H. F., 106

Rozin, P., 118, 119, 139, 199, 311
Rubin, R. D., 413
Rudy, J. W., 441
Russell, E. S., 95

Sachs, B. D., 174, 254
Sackett, R. S., 212
Saltzman, I. J., 212, 248, 453, 461
Salzberg, C. L., 169
Sanders, G. H., 228
Santos, J. R., 351
Sardello, R. J., 455
Scagliosi, G., 154
Scarborough, B. B., 284
Schachter, S., 94
Schaeffer, R. W., 169, 203, 425
Schiff, B. B., 267
Schiff, D., 351
Schmidt-Nielsen, B., 162, 167
Schneider, G. E., 179
Schoel, W. M., 436
Schoenfeld, W. N., 326, 328, 467, 468
Schrier, A. M., 413
Schuster, R. H., 396, 475
Schwartz, M., 179, 337
Schwartzbaum, J. S., 152, 153
Sclafani, A., 150, 200
Scott, E. M., 118
Scott, W. W., 146
Screven, C. G., 285
Sears, G. W., 348
Seelbach, S. E., 185, 383
Seeman, W., 270
Segal, B., 285
Segall, M., 181
Seligman, M. E. P., 311, 435, 474
Seward, G., 175, 283
Seward, J. P., 175, 224, 283, 296, 297, 298, 301, 404, 420, 440
Sgro, J. A., 431, 432
Shafer, J. N., 356
Shanab, M. E., 418
Shapiro, M. M., 302
Share, I., 152
Sharp, D., 351
Sheffield, F. D., 218, 219, 258, 259, 264, 269, 307, 350
Sheldon, A. B., 233
Sherif, M., 201
Sherrington, C. S., 97
Shettleworth, S. J., 311
Shirasu, M. E., 156
Shirley, M., 218, 221
Shuford, E. H., Jr., 425

Sidman, M., 328–331, 338
Siegel, H. S., 255
Siegel, P. S., 165, 193, 194, 197, 201, 206, 222, 229, 249, 253, 255, 284, 376, 465
Siegel, S., 146
Simmons, R., 121, 423
Singer, C., 45, 48
Singer, E. A., 95
Singer, J. E., 94
Siskel, M. Jr., 425
Skinner, B. F., 2, 16, 18, 47, 139, 212, 213, 287, 386, 394, 438, 447, 461, 462, 463, 466, 468
Skucy, J. C., 442
Slater, J., 181
Slonaker, J. R., 117
Smith, F. V., 7
Smith, K. U., 203
Smith, M. F., 203, 451
Smith, M. H., 118, 152–154, 264
Smith, M. P., 260, 263, 264, 465
Smith, N. F., 381
Smith, O. A., 147, 337, 352
Smith, R. F., 352
Smith, S., 128, 286
Snowdon, C. T., 139, 156, 196, 265, 266
Solomon, L. N., 324
Solomon, R. L., 284, 301–303, 323–327, 340, 342, 344, 354, 386, 393, 407
Soulairac, A., 174
Sparks, D. L., 253
Sparling, D. L., 415
Spear, E., 201
Spear, N. E., 267, 415, 417–419, 425
Spence, K. W., 15, 211, 215, 216, 238, 244, 246, 295, 301, 412, 420, 423, 428, 429, 432, 433, 466
Spencer, H., 42, 43
Spitzner, J. H., 417, 418
Spivey, H. E., 153, 154
Staddon, J. E. R., 401–403, 464
Staudt, V. M., 23
Stein, L., 267
Steinberg, M., 229
Steinman, F., 417
Stellar, E., 139, 151, 203, 204
Stenmark, D., 374
Sterritt, G. M., 255, 263
Stettner, L. J., 231
Stevens, S. S., 13, 186
Stevenson, J. A. F., 224
Stevenson, S. S., 400

Stevenson-Hinde, J., 311
Stewart, C. C., 115
Stewart, C. N., 224
Stewart, D., 33
Stocking, R. L., 375
Stokes, L. W., 222, 277, 334
Stone, C. P., 121, 139, 142, 175, 177, 178
Stone, G. R., 369
Storms, L. H., 381
Stout, G. F., 35, 90
Strange, J. R., 253
Strassburger, R. C., 212, 240
Stretch, R., 377
Stricker, E. M., 160, 161, 208
Strominger, J. L., 153
Strong, T. N., 228
Strutt, G. F., 224
Stuckey, H. L., 165
Sturman-Huble, M., 121
Swanson, A. M., 285, 355
Szymanski, J. S., 115, 214

Tacker, R. S., 401
Tallon, S., 193, 196
Tang, M., 206
Tarpy, R. M., 224
Tarttelin, M. F., 254
Taylor, C. J., 156, 260
Taylor, G. T., 231
Teel, K. S., 216, 244, 252, 276
Teghtsoonian, R., 220
Teitelbaum, P., 146, 149, 151, 155, 169, 195, 252, 265
Telegdy, G. A., 216
Tellish, J. A., 381
Temmer, H., 350
Tenen, S. S., 351
Thach, J. S., Jr., 185
Theios, J., 241, 339, 347, 351, 383
Thilly, F., 23
Thomas, D. R., 244, 473
Thomas, D. W., 195, 196
Thomas, J. R., 469
Thompson, T., 402
Thompson, W. R., 105, 182, 231
Thomson, C. W., 265
Thorndike, E. L., 286, 367, 368, 371
Thornton, L. W., 158
Thurstone, L. L., 99
Timberlake, W. D., 201
Tinbergen, N., 104, 105, 107
Tinklepaugh, O. L., 424
Tolliver, G., 166

Tolman, E. C., 17, 47, 92–
95, 99, 215, 236, 281,
314, 424, 449
Tombaugh, T. N., 432
Towbin, E. J., 154, 165
Trankina, F., 160, 162
Trapold, M. A., 210, 214,
301, 427, 437, 438, 439,
441–443
Traupman, K. L., 408
Treichler, F. R., 141, 169,
226, 227
Troland, L. T., 43
Trost, R. C., 285
Trowill, J. A., 268, 269,
425, 426
Trumble, G., 413
Tsai, C., 121
Tsang, Y. C., 112
Tuchapsky, S., 160
Tulving, E., 435
Turner, L. H., 340, 354

Uexküll, J. von, 103

Valenstein, E. S., 260, 268,
269
Vaughn, J., 375
Verney, E. L., 118
Verplanck, W. S., 100, 153,
165, 252
Verworn, M., 110
Vogel, J. R., 426

Wada, T., 116
Wagman, W., 465
Wagner, A. R., 404, 407,
414, 415, 421, 422
Wahlsten, D., 351, 352,
372
Wald, G., 117, 226, 227
Walike, B. C., 147
Walker, D. W., 148
Walker, K. C., 437
Wallace, R. B., 454
Waller, T. G., 414
Walloch, R. A., 377
Walter, N., 369
Wampler, R. S., 151
Wang, G. H., 117
Wangensteen, O. H., 112
Ward, H. P., 152, 153
Warden, C. J., 41, 120,
121–123, 375, 426
Warner, L. H., 175

Warren, H. C., 32, 33
Warren, J. A., Jr., 339,
352, 353, 354, 384
Washburn, A. L., 110
Washburn, M. F., 41
Waters, R. W., 408
Watson, J., 24
Watson, J. B., 99, 285,
286, 427, 433
Watt, H., 69, 70
Way, J., 401
Wayner, M. S., 227
Weasner, M. H., 227
Webb, W. B., 184, 208,
209, 216, 251–253, 275,
278, 461
Weber, M. L., 260
Wedeking, P. W., 351
Weijnen, J. A. W. M., 169
Weiner, B., 94
Weinstein, L., 426
Weinstock, R. B., 142, 417
Weinstock, S., 431, 432
Weir, L. G., 113
Weisinger, R. S., 414
Weisman, R. G., 349, 350
Weiss, B., 212
Weiss, S. J., 470
Weissman, A., 284
Welker, W. I., 200, 231,
232
Wells, W. R., 99
Westbrook, W. H., 176
Wetzel, R. J., 192
Whalen, R. E., 174, 177,
259, 353
White, R. T., 456, 457,
471
Whittleton, J. D., 338
Wickens, D. D., 274, 413
Wike, E. L., 185, 285, 424,
431, 432, 454, 455
Wike, S. S., 185
Wilder, D. H., 272
Williams, D. R., 169, 252,
312, 318
Williams, H., 270
Williams, H., 312, 318
Williams, J. L., 442
Williams, K. A., 447
Williams, R. A., 142, 144,
192, 205
Williams, S. B., 130–132
Wilm, E. C., 41
Wilson, E. H., 388

Wilson, M., 429
Wilton, R. N., 475, 476
Winnick, W. A., 272
Winokur, S., 438
Wischner, G. J., 378
Wist, E. R., 431
Witte, R. S., 302
Wolf, G., 118, 265
Wolf, S., 113
Wolfe, J. B., 426, 449, 450,
455, 460, 477
Wolff, H. G., 113
Wolpe, J., 128
Wong, R., 433
Wood, L., 23
Woodbury, C. B., 272
Woods, P. J., 185, 211, 232
Woods, S. C., 146, 148,
198
Woodworth, R. S., 47, 48,
96–98, 282
Work, M. S., 220
Wright, J. H., 191, 226,
227, 285
Wyckoff, L. B., 460, 470,
474, 475
Wynne, L. C., 324–326,
342

Yamaguchi, H. G., 212,
276
Yerkes, R. M., 374
Young, P. T., 48, 118, 126,
192, 425
Young, W. C., 174, 178
Younger, M. S., 220, 334

Zamble, E., 442
Zaretsky, H. H., 415
Zeaman, D., 252, 412
Zeigarnik, B., 74
Zeigler, H. P., 107, 150,
197, 198, 200
Zeller, E., 22
Zener, K. E., 214, 248
Zigler, M. J., 99
Zilboorg, G., 34, 35, 66
Zimbardo, P. G., 182, 200,
231
Zimmerman, D. W., 454
Zimmerman, J., 469, 470
Zimmerman, R. R., 283
Zoloth, S. R., 178
Zucker, I., 177
Zweig, S., 66

INDEX
OF SUBJECTS

Abnormal psychology, 34, 63, 64
Acquired drive, 264, 281–290
  acquired drive studies, 289, 350, 357, 360
  theory of avoidance, 287–289, 323–326, 344
  theory of frustration, 401–403
Activity. See General activity
Activity cycles. See Cyclicity
Adrenalectomy, 118
Aggression, 363, 400
Amount of reinforcement, 292, 294
  in acquisition, 413, 414, 421–423, 441
  contrast effects, 416–419
  discrimination of, 419, 420
  extinction effects, 414–416
Antecedent conditions, of drive, 132, 264
  hunger, 136–157
  of other drives, 179–186
  of sex, 173–179
  of thirst, 157–167
Anticipation of feeding, 221–223, 230, 277
Anxiety, in psychoanalysis, 63. See also Fear
Appetite, 111. See also Incentive
Arousal theory, 254
Associationism, British, 29–32
Associative explanations
  of acquired drive, 282
  of displacement, 106
  of frustration, 400, 402
  of motivation, 127–129, 292, 307
  of punishment, 382, 383
  of purpose, 292
  of secondary reinforcement, 455–459
Autoshaping, 312, 313, 318
Aversive stimulus, 185, 186. See also Escape
Avoidance learning, 287–288, 323–366

associative effects, 337, 338
energizing effects, 338–340
extinction, 324–326, 346, 350
Sidman, 329–331
situations
  bar pressing, 351–356
  freezing, 357, 360–363
  one-way, 350–351

Bar pressing
  in avoidance, 351–356
  drive effects, 212, 213
  drive-shift effects, 338–341
  incentive effects, 413, 425
  punishment of, 378–381
  suppression of, 393–399
Behavior sampling, 229–230
Biological clocks. See Cyclicity
Biological needs, 117, 119, 129, 183
Blood sugar, 138, 145, 146, 224, 260

Caloric regulation, 137–139, 197–199
Carry-over effects, 242, 243
Causation
  Aristotalian, 3, 59
  varieties of, 3, 7
CER. See Conditioned suppression
Chain schedules, 461–464
Circadian cycles. See Cyclicity
Classical conditioning, 340–343
Click, as a secondary reinforcer, 447, 455–459, 471
Columbia obstruction box, 120–124
Comparative psychology, 40, 101–103
  and activity, 227, 228
  and drinking, 167
  and feeding, 198–199
  and learning, 311
  and sex, 171–173, 175
Conditioned negative reinforcement, 327–331, 345–347, 356, 407

Conditioned reinforcement. See Secondary reinforcement
Conditioned suppression, 385, 386, 393–399, 474
Conditioning
  of fear, 285–290
  of hunger, 282–285
  of somatic reactions, 113, 146, 260
Conflict
  in psychoanalysis, 58
  in rats, 379
Constraints on learning, 310, 311, 319, 320, 352, 357–360
Constructs
  compromise character of, 19
  empirical, 12, 13
  theoretical, 15–19
Consummatory behavior, 97. See also Eating, etc.
  dimensions of, 424
Contrast effects, 292, 416–419, 425, 426, 431
Coolidge effect, 174, 175
Crespi effect, 292, 293, 412
Cues. See Predictive cues
Curiosity. See Exploration
Cyclicity, diurnal
  of drinking, 205, 206
  of eating, 193–196, 277
  of general activity, 221–223, 277
  short feeding cycles, 117, 195, 196

Data language, 13
Defensive behavior, 185, 357, 358
Definitions of constructs, 12, 16–18
  overrigid, 12, 112, 122, 125
Delay of reinforcement
  in acquisition, 426–431
  and discrimination learning, 427–429
  in extinction, 432
  with long delays, 433–435
Deprivation
  and activity, 183
  and contrast effect, 431
  and drive, 140

Deprivation (*Continued*)
  effect on incentive, 264,
    297
  of exploration, 182
  of food, 143
  prior experience with,
    141, 142, 192
  of sex, 175, 176, 208, 210
  of sleep, 208, 209
Deprivation schedules,
  136, 137, 194, 205
Derived drives. *See*
  Acquired drive
Determining tendencies,
  69–71
Determinism, 6, 21–51
  in biology, 36–40
  empirical, 44–48
  and mechanism, 23–29
  in psychology, 53
Dietary dilution, 138, 139
Direct placement, 440, 441
Discrimination
  in avoidance, 355
  drive effects, 215–217,
    244
  of incentive, 419
  incentive effects, 413,
    414
  in punishment, 394–399
Displacement, 104–106
Diurnal cycles. *See*
  Cyclicity
Drinking, 113, 203–208.
    See also Thirst
  associative factors in, 204
  energizing of, 206
  in hungry animals, 165–
    167
  learning to drink, 205
  lick rate, 203
  nonregulatory, 168–170
  sham, 113, 152
  temporal factors in, 205,
    206
Drive, acquired. *See*
  Acquired drive
  antecedent anchoring of,
    135–187
  combination with habit,
    130–133, 236–247
  combination with incen-
    tive, 420, 421
  definitions of, 112, 122–
    126
  early concepts of, 109–
    126
  effects on, discrimina-
    tion, 215–217, 244
    generalization, 244
    resistance to extinc-
      tion, 133, 212
    response latency, 210–
      212, 243
    response rate, 213

response vigor, 213,
    214, 241–243
  etymology of word, 48,
    97
  evolution of concept,
    108–126
  externalized, 284
  Hull's construct, 129–
    133
  and instinct, 59, 100,
    108
  irrelevant, 247–257, 274
  and need, 117–120, 128,
    132, 170, 257–264
  sources of, 129
  syntactical problems,
    112
  without need, 172, 184,
    259
Drive discrimination, 270–
  273
Drive interaction
  hunger and thirst, 165–
    167
  other, 253–256
Drive-reduction hypothe-
  sis, 260–264, 324
Drive-shift studies, 238–
  244
Drive stimuli, 128, 129,
    132, 270–278, 307
Drive substitution, 250–
  253
Drive summation, 248–
  250, 253–256

Eating, 189–203. *See also*
    Hunger
  anticipatory, 193, 221–
    223
  associative factors in,
    192–195
  cyclicity of, 193–196,
    277
  energizing of, 200–202
  learning to eat, 192
  non-regulatory, 197–
    199, 203
  sham, 155, 257
  and specific hungers,
    117–120
  and temperature, 154
  temporal factors in, 193
  in thirsty animals, 153,
    154
Electrical brain stimula-
  tion, 266–269, 427
Elicitation theory, 371–372
Emotion, 26, 89, 91, 94
Emotionality, 255–256
Empirical determinism,
  7–10, 44–48
Energizing effect, 131–133.
    See also Drive
    effects

on consummatory be-
    havior, 189–210
  on general activity, 217–
    233
  on instrumental be-
    havior, 210–217
  of stimuli, 307
Energy, in behavior, 97
  of fixed action patterns,
    103–106
  versus structure, 68–70,
    106, 107
Escape learning, 185, 214,
    238, 253, 287
  in avoidance, 334, 335,
    356
  in punishment, 383, 384
Estrus cycle, 117, 230
Ethology, 101–107
Evolution, 37–40, 102
Expectancy, 316–320
Exploration, 121, 231–233
  as a drive, 180–182, 269
  effect of hunger, 120,
    231
Externalization of drive,
  284

Faculty psychology, 33
Fear
  as an acquired drive,
    285–290, 299
  and avoidance, 288,
    323–325, 339–344
  empirical status of, 303
  and punishment, 384–
    386, 393–399
Feedback cues, 347–350
Field theory, 71, 80
Forces, 48
  psychological, 48, 49
Fractional anticipatory
    goal response. *See* r$_G$
Free will, 22, 28, 30, 49,
    65, 77, 89
Freezing, 352–355, 357,
    360–363
Frustration, 400–409
  in amount of reinforce-
    ment, 404, 405, 415,
    421–423
  and contrast effects, 405,
    417
  in delay of reinforce-
    ment, 405, 431, 432
  history of concept, 400,
    401
Functional autonomy, 65

Garcia effect, 119, 309,
    310, 434, 435
General activity, 115
  anticipatory, 116, 221–
    223, 230, 277
  artifacts due to, 253, 460

cyclicity of, 221–223, 277
effect of drive, 115–117
effect of food cue, 219,
    442
learned aspects, 183,
    219, 233–236
specificity of, 227, 228
Generalization, motivation
    effects, 244–246

Habit, 88, 130–133, 298
Hedonism, 23, 28, 31
ethical, 23
psychological, 28, 31
Spencer's 41–43
Homeostasis, 56, 57, 81,
    85, 118, 129
Hormones
hunger, 146–149
satiety, 147, 148
sex, 171, 176–178
Hunger. *See also* Eating
antecedents of, 136–157
conditioned, 283–285
definition of, 136
hormone, 146–149
introspective accounts,
    111
pangs, 110
physiological basis of,
    112, 114, 144–156
sensations of, 110
specific, 117–120
as weight loss, 143, 144
Hunger-thirst interaction,
    165–167, 252
Hyperphagia, 149–151,
    195
Hypothalamus centers,
    114
in hunger, 149–151
for reinforcement, 266–
    269
and sensory deficits, 150
in thirst, 168
Hypovolemic thirst, 160,
    161, 208, 227

Imprinting, 102, 104
Inanition, 137
Incentive. *See also* Amount
    of reinforcement
combination with drive,
    420, 421
and drive, 122, 295–297
problem of equating,
    123, 275
theories of, 291–300
theory of delay of re-
    inforcement, 430,
    431
theory of frustration,
    403–407
Independence of drive
    and habit, 131, 132,
    236–247

Inhibitory conditioning,
    342
Instinct, 88–107
compromise character of,
    31, 86, 101
and drive, 59, 100, 108
early concepts of, 27,
    31, 37
in ethology, 101–103
in psychoanalysis, 59–61
versus intelligence, 27,
    40, 87
Instinct controversy, 91–
    93, 99
Insulin and hunger, 146
Interaction. *See* Drive in-
    teraction
Intervening variables, 17
    See also Constructs
Irrelevant drive, 247–257,
    274

K. *See* Incentive

Latent learning, 440
Learning curves, 131, 236–
    238
Learning to eat and drink,
    192, 205, 435
Lick rate constancy, 203
Local theory of motiva-
    tion, 110–112

Maintaining stimuli, 128,
    132, 270–278
Maintenance schedules,
    137
Materialism, 27–29. *See
    also* Mechanism
and psychoanalysis, 55,
    56
Maze tasks
drive effects, 215, 216
drive-shift effects, 244
incentive effects, 413,
    426
Meal patterning, 195–199
Mechanistic philosophy,
    5, 6, 16, 23–29, 45,
    46, 100
and Freud, 55
opposition to, 7, 32, 44,
    314
Motivation concepts
compromise nature of,
    31, 33, 86, 101
early history of, 23–43
Mouth meter, 165
Multiplicative law for
    drive and habit. *See*
    Independence
Need
and drive, 117–120, 129,
    132, 170
without drive, 184

Lewin's construct, 74
Murray's construct, 81
Negative incentive. *See*
    Frustration
Neural pathways
in cue learning, 296
in hunger, 113, 149–
    151
in sex, 114
in thirst, 150, 161, 168
Noncontingent techniques,
    437–444
Nonnutritive food, 156,
    225, 259, 260

Observing responses, 475,
    476
Obstruction box method,
    120–124
Osmotic theory
of hunger, 152, 153
of thirst, 159, 160

Percentage of reinforce-
    ment, 436
Peripheral theory of
    motivation, 109–
    114
Physiological mechanisms
in drinking, 113, 157–
    168
in eating, 112, 114, 144–
    156
in sex, 114, 173–179
Polydipsia, 169
Predictive cues, 316
in avoidance, 343, 344,
    348, 349
in general activity,
    218–220, 442
in punishment, 390–393
Promissory notes, 16, 115
Psychoanalysis, 54–68
adequacy of theory, 66,
    67
and behavior, 62–64
scope of, 64, 65
Punishment, 367–400
the contingency ques-
    tion, 393–399
defined, 369, 370
facilitating effects, 371–
    378
ineffective, 368–372
moral question, 386
suppressing effects,
    378–381, 387
theories of, 381–393
Purposive behavior, 93–
    95, 291, 298, 315

Quality of reinforcement,
    423–425
contrast effects, 425–426
Quinine acceptance, 142,
    144

Radical empiricism, 18
Random activity, 115. *See
    also* General
    activity
Rationalism
    Freud's attack on, 50,
        65
    new, 35, 36
    traditional, 2–5, 22
Realism, psychological,
    32, 71, 79
Reductionism, 46–48
Reflexes, 1, 25
Regulation of intake, 137–
    139, 197–199
Reinforcement, amount of.
    See Amount of re-
    inforcement
    contingencies of, in
        avoidance, 332–
        335, 336
    in incentive studies,
        437–444
    delay of. *See* Delay of
        reinforcement
    mechanisms of, brain
        stimulation, 266–
        269
        consummatory be-
            havior, 258, 259
        drive induction, 269,
            270
        drive reduction, 260–
            264
    partial. *See* Percentage
        of reinforcement
    quality of. *See* Quality
        of reinforcement
    secondary. *See* Second-
        ary reinforcement
    theory of motivation,
        304–313, 345–347
Relief cues, 300, 465
Reproductive behavior,
    171–173
Response measurement
    problem, 189, 190,
    238
Responsibility, personal,
    3, 24, 386
r_G, 273, 291–294. *See also*
    Incentive
    anticipations of concept,
        28, 43
    empirical status of, 301–
        303
    and frustration, 406
    and secondary reinforce-
        ment, 466

Saccharin
    as an incentive, 425, 426
    as a reinforcer, 259
    as a secondary rein-
        forcer, 264

Safety cues, 342, 349,
    391–393
Salt
    appetite for, 118, 265
    balance, and hunger,
        152, 153
    and thirst, 157–160,
        165, 207
    deficiency, 118
Satiety hormone, 147, 148
Satiety mechanisms
    for hunger, 151–156
    for thirst, 164, 165
Scaling, drive, 186
    behavior strength, 211
S_D. *See* Drive stimuli
Secondary reinforcement,
    264, 446–478
    chaining, 461–464
    and delay of reinforce-
        ment, 427–429, 461
    and discrimination, 460–
        464
    early experiments, 447–
        451
    maintenance of be-
        havior, 455–460
    negative. *See* Avoidance
    new learning with, 451–
        455
    theories of, 466–478
Selective facilitation, 294,
    295, 301
Selective learning, 308–
    312. *See also* Con-
    straints
    with drive stimuli, 272
Self-selection of foods,
    117, 118
Self-stimulation, 266–269,
    427
Semantics of a theory, 11
Set, 69
Set point for body weight,
    138, 151
Sex
    consummatory behavior,
        173–179
    as a drive, 114, 172, 173
    hormonal background,
        176–178
    as a reinforcer, 175, 176,
        259
    sensory factors, 177, 179
Sham drinking, 113, 152
Sham eating, 155, 257
Shock intensity
    in avoidance, 339
    in escape, 186, 214
    in punishment, 378, 381
Shrinkage paradox, 162, 164
Sidman avoidance, 329–331
Sleep, 208, 209
Social motives, 83, 90,
    281–282

Specific hungers, 118
Spontaneous activity. *See*
    General activity
SSDR hypothesis, 357–366
Stimuli
    aversive, 185, 186
    drive. *See* Drive stimuli
    feedback, 347–350, 357
    releasing, 102
    supporting, 317, 318
Stimulus
    deficit, 58
    etymology of, 57
Stomach contractions,
    110–111, 113, 144
    and activity, 116
Stomach loading, and
    satiety, 152–156,
    158, 164, 165
    and contractions, 115
    and reinforcement, 257,
        260–263
Syntax of a theory, 11

Teleology
    Aristotelian, 3
    behavioral, 93, 94
Temporal factors. *See*
    Cyclicity
Tension, Lewin's construct,
    73
Theoretical constructs, 12,
    16
Thiamine deficiency, 119
Thirst. *See also* Drinking
    antecedents of, 157–
        166
    definition of, 157
    physiological basis, 157–
        164
    sensations of, 111
    and weight loss, 162–
        164
Time sampling, 229–230
Token rewards, 449–451
Traditional rationalism,
    2–5, 22
Transfer of control, 339–
    343, 437–440
Two-factor theory, 286–
    290, 323–326, 344

Urges to eat or drink, 115

Vacuum activity, 96, 103,
    106, 172
Valence, Lewin's construct,
    76
Vicious circle effect, 372–
    377

Weight loss
    in hunger, 139–143
    in thirst, 162–164
Why questions, 10, 89, 97
Würzburg, 69, 70

A
NEW
ECONOMIC
ERA

GEORGE KATONA
BURKHARD STRUMPEL

ELSEVIER · NEW YORK
NEW YORK · OXFORD · SHANNON

ELSEVIER NORTH-HOLLAND, INC.
52 Vanderbilt Avenue, New York, New York 10017

Distributors outside the United States and Canada:
THOMOND BOOKS
(A Division of Elsevier /North-Holland Scientific
        Publishers, Ltd.)
P.O. Box 85
Limerick, Ireland

Library of Congress Cataloging in Publication Data

Katona, George, 1901-
  A new economic era.

  Bibliography: p.
  Includes index.
  1. Economic history—1945- 2. Consumers.
3. Economics—Psychological aspects. I. Strumpel,
Burkhard, joint author. II. Title.
HC59.K385   330.9′04   77-25842
ISBN 0-444-00258-8

CONTENTS

Acknowledgments   vii

1. Introduction   1
2. The Early 1970s—Economic Trends   11
3. The Experience of the Recession   29
4. New Trends in Consumer Attitudes   45
5. The Work Ethic   65
6. Retirement and Saving   81
7. Collective Deprivation and Societal Discontent   95
8. Change in Behavior—The Example of the Energy Crisis   107
9. The Failings of Economics   117
10. The Challenge of a Humane Economy   131
Appendix 1: Satisfactions and Subjective Welfare   147
Appendix 2: Inflation and Unemployment   161
Bibliography   169
Index   173

ACKNOWLEDGMENTS

This attempt to analyze middle-range economic trends and thus to assess the prospects for the next ten years is based on a belief in the usefulness of interdisciplinary and international studies. Thirty years of association on the part of one author (G. K.) and ten years on the part of the other author (B. S.) with the Survey Research Center, a part of the Institute for Social Research of the University of Michigan, is reflected in the joint application to economic problems of the methods, concepts, and findings of economics, psychology, and sociology.

In addition to generally available statistical data, information collected through sample interview surveys conducted over the past thirty years in the United States and in Germany aided in the comparison of people's attitudes, expectations, and values in the 1950s and 1960s with those in the 1970s. The authors did not rely just on the findings of the surveys; they also read many of the interviews and found that the ways in which survey respondents expressed their opinions and feelings about inflation, unemployment, and many other economic issues provided clues to changes in public opinion and the economic climate. The authors owe a great debt to several colleagues at the Survey Research Center as well as to hundreds of interviewers and thousands of respondents for having contributed to this book and making it possible.

Special thanks are due to Sylvia M. Kafka for editing the book. Her unerring ability to understand what the authors wanted to say but failed to express clearly made her, in effect, a coauthor of the book. We are very grateful also to Nancy McAllister for her work not only in typing and retyping the manuscript but in contributing to it by locating many useful old papers and data.

The two authors have worked closely with each other for many years. The original idea for the book came from Burkhard Strumpel, who was primarily responsible for Chapters 5, 7, 8, and 10. George Katona did a larger share of the work on Chapters 3, 4, 6, and 9. In 1977 Burkhard Strumpel left Michigan to accept an appointment as professor of economics at the Free University of Berlin, Germany.

GEORGE KATONA
BURKHARD STRUMPEL

A NEW ECONOMIC ERA

1
INTRODUCTION

In 1970 or thereabouts the Western industrial nations entered a new economic era.

The quarter century after World War II was a period of rapid growth, unprecedented in economic history. People's expectations, aspirations, and desires for more consumer goods, better jobs, and greater income security were largely fulfilled.

In the course of the 1970s, however, the economy became a cause for concern rather than a source of satisfaction. As the result of rapid inflation millions of people, even those with substantial increases in their wages or salaries, could not improve their standard of living. The market failed in its major task, to bring together potential workers with unfilled jobs; unemployment was large while many jobs were waiting for suitable applicants, and needs for private and public services were not being satisfied. The market also appeared incapable of reconciling the desire for a humane and congenial environment with the requirements of an economy that depended for its vitality on continuous growth and expansion.

Is it justified to attribute lasting significance to these changes? Or are we dealing here with nothing more than cyclical fluctuations and the one-time impact of the oil crisis, so that we should expect the problems of 1973–1977 to disappear in a few years? Analysis of the substantial changes in attitudes, beliefs, and values that have occurred between earlier postwar years and the 1970s sheds light on the answers to these questions. The certainty and assurance that prevailed in the former period have given way to disorientation and confusion. Earlier, confidence and trust in the government and big business as well as in continuous growth sustained optimistic attitudes, and participation in the "economy of more" was most satisfying. In the 1970s skepticism and mistrust developed, and belief in growth and progress was shaken. Lack of understanding of what was going on in the economy made for uncertainty and thus for volatility in attitudes and behavior.

In the last few years there were both economic changes and changes in people's attitudes toward economic processes:

- Not only did inflation become rapid, but confidence and trust in the abilitiy of government, big business, and experts in general to slow down inflation were severely weakened.

- Not only did unemployment grow greatly, but the employment situation worsened also because of changes in work ethics.

- Not only were there adverse changes in the availability and price of energy as well as of industrial raw materials, but concern with their impact on the quality of life and on the environment also increased greatly.

- Earlier we tried to avoid inflation; today we ask only whether inflation will be rapid or slow.

- Earlier we hoped for full employment; today we ask only whether unemployment will be large or small.

- Earlier we took growth and progress for granted; today we struggle to keep our standard of living at yesterday's level.

After more than two years of cyclical upswing, our economic problems seem to have become more difficult rather than less difficult to solve. The understanding of economic developments is not facilitated by conventional economic thinking. Traditional concepts restrict our attention to the business cycle and tend to confine the reasons for economic difficulties to financial factors that are studied in a national rather than a global context. In this book we shall try to show that the economic problems of this decade must be understood, analyzed, and resolved within the context of the cultural and sociopsychological changes that have taken place in mature industrial societies.

To accomplish this purpose, we shall be concerned, first, with middle-range trends. We shall attempt to discern developments that fashioned our economy over several years in the 1970s and that may foreshadow trends over several years to come. Secondly, we shall be engaged in an interdisciplinary study. Without neglecting economic-financial processes—changes in incomes, assets, debts, and, above all, prices—we shall pay attention to changes in attitudes, expectations, beliefs, and values held by the people. Finally, we shall try to shed light on economic and sociopsychological trends in America by comparing them with trends elsewhere, primarily in one of the most successful industrial countries, West Germany.

What will be done differs greatly from the short-run analysis of most economic studies and forecasting. As is well known, the understanding of business cycles and the forecasting of economic developments for the subsequent six or twelve months constitute the most engrossing preoccupation of a broad group of economists. By expressing the interdependence of its different sectors in exact terms econometricians have been successful in depicting how the economy has functioned in the past and sometimes even how it will function in the near future. Economists have developed and tested fiscal and monetary theories by applying them to short-term economic trends.

The authors of this book and the institution with which they are connected have likewise concerned themselves with short-term forecasting by attempting to show that it would be greatly enhanced by the measurement and analysis of people's expectations that shape their subsequent economic behavior. An *index of consumer sentiment* was devised in order to measure consumers' willingness to buy. The index was found

3

to have predictive value, especially regarding turning points of the business cycle. Findings made over twenty-five years support the underlying theory that willingness to buy influences consumers' discretionary expenditures, and these expenditures in turn lead and influence the entire economy in recessions as well as in recovery (see Katona 1975 Part 2).

Long-term prospects have also received some attention from economists, as, for instance, in studies of probable economic trends toward the end of this and the beginning of the next century. Extrapolation from prevailing trends represents practically the only available method for such long-term forecasting. There is no question of its usefulness, particularly in the area of population studies, in showing what would happen if processes should continue to operate as they have in the past. But, for example, when limits to growth are predicted on the basis of the exhaustion of natural resources, provided demand and supply continue to grow as they have been growing, what is demonstrated above all are the limits of methodology. Economic trends are characterized by feedback from output to input, to which it is very difficult, if not impossible, to adapt the process of extrapolation.

We shall contrast common traits of the twenty-five years prior to 1970 with those that became apparent in the 1970s. This will be done regarding economic processes as well as people's attitudes and values that influence their behavior. Man, in this approach, is the subject, not just the object of economic changes.

The years 1945 to 1970 constitute the period in which affluence originated. The term *affluence* is here given the specific meaning of "more for the many, rather than much for the few"(see Katona 1964, p. 6). In the annals of history we find periods in which nations have been called rich; they had a thin upper class that had accumulated great wealth. Even in the nineteenth and first half of the twentieth centuries the well-to-do middle class comprised much less than the majority of the people. In the post-World War II years poverty was not eliminated—although it was greatly reduced—and yet the majority of Americans were affluent in the sense that they were in a position to spend money on many things they wanted, desired, or chose to have, rather than on necessities alone. The acquisition of discretion in spending and saving by masses of people represents the essence of the new era that began in the United States in the late 1940s. A few years later affluence in this sense spread to Canada, Western Europe, and Japan.

What will be the major features of the second post-World War II period, which began around the year 1970? Logically, three possibilities are indicated: The first would be further growth and the spread of affluence, that is, the continuation of earlier trends rather than the emergence of a new era. This possibility must be considered because toward the end of the 1970s affluence was far from complete and especially because those who were deprived of opportunities because of their race, lack of skills or education, age, or the state of their health failed to participate in what they considered to be the American way of life.

A second possibility would be the decline of affluence. Some of what was achieved in the 1950s and 1960s could be lost in the 1970s and 1980s. Millions of people would again be compelled to spend all their money for the satisfaction of imminent needs, for food, shelter, transportation, and the like. Unemployment would rise and aggregate demand would be reduced.

A third and frequently mentioned possibility would be stagnation.[1] Growth would be replaced by staying where we are. This prospect, perhaps welcome to those who call it stability and who are afraid of growth, is deplored by the great majority of people, who, not having participated to their satisfaction in the generally rising standards of living, would feel deprived if they were not to get what they felt was due them.

To make no mystery of our position, let us say without delay that we do not think that any of the three possibilities describes what the next decade will bring. We expect a series of rapid fluctuations, periods of recovery alternating with recessions in fairly quick succession. Ups and downs in the

---

[1]Especially in Western Europe the expression *stagflation* is widely used. Some economists there predict that Europe is headed toward stagnation coupled with inflation.

economy brought about by optimism or even elation that is shortly replaced by pessimism or even dejection appear more probable than either stagnation, overall decline, or further growth.

Responsibility for the volatility of attitudes as well as the prevailing feeling of uncertainty was found to reside in a lack of understanding of what was going on in the economy. Cognitive schemata that could provide a basis for that understanding were found to be wanting. The enduring, substantial, and painful increases in prices as well as the rapid and wide fluctuations in business activity were both found to have surprised, even amazed, many people. The common man could not understand how either inflation or the instability of the economy had come about. This situation contrasted greatly with the one prevailing in the 1950s and 1960s, when simple concepts were at hand, thanks to which continuous growth and the betterment of one's standard of living were understood as something that inevitably had to happen.

The absence of understanding in the 1970s may be attributed to the fact that laymen received no help from the experts. Economists were most successful in the 1960s, when it was widely believed that the application of their teachings had served to make the business cycle obsolete. But in 1973 the leading economists failed to predict the great recession, and in 1974 they gave contradictory answers regarding its origin and prospects. Thus consumers as well as businessmen remained at sea. The understanding and assurance that in earlier years had produced stable behavior were missing. Lack of understanding of what is going on makes people feel uncertain and helpless and thus leads to volatile attitudes. Then, whenever there is even unimportant good or bad news, they tend to overreact in one direction or the other.

Strategies of economic policy that would be capable of dealing with the specific problems of the new era are lacking. The present worldwide difficulties generate hardly less confusion than the depression of the 1930s. What failed in both cases were the images, cognitive concepts, and political tools that had succeeded in providing an orientation to experts as well as to laymen during the preceding better times. A convincing explanation of the crisis in the thirties was presented in 1935 by John Maynard Keynes, who identified the failure of demand to utilize the production potential of the economy as the major cause of the depression. The explanation came too late to forestall the overoptimistic predictions and ineffective therapies that prevailed during the depression, undermining confidence in the expertise of economists and the strategies initiated by them. Hardly less discredited today is the claim that Keynesian fiscal and monetary policies could be used to secure monetary stability, full employment, and continuous growth by augmenting or diminishing aggregate demand as the situation required. Experts and laymen are driven to the conclusion that:

- There must be something wrong with the law of supply and demand when prices keep going up both in good times and bad times, both when demand is high and when it is low.
- There must be something wrong with Keynesian economic policies, which teach us that by increasing total demand we can reduce unemployment and by decreasing it we can slow down inflation, when inflation and unemployment appear to reflect the same sickness and the one threatens to bring about the other.

We are in urgent need of a post-Keynesian paradigm in order to understand the contemporary economy and to shape it in accordance with the objective developments as well as the subjective expectations of our decade. Such a paradigm may well focus on the concept of qualitative rather than a quantitative growth.

The symptoms of a mismatch between man and the economy—for instance, the coexistence of unemployment, job openings, and unfilled needs for personal services; citizens' protests against the construction of nuclear power plants, airports, factories, and highways in certain neighborhoods, even though they would provide employment—seem to suggest that the difficulties are indeed of a qualitative rather than a quantitative nature. It may be less the quantity of the product than its composition that has become the problem in the 1970s. Joan Robinson, in a paper entitled "The Second Crisis of Economic Theory," compared the present problems with those of the thirties, when Keynes demonstrated that a purely quantitative intervention might provide the remedy. According to Robinson, "the first crisis arose from the breakdown of a theory which could not account for the *level* of employment. The second crisis arises from a theory that cannot account for the *content* of employment. . . . Now that we all agree that government expenditure can maintain employment we should agree about what the expenditure should be for" (1972, p. 6).

Much of the failure of the labor market has been found to be of a qualitative nature. Certain segments of the labor force were unemployed during both upswings and downswings, in bad as well as in good times; others, especially white married males age twenty-four to forty-five, were primarily concerned with the lack of good jobs, that is, of jobs equal to their qualifications that would enable them to reach their desired goals.

In presenting differences between the economic era before and the era after 1970, we shall point to the decline in the proportion of people who thought that they themselves could control their own fate; feelings of dependence on the government or on luck were found to have increased. At the same time a growing proportion believed that their job should not only provide adequate earnings but also be satisfying and contribute to self-fulfillment. In this desire for a better quality of job very many people felt disappointed.

A striving for quality rather than quantity became evident also in the area of consumer behavior. Concern with the durability and the performance of products and especially with the quality of repairs and services in general began to replace the enjoyment of buying an ever-growing number of consumer goods.

The 1970s differed from the earlier period not only in the continuous pressures of inflation and recession but also in the growing attention paid to the quality of life. The environment, especially the extent of pollution, the decay of central cities, and the safety of streets, became matters of great concern. Subjective well-being became dependent on many things beyond the size of one's income.

8

The relationship between the command over material resources and the satisfaction of nonmaterial needs is very complex. Economic growth does not lead automatically to a fulfillment of people's expectations. Conversely, it would be misleading to attribute the responsiblity for the present malaise to slow growth alone. Many people are dissatisfied and insecure not because they have less or earn less but rather because they do not understand the environment, because they see things happen that they do not approve of, and because they feel they have lost control over their own fate.

The preceding considerations define the program of the book. Changes in attitudes and behavior will be considered in connection with economic changes. We begin, however, by identifying the economic trends of the 1970s.

2
THE EARLY 1970S–ECONOMIC TRENDS

In the United States the 1970s began with five quarters of recession followed by a short recovery and then another recession. While in the first postwar era prosperous periods were interrupted only by occasional short recessions, the first six years of this decade were marked by twelve quarters of recession and twelve quarters of recovery.

| | In the U.S. | |
| | RECESSION | RECOVERY |
YEAR	(Quarters per year)	
1970	4	0
1971	1	3
1972	0	4
1973	1	3
1974	4	0
1975	2	2
Six-year total	12	12

In Germany there was no equivalent of the American recession of 1970; 1969 and 1970 were boom years, following a recession in 1967. But in both countries the 1974–1975 recession was the deepest and longest since the 1930s. Declines in real GNP and real income over considerable periods made their first appearance. The recession set in much later in Germany than in the U.S., in the summer of 1974 rather than the fall of 1973.

The annual rates of growth of the most important economic indicators are presented in Table 2-1, both for the 1970s and for the preceding postwar years. In the 1970s, in the U.S. as in Germany, growth of GNP and its important parts, as well as of personal income and of production, was rather limited compared with the rapid growth in the 1950s and 1960s. The comparisons are made in constant dollars because prices, unlike the other variables, advanced only moderately in the 1960s but rapidly in the 1970s. In the 1970s inflation accelerated greatly and contributed to the deterioration of very many people's standard of living. In the 1950s and the first half of the 1960s there were a few years in the U.S. and many years in Germany with average price increases of less than 1 percent. In the U.S. before 1965 less than 2 percent per year was the most common rate of annual price rise.

✳ Wage and salary increases, which in the 1950s and 1960s greatly exceeded price increases, failed even to keep up with them in the 1970s. In some years the averages showed small declines in well-being, but they did not tell the whole story. There were many families who suffered substantial losses in real income in those years, while others continued to make gains.

✳ Price increases likewise showed great variation. The first postwar era was characterized by declining costs of energy, the supply of oil, gas, and electricity remaining abundant and inexpensive.[1] The same was true of most industrial raw materials and agricultural products as well as of capital. In the U.S. low interest rates characterized a period of easy money, which ended in 1966. Real interest rates, nominal interest rates minus the rate of inflation, were no higher in the mid-1970s than ten or twenty years earlier. But the cost of erecting, say, a

---

[1]According to calculations of the electrical industry, the average price of electricity declined by 33 percent from 1944 to 1968, in which period most other prices rose substantially. The price decline was due to economies of scale and technological progress.

TABLE 2-1 Annual Growth Rate of Major Economic Indicators (in percent)

Years	GNP	Personal Disposable Income per Capita	Expenditures on Consumer Durables (In Constant Dollars)	Fixed Business Investment (Nonresidential)	Industrial Production Index	Consumer Price Index
				United States		
1947–1957	3.9	2.2	6.9	3.1	5.8	2.6
1958–1969	3.4	3.1	8.8	5.8	6.5	2.5
1970–1975	1.7	1.8	3.8	0.9	1.1	6.4
				West Germany		
1955–1969,[a]	8.1	6.0	N.A.[b]	9.0	2.7[c]	2.3
1970–1975	2.3	1.6	N.A.,[b]	–0.2	1.0	5.7

[a] The growth rates of the German economy were not calculated from the end of World War II but from a time when economic conditions had become fairly normal.
[b] N.A. = Not ascertained.
[c] 1962 to 1969.

13

power plant went up substantially when money had to be borrowed at 9 to 10 percent rather than at 4 percent per annum, that is, when the borrower had to compensate the lender for an expected inflation rate of 5 or 6 percent over a period of twenty or thirty years.

In the 1950s and 1960s the rate of growth in Germany was exceptionally high, much higher than the likewise unusually large growth rates in the U.S. In the 1970s, however, modest gains characterized both countries.

The average rates of growth during the years 1970 to 1975 give no indication of the great fluctuations that occurred during that period and the depth of the deterioration that marked the recession of 1973–1975. In Table 2-2 we show the trend of real GNP, industrial production, unemployment, and retail prices (1) for the six months just before the great recession (first half of 1973), (2) during the depth of the recession (last quarter of 1974 and first quarter of 1975), and (3) just after the recession (last quarter of 1975 and first quarter of 1976). In the United States huge declines in real GNP and industrial production, causing high rates of unemployment, coincided with unprecedented price increases, while in Germany the same developments occurred in GNP, production, and unemployment, but not in inflation, which was slightly reduced during the worst period of the recession. Recovery toward the end of 1975 and at the beginning of 1976 was substantial in most indicators, but not in the rate of unemployment.

TABLE 2-2   Annual Growth Rate Before, During, and After the Recession of 1973–1975 (in percent)

Year and Quarter	GNP in Constant Dollars	Industrial Production Index	Unemployment [a]	Consumer Price Index
United States				
1973 I–II	5.0	5.0	4.9	8.5
1974 IV–1975 I	−8.4	−26.0	7.4	11.5
1975 IV–1976 I	6.2	11.1	8.0	8.6
West Germany				
1973 I–II	6.3	0.6	1.1	7.8
1974 IV–1975 I	−9.0	−11.0	3.7	5.7
1975 IV–1976 I	9.7	13.4	5.1	4.3

[a] Rate at indicated periods.

For two decades before 1970 unemployment was practically nonexistent in Germany; indeed, "guest" workers from other countries were needed to fill many jobs. In the United States unemployment fluctuated in most postwar years between 3 and 5 percent and rose above 5½ percent only in the middle of 1974, much later than most other indicators had denoted bad times. In the spring of 1975 the rate of unemployment rose to a high of over 9 percent in the U.S. and to 5 percent in Germany.

Figures 2-1 and 2-2 show the fluctuations in the rate of growth of the real gross national product and unemployment both in the U.S. and in Germany each year between 1950 and 1975. The ups and downs of the business cycles and the unusual severity of the last cycle are clearly indicated in the charts.

More rapid inflation and greater unemployment as well as lower rates of increase in real GNP, real incomes, and production in the 1970s than in the two preceding decades are the most obvious differences between the two economic eras. Searching for the underlying forces responsible for the unprecedented growth in the Western industrial nations following World War II until the 1970s, we may describe the constellation of circumstances that prevailed in those years as follows:

- Energy and most raw materials were readily available and their relative prices declined over time.
- A mobile labor force was available from a shrinking agricultural sector, the closing of small and inefficient enterprises, an increase in female participation in the labor force, and immigration.
- Capital was available due to a fairly constant rate of saving, high enough to provide for the needs of investors at low rates of interest.
- There was increasing availability of skills due to the rapid expansion of educational attainment.
- Private households readily absorbed the ever-increasing production of goods and services; consumers were optimistic, unsaturated, "thing-minded."[2] There was rapid popula-

---

[2]The significant role of consumer optimism in contributing to affluence has been shown in Katona (1964).

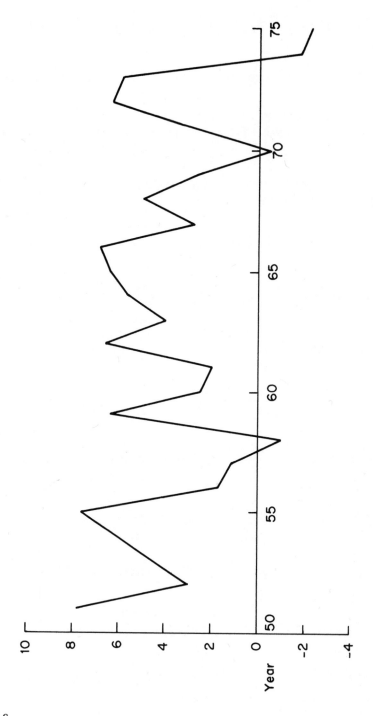

United States

Year

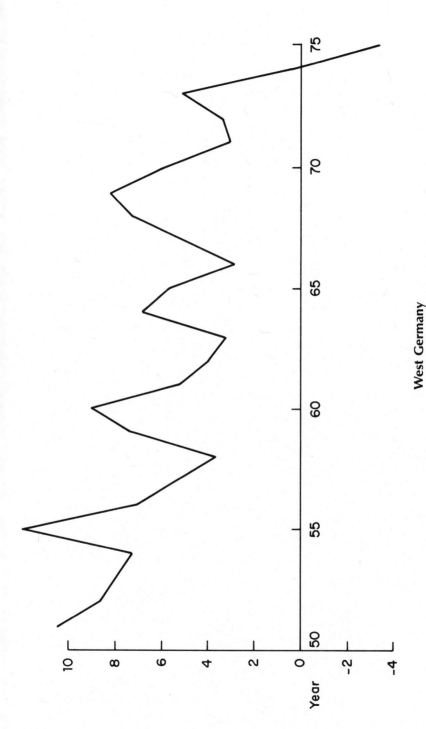

West Germany

FIGURE 2-1   Fluctuations in Gross National Product, 1950–1975 (rate of change against previous year in percent of constant dollars).

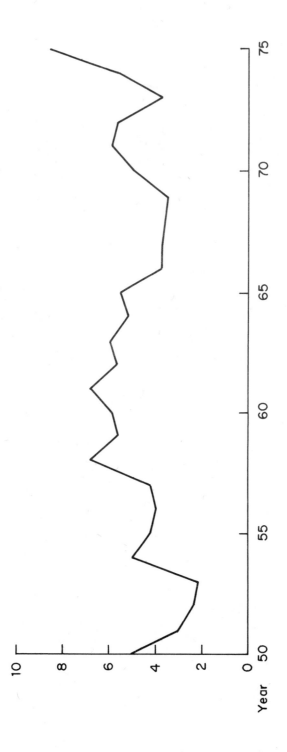

Year

United States

18

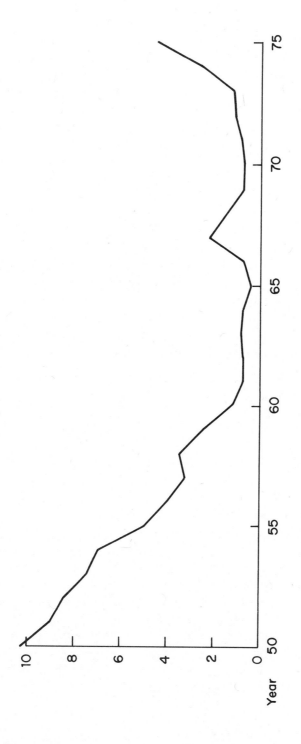

West Germany

FIGURE 2-2 Fluctuations in Unemployment, 1950–1975 (annual rate in percent).

tion growth and a growth of suburbia accelerated by government subsidies to home owners and federal highway construction. Suburbanization, in turn, led to the strong expansion of the housing and automobile industries (also, of course, to the demise of the inner cities).

The situation in the 1970s differed in the following basic respects from that of the preceding postwar period:

- The prices of raw materials and of energy rose sharply after a long period of decline relative to other prices.
- The proportion of the labor force employed by the sectors producing goods (manufacturing, mining, construction) decreased.
- Pollution control standards and other environmental constraints raised the operating costs of industry. Conserving the environment impeded certain forms of production (e.g., the erection of nuclear power plants).
- Consumer confidence and consumer expectations suffered periods of sharp deterioration.

The Consumer Economy

One significant feature of the first postwar era, the development of what may be called the consumer economy, was maintained in the 1970s. The consumer economy was characterized by a great increase in discretionary expenditures by consumers and a lead of these expenditures during the business cycle. Discretionary expenditures are those that consumers may postpone or carry out in advance of need if they so desire. The most important among the discretionary expenditures are those for durable goods, and these are the only ones for which good statistical data are available. As shown in Table 2-1, in the U.S. expenditures for consumer durables rose to a larger extent in the first era than did the other major indicators of economic activity—real GNP, personal income, or business investment. The largest of the discretionary expenditures are those made for automobiles. It is shown in Table 2-3 that in the course of each of four postwar recessions

TABLE 2-3   Movements in Real GNP and New Auto Sales in Recession and Early Recovery Periods, U.S.

	Percent Change, Peak to Trough	Percent Change, Trough to the Fourth Subsequent Quarter
1957–1958 recession		
Real GNP (dollars)	−3.2	7.1
Domestic auto sales (number)	−31.7	39.6
1960–1961 recession		
Real GNP	−1.2	6.1
Domestic auto sales	−19.9	28.6
1960–1970 recession		
Real GNP	−1.1	4.6
Domestic auto sales	−36.2	....ᵃ
1973–1975 recession		
Real GNP	−6.6	7.1
Domestic auto sales	−42.6	31.1

SOURCE: Federal Reserve Bank of Saint Louis *Review*, June 1976.
ᵃ Omitted because of automobile strike.

the number of cars purchased fell much more sharply, and in the first phase of each recovery rose much more sharply, than real GNP.

In Germany at the end of World War II there were practically no passenger cars, and automobile sales increased steadily until 1967. Fluctuations in automobile sales remained insignificant until 1973 or 1974, when the German economy for the first time participated in the basic feature of the American economy, the large decline in automobile sales during a recession. Registrations of new passenger cars fell in Germany from 1.96 million in 1972 to 1.56 million in 1974. In earlier years business investment in plants and machinery, rather than consumer investment in automobiles and appliances, represented the best indication of growth of the German economy. During the 1960s and early 1970s fixed investment amounted to approximately 25 percent of GNP in Germany and only 15 percent in the United States. The steady and substantial growth of fixed investment provided the basis for one fundamental feature of the German economy, the rise in exports, which increased in the 1950s and 1960s much faster than GNP. A decline in the rate of business investment started in Germany earlier than in the U.S., namely, in 1971, and was very substantial in outlays for plants and machinery intended for expansion rather than replacement.

The fluctuations in both business investment and consumer investment during the 1970s in America are shown in Figure 2-3 (both are expressed in constant dollars). Expenditures on consumer durables fell earlier and rose earlier than expenditures on plants and machinery, and the amplitude of the fluctuations was much larger in the former than in the latter. Expenditures on consumer durables began to decline in 1973 and continued to fall over seven consecutive quarters. Busi-

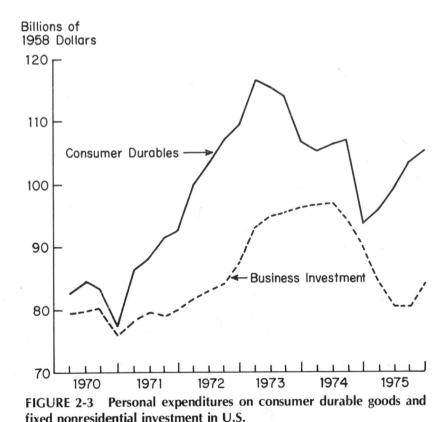

FIGURE 2-3 Personal expenditures on consumer durable goods and fixed nonresidential investment in U.S.

ness investment did not turn down until the third quarter of 1974. Prior to the recession American business investment was the highest ever reached till then and remained high during the first part of the recession. The utilization of industrial capacity amounted to only 69 percent in 1975 compared to 80 percent in the preceding years and much higher rates in the 1950s and early 1960s.

One important economic indicator that moved in the same way in the 1960s and the 1970s was the rate of personal saving. Both in the U.S. and in Germany it rose in the late 1960s and continued to rise in the 1970s, reaching unprecedented high levels at the time of the deepest recession and greatest inflation.

Personal Saving in Percent of Disposable Income

Year	U.S.	West Germany
1964–1969	6½	11½
1970–1972	7	13½
1973–1975	8	14½

Since World War II the German people have saved a much higher proportion of their income than the American people. The authors of this book have discussed the reasons for these differences in earlier publications (see Katona, Strumpel, and Zahn 1971 and Strumpel 1975a). It may suffice to say here that the difference in the respective roles of consumer and business investment was crucial in bringing about different saving rates in the two countries. In the United States a large share of automobiles and other durable goods were purchased on the installment plan, and the excess of borrowing over repayment of consumer debt consistently reduced the total amounts saved. In the 1960s about one-half of Americans both approved of and used installment credit, while only one-fourth of the Germans approved of it and only one-tenth actually had any installment debt. When asked about their purposes for saving, Americans spoke primarily of rainy days (emergencies, illness, unemployment) and of retirement. Only 10 percent mentioned saving for the sake of purchasing durable goods. In contrast, close to 60 percent of Germans said that

23

they were saving in order to be able to make large purchases later.

In spite of rising rates of saving, personal wealth declined substantially in the 1970s in both countries. This was due to a long-lasting downward trend on the stock markets, especially pronounced in the U.S., where it occurred in 1969 and 1970 and, after a recovery, again in 1973 and 1974. The Dow-Jones index of stock prices, representing stocks of the largest corporations, fell from over 1,000 in January 1973 to under 600 late in 1974. The decline in the dollar value of stocks ignores the simultaneous sharp decline in the purchasing power of the dollar. When in 1975–1976 stock prices recovered their earlier losses, they did so only in terms of the devalued dollars, and they still failed to compensate for the large price increases of those years.

The decline in stock prices represented a sizable reduction in personal wealth. The Federal Reserve Board published a chart indicating the fluctuations of the "per capita deflated net worth" of households, defined as "financial assets minus financial liabilities divided by population and the Consumer Price Index." The chart shows that this net worth was approximately 33 percent lower in 1974 than when it reached its highest value (both in 1968 and 1972). With an improved trend on the stock market the deflated net worth recovered less than one-half of its previous losses between 1974 and the spring of 1976 (*Federal Reserve Bulletin*, June 1976, p. 464).

It must be kept in mind, however, that stock ownership is highly concentrated among the rich, that a large part of the losses represented paper losses or losses of wealth gained in earlier years of stock market boom, and above all, that the increase in value of the most widely held asset of American families, the owner-occupied home, kept pace with the increase in prices in the 1970s. The real value of home ownership advanced because of the repayment of mortgage debt out of rising incomes in dollars of reduced purchasing power.

The reduction in the value of their shares made the financing of capital needs by corporations difficult. The decline in stock prices far exceeded the decline in profits. Profits in current dollars gained greatly in the early 1970s, but declined if expressed in constant dollars or percent of capital. They amounted to over 6 percent of capital in the 1950s, 8.3 percent in 1961–1965, 7.7 percent in 1966–1970, but only 5½ percent in the first few years of the 1970s. Similarly, in Germany profits in percent of sales declined from 4 percent in the first half of the 1960s to 3.4 percent in 1971–1973. Even in 1976, when there was a sizable gain in profits in real terms in both countries, the profit rate in percent of capital or sales improved very little.

On the Reasons for the Recession of 1973–1975

Up to now we have described what happened without attempting to identify the dynamic factors responsible, particularly for the recession of 1973–1975. It should be noted first that most leading economists were not aware of such forces before they became operative, and many failed to identify them even after the recession had set in. This can be indicated by their failure to predict the recession, a failure shared by those who relied on econometric models as well as of those who usually exhibited great insight. In the words of one of the latter, Arthur M. Okun, "most economic forecasters, including me, saw . . . a strong but well-balanced expansion in 1973 accompanied by an imperfect but hardly alarming record of price performance. Rarely has such a broad, bipartison professional consensus been so wrong" (1975, p. 22). In March 1975, when the first signs of recovery were already visible, Okun summarized the developments of the preceding disastrous year as follows: "In retrospect, most of 1974 was marked by a tug-of-war between business spending, which was still pulling upward, and consumer spending pulling down. The government kept predicting that businessmen would win that tug-of-war. . . . The consumers' downward pull won the tug-of-war, and then the entire economy tumbled downhill in an avalanche" (Ibid., p. 24 ff).

We may add that it was not just the government that kept predicting that "businessmen would win that tug-of-war" but also many economists because of their trust in the theory of bygone years that business investment alone had the power to fashion economic trends. In fact, there was no tug-of-war. In every quarter in 1973 consumer expenditures on durable goods, and many more of consumer discretionary expenditures, were lower than in the preceding quarter. The decline in these most volatile forms of expenditure affected general trends and, at a very late date, in 1974, caused businessmen to revise their investment plans. In these respects what happened in 1973–1974 was hardly different from what had happened in previous recessions, and the major question as to why consumers had restricted their discretionary expenditures is left unanswered.

Postponing the discussion of that question to the next chapter, we shall ask here: Was the last recession nothing but a cyclical development, or was it unique and different from earlier postwar recessions? It was widely believed that the last recession was different because it was worldwide, precipitated by the oil embargo. However, the oil embargo was imposed only toward the end of 1973 and the greatest increase in oil prices occurred only in 1974. Thus, the recession in the United States, although not in Germany or many other European countries, had already begun before the oil embargo. We shall indicate again in the next chapter why it is very probable that we would have had a recession even without any disturbance in the oil market, though in that case it might well have been milder and shorter than it was.

Inflation was accelerated in 1974 by what may be called OPEC's "excise tax" on oil, but prices had already begun to rise sharply in the spring of 1973, likewise as the result of foreign developments. Food prices skyrocketed when large Russian purchases of American wheat were disclosed. There can be no doubt that bad harvests abroad and foreign grain purchases, mishandled by American authorities, contributed to inflation. But in spite of sharply rising food prices, the consumer price index advanced in the second quarter of 1973 by only somewhat over 5 percent, in the third quarter by less than 7 percent, and in the fourth quarter by 8.4 percent. Personal income advanced at a somewhat faster rate—on the average by 12 percent in current dollars in 1973—so that in each

26

of the four quarters of the year average real incomes were still rising. But the gains in real income were smaller than in earlier years, and, as is not shown by the averages, a sizable proportion of the population had no gain at all or suffered losses because of the huge increase in the prices of necessities. Nevertheless, it may be questioned whether these developments, or even the real diminution of purchasing power of the American people in 1974, suffice to explain the extent of the decline in consumer demand and therefore of the recession. It was, as we shall argue in the next chapter, primarily people's subjective experience that was responsible for the change in demand. The 1973–1975 recession was not just another cyclical fluctuation but rather a crisis of confidence.

The lowest point of the 1973–1975 recession was reached in the first quarter of 1975 in the U.S. and several months later in Germany and the other industrialized countries. Recovery was ushered in by consumer purchases, and the consumer was celebrated as the hero. Most conspicuous was the jump in sales of domestic automobiles, in America a jump of 31 percent from the first quarter of 1975 to the first quarter of 1976 (see Table 2-3). The rate of price increases also abated in the course of 1975, as did unemployment rates early in 1976. Nevertheless, inflation and unemployment remained substantial. The cyclical disturbance was overcome, and yet the economic situation was considered to be far from satisfactory. The crucial question is: Is it permissible to use the developments of 1970–1976 as a basis for conclusions about things to come? This question will be taken up in the following chapters, where we shall present weighty evidence for the proposition that in the 1970s a new economic era started, different from the first postwar era of the preceding twenty-five years.

3
THE EXPERIENCE
OF THE RECESSION

The previous chapter told much less than the complete story of the recession of 1973–1975. Economic and financial statistics alone are not sufficient for us to fully assess the recession or to understand its course. In the light of survey data about how the American people felt and what they were thinking during those years, it becomes clear that other important factors must be taken into account. To cite but three examples:

- The sudden increase in food prices in the spring of 1973 represented for millions of housewives the traumatic experience of being compelled to leave food stores without being able to buy all the items on their shopping lists.

- What economists spoke of as an oil embargo was experienced by millions as an "oil shock" when they suddenly realized that, rather than belonging to the most powerful country in the world, they were dependent on the whims of a few oil sheikhs.

- In 1974 millions of people had given up hope and were more dejected than at any time since the 1930s.

Even these three dramatic instances fail to convey the essential feature of the recession, namely, the crisis of confidence. After Vietnam and Watergate the government was no longer trusted and was thought to be incapable of keeping employment up or inflation down. At the same time big business was thought to be profiteering or even corrupt, and the esteem even of judges and physicians, who had previously been most trusted and respected, was greatly reduced.

Psychological data were useful not only to understand the recession; they also served to predict it long before it began. Several months after quarterly surveys carried out with representative samples indicated a deterioration in consumer sentiment, discretionary demand turned down and economic conditions began to worsen. The predictive success of consumer attitudes would not have been possible unless a change in these attitudes contributed to bringing about economic fluctuations.

Change in Short-Term Expectations

Figure 3-1 shows the movements of the Survey Research Center's index of consumer sentiment from 1969 to 1977 and their relation to the two recessions that occurred during those years in America. The index is a summary measure derived from quarterly surveys of consumer attitudes and expectations about personal finances, business trends, and buying conditions. It is based on five questions, but each survey contains about thirty questions, some identical over many years and some changed according to changing conditions, which yield much additional information. The surveys are an attempt to find out not only what people think but also why they think as they do at a given time. First, however, restricting ourselves to the index, we note that it

- Declined steadily all through 1969 (when GNP, personal incomes, and retail sales remained on a high plateau);
- Bottomed out in 1970 (when the recession kept getting worse);
- Advanced in 1971–1972 to the 1969 level, but not to the level of the mid-1960s;

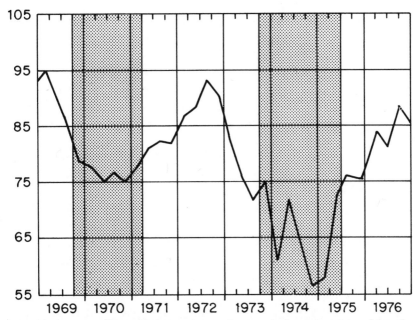

FIGURE 3-1 Index of consumer sentiment. Index constructed by the Survey Research Center, University of Michigan. February 1968 = 100. Shaded portions indicate recessions.

- Declined steadily in 1973, indicating in the early spring of that year the threat of a recession and enabling the survey directors to write in the fall of 1973, before the oil embargo, that "a general recession is imminent."

Following Figure 3-1 further, we find that the index

- Showed some zigzag movements during the oil embargo but resumed its sharp decline in the second half of 1974;
- Reached its lowest point, by far the lowest in twenty-five years, in December 1974;
- Recovered considerably all through 1975 and early 1976.

Comparable German data provide additional evidence of the predictive value of attitudes. The Common Market Organization decided in the early 1970s to finance sample interview surveys in each of its member countries so as to apply the approach of the Survey Research Center to the prediction of business cycles. Several of the Survey Research Center's questions were used, as shown in Table 3-1, which compares American and German data.

In one respect, which is of paramount importance, American and German trends are identical. Consumer attitudes and expectations declined sharply in the twelve months prior to the beginning of the last recession, long before the deterioration in economic trends set in.

Table 3-1 also indicates some differences between the two countries. First, in America the worsening of attitudes occurred in two phases: one before the onset of the recession and another, in 1974, following the oil embargo and coinciding with the deterioration in economic conditions. In Germany there was an advance deterioration in consumer expectations but hardly any when conditions actually worsened; by the beginning of 1975 most expectations showed an improvement.

Second, the German attitudinal data show a lower starting point in 1972 and a greater decline in the subsequent period than the American data. The difference is due to the lesser frequency of optimistic answers ("will be better," "will be good") given by German consumers, and a greater proportion of answers reflecting the middle position, rather than to a greater frequency of pessimistic answers. In 1973–1975 pessimism was very widespread in both countries. Supplementing the data in Table 3-1, we may report that at the time of the low point of the depression in the U.S. 87 percent and in Germany 74 percent of respondents said that business had deteriorated; in the U.S. 68 percent and in Germany 59 percent said that business conditions would continue to deteriorate during the next twelve months.

In both countries consumers' evaluations of their own personal financial situation fluctuated less than their evaluations of general economic conditions. Yet the deterioration of the former was still substantial, as may be indicated by the answers to a survey question about major changes in the respondents' economic situation during the recession. About 33 percent of Americans (according to Yankelovich surveys, early 1976) and 29 percent of Germans (Allensbach surveys, late

1975) reported that during the recession their situation had worsened. Still higher proportions, namely, 44 percent in the U.S. and 49 percent in Germany, said that they had found it necessary to cut down on their expenses or to economize.

Reasons for Pessimism—As the People Report Them

In analyzing survey data on the reasons given for changes in attitudes and expectations we shall neglect the recession of 1970 and its aftermath. One of the authors devoted a chapter of a recent book to this topic (Katona 1975, Chapter 8). Because of the similarity of the situation in 1973, however, it may be recalled that one of the crucial factors in 1969 was people's perception of the goals of the government's economic policies. While the government had committed itself to fighting inflation through restrictive monetary and fiscal policies, the people appeared to have gotten the message that the government had decided to control the inflation by promoting a recession and bringing about unemployment. We should also note that the recovery from the recession of 1970 was incomplete, particularly in terms of consumers' long-term expectations about business trends. In 1972, at a time when consumers generally thought that it was a good time to buy and the index of consumer sentiment was as high as in 1968, their attitudes regarding prospects over five years were quite pessimistic. But, at that same time, confidence in their own ability to fashion their economic future was high, and expectations about personal finances over several years were favorable.

In the spring of 1973 the shock of a sudden, unexpected, and large increase in food prices resulted in a substantial change. The American people's reaction to inflation changed radically from what it had been in the preceding years. To explain briefly: The usual consumer response to price increases, as observed most of the time between the end of World War II and 1973, had been to feel worse off because of higher prices and therefore to postpone or abstain from some purchases. Worries about how to pay for necessities in the future at their higher prices had increased motives to save.

TABLE 3-1 Trend of Attitudes, 1972–1976

	High Point Before Recession [a]	Immediately Preceding Recession [b]	Toward the End of Recession [c]	A Year After the Recession [d]
	(Percent of Favorable Minus Unfavorable Answers)			
Expectations				
Economic conditions in 12 months				
U.S.	+16	−5	−19	+18
West Germany	−1	−54	−20	+20
Unemployment in 12 months				
U.S.	−2	−20	−35	+8
West Germany	−5	−58	−14	+18
Personal financial situation in 12 months				
U.S.	+22	+6	−1	+18
West Germany	+8	−20	−8	+4

	[a]	[b]	[c]	[d]
Good or bad time to make large purchases[e]				
U.S.	+24	+27	−4	+24
West Germany	+29	+2	+9	+20
Economic conditions in 5 years				
U.S.	+9	−32	−53	−24
West Germany	....[f]	....[f]	....[f]	....[f]
Perceptions				
Current economic conditions compared to a year ago				
U.S.	+30	−17	−63	+24
West Germany	−15	−70	−67	+5
Personal finances compared to a year ago				
U.S.	+15	−7	−17	0
West Germany	+5	−25	−17	−6

[a] Fall 1972 in both countries.
[b] August 1973 in U.S., January 1974 in West Germany.
[c] October 1974 in U.S., January 1975 in West Germany.
[d] Spring 1976 in both countries.
[e] Wording in the U.S., "durable goods"; in Germany "Anschaffungen."
[f] Figures not available.

35

Thus the response to creeping inflation had been to save more rather than to spend more (see Katona 1975, Chapter 9).

On the other hand, it has been observed in many countries in the past that the response to runaway inflation and the expectation of much higher prices has been a sharp increase in spending. It was often postulated that the rational man, when he expected prices to go up, would spend in excess and in advance of his needs, stocking up and hoarding goods at the prevailing "lower" prices. This shock reaction to inflation was observed in the U.S. for a short time in 1950 following military defeat in Korea, when the recurrence of wartime shortages was widely expected. The shock response was also observed in 1973, when the increase in food and especially meat prices confused and disoriented American consumers.

We shall cite a few survey findings: While at the end of 1972 only 7 percent of a representative sample expected the prices of things they would buy to rise by more than 5 percent during the next twelve months, by February 1974 28 percent expected prices to go up by more than 10 percent. At that time two out of every five respondents explained spontaneously that they felt worse off because of the higher prices. Instead of saying, as the majority had earlier, that inflation hurt them only a little, more than one-third of all consumers averred that inflation hurt them greatly. In the earlier years only a handful of consumers could be found who reported that they had made any purchases in advance in order to beat inflation. Toward the end of 1973 one out of every four respondents said so.

Whether it was a good or bad time to buy durable goods has for more than twenty years been one of the most useful questions asked of respondents by the Survey Research Center. (The answers to this question are included in the index of consumer sentiment.) Before the 1970s the answer "This is a bad time to buy" was more frequent during times of accelerated but still limited inflation, and respondents would explain that prices were "too high" and they were priced out of the market. In 1973 the opposite argument was much more common. "Good time to buy" was the response of two out of every five respondents, and most of them explained that prices were low compared to what they would be in the future. This change in response explains why the American data about "good or bad time to buy" in Table 3-1 show a small "improvement" rather than a deterioration from 1972 to 1973 (from +24 to +27).

In giving reasons for their attitudes toward inflation people made reference to the government and to government policy as frequently in 1973 as in earlier years. In the 1950s and 1960s inflation was not a major worry because many people thought that "what goes up will come down." When asked why this would happen, most respondents simply referred to some kind of government action, indicating that they trusted the government to help. In 1973, on the other hand, the inability and even the unwillingness of the government to slow down price increases was frequently mentioned. The abandonment of price control and the notion that the government was inactive were linked in many people's minds with Watergate and the growing disillusionment with government.

Later in 1973 and in 1974 public attitudes toward government policies worsened further. When survey respondents were asked about economic news heard in the recent past, they frequently spoke of an impending recession and growing unemployment brought about by government policies intended to fight inflation. Instead of accepting the official notion that reduction of demand was a justified price to pay for lesser inflation, a credibility gap developed, and people argued that we would have a recession and high unemployment as well as inflation.

In the late fall of 1973 came the oil embargo. For the first time since World War II shortages developed, and the threat of still greater shortages became universal. The decline in the index of consumer sentiment, as shown in Figure 3-1, was substantial. So was the improvement in the index when the embargo was lifted, but within a short time inflation accelerated again and pessimism spread further.

In the second half of 1974 the American people were again disappointed. President Nixon resigned, but President Ford failed to reverse the course of the economic policy of his predecessor. Ford followed Nixon in declaring that inflation was the major enemy to be fought. Many survey respondents as-

37

serted that the government was reducing incomes and employment in order to fight inflation and, in the same interview, that the government was unable or unwilling to act.

Early in 1975 President Ford made a 180-degree turn in his economic policy by proposing a small cut in income taxes for the purpose of arresting the recession. At the same time the recession reached its trough. Although the American people did not greet the tax cut with enthusiasm and continued to mistrust government action, habituation to bad news brought about a change. Inflation and unemployment were no longer new at that time. Moreover, they did not get worse. By the spring of 1975 there was even some reduction in the rate of price increases. Survey respondents continued to refer to price increases and unemployment as adverse factors and worries, but less frequently than at earlier times. In the course of the year 1975 the frequency of bad news as reported by survey respondents declined and that of good news began to rise.

In Germany the recovery set in later than in America. The improvement in expectations about economic trends and unemployment was, however, at least as strong in that country as in the U.S. (see Table 3-1). In 1976 Germany was the Western country with the least inflation and the strongest currency. Yet the old situation of full employment and absence of economic worries has not as yet returned.

To What Is Pessimism Related?

In the preceding section we indicated some of the forces that influenced negative consumer attitudes in 1973–1974 by reporting what survey respondents themselves said about why they were pessimistic. Another method of seeking out reasons for the sharp deterioration in consumer sentiment is to relate changes in consumer sentiment to data on changes in other economic or political indicators.[1]

We shall study the relation of sentiment to (1) past price increases, (2) price expectations, (3) changes in real income,

---

[1]The discussion in this section is based on Katona (1976a).

38

(4) unemployment, and (5) attitudes toward the government. Strong positive correlations were found in the first and fifth instances, but only weak ones in the second, third, and fourth.

Inflation represents the most obvious antecedent to changes in consumer sentiment. When the monthly consumer price index was tabulated to show the rate of increase against the preceding year for the three years 1973, 1974, and 1975, a very high negative correlation was obtained between that series and the quarterly data of the index of consumer sentiment (see Strumpel 1975b and Katona 1976a). The deterioration of sentiment and the acceleration in the rate of consumer prices began at about the same time, in the spring of 1973. Later in 1973 as well as in 1974 the rate of price increases was more pronounced than the worsening of sentiment. The highest rate of price advance, 12.2 percent, occurred in December 1974, about the same time the index of consumer sentiment reached its lowest level. The similarity of movements between the two series is hardly surprising, since consumers themselves referred to inflation as the major explanation of their pessimism in those years.

But there are good reasons to believe that rising prices were not the sole cause of the deterioration in sentiment in 1973–1974. If they had been, this period would be unique in that respect. Prior to 1973 the correlation between the price index and the sentiment index was much weaker. In 1967–1968, for instance, when price advances accelerated, sentiment was fairly stable at a high level. Again, in 1969, when the rate of price increases was quite stable, sentiment deteriorated greatly.

We should also note that the underlying logic of seeking an explanation for worsening sentiment by examining actual price increases is far from clear. It would be much more understandable if change in sentiment were a function of price expectations. The expectation of higher prices might well result in worry about the future, about loss in real income and thus about a decline in purchasing power. In fact, however, the correlation between price expectations and the index of consumer sentiment was found to be very much weaker than that between consumer sentiment and past price changes.

True, survey respondents who expected considerable price increases tended to believe that business conditions would be bad or would worsen. In contrast, those who expected small price increases (less than 5 percent) or no price increases at all were more optimistic about the economy. But this association helps little to explain the sharp decline in opinions about the business outlook late in 1973 and in 1974. Price expectations worsened only to a small extent in those years, and at all times the majority of respondents expected small price increases. When price expectations were most pessimistic, as reported before, less than one-third of consumers thought that prices would go up by 10 percent or more over the next twelve months. Thus during the worst inflation two-thirds of Americans thought that prices would go up more slowly in the future than they had in the recent past.

Changes in real income helped not at all to explain the onset of the deterioration of consumer sentiment. In the winter of 1972–1973, when sentiment began to worsen, gains in real income reached high levels. The downturn in the annual advance of real income began only in the fourth quarter of 1973. To be sure, in 1974 both consumer sentiment and real income declined sharply, and both advanced in 1975.

While the drop in real income lagged by six to nine months behind the drop in sentiment, unemployment showed a still longer lag in 1973–1974. Bad news about the unemployment situation cannot serve as an explanation for people's expectations either about the business situation or even about future trends in unemployment. Unemployment was fairly stable at a level of around 5 percent not only in 1973, but also in the first half of 1974. The rate of unemployment continued to increase in the first half of 1975, when people began to expect an improvement in the economic situation.

Survey respondents frequently discussed government policy, as well as Watergate, when they explained their pessimistic attitudes. Quarterly survey data are available regarding attitudes toward the government's economic policies. Respondents were given three choices, namely, to characterize the government's policy toward inflation and unemployment as good or as bad or to take a middle position. Fluctuations of these evaluations are presented in Figure 3-2 together with the movements of the index of consumer sentiment. The closeness of the fluctuations of the two attitudes before and during the recession is quite remarkable.

Additional information on the relation of attitudes toward government policy to expectations about business conditions is presented in Table 3-2. By comparing the data in each row we find that respondents who thought that the government was doing a good job were consistently much more optimistic regarding expected business conditions than respondents who thought that the government was doing a poor job. For instance, in September 1972 favorable one-year expectations exceeded substantially the unfavorable ones (+45 percentage points) among those approving the government's policies, while favorable and unfavorable expectations were almost

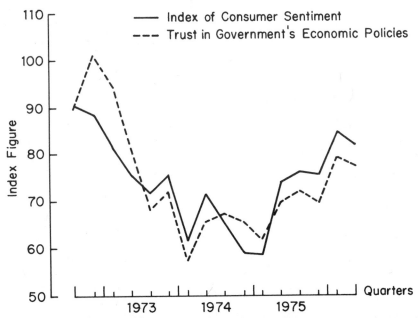

FIGURE 3-2   The index of consumer sentiment and trust in government (Trust in Government's Economic Policies = difference between good and bad opinions of government's policy on inflation and unemployment.)

equal (+4) among those who disapproved of the government's policies. It is true for all ten comparisons that those who thought the government was doing a good job were more optimistic than those who thought the government was doing a poor job. Nevertheless, we again have good reasons for believing that the deterioration of consumer sentiment over the years 1973 and 1974 was not due to attitudes toward government policy alone. Following each of the four columns from 1972 to 1975, we find a steady and substantial worsening of business expectations irrespective of attitudes toward government policies.

Toward the end of 1975 and in the first half of 1976 the relationship between attitudes toward the government and business expectations changed somewhat. At that time the index of consumer sentiment continued its substantial advance while attitudes toward the government improved very little. In May 1976, for instance, 32 percent of the sample still thought that the government was doing a bad job and only 9 percent that it was doing a good job. (The majority of respondents took a middle position.) At that time Americans in gen-

TABLE 3-2   Relation of Attitudes Toward Government Policy to Expectations About Business Conditions

	Government in Its Economic Policy Is Doing a			
	Good Job [a]		Poor Job	
	One-Year	Five-Year	One-Year	Five-Year
Date of Survey	Business Expectations [b]			
September 1972	+45	+24	+4	−19
December 1973	+12	+5	−40	−52
September 1974	+1	−6	−57	−58
February 1975	−16	−28	−74	−63
September 1975	+35	+6	−30	−43

[a] Based on a small proportion of respondents in 1974 and 1975.

[b] Positive figures in the table show the excess of "good time" over "bad time" answers in percentage points; negative figures show the excess of "bad time" over "good time" answers. For instance, among those who said in September 1972 that the government was doing a good job 45 percent more respondents said that in one year business conditions would be good than said that they would be bad. At the same time among those who said the government was doing a poor job 19 percent more respondents said that in five years business conditions would be bad than said that they would be good.

eral were well aware of the recovery in business conditions. On the whole, both those who thought that the government was doing a good job and those who thought that it was doing a bad job agreed that business conditions had improved. Thus we find that government policies were most commonly blamed for the recession but were not credited with bringing about the recovery.

In summary, the findings indicate that the antecedents of changes in sentiment are manifold and vary from time to time. After the fact it is usually possible to find out what developments or opinions were responsible for changes in consumer attitudes. For instance, as we have just seen, the 1973–1974 deterioration of sentiment can be attributed primarily to the experience of inflation jointly with growing mistrust of the government.[2] Before the fact, however, this could hardly have been known, and thus there is no substitute for the frequent measurement of consumer attitudes for the purpose of finding out what news is influential and detecting how willingness to buy is changing.

Past experience, of course, enables us to make "conditional forecasts" that are of great practical significance. Having observed that certain things have consistently had similar effects in the past—for instance, that a sudden acceleration in price increases tended to dampen confidence—we are in a position to make generalizations valid for the future. Their usual form will be, "If such-and-such developments occur, then such-and-such change in sentiment will arise and influence demand."

The relation between the two principal economic worries is complex. At certain times inflation and at other times unemployment was the principal worry, both among upper- and lower-income people. Developments at the time of question-

---

[2]The correlation over the period 1971 to 1975 between past changes of the retail price index and the index of consumer sentiment was .930; the correlation between attitudes toward the government's economic policy and the index of consumer sentiment was .902. Obviously, correlation does not prove causation. While the deterioration of consumer sentiment may partly be attributed to the growing distrust in the government's ability to fight inflation and unemployment, the latter may have partly resulted from the worsening notions about economic trends and personal finances.

ing appear to be responsible for the one or the other evil becoming salient. But at all times between 1973 and 1976 the American people were greatly concerned with both inflation and unemployment. Although most of them believed that the two bad things went together and did not accept the idea that it was possible to trade off one for the other, the relation between the two remained unclear to most Americans.

4
NEW TRENDS IN CONSUMER ATTITUDES

Will the recessions of the early 1970s soon be forgotten and will the economy resume where it left off in the 1960s? Or will the early 1970s be remembered as a period of transition from an era of rapid economic growth, rising affluence of the masses, and confidence in the future to an era of quite different characteristics? In this chapter we shall discuss developments—economic, sociological, and psychological —that reveal new trends. These trends continued even after the economy had recovered from the severe recession.

Inflation has become a permanent threat rather than a result of occasional bursts of demand or money supply. This change has sometimes been attributed to the impact of the rising cost of energy and the large amounts of money spent for the control of pollution. These important developments do not suffice to explain the great increase in inflationary pressures. A major change took place in what may be called inflationary ideology. What is meant by inflationary ideology is, first, that businesses no longer hesitate to raise prices. Instead of fearing adverse consequences of higher prices on their sales, many business firms resort to "anticipatory pricing" by incorporating expected cost increases in their prices. Secondly, as a legacy of inflationary experiences consumers exhibit little resistance to rising prices. In contrast to earlier times in 1976–1977 they responded to price increases only rarely and for brief periods by reducing their purchases. The acceptance of inflation as something inevitable represents the new ideology.[1] The question is no longer whether or not there would be further inflation but rather at what rate it would occur. Survey respondents said, and most experts agreed, that the best one could hope for over the next five or ten years would be a slowing down of inflation rather than a stabilizing of prices. Expectations about the future course of unemployment were similar; the hope for full employment has practically disappeared.

In the twenty-five years after World War II continuing economic growth and a steady improvement in our standard of living were viewed as our natural destiny. In those years thousands of people reported to interviewers that their standard of living was better than that of their parents and grandparents, and they expressed confidence that it would continue to improve both for themselves and for their children. In the 1970s, on the other hand, most people recognized the possibility, even the threat, that the process of improvement might not continue. They were fully aware of the fact that they had to run just not to lose ground, that is, that they had to earn considerably more money just to keep even in terms of purchasing power. In the first period Americans went so far as to ask, "Is the business cycle obsolete?" while in the 1970s they wondered when the next recession would occur.

In the late 1960s it became questionable whether material progress would suffice to enhance people's sense of well-being. Scholars began to interest themselves in the "quality of life" and to look for social indicators. It had long been recognized that there was a discrepancy between growth in the GNP and improvement in people's satisfactions or happiness. Survey findings in the early 1970s demonstrated that subjective well-being was much less dependent on the absolute level of

------

[1]Fritz Machlup (1975) emphasized that it is not inflation itself but inflationary ideology that is transmitted from country to country. In writing of ideology, Machlup thinks chiefly of expansionary public policy.

income than on changes in income (see Strumpel 1974). Increases in income—regardless of the level of the income —were found to be strongly associated with feeling better off and decreases with feeling worse off. At the same time, over several years in the late 1960s and early 1970s, incomes and the quantity of consumer goods possessed increased, but there was no increase in satisfaction either with incomes, standard of living, or life in general. It appears that a gap between people's aspirations and their assessment of their actual situation brought about feelings of dissatisfaction.[2] The constant and substantial rise in aspirations that accompanied improvements in the standard of living contributed to the lack of improvement in people's sense of satisfaction with their lives. A change in many people's focus of attention from material considerations and consumer goods to nonmaterial problems and goals—safety in the streets, equality in health care and education—was an additional important reason for the divergence between trends in income and trends in satisfaction.

In America as well as in Western Europe people entered the 1970s with high aspirations and were bitterly disappointed. The very fact that economic developments in the 1960s were exceptionally favorable and generated great expectations had the result that the subsequent experience in the 1970s of reduced purchasing power, difficulty in getting appropriate jobs, and disappearing opportunities was most strongly felt.

Attitudes, expectations, and aspirations are closely related. As Likert and Likert argued, and demonstrated in studies of management, "attitudes reflect experiences in relation to expectations" and "unrealized expectations [are] a source of conflict" (1976, p. 3).

---

[2]"A level of satisfaction derives from some greater or lesser gap between our estimate of an actual situation and one which the actor prizes or aspires to" (Campbell, Converse, and Rodgers 1976, p. 184). These authors present measures of satisfaction with a variety of domains of life as well as of the general sense of well-being. A study of economic satisfactions is presented in Appendix 1 in this book. The importance of supplementing objective social indicators (for instance, on the number of physicians or hospital beds per capita) with subjective social indicators has been shown earlier by Campbell and Converse (1972).

Long-Range and Short-Range Expectations

Nobody will doubt that what has just been said about the changed attitudes toward inflation and growth was true in 1974, at the time of the deep recession. But what about two or three years later? At that time consumers increased their purchases of cars and a variety of other consumer goods, the rate of inflation slowed down, and even the rate of unemployment declined somewhat. As indicated in the previous chapter (Table 3-1), both in the United States and in Western Europe consumer attitudes recovered sharply by the spring of 1976. The advance was particularly large in the proportion of consumers who expected an improvement in business conditions during the following few months and thought that it was a good time to buy durable goods. But Table 3-1 also presents American data about economic conditions expected in five years. The latter show the only instance of pessimistic expectations exceeding the optimistic ones (minus sign) for the spring of 1976.

Table 4-1 shows the difference in the U.S. between trends in people's long-term and short-term business outlook. Even at the best time, 1965, short-term expectations were more optimistic than long-term expectations, but the proportion of pessimists was similar in the two instances. By 1976 all business expectations were less favorable than in 1965, and five-year expectations lagged far behind one-year expectations.

TABLE 4-1   The Differential Between People's Short-Term and Long-Term Economic Outlook

EXPECTATIONS ABOUT BUSINESS CONDITIONS	NEXT 12 MONTHS (Percentage of Respondents)		NEXT 5 YEARS	
	SPRING			SPRING
	1965[a]	1976	1965[a]	1976
Good	71	46	47	16
Uncertain	13	28	39	44
Bad	16	26	14	40
Total	100	100	100	100
Index	55	20	33	−24

[a] The 1965 figures are the highest recorded in that year.

Uncertainty grew even regarding one-year expectations; looking ahead over five years, only one out of seven consumers was optimistic.

The recovery of long-range expectations from 1974 to 1976 was incomplete regarding people's personal financial outlook as well. In Table 4-2 we show how Americans in the years 1972–1976 assessed the development of their personal financial situation over the preceding five and the following five years. It should be noted that in 1972 these data were as favorable as at any time in the 1960s. Optimism about personal finances was solidly grounded in the appreciation of one's own ability, which, in the opinion of many, would assure progress and improvement. At that time one of the authors wrote about the persistence of belief in personal financial progress and considered those findings as justifying an optimistic outlook (Katona 1976b). As Table 4-2 indicates, people's optimism about their personal financial situation declined greatly during the subsequent recession and recovered incompletely by 1976.

Large differences are found between the opinions of high-income and low-income families.Most of those who, according to their income, belonged roughly in the upper one-third of the distribution, reported good experiences and expected further progress. It is hardly surprising that those in the low-income brackets reported overwhelmingly that they were

TABLE 4-2   Assessment of Personal Financial Situation, Past and Future

	1972-II	1974-I	1974-III	1975-I	1976-III
	(Percent Difference Between "Better" and "Worse")				
Compared to 5 Years Earlier					
All families	39	34	23	18	22
High income[a]	62	52	44	43	56
Low income[b]	15	9	−5[c]	−14[c]	−15[c]
Expected in 5 Years					
All families	43	22	24	33	35
High income[a]	50	25	26	44	47
Low income[b]	28	10	20	15	19

[a] $15,000 and over (in 1976).

[b] $5,000 and under (in 1976).

[c] Minus signs indicate that answers of "worse" exceeded answers of "better."

worse off than five years earlier. What is noteworthy is that among these only a small proportion (one out of four) expected improvement during the following five years. The difference between the data obtained in 1976 and 1972 for high- and for low-income families is striking. Low-income people hardly participated in the recovery of the sense of well-being.

Of interest is the proportion of families who had experienced improvement in the past and also expected further improvement. The frequency of this "better-better" group was 34 percent in 1972 and only 29 percent in 1976. Yet, just as in earlier years, younger family heads (under forty years of age) belonged disproportionately to this group, which, as shown in earlier publications, represents a very high proportion of buyers of consumer goods.

We have already mentioned that, in contrast to long-range expectations, those relating to the near future recovered fairly rapidly after the recession of 1974. Following a low point of 53.7 in December 1974, the Survey Research Center's index of consumer sentiment, designed to measure changes in consumers' willingness to buy, advanced to 88.8 in September 1976 and thus reached the level of late 1972. How can the difference between the trend of short-term and long-term expectations be explained? We may find an answer to this question by searching for other attitudes that remained depressed in the course of the year 1976, when Americans in general were sufficiently optimistic to say that it was a good time to buy automobiles and other durable goods.

One of the questions repeatedly asked in the Survey Research Center's quarterly surveys is intended to find out whether people think that their savings and reserve funds are adequate or whether it is more important than usual to add to them. We shall cite the detailed findings in Chapter 6; it may suffice to report here that in 1976, at a time when recovery from the recession was well advanced, people's desire to save was unusually high. This finding is in line with heightened uncertainty about the more distant future.

The decline in confidence that the government's economic policies would bring about recovery was amply discussed in the preceding chapter. In the spring of 1976 one-third of survey respondents condemned and less than one-tenth praised the government's policies to fight inflation and unemployment. (The majority took a middle position; see also Figure 3-2.) These opinions were in accord with the mistrust expressed at that time in practically all institutions. In the 1950s and early 1960s the terms *government* or *Washington* stood for something respected and trusted. In those years people were not much disturbed either by rising prices or news about corruption because they believed that the government would take suitable countermeasures. Most Americans were not even concerned with what the government would do; it sufficed to know that there was an institution that in case of any adverse developments would act and restore things as they should be. In contrast, in the early 1970s there developed what has rightly been called political alienation or even political cynicism. An index of trust in the government, constructed by the Institute for Social Research and consisting of questions not related to the economy, stood at +50 in 1958, at +20 in 1968, and −26 in 1973. In 1976, after the presidential election, a measure of −28 was obtained.[3]

The Vietnam War and the inability to deal with riots, protests, and other indications of dissatisfaction slowly eroded people's confidence in the government and created doubts about its power to correct the evils of society. Then came Watergate and with it widespread mistrust of government. Following the great recession, both Carter and Reagan derived support from anti-Washington feelings in the primaries of 1976. Survey questions indicated that the absence of confidence extended from the presidency to the Congress and even to the Supreme Court. While in the 1960s people joked about the anti-Establishment attitudes of the hippies, in the 1970s

---

[3]The above figures are those obtained from whites. The corresponding figures for blacks are: +50, +40, −47 and, for 1976, −56. The plus signs indicate that expressions of trust were more frequent than expressions of distrust, and the minus signs that the reverse was true. The following is an example of the questions used in constructing the index: "Do you think that quite a few of the people running the government are a little crooked, not very many are, or do you think hardly any of them are crooked at all?" See Miller (1974); the 1976 data are from personal communication.

the old as well as the young criticized all forms of the Establishment.

A common polling device consists of having respondents rank a list of occupations according to which ones they respect or which they would most like their children to pursue. For many years physicians were ranked at the top of such lists. Not only were they highly esteemed; it was also thought that they fully deserved the large amounts of money they made. In the last few years complaints have become increasingly frequent not only about their high fees but also about the quality of their services. The latter was evident in the increased number of malpractice suits and the finding that many people considered substantial payments made to the plaintiffs as justified. Instances of medical malpractice probably did not increase from the 1950s to the 1960s and 1970s. What did increase were dissatisfaction with medical practices and actions taken to remedy alleged mistreatment. Just as in former times the purchaser of a new automobile considered it his bad luck when the car had many defects, so did patients who felt worse after medical intervention think that there was no remedy for what had happened to them. In the 1970s, when respect for physicians as well as for big business diminished, both the patient and the car buyer sought and accepted the help of lawyers to receive compensation.

Attitudes toward big business suffered from more than just growing skepticism toward powerful institutions in general. There were also specific reasons for people to believe that large business firms did not operate in the public interest and to speak of them as profiteering and corrupt. The name Lockheed was frequently used by survey respondents to illustrate corrupt practices. Even though bribes paid to foreign governments were the most highly publicized, many people believed in the prevalence of corrupt practices in domestic dealings as well. Even twenty years ago some ambivalence in American attitudes toward big business was detected because of compassion toward the small businessman—perhaps most particularly the neighborhood grocer—and the self-made man who had had to give way to chain stores and other forms of big business. On the whole, however, the spread of supermarkets and the predominance of large firms over all markets were considered to represent progress, and big business was admired, with growing sales and profits being just as proudly cited as records in the sport world. As late as in the early 1960s products of large corporations were thought to be the best buys, and employment of one's children by a large corporation was believed to be very advantageous.

All that changed in the 1970s. An index of attitudes toward big business dropped from 55 to 16 in the ten years prior to the mid-1970s. To the question whether big business helped or hurt the American economy, in 1975 unfavorable answers far outweighed the favorable ones. One could argue that such verbal expressions should not be given great weight because at a time of rapid inflation and high unemployment one could hardly expect praise for business leaders. But the underlying attitudes had some effects on people's behavior: Savers refrained from buying common stock in the 1970s; the number of individual shareholders declined slightly but continuously. Apparently brand loyalty became less widespread than before, and complaints and protests against unsatisfactory goods purchased became more frequent.

The widespread antibusiness feeling may have further grave consequences for big business unless it is reversed. Instead of being proud of their country's having the largest and most powerful multinational corporations, an increased proportion of Americans now support the breaking up of some of the largest ones, as, for example, some oil and automobile companies. Rising profits are viewed by many as signs of wrongdoing rather than as indications of success. Such attitudes may, of course, influence future legislation.

Volatility of Consumer Attitudes

One of the major changes from the first postwar era to the 1970s has been an increase in the volatility of consumer attitudes and expectations. Some indications of this volatility were presented in the previous chapter. It was shown in Figure 3-1 that both the decline of the index of consumer senti-

ment in 1973–1974 and its recovery in 1975–1976 were interrupted several times, producing a zigzag movement. In contrast, advances and declines in the first postwar era, before
and after the recession of 1958, for instance, were steady and
continuous: Once a trend set in, it continued until it reached
either a peak or a trough.

The volatility of expectations is expressed not only in frequent reversals of direction but also in a greatly increased
amplitude of change. The absolute quarterly changes in the
index of consumer sentiment amounted, on the average, to
2.28 percentage points in 1965–1968 and 2.78 percentage
points in 1969–1971. But they rose very sharply to 6.05 percentage points in 1972–1976 (see Curtin 1977).

The increase in the range of the quarterly movements of the
index is also shown in Figure 4-1. While between 1965 and
1973 the quarterly changes rarely exceeded 2 or 3 percentage

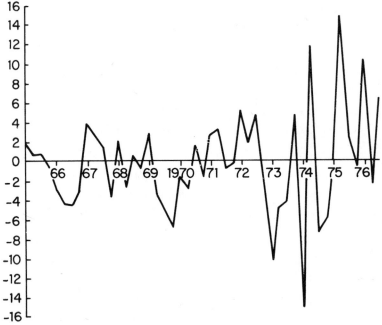

FIGURE 4-1   Quarterly fluctuations of the index of consumer sentiment (changes in index points from quarter to quarter), 1965–1976.
(Source: Survey Research Center, University of Michigan)

points, in the following few years much larger changes were the rule.

A further survey finding related to the volatility of consumer attitudes was mentioned earlier in this chapter: The frequency of "uncertain," "don't know," or "can't say" answers received to questions about the economic outlook increased substantially in the 1970s. Noteworthy also is the finding that in reply to the question regularly asked in the Survey Research Center's surveys—"During the last few months have you heard of any favorable or unfavorable changes in business conditions?"—the proportion giving negative answers, denying that they had heard any such news, declined greatly in the 1970s. The proportion of Americans saying that they had not heard or could not recall any economic news at all was as high as 60–70 percent in the 1960s, but only 25–30 percent in 1975. This, of course, is understandable in view of the strong impact of inflation and recession on people's lives. Even though less credibility of the government and of authorities and experts in general has made people skeptical and added to their uncertainty, more of them were listening to economic news than ever before. Thus a great variety of news, both good and bad, could influence American consumers in the mid-1970s.

The strongest evidence of volatility is obtained from a study of attitude changes by individuals. When the same question about personal financial or general economic expectations is asked twice from the same sample, the second time several months after the first time, it has been generally assumed, and was confirmed in the 1950s and 1960s, that there would be a fairly high correlation between the two answers by the same people. In the summer of 1976, however, the answers to the same survey questions asked six months apart yielded no correlation at all: Knowing the first answer of an individual gave no clue whatsoever to his or her second answer.

A large turnover in attitudes of individuals does not in itself suffice, however, to indicate uncertainty or instability of attitudes. The matter must be studied more closely. Different answers obtained in successive interviews with the same respondents may have three causes:

1. Misclassifications. Change in response may be due to clerical errors, reporting errors, or even a change in the mood of a respondent; these random changes are expected to cancel out.

2. Instability or uncertainty of the response. If respondents are guessing the answer to a question or are very uncertain about what response to give, it is probable that their second response, given some months later, will be different from the first one.

3. Acquisition of experience or learning. Change in response may be due to the acquisition of new experiences or new information in the interval between two responses. Regarding the economic questions discussed here, the learning process may have taken place either because of personal experiences or because of news transmitted by mass media and received by very many people at the same time. Personal financial experiences may, of course, differ widely from individual to individual: At any given time some respondents or some members of their families may, for example, get a new or better job or may lose a job, or may fall sick or may recover from illness. General economic news, however, is usually unidirectional, provided there is significant and salient news at all. Then the mass media all over the country uniformly report the same information, as for instance, that inflation has slowed down or accelerated, or that times have gotten better or worse.

Of crucial importance is the relation between aggregate change and individual turnover. Aggregate change is determined by comparing the findings obtained from two successive samples. This is the only change usually studied and reported; it indicates, for instance, greater or lesser optimism of the sample or of all consumers from one time to the next. Individual turnover represents a different kind of statistic. In the simplest manner it can be measured by determining the proportion in the sample that gave the same answer on two successive occasions and the proportion that changed their answers. These figures do not suffice, however, to explain what is going on. For that purpose the changers must be divided into two groups, those who changed in the direction of the aggregate change (the majority) and those who changed in the opposite direction and, so to speak, swam against the current. The proportion of changers in the direction contrary to that of the aggregate change provides the most relevant information, as will be apparent from the differentiation of four cases, the extremes of which are illustrated in Table 4-3.

In Case 1A in the table, the proportion of changers is just sufficient to bring about the small aggregate change from a 50–50 to a 55–45 distribution; there are no changers in the reverse direction. In Case 1B the proportion of changers in the direction opposite to the aggregate change is maximal, consistent with the small aggregate change. Substantial aggregate changes from a 50–50 to a 70–30 distribution are shown in

TABLE 4-3   Extreme Cases of Individual Turnover

1A

Second Response	First Response	O	P	Aggr.
O		50	5	55
P		0	45	45
Aggr.		50	50	100

1B

Second Response	First Response	O	P	Aggr.
O		5	50	55
P		45	0	45
Aggr.		50	50	100

2A

Second Response	First Response	O	P	Aggr.
O		50	20	70
P		0	30	30
Aggr.		50	50	100

2B

Second Response	First Response	O	P	Aggr.
O		20	50	70
P		30	0	30
Aggr.		50	50	100

NOTES: O = Optimistic, P = Pessimistic.

Each case is a 2-by-2 table for a question asked from identical respondents on two successive occasions. In Cases 1A and 1B there is a small, and in Cases 2A and 2B a substantial, aggregate change. In the A cases the individual turnover is as small, and in the B cases as large, as is consistent with the aggregate change.

The actual survey findings present a somewhat more complicated picture. Respondents' attitudes and expectations are tabulated in three categories (better or good, same or pro-con, worse or bad), so that 3-by-3 rather than 2-by-2 tables are constructed.

Cases 2A and 2B. In 2A the proportion of changers in the opposite direction is minimal, in 2B it is maximal.

What are the circumstances in which we should expect each of these situations, or situations resembling the four extreme cases, to occur?

Case 1A   Small aggregate change and small individual turnover. We may expect to find this case when twice in succession the same respondents are asked simple factual questions (for instance, about the education of the respondents) that are not expected to change between the two interviews. The changes observed will be due primarily to misclassifications that cancel out. Questions about simple and stable attitudes may yield similar results.

Case 1B   Small aggregate change and large individual turnover. Suppose the answer to a question is not known to the respondent and is guessed in both instances. It may then be expected that many people would make different guesses each time and thus show large individual turnover, but the changes would cancel out, so that the two aggregate distributions would not differ substantially. We may expect a similar situation in the case of changes brought about by diverse personal experiences in the absence of major unidirectional news.

Case 2A   Large aggregate change and small individual turnover. A basis for this case would be effective learning by the entire sample. Suppose that after the answer to a question had been guessed correctly by one part and incorrectly by another part of the sample, the entire sample learns the correct answer. In this case there will be a large aggregate change, and yet the individuals will fall into two groups only: those who gave unchanged answers (because they guessed correctly the first time) and those who changed their answers from the incorrect to the correct one. No one (except, of course, for possible misclassifications) will be found swimming against the current.

A similar situation is to be expected whenever there is news of substantial importance and generality. News about rapid inflation or a large increase in unemployment, for instance, may result in substantial aggregate change in people's economic outlook with an insignificant proportion of individuals changing their attitudes and expectations in a direction contrary to the majority.

Case 2B Large aggregate change and large individual turnover. The presence of divergent news, with one kind being more frequent than the other, coupled with the presence of a great amount of uncertainty, doubt, or misorientation would bring about this result. Paul Lazarsfeld obviously thought of this case alone when he assumed that large turnover always indicates instability of opinions: "If the turnover is large, it indicates that the opinion or behavior is unstable. We know that people feel uncertain and that propaganda may be effective, or that clarification and education are required" (see Introduction to Lazarsfeld, Berelson, and Gandet, 1948).

The following generalizations were made by one of the authors as the result of surveys in the 1950s (see Katona 1958):

1. Small aggregate changes usually result from many individuals changing their opinions or attitudes and the changes in different directions canceling out, rather than from most individuals giving the same answer twice in succession. This is illustrated in the first column of Table 4-4, which reproduces data obtained in the 1950s. A rather substantial proportion of the sample changed in both directions when the aggregate change was small.

2. When aggregate change is large, unidirectional individual changes are common. The sample then could be divided into two large groups: those who changed their attitudes in the direction of the aggregate change and those who did not change their attitudes. The third possible group, those with reverse changes, was found to be small. In the case of a fairly large aggregate change (middle column of Table 4-4) only 10 percent, and in the case of a very large aggregate change (right-hand column) only 8 percent, of the sample were found to have changed their attitudes in the direction opposite to the aggregate change.

TABLE 4-4   Fluctuation of Opinions of Identical Individuals in the 1950s (in percent)

DIRECTION OF CHANGE FROM FIRST TO SECOND INTERVIEW	PERSONALLY B/W THAN YEAR AGO[a]	BUSINESS B/W A YEAR[a] FROM NOW	BUSINESS DURING NEXT 12 MONTHS
Shift toward optimism	20	10	38
No change	62	65	54
Shift toward pessimism	18	24	8
Total	100	100	100
Aggregate change	2	−14	30

NOTE: Taken from Katona (1958) from surveys conducted between 1955 and 1957. Illustrated above are small aggregate change (first column), sizable aggregate change (second column) consisting of a shift toward pessimism, and very large aggregate change (third column).

[a] B/W = better/worse.

The generalization regarding the unidirectional changes in attitudes toward economic developments was in line with a basic hypothesis of psychological economics. It states that waves of optimism or pessimism spread over a great many people at about the same time. "Because the same information, or very similar information, reaches millions of people at the same time, changes in attitudes resemble contagious diseases rather than movements in different directions, which cancel out" (Katona 1975, p. 56).

In Table 4-5 we present data from recent surveys in which the same sample was interviewed twice, in February and September 1976. In those seven months consumers became more optimistic and the index of consumer sentiment advanced. Those who changed their opinions are divided into two groups. The row "Shift toward optimism" indicates the proportion of individuals who gave a more optimistic answer in the second than in the first interview, thus changing in the direction of the aggregate change; and the row "Shift toward pessimism," the proportion giving a less optimistic answer, thus changing in the opposite direction. (Of all the questions asked, the only exception was found in the answers about "favorable or unfavorable news heard," where the frequency of favorable news reported declined slightly.) The large individual turnover in the instances in which the aggregate change amounted to but 1 or 2 percentage points is not surprising, although the proportion of changers was larger in 1976 than in the 1950s. What is contrary to any finding of the 1950s is shown, for example, in the columns "Business B/W Than Year Ago" and "Business During Next 12 Months." We find here that there was a considerable improvement in the opinions expressed by the entire sample: In September 1976 as compared with February 1976 many more Americans thought that business conditions had improved during the preceding twelve months and that business conditions would be good in the next twelve months. Nevertheless, the proportion of changers who "swam against the current" was in both cases 27 percent of the sample; in other words, more than one-quarter of all individuals changed their opinions in the direction contrary to the majority. In many studies conducted in the 1950s and 1960s, not a single such instance was found of both large aggregate change and large individual turnover.

By far the smallest frequency of "reverse" changes and by far the greatest consistency in the two answers was found regarding the direction of price expectations. In this case 59 percent gave the same answer in September as in February. Nevertheless, two fairly large groups shifted and became either "more" or "less" inflation minded in those months. A much greater proportion changed their answers when asked about economic news heard during the preceding few months: In September 31 percent reported that they had heard favorable news, whereas in February they had reported unfavorable news or no news at all; likewise 31 percent reported in September having heard unfavorable news and in February having heard favorable or no news at all. In addition, 26 percent reported having heard no news either time, and only 12 percent reported the same kind of news both times.

When we study the differences between respondents whose attitudes improved and respondents whose attitudes deteriorated from February to September 1976, we find that the former reported overwhelmingly in September that they had heard favorable economic news, while among the latter reports of having heard favorable or unfavorable news were made in similar proportions. The answers of the two groups about their past financial experiences and even about past trends in the

TABLE 4-5 Fluctuation of Opinions of Identical Individuals, 1976 (frequency in percent)

DIRECTION OF CHANGE FROM FIRST TO SECOND INTERVIEW	PERSONALLY B/W THAN YEAR AGO[a]	PERSONALLY EXPECT B/W IN A YEAR[a]$_{l,3}$	PRICES UP/DOWN IN A YEAR	GOVERNMENT DOES G/P JOB[b]	FAVORABLE UNFAVORABLE NEWS HEARD
Shift toward optimism	37	31	23	34	31
No change	33	41	59	44	38
Shift toward pessimism	30	28	18	22	31
Total	100	100	100	100	100
Aggregate change	7	2	8	15	−1

	BUSINESS B/W THAN YEAR AGO[a]	BUSINESS B/W A YEAR FROM NOW[af]	BUSINESS DURING NEXT 12 MONTHS	BUSINESS DURING NEXT 5 YEARS	G/B TIME TO BUY HOUSEHOLD GOODS[a]	G/B TIME TO BUY CARS[c]
Shift toward optimism	34	32	39	39	37	38
No change	39	37	34	33	33	28
Shift toward pessimism	27	31	27	28	30	34
Total	100	100	100	100	100	100
Aggregate change	20	2	20	17	15	7

N = 694 respondents interviewed twice.

NOTE: Shift toward optimism = proportion giving a more optimistic answer in the second than in the first interview. Shift toward pessimism = proportion giving a more pessimistic answer. The difference between one-step changes (e.g., change from same to better) and two-step changes (e.g., from worse to better) is disregarded. This difference is taken into account in the row "Aggregate change," the change between the marginal distribution at the two dates. The aggregate changes shown here differ slightly from those published by the Survey Research Center in the fall of 1976 because those publications were based on much larger weighted samples.

[a] B/W = better/worse.
[b] G/P = good/poor.
[c] G/B = good/bad.

economy likewise differed substantially. Apparently in 1976 the American people were divided not only regarding their personal financial experiences, but also regarding their perceptions and understanding of prevailing economic trends. The generalization made in the 1950s and 1960s that economic news heard resembled a contagious disease that uniformly spread over the country was no longer valid.

While the data presented in Table 4-5 were collected in a single year (1976), the persistence of the volatility of attitudes may be illustrated by referring to an earlier article that contains 1975 data (see *Economic Outlook USA,* Summer 1975), and by mentioning some findings obtained in 1977. In February 1977, when aggregate changes were somewhat smaller than those shown in Table 4-5, the proportion of respondents giving the same answer as nine months earlier to questions about business conditions during the next twelve months and during the next five years was 32 percent, and of those "swimming against the current" was close to 25 percent.

Lest the reader think that volatility has replaced unidirectional changes, that is, the contagious-disease syndrome, regarding every one of the economic attitudes studied, one divergent finding should also be mentioned. In February 1977, at the height of what may be called the Carter honeymoon, people's opinions about the government's economic policies improved greatly (more people saying that the government was doing a good job and fewer that it was doing a bad job). At that time two large groups of individuals, those who gave the government a better mark than nine months earlier and those who gave it a good mark both times, comprised close to 90 percent of the sample. Reverse changes were infrequent. These data show that at a time when the expectations of individuals were much more volatile than they had been in earlier decades, it was still possible to detect the phenomenon of masses of people acquiring a new opinion or attitude at about the same time.

It appears that as a result of their experience with inflation and recession, in the mid-1970s Americans listened to economic news with greater interest than in earlier years. Even trivial and unimportant news was frequently noticed and promptly influenced people's attitudes. The resulting fluctuations in consumer sentiment were reflected in ups and downs of consumer expenditures and sharp fluctuations in the rate of personal saving. The volatility of economic behavior may be illustrated by citing the great variations in the years 1975–1977 in the gains of the most comprehensive economic statistic, the gross national product. The rate of increase of GNP against the previous year was 11.4 percent in the third quarter of 1975, 3.3 percent in the fourth, but 8.8 percent in the first quarter of 1976. Then followed a decline in growth rates to a low of 1.2 percent in the fourth quarter of 1976 and a subsequent rise to 7.5 percent in the first quarter of 1977. Volatile economic attitudes and volatile economic behavior characterized the recovery from the great recession.

In Chapter 9 we shall discuss an additional factor that contributed to the volatility of attitudes, namely, the absence of understanding of economic developments. As to the future impact of volatility, it may suffice to say here that a quick succession of waves of consumer optimism and pessimism would make a fairly rapid series of economic fluctuations probable. Before saying more about that crucial question, we shall proceed with our analysis of the changing 1970s.

5
THE WORK ETHIC

Recently changes in values and life-styles have become of great interest to businessmen, planners, government officials, and the public at large. Gloomy pronouncements abound to the effect that the motivation to work and the work discipline have deteriorated, that consumers live beyond their means, that demands for government services are on the increase, that an early retirement mentality is spreading, that the young generation has even started to question the institutional and moral bases of our society. Deviations from the ethic of thrift, discipline, and duty are being described as serious erosions of traditional virtues. There is indeed little doubt that changing values are often translated into behavior and thus lead society to change. Should it be true that, for example, being promoted to foreman is no longer appreciated as a desired reward for competent services, other incentives, perhaps even new principles of organization and leadership, may become necessary.

Change in Values

Values are relatively stable personality attributes, affective states, and generalized concepts and thus differ from attitudes which are more frequently changing. A person possesses considerably fewer values than attitudes (see Rokeach 1973). Values must also be differentiated from aspirations. Aspirations can be described as the images a person holds about a good or desirable life, for instance, with respect to the kind of dwelling he prefers, his career achievement, or his savings. Aspirations tend to grow with accomplishment; they are formed in interaction with the social environment, particularly the "reference groups." Values, in contrast, are more durable and less influenced by the immediate environment. Nevertheless, they also are shaped by external events and circumstances. In a society characterized by poverty and need the procurement and defense of food and shelter, in brief, command over material resources, are accepted as the central values and goals. Both individual norms of behavior and the collective goals of organizations are geared to these priorities. Spiritual and intellectual pursuits are mainly reserved for those individuals and societal strata that are relieved from the pressing concern for food and shelter.

The transition from materialistic or acquisitive values to postindustrial values of self-actualization has been set forth by Ronald Inglehart (1977). He adopted Maslow's theory that there is a hierarchy of motives and postulates that people's values change with growing affluence and security: People who are relatively well supplied with consumer goods, well-to-do and secure, place particular importance on nonmaterial values. Believing further that values are the result of acculturation during the formative years of childhood, Inglehart compared the values held by different age groups. People who grew up under prosperous conditions were expected to have different values from those who grew up under conditions of economic distress. In surveys conducted in 1973, prior to the last recession, respondents were asked to choose the three goals most important to them from a list of twelve. Three of these goals Inglehart called economic, for instance, the goal of fighting rising prices or of economic growth. In the middle he listed three goals in the category of "safety" (e.g., fighting crime) and three in that of "belonging" (e.g., more say on the job). Goals of "self-actualization" (protection of free speech, protecting nature from pollution, or believing that ideas count) constituted the other extreme.

Table 5-1 summarizes the choices expressed by respondents in the largest countries of Western Europe and in the United States. In most countries preoccupation with the value of money was prevalent at the time of the survey. The Americans differed from the Western Europeans in that they accorded higher priority to nonmaterial values and lower importance to material or economic values. This was interpreted by Inglehart as the consequence of the relatively high economic achievement and the high living standards enjoyed by Americans for a longer time than by Europeans. The Germans differed not only from the Americans but also from their European neighbors by an extraordinarily strong fixation on economic security, a characteristic noted as early as the late 1960s. (See Katona, Strumpel, and Zahn 1971.)

Inglehart found substantial and regular differences among different age groups in all countries studied. Economic values increase and self-actualization values decrease consistently as one proceeds from younger to older ages. Only one-fourth or

TABLE 5-1   Preferred Goals in Western Europe and the United States, 1973

GOAL	UNITED STATES	BRITAIN	WEST GERMANY	FRANCE
	(percent choosing given goal as first or second most important of 12)			
Fight rising prices (E)	25	50	44	43
Economic growth (E)	16	29	24	18
Fight crime (S)	22	17	21	20
Stable economy (E)	21	25	39	12
Maintain order (S)	20	11	18	21
More say on job (B)	16	15	12	13
Less impersonal society (B)	12	12	11	28
More say in government (B)	16	15	9	9
Protect free speech (A)	10	11	11	14
Protect nature from being polluted (A)	18	6	4	9
Believing that ideas count (A)	8	4	3	11
Strong defense forces (S)	16	6	5	3

SOURCE: Inglehart (1977).

NOTE: Letters in parentheses indicate category of the given goal: (E) = economic, (S) = safety, (B) = belonging, (A) = self-actualization.

less of those under twenty-nine years of age considered materialistic values most important, while in Germany about 60 percent and in the U.S. close to 40 percent of those over sixty-five did so (Table 5-2).

The results conform to popular notions about differences between young and old people. It is often thought that old persons tend to be rather conservative and concerned with the preservation of the status quo; young persons are inclined to favor change. Could it be that the quoted data result from an age effect rather than a generation effect and thus do not reflect specific experiences of today's young generation? Is it likely that materialistic values will be held by the young of today, once they reach middle or old age? These questions cannot be conclusively answered in the negative. Reliable answers could only be given if comparable surveys were to be made in the future. Yet there are several indications that the conspicuous differences in values between the generations are indeed an expression of cultural change and not just an artifact of the life cycle.

Let us start with indirect evidence. According to Inglehart's hypothesis the generation gap in values should be greater in countries with a relatively fast rate of economic growth. It should be greater also in countries in which the economic experiences of younger people during their formative years differed drastically from those of older generations (e.g.,

TABLE 5-2   Preferred Goals by Age Groups in Western Europe and the United States (in percent)

AGE GROUP	UNITED STATES		BRITAIN		WEST GERMANY		FRANCE	
	E	A	E	A	E	A	E	A
19–28	24	17	27	11	24	19	22	20
29–38	27	13	33	7	39	8	28	17
39–48	34	13	29	6	46	5	39	9
49–58	32	10	30	7	50	5	39	8
59–68	37	6	36	5	52	7	50	3
69+	40	7	37	4	62	1	55	2
Total spread	26[a]		17[a]		56[a]		51[a]	

SOURCE: Inglehart (1977).

NOTE: E = economic; A = self-actualization (see Table 5-1).

[a] Difference between E and A as obtained in the oldest and youngest groups in percentage points.

European countries, where World War II had radically different effects on the different generations) than in countries where there were no such drastic differences (e.g., the U.S.). The first point is borne out by the great difference in the spread between the proportion of people in older and younger age groups having either materialistic or nonmaterialistic values in Germany and France, with their rapid economic growth, and the small difference in the spread in Great Britain, with its slow growth. The second point seems to be confirmed by the small increase in materialistic values with age in the United States, compared with Germany and France.

The question of whether changes in values are related to age or to cultural change is susceptible to fairly direct testing, such as was done by the Survey Research Center of the University of Michigan in 1965 and in 1972. Male workers were asked in each of those years to list their occupational goals in order of importance. The same questions were also asked in 1968 and 1973 in Germany. It appears (see Table 5-3) that within less than one decade the occupational goals considered most important shifted significantly from income security toward "intrinsic" rewards, such as a sense of accomplishment. This was the case both in the United States and in Germany. What respondents meant by a "feeling of accomplishment" was often described as doing important work, something which was worthwhile, or, at least, doing the job well.

In the United States changes were particularly evident among younger respondents, including those who entered the labor force between 1965 and 1972. While blue-collar workers placed the highest emphasis on income-related considerations in judging a job, white-collar workers and the self-employed placed "feeling of accomplishment" and "good chance for advancement" high on the list.

Further insights about the value changes of the younger generation can be gained from a series of surveys conducted by Daniel Yankelovich in the late 1960s and early 1970s in the United States among Americans sixteen to twenty-five years old (1974). His results confirm that changes are indeed taking place and that they are particularly pronounced among young people. The growing desire for self-expression on the job ex-

TABLE 5-3 Most Important Job Characteristics (in percent)

	STEADY INCOME	NO DANGER OF BEING FIRED	LOTS OF FREE TIME	HIGH INCOME	GOOD CHANCES FOR ADVANCEMENT	FEELING OF ACCOMPLISHMENT	TOTAL
American Male Workers							
All respondents							
1965	46	9	3	10	11	21	100
1972	35	12	3	10	11	29	100
Blue-collar workers							
1965	52	12	3	11	9	13	100
1972	45	15	2	11	12	15	100
White-collar workers							
1965	37	6	2	9	14	32	100
1972	24	8	3	9	10	46	100
Younger workers (under 30)							
1965	41	9	2	13	18	17	100
1972	27	12	2	15	17	27	100
Older workers (over 30)							
1965	47	9	3	9	10	22	100
1972	38	12	3	8	9	30	100
West German Male Workers							
All respondents							
1968	70	N.A.[a]	7	14	5	10	100
1973	52	N.A.[a]	3	18	3	24	100

SOURCE: Surveys directed by B. Strumpel; American surveys conducted by the Survey Research Center of the University of Michigan.
NOTE: The question was: "Would you please look at this card and tell me which thing on this list about an occupation you would most prefer? [Interviewer shows card] Income is steady; income is high; there is no danger of being fired or unemployed; working hours are short, lots of free time; chances for advancement are good; the work is important, gives feeling of accomplishment."
[a] N.A. = not asked.

tends beyond an insistence on interesting work. It is also directed toward more autonomy and less strict supervision and is associated with less emphasis on monetary rewards. It was found, however, that young workers often fail to find what they desire. There are disquieting symptoms of a fading sense of being appropriately rewarded for one's work effort.

Germany in recent years has witnessed great changes in the work ethic, which are related to the changing goals in the U.S. (see Table 5-4). The traditional virtues of polite demeanor, subordination, diligence, modesty, and respect for private property have lost ground. In both countries there has been a lessening of the feeling of being in control of one's own fate and of the conviction that hard work pays off; the proportion of those who prefer "a life without work" has grown.

What does this mean for the relationship between man and the economy? One might be tempted to take the manifest shift in goals and attitudes about work at face value. If people do not seek fulfillment mainly in material goals, in consumption

TABLE 5-4   Attitudes Toward Hard Work

United States, Entire Population	1968	1976
	(Percent Agreeing)	
Hard work will always pay off if you have faith in yourself and stick to it.	58	43
Hard work alone will not guarantee success, but if you don't work hard you don't have a chance of succeeding.	35	42
The idea that hard work leads to success is a lie. Nowadays you have to know someone or be just plain lucky.	7	14

SOURCE: American Council of Life Insurance.

West German Workers	1962-1963	1972	1975
	(Percent Agreeing)		
Each person is the master of his own fate.	55	51	52
Some are simply on the top and some are on the bottom.	33	35	39
Undecided.	12	14	9

SOURCE: E. Noelle-Neumann, *Die Zeit*, April 30, 1976.

and production, but rather in those areas generally referred to as the "quality of life"—a humane work environment, friendly treatment by supervisors and coworkers, perhaps artistic and educational activities—one might surmise that they would demand more free time, do more for their education, be less willing to change their residence in the interest of their career, and be less motivated to work for the purpose of acquiring more consumer goods. Alternatively, a diminution of material attractions, instead of shifting involvement from the realm of work to the realm of leisure, might simply lead to a different kind of work motivation. A worker who has as his goal an interesting job might be more inclined to do good work for its own sake rather than for the sake of higher compensation.

More than one study has provided evidence of a diminution in the degree to which workers feel able to control their own fate. A survey among German workers, for example, showed that the proportion who considered success in life as dependent on luck rather than on their own actions had increased over the last ten years (see Table 5-4). Again, the conviction that hard work always pays off diminished significantly among American college students from 1969 to 1973 (from 56 to 44 percent), and even more drastically among young people who did not attend college (from 79 to 56 percent, see Yankelovich 1974). Table 5-4 exhibits a similar shift for the entire American adult population.

Blue-Collar Ethic and White-Collar Ethic

A work ethic is not generated in a social vacuum. It is systematically rooted in differences between subgroups of the population, as defined by social status and available opportunities. There is a tradition that establishes distinct economic choices, life-styles, and ideologies for different social strata according to their actual opportunities and the constraints of reality. Werner Sombart (1921), in distinguishing between "handicraft" and "business," offers a clue to the psychology of "manualists." The latter, in his words, "are animated by the motive of securing a livelihood . . . and act according to rules prescribed by a common organization." Selig Perlman elaborates:

> There is a separation between those who prefer a secure, though modest return—that is to say, a mere livelihood—and those who play for big stakes and are willing to assume risks in proportion. . . . The limited or unlimited purpose is, in either case, the product of a simple survey of accessible economic opportunity and of realistic self-appraisal. The manual worker is convinced by experience that he is living in a world of limited opportunity. . . . The businessman, on the contrary, is an eternal optimist. [1928, pp. 238–239]

In the half century since these words were written, the occupational structure of industrial societies has changed considerably. It is no longer the manual-entrepreneurial split that is most important in defining economic opportunity. There has been a phenomenal growth in the clerical, managerial, technical, and professional occupations, to which none of the characteristics described by Perlman seems to fit. Whereas the opportunities of clerical workers in many respects hardly exceed those of blue-collar workers, professional and managerial workers command considerably richer opportunities.

It is then not surprising that the achievement of progress is viewed by blue-collar workers primarily in terms of increasing their working time, while white-collar workers, particularly those with higher occupational status, view career progress less in terms of a quantitative expansion of their work than in terms of a qualitative improvement or change.

Table 5-5 shows that blue-collar workers, to get ahead, would be more willing than white-collar workers to sacrifice their vacations or leisure time. White-collar workers, particularly those of higher status, think first of changing their place of residence. Among the latter, willingness to accept less secure jobs is more common than among blue-collar workers. White-collar workers with little education share some attitudes with each of these two groups.

Inquiring further about characteristics that determine willingness to do something toward occupational advancement, we again found distinct differences. For blue-collar workers

TABLE 5-5   Incentives of White Employed Males by Occupation and Education (in percent)

| | In Order to Get Ahead, Would You | | | |
RESPONDENTS WITH	GIVE UP VACATIONS?	GIVE UP LEISURE?	TAKE LESS SECURITY?	MOVE FAMILY?
Blue-collar job	63	64	28	38
White-collar job, low education	53	61	36	43
White-collar job, high education	46	55	46	66

SOURCE: Survey Research Center study directed by B. Strumpel in 1972.

special efforts to work more were found to be mainly a result of financial pressures. Those short of cash were more likely to be inclined to exert additional work effort. For white-collar workers, on the other hand, it was their value orientation, the relative attraction of the nonmaterial characteristics of a job, the intrinsic satisfaction, that was significantly related to the inclination to invest more in their career. Those who place great importance on interesting activity are more likely than others to move and to take risks.

While the productive reserves of this latter group tend to be mobilized by the "carrot" of a broad range of rewards, the incentives of blue-collar workers and those in the lower half of the socioeconomic scale are heavily tied to the "stick" of material necessity. Here the inclination to do more work is contingent on immediate reward—working more hours provides instant cash.

Many blue-collar workers are then worse off than the elite of white-collar employees: first with respect to perceived material well-being, and second with respect to the "psychic costs" of work. Although these are subjective terms, it is easy to identify economic status and quality of employment as their objective correlates. A variety of data suggest that a low quality of employment depresses incentives. The failure of the modern work environment to respond to the rising aspirations for intrinsic rewards has indeed been responsible for the scattered symptoms of declining work discipline (see Strumpel 1974 and U.S. Department of Health, Education and Welfare 1973).

"Good" work ethic means something different for different

groups of workers. A "diligent" blue-collar worker shows the traditional virtues of punctuality, discipline, and honesty. He is capable and willing to perform simple, repetitive tasks regularly, routinely, and reliably by exactly following the written and unwritten rules. What counts more in the higher-status and occupational groups is risk taking, flexibility, versatility, mobility, and adaptability. What is required are ideas, solutions to problems, and innovations rather than a given quantity of output or of time worked. The stereotype of "hard work" is more appropriate for the successful blue-collar worker, less so for the high level managerial employee. This is so, first, because, for the latter the job in itself offers more fulfillment and, second, because, contrary to prevailing opinion, higher-level workers spend less time working than do those at lower levels.[1] Even the norms of honesty are interpreted more generously for higher-level occupations: The gray area between business and personal expenses—for instance, personal phone calls on the business line, entertainment on the expense account, private use of the company car —typically exists for the higher-status groups but not for blue-collar workers.

When we consider these data in a broader context, it becomes clear that the shift in work-related values represents a departure not so much from the work ethic as from the traditional norms of the blue-collar worker. Subject to erosion have been the characteristics of the disciplined, obedient, subordinate manual worker. A basic alienation from work cannot be observed in either the U.S. or Germany. To be sure, as we shall note in the next chapter, older workers in both countries, supported by more generous social security and old age pensions and private savings, more often take advantage of the possibility of early retirement. The trend toward earlier retirement is counterbalanced in the United States and more recently also in Germany by the rising participation of married women in the labor force.[2]

---

[1]The above statement has been documented in comparative international time studies; see Szalai (1972).

[2]The rate of female labor participation in the U.S. rose from 32 percent in 1947 to 46½ percent in 1975.

At the same time we must not lose sight of the high unemployment figures as well as a variety of signs of disillusionment with work. There is no harmony between trends in values and trends in job characteristics. We found among workers at all levels in both countries some loss in their sense of control over their own fate (documented further in Chapter 10, Table 10-1) and a growing desire for more self-fulfillment in their work. Unfortunately, their changed aspirations are not being met by a corresponding enrichment in the nature of most occupations. More and more often people are being disappointed by their jobs.

It is young people particularly who approach the job world with rising aspirations. Work must offer more than just good pay. The traditional worker tended to sacrifice his working time to the company and looked for satisfaction in his family and leisure. The typical young employee today who is shaped by new values is hardly less willing to get involved in his work. Yet he does this more often with the expectation of working at the level of his potential and finding fulfillment on the job.

Unemployment and Underemployment

The new occupational values have been largely frustrated by the unfavorable labor markets of the 1970s. There are not sufficient jobs of high enough quality available to satisfy the new aspirations. The increased output of graduates from institutions of higher learning, which during the first phases of the educational revolution diminished the supply of workers, is now providing an oversupply. One result has been that between 1969 and 1975 starting salaries of college graduates in the United States declined greatly in real terms. More highly educated people have been forced to accept lower-paid jobs otherwise occupied by individuals with less education. Underemployment tends to trickle down. According to Richard Freeman and J. Herbert Hollomon:

> College placement data show a decline of 23 percent in the real starting pay for men with social science and humanities degrees between 1969 and 1975, a fall of 21

percent in the real pay for beginning BS mathematics majors; and of 17 percent for beginning electrical engineers with doctorates. . . . New college graduates are having severe problems obtaining desirable work. Over 30 percent of the graduating men and 25 percent of the women in the class of 1972 were holding nonprofessional, nonmanagerial jobs in the early seventies, compared with just over 10 percent of graduates in a roughly similar status in the class of 1958. Between 1969 and 1974, the relative number of male college graduates working as salesmen and the proportion of female graduates employed in clerical positions both increased by 30 percent. [1975, p. 25.]

The other side of the coin is that workers do not have an unlimited willingness to adjust to the opportunities in the labor market. The average unemployed or underemployed worker is more choosy now. Some of what Martin S. Feldstein wrote just before the last recession is still valid:

The picture of a hard core of unemployed persons unable to find jobs is an inaccurate description of our economy and a misleading basis for policy. A more accurate description is an active labor market in which almost everyone who is out of work can find his usual type of job in a relatively short time. The problem is not that these jobs are unavailable but that they are unattractive. Much of the unemployment and even more of the lost manpower occurs among individuals who find that the available jobs are neither appealing in themselves nor rewarding as pathways to better jobs in the future [1973, p. 11].

Unemployment is no longer tantamount to poverty. The unemployed are not much more likely to fall below the officially stipulated poverty line than the rest of the population. Conversely, employment is not completely effective in guaranteeing a decent level of consumption. In 1974 13 percent of family heads with wage incomes (calculated on an equivalent full-time basis) did not earn enough to lift a family of four above the poverty level.[3] Even in times of high unem-

---

[3]The source of the statements about the relation of the incomes of the unemployed and of wage earners to the poverty level is the Longitudinal Survey of Income Dynamics (directed by J. N. Morgan), Survey Research Center, University of Michigan.

ployment there are numerous job vacancies. Many jobs are badly paid, offering wages little higher than the available government support. Furthermore, government programs of income maintenance permit unemployed workers to hold out for an attractive job opportunity rather than forcing them to accept the first offer.

In Germany even jobs that are well paid but require heavy manual labor have been losing their attractiveness and cannot be filled by the substantial number of Germans unemployed. This became manifest in 1976 through a controversy of the automobile and steel industries with the government concerning foreign workers. The industry was urging the government to lift the restrictions on the immigration of, primarily, Turkish, Greek, and Yugoslav workers that had been imposed during the recession and maintained subsequently in the light of the persistent high unemployment.

The question arises: Are there mechanisms in sight that are capable of closing the gap between aspirations and job characteristics? Do disappointed expectations lead to a rapprochement with reality? In other words, will there be a return to the old, traditional work ethic?

The satisfaction of some observers who see on the horizon a quick restoration of the traditional virtues appears to be premature. Whatever adaptation to the recession is apparent represents outward, almost hypocritical, conformity. Yankelovich (1974) reported a slightly increased willingness of young American college students, toward the end of 1973, to conform to the exigencies of the job in the interest of their career. But there was little willingness to compromise where basic values were concerned.

Value changes do have behavioral consequences. Young workers who are confronted with a difficult labor market and, moreover, tend to be disappointed by their jobs, and who can expect sizable financial benefits in case of unemployment, may well be tempted to accept longer periods of unemployment. The combination of lower rates of economic growth, increasing female participation in the labor force, and a high proportion of college graduates entering the labor market tends to narrow the supply of attractive jobs for persons without high school diplomas or other academic credentials. The unruly years of the late 1960s did indeed bring with them the alienation of many students from the occupational values of the Establishment. This form of alienation has ceased to be typical. If the labor market at present does not offer satisfactory opportunities, the better educated can sometimes fall back on the next best jobs, thereby pushing a step down those just qualified for those jobs. Thus underemployment spreads and is finally converted into a bottom layer of unemployed with little education or skill.

In sum, the recessions of the 1970s and their aftermath have reinforced or even created grave inequalities of opportunity. Young people and labor force entrants, recent college graduates, women who reenter the labor force, and middle-aged and older people who happen to lose their jobs have to bear the brunt of the costs through unfavorable career and employment opportunities or sharply reduced wages. In 1976 close to one-half of the unemployed in the U.S. were twenty-five years old or younger. In contrast, most twenty-five to fifty-year-old workers who have held jobs for long periods find their status maintained; prevailing or informal job arrangements usually safeguard the status quo and immunize them against the market. This makes it inevitable, however, that the market hits those hardest who most want to change their situations. It was very different in the era of expansion in the first postwar decades when opportunities were available to almost everyone and career advancement to many. There is now a generation gap in opportunities. Many recent college graduates must take jobs that could have been filled by high school graduates. This strangulation of opportunities must weigh heavily on Americans, who, unlike Europeans, are still entering the labor force in growing proportions. It is because of considerations related to both economic growth and justice that reestablishing a reasonable level of job and career opportunities for those deprived of them deserves highest priority on the agenda of economic reform.

There is little doubt that underemployment, perpetuated by the new choosiness and the new aspirations for better jobs, has started to challenge the traditional methods of management and generates the risk of dissatisfaction and alienation. What may appear on the surface as a problem of the changing work ethic must therefore be identified as a challenge to business and government, and primarily as a warning to them to face rising aspirations for good, interesting work. Strategies of economic policy that will be considered in the final chapter of this book include the creation of such jobs and the upgrading of existing jobs. The new aspirations are not frivolous. Yet they start to threaten the pursuit of the traditional ways of progress and growth that made them possible. Rather than deploring these values or trying to legislate them away, we would do far better to adapt to them and structure our future accordingly.

6
RETIREMENT
AND SAVING

Any enumeration of the differences between the first postwar era and the one that began in the 1970s must contain a discussion of changes in the position of retired people. Since World War II the population sixty-five years of age or older has increased more rapidly than the population as a whole. In 1975 in the United States it exceeded 10 percent of the entire population and is continuing to grow. In addition, over the last several decades the number of years lived in retirement has increased substantially, because of both greater longevity and earlier retirement than in the past.

At the same time public and private provisions for financial security during retirement have improved considerably. Even so, a great many people still suffer from not having what they would consider adequate reserve funds. The discussion in this chapter will start with a study of provisions for retirement and continue with a consideration of savings and reserve funds. Because retirement is one of the most important purposes of saving, there is a close link between the two.

Provisions for Retirement

In the U.S. a fairly universal old-age pension system is of recent origin, in contrast to the long-established system in Germany, which, however, was greatly improved in the postwar years and now fully compensates for losses due to inflation. The price paid in both countries is high taxation. In fact, a very large part of the recent increase in the share of taxation in GNP stems from increases in social security taxes. The latter were raised most recently in January 1977.

Table 6-1 shows the sizable increase in social security taxes and in government expenditures for education in the U.S. and in Germany from 1960 to 1974. These outlays, together with those for retirement and welfare, explain practically the entire increase in the course of those years in the share the government took from the national product. Therefore, it is hardly appropriate to speak of a growing encroachment by the public sector on the proper activities of the private sector. Expenditures for education stem from the postwar baby boom and increased demand; they result in the formation of human capital.

Even though the American social security system was established in 1935, it is only since the 1960s that it has provided sizable old-age benefits to practically everyone who worked during their productive years. In 1975 the old-age benefits

TABLE 6-1 Taxation, Social Security Taxes, Government Expenditure for Education as a Proportion of Gross National Product (in percent)

	United States			West Germany		
YEAR	ALL TAXES	SOCIAL SECURITY TAXES	GOVERNMENT EXPENDITURES FOR EDUCATION	ALL TAXES	SOCIAL SECURITY TAXES	GOVERNMENT EXPENDITURES FOR EDUCATION
1960	27.8	4.1	5.4	31.8	9.2	. . .
1965	28.9	4.3	6.6	32.4	9.5	3.4
1970	31.0	5.9	7.7	33.1	10.4	4.0
1973	. . .	. . .	. . .	36.6	12.3	4.8
1974	34.0	7.3	7.8	. . .	. . .	5.3

NOTE: The data, taken from official statistics, include federal, state, and local taxes and expenditures.

paid out by the system were practically equal to the contributions (taxes) to the system, so that it operated in a pay-as-you-go manner. The annual contributions of more than 80 billion dollars paid by employers and employees were similar in size to the entire amount of private saving.

Recent changes in the social security system resulted in an outcry about its impending bankruptcy, provoked by the prospect that, increasingly, fewer and fewer working people will have to take care of more and more retired people. True, due to the spread of early retirement as well as longevity, the proportion of contributions to beneficiaries has undergone an unfavorable change[1] that may continue in the future. The underlying idea of the argument that today the younger generation takes care of the older generation has, however, been challenged by J. N. Morgan (1977), who argues that each generation of retirees pays its social security taxes and hence consumes less than it would if these taxes had not been levied; therefore it has a right to a fair return, both interest and principal, on its contributions. If 3 percent interest in real terms were added to an average contribution over forty years, and fifteen years of retirement is assumed, more than half of the benefits would represent interest. The prevailing pay-as-you-go system simply implies that the government, because it does not actually invest the accumulated funds, fulfills its obligations to those who have made contributions out of its current rather than past revenues. Thus there is no reason to restrict the source of the funds to social security taxes.

Since the early 1960s social security has increasingly been supplemented in the U.S. by private pension plans. From small beginnings these plans have grown so fast that by 1980 they are expected to cover about two-thirds of the labor force. These plans accumulate sizable reserves year after year. In 1975 contributions to private pension plans, mostly on the part of employers, amounted to 15½ billion dollars compared with 10 billion dollars benefits paid out. The private pension

---

[1] In 1975 there were 18 people over sixty-five years of age for every 100 people ages eighteen to sixty-four; in 1950 there were only 13 older people per 100 people of working age.

reserves of close to 200 billion dollars were invested mostly in common stock and represented approximately 20 percent of the total value of all outstanding stocks of publicly held corporations.

How have these developments affected people's behavior? Regarding the behavior of the retired people the answer is clear: They live better than at earlier times. The average income of retirees has increased greatly—from social security, other pensions, dividends, and interest, as well as from the occasional work that many of them do. According to recent findings, many retired people in their sixties even save some of their income; looking forward to many years of retirement, they are strongly motivated to do so.

The lengthening of the retirement period is one of the important changes that have occurred recently. To a small extent it is due to increased longevity, mainly, however, to a trend toward early retirement. Surveys disclose that most Americans consider sixty-five the "normal" retirement age. Yet the majority of those who in the recession year of 1975 applied for retirement benefits for the first time were sixty-two to sixty-four years old. Nationwide sample surveys of the Survey Research Center indicate that, among family heads thirty-five to sixty years of age, in 1966 42 percent and in 1976 even 46 percent indicated that they planned to retire before they were sixty-five years old. Interestingly, the proportion of those who planned to retire early was smaller in older than in somewhat younger groups. The prevailing retirement provisions apparently look more promising when retirement is far away than when it is imminent.[2]

It is not permissible to conclude that it has been the improvement of retirement prospects that has caused people to retire early. To say so would be equivalent to calling the pill the cause of reduced birth rates; in fact, the pill only made it possible for people to do what they desired to do for other reasons. Similarly, social security and private pensions made it possible for many people to realize what they desired,

[2]See Barfield and Morgan (1969) for older data; unpublished Survey Research Center tabulations for 1976 data.

namely, not to continue with their strenuous and often monotonous work for too many years.

At the same time, however, many individuals bitterly complained about being compelled to retire at the age of sixty-five. Satisfied with their job and in good health, they wished to continue to work, and the enforced idleness made them unhappy. Sample surveys disclosed that the majority of Americans were opposed to compulsory retirement at a fixed age.

Planning to retire early is not the only effect of changes in pensions on people who have not yet retired. We must also ask how their patterns of spending and saving have changed. In this respect there exists an oft-repeated theoretical position postulating that wealth, meaning social security as well as any other wealth, reduces saving.[3] In essence this theory maintains that the government by providing old-age insurance is responsible for the shortfall in saving and therefore in investment. Because of the importance of this position, it is necessary to interrupt our discussion of recent developments and discuss, briefly, differences between traditional economic theories about saving, on the one hand, and psychological principles and recent survey findings about saving patterns, on the other.

On the Theory of Saving

Three equations relating to spending and saving are to be found in introductory textbooks of economics. The first,

$$S + C = Y,$$

says that saving and consumption together make up incomes and represent the two uses of income. It does not follow, how-

---

[3]Many years ago Milton Friedman wrote about the retirement provisions of the social security system: "The availability of assistance from the state would clearly tend to reduce the need for private reserves and so to reduce planned saving" (Friedman 1957, p. 123). More recently Martin Feldstein wrote that "the social security program, by providing relatively substantial retirement income to middle- and low-income families, has reduced their need to accumulate fungible wealth" (Feldstein 1976a, p. 800).

ever, that saving and consumption are alternatives in people's minds. Most people desire both and even an increase in both. When income went up, as happened in the postwar era to the majority of families in most years, people achieved their desires by using part of their income increment to increase spending and part of it to save more.

The second equation says that consumption is the function of income:

$$C = f(Y).$$

True, the higher the income, the larger are the consumer expenditures. But at the same time it is true that the higher the income, the larger also are the amounts saved. In fact, in the U.S. low-income people save nothing or very little, and most of the amounts saved are saved by upper- or high-income families.

The third equation,

$$C = f(Y,W),$$

expands the second by assuming that consumption is a function not only of income but also of wealth. The larger the wealth, the higher are the consumer expenditures. From this it is deduced that wealth depresses saving: If you are wealthy, you are not motivated to save.

True, large assets and especially large liquid assets represent an enabling condition for spending and thus may lead to a reduction of savings. But this tendency is opposed by two factors that stimulate saving by people who have substantial assets. First, repeated measurements indicate that savers' levels of aspiration increase with accomplishment. Surveys revealed that, after the savers had accumulated savings that they had originally considered ideal and the need for which had greatly stimulated thrift, the amount appeared insufficient, and the savers felt the need for still larger reserve funds. Second, there is the influence of habitual saving patterns. Most Americans' accumulated reserve funds result from their own saving during their lifetime. The habitual saving process that results from the saver's income, expenditure patterns, and habits of thriftiness may occasionally be interrupted by a year of large expenditures but may be expected to continue even after the saver has accumulated sizable assets. Cross-section studies revealed that the owners of substantial amounts of savings were the largest savers.[4] The validity of the argument that the greater the assets, the smaller the amounts saved and that wealth depresses saving is therefore subject to doubt.

A widely accepted theory of saving is based on a life-cycle model and maintains that people save during working years for the purpose of consuming the savings during their retirement. Since workers who save are more numerous and have higher earnings than retirees, it follows that aggregate personal saving will be positive. It has been part and parcel of this theory that old-age insurance and private pension plans reduce or may even eliminate the *need* for individual saving.

Empirical studies of the behavior of American savers confirm one part of the theory: Most people do save for the purpose of using the accumulated savings during their lifetime. Inheritance is, in most cases, unintentional rather than planned. There is, to be sure, one exception relevant for the aggregate volume of saving and dissaving: The rich, who are the owners of a substantial proportion of all personal assets, frequently plan to bequeath an estate to their children and grandchildren. Following further the empirical studies of American savers, we find that most of them have two major purposes in mind. When asked about their reasons for saving, in addition to retirement, they speak of "rainy days." They are aware of the uncertainty of the future and the possibility of emergencies that might make it necessary to fall back on savings.

Some additional broad and widely accepted generalizations about the saving process have occasionally been contradicted by recent empirical studies. That amounts saved should be larger in periods of recession than in periods of prosperity is frequently postulated. True, motivations to save are particularly large when recession or unemployment threaten. Most

---

[4]Detailed findings mentioned in this and the following paragraphs may be found in Katona (1964 Part 5; 1975 Part 5).

importantly, recessions are characterized by lower purchases of durable goods and other discretionary expenditures, so that both cash withdrawals from liquid assets and installment borrowing are reduced. On the other hand, this generalization does not take into account the fact that rising incomes represent the most propitious factor in bringing about large increases in saving. Thus an important stimulus to saving is present in prosperous times and missing in periods of recession.

We may also recall here that, as already discussed in Chapter 3, according to traditional assumptions inflation and the expectation of inflation should induce consumers to buy in advance and in excess of their needs. Therefore, inflation should stimulate spending and curtail saving. But over the last several decades, uncertainty associated with inflation and the knowledge that expenditures on necessities would increase with rising prices induced many people to react to inflation by saving more rather than by spending more. To be sure, this happened only in periods of creeping inflation. Twice in recent American experience, in 1950 and again in 1973–1974, many people were so greatly disturbed by fear of inflation and of shortages that they abandoned their old habits of spending carefully and began to stock up and hoard a variety of goods.

The conclusion to be drawn from this analysis is: Little reliance should be placed on a theory of saving based on a priori considerations. The circumstances prevailing at a given time must be studied at that time if we are to understand and predict people's saving behavior.

We return now to the discussion of the impact of greatly improved retirement prospects on the saving performance of Americans before retirement. Feldstein argued that two forces impinge on working people: First, wealth, including social security wealth, "unambiguously reduced the amount of personal saving." Second, the "reduction in working years and the resulting increase in the period of retirement induce additional saving." Therefore "the net effect of social security on the saving of the non-aged is indeterminate" (1976b p. 78).

On the other hand, Katona (1965) has argued that wealth

does not necessarily reduce saving motives, and social security and private pension wealth may even increase the desire to save because being closer to one's goal represents a psychological force that enhances motivation (while motivation is weakened when it appears impossible or very difficult to reach a goal).

When private pension plans began to spread in the early 1960s, a unique opportunity presented itself to find out which of the two theories was correct, the theory of the alleged rational behavior or the psychological theory. At the time the American working population was divided into two large and comparable segments, one covered by fairly recent private pension plans and the other not so covered. (It should be noted that both segments were covered by social security or government pensions and, therefore, even in the early 1960s it was not possible to determine, by means of surveys, the impact of social security coverage on saving.) The results of the investigation revealed unequivocally that the expectation of private pension benefits did not reduce the amounts saved by working people.[5]

These findings have frequently been called surprising or paradoxical.[6] This characterization is understandable only if one starts with the assumption that wealth must of necessity reduce amounts saved.

Of course, what was true in the early 1960s may not be true in the 1970s, and Katona wrote in 1965 that in future years, if social security and private pensions provide higher benefits, their effect on saving may be different from what it was when the survey was conducted in 1963. But it is hard to accept Feldstein's argument that social security and longer retirement exert contradictory influences on saving. Yet his conclusion, that the net effect on saving is indeterminate, may be correct. To determine this effect by empirical methods would

---

[5]See Katona (1965). Some findings presented in that monograph even showed that private pension plans may have stimulated amounts saved. Philip Cagan (1965) published similar results at the same time.

[6]For instance, by Feldstein (1976a, 1976b) as well as Munnell (1974). Feldstein called Katona's arguments "a dramatic departure from the usual assumptions of economic analysis" (1976b, p. 81).

be very difficult. Cross-section studies no longer suffice because no comparable groups can be found without either social security or private pension plans.[7]

Are Amounts Saved and Reserve Funds Adequate?

The main question regarding amounts saved in the recent past and the near future is: Are people interested in saving and are they able to save and thus supply the funds needed for investment? Our findings are that neither social security nor the improvement of retirement prospects, nor any other development, has diminished the felt need or the motives to save.

We mentioned in Chapter 2 that in the late 1960s and early 1970s the proportion of income saved increased both in the United States and in Germany. The 1975 saving rates of over 8 percent of disposable income in the U.S. and over 15 percent in Germany were the highest reached in any postwar year. It does not follow, of course, that the more adequate retirement provisions of recent years stimulated the saving process, but the facts do cast some doubt on the assertion that incentives to save were blunted by increases in pensions. The major empirical finding is that people in the mid-1970s felt insecure, more so than earlier. First of all, the maintenace of the living standards of working people became uncertain. Awareness of extended periods of recession and large unemployment, even on the part of people with good jobs, as well as uncertainty about economic and political prospects enhanced the felt need for reserve funds. Very many people also felt that the pensions they could expect, even though much higher than in the past, would not suffice to cover their needs and would have to be supplemented from other sources.

Surveys provided evidence that the need for saving *felt* by the American people in the mid-1970s was greater than in

---

[7]Even in the early 1970s the self-employed represented the only significant group without private pensions. Their saving performance is different from other people's for a variety of reasons. Therefore, and because they are based on assets rather than amounts saved, the cross-section studies by Munnell (1974, 1976) are far from convincing, and the results of her regression equations are not impressive.

earlier years. One of the questions included in the Survey Research Center's quarterly surveys reads: "Do you think it is more important now than usual for you to try to add to your savings and reserve funds, or are you fairly well satisfied with your savings?" In 1975 and 1976 as many as 70 percent of representative samples said that it was more important than usual to save and/or that they were dissatisfied with the size of their savings. In 1972, before the great recession, this proportion was less than 40 percent. It is not so much that satisfaction with their savings declined, because few people ever expressed satisfaction with their savings, but that people felt a greater need for additional security. In 1972 many more respondents than in 1976 said that they didn't know or had no opinion on the subject. It appears that the rate of saving was high in the mid-1970s because people felt an increased desire to save.

Should one argue, then, that it is the total of accumulated savings rather than the amounts saved each year that are insufficient for present needs? Obviously, a statement that the U.S. or Germany had not enough savings would be equivalent to saying that these most affluent countries of the world were too poor. Nevertheless, there are good reasons to argue that for very many families in the United States, their accumulated savings are inadequate. Total savings are large, but the majority of Americans have no savings or very little savings. Personal assets are highly concentrated among a relatively small proportion of people, the rich. Wealth is much more concentrated than income. In 1972, according to data prepared by the Internal Revenue Service, 6 percent of Americans owned 52 percent of all net personal wealth.

	Shares Held by the Richest	
U.S. ASSETS IN 1972	1 PERCENT	6 PERCENT
Net worth	26%	52%
Real estate	15	43
Corporate stock	57	72

SOURCE: Joint Economic Committee of the U.S. Congress 1976.

Of the estimated 4.3 billion dollars market value of total

personal assets in 1972, and 3.5 billion dollars net worth (assets minus liabilities), real estate and corporate stock are the two largest components. Real estate is not highly concentrated, because it includes the value of homes, which are owned by two-thirds of all American families. Common stock, on the other hand, is concentrated to the extent that the richest 1 percent own more than half of the total. To go beyond the fact that 94 percent of Americans own less than one-half of all net worth, it is probable, although the data are far from exact and not up to date, that one-half of all American families have very few assets beyond the value of their homes. They do have some wealth in the form of claims for social security and other pensions after retirement, but they do not regard these claims or their homes as reserve funds because they cannot be used in case of an emergency. Having such liquid reserve funds in amounts as large as their annual income, which is greatly desired but still would hardly be sufficient, characterizes less than one-half of all families.

Why is wealth highly concentrated? The first and most obvious answer is that the poor do not save. Sometimes it is argued that they do not save because they have social security and therefore do not need to save for retirement. We have already dismissed this argument and must also dismiss the argument that absence of saving, not only on the part of the poor but also of very many middle-income families, is due to not being motivated to save.[8] When these people are asked in surveys whether they plan to save the following year, the proportion giving affirmative answers is always very much higher than the proportion reporting a year later that they had actually saved in the previous year. Good intentions to save are often not realized because, except in the case of upper-income families, expenditures, expected as well as unexpected, have priorities and may exhaust the entire income. The high and rising social security taxes, which are regressive and hurt lower-income people more than upper-income peo-

---

[8]It should be noted that millions of middle-income people do save by repaying what they owe on mortgage and installment debt; the statement that they do not save is correct in the sense that they do not accumulate any liquid reserve funds.

ple, also contribute to the inability of a large group of families to save.

Thus the major reason for the great concentration of wealth is the absence of, or very small extent of, accumulation of bank deposits and stocks by those in the lower half of the income distribution and those in the younger age groups. Those who failed to save a proportion of, say, 10 percent of their income over many years have no significant liquid assets.

Only relatively few Americans have inherited sizable sums of money, and only relatively few have acquired wealth through substantial capital gains. Clearly, large capital gains can be made only if one can make a sizable initial investment in business, stocks, or real estate. Spending less than one earns—when the repayment of mortgage and installment debt is thought of as spending, a view shared by most Americans—is very difficult for very many people. The size and diversity of expenditures that are considered necessary is too great.

Little can be done in a short period of time to reduce the high rate of concentration of wealth. Taking away from the rich through higher income or inheritance taxes would not solve the problem. The opening up of ownership and control of industry to broad groups of people has frequently been discussed, but no good ways of setting that process in motion have yet been found. Neither in the U.S. nor in Germany have employee stock-ownership plans been successful. In the 1970s the number of individual owners of stock even declined in the U.S.

There is one more point to be made. It is true that during the last few years the ownership by two-thirds of American families of the one-family homes in which they live has greatly mitigated the adverse impact of inflation on their assets. But in the mid-1970s the continuation of a high rate of home ownership has become doubtful. The median price of new houses sold went up from the beginning of 1972 to the end of 1976 from twenty-five thousand dollars to forty-five thousand dollars and of existing houses from twenty-five thousand dollars to forty thousand dollars (see *Federal Reserve Bulletin*, March 1977, p. 191). While most home owners have gained little from the (unrealized) appreciation of the value of their houses, these price increases, far exceeding the gains in people's incomes, threaten to make it impossible for a large proportion of young married couples to acquire a one-family house and thus may disrupt what has been a major asset of American life.

We conclude the discussion of the saving process by repeating that in spite of substantial gains in pensions for retirement, the accumulation of reserve funds is felt to be insufficient on the part of a substantial segment of the population. This fact contributes greatly to the prevailing feelings of lack of security.

7
COLLECTIVE DEPRIVATION AND SOCIETAL DISCONTENT

In a discussion of the social consequences of the economic difficulties of the 1970s several points of view emerge. Some observers believe that the interruption of rapid economic growth would inevitably lead to a period of aggravated social tension. They hold, first, that the continuously increasing production of goods in the postwar era succeeded in disguising the latent social costs of growth, such as the deterioration of the environment and of the quality of life, bottlenecks in the provision of public services, and the diminution of raw material reserves. Second, they assert that the lower-income groups, as long as they profited from rising real incomes, ignored their relative position in the economic hierarchy but that a slowdown of growth reveals the inherent inequities of the prevailing income distribution.

There is a contrasting opinion holding that bad times and concomitant threats to the prevailing standard of living and job security revive the traditional virtues of thrift and work discipline and thus lead to a reduction in demands for greater satisfaction with existing levels of living, and even to national solidarity and return to the basic values of life.

Neither of these hypotheses has been empirically tested or

ever phrased in such a way that it could be tested. Each of the two can be "proved" or "disproved" by citing examples. But the very simplicity of the examples that seem to validate each point of view suggests that they do not adequately reflect actual conditions. The question is not whether but rather under what conditions economic deterioration may either create or reduce conflict. Although the data on which such a theory could be constructed are not yet at hand, the development of social indicators has prepared the ground by generating both theoretical approaches and empirical data that will ultimately serve that purpose.

History provides no evidence of any clear-cut relationship between economic deterioration and political unrest. Rather, the examples frequently cited indicate varied reactions to economic adversity. It has been noted, for instance, that the solidarity of the British during the hard times of World War II contrasted sharply with the intensity of economic conflict in the same country during the 1970s. It has also been noted that the struggle for civil rights and racial unrest in the United States in the 1960s occurred at a time when the social and economic position of the protesting groups was improving.

The basic question, it would seem, is not what economic developments occur at a given time but rather how they are perceived and interpreted and, in particular, what kind of expectations they engender. Social conflict presupposes, first, that the deteriorating economic situation is experienced as unsatisfactory, disappointing, or threatening. Second, the difficulties must be seen as not being justified or as not being equitably distributed because they do not place an equal burden on everybody. In order for inequity to be perceived, it is often enough for the position of a person to deteriorate relative to other persons or groups rather than absolutely.

Besides disappointment and inequity the sociopsychological literature identifies a third factor in the potential for conflict, namely, the presence or absence of "instrumentality," that is, of actions or avenues to change the situation open to those affected by the absolute or relative deterioration. The actions available must represent realistic options with a chance of success. This is particularly so when people must sacrifice immediate benefits for the sake of distant rewards, as in the case of strikes or illegal protests. The chance of success is obviously less important in the case of such a possible instrument of protest as voting. Voting for a radical candidate, for example, involves no personal courage or sacrifice.

Under what circumstances does economic adversity meet the three conditions that spur people to protest? As to the first, one may safely assume that the deterioration of the economy disappoints the expectations and aspirations of many people. With respect to the absence of justification for the situation, a generalization is more difficult. People may be able to justify economic deterioration if comparison with other individuals or groups does not indicate an inequitable distribution of the burden and if the national leadership is not held responsible and lives up to the situation; in short, if a climate of solidarity and competence prevails. With respect to the third condition, namely, the availability of potential action to change the situation, economic adversity usually fails to allow for such action, at least apart from the extreme case of radical upheaval. Strike threats tend to be ineffective in a recession, when due to overproduction the chances of success are reduced and due to unemployment the risks of making demands and protests are high.

To illustrate the circumstances under which social protest arises, we may briefly recall the racial unrest in the United States between 1964 and 1968. These events took place in a general setting of economic prosperity. Government pronouncements had drawn public attention to the discrimination against a racial minority, and civil rights legislation of the Johnson administration had done away with the institutional forms of discrimination on the legislative level. Even the income differences between the races had begun to diminish at that time. The Institute for Social Research of the University of Michigan conducted a survey immediately following the riots in Detroit and Newark. It was found that the rioters had more education than the nonrioters in the same community, were politically and socially more committed, and more often felt that they had been discriminated against. Accordingly Nathan Caplan and Jeffrey M. Paige (1968) rejected the "riffraff theory," that those who riot are irresponsible deviants or criminals, and favored what they called the "blocked-opportunity theory." A third possible explanation, the "relative deprivation theory," holds that the closer one comes to reaching a goal, the greater the frustration when it is not attained. Even though a study of the personal progress of individual rioters failed to confirm the latter theory, the general circumstances of the 1967 riots appear to be in line with it.

In the 1960s the political scientists Gabriel Almond and Sidney Verba (1963) characterized Americans as fairly ideal democrats. An international comparison of political behavior based on surveys in several countries demonstrated that personal participation in community affairs (membership in political organizations, parent–teacher organizations, community groups, etc.) was more frequent among Americans than among Germans or Italians. Early in the 1960s three-quarters of American adults, but only one-third of the Germans and one-quarter of the Italians, classified themselves as participants in political affairs. The past decade seems to have changed the picture, at least to some extent. There has been a long-term continuous decline in political trust in the United States, which has been even more pronounced among non-whites than whites (see Chapter 4). Uneasiness and alienation have become common. Also the voter turnout has declined continuously, from 68 percent in 1960 to 55 percent in 1976. As to the reasons for these changes in the 1960s it may suffice to refer to the Vietnam War, racial and student unrest, and the increase in criminality, which were all frequently blamed on the government. Then came the Watergate scandal, as well as the inability of the government to forestall or, for a long time, even to moderate inflation and unemployment. As a result, candidates for political office who opposed the government in Washington or who had not previously participated in it, found favor among the voters.

One major source of the increased distance between Americans and their political system was disclosed in our studies. This is the rising doubt about the equity of the income distribution, an increase in people's sense of being underpaid compared with others, for which we have chosen the term collective deprivation. This is an important sociopsychological variable linking economic adversity to social conflict. In order to experience deprivation it is not enough to be dissatisfied; one's condition must also be considered inequitable or unjustified. The standards that are used to gauge the equity of a condition are based on both self-interest and social norms. These norms can legitimize even an unsatisfactory situation and thus diffuse the situation so that it is not translated into social conflict. According to W. G. Runciman (1966) a distinction must be made between individual and collective deprivation.[1] The latter is particularly important in our context. An example of individual deprivation is the young executive who has been disappointed in his hopes of being promoted. He does not believe that executives in general are less adequately rewarded than they deserve. Rather, he feels that he personally is being inequitably treated compared with other members of his subgroup. An example of collective deprivation is the class-conscious worker who is convinced that not only he but other workers as well are being inadequately rewarded by the society to whose welfare they contribute.

The Survey Research Center conducted surveys in an attempt to measure collective deprivation by asking workers and employees to say whether they thought they got more or less than they deserved compared with people in other occupations. The main use of the findings from repeated surveys of this kind is to demonstrate changes in felt inequity from one time to the next. Table 7-1 shows that during the eighteen months between the spring of 1972 and the fall of 1973 there was a substantial increase in dissatisfaction as well as in the extent of felt inequity. In addition, it is worth noting that in 1973 and 1974 approximately one-half of working Americans described their financial rewards as inequitably low compared to those of workers in other occupations. This is remarkable, since American society has traditionally accepted the inequality of incomes by invoking the concept of the equality of opportunity and the prospect of rising mass affluence.

---

[1]Runciman speaks of fraternal rather than collective deprivation.

TABLE 7-1 Deterioration of Satisfaction and Felt Equity (Percent of Employed Persons, U.S.)

A. Satisfaction with Income[a]

OPINION	SPRING 1972	FALL 1973	FALL 1974
Delighted, pleased, mostly satisfied	73	60	53
Mixed	15	20	22
Mostly dissatisfied, unhappy, terrible	12	20	25
Total	100	100	100

SOURCE: Survey Research Center, University of Michigan.

[a] The instruction was: "Please tell me what number on this card best says how you feel about ... the following: How satisfied are you with the income you (and your family) have?" (The seven-point scale on the card contained the following entries: delighted, pleased, mostly satisfied, mixed, mostly dissatisfied, unhappy, terrible.)

B. Collective Deprivation[a]

	SPRING 1972	FALL 1973	FALL 1974
Work Income Is			
About as much—or more—than deserved	61	47	51
Somewhat less than deserved	31	33	33
Much less than deserved	8	20	16
Total	100	100	100
Work Income Is Less Than Deserved			
White-collar workers under 35 years	41	51	42
White-collar workers 35 years and older	40	48	52
Blue-collar workers under 35 years	37	49	54
Blue-collar workers 35 years and older	36	62	50

SOURCE: Survey Research Center, University of Michigan.

[a] The question was: "How fair is what people in your line of work earn in comparison to how much people in other occupations earn? Do you feel that you get much less than you deserve, somewhat less than you deserve, about as much as you deserve, or more than you deserve in comparison to how much people in *other* occupations earn?"

The sharpest increase in the feeling of inadequacy of income was found among blue-collar workers over thirty-five years of age (from 36 to 62 percent, as shown in Table 7-1). Indeed, it is known that earnings during the 1970s varied greatly even within blue-collar and white-collar categories. Tabulations of the Bureau of Labor Statistics show, for instance, that the weekly wages of automobile and steel workers advanced by approximately 30 percent between October 1973 and October 1976, while those of textile and hotel workers rose only 22 percent (in current dollars). Thus long-prevailing wage differences were accentuated rather than reduced. In absolute amounts steel and auto workers enjoyed a weekly wage of close to $300 in the fall of 1976, as against an average wage of $150 for textile workers and less than $100 for hotel workers. No statistical data are available about salary discrepancies among white-collar workers. But the published figures on very high remunerations of executives of large corporations were well known to many badly paid employees, who repeatedly said in surveys that "the rich get richer, and the poor get poorer."

To return to the large changes in the proportion of people experiencing collective deprivation, as shown in Table 7-1, one cannot attribute these shifts simply to the objective economic deterioration over the period of the three surveys. (Real aggregate incomes still increased by 3 percent in 1973 and decreased only in 1974, while the feeling of deprivation increased in 1973 and remained stable on a high level in 1974.) Rather, the special circumstances of the recession in 1973 have to be considered. In Chapter 3 we spoke of the shock millions suffered because of the sudden, unexpected, and unexplained substantial inflation. Now we must add that apparently very many Americans felt that the ravages of inflation did not affect everyone equally.

As to the polarization of income experience, we must note that the downswing of 1973 stood out from earlier downturns in that it generated drastic differences in its effects. Usually bad times had been brought about by a contraction in the size of the economic pie, which had affected almost everybody, the rich and the poor, capital as well as labor. This time, however, bad times were being accompanied by a redistribution of the pie: In addition to oil companies and owners of gold, many farmers and entrepreneurs increased their share, while laid-off workers as well as people on fixed incomes suffered losses. Selective price increases, that is, changes in the prices of certain consumer goods or services relative to changes in other prices, were particularly frequent and steep in 1973–1974 and occurred repeatedly in quick succession. They were resented as illegitimate by those who had to pay them. The clamor over the "windfall profits" of the oil industry is a case in point. Inflation and shortages led to results considered inequitable by the people: Many suffered losses in real incomes and relative status while others profited. The polarization of these experiences is reflected in Table 4-2 (page 49), which shows the great differences in the personal financial experience of those in upper-income as against lower-income groups.

In addition, our surveys indicate that broad groups of people felt they had less chance than they once had to improve their income. Earlier, there were two avenues toward improvement: social mobility, implying an advance in one's position relative to others in society, and rising affluence, that is, increasing real incomes per capita due to economic growth. Mobility is either facilitated or obstructed by the individual's initial standing as defined mainly by education and occupation, supplemented by age. Once formal schooling is ended and an occupation chosen, the material future, relative to others in society, is largely determined by age and seniority. The other avenue for income progress, the one dependent on the growth of the economy, was long open to the large majority of the population, including those whose social status remained stable. The first decades after World War II were very generous in providing real income increases. In the 1970s, however, several years of absence of any gain in real income deprived the nonmobile worker of his only and highly cherished source of participation in material improvement. Conversely, the prospect of improvement remained real (albeit somewhat diminished) to those who by virtue of their mobility could expect relative increments in their economic position, mainly young white-collar employees who had a career ahead of them. This may partly explain why between 1972 and 1974 these people, as our data show, were hardly affected by the strong momentum toward felt inequity.

The role of inflation in magnifying the increased sense of inequity must be further clarified. In the 1950s and 1960s even income gains caused by productivity changes that were shared by millions of others were considered to be deserved and were seen by workers as resulting from their own performance rather than as windfalls (see Katona, Strumpel, and Zahn 1971, p. 53 ff). In the highly inflationary environment of the early 1970s nominal income increases were generally maintained, thus reinforcing the anticipation of continuing gains. The unexpectedly large inroads of inflation into real income, then, were deeply resented. In the language of equity theory the individual, on the basis of earlier learning experiences, revised upward the notion about the value of his own work without seeing his rewards being adjusted correspondingly. Moreover, surveys disclosed that very many people believe that if everything becomes more expensive, someone must be profiting from the price increases. Thus, others, even if they may actually do no more than keep up with inflation, are perceived by them as gaining, thereby accentuating their own sense of deprivation.

The economic aspirations of the American people remained at a high level even at a time when long-range expectations were sharply reduced (see the data in Chapter 4). The majority of Americans said in 1976 that they would *not* be satisfied if their economic situation and standard of living were to remain unchanged (Table 7-2). Past experience with continuous improvements, perhaps coupled with American traits of dynamism and optimism, makes continuous advances a necessity, the absence of which is unacceptable.

Despite the degree of dissatisfaction and the extent of felt inequity disclosed by our surveys, the fact remains that they did not serve to foster social conflicts. The great recession passed without actions that would have endangered either the productive system or the political process. This may be explained by the lack of instrumentality. The recession, marked by an ebb in the flow of both private and public funds, di-

TABLE 7-2   Reaction to No Change in Personal Economic Conditions in the Next Several Years (in Percent)

OPINION[a]	UNITED STATES		WEST GERMANY	
	1971	1976	1965	1975
Would be satisfied	42	40	67	69
Don't know, undecided	1	5	6	5
Would be dissatisfied	57	55	27	26
Total	100	100	100	100

SOURCE: Survey Research Center and Yankelovich (American data), Institut für Demoskopie (German data).

[a] The question was: "Suppose five to ten years from now your (family's) personal economic situation was the same as now, would you be satisfied or dissatisfied?"

minished the chance for the success of strikes and other protest actions.

Likewise, in Germany no signs of social conflict were visible. In contrast to the aftereffects of the minirecession of 1966–1967, there was neither a manifest turn toward political radicalism nor a wave of strikes. Instead, the prevailing desire for stability made people ready to cut down their demands, both in the personal realm of income aspirations and in the realm of demand for public spending. As can be seen from Table 7-2, the proportion satisfied to have economic conditions remain the same, that is, not to improve in the future, was very large in Germany in both 1965 and 1975.

Additional survey data may serve to illustrate this point. Toward the end of 1974 a representative cross-section of Germans were asked the following question by the Institut für Demoskopie, Allensbach: "Experts say that the economy can only return to normal if everybody tightens his belt. Would you favor that in 1975, if necessary, wages and salaries not be raised, or should wages and salaries be raised in any case, even if prices would have to rise even more this way?" Answering this somewhat suggestive question, 61 percent of the respondents advocated not raising wages, while 22 percent demanded wage increases in any case. Eleven percent (contained in the 22 percent), however, would have consented to smaller wage increases than in the preceding year. On the basis of this undercurrent of willingness to sacrifice, the government was able to maintain its popularity not by minimizing but rather by dramatizing the recession, as became evident from the emphasis Federal Chancellor Schmidt repeatedly placed on the international nature of the economic crisis.

Indeed the Germans in 1975 maintained a considerably more favorable opinion of their governmental system than either the Americans or the British. In answer to a question asked in the three countries, 69 percent of the Americans interviewed and 56 percent of the British, but only 31 percent of the Germans, expressed the opinion that their country was governed in the interest of certain groups rather than in the interest of the whole population.

As we have seen, the Germans were more able than the Americans to reduce the level of their aspirations. To be sure, their expectations were disappointed by the recession, yet their aspirations seem to have diminished at a pace equal to their expectations. In addition, the government apparently was able to convince the German public that the responsibility for the recession lay in external circumstances: the oil crisis, the appreciation of the Deutsche Mark making German exports less competitive abroad, and the impact of the worldwide recession. Finally, and importantly, the government at least partially succeeded in distributing the burden caused by the economic crisis to all population groups. For instance, when the civil service was heavily criticized for ignoring the plight of the private sector and further expanding its scope, governmental positions were eliminated and promotions reduced. The drastic increase in the price of heating oil was counteracted by subsidies to low-income recipients.

In spite of the differences between Germany and the United States, it is true of both countries that the economic adversity failed to aggravate social conflict. It should not be concluded, however, that economic difficulties persisting over extended periods would not arouse adverse societal reactions. Should unemployment and inflation remain high during a period of increases in sales and profits, the potential for acts of protest, especially strikes, would certainly increase.

8
CHANGE IN BEHAVIOR– THE EXAMPLE OF THE ENERGY CRISIS

In this chapter we shall analyze the conditions under which cooperative rather than competitive behavior may be expected to help solve a problem or avert a crisis. People's reactions to the energy crisis of 1973–1974 will serve as our major example. In earlier years continuous and sharply rising demand for material goods required an ever-growing energy consumption and use of raw materials. In the consumer budget it is primarily the dwelling and the automobile that determine the degree of use of energy. The migration from the inner cities to the suburbs has been accompanied by a spectacular increase in energy consumption. Dispersed dwellings increase the use of energy both for heating and transportation. Because the rate of increase in the consumption of energy and raw materials that prevailed prior to 1973 cannot be perpetuated, it becomes particularly important to understand the conditions prerequisite to cooperative behavior and to changes in consumption, perhaps even in life-styles.

People who buy less of a scarce item help others and contribute to economic stability. In contrast, those who compete against others by trying to buy or even hoard scarce goods help drive prices up. The composition and price elasticity of consumer demand is of decisive importance for crisis management and, in addition, for monetary stability. Both could be achieved more easily if consumers, instead of buying goods that are in relatively limited supply or the costs of which keep rising, were to turn toward goods or services that are relatively abundant or the supply of which can easily be expanded and that are less demanding in terms of the depletion of non-renewable resources. For instance, people might buy an education instead of a car for a teen-ager, or cross-country skis instead of a snowmobile. This kind of reaction would be price elastic and flexible and would constitute an act of solidarity. In contrast, the determined attempt to stick to the customary demand for material goods would aggravate the underlying condition. Competition among buyers for available goods regardless of cost or the general welfare would force price increases and do harm to the society that could be avoided by more adaptive behavior.

Economic thinking usually considers price as a sufficient mechanism for the regulation and allocation of goods. Yet leaving the task of allocating scarce goods exclusively to the price mechanism would be unacceptable to many people and would thus lead to undesired social and political consequences. Because consumption habits are not flexible, prices in some cases would have to rise to such an extent that a large proportion of people would be excluded from levels of consumption considered customary and necessary. Sudden, unexpected, and substantial price increases not only might result in reduced purchases but might also provoke anger and a sense of inequity. Therefore there are good reasons to look for an alternative way to allocate goods.

A second reason why the allocation of scarce goods should not always rely on prices alone has to do with the emergence of the affluent society. Today, for example, for many millions of American families, even a ten-cent increase in the price of a gallon of gasoline would represent a hardly noticeable difference in their total household expenditures. They might then reduce their gasoline consumption only if suitable alternatives were available. But for many people the absence or inadequacy of public transportation, as well as long-standing

108

habits, make a reduction in gasoline consumption very difficult. The allocative influence of prices is greatly reduced when the possession of discretionary income has become the rule rather than the exception.

When influencing consumer behavior is considered as a political strategy, an ethical question is raised. Should we not accept existing tastes and preferences even if the resultant behavior aggravates economic problems? Doesn't the alternative represent manipulation and regimentation? The answer lies in the distinction between manipulation and influence or persuasion. Persuasion in itself is neither good nor bad provided those to whom it is directed have a choice, can listen or not, and agree or disagree as they desire. In a democracy that relies largely on market allocation, consumer preferences and tastes should, of course, be accommodated if at all possible. But tastes, though generally rather fixed, are not immutable. Even though they are frequently shaped early in life and are the product of the social and economic environment, they do change and can be changed. For example, the government showed respect for public tastes while still trying to influence them in the case of tobacco and alcohol. They remain available on the marketplace even while their consumption is discouraged through taxation and public information campaigns.

The expansion of consumer wants for material products, mainly consumer durables, has been stimulated in the past several decades by declining relative prices for these goods. It has been facilitated by intervention by the government, such as the federal highway program and the deductibility of interest payments on mortgages. It has been facilitated as well by the absence of intervention, such as the failure to compel people to account for environmental damage and resource depletion. Unfortunately, today's changed economic and environmental conditions cannot, in themselves, be counted on to bring about appropriate changes in consumer behavior. Behavioral adaptation requires different inducements.

Three prerequisites of behavioral change can be identified: First, the situation must be serious and must be recognized as such. Second, there must be a climate of legitimacy, equity, or solidarity. Cooperative behavior is facilitated when the problem and the measures taken to deal with it are well understood and the burden is shared equitably by all. Third, the new behavior must be seen as conforming to the criterion of instrumentality (as defined in Chapter 7). It must be adequate to accomplish its purpose, and it must not "hurt" people excessively, that is, its costs and benefits must be in a reasonable relationship to one another. For example, conservation behavior would have to be viewed as a genuine contribution to the solution of the problem, and a reduction in purchases because of price increases would have to be rewarded by noticeable savings.

Response to the Oil Crisis

Consumer reaction to the oil embargo was studied in surveys made in both the United States and Germany at the height of the energy crisis in 1973–1974. The embargo caused, at least temporarily, an acute threat to the supply of energy that was immediately recognized by the people in both countries. Shortly after the embargo more than half of American survey respondents felt that the energy problem was very serious. Half of these even considered it to be the most important problem confronting the nation at that particular time. At the same time approximately three-quarters of German respondents believed that within two or three months gasoline might become so scarce as to cause serious supply problems. The measures taken by the two governments, such as the prohibition of driving on Sundays in Germany or the imposition of a speed limit of fifty-five miles per hour in the United States, imposed the same restrictions on everyone. At the same time, drastic price increases made conservation rewarding. It is therefore not surprising that the govermental measures were well accepted and that a substantial proportion of both Americans and Germans decided to save energy, as indicated by their responses in surveys (Table 8-1).

The sense that the problem was of considerable national importance favored the change in behavior. Among Americans who considered the energy situation as the most serious problem 61 percent said that they had restricted their con-

TABLE 8-1 Extent of Energy Conservation During the Winter of 1973–1974 (in Percent)

A. United States

EXTENT OF CONSERVATION	HEAT[a]	ELECTRICITY[b]	GASOLINE[c]
Very much	13	14	23
Somewhat	49	50	37
Not very much	18	20	19
Not at all	14	15	19
Not ascertained	6	1	2
Total	100	100	100

SOURCE: Survey Research Center, University of Michigan.

NOTES: $N = 1,353$. Excluded from the percentage distributions for heat and electricity were those respondents who neither owned nor rented a home; respondents whose families did not own a motor vehicle were excluded from the percentage distribution for gasoline conservation.

The questions below were preceded by the statement: "As you will remember, there were some shortages of gasoline and energy last winter. Some families were able to cut down on the energy they used, while for other families this wasn't possible."

[a] "How much were you (and your family) able to lower the heat in your home last winter compared to the winter before: were you able to lower it very much, somewhat, not very much, or not at all?"

[b] "How about cutting down on the amount of electricity you (and your family) use in your household? Have you cut down very much, somewhat, not very much, or not at all?"

[c] "How about cutting down on driving this year compared to last? Have you (and your family) cut down on that very much, somewhat, not very much, or not at all?"

B. West Germany

EXTENT OF CONSERVATION	Respondents in Households Heating with				
	COAL	OIL	GAS	ELECTRICITY	TOTAL
Made use of methods to save energy	26	53	35	26	43
Reduced heat	16	45	20	11	33
Used less electricity	16	21	25	17	20
Used less hot water	6	13	7	9	11
Did not save energy	74	47	65	74	57
Total	100	100	100	100	100

SOURCE: Institut für Demoskopie, Allensbach.

$N = 2,000$.

sumption of energy, while among those who thought it not a serious problem only 37 percent had done so. Furthermore, approval or disapproval of government policies was found to be significantly correlated with conservation efforts (see Curtin 1976).

It appears that in 1973–1974 rationing would have been acceptable to a large proportion of the population. In response to a question asked by the National Opinion Research Center, (NORC), "Do you think gasoline rationing throughout the nation is necessary?" 35 percent of the respondents answered in the affirmative, 50 percent in the negative, and 15 percent were undecided. In response to an open-ended Survey Research Center question, "If enough energy is not saved by voluntary actions, what do you think should be done?" not fewer than 61 percent of the sample mentioned gasoline rationing. Somewhat later in response to the NORC question "What three actions would you most like federal, state, or local government to take in order to cut fuel consumption?" 81 percent referred to speed limits as the most desirable of the choices, followed in popularity by the improvement of mass transit (51 percent), encouragement of car pools (48 percent), and gasoline rationing (32 percent). The relaxation of antipollution standards was approved of by only 23 percent of the respondents.

It is obvious that the approval of rationing is contingent on the recognition of the seriousness of the situation. When those respondents who had said they thought rationing was not necessary were asked why, 75 percent answered, "There is no gasoline shortage." Apparently there are few opponents of rationing as a matter of principle (see Murray et al. 1974).

The years after the oil embargo revealed considerable differences between the U.S. and Germany. After the embargo had ended, the Germans considered the energy crisis a thing of the past, while most Americans thought more in terms of a temporary reprieve. In 1976 a return of the crisis was considered probable by only 10 percent of the Germans but 58 percent of the Americans.

The Survey Research Center asked the following question in the United States late in 1974: "There have already been some shortages of energy and other resources in this country, and others are predicted for the future. In general, do you think most of these shortages can be avoided by new scientific discoveries or will we have to learn to consume less?" Thirty-five percent of the respondents believed shortages could be avoided by additional supplies, while 44 percent thought we would have to learn to consume less. An additional 16 percent considered both answers appropriate, that is, technology could help but we would still have to save. In the opinion of the majority the supply situation not only was serious but also would remain serious, and demand would have to give.

The difference between the impact of the energy crisis in the two countries is probably related to the brief duration of the experience of the oil shortage in Germany. For the Germans the events represented only a brief, temporary episode. In contrast, the world view of Americans changed lastingly after their supplies were challenged by a group of hitherto little-known countries. Furthermore, a part of the responsibility for the crisis was attributed by Americans to their own government as well as to the American oil companies. It is not surprising, then, that in Germany the abatement of the crisis led to a rapid decline in the sense of urgency, while Americans continued to worry about energy even after 1974. Nonetheless, even in the U.S. the proportion of people understanding the need to conserve energy as well as the proportion conserving declined greatly in 1976.[1]

Change in Behavior

In the previous chapter we found no valid argument that would lead us to expect a direct and necessary relationship between economic adversity and social conflict. By the same token, there is no reason to expect cooperative behavior to emerge during a crisis when customary ways of thinking and

---

[1] In the weeks before April 1977, when President Carter announced his energy policy and called upon the American people to make sacrifices, only a small proportion of Americans thought that there was an acute energy crisis. The response of the people to Carter's announcement and the subsequent legislation cannot be discussed in this book.

behaving are abandoned. In such a setting many things are possible—a spirit of solidarity or cynical egotism, patriotic sacrifice or protest, acceptance, or even rebellion.

We may enumerate the conditions for the one or the other outcome by summarizing the previous discussion. Change of behavior, and the emergence of cooperative behavior, will take place, first, only if people feel that most others will act in the same manner. People will not be willing to curb their own consumption if they think that the wealthy, who can more easily afford to pay a higher price, will act differently. In addition to the equitability of restrictions common understanding of the need for a change represents a requirement for change. Finally, an alternative response must be available if a change is to take place. The greater the sacrifice involved in the changed behavior, the greater the need for the first two requirements to be fulfilled.

Well-known reactions to wartime shortages and restrictions provide additional evidence supporting these conclusions. When the war ended—and even somewhat earlier, when the end was in sight—people's adherence to price controls and rationing weakened greatly. They then questioned both the need for further sacrifices and the adherence of others to the restrictions.

The possiblity of change, even of radical change, in mass behavior may no longer be doubted. Recent changes in fertility behavior have resulted within ten years in the size of American families being reduced to such an extent that the "population explosion" has given way to "zero population growth." In 1960 there were 118.0 births per 1,000 women age fifteen to forty-four; in 1975, 66.7. Table 8-2 shows the rapid decline within ten years in the number of children desired.

The three reasons for the radical reduction in the number of

TABLE 8-2 Lifetime Births Expected by Wives, United States

	18–24 YEARS OLD	25–29 YEARS OLD	30–34 YEARS OLD
1965	3.1	3.4	3.6
1975	2.2	2.3	2.6

SOURCE: Bureau of the Census, P20-301, November 1976.

children born and wanted are well known. People understood the need for and the advantages of having fewer children; they viewed having small families as the rule accepted by most others, rather than an exception; and the pill provided a means for accomplishing the desired goal.

The present need to change consumer behavior is obvious. In the thirty years following World War II progress and advancement were achieved by means of the acquisition of an ever-larger quantity of consumer goods. Now shortages in energy and natural resources in general, as well as considerations of preserving the environment, call for different patterns of consumption. Clearly, changes in consumption cannot be expected unless and until alternatives are available. Smaller cars, public transportation, and consumer goods of high durability, for example, would have to be within the reach of the average consumer. The problem then will be to make the public fully aware of the seriousness of the changed economic and environmental situation and the real need for their cooperation. Indeed, it may be necessary to arouse a new image of the role of consumption in society and of what constitutes an improvement in the quality of life.

9
THE FAILINGS
OF ECONOMICS

We now turn to a study of underlying reasons for the changes in people's attitudes and expectations in the middle 1970s. We shall conclude from survey findings about the American people's disorientation and confusion concerning economic matters that experts and scholars failed to transmit suitable guidelines that would have enabled the layman to comprehend what was going on. We shall begin with a few references to the psychology of learning and thinking, which may serve to place the change from assurance to uncertainty in its proper perspective.[1]

In order to arrive at genuine understanding, information received must be organized in such a manner as to permit the solution of a problem. Memorizing specific statements of explanation or being indoctrinated with a set of dogmas and theories can hardly bring about real understanding. Problem solving consists of a process of reorganization, which ends when all of the pieces fall into place. This end point may

---

[1]George Katona conducted and published psychological studies on learning and thinking long before he turned to the analysis of economic behavior (see Katona 1940). During the last few years he has expanded these studies from individual to mass learning processes. The following considerations are based on his article "Cognitive Processes in Learning" (Katona 1973).

sometimes be reached when one finds oneself in agreement with others in one's sphere of contact or feels, rightly or wrongly, that one is in agreement with many other people in the country.

The emergence or formation of broad notions or theories constitutes the most satisfactory conclusion of the process of organizing information. It is not enough that question marks disappear; new cognitive schemata must emerge that integrate various pieces of information. This is the traditional function of a theory, to integrate what is known and at the same time to go beyond the available data by providing the means to answer other questions that may arise.

The schemata or theories constructed in the process of learning by broad groups of people are rather simple. Clarity results from the simplification and even the suppression of information. Numerous complexities, puzzling or contradictory in earlier stages, disappear. When complexities are disregarded, the large and diverse amount of information received ("information overload") is satisfactorily handled and fitted into a limited number of simple cognitive schemata.

These psychological principles may easily be applied to the first postwar era. Rapid growth and improvement, in industrial production as well as in personal standards of living, represented nothing surprising or strange even when compared to the deep depression before the war. On the contrary, survey respondents indicated that the favorable changes had been expected and were seen as necessary developments. During the war many people understood that it was the production of guns, tanks, and planes that kept people employed and prosperous, and after the war that it was the production of the many things needed and wanted by consumers that made the wheels turn and put money in people's pockets. Personal progress was attributed to what the people themselves did and was viewed, therefore, as nothing more than they deserved for working hard and progressing in their careers.

The way in which simple formulations or schemata serve people to arrive at an understanding even of new and surprising developments was again revealed in the analysis of people's responses to the tax cut proposal made by President

Kennedy in 1962. Surveys showed that at the time the proposal was made, it appeared to millions of people to be a mistaken and even a preposterous way to respond to the economic needs of the time. At a time when the government was taking in less than it spent and when very large additional expenditures were needed, the government surely could not and should not reduce its revenues! It took a year and a half until these notions gave way to a newly formed association between a tax cut and improvement in business conditions. In this period of time people arrived at the oversimplified formula that by paying less taxes they would be put in a position to spend more and that thus business would improve and with it government finances. They thus generally came to approve the tax cut (see Katona and Mueller 1968).

Similarly, inflation was easily "dealt with" prior to the 1970s. It was considered to be a "bad" thing even by the great majority of people whose wages and salaries at that time rose much more than did prices. "Inflation deprives us of the well-earned fruits of our labor," was the common feeling of most Americans. It was a most unwelcome development but not a catastrophe. Thus it is understandable that in the 1960s, when asked directly, most people said that inflation had hurt them a little, and only a few said that it had hurt them badly. Regarding the value of their assets, most people expressed no concern. Putting money in savings accounts remained popular and savers were satisfied with the "high" interest rates they received. The value of the most important asset of most people, the one-family home owned by two out of every three American families, did not suffer and may even have appreciated with inflation.

As to the origins of inflation, some people blamed business, others the labor unions, and still others the government, but these opinions were far from strong and did not contribute to social conflict. About how to arrest or slow down inflation, clear notions developed with which 60 to 80 percent of Americans agreed. In 1969, for instance, they said no to the suggestion that income taxes should be raised or that consumers should spend or borrow less. Practically unanimously they approved proposals that the government should spend less or that increases in wages and salaries should exceed increases in prices and also, later, that prices should be controlled.[2]

These simple schemata sufficed in the 1960s to remove inflation from the category of problems that were not understood and were therefore disturbing. That the crystallization of opinions was rudimentary and incomplete became apparent only in the 1970s. Prior to that time most economic developments were not worrisome. When people were asked about their worries or when, for instance in 1968, a representative sample of Americans was asked, "What would you say are the most important things that might influence business conditions during the next twelve months?" noneconomic developments were overwhelmingly mentioned. Not fewer than 60 percent of heads of families referred to the war in Vietnam, 25 percent to the forthcoming elections, and sizable proportions to riots and urban problems. Only a few references were made either to taxes or to inflation and unemployment.[3]

What happened in the 1970s has already been amply discussed. Surveys revealed that many people, even among those with extensive education and good positions in business, threw their hands up in frustration when asked about the origin of the most important developments of the day. This was true first of all of inflation. Why do prices go up? Why are they going up much more now (question asked in 1974) than at earlier times? What should be done to slow price increases down? A common answer to all these questions was, "Nobody knows." Of course, many people knew that two-digit inflation had not occurred during World War II or the Vietnam War. Profiteering by the Arab oil cartel was frequently mentioned in answer to a question about the origin of inflation, but many people found it difficult to blame the Arabs for the high prices of milk and bread or the sharply rising charges of physicians.

In the 1970s the proportion of respondents saying that infla-

---

[2]Wage control, however, was not approved by the American people in 1971 or 1972. Regarding government spending, dissonance was apparent, although the people themselves were hardly aware of it. The same people who said that on the whole the government should spend less also approved proposals that the government should spend more for such purposes as education and medical care (see Katona 1975, Chapter 22; see also Chapter 10 of this book).

[3]Out of 86 percent of the sample who answered the question, 36 percent mentioned one and 50 percent two factors. More than two mentions were not counted.

tion hurt them greatly increased substantially (see Chapter 3). That most esteemed signal of stability and assured value, the dollar, became subject to a doubt that enveloped not just the purchasing power of income but money in the bank as well. A new form of behavior appeared profitable, not shopping carefully after comparing prices at several places, but rushing to buy in advance and in excess of needs before rising prices put the desired items out of reach. Those who acted this way were sometimes criticized as speculators, and yet it was difficult to condemn them. It was widely assumed that some business firms reaped large profits from inflation. The felt injustice greatly added to personal suffering.

The second great problem, the mention of which brought forth replies indicating confusion, was the instability of the economy. Domestic automobile production fell in the course of little more than a year from 10½ million cars to less than 6 million. Very many people, not only the automobile workers in Detroit, were aware of the great decline in car production (without knowing the figures, of course) and were unable to explain how it came about. "People are not buying cars" or "Gas prices have gone up too much," survey respondents answered in 1974–1975, but they themselves appeared to feel that their explanation was incomplete or insufficient to account for the extent of layoffs and unemployment. After another year had passed and gas prices had risen still further, automobile production, at a rate of almost 10 million, failed to satisfy demand! Why economic conditions and prospects appeared hopeless one year, while a year or two later they seemed to be rosy, could not be understood, and the news media offered no answers.

Difficulties of comprehension were apparent in many other areas. It was obvious to most people that large government spending and big deficits were bad, and yet substantial majorities advocated spending more on medical care, on payments to the umemployed, on education, and, although in this respect there was much opposition, also on defense. Ambivalence prevailed even about taxes. High taxes were disapproved of because they hurt badly, but they were sometimes recognized as necessary.

Let these examples of the disorientation and lack of understanding on the part of the American people suffice. The question is, Why did the "experts" offer no help? Scientific insights commonly filter down to the masses. Theories developed by scholars are generally popularized in simplified form and thus provide a tool that helps laymen to master or at least to handle new developments.

This was the case in the 1950s and 1960s, when economic growth reigned supreme. Certainly there were controversies among experts, for instance between Keynesians and monetarists, but their differences appeared insignificant compared to their widely known areas of agreement. The extent of the confidence in theory may be sufficiently illustrated by recalling that in the 1960s serious thought was given to the possibility of the complete elimination of the business cycle through economic policy, and the ironing out of small fluctuations by "fine tuning" the policy was thought to be the probable next step.

When we look at the writings of economists in the mid-1970s, we may mention again the failure of leading econometricians to predict the severe recession that began in 1973 and lasted until 1975. Even at a time when, as it became known later, America was already in a recession, several economists proclaimed that there would be no recession. Traditional economic dogma firmly held that given the high level of business investment early in 1974, a recession was just not possible. Then followed a cleavage in explanations and proposed policies so complete and so fundamental that laymen were left bewildered and without any guidance.

We shall present two major examples of the absence of cognitive schemata in the form in which the discussion filtered down to intelligent laymen rather than in the usual mathematical language of economists. Our purpose here is to indicate that in the 1970s the common man received no help from professional scholars in trying to understand the most important economic developments.

The first example concerns the relation of unemployment to inflation. The pre-1970 doctrine was expressed by the Phillips curve, according to which unemployment and inflation were opposites: When the one increases or accelerates, the other

declines or slows down. Both the demand–pull and the cost
–push theories of inflation postulate that less money in the
possession of consumers, as necessarily occurs in a recession
and especially as a result of widespread unemployment, must
slow down the increase in prices. Thus it has traditionally
been held that it would be effective economic policy to substitute unemployment for inflation.

In sharp contrast, we read in the *Economic Report of the
President*, transmitted to Congress in January 1976, that "inflation and unemployment are not opposites, but related symptoms of an unhealthy economy" (p. 4). Several economists
changed their opinions and in the mid-1970s expressed doubt
that inflation might be traded off against unemployment (see
Public Agenda Foundation 1976). The authors of this book
fully agree with the statement cited from the President's Report and emphasize that both rapid price increases and rising
unemployment represent bad news that affect the psychological predispositions of consumers, and thereby the economic
climate, in similar ways. (This point is elaborated on in Appendix 2.) But the statement in the President's Report may
hardly be viewed as having represented accepted knowledge
even at the time when it was enunciated—barely two years
after the government had embarked upon a program of fighting inflation by generating a recession! Similarly, in 1976 a
broad group of economists continued to argue that a quick
reduction in unemployment would be dangerous because it
would resurrect rapid inflation. In April 1977 President Carter, when withdrawing his proposal to stimulate the economy
by granting tax rebates, argued that they would foster inflation. Thus the experts were divided and failed to provide
guidelines that would have enabled laymen to understand
how inflation and recession are related to each other.

Much more could be written about the confusion among
experts as well as among people in general. For instance, both
of the following statements have been widely circulated in the
economic literature and in popular articles: first, that inflation
causes recession and, second, that inflationary fever induces
people to stock up, and this increased demand makes wheels
turn. Similar conflict exists as to business investment, which

was long thought to be stimulated by inflation because business firms would build new plants and acquire new machinery in the expectation of still higher prices. But during the most rapid inflation of 1974 business investment turned down and remained low in 1975 and 1976, when the economy recovered and inflation continued. Last, but not least, the relation of inflation to the stock market proved very confusing to many people. It had been argued for many years that stocks represented a hedge against inflation because the owners of business firms, in contrast to their creditors, were immune to the depreciation of money. This belief was exploded in the 1970s. At that time of rapid inflation the prices of stocks went down. The uncertainty and malaise generated by inflation, recession, and mistrust of the government led to abstention from investing in common stocks, as well as in plants and machinery and in consumer durables. But the economists failed to explain, and the people kept wondering why what was so long proclaimed to be true became false when it really mattered.

These instances of failures of expert opinion have all been related to inflation. The second principal area in which accepted knowledge about economic processes and their origins have failed to provide answers has been that of business investment and its role in generating employment and prosperity. Here again brief and simplified statements about prevalent economic theory may suffice to set the scene. One position that may be called the classic dogma was expressed concisely in the major plank of the German Christian Democrat Party platform, proclaimed prior to the 1976 elections: "The investments of today are the jobs of tomorrow." Similarly, a newspaper advertisement placed in New York by a large American corporation declared in bold type: "To create new jobs in the future, American business must start laying money aside now." The ad continued to say that new plants and machinery were needed to provide jobs. In order to have funds for these investments, corporate profits would have to grow and taxes on dividends and generally on wealthy people, who are the largest savers, would have to be reduced.

"We must achieve a basic shift in our domestic policies

away from personal consumption and enormous government spending and toward greater savings and capital formation," declared William A. Simon, Secretary of the Treasury at that time (Simon 1975). He explained that "increased production is the only way to increase our standard of living, and yet in recent years we have not adequately met the capital investment requirements of this nation." References to American saving and investment rates as lower than those in other highly industrialized countries complete Simon's argument.

The primacy of business investment in generating change in economic trends is an old theorem of economics. In early capitalism investment in plants and machinery was equivalent to innovation and served to raise productivity as well as to stimulate growth. The theory of the "multiplier," that expenditures for capital goods reverberate through the economy by generating a chain of income, contributed further to sanctifying investment.

To many laymen the argument that "more factories mean more employment" appeared persuasive. How could one take exception to the news that after the Volkswagon Company had invested in an unfinished factory in Pennsylvania and equipped it with new machinery, employment would increase greatly in that county?

But it was still easier to approve the opposite view. To continue in the layman's language, the proposition "to help the unemployed, favor investments by the rich" appeared to many as unacceptable or even ridiculous. Proposals to create public-service jobs and thus give work to the hard-core unemployed, rather than to pay them for not working, made much better sense. In the summer of 1976 when President Ford vetoed in vain a bill taking some steps in that direction, his argument that makeshift jobs would be temporary, while capital formation would provide lasting employment, was less than convincing.

In the discussion of whether or not capital investment should be stimulated, several further arguments were made and will be mentioned in the next chapter. From the point of the general understanding of the problem, arguments about methods of pump priming or the rate of capacity utilization are much less important than the widely discussed emergence of what has been called the postindustrial society in place of the traditional production society. The belief in constantly growing production as the major means toward greater well-being has become doubtful and open to suspicion. If improvement in the quality of our lives and the creation of a better environment are to be our principal goals, it makes little sense to consider the production of more and more goods—of just any goods rather than "better" goods—*the* objective of economic policy.

We conclude that people's understanding of ongoing economic developments was not promoted by the experts, whose analyses and recommendations were found to be contradictory and confusing. The shortcomings of economic theory did not remain unnoticed. We already mentioned in Chapter 1 the 1972 paper by Joan Robinson, who wrote of the "evident bankruptcy of economic theory which for the second time has nothing to say on the question that, to everyone except economists, appear to be most in need of an answer" (Robinson 1972, p. 10).

Disorientation and confusion have been apparent not in the economic area alone. Let us mention, for instance, the question of the approval of erecting nuclear power plants. From an economic point of view the need for nuclear power was easy to understand, but doubts about the safety of nuclear plants and fear of too much interference with nature caused millions of people to become skeptical or even antagonistic. To illustrate the extent of the feeling of helplessness and powerlessness that pervades the broad masses, including many highly educated people, it is enough to mention the problem of crime prevention. Should crime be fought by massive efforts to rehabilitate criminals or stern measures of long prison sentences without parole? Choosing among arguments for the one or the other point of view has become as difficult as choosing between contradictory programs for fighting inflation or unemployment.

Lack of understanding breeds uncertainty and stress. It also provides the basis for quick and excessive reactions to new developments. A steady course of action and adherence to long-run plans are possible only when the future is seen with some degree of assurance. In the economic area disoriented consumers may easily shift from elation to dejection and thus from buying waves to abstinence in spending according to the fleeting news of the day.

Sizable economic fluctuations following one another in rapid succession would differ greatly from a period of stagnation. In the first case some people at certain times would have great opportunities for advancement and even the acquisition of wealth; some people at other times would suffer greatly and, provided they are not the same ones who gained most in good times, as is probable, they would rightfully claim that they had been excluded from what was due them. On the other hand, stagnation might ensue only when consumers and businessmen were indifferent or even lethargic, which in the 1970s they were not. In spite of these large differences, the two scenarios have in common that growth over several years would be nonexistent or much smaller than in the 1950s and 1960s. However, absence of growth from peak to peak, or from a middle position in one cycle to the middle position in the next, results from different circumstances in a period of volatility than in a period of stagnation.

Persistence of the volatility of attitudes is probable, at least in the absence of the restoration of trust in goverment and a better comprehension of economic developments, because in an inflationary era people become easy prey to a great variety of news reports. At certain times information on increased inflationary pressure will spread because of what transpires from the oil cartel or domestic energy policies, or because of occasional shortages of food products or industrial raw materials. At other times anti-inflationary policies may appear to have made progress both at home and in Western Europe. Similarly, attempts to reduce unemployment may hardly be expected to progress smoothly. Finally, it should be mentioned that the huge amounts of available petrodollars and Eurodollars may tend to bring about frequent and rapid movements of funds, which may occasionally disrupt the functioning of the international banking system. Thus the volatility of consumer attitudes and behavior may easily be reinforced by an increased volatility in the financial markets.

Appendix—Note on Popular Opinions

Supplementing our discussion of the American people's disorientation and confusion about economic matters, a few data will be presented here on the frequency with which various opinions were held. The Survey Research Center of The University of Michigan interviewed a representative sample of 1,214 respondents in the summer of 1977. Questions were formulated by George Katona and Richard Curtin in order to find out what people thought about the reasons and remedies for inflation and unemployment.

The question about the origin of inflation was introduced by the statement "During the past several years prices have gone up faster than in the early 1970s and 1960s." Respondents were then asked to agree or disagree with several assertions containing "reasons why this might have happened." Practically all respondents disagreed with the suggestion that prices have gone up rapidly because the government did not tax enough; substantial majorities agreed on blaming (1) business firms for raising prices too much, (2) labor unions for demanding too large wage increases, and (3) the government for spending too much; more people disagreed than agreed with attributing price increases to certain goods being in short supply. These findings have changed very little from those obtained in 1969 when price increases were much smaller.

The same is true of answers on the preferred remedies to inflation. When asked, "What should be done to slow down inflation," most respondents disagreed with the proposal that the government should raise income taxes. The majority also disagreed with the suggestion that scarce goods be rationed, while the respondents were almost equally divided about approving or disapproving price and wage controls. Two proposals were approved by substantial majorities and often by the same people, although the first would require additional expenditures and the second reduced expenditures:

To Slow Down Inflation	Agree	Disagree
The government should encourage more employment	82%	14%
The government should spend less	65%	25%

An open-ended question was asked about the reasons for the prevailing high levels of unemployment. Some twenty different answers could be identified, yet none was given by more than 10 or 20 percent of the respondents. For instance, inflation, population trends, and absence of desire to work were mentioned as responsible for unemployment. Close to one-fifth of respondents said that they did not know why unemployment was high.

When asked what should be done to reduce unemployment, most respondents agreed with the suggestion that the government should train people to make them more employable. That taxes should be lowered and that government should hire those who cannot find jobs also received majority approval, while the suggestion that the government should spend more to stimulate the economy was approved by one-half and disapproved by the other half of respondents.

Some answers received sound as if inflation and unemployment were seen as opposites and should be cured by different or even contradictory methods. For instance, that the government should spend less to slow down inflation and that it should hire those who cannot find jobs so as to decrease unemployment, are prescriptions of a very different nature. Nevertheless, when asked whether the respondent expected more or less unemployment if prices were to rise fast, 55 percent answered "more" and 29 percent "less" unemployment. In other words, the majority thought that inflation and unemployment rise together.

These findings appear to indicate that most people do not know and do not understand what makes for high inflation and unemployment and how the two great evils should be fought. Apparently any proposition that sounds good (e.g., the government should hire unemployed people) is approved and any proposition that sounds bad (e.g., taxes should be raised) is disapproved. Willingness to make sacrifices is not apparent.

10
THE CHALLENGE
OF A HUMANE ECONOMY

As we have said before, it is not so much the stagnation of incomes, assets, and investments that make people dissatisfied and fearful, but rather the uncertainty created by the threat of unemployment and the depreciation of savings and old-age incomes. Furthermore, to repeat the thesis of the last chapter, people in Western societies are confused and disoriented because the prevailing ways of thought do not help them to understand current economic developments, to anticipate changes, and to derive appropriate guidelines for economic policy. Finally, their anxiety is aggravated by an inadequate adjustment of production to a broad range of human needs and values.

Were it true that economic success or failure, satisfaction or dissatisfaction, depended on the size of production and consumption alone, then a return to quantitative growth of the old type could solve our problems. Yet, and this is the recurring theme of the preceding chapters of this book, sociopsychological developments greatly influence people's reactions to economic trends. In order to respond properly to changed attitudes and values, economic policy must be oriented not toward the quantity but rather toward the quality of production; it must devote its main attention not to a further expansion of productive potential but rather to the question of how to organize our economy so as to better accommodate the human needs for security, continuity, equity, and self-actualization within the limits imposed by the environment and the available natural and human resources.

During the last ten years there have been changes in people's priorities. We are no longer concerned exclusively or even mainly with an increase in the level of consumption. On the list of priorities of the average family other concerns have gained in importance: a secure job; continuous income even in case of sickness, disability, and old age; appropriate forms of job and career; safety in one's home and on the street; and neighborhoods that do not deteriorate as the result of rapid changes in the human or physical environment. Many people have also turned their attention toward such issues and amenities as their treatment as patients; shopping facilities, public services, and helpful neighbors within easy reach; less regimentation on the job. They are also concerned with their freedom to make important decisions for themselves—for instance, about the time of retirement, the timing of vacations, or work hours—and with their ability to correct a mismatch between themselves and their jobs—for instance, by way of adult education and retraining. One can see from the public protests in all large industrial countries against the construction of nuclear power plants and superhighways that people do not want to be exposed to a barrage of innovations they consider undesirable, nor do they want to be confronted with involuntary changes in their physical or social environment. These new desires are more than a passing fad. They compete with the pursuit of traditional ways of progress and growth. Much thinking and debate will be required to strike a balance between an expansion of production that ignores the new priorities and an attempt to create a humane economy regardless of its consequences for production.

The success of the Keynesian paradigm in the past was based on the congruence of the economic goals proclaimed by Keynesian economists—full employment, monetary stability, growth—with people's priorities, hopes, and concerns, as well as on the availability of instruments, that is, fiscal and monetary policies capable of achieving the desired goals. Most conspicuously, budget deficits incurred by expansionary policies were reduced if not balanced by rising tax revenues that emerged as a byproduct of growth; jobs lost through the industrialization of agriculture and the disappearance of small crafts and trades were readily compensated for by expanding industrial and, later, administrative and service occupations.

Traditional economic goals are no longer in harmony with present priorities. All of them require expansion and reformulation. The concept of monetary stability must be broadened to encompass continuity. People want to rely not only on the value of their money but also on the security of their income and their old-age pensions. They are also eager to maintain their social relations and social status. Full employment begins to take on a new meaning. It is no longer enough to have a job; the job should make use of a person's skills and abilities. Not only should it pay well, it should also allow some self-determination. The meaning of economic growth has also changed. What matters more than an increase in the quantity of goods and services produced is an improvement of well-being. Improving the standard of living must not be at the expense of a deterioration of the environment.

An integrated picture of new strategies that would be appropriate to changed goals and priorities has not yet developed. This is the main reason why the strategies for a humane economy that have been publicly discussed threaten to get lost in conflicts about goals and priorities and do not elicit enough official or public support. For instance, opponents of nuclear power are still helpless in the face of the claim of its supporters that nuclear power is necessary to provide adequate energy for national needs and ultimately to create jobs. Policies appropriate to the new era will have to be based on a paradigm different from that of Keynesians.

Induced Investment or Induced Employment

In the past, growth served to perfect the mastery of man over nature.[1] The utilization of natural resources was the fron-

---

[1]This and the next section are based on Burkhard Strumpel's paper commissioned by the Joint Economic Committee of the U.S. Congress (Strumpel 1976b).

tier during the period of industrialization. Human ingenuity, combined with abundant energy and raw materials, made exponential growth in production possible. Recently, the mastery of man over nature has started to yield fewer additional benefits because of the declining accessibility of raw materials and the danger of pollution to the environment coupled with decreasing public tolerance of ecological damage.

There are some who feel challenged to overcome such barriers to growth in production by trying harder to create conditions that would make further growth possible. To this end they argue that the most urgent need is a boost in capital investment, mainly to increase the production of energy and the processing of raw materials. It is believed that, once those resources are again abundant, high employment must inevitably follow and that, even before that time, the investment program itself will absorb labor. Employment is considered to be a by-product of investment in plants and machinery, which in turn is induced through capital infusion.

The beliefs implied in this position are based on traditional criteria of (1) employment, (2) efficiency through technical progress, and (3) the utility of the product.

Employment   Induced investment is assumed to create additional employment mainly by virtue of its income effect. Those who supply the goods and services needed for the production of investment goods receive (additional) income. Their (added) demand reverberates through the economy to create further employment and income (multiplier effect.).

Efficiency   Induced investment, it is held, leads to increased productivity. Mechanization substitutes machine power for manpower and the replacement of old machines by new machines represents a technological advance.

Utility of the Product   It is assumed that the public would be receptive and provide the necessary market for the goods produced by the additional capacity created by induced capital investment.

These beliefs have been reinforced by the success story of

postwar growth, which still shapes economic thinking about the leading role of investment by the private sector.

Economic activity is generated by a complex interaction of demand conditions with a variety of productive factors: resources, labor, capital, management. A particular factor becomes the more important or central the scarcer it is in comparison with the other factors. Thirty years ago the phenomenal success of the Marshall Plan in stimulating the economic resurgence of Western Europe was due precisely to the fact that capital, along with superior technology, was infused into economies that were well equipped with labor, resources, and management skills and that were full of people hungry for goods.

For the United States today, in contrast, there is little reason to identify investment as the foremost strategic factor that would make the economy grow. If we look to the sequence of events during business cycles, we see that business investment over the past thirty years has tended to lag behind consumer expenditures for durable goods (see Chapter 2). True, in the 1950s and 1960s large growth rates of private investment in plants and equipment, necessitated by an expansion of the production of goods, did contribute to a high degree of employment as well as to a rapid rise in productive efficiency, much of it consisting in the transfer of resources from places with lower to places with higher productivity. Reasonably high levels of employment were maintained through an expansion in overall production. Human labor was made more efficient by energy operating through machines, while investment both in human know-how and materials made mechanization possible. As to the utility of the output, Americans readily adapted to the availability of more goods. They were thing-minded, willing to invest in consumer durables and to incur debt.

The question of whether such a capital-oriented interventionist strategy would be appropriate for the present time mainly revolves around the criterion of the utility of the product. Would induced investment today conform to people's needs and to market demand? The weight of the evidence provides a negative answer to this key question, which is crucial for investment in private industry. In Chapter 2 we pointed out that industry operated much below capacity not just during the recessions but also during the good years of the 1970s. In 1975–1977 only a few industries with sharply rising sales, as for instance the producers of automobiles, made any substantial increase in the amounts of money they spent on new plants and machinery. Even including those increases, the total amount of business investment remained low, because even companies with large profits and sizable funds at their disposal felt no need for expansion. There are hardly any reasons to expect a great change in the near future. Sluggishness of business investment in the United States, as in Germany and Japan, is a consequence of the declining attractiveness of the material-intensive production that is characteristic of the present stage of industrial development. Any large-scale capital injection into the manufacturing sector would run counter to the lack of consumer interest in the resultant additional products.

As to the belief that increasing investment would create more employment, it must be noted first that the substantial upswing of 1975–1976 in the major industrial countries failed to make a substantial dent in the unemployment rates. There are other reasons as well why induced investment would fail to reduce unemployment substantially. It has been shown in Germany and is probably true of the U.S. as well that a growing proportion of the investment outlays in the 1970s was used not for the expansion of plants and production facilities but for modernization in order to replace men by machinery. True, such modernization may generate greater productivity, but even that is likely to be at a lower rate than in the golden age of rapid economic growth. There is some evidence that the marginal costs of capacity expansion have risen considerably in relation to average costs and that the blessings of increasing the size of production and plants have greatly diminished.[2]

Those who believe in the necessity to increase capital ex-

---

[2]For instance, A. E. Kahn (1976) reports that the economies of scale were "suddenly exhausted" in the production of electricity. We do not know how general this development is.

penditures in the United States frequently cite the example of West Germany. In Germany capital investment represents a much larger proportion of GNP than in the U.S., and for many years sharp increases in it coincided with increases in prosperity and well-being. The discussion of the American-German differences may be kept very short because a few years ago the authors devoted a large part of a book to demonstrating the fundamental differences in the economic development of the two countries.[3]

Since the end of World War II Americans have been consumption-oriented; they felt better off than in the past, expected to be better off in the future, and expressed their optimism and their aspirations by continuously increasing their purchase of consumer goods. They did so very frequently by buying on the installment plan, and the continuous increase in borrowing resulted in a low net rate of saving. In contrast, the Germans even in the best of years were fairly skeptical about their own progress, expressed feelings of saturation, and were security-oriented. A continuous increase in productive capacity and in the export of manufactured goods was considered the basis of the economic progress of the country.

In the 1960s, while almost every second American boy or girl eighteen years of age was in college, in Germany only every tenth youngster of that age went to school full time. At that time more than two-thirds of American fathers expected their boys to go to college, while only one-third of German fathers approved of boys staying in school beyond the age of eighteen, because they wanted them to have jobs at that age.

A greater contrast between two highly developed economies and the economic belief systems of two people could hardly be envisaged than was observed in the 1950s and 1960s in the U.S. and Germany. Apparently Americans chose a form of economic development appropriate to their priorities, and the Germans a different form according to the

---

[3]See Katona, Strumpel and Zahn (1971). The trend of consumer demand for automobiles and of business investment in Germany was already mentioned in Chapter 2 of this book.

traits of thriftiness and diligence for which they had long been known. During the last ten years, however, the interest of Germans in the acquistion of consumer goods has greatly increased, German capital expenditures have declined, and the proportion of young Germans entering universities has risen sharply. While some American experts still point to Germany as a country that relies on large capital investment for progress, the Germany of today has embarked on a policy that sees recovery dependent to a large extent on consumer spending, and on public works as well.

Employment Policies for the New Era

The task emerges to outline alternative goals. They must lead to strategies that are feasible and politically realistic, that is, have a fair chance of favorable reception in the process of public opinion formation and political decision making. The existing productive structure must be changed cautiously, first of all by way of a redirection of the increments of GNP. The changes must also be compatible with the interests of the larger social groups and factions.

The frontier of economic growth has shifted from natural resources to human resources. While an increase in the production of goods that require a great amount of raw materials encounters increasing barriers, manpower has become more abundant, both quantitatively and qualitatively. In order to achieve growth, we must make more intensive use of amply available human resources while we husband scarce physical resources.

When the accumulation of material goods ceases to be an attainable and desirable goal, what else is there to move toward? Does it mean that we must do without growth altogether?

Our vision includes continuous growth in what is customarily measured as GNP. Whether or not America will succeed in maintaining growth depends only partly on technological ingenuity in meeting the challenge from an increasingly recalcitrant physical environment. It depends largely on the ability to use idle resources to produce output that conforms to people's evolving tastes and aspirations, just as the combination of technical progress, ready availability of natural resources, and the "thing-mindedness" of the consumer, as we noted earlier, led to the mass consumption society of the past quarter century. We must bring together new frontiers of production with new frontiers of consumption.

At present two kinds of underutilized resources meet the eye: plants and equipment, as measured by idle capacities, and people, as measured by unemployment. The overcapacity in physical capital will be only temporary, given the depreciation of the existing stock. Matters are different with respect to the underutilization of people, as is evident from the prevalence of high unemployment in periods of rising demand.

Americans, unlike Western Europeans, have chosen not to reap the fruits of affluence in the form of more leisure and less paid work. Notwithstanding a trend toward early retirement, ever higher proportions of adults, especially women, are flocking into the labor force. The quality of the labor force is also increasing, due to rising educational attainment. It is not likely that continuing underemployment will change these revealed preferences of people to work and to improve the quality of their work. Labor is a resource that is lastingly underutilized.

There is no hope for absorbing into our economy most of the labor now idle unless we shift our tastes toward consuming final products that incorporate more labor and fewer materials, or from buying more goods toward buying more services. The belief that today's consumption level of the rich will be the mass consumption of tomorrow is no longer valid. In 1940 refrigerators, washing machines, and automobiles were owned only by the well-to-do. Today they are in most households. Yet the second home in Florida, the private plane, the heated swimming pool, and the vacation trip around the world cannot be for everybody; space and energy constraints intervene. What political power will be able to find sites for scores of new airports and power stations against the resistance of the adjoining communities? And how could our world tolerate much greater expansion of energy-intensive long-distance travel and other mass pursuits that go considerably beyond present levels of resource utilization?

In changing its direction, an economy on the way toward qualitative growth must search for expansion of a kind that

- Creates a relatively large number of jobs, in other words, that is labor intensive;
- Satisfies urgent human needs and aspirations the supply of which is not strongly limited by natural constraints, but which contains a high proportion of human capital;
- Places a minimal burden of pollution on the environment;
- Creates interesting, rewarding jobs;
- Requires no involuntary geographic mobility.

In accordance with these goals, the manufacturing sector would have to change its emphasis from expansion to consolidation. Instead of faster cars, lighter and more durable cars would be produced that would require fewer raw materials for their use. Instead of replacing old sections of our cities with new buildings, existing buildings would be renovated. It would be necessary to

- Revive the railway system;
- Increase the energy efficiency of appliances;
- Use the waste heat of power plants;
- Create recreational facilities in neighborhoods;
- Provide public offices and services that can be reached by public transportation.

New employment in the private sector would be promoted, for instance, by training unemployed workers in such skills as repairing houses, performing paramedical services, providing child care, and so on. Yet it is public employment that must qualify as the "pump primer" for the economy of the next decade, just as private investment served as an effective stimulus in the past. It would take too long for consumer demand to shift vigorously enough from goods to services to make a real dent in unemployment. The government, subject to the constraints of public approval, is in the best position to take the initiative by introducing such services for the people as could be expected in time to become popular.

The required program would have to attract the labor that is available, focusing on their specific skills and locations, and paying wages comparable to those of employed workers with similar skills and performance. Workers should, of course, be hired only if the services rendered clearly fulfill perceived needs. Work that would not create a clearly perceptible and appreciated output would satisfy neither the public nor the workers engaged in it. There is little indication of saturation of the market for such work. Perceived needs for such things as social and community services; health care; nonconventional types of education; care for the sick and aged; and municipal services such as fire protection, police, sanitation, and home services are immense.

The following considerations define the principles on which a massive public employment program should be based:

1. It should be highly decentralized and offer jobs to workers in specific locations who have specific skills.

2. Rather than confining itself to providing low-paid jobs, it should recruit at all levels.

3. The program should not be planned as a stopgap measure; it should be set up with the idea of remaining in effect and yielding valuable continuous services.

4. It should aim not at the elimination but, more realistically, at the drastic reduction of unemployment. It would most likely fail to employ many marginal workers as well as those who cannot or do not want to be integrated into the production of services that are considered valuable or needed.

5. It should aim particularly toward providing employment for younger people.[4]

6. It should be highly undogmatic with regard to who runs a particular project: the federal government, local government, private business, or combinations of these.

In sum, the program should serve two goals of equal impor-

---

[4]Not fewer than 40 percent of those unemployed in 1976 were under twenty-five years old. This was the case both in the U.S. and in Western Europe.

tance: a high level of employment and the provision of badly needed services.

There is great awareness today of four major areas of public need: (1) slower inflation; (2) income maintenance; (3) education, health care, and community services, and (4) employment. The first two areas are traditional and undisputed preoccupations of government. The latter two complement each other in supporting the case for a combined employment and public service program.

On the Acceptance of Government Programs

No discussion of different concepts of economic policy for a changing world would be complete without assessing the potential public acceptance of the idea that government should play an active role in providing employment. We cannot predict the popular support of concrete pieces of legislation. We can say, however, that survey data collected between 1968 and 1975 on economic expectations and orientations toward government intervention indicate that, along with disenchantment with government policies and grave fears with regard to all matters economic, there is growing ferment favoring a reorientation from a laissez-faire to an activist government stance. Let us briefly review these data.

The first three columns of Table 10-1 indicate a fairly low level and a decrease in the 1970s in the extent to which individuals felt that they could control their own fate. As we showed in Chapter 5, society and unknown forces are now seen as more powerful than before, as wielding increasing influence over the individual's situation. That this should be so regarding the delivery of medical care or the improvement of neighborhoods is hardly surprising. It may perhaps also be expected that the provision for college education and the accumulation of funds for retirement are considered by half of all Americans to be beyond their personal control. But in 1975 two-thirds of American adults averred that getting a better-paying job was a matter over which they had no great control.

The right-hand side of the table presents the reverse side of the picture. The answers to the second question asked indicate

TABLE 10-1   Fate Control and Preference for Government Intervention

	Percent Feeling a Great Deal of Individual Control			Percent Feeling Government Should Do More		
	1968	1973	1975	1968	1973	1975
Improving the availability and quality of medical care	17	10	13	49	62	65
Providing for your children's college education	63	52	51	35	30	43
Accumulating funds for your retirement	58	44	46	52	64	71
Improving the neighborhood you live in	38	23	22	28	42	36
Buying your own home	69	N.A.[a]	52	20	N.A.[a]	21
Getting a better-paying job	44	37	34	54	64	72

SOURCE: Mathew Greenwald and H. T. Schrank, "Demands on Institutions and Perceived Personal Control" (Draft discussed at Conference on Family Economic Behavior, Institute of Life Insurance, January 1976.) In 1968 and 1973 the data were collected by Daniel Yankelovich, Inc., and in 1975 by Research 100.

NOTE: The questions were: "There are differences in opinion about how much control a person has today over what happens to him during his lifetime. This card lists some of the more common problems and needs that people may have at one time or another.

"For each one, tell me whether you, as an individual, feel you have a great deal of control over what happens, some control, or very little control.

"Now let's go through the list once again. This time, for each problem or need, tell me which you yourself feel the government should do more about than it now does, which you think the government should not get involved in at all, and which you think the government is now doing just about enough."

SAMPLE: The data are based on nationwide attitude surveys of people age eighteen and over, conducted in 1968, 1973, and 1975 sponsored by the Institute of Life Insurance. Sample size was 3,023 in 1968, 2,007 in 1973, and 1,404 in 1975. The area probability sampling method was used in all three surveys.

[a] N.A. = not available.

that demands for government involvement and government spending were widespread and increased in frequency from 1968 to 1975. This was true for all items discussed, and particularly for the problem of getting a better job. Thus it can be seen that malaise and declining trust in government are not being translated into apathy or preference for "less government."

We know from other evidence (see Katona 1975, Chapter 22, and Curtin and Cowan 1975) that the American people, though opposed in principle to government spending, are in favor of it for a variety of fiscal programs of which they approve. George Katona and his colleagues conducted three studies between 1961 and 1973 on public attitudes toward fiscal programs. At each of these times the majority of people expressed the opinion that the government should spend more than it had been on a variety of important fiscal programs. Thus, for instance, in 1973 57 percent of American adults said that more, 35 percent that the same amount, and only 8 percent that less should be spent on education. Similar data were obtained with regard to government expenditures for hospital care, public housing, mass transportation for cities, reduction of pollution, and highway construction. Only for foreign aid and space exploration did the great majority of people advocate reduced expenditures, while an increase in welfare payments, favored in earlier times, was opposed by a small majority in 1973. There were no substantial shifts between 1961 and 1973 in the direction of desiring either larger or smaller government expenditures.

After completion of this inquiry respondents were asked whether they would agree to increased expenditures even if their taxes had to be raised. Some people changed their opinion, but the majority expressed willingness to pay higher taxes for the programs they favored.

In sum, a large and increasing proportion of Americans believe in the necessity of the government to deal actively and effectively with the nation's principal trouble spots, be they unemployment, health care, or municipal services. To refuse to act on ideological grounds, or to wait for the "self-healing forces" of the economy, would serve to reinforce a mood of pessimism or even cynicism. The majority of Americans are aware that there are urgent needs for both additional employment and public services.

Would a public employment program be inflationary? As we have said, it can no longer be assumed that an increase in employment inevitably increases inflation, particularly at a time of large unused human resources. Yet the additional income of those formerly unemployed might well result in a substantial increase in aggregate demand. Therefore the eventual need for additional taxation—some time after the program has been instituted—must be anticipated.

The absence of a highly visible goal represents one major reason for people's present state of disorientation and confusion. Qualitative growth might provide the much-needed positive goal toward which people might strive. It could thus help to overcome the prevailing sense of uncertainty and instability.

A variety of additional developments might well render invalid our expectation that predictability will be reduced as the result of volatile economic behavior and sharp and frequent economic fluctuations. One such development would be the restoration of public confidence in the ability of the government, or of big business, to put an end to persistent inflation and unemployment. Alternatively, feelings of uncertainty could possibly be allayed if new or improved economic theories were to filter down to the general public and reestablish their understanding of economic developments, so that they might once again hold stable and confident expectations. Both of these changes are difficult to achieve and may hardly be expected to be accomplished in a short time. Our best hope lies in the development of a belief system that centers around qualitative growth. The restoration of faith in people's ability to control their own fate, as well as the restoration of comprehension of economic developments and even of confidence in the government, may become easier with the emergence of a positive public image about economic goals.

Our analysis of the turbulent decade of the 1970s gives rise to an awareness of new and difficult problems that confront the postindustrial society. Economics presents us with many examples of failure, but also with some proof of remarkable adaptability. Slower growth in the production of goods is not tantamount to a sentence of social conflict, diminishing well-being, or absence of progress. What is needed is a redefinition of what constitutes well-being and progress. Very probably, this process has not only begun, but, perhaps more than we realize, public opinion has already been carrying it forward.

APPENDIX 1:
SATISFACTIONS
AND SUBJECTIVE WELFARE

Systematic knowledge about the satisfactions of individuals with the various aspects of their economic situation, both current and future, is greatly needed. If such knowledge were available and especially if changes over time in satisfactions and aspirations were known, economic policy would rest on more solid foundations. As a starting point for the acquisition of such information, a survey was carried out in the early 1970s. Data obtained in this survey about people's satisfactions and dissatisfactions with the economic aspects of their lives will be summarized here.

The understanding of national trends in people's satisfactions requires an analysis of differences among subgroups in society. Social change is a process of diffusion. Sometimes it starts with the young—with accelerated rates of societal change, age differences widen into generational gaps (Katz 1972)—or it may start with those people who are best adapted to or favored by change. Economic historians point to the

---

This appendix is based on "Economic Life-Styles, Values, and Subjective Welfare" by B. Strumpel (with the assistance of R. T. Curtin and M. S. Schwartz) in Strumpel (1976a). That article contains additional data on satisfactions and economic life-styles.

pioneer role of the entrepreneurial class in early industrialization. Today perhaps professionals or college graduates are most likely to be innovators in economic life-styles and behavior. In any event, the economic needs and desires of subgroups whose status is changing either relatively or absolutely merit particular attention.

The individual choices underlying differences and trends among subgroups are not made frequently or suddenly. They are the product of past experiences and information gathering and are reflected in values, goals, and aspirations, which are formed in advance of action. The most crucial behavior patterns—educational and career decisions and, to a lesser degree, consumption and saving habits—are formed early. It is particularly important to explore the minds of younger adults, for whom the conflicting pressures and aspirations in the worlds of work, consumption, and leisure operate with full force and are not yet tempered by the accommodation to reality and the lowering of goals characteristic of older people. Accordingly, the sample survey data collected and analyzed in this appendix have been drawn from a universe of young households.[1]

A set of questions, as indicated in Table A-1, were designed to permit the rating of respondents' feelings about various aspects of their economic lives. Presumably, satisfaction is inversely proportional to the distance between aspiration and reality. But there are several reasons why satisfaction ratings alone should not be used as estimates of individuals' sense of well-being in a particular area.

Economic satisfaction is, for example, not necessarily considered desirable. It is considered undesirable by many if it represents accommodation or acquiescence to a constraining reality. Dissatisfaction, on the other hand, may represent an attitude developed in response to opportunities, so that it may be the concomitant of optimism.

---

[1] Birth records and other official sources were used to obtain a random sample of households whose first child was born during the 1960s (i.e., the oldest child was ten years old or younger) from the Baltimore and Detroit standard metropolitan areas. Only family units with employed heads were interviewed. The final sample consisted of 574 male heads and their wives, only 6 percent of whom were over forty years of age.

Many people already know that they would not be satisfied tomorrow with what would satisfy them today. If they have made progress, they most probably would not be satisfied now with what they had or wanted to have yesterday. If they have lost ground or discovered that their earlier goals were unrealistic, they may have reduced their goals. Furthermore, dissatisfaction may as often be a symptom of impending success as it is of failure or maladjustment.

The degree of dissatisfaction an individual feels does not yield any quantitative information about his goal. If somebody expresses dissatisfaction with an income of ten thousand dollars, we do not know the amount of additional income that would satisfy him. We also know little about the importance he attaches to his not having the income he would like.

A tested theory of goal formation and adjustment does not yet exist; there are only fragments of theories, each capturing certain aspects of what really occurs. One hypothesis is that tastes or preferences are independent of income changes. If preferences do indeed remain constant, then rising accomplishment can only increase satisfaction.

Goals are related not only to accomplishments but also to expectations. Those expecting financial progress are likely to raise their aspirations further than those who expect financial stagnation. On a more general level, perceived chances for remedying an unsatisfactory situation may accentuate its importance and reduce the patience to endure it. De Tocqueville remarked 150 years ago: "The evil which is patiently endured as long as it is considered inevitable becomes intolerable as soon as a remedy is in sight. And after substantial improvement has set in, there is more clamor than ever before."

Changes in expectations may be prompted by shifts in ideology or by trends in public opinion. Aspirations, goals, and satisfactions, as well as estimates of their importance, may occasionally be formed, shaped, and changed with no manifest relationship to changes in the economic environment. There is little hope, therefore, that a parsimonious hypothesis relating present or past economic or environmental variables to goals or satisfactions may alone explain various people's satisfaction with their well-being. Such a hypothesis would have to be supplemented by psychological and sociological

149

explanations relating to values, aspirations, and expectations, which in turn are culturally determined.

The respondents in our surveys were men in their most productive years who were accustomed to income increases. Almost three-quarters of them reported being better off financially than they had been the previous year, although the interviews were conducted during a recession. Job satisfaction was very pronounced; only 8 percent of all respondents and only 13 percent of black respondents said that they were not satisfied with their jobs.

A recent American study based on interviews with a representative cross-section of members of the labor force may provide a clue to why such a high proportion of workers were satisfied with their jobs. It revealed a significant positive relationship between change in technology and job satisfaction (Mueller et al. 1969). Working conditions in industrial economies have steadily improved in the last fifty years; there has been a trend toward reduced physical effort, improvement in the work environment, increased security against personal injury, and more rewarding social relationships with supervisors and fellow workers. These have resulted partly from the specific efforts of government, unions, and employers and partly from intersectoral shifts in employment and technological changes. Of course, it is also possible to view the high extent of job satifaction as a symptom of goal reduction or withdrawal rather than simply as a product of a favorable working environment.

As shown in Table A-1, satisfaction with income was much lower; 57 percent of the sample did not feel their income was large enough for them to live as comfortably as they would have liked at the time. Although the large majority reported that they were better off than they had been a year earlier, less than half of those were satisfied with the changes in their financial situation. Still, only 14 percent said that their income was not sufficient to meet bills and necessary expenditures. Among blacks, however, the latter proportion was as high as 31 percent.

TABLE A-1 Satisfaction with Job, Income, Standard of Living, and Education by Race and Occupation of Family Head, 1971 (in Percent)

	ALL RESPONDENTS	RACE AND OCCUPATION		
		WHITE		
		WHITE-COLLAR[a]	BLUE-COLLAR[b]	BLACK
Satisfaction with job				
Satisfied	62	66	59	61
Moderately satisfied	30	29	32	25
Not satisfied	8	5	9	13
Not ascertained; don't know	...[c]	...[c]	...[c]	1
	100	100	100	100
Family income sufficient to live comfortably				
Yes	42	48	42	25
No	57	52	57	74
Not ascertained; don't know	1	...[c]	1	1
	100	100	100	100
Family income sufficient to meet bills				
Yes	86	91	88	68
No	14	9	12	31
Not ascertained; don't know	...[c]	...[c]	...[c]	1
	100	100	100	100
Satisfaction with standard of living				
Satisfied	34	39	36	21
Moderately satisfied	50	50	50	48
Not satisfied	16	11	14	31
	100	100	100	100
Satisfaction in case standard of living 5 years hence is not better				
Satisfied	15	14	19	11
Moderately satisfied	27	25	30	17
Not satisfied	58	61	71	72
	100	100	100	100
Concern with future standard of living				
Very concerned	41	31	43	60
Somewhat concerned	36	42	35	26
Not too concerned	18	24	16	8
Not at all concerned	4	3	5	5
Not ascertained; don't know	1	...[c]	1	1
	100	100	100	100

TABLE A-1 continued on next page

	ALL RESPONDENTS	RACE AND OCCUPATION		
		WHITE		
		WHITE-COLLAR [a]	BLUE-COLLAR [b]	BLACK
Satisfaction with education				
Satisfied	31	47	19	16
Moderately satisfied	35	36	34	30
Not satisfied	34	17	47	54
	100	100	100	100
Work is just a way of making money				
Agree	37	20	45	61
Disagree	62	79	53	38
Not ascertained; don't know	1	1	2	1
	100	100	100	100
Worry about unemployment				
Yes	23	17	30	24
No	75	82	69	73
Not ascertained; don't know	2	1	1	3
	100	100	100	100

SAMPLE: Younger people in two metropolitan areas (see text, n. 1, page 148). Survey Research Center study directed by Burkhard Strumpel.

[a] White-collar workers include professionals, managers and officials, and clerical and sales workers.

[b] Blue-collar workers include craftsmen, foremen, and laborers.

[c] Less than 0.5 percent.

The question about respondents' satisfaction with their standard of living was most commonly answered by choosing a middle position ("moderately satisfied"), with more people being fully satisfied than dissatisfied.

Felt needs increase rapidly in this early stage of the life cycle. Rising wants are projected into the future and readily translated into a sliding level of aspirations expanding over time. What is enough today will not be satisfactory tomorrow, and what is already unsatisfactory today will be much more so tomorrow. There are great differences in different population groups' satisfaction with their present level of living and their concern about the prospect of that level not improving over the next five years (Table A-1).

The proportion of blacks, many of whom are not well off,

and the proportion of white-collar whites, many of whom are very well off, who would be dissatisfied if their standard of living did not improve during the next five years, are similar, 72 and 61 percent, respectively. Americans, much more than Europeans, demand and expect progress and change. Impatience goes along with optimism and is conducive to the reinforcement of wants. This pattern does not prevail in other affluent societies (Katona, Strumpel, and Zahn 1971).

Satisfaction with education is not pronounced. The proportion who say they are dissatisfied is as high as the proportion fully satisfied. In this respect there are substantial differences between whites and blacks and also between whites with white-collar and whites with blue-collar occupations. Those who had the least education expressed the greatest dissatisfaction.

Over 60 percent of all respondents disagreed with the proposition that work is just a way of making money. The proportion was largest among white managers and professionals and smallest among the blacks.

Finally, it is shown in Table A-1 that in 1971 among younger American family heads worry about unemployment was not pronounced. But even at that time in a sample not containing any unemployed about one out of four expressed such worries.

What determines economic satisfaction? First of all, expressed satisfaction increases with socioeconomic status. Satisfaction with one's job and living standard responds to reality; actual income correlates positively with measured satisfaction in standard of living; and job satisfaction correlates with the objective "quality" of a job, working conditions, job status and autonomy, and monetary rewards.

There is a strong correlation between individuals' satisfaction with their standard of living and with recent increases in their income. The increases move the individual closer to his goals, and although he tends to respond to improvement by increasing his level of aspirations, this increase is a slow and gradual process. Recent improvements, then, are particularly likely to be greeted with satisfaction, if only temporarily.

While blue-collar workers receive their peak income early

in life and may suffer income losses as early as in their forties or fifties, white-collar workers, especially professional workers and managers, begin their working life at relatively low salaries and reach their peak income only late in life, often just before retirement. They are permanently on the rise financially, and their ranks are expanding. In 1950 the number of blue-collar workers in the United States was slightly higher than that of white-collar workers. In 1965, however, the latter outnumbered the former by 20 percent.

Satisfaction with standard of living in the United States is largely a response to the change in the level of both income and standard of living rather than to the level itself. The more affluent segment of society (professionals and managers) harbors the most dynamic orientation. Although these people are most satisfied with the present, the prospect of no improvement in their standard of living during the next five years is particularly disturbing.

Among managers 73 percent and among professionals 60 percent said that they would not be satisfied if five years hence their standard of living would not be higher. The psychological dependence on improvement in living standards may raise serious threats to the subjective sense of well-being during a period of protracted economic stagnation or declining growth rates.

The older our respondents, the more satisfied they were, both with their living standards and with their job, irrespective of income level. Age seems to be a proxy for realism. The options of the young become the constraints of the old, and they are perceived that way. Unattainable goals are abandoned or modified as time passes.

There is considerable virtue in linking measures of economic well-being to various aspects of the environment or the economic situation rather than to psychological predispositions. Yet after the situational variables have been introduced, there is still much unexplained variation in people's expressed satisfactions. With the loosening of social control and the satisfaction of physiological needs, people's goals and behavior are increasingly freed from economic and role constraints. Environmental data consequently do not suffice to predict their reactions.

Substantial differences in satisfactions between occupational subgroups with similar social status are another indication of systematic differences in goals. For instance, white managers were found to be more dissatisfied with their standard of living than white professionals, and they also had a much more negative attitude toward the prospect of income stagnation over the next five years. Black blue-collar workers were considerably more dissatisfied with their living standard than white blue-collar workers with the same income.

Various occupational subgroups also structure their environment and perceive the choices open to them in different ways. This is not to deny that differences in occupation within the white-collar and the blue-collar strata represent somewhat different environments. However, these environments are only partly determined by income and income trends, and partly by occupational opportunities, availability of housing, transportation, and the like. There are many reasons rooted in the individuals' background, past experience, and present affiliation that explain why different people react differently to the same reality. Even if we cannot hope to capture many of these rather diffuse and interpersonally heterogeneous sources of influence, we can identify their effects as they are reflected in people's values and orientations.

Table A-2 presents rankings of job attributes. The rankings made by heads of younger families in Baltimore and Detroit differed from those obtained in a national cross-section study presented in Chapter 5 (Table 5-3) only insofar as the younger people put less emphasis on "steady income" than the other segments of the population. Table A-2 shows that steady income is most appreciated by those with little formal education or by manual, clerical or sales workers. On the other hand, a "feeling of accomplishment" is the most cherished job characteristic for those with a college degree or for professionals and managers.

Further analysis supports the notion of dividing the population into three groups. White blue-collar workers are strongly attracted to values related to material security; white professionals to nonmaterial values such as an important or exciting life. The blacks in our sample, most of them operators and laborers, were clearly oriented toward "prosperous life" and

TABLE A-2 Most Important Job Characteristic Within Demographic Groups, 1971 (in Percent)

	Job Characteristic Ranked First by Family Head							
	Income Steady	Income High	No Danger of Being Fired	Hours Short	Chance for Advancement Good	Feeling of Accomplishment	D.K., N.A.[a]	N
All family heads	29	14	10	1	17	29	…	574
Age of family head								
19–25 years	27	17	16	1	17	22	…	140
26–30 years	30	11	9	1	21	27	1	214
31 years or older	30	16	7	1	11	35	…	220
Education of family head								
0–11 grades	39	24	19	1	7	10	…	134
High school	39	10	9	1	17	23	1	177
College, no degree	24	16	11	1	23	25	…	140
College	8	8	1	1	18	63	1	121
Race and occupation of family head								
White professionals	11	7	4	1	20	56	1	122
White managers	9	13	4	2	27	45	…	55
White clerical, sales	36	20	5	3	14	22	…	59
White craftsmen, foremen	37	9	12	1	15	26	…	113
White laborers, operators	39	23	19	2	9	8	…	107
Black professionals, managers, clerical, sales, craftsmen, foremen	28	25	14	…	16	17	…	36
Black operators, laborers	42	14	16	…	16	10	2	50

NOTE: Response categories total 100 percent for each subgroup.
SAMPLE: See Table A-1.
[a] D.K. = don't know; N.A. = not ascertained.

"high income." They also tended to emphasize affiliative values like "being helpful" and "being well liked," although these differences are far less pronounced. Professionals and managers differed significantly from the rest of the sample by referring much more frequently to self-actualizing values and job advancement, somewhat less frequently to high income, and much less frequently to income or job security.

Implications for Society

The economic orientations we are concerned with may be viewed as measures of individual adaptation to societal resources. The variables we examined have manifest behavioral consequences for consuming, saving, working, and choosing an occupation. Some of those relationships with implications for aggregate consumer demand have been discussed earlier (Katona, Strumpel, and Zahn 1971). Here we shall be concerned with implications for society as a whole, especially with regard to the incentives to work.

The 574 young American people in our sample were highly satisfied with their jobs but less satisfied with their standard of living and education. Aspirations were clearly centered in the sphere of consumption and domestic living. Perhaps the high job satisfaction is the result of a relative stagnation of vocational goals in a setting of improved working conditions, a relative increase in the proportion of comfortable white-collar and related jobs, and rising real incomes, even for the nonadvancing employee. This type of satisfaction appears to be of a fairly passive variety. Only 17 percent of the sample considered chances for advancement the most important attribute of a job. In contrast, 39 percent listed job and income security. Asked what would tempt them most to change their jobs, most individuals chose higher income; fewer people chose career advancement.

The classic mechanism for coping with high and unfulfilled consumption aspirations is the stepping up of effort, working more or striving for advancement. Yet in the blue-collar strata, respondents seemed to expect progress in the form of general increases in wage and salary levels rather than from changes in the individual roles within the production set up. Work was seen primarily in an instrumental way, and those subgroups most dissatisfied with their standard of living and most desirous (and in need) of higher incomes were least actively oriented toward goal attainment. Higher status groups were more achievement-oriented and appeared to be motivated by nonmaterial rewards.

Apparently, the link between the need for or the expectation of financial gains and the motivation to work for these increases has become somewhat tenuous. Weak goals for advancement and high expectations for income increases constitute a potentially explosive combination in a period of declining growth rates. Future data are needed to test the hypothesis that claims upon the system are rising faster than the willingness to provide the necessary effort.

How did the people in our sample adapt to their environment? The data warn us against establishing summary indices of well-being for comparison among cross-sections. The main argument against doing so is provided by a factor analysis of satisfactions within occupational and racial subgroups,[2] which suggests that satisfaction with various aspects of economic life has different meanings to different groups. The same thing must be said about variables such as job involvement, concern with the future, and satisfaction with education.

Our data permit us to draw the conclusion that higher socioeconomic status provides a fuller sense of well-being. The belief in a humble but happy life could not be identified in any segment. High-status people, mainly professionals, were generally more satisfied with what they had and more confident about their future. Even managers, who were somewhat more likely to be dissatisfied than professionals, tended to be optimistic about their ability to improve their situation. Lower-strata respondents in our sample of men in their most productive years were not only frequently dissatisfied with virtually all aspects of their economic situation, but

---

[2]Not included in this appendix. See Chapter 2 of Strumpel (1976a).

many of them were also worried about their well-being, not involved in their work, and not confident of their ability to master their fate.

Higher-status people were subjectively better off partly because they were more likely to experience substantial real income increases. These increases, as we know from other research (Katona and Mueller 1966), are only slowly incorporated into the individual's routine level of living and current expenditures so that they tend to provide a sense of financial latitude. Large income increases are often used for purchasing durables and for saving. The former use plays a large role in the representation of high standard of living, the latter in providing a sense of security.

Americans, in contrast to Western Europeans, place an unusually heavy emphasis on progress. No less than 84 percent of our sample of young heads of household expected they would be better off a year from the time of the survey. If five years hence their standards of living were to remain the same, 58 percent said they would be outright dissatisfied. The expectation of progress made them quite vulnerable to even small setbacks. The absence of progress experienced by many more blue-collar than white-collar workers must already have had a detrimental effect on their economic satisfaction. If stagnation is considered bad news, then good news may become a scarce commodity.

The nonattainment of goals can be handled in several ways. Individuals can step up their efforts to bring reality in line with their goals, or they can reduce their goals. If they do neither, their recognition of failure can still coexist with a sense of self-efficacy and optimism: Things will be better tomorrow. Dissatisfaction has many more serious psychological, behavioral, and systematic consequences when none of these avenues is open. It appears that people of low status are severely limited in their means and opportunities for getting out of an unsatisfactory job, neighborhood, or financial situation. If they are dissatisfied, then they are, rightly or wrongly, less confident in their ability to do something about it. They also have less reason to view the future with optimism. They remain more worried about changes even if they reduce their goals so that they will be satisfied with what they have—a trend observed among white blue-collar workers.

While our concern with subgroup differences in economic motivation and subjective welfare appears to be justified, it is by no means clear to what extent these variables are amenable to change through public policy. If time series data were available, changes in the environment could be related to their subjective and motivational consequences. This would be a first step toward identifying sources of motivation and satisfaction. The monitoring of people's economic wants, aspirations, and satisfaction can play an important role as a sensitive feedback and warning mechanism for public policy.

APPENDIX 2:
INFLATION
AND UNEMPLOYMENT

Milton Friedman's Nobel Lecture on inflation and unemployment (1977) has two features that are very much in line with major arguments of this book. Friedman (1) put psychological concepts—perceptions, expectations, surprises—in the center of his explanatory scheme, and (2) reported on the contradictory and confusing positions taken by economists and policy makers about the relation of inflation to unemployment. Both points call for additional discussion.

Friedman began his essay with a consideration of methodological issues. He acknowledged that a "drastic change . . . has occurred in accepted professional views" and argued that it "was produced primarily by the scientific response to experience that contradicted a tentatively accepted hypothesis" (1977, p. 453). That hypothesis stated that the negatively sloping Phillips curve, offering a stable trade-off between inflation and unemployment, explained the relation between these two major evils of our time. Friedman wrote that "The phenomenon of simultaneous high inflation and high unemployment increasingly *forced* itself on public and profes-

---

This appendix was prepared by George Katona.

sional notice" (p. 455, italics not in original). Experience contradicting tentatively accepted hypotheses is in Friedman's view "the classical process for the revision of a scientific hypothesis" (p. 453). This process applies to economics as it does to natural sciences. The evidence presented by Friedman consists of data on annual changes in the rates of inflation and unemployment in seven countries from 1956 to 1975. In the first part of these twenty years, as postulated by the Phillips curve, the two sets of changes moved (mostly) in opposite directions, but in the 1970s in the same direction.

Friedman's formulation of the principles of scientific methodology is hardly the most fortunate one. It is not the rule that unexpected events provide the impetus for the revision of an accepted hypothesis. More usually, alternative hypotheses formulated by scientists suggest the tests that the scientists themselves develop in order to find out which hypothesis is valid. Or new ideas lead to the reformulation of the old hypothesis that makes it possible to discern the circumstances under which the expected outcome does or does not arise. In disciplines where experimentation is not possible this may be done by breaking down the aggregate effect into its various parts or analyzing it under different circumstances and among different population groups.

Use of Psychology in Economics

In explaining the revision of the original hypothesis Friedman discussed how "a rise in nominal wages is perceived by workers as a rise in real wages" and how differently "it is perceived by employers" as well as "how perceptions will adjust to the reality" (p. 457). He stressed "the importance of surprises—of differences between actual and anticipated magnitudes" of price increases (p.469). He also referred to "the habits and attitudes of . . . citizens" (p. 465) in order to explain certain economic developments.

Unfortunately, Friedman made use of psychological terminology but not of the psychology of perceptions and expectations. Even though behavioral economists have measured people's expectations of incomes, prices, and some other variables for the past thirty years, Friedman stated a priori what kind of perceptions, expectations, habits and attitudes prevailed at certain times.

The following example illustrates how Friedman's psychological preconceptions contradict observations. Friedman wrote that "in the immediate post-World War II period, prior experience was widely expected to recur.... The expectation in both countries [U.S. and U.K.] was deflation" (p. 465).[1] However, we know from extensive surveys conducted by the Division of Program Surveys in Washington and its successor, the Survey Research Center at Michigan, under the direction of this author, that in 1945–1946 the American people—in contrast to a few experts—were optimistic, expecting good times with small price increases. Deflation, the experience of the 1930s with declining prices and demand, had been erased from the minds of the majority of people, who believed that nothing like what they had experienced in the 1930s could happen again. World War II was not seen as an interruption after which the economy would resume where it had left off before the war. For most people, the end of the war signified a new beginning. Consumers and businessmen behaved in line with their optimistic expectations, and there was no postwar recession. Only later, in 1949, did a substantial proportion of people expect a decline in prices (and viewed it as a "good thing").[2]

Friedman followed in his article the basic ideas of recent work on "rational expectations" and referred to them with approval (p. 459). The observation and the measurement of expectations are seen as unnecessary by some theorists because they postulate that expectations are formed rationally. Expectations are made an endogenous variable that may be deduced from data already included in the system. In earlier

---

[1]Friedman did not say whether he meant the expectations of economists, businessmen, or the public at large. But the statement followed a reference to the habits and attitudes of American and British citizens.

[2]The survey data for 1945 to 1949 were published in articles entitled "Surveys of Consumer Finances" in the Federal Reserve Bulletin. The developments described above were discussed by Katona (1951), pp. 278–281 and Katona (1960), pp. 31–36, 174–177.

times this meant that people expected that to happen which had happened in the past. Therefore, recent past price trends were simply substituted for price expectations (for instance, in the models of the Federal Reserve Bank of Saint Louis). I called these expectations "extrapolative" and showed under what conditions they do and under what conditions they do not arise (see Katona 1972).

More recently some writers have assumed that rational expectations are modified by the consideration of past forecasting errors, that is, that people take into account deviations of actual developments from what was expected. But a variety of studies indicate that economic attitudes and expectations change radically when new developments are widely perceived as influential and alter people's frame of reference. Whether or not this is the case and what the expectations are at a given time must be found out through systematic observation of representative samples.

Confusion About Economic Developments

It has been argued in Chapter 9 that the currently prevailing uncertainty and volatility of attitudes arose partly because most people found it very difficult to understand what was going on and were not helped by experts in their search for answers. The relation between inflation and unemployment was a foremost example of the confusion. These arguments are supported by Friedman's discussion.

Friedman suggested that "the apparent positive relation between inflation and unemployment has been a source of great concern to government policy makers" (p. 460). He quoted statements issued by high British and Canadian officials about rapid inflation being followed by higher levels of unemployment and concluded that "these are remarkable statements, running as they do directly counter to the policies adopted by almost every Western government through the postwar period" (p. 460). Friedman argued that the rate of inflation is not likely to be steady. The increased "volatility of inflation" creates uncertainty and preempts the formation of stable or single-valued anticipations. "The public has not adapted its attitudes and its institutions to a new monetary environment" (p. 470).

Friedman described recent developments as follows: "The data strongly suggest that . . . rising inflation and rising unemployment have been mutually reinforcing, rather than the separate effects of separate causes. The data are not inconsistent with the stronger statement that, in all industrial countries, higher rates of inflation have some effect that, at least for a time, make for higher unemployment" (pp. 463–464). The length of that time, he stated later, may be measured "by quinquennia or decades not years" (p. 470).

Following his descriptive statements, Friedman presented a "tentative hypothesis" that represented a "modest elaboration" of the hypothesis that he had held earlier. According to the new hypothesis, "the rate of unemployment will be largely independent of the average rate of inflation" and "high inflation need not mean either abnormally high or abnormally low unemployment" (p. 464). The hypothesis fails to specify the forces that make for a positive and those that make for a negative relation between unemployment and inflation. It is difficult to see how the hypothesis would serve to solve the problem or help the public to arrive at an understanding of the relation between inflation and unemployment.

Psychological Hypotheses

When traditional theory fails to yield correct predictions of things to come, or to explain what has been going on, a small patchup job will often not suffice. Radical changes involving the restructuring of basic assumptions may be required. A few words will be said here about how a radical change, consisting of the incorporation of established psychological principles into economic theory, may help to clarify the relation between inflation and unemployment.

The first principle to be used has been called by the author the "generalization of affect." What is considered to be good is seen as having only good effects and what is considered to be bad as having only bad effects (see Katona 1964, p. 160 ff.). For instance, in 1945–1946 most people were found to believe that the end of World War II could not possibly cause such bad things as recession and unemployment. Nor could inflation, a bad development in the opinion of the majority of Americans, have such favorable effects as increasing employment and improving business conditions. The author reported that "rarely do many people mention both favorable and unfavorable business news at the same time; according to whether they feel that business conditions are improving or deteriorating, only good news or only bad news are salient to them" (Ibid., p. 162).

Thus for most people—not only for the masses of consumers but also for the business leaders—it is easy to see how two great evils, inflation and unemployment, go together. Inflation is associated with uncertainty and doubt, even for those whose incomes increase at a greater rate than prices, and represents a bad time to spend or to invest. In inflationary times, so many people argue, one has to save more than before so as to be able to pay for necessities in the future, when they will cost more. (Juster and Wachtel 1972 confirmed that in the postwar decades in the U.S. inflation was associated with increased saving.) Similarly, inflation usually affects business behavior in the direction of hesitancy.

But, as has also been shown, people's attitudes and behavior do change under the impact of strong stimuli. In 1950 news of military defeat in Korea and in 1973 news of sudden and rapid increases in food prices made for the expectation of shortages. Many people turned to purchasing goods in advance and in excess of their needs. Fear of serious adverse developments resulted in a break with past habits. Instead of shopping carefully and comparing prices at different places, as they used to do, some people hurried to stock up before the goods became unavailable or their prices rose further. Business firms behaved similarly by stocking up on raw materials far beyond their immediate needs.

There is much psychological evidence that the giving up of long-established habits is accompanied by disorientation and stress. Under stress the hectic activity of rush buying will have different consequences from those of other instances of rising demand: Business firms would not expect good times to continue and would not be inclined to increase their production and hire workers.

In the U.S. between 1975 and 1977, although there was no runaway inflation, prices advanced at a fairly quick pace. This development ensued because certain attitudes toward inflation greatly strengthened economic forces pressing toward higher prices. In these years inflation was seen as being inevitable. Therefore there was hardly any consumer resistance to price increases, and business firms no longer hesitated to raise prices for fear of adverse customer reactions. This kind of mentality stimulated employment to a small extent only because consumers' advance buying was restricted to purchases of houses and cars.[3]

The psychological principles involved must of course be elaborated and tested in the context of economic developments. The psychological factors representing the extent of uncertainty are measureable. Their strength must be determined because the final outcome depends on whether the psychological forces or the economic forces, as expressed in the Phillips curve, are stronger at a specific time.

---

[3] In the spring of 1977 the proportion of survey respondents with the opinion that it was a good time to buy a house jumped to 62 percent; most of them explained their opinion by saying that house prices would go up further.

BIBLIOGRAPHY

Almond, G. A., and Verba, Sidney. 1963. *The Civic Culture: Political Attitudes and Democracy in Five Nations.* Princeton, N.J.: Princeton University Press.

Barfield, Richard, and Morgan, J. N. 1969. *Early Retirement: The Decision and the Experience.* Ann Arbor, Mich.: Institute for Social Research.

Cagan, P. D. 1965. *The Effect of Pension Plans on Aggregate Saving, National Bureau of Economic Research, Occasional Paper 95.* New York: Columbia University Press.

Campbell, Angus, and Converse, P. E., eds. 1972. *The Human Meaning of Social Change.* New York: Russell Sage Foundation.

Campbell, Angus, Converse, P. E., and Rodgers, W. L. 1976. *The Quality of American Life: Perceptions, Evaluations, and Satisfactions.* New York: Russell Sage Foundation.

Caplan, Nathan, and Paige, J. M. 1968. A Study of Ghetto Rioters. *Scientific American,* August, pp. 15–21.

Curtin, R. T. 1976. Consumer Adaptation to Energy Shortages. *Journal of Energy and Development* 2:38–59.

———. 1977. The Consumer Outlook: Optimistic but Vulnerable. In *The Economic Outlook for 1977,* pp. 61–75. Ann Arbor, Mich.: Department of Economics, University of Michigan. (From Twenty-Fourth Annual Conference on the Economic Outlook, November 1976.)

Curtin, R. T., and Cowan, C. D. 1975. Public Attitudes Toward Fiscal Programs. In *Surveys of Consumers 1972–73,* ed. Burkhard Strumpel,

Charles Cowan, F. T. Juster, and Jay Schmiedeskamp, pp. 57–74. Ann Arbor, Mich.: Institute for Social Research.

Feldstein, M. S. 1973. *Lowering the Permanent Rate of Unemployment.* Washington, D.C.: U.S. Government Printing Office.

———. 1976*a*. Social Security and the Distribution of Wealth. *Journal of the American Statistical Association* 71:800–807.

———. 1976*b*. Social Security and Saving: The Extended Life Cycle Theory. *American Economic Review* 66:77–86.

Freeman, Richard, and Hollomon, J. H. 1975.. The Declining Value of College Going. *Change,* September, p. 25.

Friedman, Milton. 1957. *The Theory of the Consumption Function, National Bureau of Economic Research.* Princeton, N.J.: Princeton University Press.

———. 1977. Nobel Lecture: Inflation and Unemployment. *Journal of Political Economy* 85:451–472.

Inglehart, Ronald. 1977. *The Silent Revolution: Changing Values and Political Styles Among Western Publics.* Princeton, N.J.: Princeton University Press.

Joint Economic Committee of the U.S. Congress. 1976. *Broadening the Ownership of New Capital, a Staff Study.* Washington, D.C.: U.S. Government Printing Office.

Juster, F. Thomas, and Wachtel, Paul. 1972. Inflation and the Consumer. *Brookings Papers on Economic Activity,* pp. 71–114.

Kahn, A. E. 1976. Recent Developments in the Regulation of Electric Utilities. *Challenge,* November–December, pp. 42–43.

Katona, George. 1940. *Organizing and Memorizing.* New York: Columbia University Press. (Republished in 1967 by Hafner Publishing Company, New York.)

———. 1951. *Psychological Analysis of Economic Behavior.* New York: McGraw-Hill.

———. 1958. Attitude Change: Instability of Response and Acquisition of Experience. *Psychological Monographs* 72:1–38.

———. 1960. *The Powerful Consumer.* New York: McGraw-Hill.

———. 1964. *The Mass Consumption Society.* New York: McGraw-Hill.

———. 1965. *Private Pensions and Individual Saving.* Ann Arbor, Mich.: Institute for Social Research.

———. 1972. Theory of Expectations. In *Human Behavior in Economic Affairs,* ed. Burkhard Strumpel, J. N. Morgan, and Ernest Zahn. pp. 549–590. Amsterdam–New York: Elsevier.

———. 1973. Cognitive Processes in Learning: Reactions to Inflation and Change in Taxes. In *Surveys of Consumers 1971–72,* ed. Lewis Mandell,

George Katona, J. N. Morgan, and Jay Schmiedeskamp, pp. 183–203. Ann Arbor, Mich.: Institute for Social Research.

———. 1975. *Psychological Economics*. New York: Elsevier.

———. 1976a. Understanding Consumer Attitudes. In *Surveys of Consumers 1974–75*, ed. R. T. Curtin, pp. 203–219. Ann Arbor, Mich.: Institute for Social Research.

———. 1976b. Persistence of Belief in Personal Financial Progress. In *Economic Means for Human Needs*, ed. Burkhard Strumpel, pp. 83–105. Ann Arbor, Mich.: Institute for Social Research.

Katona, George, and Mueller, Eva. 1968. *Consumer Response to Income Increases*. Washington, D.C.: Brookings Institution.

Katona, George; Strumpel, Burkhard; and Zahn, Ernest. 1971. *Aspirations and Affluence*. New York: McGraw-Hill.

Katz, Daniel. 1972. Psychology and Economic Behavior. In *Human Behavior in Economic Affairs*, ed. Burkhard Strumpel, J. N. Morgan and Ernest Zahn, pp. 57–81. Amsterdam–New York: Elsevier

Lazarsfeld, P. F., Berelson, Bernard, and Gaudet, Hazel. 1948. *The People's Choice*. 2nd ed. New York: Columbia University Press.

Likert, Rensis, and Likert, J. G. 1976. *New Ways of Managing Conflict*. New York: McGraw-Hill.

Machlup, Fritz. 1975. How Inflation Is Transmitted and Imported. *Euromoney*, September. (London.)

Mandell, Lewis; Katona, George; Morgan, J. N.; and Schmiedeskamp, Jay. 1973. *Surveys of Consumers 1971–72*. Ann Arbor, Mich.: Institute for Social Research.

Miller, A. H. 1974. Political Issues and Trust in Government: 1964–1970. *American Political Science Review* 68:951–972.

Morgan, J. N. 1977. An Economic Theory of the Social Security System and Its Relation to Fiscal Policy. In *Income Support Policies for the Aged*, ed. G. S. Tolley and R. V. Burkhauser, Cambridge, Mass.: Ballinger.

Mueller, E. L.; with Hybels, Judith; Schmiedeskamp, Jay; Sonquist, John; and Staelin, Charles. 1969. *Technological Advance in an Expanding Economy: Its Impact on a Cross-Section of the Labor Force*. Ann Arbor, Mich.: Institute for Social Research.

Munnell, A. H. 1974. *The Effect of Social Security on Personal Savings*. Cambridge, Mass.: Ballinger.

———. 1976. Private Pensions and Saving; New Evidence. *Journal of Political Economy* 84:1013–1032.

Murray, J. R.; Bradburn, Norman; Cotterman, Robert; Minor, Michael; and Pisarski, Alan. 1974. *The Household Impact and Reponse to the Energy Crisis*. Chicago, Ill.: National Opinion Research Center.

Okun, A. M. 1975. *What's Wrong with the U.S. Economy? Diagnosis and Prescription.* Washington, D.C.: Brookings Institution General Reprint 305.

Perlman, Selig. 1928. *A Theory of the Labor Movement.* New York: Kelley.

Public Agenda Foundation. 1976. *Inflation and Unemployment.* New York: Author.

Robinson, Joan. 1972. The Second Crisis of Economic Theory. *American Economic Review, Papers and Proceedings* 62:1–10.

Rokeach, Milton. 1973. *The Nature of Human Values.* New York: Free Press.

Runciman, W. G. 1966. *Relative Deprivation and Social Justice.* Berkeley, Calif.: University of California Press.

Simon, W. E. 1975. Shaping America's Economic Future. *The Conference Board Record,* August, pp. 21–23.

Sombart, Werner. 1921. *Der Moderne Kapitalismus.* Vol. 1. Berlin: Duncker and Humblot.

Strumpel, Burkhard. 1974. Economic Well-Being as an Object of Social Measurement. In *Subjective Elements of Well-Being,* ed. Burkhard Strumpel, pp. 75–122. Paris: Office of Economic Cooperation and Development.

———. 1975*a*. Saving Behavior in Western Germany and the United States. *American Economic Review, Papers and Proceedings* 65:210–216.

———. 1975*b*. Stagflation und Verteilungskonflikt. *Wirtschaftsdienst* 4:189–194.

———. 1976*a*. *Economic Means for Human Needs.* Ann Arbor, Mich.: Institute for Social Research.

———. 1976*b*. Induced Investment or Induced Employment—Alternative Visions of the American Economy. In *U.S. Economic Growth from 1976 to 1986: Prospects, Problems, and Patterns.* Capital Formation: An Alternative View, December 27, 1976, vol. 8, pp. 33–55. Washington, D.C.: U.S. Government Printing Office.

Strumpel, Burkhard; Morgan, J. N.; and Zahn, Ernest; eds. 1972. *Human Behavior in Economic Affairs.* Amsterdam–New York: Elsevier.

Szalai, Alexander, ed. 1972. *The Use of Time.* The Hague: Mouton.

U.S. Department of Health, Education and Welfare. 1973. *Work in America.* Cambridge, Mass.: MIT Press.

Yankelovich, Daniel. 1974. *The New Morality—A Profile of American Youth in the 1970s.* New York: McGraw-Hill.

INDEX

affluence, 4–5, 66
Almond, G.A., 98, 169
aspirations, 47, 66, 76, 80,
    103–104, 148 (see also
    expectations, Index of
    Consumer Sentiment)
attitudes, 46–48, 53
attitudes, change, 55–63
automobiles, 21, 27, 121

Barfield, Richard, 84, 169
behavior, change in, 108–110,
    113–115
blacks, 151, 153
blue collar versus white collar,
    72–75, 101, 154–156
Bureau of Labor Statistics, 101
Bureau of the Census, 114
business
    big, 52–53

cycle, 3–4, 46, 122
    investment, 21–22, 122,
    124–125, 134–136

Cagan, P.D., 89, 169
Campbell, Angus, 47, 169
Caplan, Nathan, 97, 169
Carter, President Jimmy, 63, 113,
    123
conflict, social, 96, 97, 105
consumer economy, 20–22, 137
consumption, 85–86
Converse, P.E., 47, 169
Cowan, C.D., 144, 169
Curtin, R.T., 128, 144, 147, 169

deprivation, 95, 98, 99, 101
discontent, societal, 95, 96, 97
discretionary expenditures, 20

Division of Program Surveys, U.S. Department of Agriculture, 163

Economic Report of the President, 123
economics, 122, 125, 126
  psychological (behavioral), 162, 165, 167
education, 76–77, 152, 153
employment, public, 140–143 (see also unemployment)
energy, 15, 107, 111–113
entrepreneurs, 73, 148
environment, 132–133
equity (and inequity), 99–100, 103, 109, 114
expectations, 30, 32, 33–35, 47
  changes in, 33, 38–43, 149
  long-range versus short-range, 48–49
  rational, 163, 164

fate control, 72, 76, 142–143
Federal Reserve Bank of St. Louis, 21, 164
Feldstein, M.S., 77, 85, 89, 170
female labor participation, 75, 78
forecasts, 25, 31, 43
Freeman, Richard, 76, 170
Friedman, Milton, 85, 161–165, 170

GNP (Gross National Product), 13–14, 16–17, 21, 64
goals, 199
government
  attitudes toward, 37, 40–43, 51, 98
  economic policy of, 33, 37–38, 109, 112, 128–129

government programs, attitudes toward, 120, 121, 142–144
Greenwald, Mathew, 143
growth, 2, 46, 95, 102, 127, 134–135, 138
growth rates, 12–14

Hollomon, J.H., 76, 170
home ownership, 92–93
humane economy, 132–133

income, 40, 85–86, 99–102, 150–151, 157
  groups, 49–50, 95
Index of Consumer Sentiment (of the Survey Research Center), 30–31, 41, 50, 54
inflation, 2, 40, 43–44, 45–46, 88, 103, 119–121, 166 (see also price increases)
  reactions to, 33, 36, 123
  and unemployment, 124, 128, 144, 161–167
Inglehart, Ronald, 66–68, 170
Institute for Social Research (ISR), The University of Michigan, 51, 97 (see also Survey Research Center)
Institut fuer Demoskopie, Allensbach, 104, 111
Institute of Life Insurance, 143
instrumentality, 110, 115

jobs, 70, 72, 150–151, 155–156
Joint Economic Committee, U.S. Congress, 91, 133, 170
Juster, F. Thomas, 166, 170

Kahn, A.E., 136, 170
Katona, George, 4, 23, 33, 39, 49, 59–60, 63, 67, 87, 88–89,

174

103, 117, 119–120, 128, 137,
144, 153, 157, 159, 161,
163–165, 170–171
Katz, Daniel, 159, 171
Keynes, J.M. (Keynesian
policies), 7–8, 132–133

Lazarsfeld, P.F., 59, 171
learning, 56
psychology of, 117–118
Likert, Rensis, and Likert, J.G.,
47, 171

Machlup, Fritz, 46, 171
managers, 154, 159
Mandell, Lewis, 171
Maslow, Abraham, 66
middle-range trends, 3–4
Miller, A.H., 51, 171
mobility, social, 102
Morgan, J.N., 77, 82, 84, 169,
171–172
Mueller, E.L., 119, 150, 159, 171
Munnell, A.H., 89–90, 171
Murray, J.R., 112, 171

National Opinion Research
Center (NORC), 112
Noelle-Neumann, Elisabeth, 71

oil embargo (oil crisis), 26, 29,
37, 110–113
Okun, A.M., 25, 172
OPEC, 26

Paige, J.M., 97, 169
pension plans, private, 88–89
Perlman, Selig, 73, 172
Phillips curve, 122, 161–162,
167

population growth, 114
poverty, 77
price increases, 12–13, 26, 36,
39–40, 102, 108 (see also
inflation)
priorities (of the people), 132
professionals, 154, 157
profits, 24–25
Public Agenda Foundation, 123,
172

quality versus quantity, 7–8, 131,
140, 145
quality of life, 46–47, 72

rationing, 112
recession of 1973–1975, 25–27,
29–44, 101, 103
retirement, 75, 81–85, 88
Robinson, Joan, 7–8, 126, 172
Rodgers, W.L., 47, 169
Rokeach, Milton, 66–67, 172
Runciman, W.G., 99, 172

satisfactions (and
dissatisfactions), 46–47, 100,
104, 131, 147–155, 157, 159
saving, personal, 23, 81, 85–89,
90, 92–94, 125
savings (reserve funds), 90–93
Schmiedeskamp, Jay, 171
Schrank, H.T., 143
Simon, W.E., 125, 172
social indicators, 47
social security, 82–84, 88–89
solidarity, 97, 108–109
Sombart, Werner, 72, 172
stagflation, 5
stagnation, 5, 127
standard of living, 1–2, 5,
151–154

stocks, common, 24, 91–93, 124
Strumpel, Burkhard, 23, 39, 67, 70, 74, 103, 133, 137, 147, 153, 157, 158, 171–172
Survey Research Center (SRC) of The University of Michigan, 30–32, 36, 55, 69, 70, 77, 84, 91, 99–100, 104, 111–112, 128, 163
Szalai, Alexander, 75, 172

taxation, 82, 144–145
tax cut, 119
de Tocqueville, Alexis, 149

uncertainty, 55–56, 59, 117, 126
underemployment, 76, 79
understanding economic processes, 6, 115, 117–118, 121, 126, 129
unemployment, 2, 15, 18, 19, 40, 43–44, 76–79, 128, 139, 141, 152

U.S. Department of Health, Education and Welfare, 74, 172

values, 65–68, 69, 75, 78
Verba, Sidney, 98, 169
volatility, 6, 53–64, 127–128

Wachtel, Paul, 166, 170
wealth, 24, 86–87, 91–93
work ethic, 65, 71, 74–76, 95, 99, 100

Yankelovich, Daniel, 69, 78, 104, 172
young (and old) 68–69, 79, 141, 147

Zahn, Ernest, 23, 67, 103, 137, 153, 157, 171–172